Residential Design Using AutoCAD 2027

Daniel John Stine

SDC PUBLICATIONS

SDC Publications
P.O. Box 1334
Mission, KS 66222
913-262-2664
www.SDCpublications.com
Publisher: Stephen Schroff

ISBN-13: 978-1-63057-818-3
ISBN-10: 1-63057-818-5

Printed and bound in the United States of America.

Foreword

To the Student:

The intent of this book is to provide students with a well-rounded understanding of Computer Aided Drafting (CAD) tools and techniques for use in both school and industry.

It is strongly recommended that this book be completed in lesson order. Many (if not all) exercises use drawings from previous lessons.

This textbook starts with a basic introduction to AutoCAD 2027 and then begins a house floor plan. Using step-by-step tutorial lessons, the residential project is followed through to create elevations, sections, details, etc. Throughout the project, new AutoCAD commands are covered at the appropriate time. Focus is placed on the most essential parts of a command rather than on an exhaustive review of every sub-feature. Many instructors and students have expressed satisfaction with the "project" approach and the sense of accomplishment at the conclusion of this textbook.

The videos that complement the material in this book can be downloaded from the publisher's website, along with exclusive bonus content.

To the Instructor:

An Instructor's resource guide is available for this book. It contains:

- Answers to the questions at the end of each chapter
- Outline of tools & topics to be covered in each lesson's lecture
- Suggestions for additional student work (for each lesson)

Errata:

Please check the publisher's website from time to time for any errors or typos found in this book after it went to the printer. Simply browse to www.SDCpublications.com, and then navigate to the page for this book. Click the **View/Submit errata** link in the upper right corner of the page. If you find an error, please submit it so we can correct it in the next edition.

About the Author:

Dan Stine is a registered Architect (WI) with over twenty years of experience in the architectural field. He is the Director of Design Technology at the top-ranked architecture firm Lake|Flato in San Antonio, Texas. Dan has worked in a total of five firms. While at these firms, he has participated in collaborative projects with several other firms on various projects (including the late Cesar Pelli, Weber Music Hall – University of Minnesota - Duluth). Dan is a member of the *American Institute of Architects* (AIA), *Construction Specification Institute* (CSI), and has taught *AutoCAD* and *Revit Architecture* classes for 12 years at Lake Superior College; he currently teaches Revit and AI to graduate Architecture students at North Dakota State University (NDSU); additionally, he is a Certified Construction Document Technician (CDT). He has presented at *Autodesk University* in Las Vegas (http://au.autodesk.com) and internationally via the *Revit Technology Conference* (http://www.dbeinstitute.org).

Mr. Stine has written the following textbooks (published by SDC Publications):

- *Autodesk Revit 2021 Architectural Command Reference (with co-author Jeff Hanson)*
- *Residential Design Using Revit Architecture 2027*
- *Commercial Design Using Revit Architecture 2027*
- *Design Integration Using Revit 2027 (Architecture, Structure and MEP)*
- *Interior Design Using Revit Architecture 2027*
- *Commercial Design Using AutoCAD 2027*
- *Chapters in Architectural Drawing (with co-author Steven H. McNeill, AIA, LEED AP)*
- *Interior Design Using Hand Sketching, SketchUp, and Photoshop (also with Steven H. McNeill)*
- *SketchUp 2024 for Interior Designers*
- *Microsoft Office Specialist, Excel Associate 365/2019, Exam Preparation*
- *Microsoft Office Specialist, Word Associate 365/2019, Introduction & Exam Preparation*
- *Microsoft Office Specialist, PowerPoint Associate 365/2019, Introduction & Exam Preparation*

You may contact the publisher with comments or suggestions at service@SDCpublications.com.

Many thanks go out to everyone at SDC Publications for making this book possible!

Table of Contents

Exclusive Bonus Content

Instructions for download on inside front cover of book

Videos

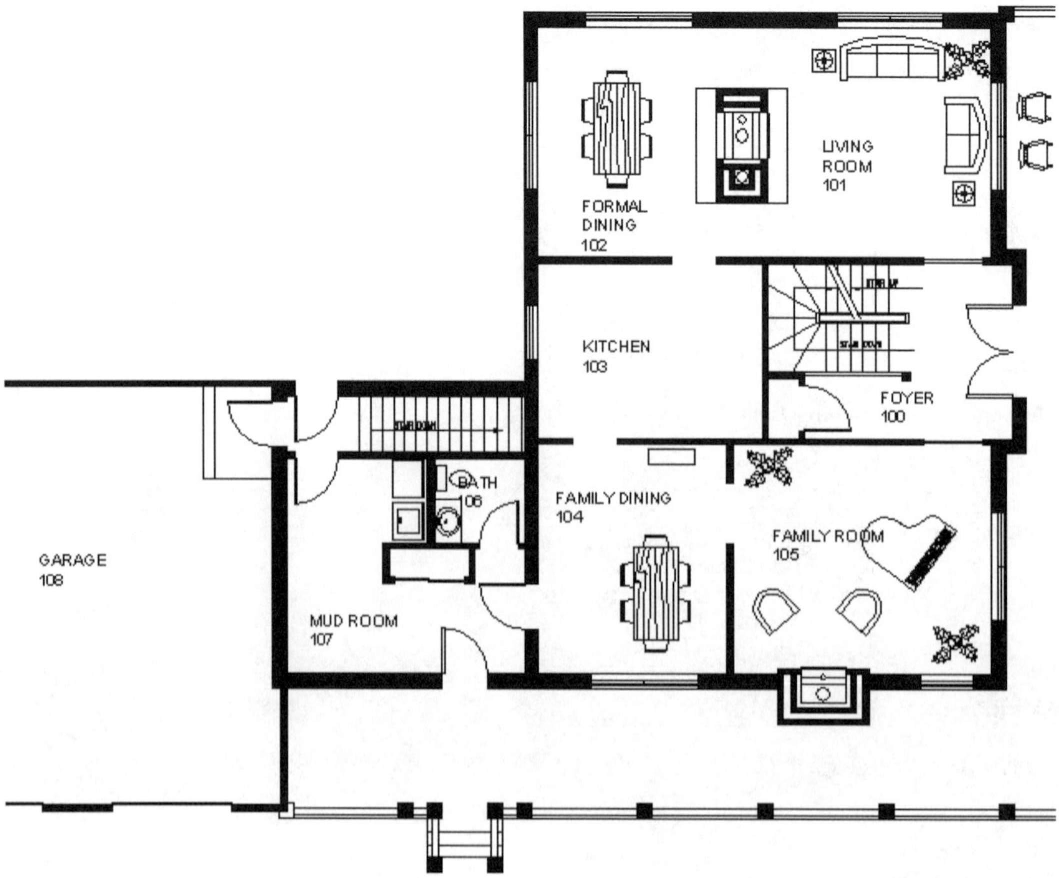

Floor plan created in Chapter 4, utilizing blocks, hatching, layers, dimensions and text.

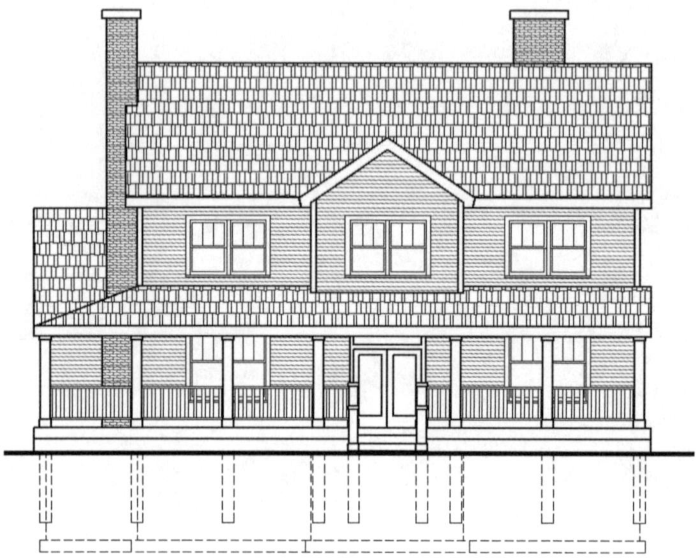

Exterior Elevation created in Chapter 5, utilizing blocks, hatching, lineweights and line types.

Lesson 1
Getting Started with AutoCAD 2027:

This chapter will introduce you to AutoCAD 2027. You will study the User Interface (UI); you will also learn how to open and exit a drawing and adjust the view of the drawing on the screen. It is recommended that the student spend an ample amount of time learning this material, as it will greatly enhance your ability to progress smoothly through subsequent lessons.

Exercise 1-1:
What is AutoCAD 2027?

What is AutoCAD 2027?
AutoCAD 2027 is the world's standard 2D Computer Aided Design (CAD) software. AutoCAD 2027 is a product of Autodesk, which also makes Revit, AutoCAD Architecture and 3DS Max to name a few. The Autodesk company web site (www.autodesk.com) claims more than 8 million users in over 100 countries. Autodesk's thousands of employees create products available in many languages.

What is AutoCAD 2027 used for?
AutoCAD 2027 is used by virtually every industry that creates technical drawings.

Just a small sampling of AutoCAD users includes industries like these:

Construction	Automotive
(Architects, Manufacturers and Contractors)	Ship Design
Aviation	Facilities
Management	Media and Entertainment

Why use AutoCAD 2027?
Many people ask the question, why use AutoCAD 2027 versus other programs? The answer can certainly vary depending on the situation and particular needs of an individual/organization.

Generally speaking, this is why most companies use AutoCAD:

- Many designers and drafters are using AutoCAD to create highly accurate drawings that can be easily modified.
- As the "standard" CAD software among many industries, transferring drawings (i.e., sharing) is very simple.
- AutoCAD's large set of features and ability to handle very large, complex drawing projects.
- Many people are trained to use AutoCAD, whether at a previous job or in school. An employer is more likely to find an employee trained in the use of AutoCAD than any other CAD program.

Many universities and colleges teach AutoCAD. Many companies require potential employees to know how to use AutoCAD.

Architecture and AutoCAD:

The Architectural profession heavily uses AutoCAD, or AutoCAD Architecture, to create drawings, schedules and presentation materials. A seasoned AutoCAD user can quickly generate several design options for a reception area, for example, and then even create a photo-realistic 3D rendering to show the client.

What about the Architectural Software Programs?

Many architectural firms still use AutoCAD even though there are several software packages that are specifically designed for architecture. The general reason has to do with design tools needed, cost, and staff knowledge of the software.

The architectural programs, like Autodesk Revit and AutoCAD Architecture (ACA), cost quite a bit more than AutoCAD, and for good reason. For example, ACA is built on top of AutoCAD. That means that ACA has everything AutoCAD has plus many additional features geared specifically towards architecture; it stands to reason that ACA would be equal to the cost of AutoCAD plus something for the additional features.

In any case, students are typically first trained using AutoCAD and then they are exposed to the more advanced programs (either in school or industry). This is similar to other programs such as Computer Science, where the student first learns a popular/industry standard program (to focus on the basics) and then, later in the program, tackles advanced languages such as Microsoft .Net.

Installation:

This book is not intended to cover installing AutoCAD on your computer. All the steps and screenshots in this book are based on the default installation, with no modifications unless noted. If needed, in the Windows **Start menu**, under AutoCAD 2027, you can use the **Reset Settings to Default** tool, which will make the program look like it would if just installed from scratch.

New features:

Every version of AutoCAD is usually packed with new features. The goal of this text is to teach you the basics and if those fundamental tools have changed you will then be learning something unique to this version of the software. But this book is not going to cover a new feature just because it is new – many new features are often intermediate to advanced tools such as the recently added "organic" 3D modeling tools. A new user needs to focus on the basics before jumping in the deep end!

Exercise 1-2:
Overview of AutoCAD 2027 User Interface

AutoCAD is a powerful and sophisticated program. Because of its powerful feature set, it has a measurable learning curve. However, when broken down into smaller pieces, you can easily learn to harness the power of AutoCAD; that is the goal of this book.

This exercise will walk through the different sections of the User Interface (UI). Understanding the user interface is the key to using any program's features.

> ***NOTE:** Make sure the Workspace feature is set to **Drafting & Annotation** (see pg. 1-10); this will help ensure your screen matches the book images.*

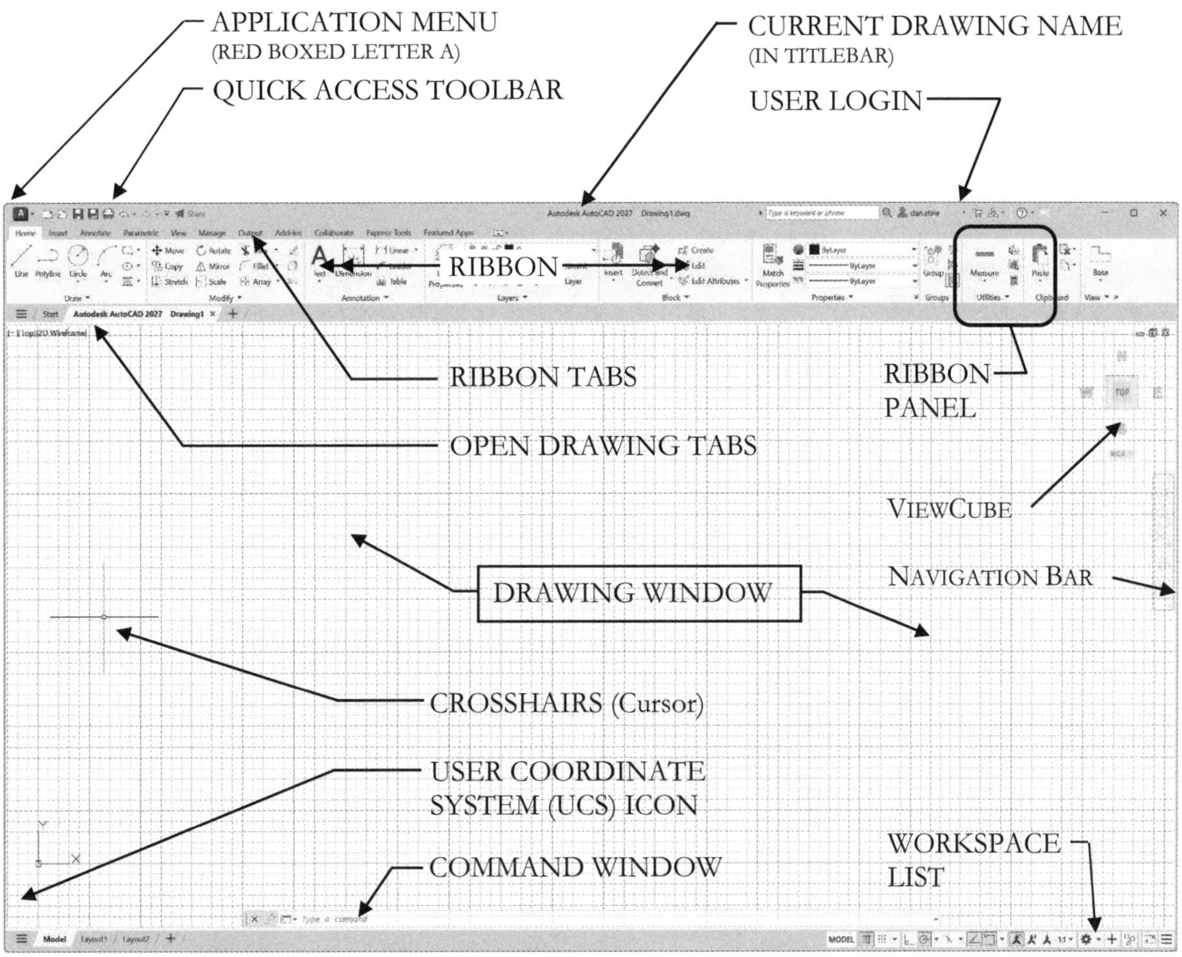

FIGURE 1-2.1
AutoCAD User Interface

The AutoCAD User Interface (the details):

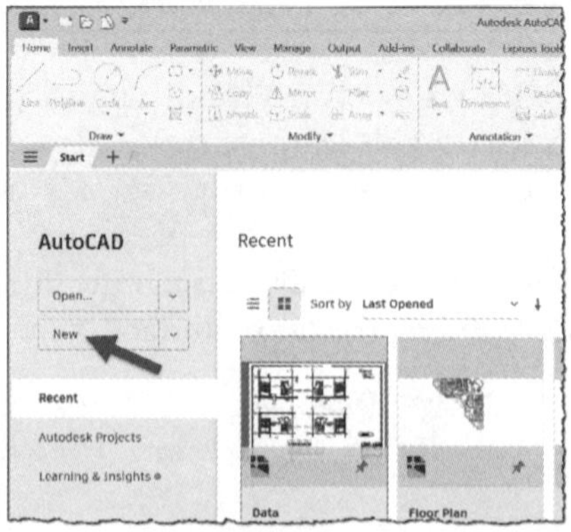

To follow along in this section, you will need to open a drawing from the **Start Tab**—for now, simply click on the **New** button on the left (see image to right). Also note that all the images in this book are based on AutoCAD's **Light** *Color Scheme*, which will be discussed at the end of this section. By default, AutoCAD uses the **Dark** *Color Scheme*; use whichever you prefer.

Application Menu:

Clicking the red "A" in the upper left reveals several menus and tools. AutoCAD has a series of menus on the left. Click on each of the menus (with an arrow to the right) to explore their contents. The options shown vary depending on whether a drawing or the home screen is active.

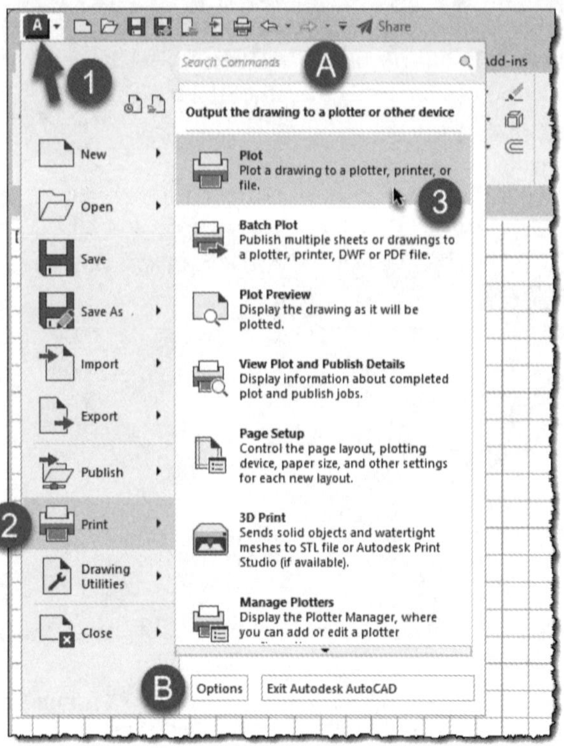

The *Open, Save and Close* commands will be covered in the next exercise.

The numbered clicks, 1-3 in the image, show how to start the **Plot** (aka Print) command – you do not need to click Plot at this time.

Item A:
The *Search* box, highlighted by the letter A, allows you to type in a word to find related commands. For example, try typing "arc" (no need to press Enter) and you will see several items appear. Click the "X" to the right of the search box to clear the search.

Item B:
The *Options* button opens a dialog with a plethora of settings; the new user would do well to avoid changing settings here.

Next, you will explore the *Ribbon* and how the various *Tabs* control the tools displayed there. Again, if your screen does not display these graphics, make sure the "Workspace" is set to **Drafting & Annotation** (see pg. 1-10 for more information).

> ***FYI:** You should know that some of the graphics you see in this textbook for the User Interface are new to this version of AutoCAD, so if you are using an older version of the program, you will not have access to the same graphics. (You should use the version of this textbook that matches the version of your software.)*

Now, you will just look at a few of the *Panels* on the **Home** tab.

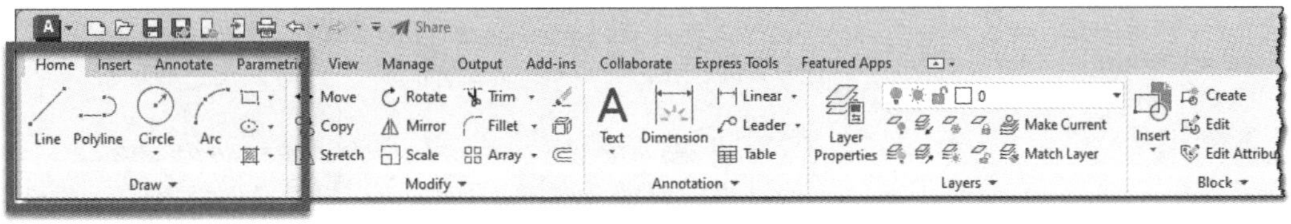

Home → **Draw**:

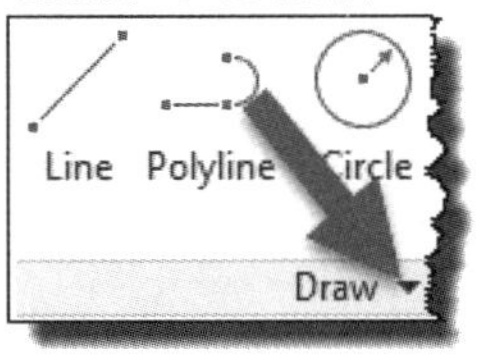

The *Draw* panel, on the *Home* tab, contains commands that allow you to draw basic 2D lines and shapes as well as hatching (hatching is a type of object that fills an area with a pattern).

Expanding panels

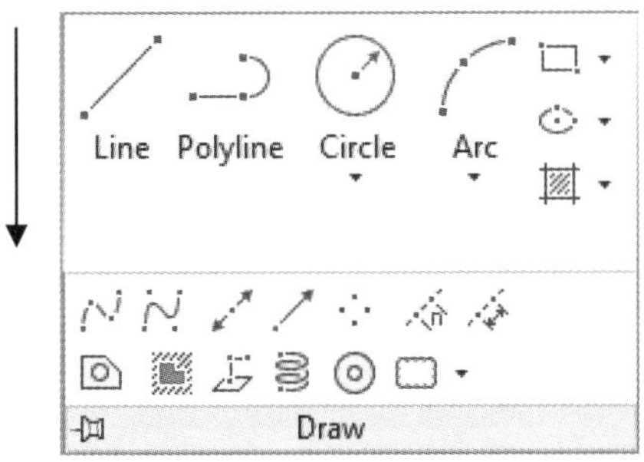

Many *Panels* have additional, but less-used tools, available in a fly-out portion of the *Panel*; you can tell if a *Panel* can be expanded by the little down-arrow (triangle) next to the panel name (see upper example to the left). Clicking anywhere in the bottom "title bar" will expand the *Panel* as shown to the left. Once you click away from the *Panel,* the extended portion will close – unless you click the "pin" icon in the lower left, which will keep the *Panel* expanded until you un-pin it. The remaining example images in this section will only be shown expanded (if available) to save space in this book.

Home → **Modify**:

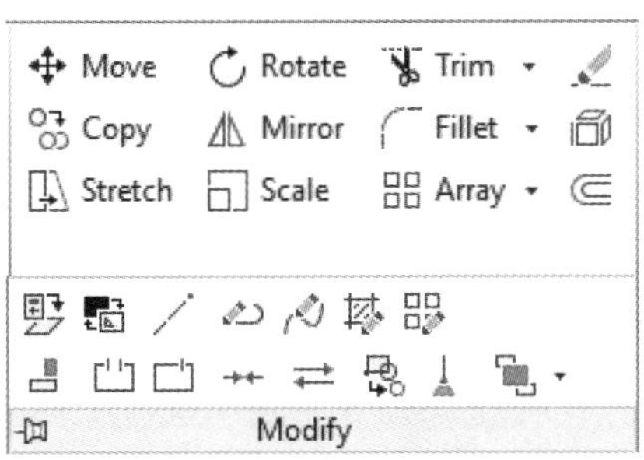

This *Panel* contains commands that modify objects in your drawings: Move, Mirror, Array, Stretch, Copy, Offset, Rotate and Erase.

This book spends a significant amount of time helping you develop a solid understanding of how these tools work; you use these commands throughout the book – practice makes perfect!

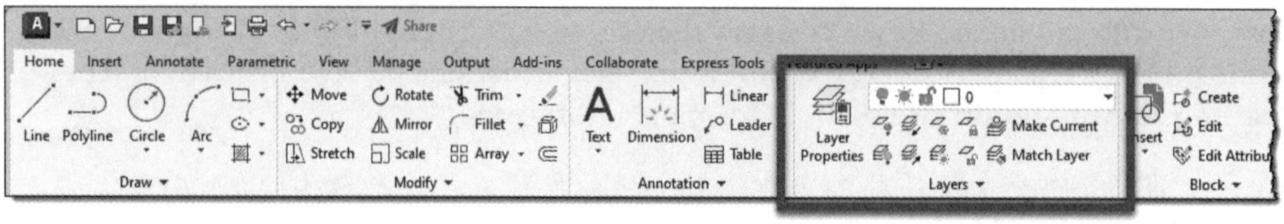

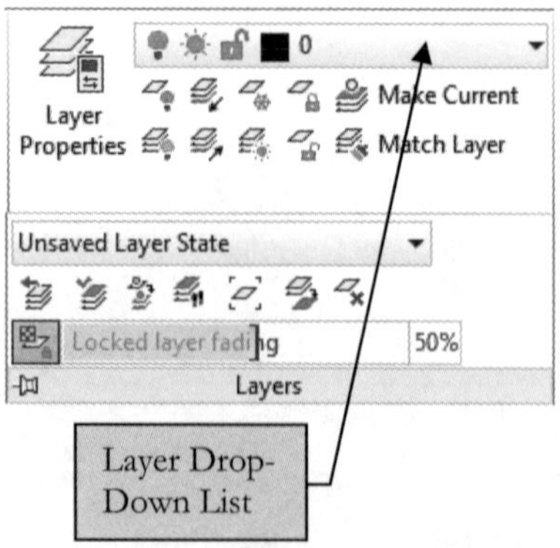

Home → **Layers**:
This *Panel* contains tools for creating and managing drawing *Layers*.

FYI: *Layers allow you to manage the display and the organization of drawing entities; more on this later.*

TIP: *When nothing is selected, the Layer drop-down list displays the current layer; when something is selected, it displays which layer the selected entity is on. (If objects on multiple layers are selected, the display is blank.)*

Drawing Tabs:

Each open drawing file is represented by a tab just below the *Ribbon* (see image below). This allows you to quickly switch between drawings. You can click the "X" to the right of the drawing name to close the file; if the drawing has unsaved changes (indicated by an asterisk next to the name), you will be prompted to save. The plus icon to the right of the last tab allows you to quickly start a new drawing. A right-click presents several options. The Start tab is always visible by default. Finally, hovering your cursor over a tab shows a model/paper space thumbnail preview.

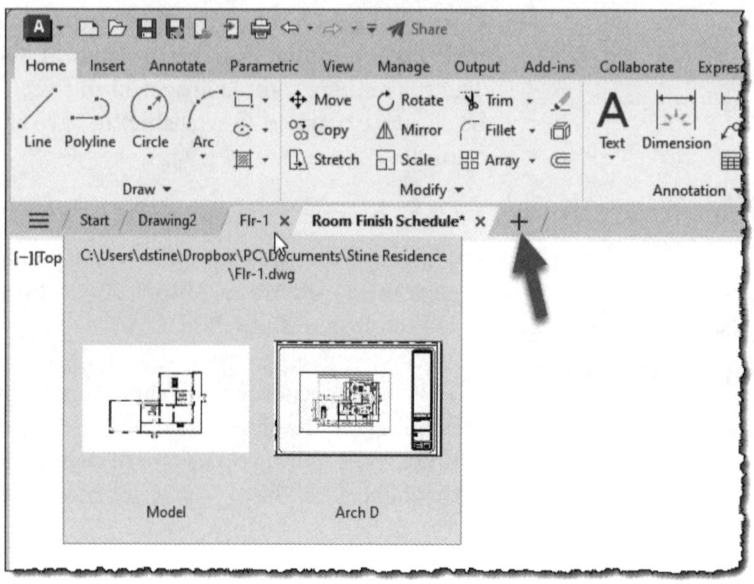

Command Window:

The *Command Window* allows you to type in commands; suggested commands will be listed as you type (Auto Complete). AutoCAD displays options and prompts for specific input for a command. When the main line says, "*Type a command,*" as in the image below, you know there are not any commands active or running. Command history is displayed above the *Command Window.*

TIP: If you accidentally close the Command Window, you can restore it by pressing **Ctrl + 9** *(i.e., press both keys at the same time) on the keyboard.*

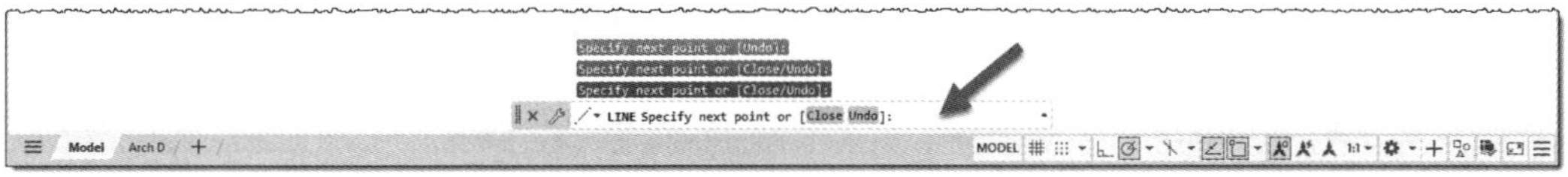

Status Bar:

This area indicates the status of various settings plus the current drawing scale. The icons are buttons which toggle whether that feature is on or not; a blue fill means the tool/feature is active. You can also right click on the buttons to adjust some settings associated with that tool. You may wish to click the **Display Drawing Grid** icon to toggle it off as it is not needed now. The last icon, to the far right, gives you several options related to what tools are displayed on the *Status Bar.*

TIP: When you hover over an icon, a tooltip will appear telling you the name of the icon; this is handy until you learn what the icon for each tool looks like.

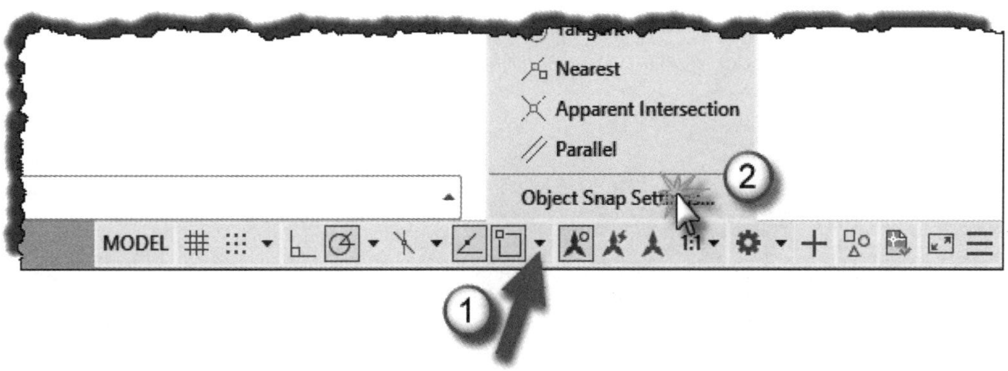

Title Bar: The *Title Bar* lists the program name, when space permits, and then the name of the drawing that is active. The *Quick Access Toolbar*, on the left, gives you convenient access to often-used commands: New, Open, and Save drawing, plus Print, Undo, Redo, & Share (for external collaboration). The area on the right provides quick access to search the *Help System* and App login.

UCS Icon: This symbol helps to keep track of your drawing's orientation relative to the X, Y, Z coordinate system. It also serves as a visual indicator of the current display mode: 2D view, 3D view, perspective, or shade mode, for example.

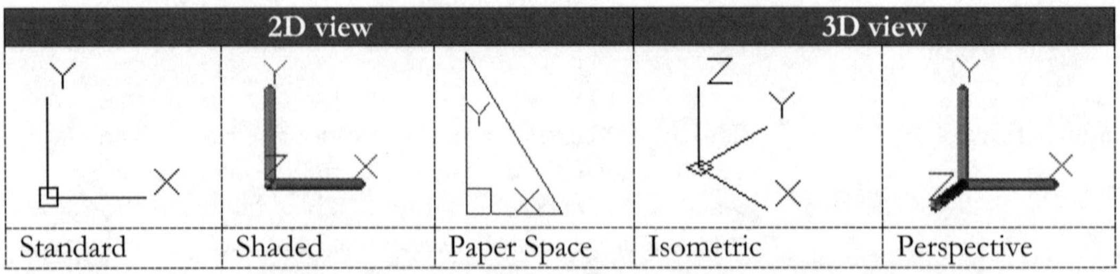

Start Tab: The Start Tab, always available, provides access to relevant information from Autodesk and easy access to recently opened documents. Clicking the large "New" button will open a new drawing based on the default template. Autodesk *Connect* is listed on the right. Finally, helpful links are located in the lower-left corner.

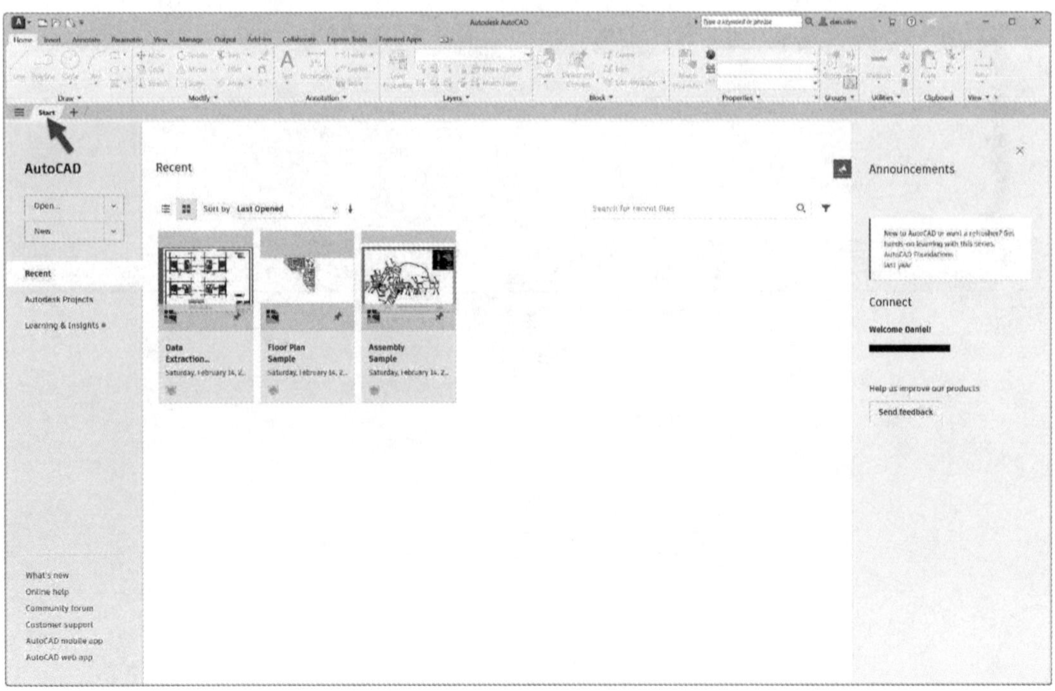

Color Scheme:

By default, AutoCAD will start with a "dark" color scheme (see second image below). The author has chosen to use the "light" color theme for the images in this textbook. You are encouraged to use whichever color theme you prefer. If you wish to change it, go to **Application Menu → Options (button) → Display (tab) → Color Scheme** (see image below). Note: the title bar is controlled by the operating system (i.e., Windows); you can right-click on your desktop and select *Personalize* to change it.

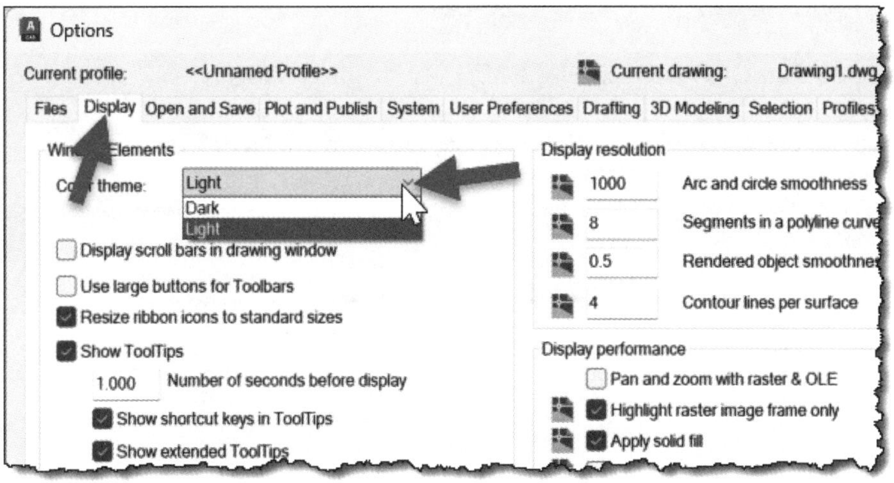

Adjusting the color theme via Options

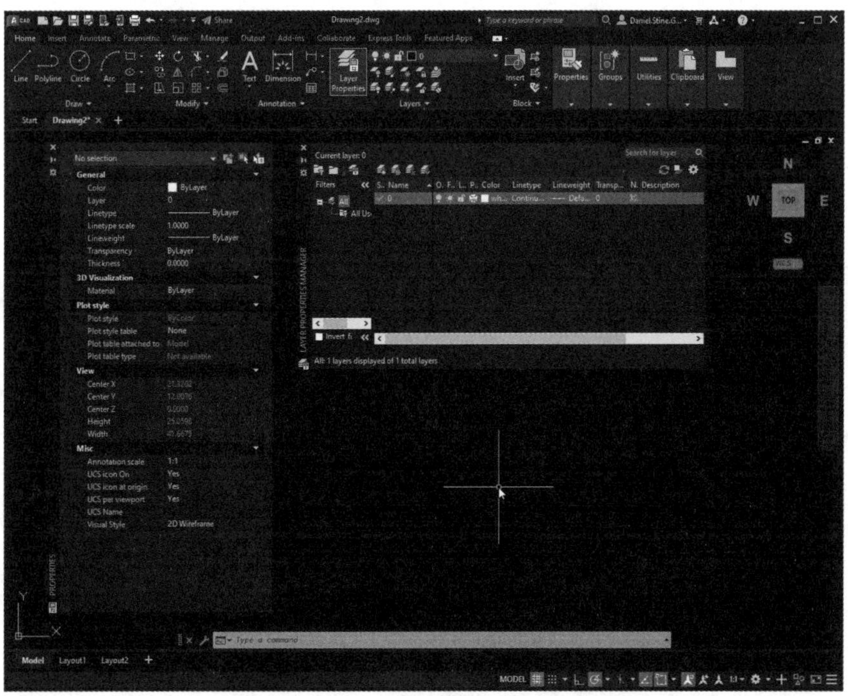

Example of the default dark color theme

Resetting the User Interface:

If the *User Interface* shown in Figure 1-2.1 does not match your computer's display, you can reset it. You, or someone who uses your workstation, may have customized some settings (although settings should be saved by user login). The next steps will describe how to reset the screen configuration.

> ***NOTE:** This step is not necessary to work through this book. It is simply offered for individuals who may have an extremely customized display and want to reset it to make comparing the images in the textbook easier.*

1. **Open AutoCAD** (see Exercise 1-3 for instructions on this).

2. Locate the **Workspace Switching** icon, as shown in Figure 1-2.2.

> ***NOTE:** The* Workspace Switching *icon is located on the* Status Bar *in the lower-right corner of the screen.*

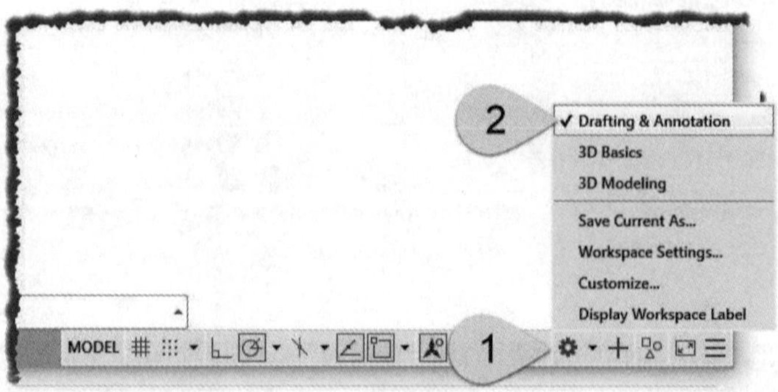

FIGURE 1-2.2 Workspace switching menu – menu shows after clicking down-arrow

3. Click the down arrow and select **Drafting & Annotation** from the pop-up menu.

> ***FYI:** Another option is* **3D Modeling**, *which reorganizes the screen to make the 3D commands readily available (not used in this book). You can try switching to another Workspace to see what it does, just switch back to Drafting & Annotation before moving on.*

Your screen should look similar to Figure 1-2.1. You can reset this at any time to return to a clean slate.

If you are still having problems, you can try resetting the program to its default settings. This will remove any customization applied to the user interface. The tool to reset AutoCAD is found in the *Windows* **Start** menu, not in AutoCAD. With AutoCAD closed, click Start → All → Autodesk → AutoCAD 2027 – English →**Reset Settings to Defaults**. This command is shown in the image on the next page.

This concludes our brief overview of the AutoCAD user interface.

Exercise 1-3:
Open, Save and Close an Existing Drawing

Open AutoCAD 2027:

Start → All Apps → AutoCAD 2027 - English → **AutoCAD 2027 - English** (Figure 1-3.1) – see notes below. Or double-click the AutoCAD icon on your desktop.

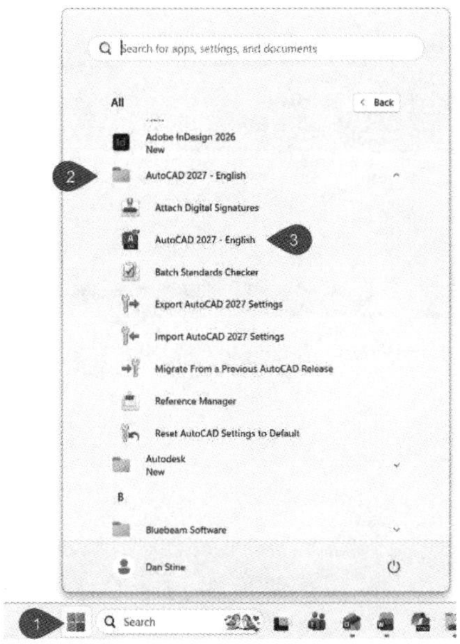

FIGURE 1-3.1 Start Menu

Notes on starting AutoCAD:

- Steps shown are for Windows 11.
- Click the items in the order shown.
- You may also simply type "autocad" in the search box. A link to start AutoCAD 2027 will appear at the top of the list.
- You can also start the program by double-clicking on a DWG file via your file browser (i.e., My Computer, File Explorer, Computer).
- Right-click on the AutoCAD icon and select one of the "Pin" options for quick access from the task bar or the start menu.

Open an AutoCAD Drawing:

By default, AutoCAD will open to the *Start* tab.

1. Open AutoCAD as described previously.
2. On the *Start* tab, click the **Open…** button (Figure 1-3.2).

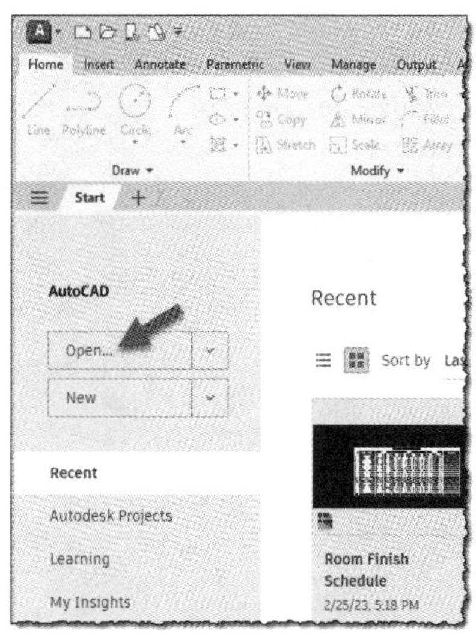

FIGURE 1-3.2 Click Open…

TIP: *You can also open drawings via the Open icon on the Quick Access Toolbar* (Figure 1-3.3). *Many users prefer using keyboard shortcuts; you can select a drawing to open by pressing Ctrl + O on the keyboard (hold down the Ctrl key and then press the letter O).*

FIG 1-3.3 Open icon on the QAT

The icon to the right of open is **Open from Web & Mobile** for files which might be saved in the cloud.

3. Browse to the following folder: **C:\Program Files\Autodesk\AutoCAD 2027\Sample\Sheet Sets\Architectural\Res** (see Figure 1-3.4A).

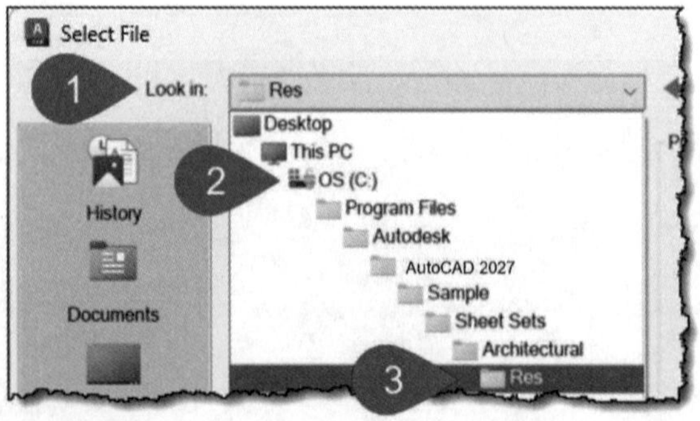

FIGURE 1-3.4A Browse to sample files

4. Select the file named **Exterior Elevations.dwg** and click **Open** (Figure 1-3.4B).
   a. Click **Yes** for any prompts about the file being "read only."

The *Exterior Elevations.dwg* file is now open, and the last saved view is displayed in the *Drawing* window.

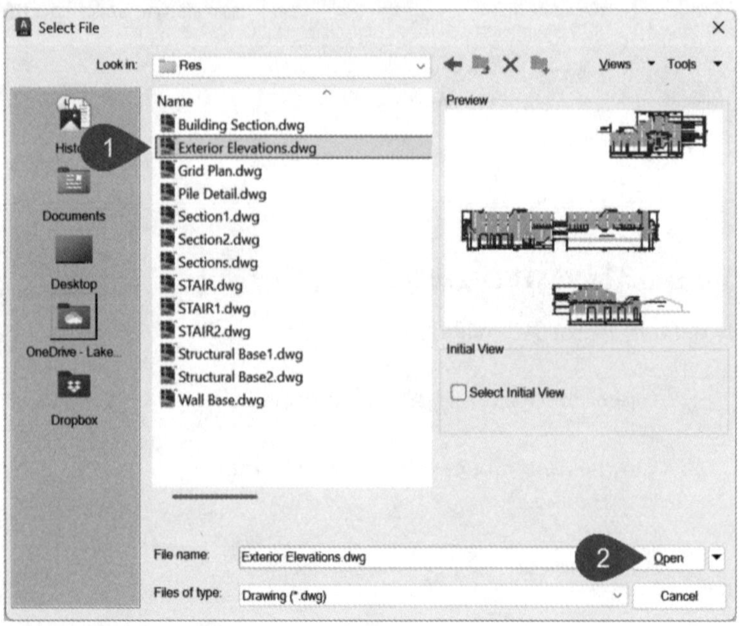

FIGURE 1-3.4B Selecting a file to open

The *Open Documents* list, via the ***Application* Menu**, are the drawings currently open on your computer.

5. Click the *Application* menu and then select the **Open Documents** icon (Figure 1-3.5).

Notice that *Exterior Elevations.dwg* is listed. You can toggle between opened drawings from this menu; however, it is more convenient to do so via the document tabs below the Ribbon.

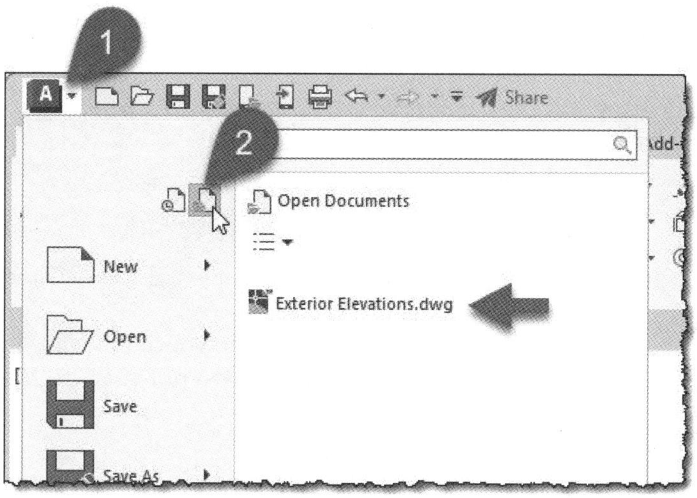

FIGURE 1-3.5 Open Documents list – one file shown to be open

Open Another Sample AutoCAD Drawing:

AutoCAD lets you open more than one drawing at a time.

6. Using the steps just described, open the following file: **C:\Program Files\AutoCAD 2027\Sample\Sheet Sets\Architectural\A-03.dwg**.
    a. If the **Sheet Set Manager** palette opens, click the "X" to close it.

Notice that the *A-03* tab is now shown (see Figure 1-3.6). Try toggling between drawings by clicking on *Exterior Elevations* tab. This is similar to switching websites in a web browser such as *Chrome* or *Edge*.

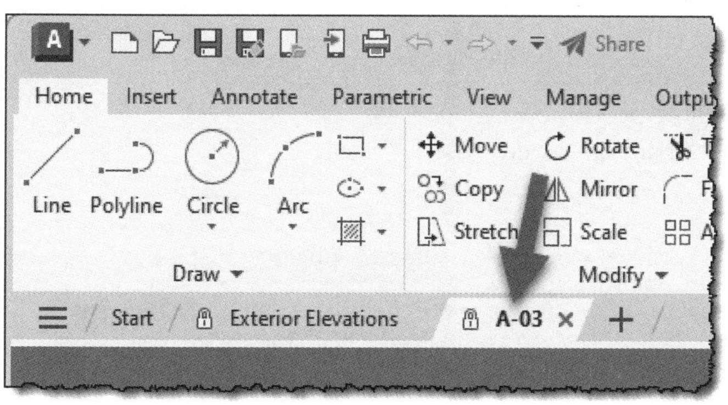

FIGURE 1-3.6 Document tabs

TIP: *Press* ***Ctrl + Tab*** *to cycle through open drawings quickly.*

Close an AutoCAD Drawing:

7. Click the **X** next to **A-03** in the *Drawing Tab*. Do <u>not</u> save if asked (see image to right).

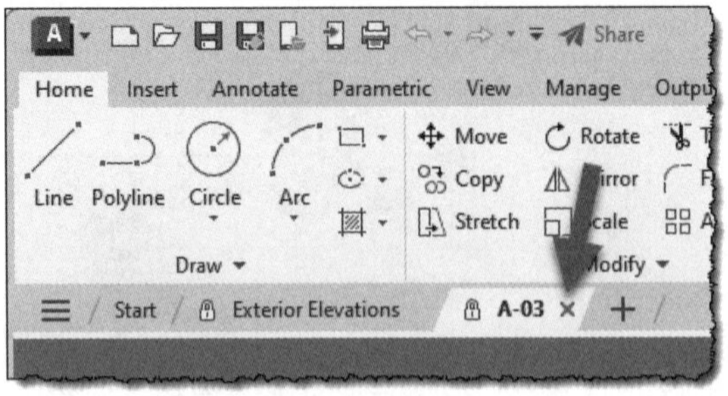

Only the specific drawing will close unless you right-click and select *Close All*. Another option via the right-click is **Close All Except This Tab**.

8. Repeat the previous step to close the other open drawing file – **Exterior Elevations**.

Whenever you try to close a drawing, if you have not saved your drawing, you will be prompted to do so before AutoCAD closes the drawing. **Do not save at this time.**

Saving an AutoCAD Drawing:

At this time you will <u>not</u> actually save a drawing.

To save a drawing, click the **Save** icon - looks like an old floppy disk - from the *Quick Access* toolbar (see image to right). The next exercise shows you how to save your files to the *Cloud*; this is a safe and secure way to back up your files and access them from anywhere. TIP: **Ctrl+S** will save as well.

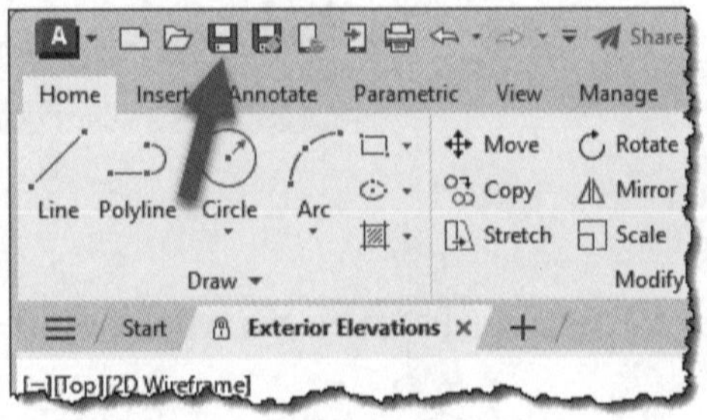

FIGURE 1-3.7 Save icon

You should get in the habit of saving often to avoid losing work due to a power outage or program crash.

> ***FYI:*** *The program does perform automatic saves that are available only if AutoCAD closes abnormally – that is, it crashes. See HELP for more information on this (type 'savetime' to set auto-save time interval).*

Closing the AutoCAD Program:

Finally, from the *Application Menu*, select **Exit AutoCAD**. This will close any open drawings and shut AutoCAD down. Again, you will be prompted to save (if needed) before AutoCAD closes any open drawings. Do not save at this time.

> ***TIP:*** *To close AutoCAD, you can also click the **X** in the <u>upper</u> right corner of the AutoCAD window (see image to the right); clicking the <u>lower</u> "X" closes the current drawing file.*

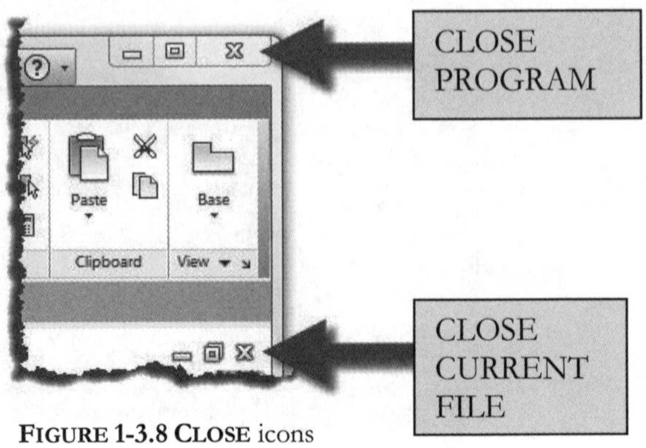

FIGURE 1-3.8 CLOSE icons

Exercise 1-4:
Creating a New Drawing

Creating a New Drawing File:

The steps required to set up a new AutoCAD drawing file are very simple. The important thing to remember is to start with the correct template file, as this will save you lots of work!

To manually create a new drawing (maybe you just finished working on a previous assignment and want to start the next one):

1. Click the **Start** tab (Figure 1-4.1. – Step #1).
2. Click the **New** down-arrow (Step #2) and then select **Browse templates** (Step #3).
3. Select **Architectural Imperial.dwt** from the SheetSets folder and then click **Open**.

   IMPORTANT: This is the file you will use to start all drawings created in this book. The Sheet Sets *feature will be covered later in this book.*

   *FYI: The word "Imperial" simply refers to a drawing based on **feet and inches** rather than metric unit of measure.*

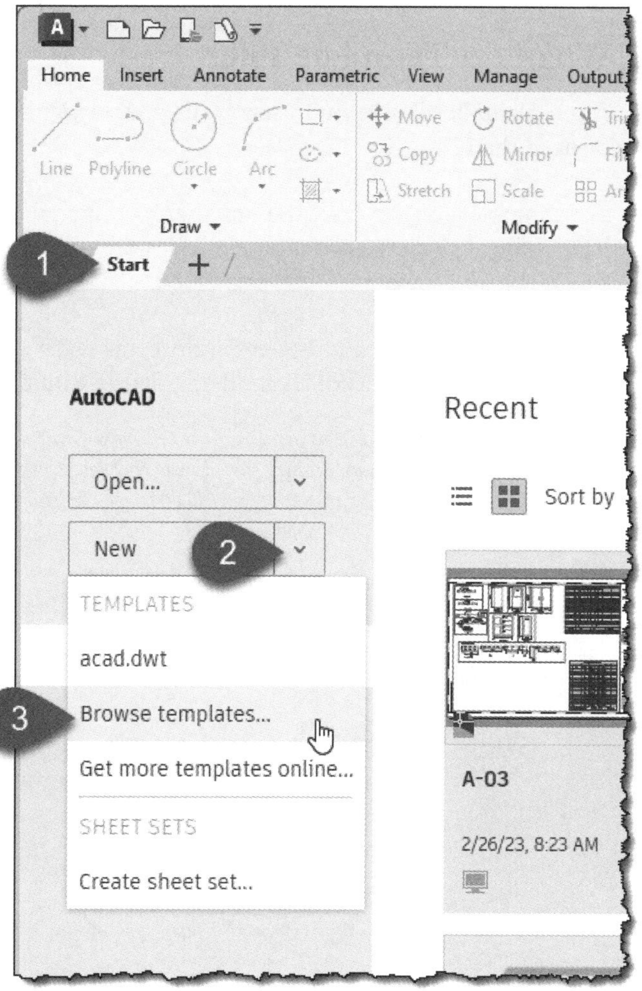

FIGURE 1-4.1 Creating new drawing

To name an unnamed drawing file, you simply save it. The first time an unnamed drawing file is saved, you will be prompted to specify the **name** <u>and</u> **location** for the drawing file.

4. Select the **Save** icon from the *Quick Access Toolbar*; you do not have to actually save your drawing at this time.

5. Specify a **name** and **location** for your new drawing file. *Your instructor may specify a location or folder for your files if you are in a classroom setting.*

   TIP: *You can also select the New Drawing icons on the Quick Access Toolbar or Drawings tab (Figure 1-4.2).*

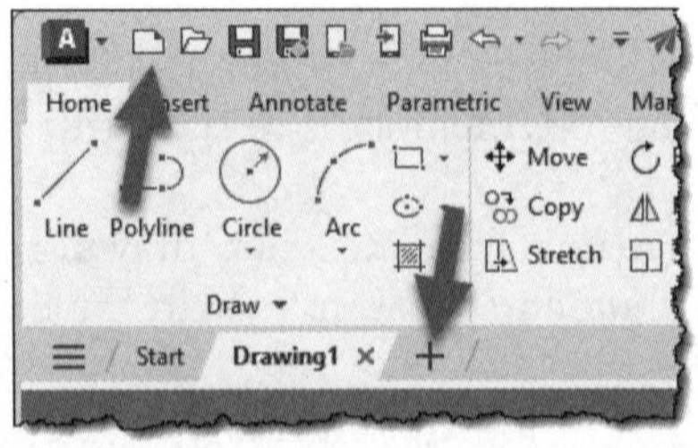

FIGURE 1-4.2 New drawing icon (QAT)

What is a Template File?

A template file allows you to start your drawing with certain settings preset the way you like or need them.

For example, you can have the units set to Imperial (i.e. feet and inches) or Metric. You can have things like dimension and text styles preloaded, etc. You can also have your company's title block and standard *Layers* preloaded.

A custom template is a must for design firms using AutoCAD and will prove useful to the student as he or she becomes more proficient with the program.

> ***BE AWARE:*** *It will be assumed from this point forward that the reader understands how to create, open and save drawing files. Please refer to this section as needed. If you still need further assistance, ask your instructor for help or search the AutoCAD Help system (more on how to do this at the end of the chapter).*

Exercise 1-5:
Using Zoom & Pan to View Your Drawings

Learning to *Pan* and *Zoom* in and out of a drawing is essential to accurate and efficient drafting and visualization. You will review these commands now so you are ready to use them with the first drawing exercise.

Open AutoCAD 2027:

You will select a sample file included with the files that came with the book.

1. Select **Open** on the *Quick Access* toolbar.

2. Open a file provided with this book: Browse to the following folder: **Sample Files\Residence**. See the inside front cover of this book for instructions on accessing the required custom sample files.

3. Select the file named **A1 - First Floor Plan.dwg** and click **Open**; your *Drawing* window should look similar to Figure 1-5.1.

   FYI: *If they are open, you can close the Tool Palette, Properties and Sheet Set Manager for now; just click the "X" in that palette's titlebar. These are like dialog boxes floating within the drawing area, which can remain open while you work.*

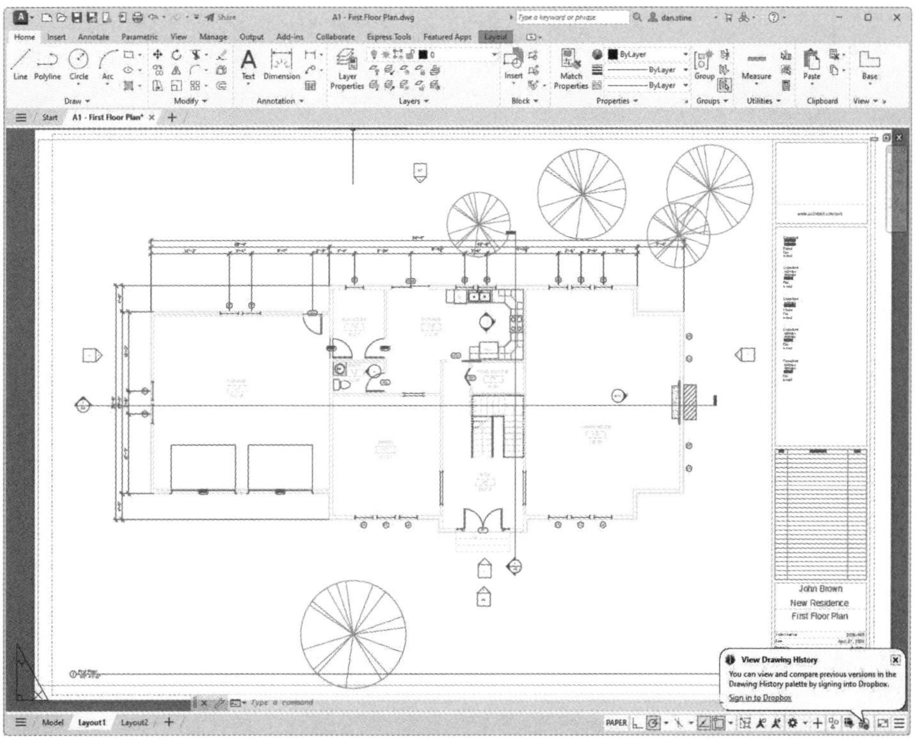

FIGURE 1-5.1 A1 - First Floor Plan.dwg drawing

Switching to Model Space:

The ***Layout* tab**(s) to the right of the ***Model* tab** is primarily used for printing sheets with drawings, details and title blocks composed on them.

> The *Model* tab (i.e., *Model Space*) is really where all the drawing is done. Then the drawings are arranged in *Layout Views* on sheets (e.g., 8 ½″ x 11″ or 24″ x 36″) for printing.

The *A1 - First Floor Plan* drawing should have opened with the ***Layout1*** tab current.

NOTE: Layout Views *can be named (or renamed) to anything you want; simply right-click on the tab and select* Rename.
(Exception: *You cannot rename the* Model *tab.)*

Next you will switch to the *Model Space* where you will learn to *Zoom* and *Pan* in a drawing.

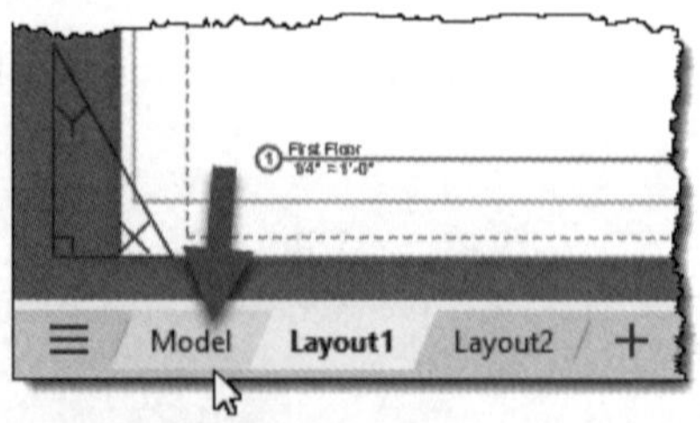

FIGURE 1-5.2 *Model* and *Layout* tabs below the *Drawing Window*

4. Click on the ***Model*** tab directly below the *Drawing Window* (Figure 1-5.2); you are now in *Model Space.*

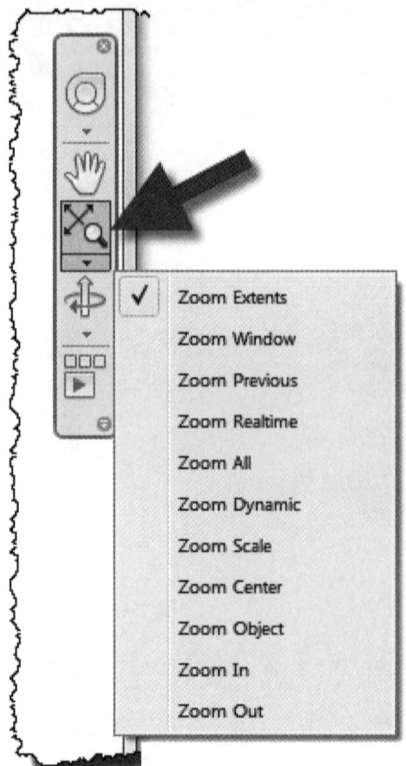

FIGURE 1-5.3 *Zoom* tools on the Navigation Bar

Using Zoom and Pan Tools:

You can access the zoom tools from the *Navigation Bar* or the *scroll wheel* on your mouse (the latter being the most used).

Click the down-arrow to see all of the options (Figure 1-5.3). The text label aptly describes what each zoom tool is programmed to do. The most used tools are **Zoom Window**, **Zoom Previous** and **Zoom Extents**. You will look at each of these plus the **Pan** tool located just above the **Zoom** icon.

Zoom In:

5. Select the Zoom **Window** tool by clicking on its icon (Figure 1-5.3).

6. Select a window over your floor plan. The dashed-line rectangle has been added to Figure 1-5.4 to describe where you should click.

   TIP: Click and release the mouse button; do not "drag."

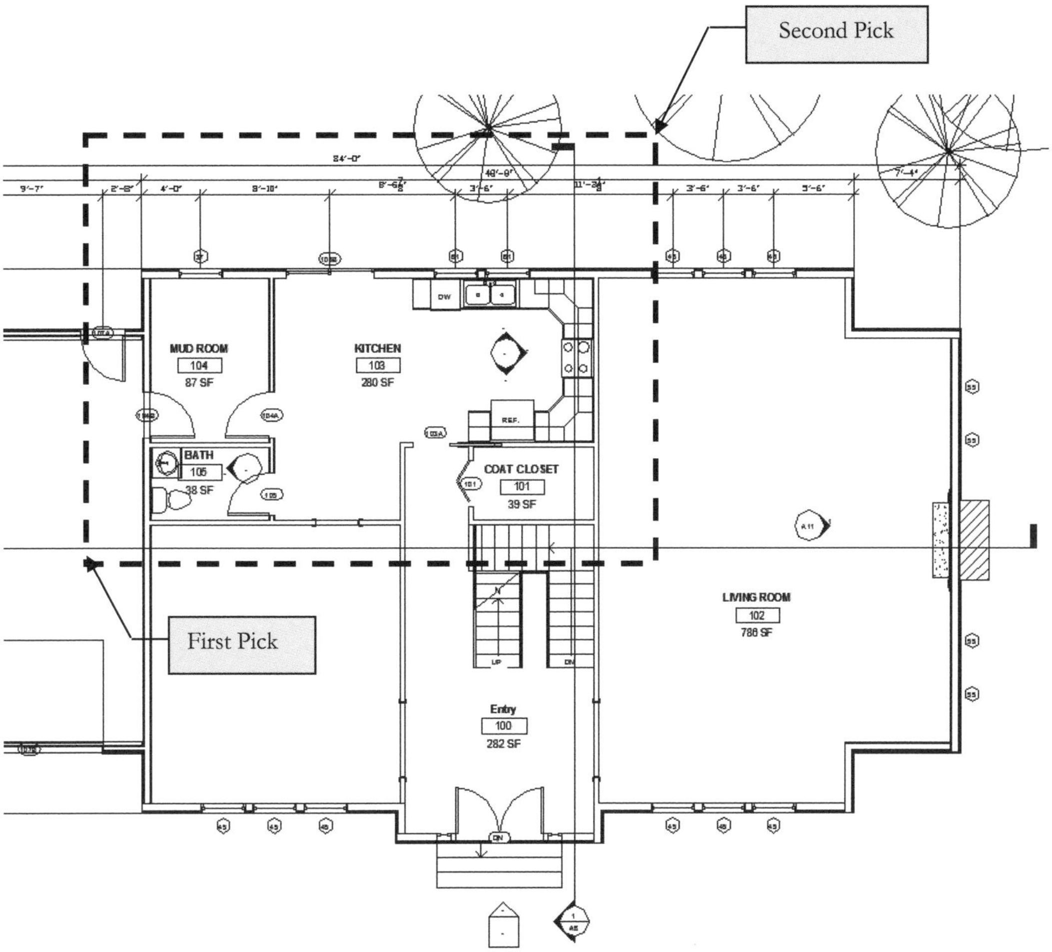

FIGURE 1-5.4 Zoom Window area

You should now be zoomed in to the specified area (Figure 1-5.5). Depending on the proportions of the rectangular area selected (and compared to the proportions of your monitor), the "zoomed in" area may be slightly larger in one direction.

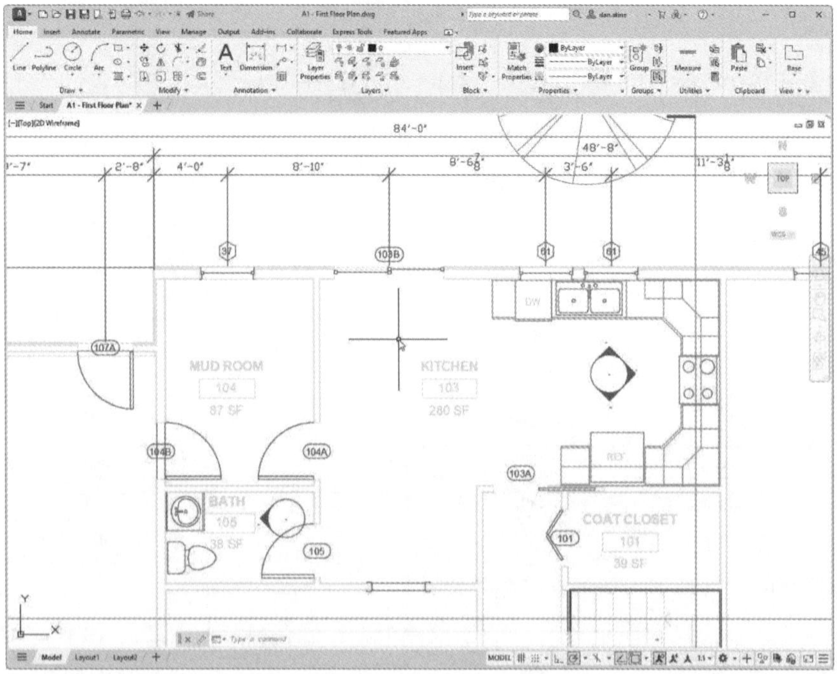

FIGURE 1-5.5 Zoom Window results

Zoom Previous:

7. Select the **Zoom Previous** tool by clicking on its icon in the *Navigation Bar* under the *Zoom* fly-out (Figure 1-5.3).

You should now be back where you started.

> *FYI: AutoCAD generates a smooth transition between zoom operations. This helps you keep track of where you are in the current drawing.*

Zoom Extents:

This tool allows you to quickly get to a view where you see everything in the current drawing; this is more useful if you are in a floor plan drawing rather than a drawing of all the utilities for an entire city (as you may essentially be zoomed too far out). If you have "garbage" lines way off to one side of your drawing, the main drawing area will not fill the screen (keep it clean!)

8. Select the **Zoom Extents** tool by clicking on its icon (Figure 1-5.3).

9. Take a minute and try the other zoom tools to see how they work. When finished, click **Zoom Extents** before moving on.

> *FYI: Whenever this book refers to clicking the mouse button, it is always referring to the left button. Any other variation will be specifically instructed. For example: Right-click on the OSNAP icon on the Status Bar.*

Pan:

The **Pan** tool allows you to slide the viewing area, in real-time, to a different part of a "zoomed in" drawing (floor plan, elevation, detail, etc.).

Panning is similar to using the horizontal and vertical scroll bars next to the drawing window (these are turned off by default), except you drag the mouse on the screen and are able to go in both directions at the same time (i.e., at an angle).

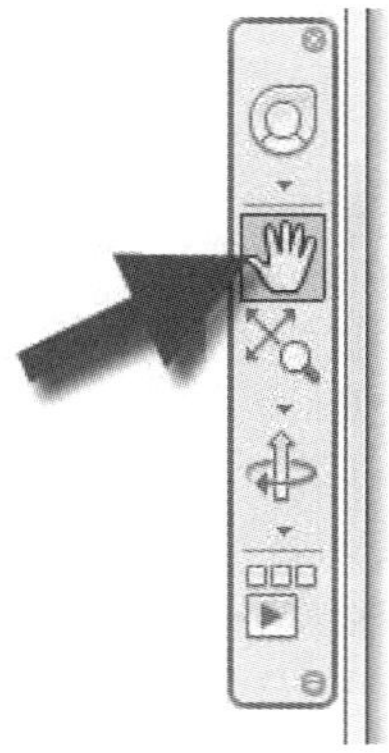

Real-time means that you see the drawing "smoothly" slide across the screen as you move the mouse. On older versions you would pick two points and then AutoCAD would move the drawing instantly from point A to point B with no "smooth" transition between.

10. Click the **Pan** icon; this icon is located in the *Navigation Bar* (see image to right).

You should now notice a **Hand Symbol** in place of the typical Arrow Pointer (or cursor). You can think of this hand as grabbing *Model Space* (when you hold down the mouse button) and "moving" it within the *Drawing* window.

11. Try panning around in the *A1 - First Floor Plan* drawing currently open on your computer; hold the mouse button down, drag the mouse, release the mouse button; drag again if you wish.

    BE AWARE: You are not moving the drawing. You are just changing what part of the drawing you see in the drawing window.

12. When you are done *Panning*, with the *Pan* tool still active, right-click anywhere in the *Drawing* window, and then select **Exit** from the pop-up menu (Figure 1-5.6), or press the *Esc* key.

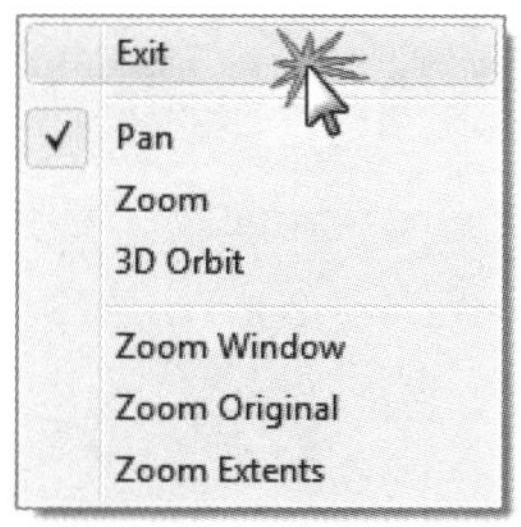

FIGURE 1-5.6 Pan right-click pop-up menu

Notice the other options you have in the pop-up menu shown in Figure 1-5.6. You can quickly toggle from **Pan** to **Zoom**, or **Zoom Window**, **Original** or **Extents**.

13. **Close** the *A1 - First Floor Plan* drawing without saving.

Using the Scroll Wheel on the Mouse:

Using a mouse with a scroll wheel is highly recommended for AutoCAD users. You can seamlessly perform most of the commands covered in this exercise without typing a command or clicking on any icons. Learning to use the wheel is so straightforward and intuitive that the following paragraph should be all that is required for you to start using the wheel productively!

The scroll wheel on the mouse is essential for CAD users. In AutoCAD you can Pan and Zoom without even clicking a zoom icon. You simply **scroll the wheel to Zoom** and **hold the wheel button down to Pan**. This can be done while in another command (e.g., while drawing lines). Another nice feature is that the drawing zooms into the area near your cursor, rather than zooming only at the center of the drawing window like the **Zoom In** tool does. Finally, if you double-click on the wheel, AutoCAD zooms the extents of the drawing.

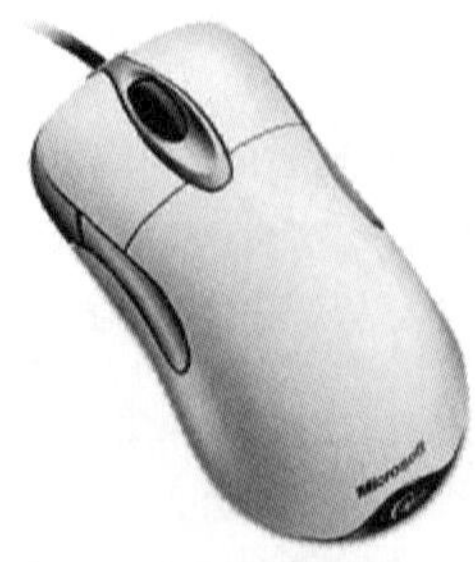

FIGURE 1-5.7 Microsoft's Optical IntelliMouse shown

The sample floor plan drawing used in this exercise is based on the residential project used in the author's textbook *Residential Design Using Autodesk Revit 2027*. The image below shows a rendering of the exterior of the building, similar to one created in that book.

RENDERING OF RESIDENTIAL PROJECT;
RESIDENTIAL DESIGN USING AUTODESK REVIT 2027

Exercise 1-6:
Using the AutoCAD Help System

The AutoCAD Help system can be very useful when you understand how it works. This exercise will walk you through the Help system user interface and the new AI-powered Autodesk Assistant.

Open AutoCAD 2027:

1. Select the **Help** icon (question mark) from the upper right corner of the program window (Figure 1-6.1).

   TIP: Click directly on the question mark; the small down-arrow reveals additional Help related items.

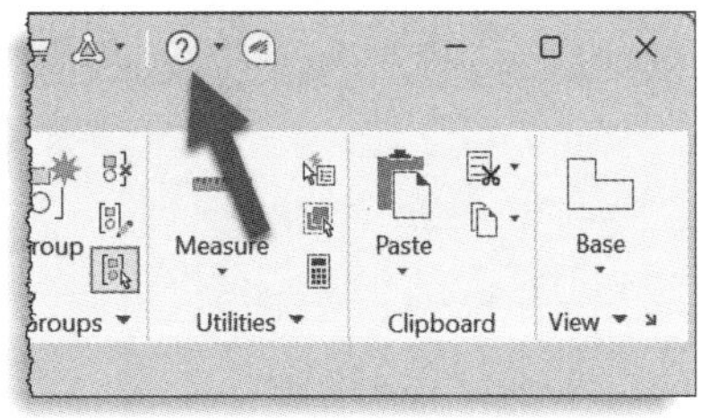

FIGURE 1-6.1 Help access icon

You should now be in AutoCAD's *Help* system window (Figure 1-6.2). The next section walks you through its various features. Note that the *Help* window is a local website that you may leave open while you return to AutoCAD. However, when you close AutoCAD the *Help* window will be closed as well. Finally, you may close the *Help* window at any time by clicking the "X" at the upper right.

Keyboard Shortcuts:

Many commands in AutoCAD have a keyboard shortcut, which means you can press a key(s) on the keyboard instead of clicking an icon or the application menu. **For example**: to start the **Line** command (and you are not currently in another command), you can type the letter **L** and then *Enter*. The Help system can be accessed by pressing **F1** on the keyboard.

Most advanced users employ a combination of keyboard and icon use. For a list of keyboard shortcuts, go to **Express Tools** (tab) → **Command Aliases**.

Exploring the Help System User Interface:

AutoCAD contains an extensive set of documentation on your computer's hard drive. This is basically your owner's manual; from this window you can research the "ins" and "outs" of the program.

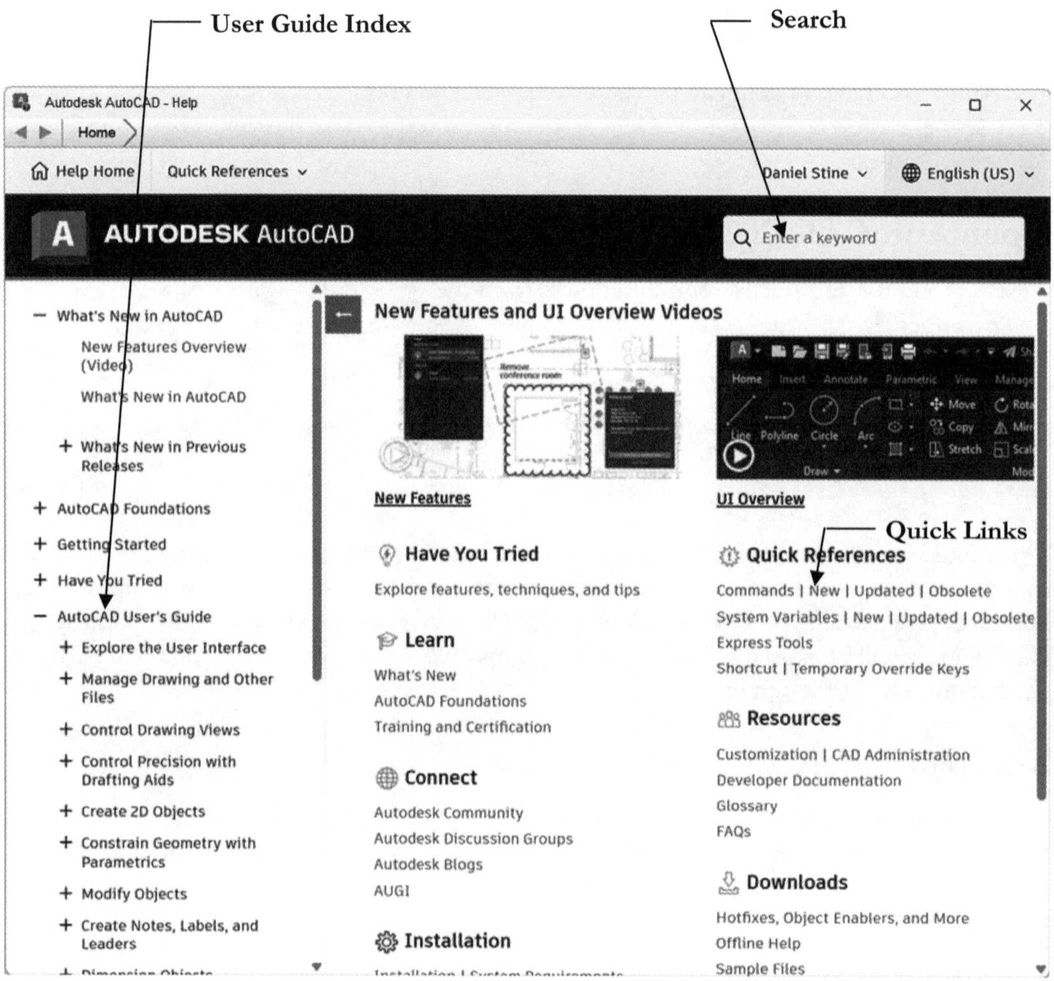

FIGURE 1-6.2 AutoCAD's Help system window

Help System in Action:

You will learn how to find information in the *Help System* on drawing *Circles.*

2. Click in the *Search* text box and enter **draw circle** (Figure 1-6.3).

3. Press **Enter**.

You should see the results shown in Figure 1-6.3. The results can be filtered using the red filter menu pointed out on the left (but, not now).

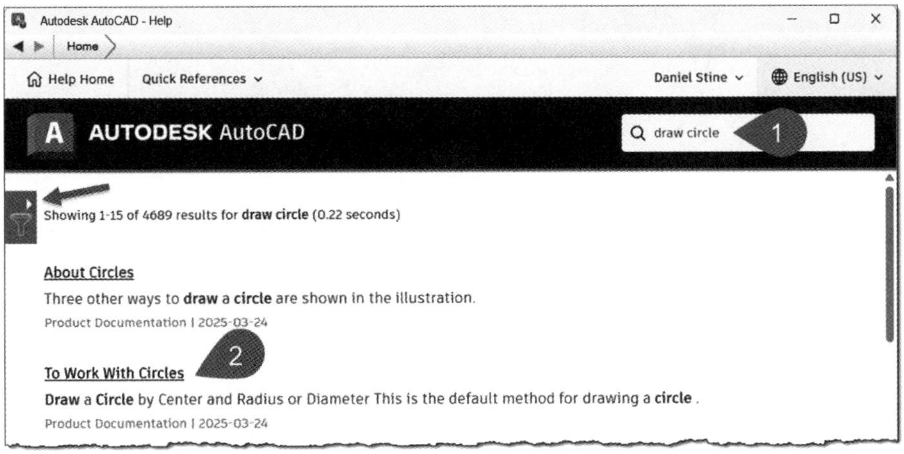

FIGURE 1-6.3 Search results

4. Click the link **To Work With Circles** (see Figure 1-6.3).

You will see specific instructions on drawing a circle in AutoCAD. Notice the various links near the bottom of the view contents window: Related Tasks, Related References, Related Concepts. These are all bits of information closely related to the main topic.

5. Click the **Home** link at the very top of the *Autodesk Help* screen to get back to the main *Help* interface (Figure 1-6.4).

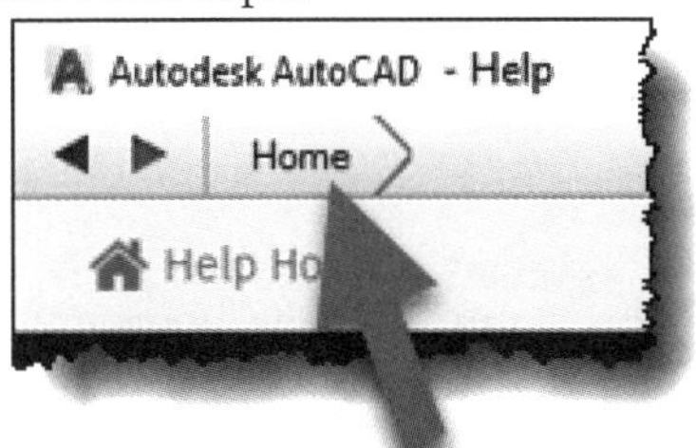

FIG 1-6.4 Help system: Home option

In some dialog boxes, like the **Plot** dialog shown in Figure 1-6.5, a Help button provides a direct link to related material in the AutoCAD Help system.

While in a command, pressing F1 will open Help with information about the current command selected.

While in Help, if you are not sure how to access a command in AutoCAD, click the **Find** icon when available (Figure 1-6.6). The command will be revealed in the AutoCAD UI with a red arrow pointing at it – this may involve a menu expanding.

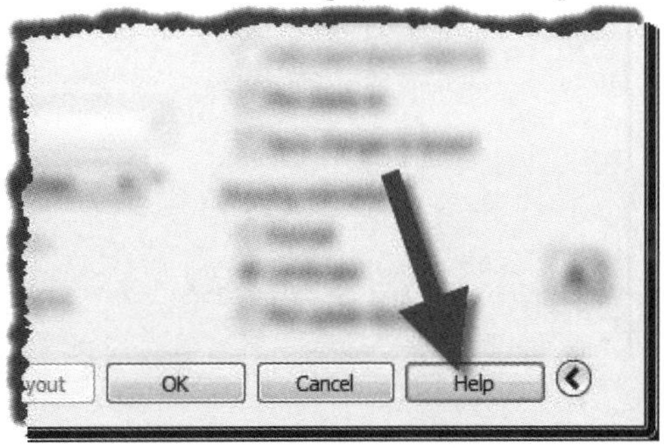

FIGURE 1-6.5 Help system: direct link

Discussion Groups:

You can also post questions in a user-to-user forum at Autodesk's website: http://forums.autodesk.com/. Here, other users can respond to your question. Sometimes you will get three ways to do the same thing. You choose which is best for you. However, beware, as not all replies will help, and some may create more problems.

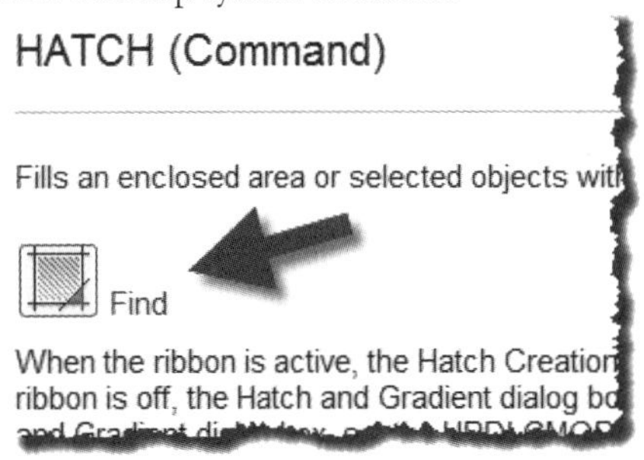

FIGURE 1-6.6 Find command in UI

Autodesk Assistant, Powered by AI:

The Autodesk Assistant is an AI-powered chatbot designed to answer questions within, and specific to, AutoCAD.

Here you are asked to describe your question in detail using complete sentences and then AutoCAD will use AI to get you to the right solution.

Here are some example questions:

- "Unhandled exception has occurred in a component"
- "Display file tabs was turned off"
- "How to create a Torus?"

When you type a question, such as "How do I draw a circle?", you will get a detailed response like the one shown in Figure 1-6.7. Below the response, it also lists the sources that can be used to verify the answers.

The box below the prompt input box says "Powered by AI. Mistakes are possible. Please double-check the responses."

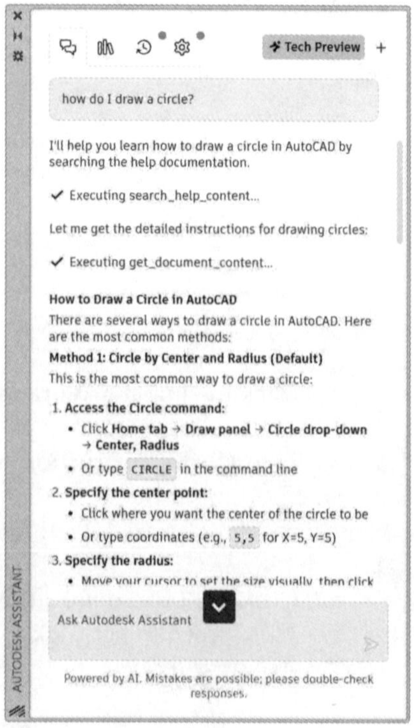

FIGURE 1-6.7 Autodesk Assistance

The example below shows how the Tech Preview, when enabled, can interact with your current drawing.

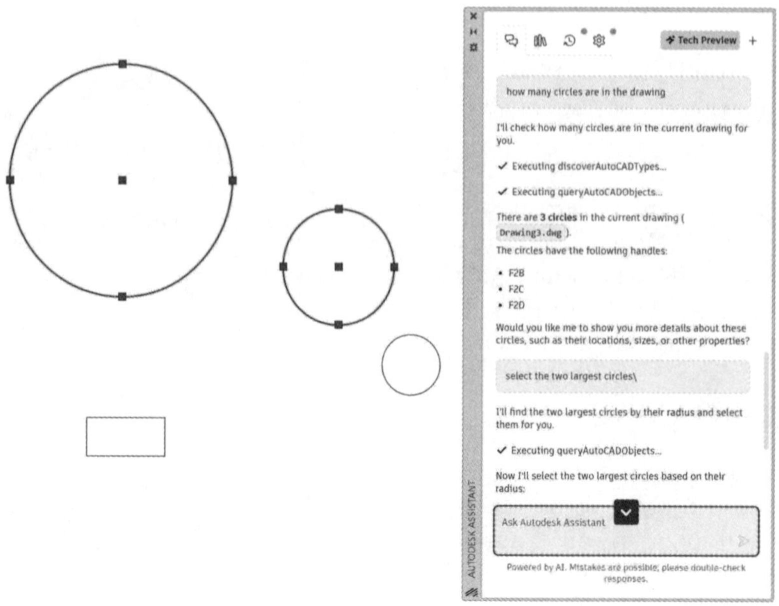

The feature will continue to develop and become more robust, so it is worth monitoring it.

Exercise 1-7:
Introduction to Autodesk Drive

We will finish this chapter with a look at Autodesk Drive, which is an integral foundation for much of Autodesk's **Cloud Services**. You do not necessarily need to use Autodesk's cloud services to complete this book successfully.

AUTODESK® **DRIVE**

Here is how Autodesk describes *Autodesk Drive* on their website:

Autodesk Drive is a cloud storage solution that allows individuals and small teams to organize, preview, and share any type of design or model data.

You can use Autodesk Drive to:

- Upload data to a personal cloud drive.
- Organize and manage your data into folders.
- View 2D and 3D designs and models within the browser on any device.
- Share files & folders with others for viewing, editing, uploading, and managing data.
- You can also access, view, and edit data that others have shared with you.
- With Desktop Connector installed, you can also view and organize files stored in Drive from your desktop and desktop applications.

The Cloud, Defined

Before we discuss *Autodesk Drive* with more specificity, let's define what the *Cloud* is. **The Cloud is a service, or collection of services, which exists partially or completely online.** This is different from the *Internet*, which mostly involves downloading static information, in that you are creating and manipulating data. Most of this happens outside of your laptop or desktop computer.

The cloud gives the average user access to massive amounts of storage space, computing power and software they could not otherwise afford if they had to actually own, install and maintain these resources in their office, school or home. In one sense, this is similar to a *Tool Rental Center*, in that the average person could not afford, nor would it be cost-effective to own, a jackhammer. However, for a fraction of the cost of ownership and maintenance, we can rent it for a few hours. In this case, everyone wins!

Creating an Autodesk Account

The first thing an individual needs to do in order to gain access to *Autodesk Drive* is create a free Autodesk account at drive.autodesk.com. If you are already using an Autodesk product, you likely already have an Autodesk account.

This account is for an individual person, not a computer, not an installation of Revit or AutoCAD, nor does it come from your employer or school. Each person who wishes to access *Autodesk Drive* services must create an account, which will give them a unique username and password.

Generally speaking, there are two ways you can access *Autodesk Drive* cloud services:

- Autodesk Drive website
- Within Revit or AutoCAD; local computer

Autodesk Drive Website

When you have documents stored in the *Cloud* you can access them via your web browser. Here you can manage your files, view them without the full application (some file formats are not supported) and share them. These features use some advanced browser technology, so you need to make sure your browser is up to date; Chrome works well.

Using the website, you can upload files from your computer to store in the *Cloud.* To do this, you create or open a **Folder** and click the **Upload** option (Fig. 1-7.1).

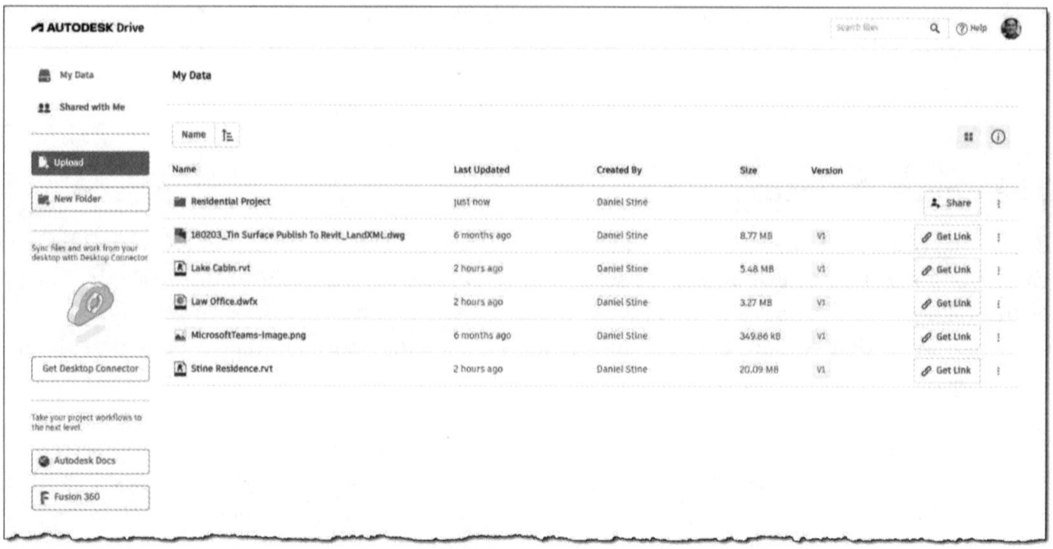

FIGURE 1-7.1 Viewing files stored in the cloud

Tip: If using a modern browser, you can drag and drop documents onto the window. This is a great way to create a secure backup of your documents.

You can share files stored in the *Cloud* with others. Simply hover over a file within *Autodesk DRIVE* and click the **Get Link** icon to see the Share dialog (Figure 1-7.2). Anyone who has this link can view and download (if Allow Downloads is toggled on) the files shared.

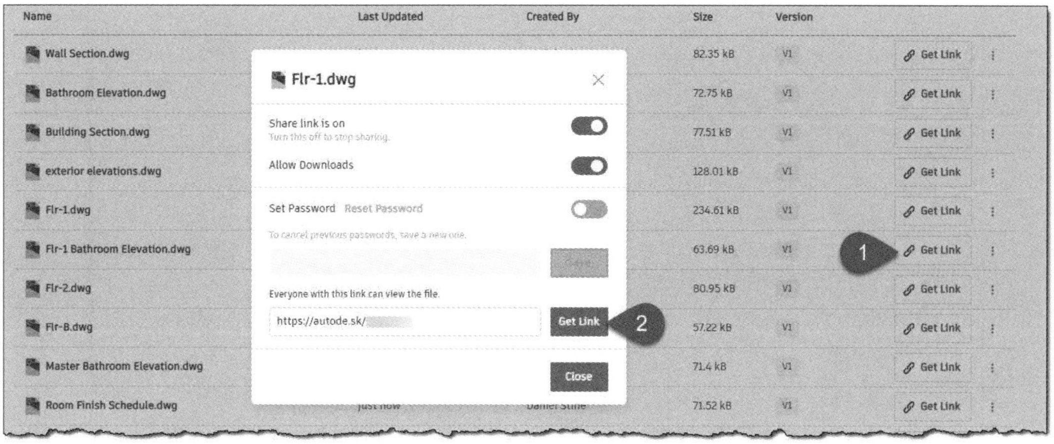

FIGURE 1-7.2 Sharing files stored in the cloud

Installing Autodesk Desktop Connector

To sync the Autodesk Drive files with your local computer and work directly on the files, you must first download Autodesk Desktop Connector. This tool creates an environment similar to OneDrive or Dropbox but with enhanced features supporting Autodesk-specific CAD and BIM workflows.

To install Desktop Connector, first close any open Autodesk products, such as AutoCAD. Then click the **Get Desktop Connector** button (Fig. 1-7.1) to access the download page. Download the latest version and install it.

Files are now synced locally and found via **This PC** within Windows Explorer (Fig. 1-7.3).

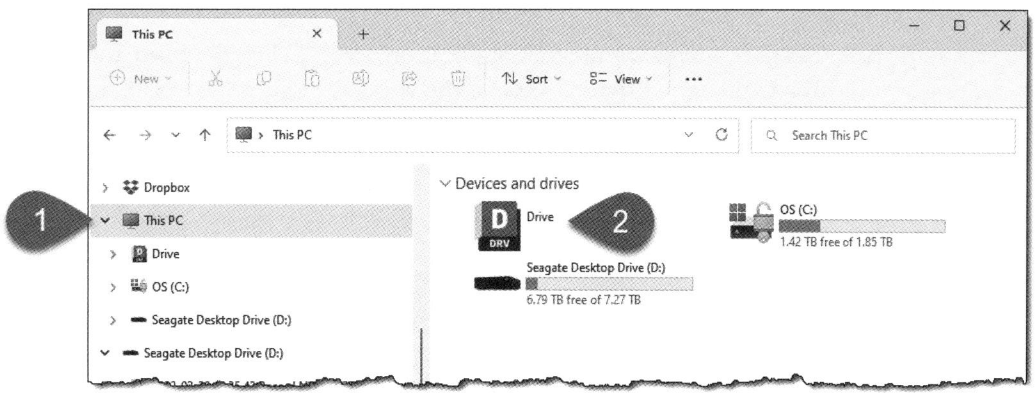

FIGURE 1-7.3 Accessing Drive files via Desktop Connector

The same cloud-based files appear locally, as shown below (Fig. 1-7.4).

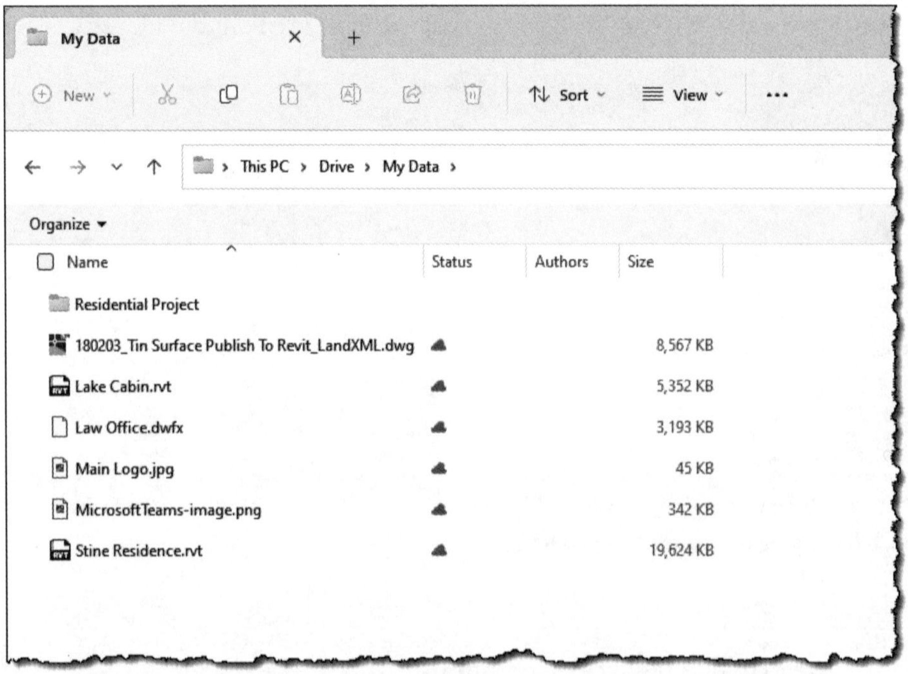

FIGURE 1-7.4 Accessing Drive files via Desktop Connector

Accessing Autodesk DRIVE within your CAD/BIM application

Another way in which you can access your data, stored in the cloud, is from within your Autodesk application; for example, Revit or AutoCAD. This is typically the most convenient, as you can open, view and modify your drawings. Once logged in, you will also have access to any *Cloud Services* available to you from within the application, such as rendering services or *Green Building Studio.*

To sign into your *Autodesk Account* within your application, simply click the **Sign In** option in the notification area in the upper right corner of the window. You will need to enter your student email address and password, or work/personal email if you are not a student. When properly logged in, you will see your username or email address listed, as shown in Figure 1-7.5 below. Note: most likely, you are already signed in, as this is required to use most Autodesk products.

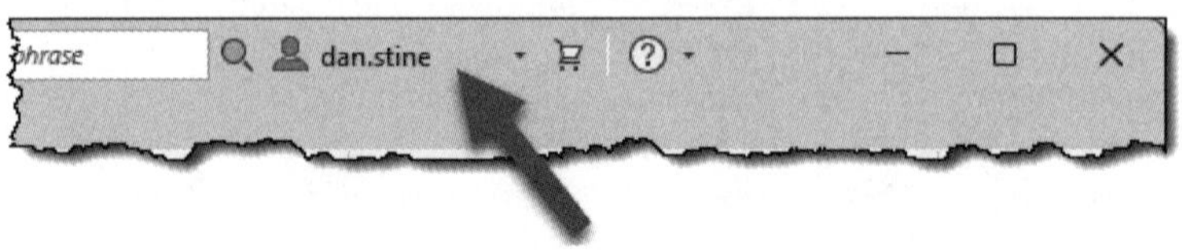

FIGURE 1-7.5 Example of user logged into their Autodesk account

The files within Autodesk Drive may be accessed via the **Open** dialog, as shown in Figure 1-7.6 below. Working on the files in this location ensures they are automatically backed up every time you save your work.

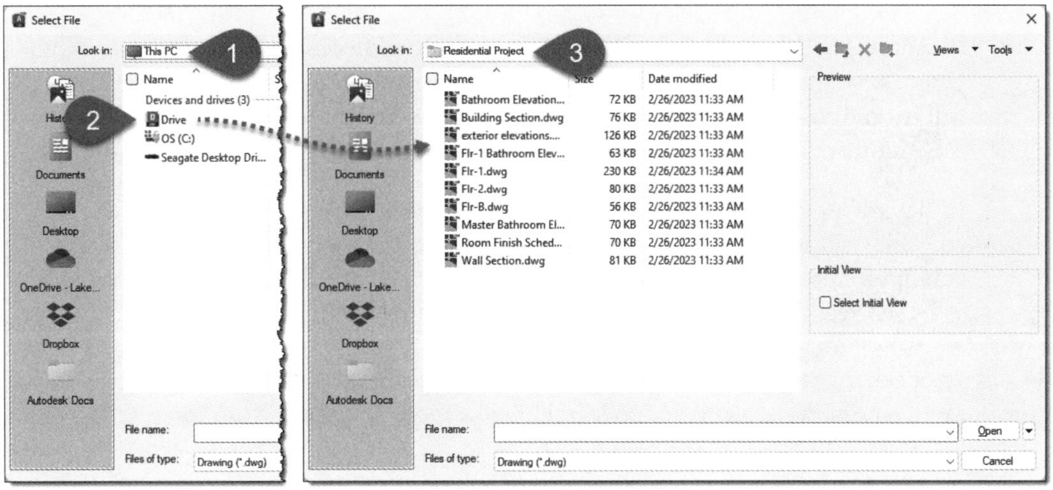

FIGURE 1-7.6 Accessing Autodesk Drive within AutoCAD or Revit

Notice that once a file has been modified, you can tell by the **Version** being incremented in Autodesk Drive when viewed in your browser, as shown below (Fig. 1-7.7).

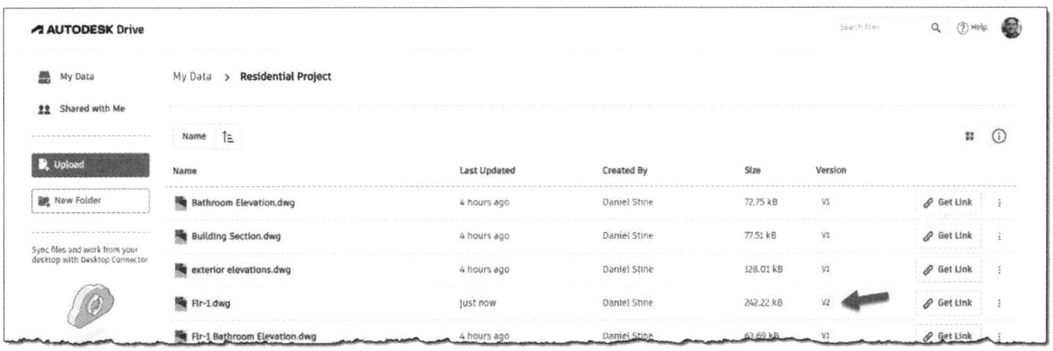

FIGURE 1-7.7 Accessing Autodesk Drive within AutoCAD or Revit

When using AutoCAD, and when sharing files with others via Drive, only one person may modify a DWG file at a time. Similarly, when working with Revit models, an additional paid service called BIM 360 Collaborate Pro is required for multiple users to work within the same BIM.

It is recommended, as you work though this book, that you save all of your work in the *Cloud*, via Autodesk Drive, so you will have a safe and secure location for your files. These files can then be accessed from several locations via the two methods discussed here. It is still important to maintain a separate copy of your files on a flash drive, portable hard drive or in another *Cloud*-type location such as *Dropbox*. This will be important if your main files ever become corrupt. You should manually back up your files to your backup location, so a corrupt file does not automatically corrupt your backup files.

TIP: If you have a file that will not open try one of the following:

- In AutoCAD: Open AutoCAD and then, from the *Application Menu*, select Drawing Utilities → Recover → Recover. Then browse to your file and open it. AutoCAD will try and recover the drawing file. This may require some things to be deleted but is better than losing the entire file.

- In Revit: Open Revit and then, from the *Application Menu*, select Open, browse to your file, and select it. Click the Audit check box, and then click Open. Revit will attempt to repair any problems with the project database. Some elements may need to be deleted, but this is better than losing the entire file.

Be sure to check out the Autodesk website to learn more about Autodesk BIM 360 Collaborate Pro and the growing number of cloud services Autodesk is offering.

Self-Exam:

The following questions can be used as a way to check your knowledge of this lesson. The answers can be found at the bottom of the next page.

1. The *Modify* panel allows you to save your drawing file. (T/F)

2. You can zoom in and out using the wheel on a wheel mouse. (T/F)

3. AutoCAD is made specifically for architectural design. (T/F)

4. A ______________ file allows you to start your drawing with certain settings preset the way you like or need them.

5. In the AutoCAD user interface, the ________________________ displays prompts for specific user input.

Review Questions:

The following questions may be assigned by your instructor as a way to assess your knowledge of this section. Your instructor has the answers to the review questions.

1. Many commands have a keyboard shortcut. (T/F)

2. AutoCAD does not provide much in the way of online documentation. (T/F)

3. The drawings listed in the *Open Documents* menu allow you to see which drawings are currently open. (T/F)

4. When you use the **Pan** tool you are actually moving the drawing, not just changing what part of the drawing you can see on the screen. (T/F)

5. To *close* AutoCAD you simply click the X in the upper right. (T/F)

6. The icon with the floppy disk image ( ) allows you to ____________________ a drawing file.

7. A *Ribbon* "panel" with a small black down-arrow to the right of the label has additional tools in an extended panel fly-out. (T/F)

8. Use the __________________________ tool to switch the view back to the one just prior to your last zoom command.

9. Holding the Scroll Wheel down initiates the _____________ command.

10. The **Model** tab (aka Model Space) is where most of the actual drafting and design is done. (T/F)

SELF-EXAM ANSWERS:
1 – F, **2** – T, **3** – F, **4** – Template, **5** – Command Window

Notes:

Lesson 2
Crash Course Introduction (the Basics):

This lesson is meant to give you a brief introduction to a few of the most used commands. You will be walked through each drawing in this lesson, step-by-step. The intent is for the user to get some of the basic concepts in mind before going through subsequent chapters.

Exercise 2-1:
Lines and Shapes

Drawing Lines:

The number one command in AutoCAD is the **Line** command. Lines in AutoCAD are extremely precise drawing elements. This means you can create very accurate drawings. Lines, or any drawn object, can be as precise as eight decimal places (i.e., 24.999999999) or 1/256.

AutoCAD is a vector-based program. That means each drawn object is stored in a numerical database. For example, a line is stored in the drawing's database as the X,Y,Z coordinates for its starting point and the X,Y,Z, coordinates for its endpoint. These coordinates are all relative to the drawing's 0,0,0 position, called the **Origin**.

When a line needs to be displayed on the screen, AutoCAD reads the line's coordinates from the drawing database and displays a line between those two points on the screen. This means that the line will be very accurate at any scale or zoom magnification.

A raster-based program, in contrast to vector based, is comprised of dots that infill a grid. The grid can vary in density and is typically referred to by its resolution (e.g., 600x800, 1600x1200, etc.). This file type is used by graphics programs that typically deal with photographs, such as Adobe Photoshop. There are two reasons this type of file is not appropriate for CAD programs:

- A raster-based line is composed of many dots on a grid (which also represents the line's width). When you zoom in (or magnify) the line, it becomes pixilated and you actually start to see each dot in the grid. In a vector file you can "infinitely" zoom in on a line and it will never become pixilated because the program recalculates the line each time you zoom in.

- A CAD program, such as AutoCAD, only needs to store the starting point and end point coordinates for each line; the dots needed to draw the line are calculated on the fly for the current screen resolution, whereas a raster file has to store each dot that represents the full length and width of the line. This can vary from a few hundred dots to several thousand dots, depending on the resolution, for the same line.

The following graphic illustrates this point:

Vector vs. Raster lines

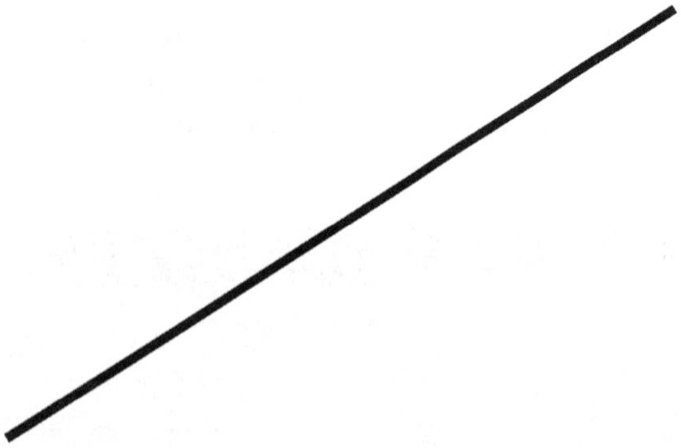

FIGURE 2-1.1 Vector Line Example
File Size: approx. 33kb

FIGURE 2-1.1A Vector Line Enlarged 1600%

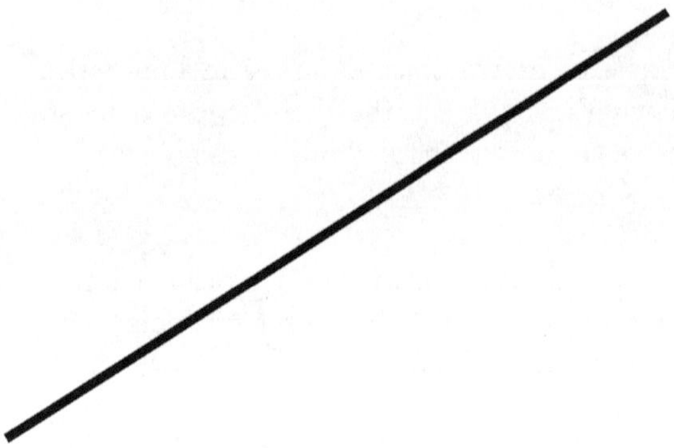

FIGURE 2-1.2 Raster Line Example
File Size: approx. 4.4MB

FIGURE 2-1.2A Raster Line Enlarged 1600%

The Line Command:

You will now study the **Line** command.

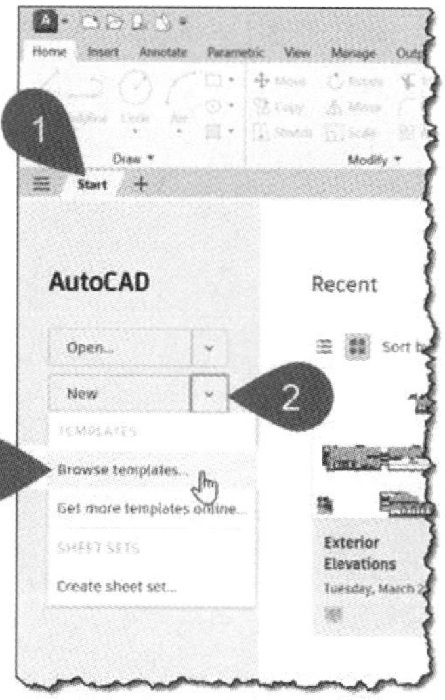

1. **Open** AutoCAD; maximize the application so it fills the screen.

2. You are on the **Start** tab.

3. Click the down-arrow next to the word **New** and select **Browse Templates…** (see image to right).

   WARNING: The default startup drawing that is opened by clicking directly in the word 'New' does not have the various variables preset for architectural CAD use. Once you select a different template, in the next step, it will become the default; this only applies to the computer you are on.

4. In the SheetSets folder, select **Architectural Imperial.dwt**.

5. In the lower-left corner of the screen, click the ***Model*** tab to switch to *Model Space* (which is where all the drawing is done as previously mentioned); see Figure 2-1.3.

   a. Turn off the *Grid Display* toggle if it is on (via the *Status Bar*).

   NOTE: Your Drawing Window *background should be black – the images in the book have it set to white for clarity in printing.*

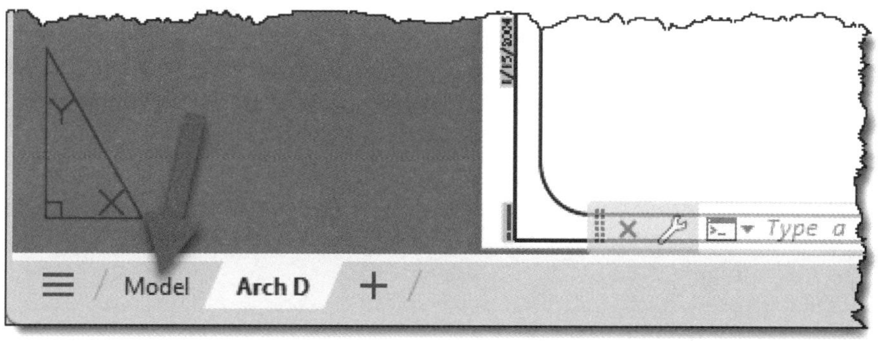

FIGURE 2-1.3 Switching to Model space

6. Select the **Line** tool (*Home* tab, *Draw* panel).

7. **Draw a line** from the lower left corner of the screen to the upper right corner of the screen (by simply clicking two points on the screen); see **Figure 2-1.4**.

   TIP: When clicking the second point, do not click on, or over, the ViewCube in the upper right. See Figure 1-2.1.

   NOTE: Do not drag/hold your mouse button down; just click.

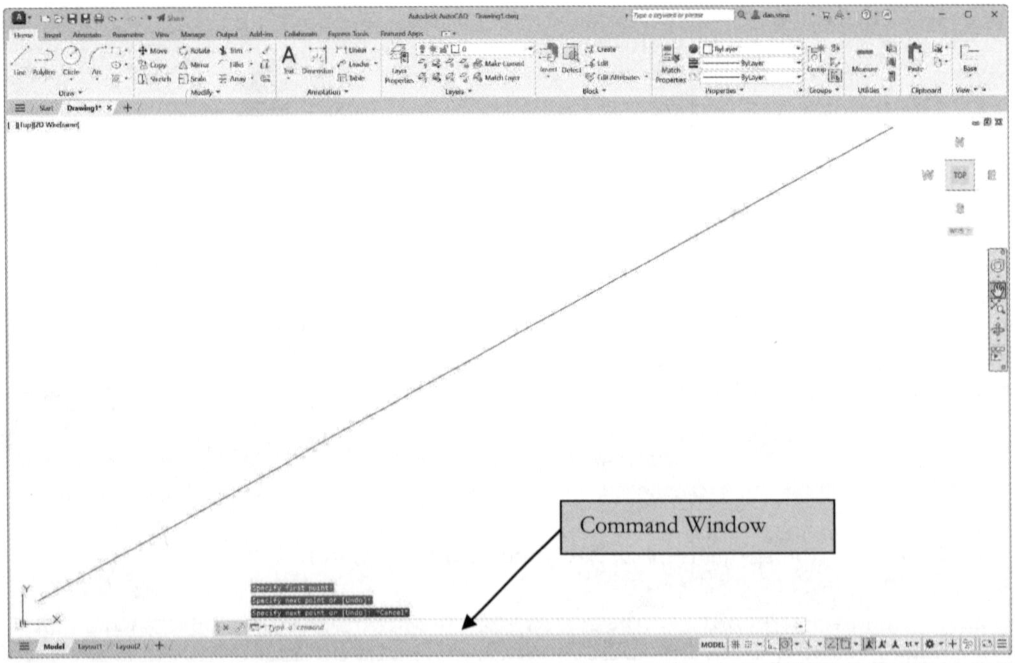

FIGURE 2-1.4 Your first line!

After clicking your second point, you should notice by looking at the *Command Window* that the **Line** command is still active. You could continue to draw lines, with the last point picked becoming the first point for the next line segment. In this case, you will end the **Line** command per the following instructions.

8. After clicking your second point (i.e., the endpoint), **right-click** anywhere on the screen and select **Enter** from the pop-up menu (Figure 2-1.5).

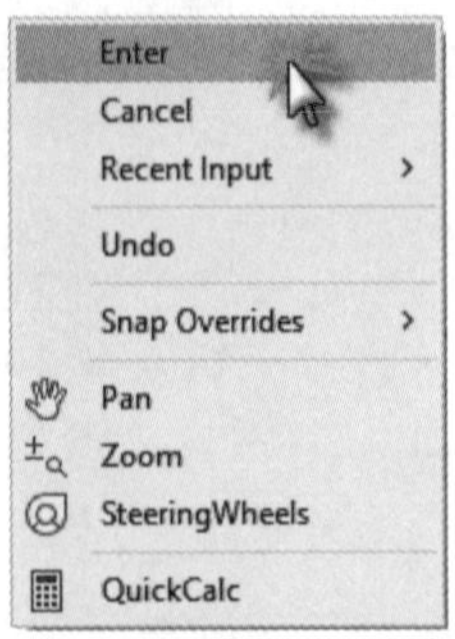

FIGURE 2-1.5 Right-click Menu; Line command active

This constitutes your first line! However, as you are probably aware, it is not very accurate in terms of length and angle.

FYI: Your line length and proportions may vary slightly from the image above and the following few steps based on your screen size and resolution. This will not negatively affect your ability to complete this section. In any case, you should maximize the AutoCAD program, so you see the largest drawing window possible.

The Properties Palette:

Typically, you need to provide information such as length and angle when drawing a line; you rarely pick arbitrary points on the screen as you did in the previous steps. Most of the time, you also need to accurately pick your starting point (for example, how far one line is from another or picking the exact middle point on another line).

> **DID YOU MAKE A MISTAKE?** LOCATION: *QUICK ACCESS TOOLBAR*
>
> Whenever you make a mistake in AutoCAD you can use the **UNDO** command to revert to a previous drawing state. You can perform multiple UNDOs all the way to your previous *Save* (and then some).
>
> Similarly, if you press **Undo** a few too many times, you can use **REDO**.

Having said that, however, the line you just drew still has precise numbers associated with its length and angle. In the next step you will use the *Properties* palette to view the line's length and angle.

9. Select the **Properties** icon (**View** tab, *Palettes* panel) or press Ctrl + 1.

Properties

You now have the *Properties* palette open on your screen. Notice that the textbox at the top says "*No selection*"; this is because no objects are selected yet (Figure 2-1.6).

TIP: If the Properties *palette is too narrow on the screen, some information may not be completely visible. You can easily resize any palette by dragging one of the three sides (opposite the palette title bar).*

Now that the *Properties* palette is open, you can select the line to display its properties.

10. **Select the Line**; hover the cursor over the line and click on it.

FYI: Notice the line highlights before you select it. This helps to select the correct line the first time.

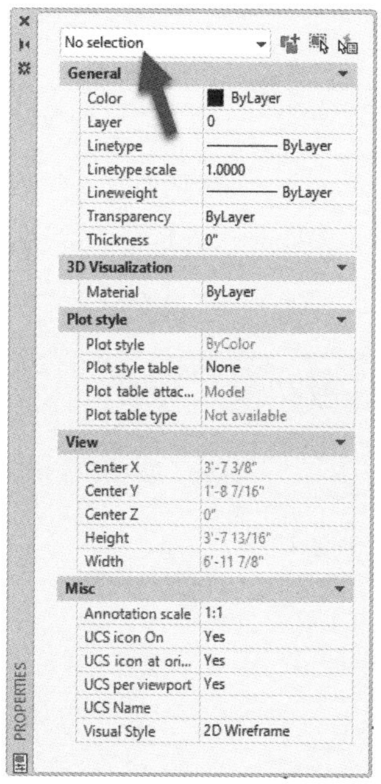

FIGURE 2-1.6 Properties Palette; No objects selected

You should now see the line's properties. Notice the textbox at the top now indicates what type of object is selected (Figure 2-1.7).

Are Your Units and Drawing Window Size Correct?

If the properties on your computer are displaying the line's data in decimals instead of feet and inches (as shown in Figure 2-1.7), that means you did not start using the correct template file.

Similarly, if your *Drawing Window* is not approximately 5′-8″ x 3′-1″ then you either started with the wrong template or your template file has been altered; if the latter is the case, which is less likely, zoom in (or out) to "correct" the screen display for this exercise.

If you started with the wrong template, you should close the drawing and start this lesson over.

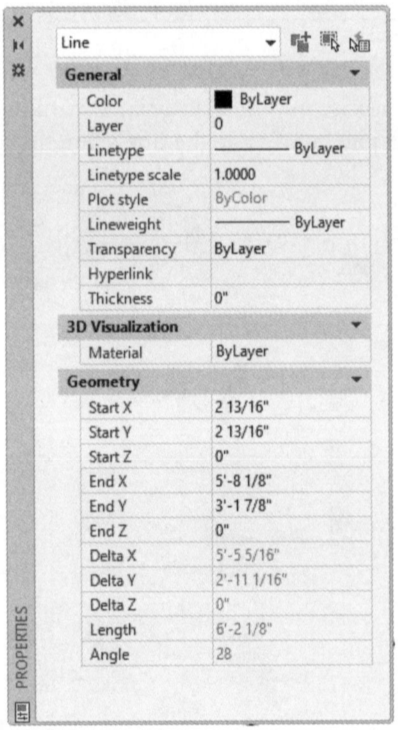

FIGURE 2-1.7
Properties palette; Line selected

Notice the information displayed for the selected line:

- The X, Y and Z coordinates are listed, relative to the drawing's origin (0,0,0), for both the start and end points.
- The line's Length and Angle are listed.
- Delta X and Delta Y; the Delta X is the horizontal distance between the start point and the end point.

The black text are editable values and the grey text are not. You cannot edit the length, for example, because AutoCAD needs more info, like what direction to make the line longer.

You should make one final observation about the line's properties and the current view: the Delta X and Delta Y represent the horizontal and vertical distances between the line's start and end points. This tells us that the drawing area, currently visible on the screen, is about 5′-8″ across (horizontally) and 3′-1″ up and down (vertically). That means that the largest item we can draw (and still see what we are doing) is something that is 5′-8″ wide x 3′-1″ tall. (See Figure 2-1.8.)

> ***RECAP:*** *At any given time you could draw a diagonal line, from one corner of the Drawing window to the other, list that line's Properties, observe the Delta X and Delta Y values, and infer from that information the current drawing area that you are zoomed into.*

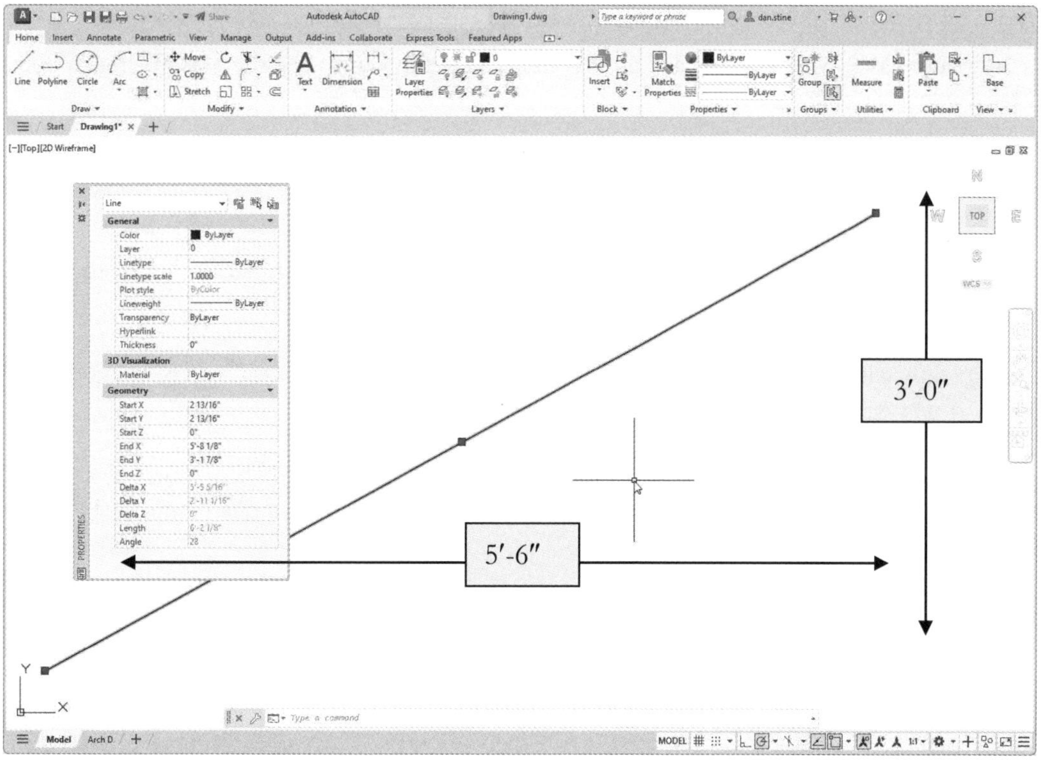

FIGURE 2-1.8 Visible area of current drawing

Everything is Drawn Full-Scale:

Even though your current view is showing a relatively small area, *Model Space* (where you do all your drafting and design) is actually an infinite drawing board.

In architectural CAD drafting, everything is drawn "real-world" size (or full-scale). ALWAYS! If you are drawing a building, you might draw a line for the exterior wall that is 600′-0″ long. If you are drawing a window detail, you might draw a line that is ⅛″ long. In either case you are entering that line's actual length.

You could, of course, have a ⅛″ line and a 600′-0″ line in the same drawing. Either line would be difficult to see at the current drawing magnification (i.e., approx. 5′-5″x3′-2″ area). So you would have to zoom in to see the ⅛″ line and zoom out to see the 600′-0″ line. You will try this next:

Draw a ⅛″ Line:

11. For now, **Close** the *Properties* palette by clicking the **X** in the upper corner of the palette.

The next steps will walk you through drawing a ⅛″ horizontal line. AutoCAD provides more than one way to do this. You will try one of them now.

You should understand that it is virtually impossible to draw a perfectly horizontal or vertical (or any precise angle) line by visually picking points on the screen. You need AutoCAD's help!

12. On the *Status Bar*, make sure **Polar Tracking** is turned on (Figure 2-1.9). *It should have a bluish highlight when turned on.*

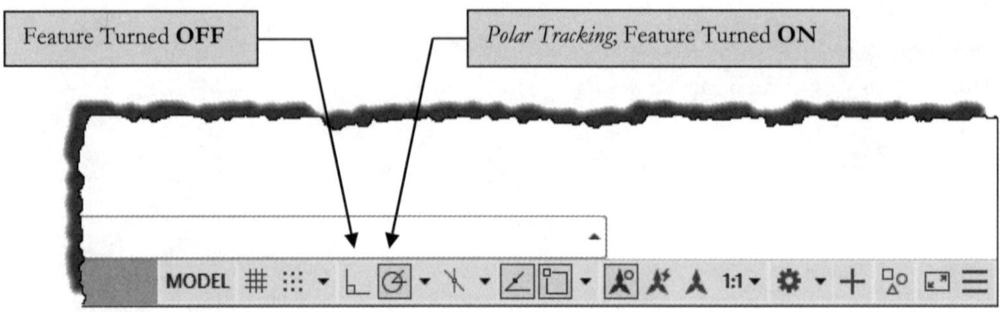

FIGURE 2-1.9 Status Bar – shown with Polar Tracking turned on.

TIP: You can adjust the Polar Tracking *settings by right-clicking on the button and selecting Tracking* Settings.

> **Polar Tracking:**
> This drawing aid feature allows you to draw lines at precise angles. When you are in the process of drawing a line, *Polar Tracking* will "snap" to certain angles in the *Drawing* window whenever your cursor comes close to that angle.
>
> A dashed line will appear on the screen giving you a visual tip that the line is "snapped" to one of the predefined angles set within the *Polar Tracking* settings. In addition to the dashed line, the tooltip (near your cursor) displays the word *Polar* and the locked angle.
>
> Clicking the mouse or entering a length while the dashed line is visible ensures the line's proper angle.

13. Using the **Line** command, pick a point somewhere in the upper left corner of the *Drawing* window.

14. Start moving the mouse towards the right and generally horizontal until you see a dashed reference line (extending off the screen in the direction you want to draw the line) appear on the screen as in Figure 2-1.10.

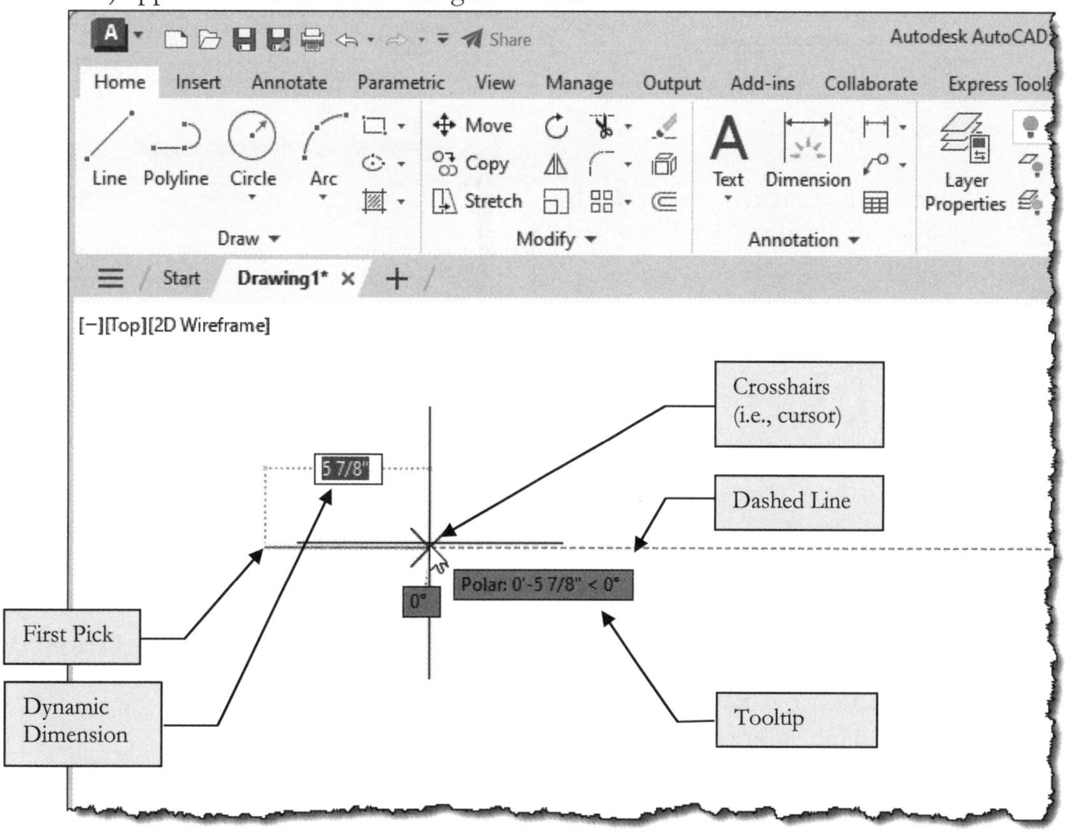

FIGURE 2-1.10 Drawing a line with the help of Polar Tracking

FYI: In order to see the on-screen dimension and the tooltip, you need to make sure the ***Dynamic Input*** *icon is toggled on, which it is by default. The toggle for this can be displayed on the Status Bar but is hidden by default. Clicking the last icon on the Status Bar reveals a list where Dynamic Input can be added to the Status Bar. Please do not chance this at this time.*

15. With the dashed line and *tooltip* visible on the screen, take your hand off the mouse (so you don't accidentally move it), type **1/8** and then press **Enter**; finish the **Line** command. **Right-click** and select **Enter** to finish the line command (you can also press the *Esc* key on the keyboard to finish).

TIP: Notice you did not have to type the inch symbol; in an "Imperial" template-based drawing AutoCAD always assumes you mean inches unless you specify otherwise. A future lesson will review the input options in a little more detail.

You have just drawn a line with a precise length and angle!

16. Use the ***Properties*** palette to verify it was drawn correctly (similar to Steps 9 and 10); check the *length* and *angle* values.

17. Use the **Zoom Window** tool to enlarge the view of the ⅛" line (or – *better* – use your wheel mouse).

18. Now use the **Zoom Extents** tool so that both lines are visible again (or double-click on the wheel button).

Draw a 600′ line:

19. Select the **Line** icon and pick a point in the lower right corner of the *Drawing* window.

FYI: Selecting a tool cancels any active command.

20. Move the crosshairs (i.e., mouse) straight up from your first point so that *Polar Tracking* activates (Figure 2-1.11).

21. With the dashed line and tooltip visible on the screen, take your hand off the mouse (so you don't accidentally move it), and type **600′** and then press **Enter**.

TIP: Notice this time you had to type the foot symbol (′) or AutoCAD would have assumed you meant 600 inches, which is only 50′.

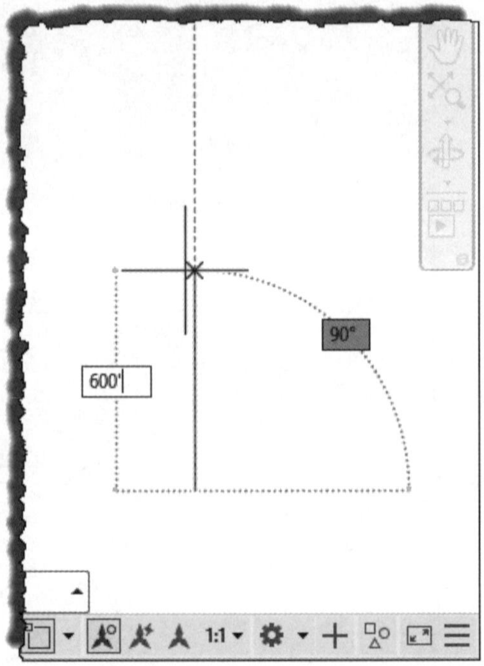

FIGURE 2-1.11 Drawing another line with the help of Polar Tracking

22. End the **Line** command *(right-click and select Enter or press the Esc key).*

Because the visible portion of the drawing area is only 3′-2″ tall (Figure 2-1.8), you obviously would not expect to see a 600′ line. You need to change the drawing's magnification (i.e., zoom out) to see it.

23. Use **Zoom Extents** to see the entire drawing (Figure 2-1.12) – the icon on the *Navigation Bar* is pointed out in the image below *(or double-click the center wheel mouse button).*

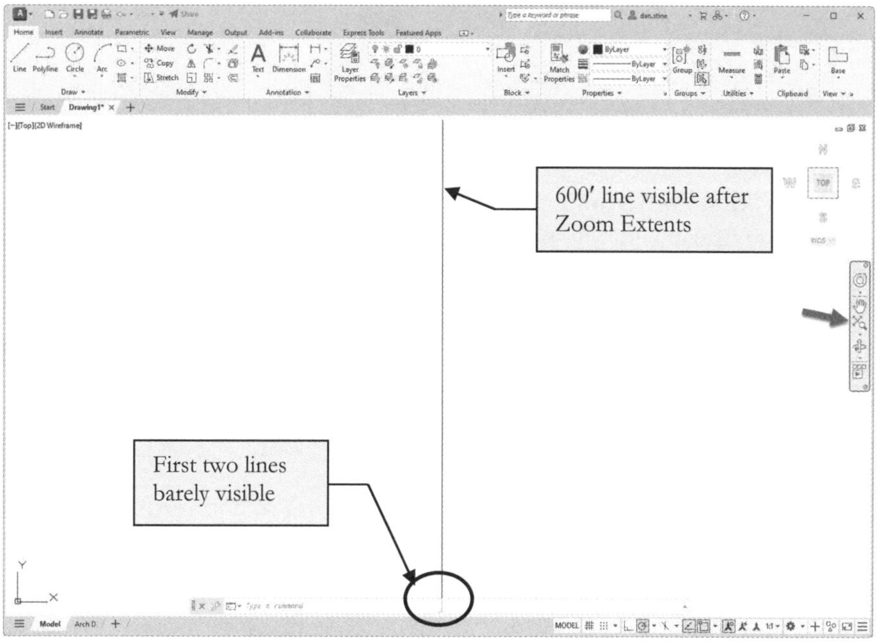

FIGURE 2-1.12 Drawing with three lines

Drawing Shapes:

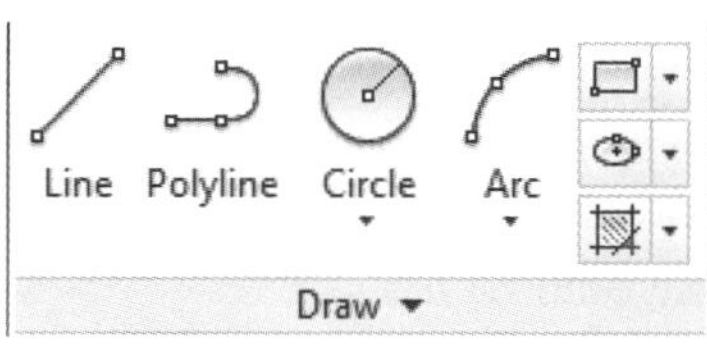

AutoCAD gives you the commands to draw common shapes like square/rectangles, circles, ellipses, and polygons. These commands can be found in the *Draw* panel on the *Home* tab. You will take a look at the **Rectangle** and **Circle** commands now.

SETTING YOUR WORKSPACE: AutoCAD has several very different looking User Interfaces. So, if your screen does not look similar to the screen shots in this book, click on the small gear icon in the lower right corner of the screen and select **Drafting and Annotation** *from the pop-up list that appears (see image to the right). Also, remember the default color theme is Dark, but the images used in the book are based on the light theme (you do not have to change this).*

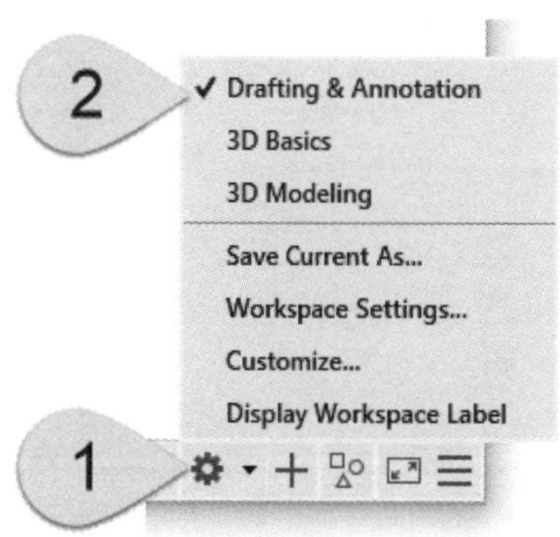

Drawing a Rectangle:

24. Use **Zoom Previous** (or **Zoom Window**) to get back to the original view.

25. Select the **Rectangle** tool from the *Draw* panel.

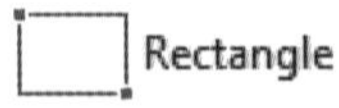

Notice the *dynamic tooltip* prompt near your cursor (your values will vary slightly):

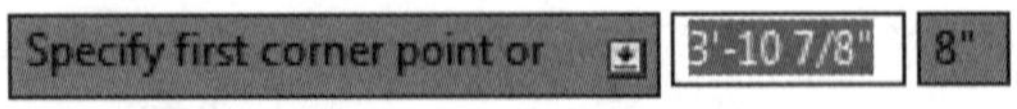

TIP: Pay attention to these prompts while you are learning AutoCAD; they tell you what information is expected/requested. Similar prompts are also displayed in the Command Window.

26. Pick your "**first corner point**" somewhere near the <u>middle-bottom</u> of the *Drawing* window (Figure 2-1.13).

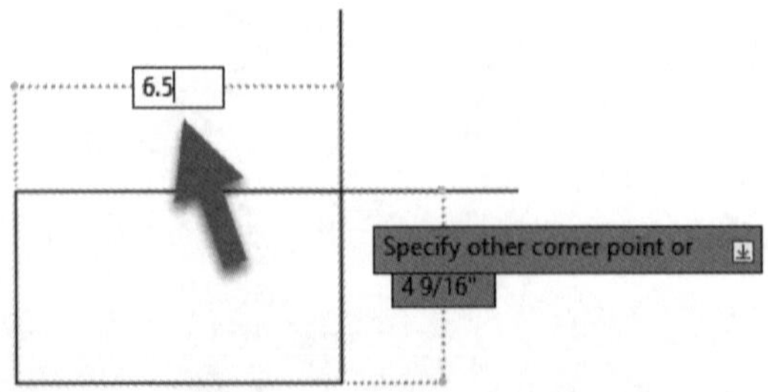

Notice the *dynamic tooltip* prompt near your cursor has changed:

At this point you can pick a point on the screen, type an X,Y,Z coordinate, or enter the dimensions on-screen via the dynamic tooltip feature near your cursor; you will use the latter method as it is easiest (*Dynamic Input* must be toggled "on" down on the *Status Bar*).

27. While being prompted for the "other corner," simply start typing (AutoCAD defaults to the *Width* tooltip for dynamic input). Type **6.5** (this equals 6½″) and then press the **Tab** key on the keyboard; <u>do not</u> press Enter.

Pressing **Tab** toggles you over to the *Height* tooltip for dynamic input (see prompt image at the top of the next page).

Notice the *Width* just entered has a padlock symbol next to it, which means that value is locked in. So, even though you will enter a numeric value for the *Height*, you could pick a point on the screen and no matter where you picked the *Width* would be 6.5″.

TIP: When drawing a rectangle, typing negative values allows you to dictate in which direction the rectangle is drawn (relative to your first pick point). When both numbers are positive, as in the previous example, the rectangle is drawn up and to the right of your first pick point.

Notice the current on-screen prompt (second value will vary slightly):

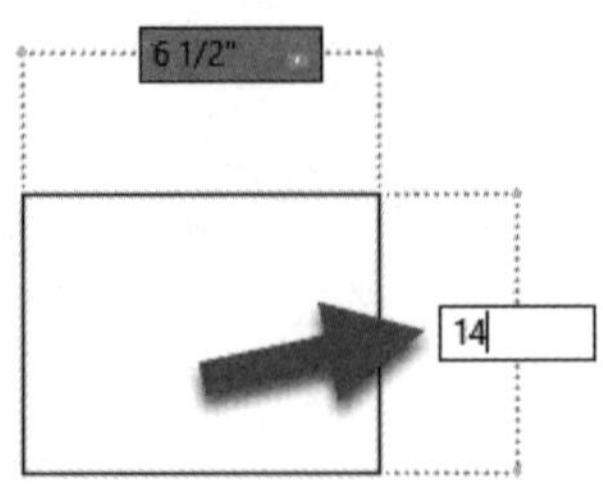

28. Type **14** and then press **Enter** (this equals 1′-2″).

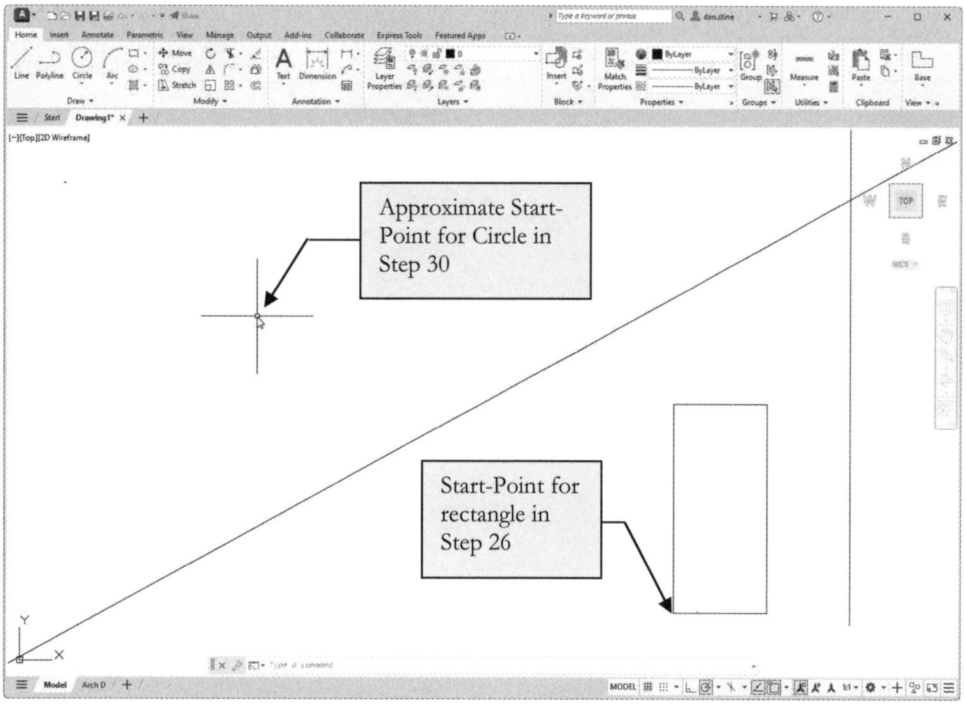

FIGURE 2-1.13 Drawing with Rectangle added

Drawing a Circle:

29. Select the **Circle** tool from the *Draw* panel—the top part of the split-button.

Circle

30. You are now prompted to pick the center point for the circle; pick a point approximately as shown in Figure 2-1.13.

    You should now see the following on-screen prompt:

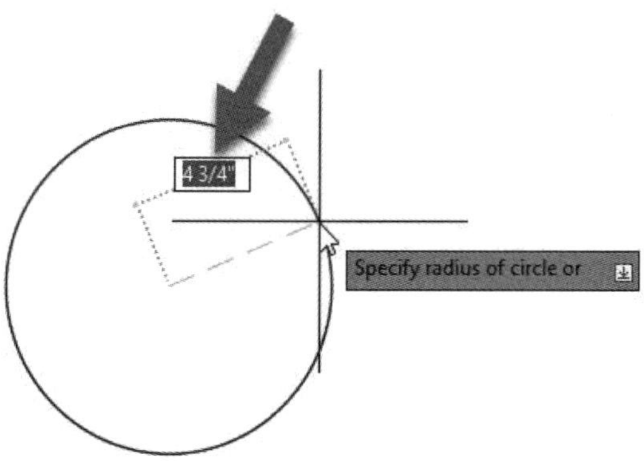

Tooltip menus:

Whenever you see a down-arrow icon within the on-screen tooltip (like the one above), you can press the down-arrow key on the keyboard to see a list of options pop up below the tooltip (see example to right). The options relate to the active command (the active command being the Circle command in this example).

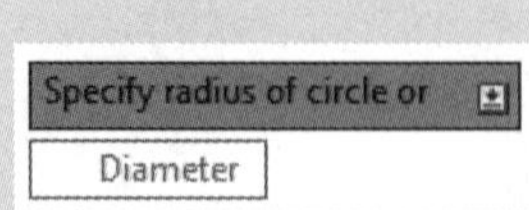

Right-click menus:

Another option is to right-click the mouse to see the same options as above plus a few standard options; this is called the context menu. If you clicked Diameter, the context menu goes away and AutoCAD expects you to enter the diameter rather than the radius.

Move your mouse around to see that you could arbitrarily pick a point on the screen to create a quick circle if needed, then proceed to the next step where you will draw a circle with a radius of $6\frac{5}{8}''$.

31. Type **6-5/8** and then press **Enter** (this equals $6\frac{5}{8}''$). (See Figure 2-1.15 on the next page.)

32. View the properties for both the Circle and Rectangle.

    NOTE: See Figure 2-1.14 for the Circle's properties; you can actually modify the Circle by entering a new Circumference or Area.

33. **Save** your drawing as **ex2-1.dwg**. Click *Save* in the *Application Menu* and then browse to a location for your file.

    TIP: If you are working on this tutorial in a school lab, you should save your files to your shared folder on the network (if you have one). In any case, be sure to back up all your files to a flash drive or cloud storage (e.g. Autodesk A360 or Dropbox).

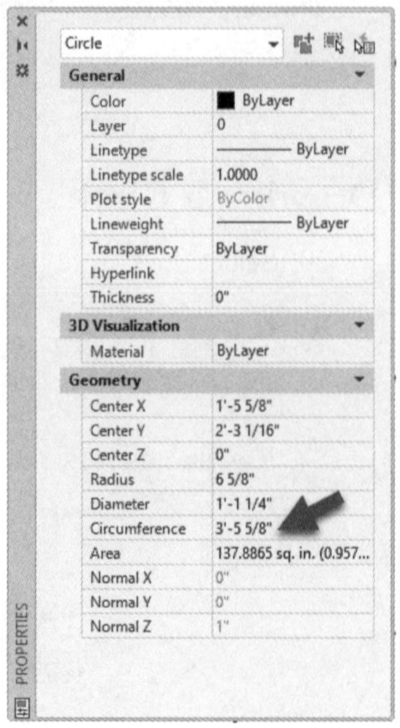

FIGURE 2-1.14 Properties for circle

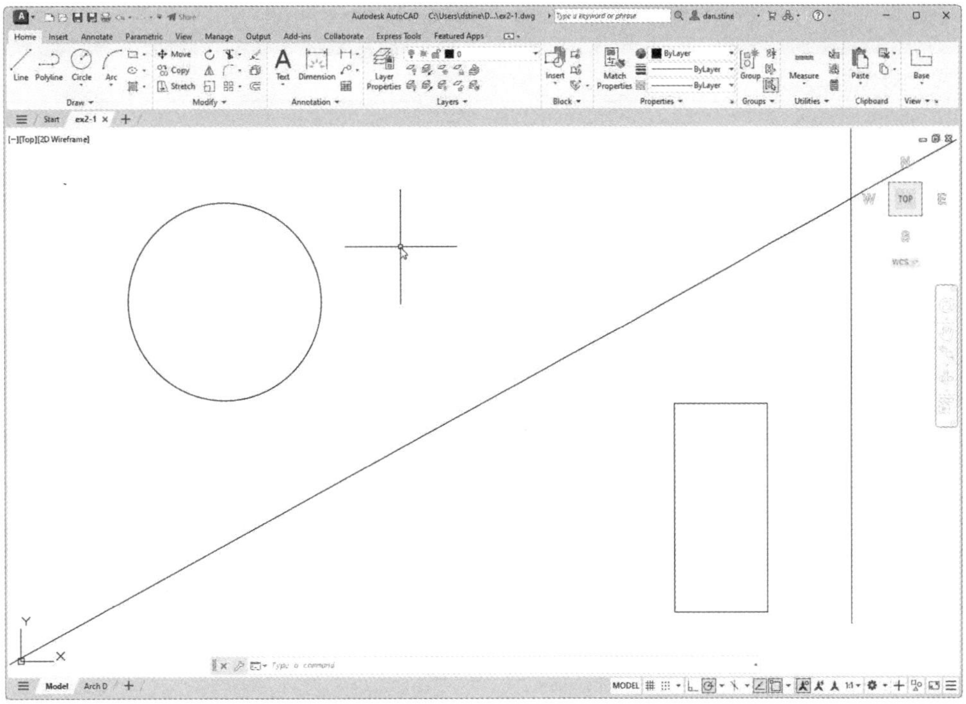

FIGURE 2-1.15 Drawing with Circle added

Where Should I Save My Files?

You should save your files to your Autodesk Drive storage space if you have set that up. Refer back to chapter one for more information on how to set up Cloud Storage.

You can also create a folder in which to save your AutoCAD files, typically a sub-folder in the Documents folder. Your instructor may specify a location for your files if you are using this textbook in a classroom setting.

Thus far you have learned how to draw accurate orthogonal lines (i.e., horizontal and vertical) and verify their accuracy using the *Properties* palette. You can also accurately draw rectangles and circles. You have also employed *Dynamic Input* and *Polar Tracking.*

Everything drawn so far has been separate, isolated items. More often than not you will want to draw lines that connect to each other, and as previously mentioned, it is virtually impossible to simply visually pick a point on the screen and have it be perfectly accurate. So, when you want to draw a new line in relation to a previously drawn one you have to use a special feature known as *Object Snaps* when drawing and modifying objects in AutoCAD. You will learn about this feature next.

Exercise 2-2:
Object Snaps

Introduction

Object Snap is a tool that allows you to accurately pick a point on an object. For example, when drawing a line, you can use *Object Snap* (*OSNAP*) to select as the start-point, the endpoint or midpoint of another line.

This feature is absolutely critical to drawing accurate technical drawings. Using this feature allows you to be confident you are creating perfect intersections, corners, etc. (Figure 2-2.1).

Object Snaps Options:

You can use *Object Snaps* in one of two ways:

- Using the *Running OSNAP* mode
- On an individual pick-point basis

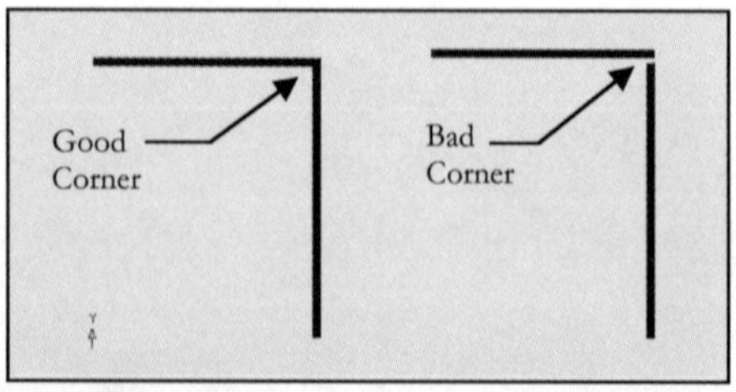

FIGURE 2-2.1 Typical problem when Object Snap is not used

Running OSNAP mode is a feature that, when turned on, constantly scans the area near your cursor when AutoCAD is looking for user input. You can configure which types of points to look for.

Using an *Object Snap* for individual pick-points allows you to quickly select a particular point on an object. This option will also override the *Running OSNAP* setting, which means you tell AutoCAD to just look for the endpoint on an object (for the next pick-point only) rather than the three or four types being scanned for by the *Running OSNAP* feature.

Enabling Running Object Snaps:

To toggle *Running Object Snap* on and off you click the **Object Snap** icon on the *Status Bar.*

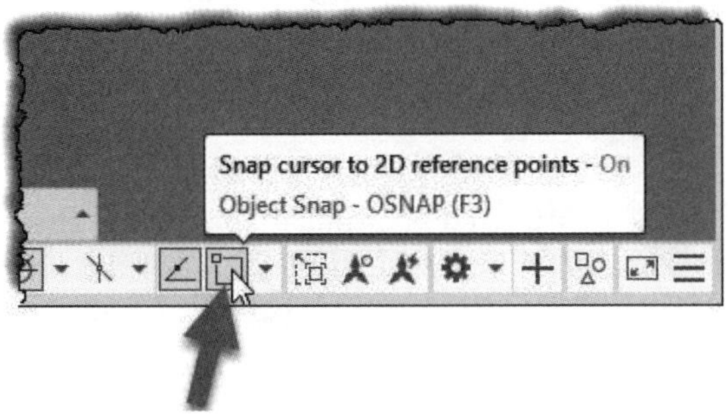

FIGURE 2-2.2 Status Bar – shown with Object Snap turned on

Snap Symbols:

When *Object Snap* is turned on, AutoCAD displays symbols as you move your cursor about the *Drawing* window (while you are in a command like **Line** and AutoCAD is awaiting your input or pick-point).

If you hold your cursor still for a moment while a snap symbol is displayed, a tooltip will appear on the screen. However, when you become familiar with the snap symbols you can pick sooner, rather than waiting for the tooltip to display.

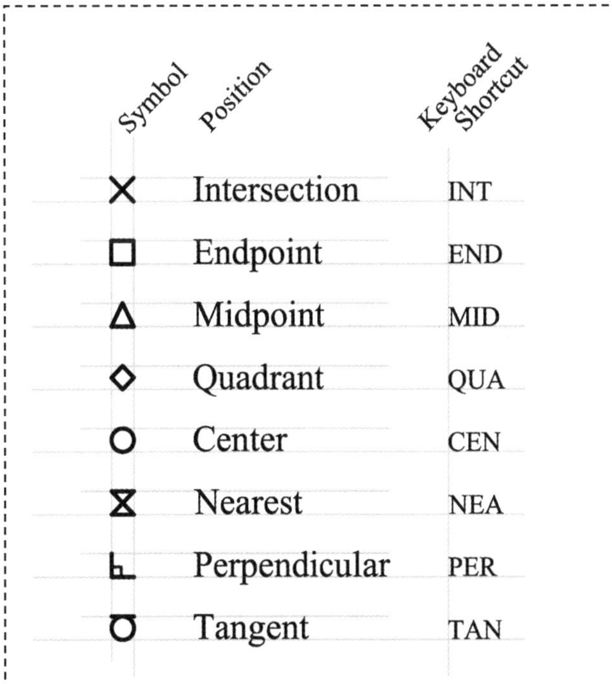

FIGURE 2-2.3 OSNAP symbols that are displayed on the screen when selecting a point.

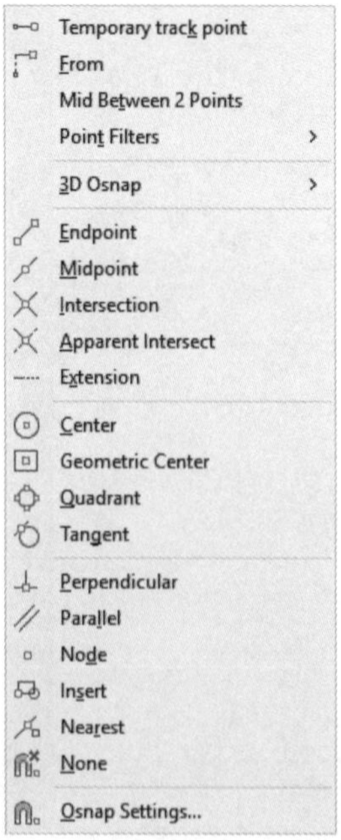

The **Tab** key cycles through the available snaps near your cursor.

The keyboard shortcut turns off the other snaps for one pick. For example, if you type *END* on the keyboard while in the **Line** command, AutoCAD will only look for an *Endpoint* for the next pick.

Finally, if you need a particular snap for just one pick, you can hold the ***Shift* key and right-click** for the *OSNAP* context menu (see image to left). If you pick **Center**, AutoCAD will only look for a Center to snap to for the next pick and then revert to the previous settings.

Setting Object Snaps:

You can set AutoCAD to have just one or all *Object Snaps* running at the same time. Let's say you have *Endpoint* and *Midpoint* set to be running. While using the **Line** command, move your cursor near an existing line. When the cursor is near the end of the line, you will see the *Endpoint* symbol show up. When you move the cursor towards the middle of the line, you will see the *Midpoint* symbol show up.
The next step shows you how to tell AutoCAD which *Object Snaps* you want it to look for.

First you need to **Open** the drawing from the Exercise files that you downloaded from the publisher's website; see instructions for download on the inside front cover of the book.

1. **Open** drawing **ex2-1 Osnap.dwg** from the online exercise files.
    a. You may also continue with your file from the previous exercise if you wish. However, this file is offered to make the result look more like what is seen in the book (given the random locations instructed in the previous exercise).

2. Next, do a **Save-As** and save to your hard drive; name the file **ex2-2.dwg**.

3. Click the down-arrow next to the Object Snap icon, on the *Status Bar*, and select **Object Snap Settings** from the pop-up menu (Figure 2-2.4).

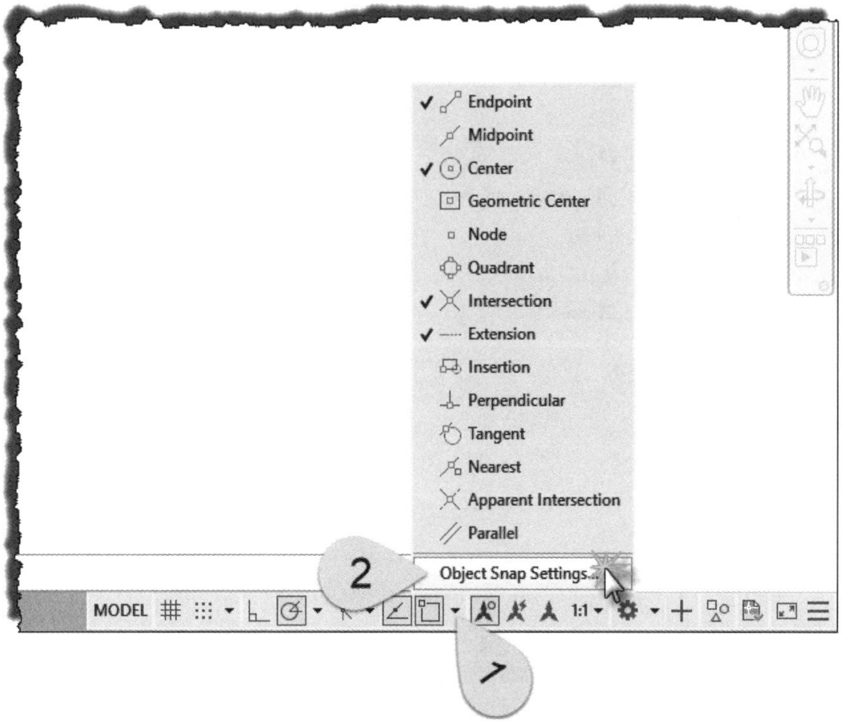

FIGURE 2-2.4 Right-click on the OSNAP button located on the *Status Bar*

You are now in the **Drafting Settings** dialog box on the *Object Snap* tab; compare to **Figure 2-2.5**.

4. Make sure only the following *Object Snaps* are checked:
   a. Endpoint
   b. Midpoint
   c. Center
   d. Intersection
   e. Perpendicular

5. Click **OK** to close the *Drafting Settings* dialog box.

FOR MORE INFORMATION: For more on using Object Snaps, search AutoCAD's Help system for ***Drafting Settings****. Then click the* ***Drafting Settings Dialog Box*** *and select the* ***Object Snap*** *link within the article.*

FYI: The running Object Snaps *shown in Figure 2-2.5 are for AutoCAD in general, not just the current drawing. This is convenient; you don't have to adjust to your favorite settings for each drawing (existing or new). Thus, each person working on this drawing can have their own preferences for Object Snaps.*

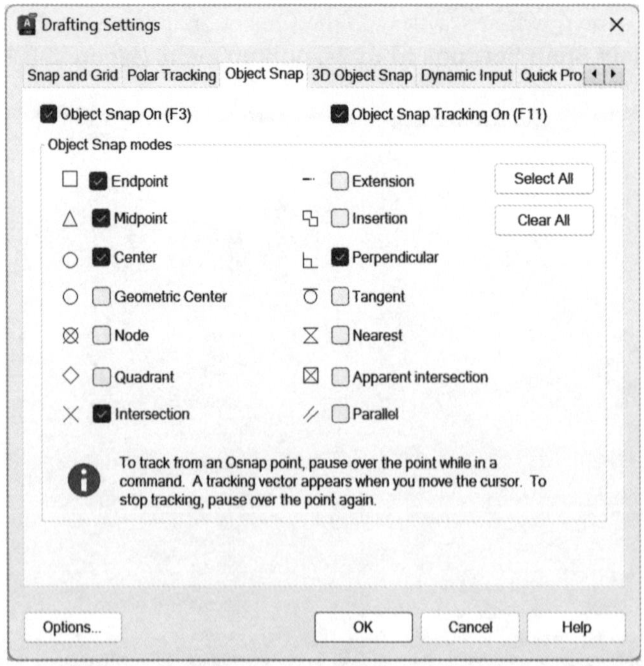

FIGURE 2-2.5 Object Snap tab on Drafting Settings dialog

Now that you have the *Running Object Snaps* set, you will give this feature a try.

6. On the *Home* tab, in the *Draw* panel, pick the **Line** command, and move your cursor to the lower-left portion of the diagonal line (Figure 2-2.6).

7. Hover the cursor over the line's endpoint (without picking); when you see the *Endpoint* symbol you can click to select that point.

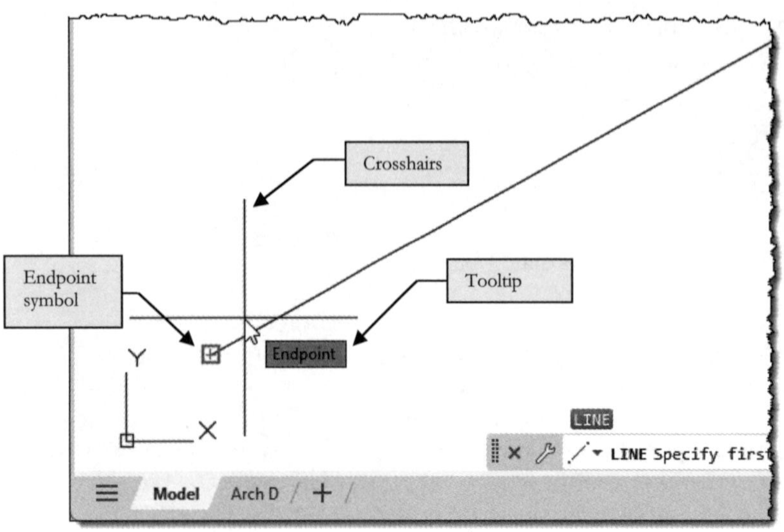

FIGURE 2-2.6 Endpoint OSNAP symbol visible

JUST SO YOU KNOW...

It is important that you see the *Object Snap* symbol before clicking. Also, once you see the symbol you should be careful not to move the mouse too much.

These steps will help to ensure accurate corners.

While still in the Line command, you will draw additional lines using *OSNAP* to accurately select the line's *start point* and *endpoint.*

8. Draw the additional lines shown in **Figure 2-2.7** using the appropriate *Object Snap* (changing the *Running Snap* as required to select the required point).

   TIP #1: When using the Line command, you can draw several line segments without the need to terminate the Line command and then restart it for the next line segment. After picking the start and end points for a line, the end point automatically becomes the first point for the next line segment; this continues until you finish the Line command (i.e., right-click and select Enter).

   TIP #2: At any point, while the Line command is active, you can right-click on the OSNAP button (on the Status Bar) and adjust its settings, or press Shift+Right-click; the Line command will not cancel.

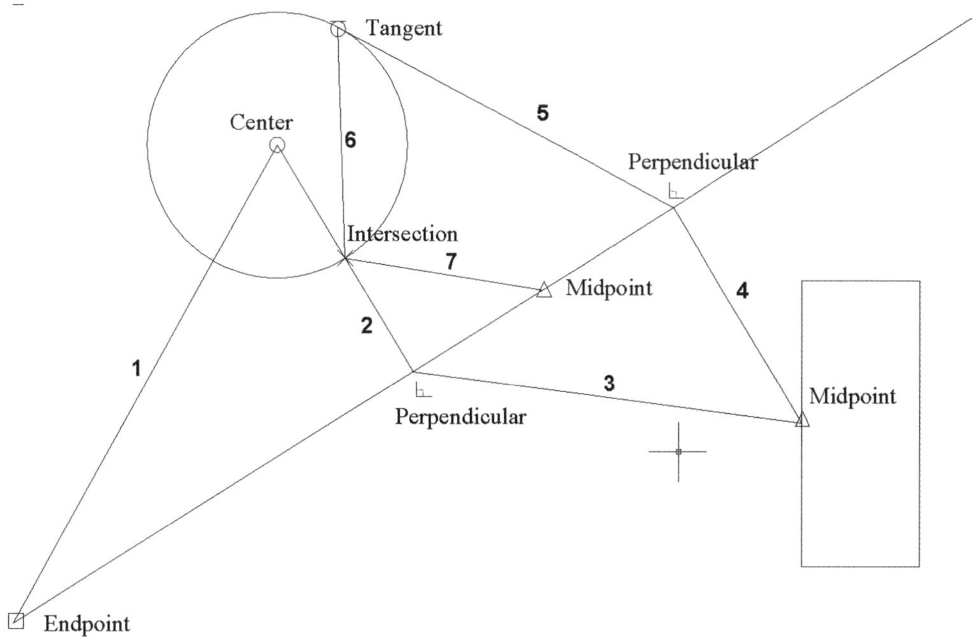

FIGURE 2-2.7 Several lines added using running OSNAPs.
The numbers indicate the order in which the lines are to be drawn.

9. **Save** your drawing as ex2-2.dwg.

This is an Architectural Example?

OK, this is not really an architectural example yet. However, the point here is to focus on the fundamental concepts, not on architecture just yet.

Exercise 2-3:
Modify Tools

The *Modify* tools are the most commonly used group of tools in AutoCAD. Much time is spent tweaking designs and making code-related revisions.

Example: Use the *Draw* tools (e.g., Lines, Circles, Rectangles) to initially draw the walls, doors, windows, and furniture. Then use the *Modify* tools to *Stretch* a room so it is larger, *Mirror* a door so it swings in the direction of egress, and *Move* the furniture per the owner's instructions.

The ability to instantly modify drawings is why CAD is so useful to architects and designers. Compared to the days of hand drawings, erasing, and redrawing, CAD is a significant productivity booster.

You will access the various *Modify* tools from the *Modify* panel on the *Home* tab as introduced in Lesson 1. This textbook focuses on the parts of a command needed to complete a specific task. If you are interested in further investigating a specific feature or command, you can use the *Help* system (or the AI-powered Autodesk Assistant); the image below (Figure 2-3.1) shows the *Select Objects* section selected.

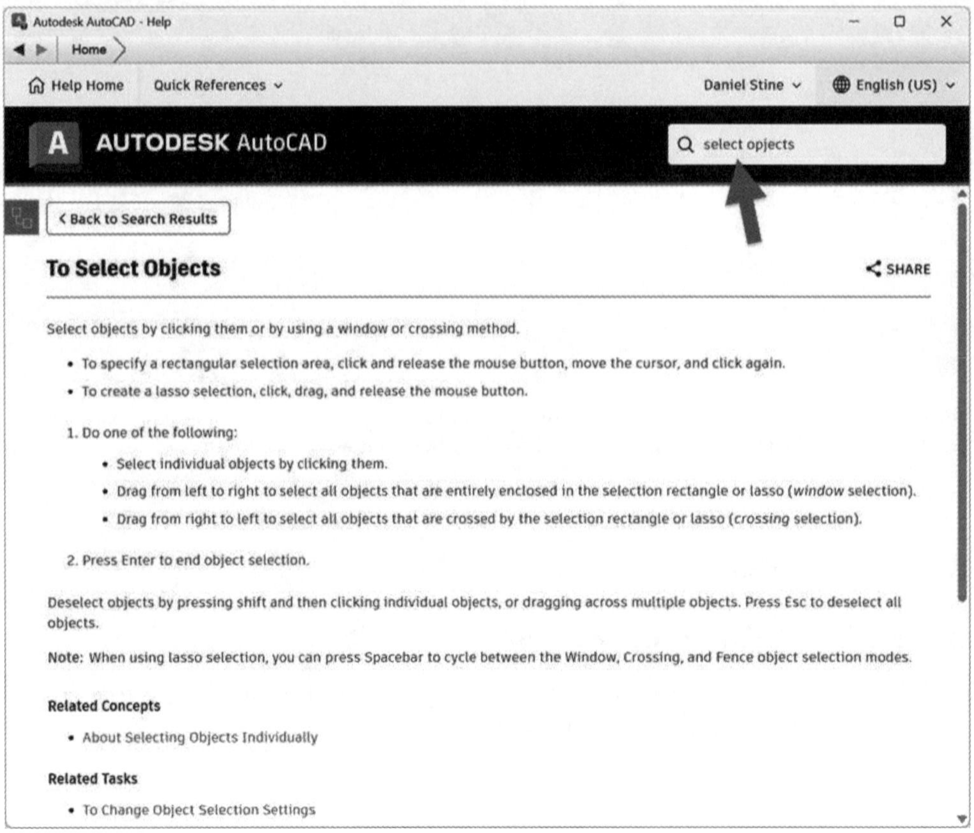

FIGURE 2-3.1 Another Help System example

In this exercise, you will get a brief overview of a few of the *Modify* tools, manipulating the "tangled web" of lines you have previously drawn.

1. **Open** drawing **ex2-2.dwg** from the previous lesson.

2. **Save As** ex2-3.dwg.

   ***FYI:** You will notice in this book that instructions or commands that have already been covered will have fewer "step-by-step" instructions.*

Erase Command:

It is no surprise that the **Erase** tool is a necessity; things change, and mistakes are made. You can erase one entity at a time or several. Erasing entities is very easy; you select the **Erase** icon, pick the objects to erase, and then right-click (which equals pressing *Enter* on the keyboard). You will try this on two lines in your drawing.

3. Select **Erase** (*Modify* panel, *Home* tab).

4. [Notice the *Command* line is prompting: **Select objects:**]
   Use the mouse to select the lines identified in **Figure 2-3.2**.

   ***TIP:** See the section on Selecting Entities on the next page.*

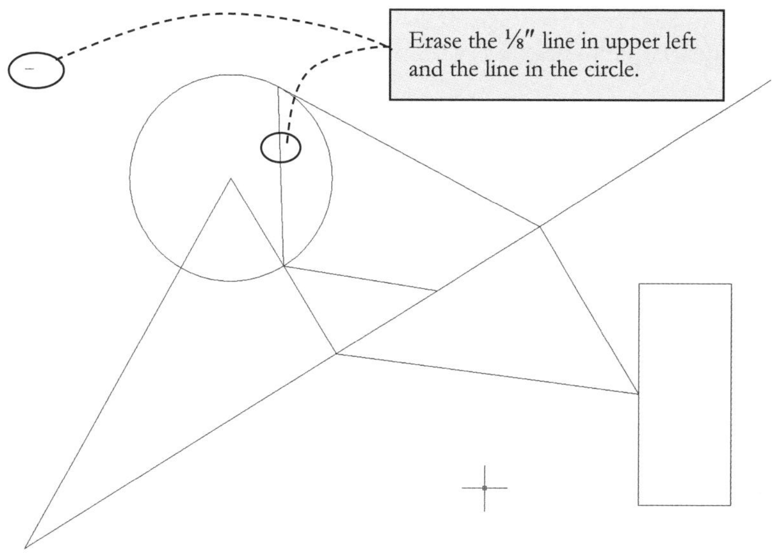

FIGURE 2-3.2 Lines to be erased

5. **Right-click** to complete the task.

Selecting Entities:

At this time we will digress and take a quick look at the various techniques for selecting entities in AutoCAD. Most commands work the same when it comes to selecting entities. As mentioned before, you need to keep your eye on the *prompts* so you know when AutoCAD is ready for you to select entities or provide other user input.

When selecting entities, you have three primary ways to select them:

- Individually select entities one at a time
- Select several entities at a time with a window
- Select several entities at a time with a lasso

You can use one or a combination of each method to select entities (when using the Copy command, for example).

<u>Individual Selections</u>:
When prompted to select entities (to copy or erase, for example), simply move the cursor over the object and click. With most commands, you repeat this process until you have selected all the entities you need (selections are cumulative), then you typically press **Enter** or right-click to tell AutoCAD you are done selecting. Holding the *Shift* key while selecting will remove items from the current selection set. Pressing the *Esc* key (1-3 times) will unselect everything and cancel the current command.

<u>Window Selections</u>:
Similarly, when prompted to select entities, you can pick a Window around several entities to select them all at once. To select a window, rather than selecting an object as previously described, you select one corner of the window you wish to select (that is, you pick a point in "space"). Now, as you move the mouse, you will see a rectangle on the screen that represents the window you are selecting. When the window encompasses the entities you wish to select, click the mouse.

You actually have two types of windows you can select. One is called a ***Window***, and the other is called a ***Crossing Window***.

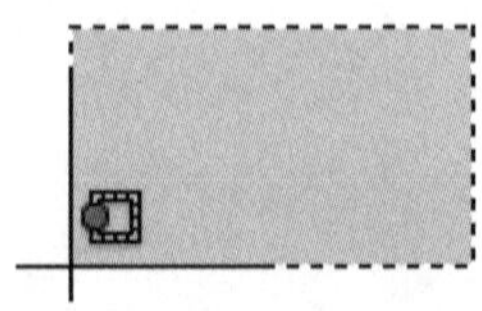

Crossing window selection

Window:
This option allows you to select only entities completely within the *Window*. Any lines that extend out of the *Window* are not selected.

Crossing Window:
This option allows you to select all the entities that are completely within the *Window* and any that extend outside the *Window*.

Using Window versus Crossing Window:
To select a *Window* you simply pick your two points from left to right (Figure 2-3.3a). Conversely, to select a *Crossing Window*, you pick the two diagonal points of the window from right to left (Figure 2-3.3b).

<u>Lasso Selections</u>:
Lasso selection lets you select an irregular area rather than a rectangular one. Simply click and hold down the mouse button to start the lasso option. You have the same *Window* and *Crossing* options as with the *Window Selection* method mentioned above.

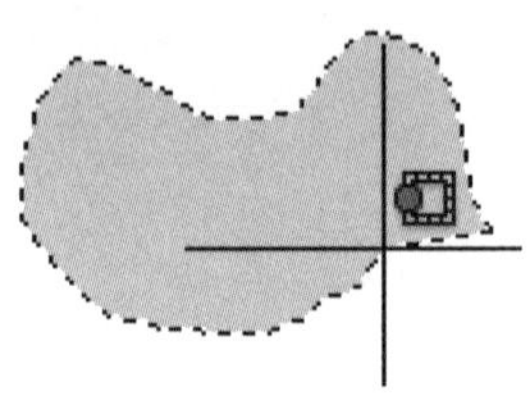

Crossing lasso selection

Below are two examples that demonstrate the difference between a *Window Selection* and a Crossing Window Selection.

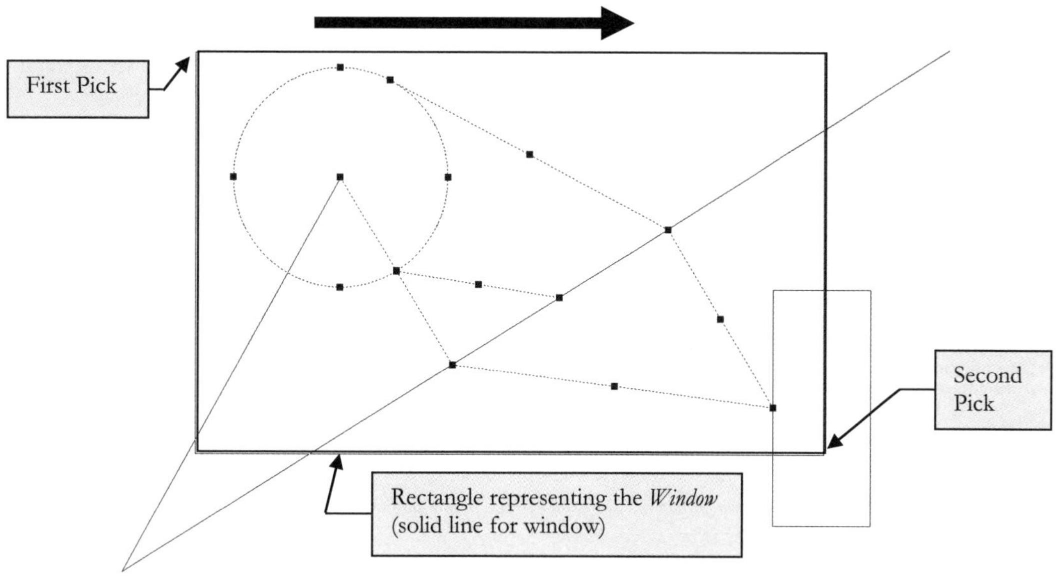

FIGURE 2-3.3A Lines selected using a *Window;* only the lines within the window are selected.

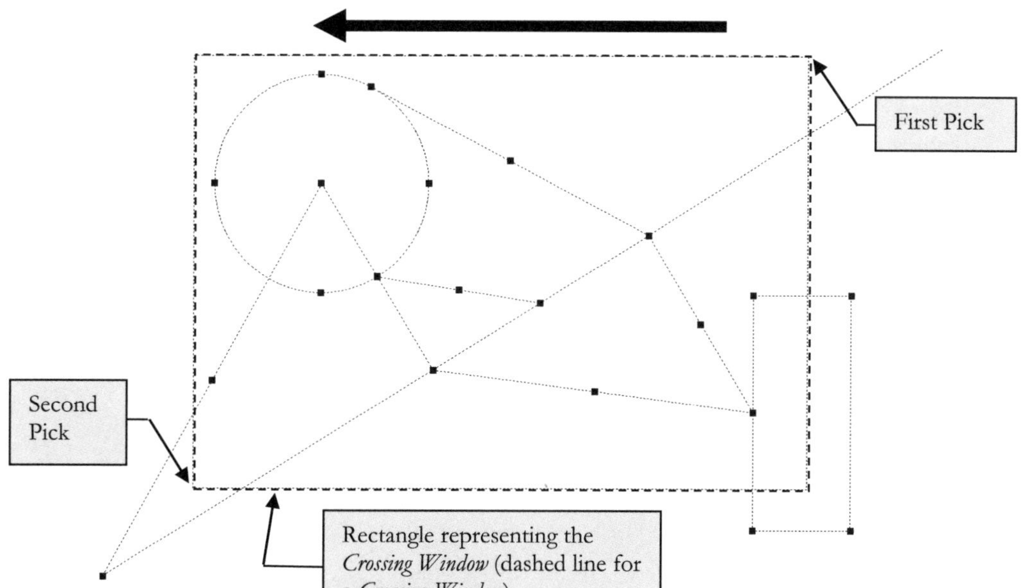

FIGURE 2-3.3B Lines selected using a *Crossing Window;* all lines are selected.

Copy Command:

The **Copy** tool allows you to accurately duplicate an entity(s). You select the items you want to copy and then pick two points that represent an imaginary vector (which provides both length and angle) defining the path used to copy the entity to; you can also type in the length and angle if there are no convenient points to pick in the drawing. You will try both methods next.

6. Select **Copy** (*Modify* panel, *Home* tab). Copy

7. **Select the circle** and then **right-click**. *This signals to AutoCAD that you are finished selecting entities to copy.*

   Notice the prompt: Specify base point or 1'-9 3/16" 3'-6 3/16"

8. Pick the ***Center*** of the **circle** as the base point (Figure 2-3.4).

   FYI: *You actually have three different OSNAPs you can use here: Center, Endpoint, and Intersection. All occur at the exact same point.*

   Notice the prompt: Specify second point or 2'-1 1/8" < 265"

9. Pick the ***Endpoint*** of the angled line in the lower left corner. (See Figures 2-3.4 and 2-3.5.)

   FYI: *At this point, you could continue copying the circle all over your drawing; AutoCAD will remain in copy mode until you press Esc or Enter.*

10. Press **Enter** to finish the command.

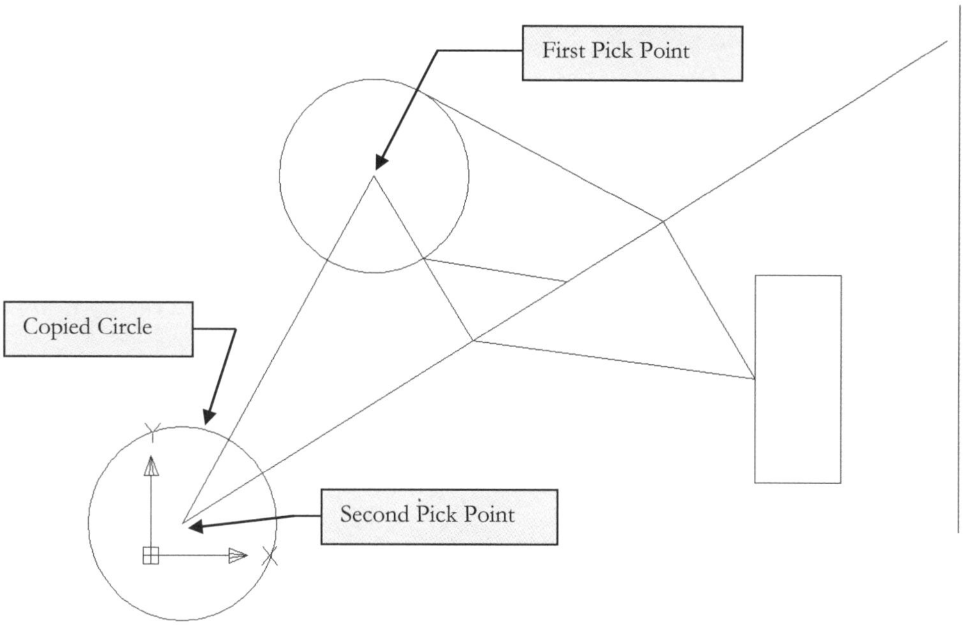

FIGURE 2-3.4 Copied circle; also indicates points selected

TIP: You may need to zoom out to see the entire circle just copied.

11. Select **Copy** again.
12. **Select the rectangle** and then **right-click**.
13. Pick an arbitrary point on the screen and then start moving your cursor up and to the right; your line cannot be "snapped" to the horizontal. *(In this scenario, it makes no difference where you pick; you will see why in a moment.)*

At this point, you will type in the displacement data (i.e., distance and angle), rather than picking a second point on the screen.

14. *The following will be entered via the on-screen Dynamic Input:* Type **18**, press **Tab**, then type **45** and press **Enter**. (See Figure 2-3.5 and on-screen prompts below.) Finally, press **Enter** to finish the command.

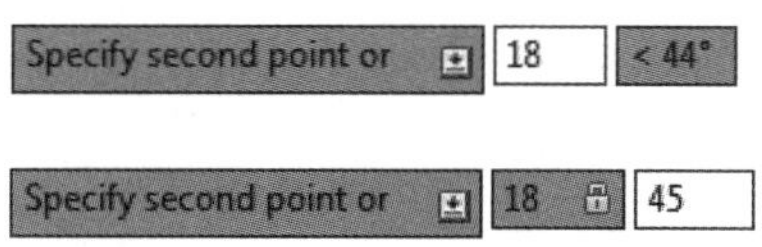

What does 18 Tab 45 mean?

When you need to *Move* or *Copy* something to a very specific location, you can type in the distance and angle from the original entity (i.e., use the first point as displacement). This is very useful when you do not have any entities drawn that represent this distance and angle (e.g., as per the steps when you copied the circle, Figure 2-3.4).

The **18** represents the distance, in this case 18 inches. Remember, if you do not specify feet or inches, AutoCAD assumes inches. So in this example, you would not have to press the extra key for the inch symbol, although 18″ would work.

Here are some other valid distances:

1′4	*equals*	1′-4″	16	*equals*	1′-4″
3′	*equals*	3′-0″	36	*equals*	3′-0″
0-3/4	*equals*	¾″	.75	*equals*	¾″
3-5/8	*equals*	3⅝″	1′3-5/8″	*equals*	1′-3⅝″

Tab toggles to the angle parameter (a second Tab returns you to length).

The **45** represents the angle (or direction) the entities will be Moved or Copied; the angle is based on the positive x-axis in a counterclockwise direction.

Here are some angles and a graphical representation of their direction:

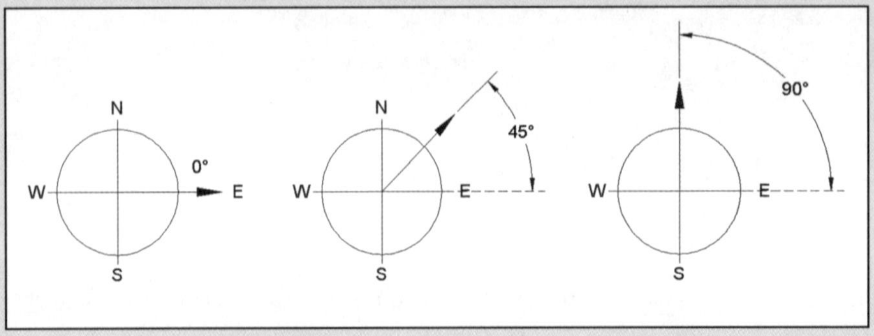

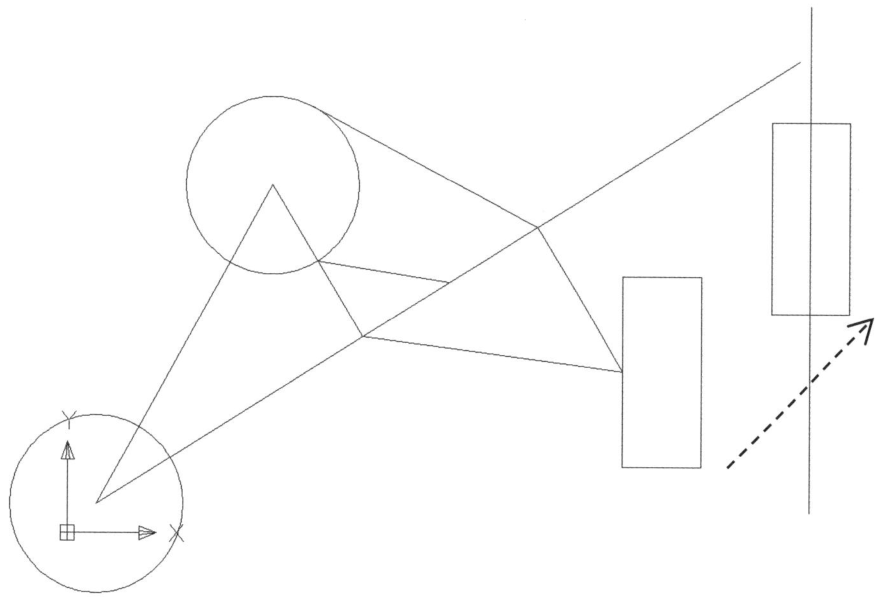

FIGURE 2-3.5 Copied rectangle. Dashed line represents the distance and angle of displacement.

> ***NOTE:*** *Your drawing may look a little different than this one because your drawing is not to scale.*

Move Command:

The **Move** command works exactly like the **Copy** command except, of course, you move the entities rather than copy them. Given the similarity to the previous command covered, the **Move** command will not be covered here. You are encouraged to try it yourself. Use the **Undo** command to get back to the drawing shown in Figure 2-3.5 before proceeding if you decide to try the **Move** command.

Rotate Command:

With the **Rotate** command, you can arbitrarily or accurately rotate one or more entities in your drawing. When you need to rotate accurately, you can pick points that define the angle (assuming points exist in the drawing to pick), or you can type a specific angle. The architectural template you are using in this book has the degrees "type" set to decimal. Other types are available, such as Deg/Min/Sec and Radians, but architects typically use decimal angles unless drawing a site plan from a surveyor's drawing that has angles listed in another format.

15. Select **Rotate** (*Modify* panel, *Home* tab). 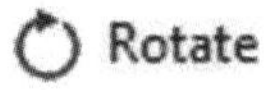

16. **Select the rectangle** you just copied (i.e., the new one) and then **right-click**; *this tells AutoCAD that you are done selecting entities to rotate.*

You are now prompted: 

This is the point about which the rotation will occur.

17. Pick the *Midpoint* of the vertical line on the left side of the rectangle (Figure 2-3.6).

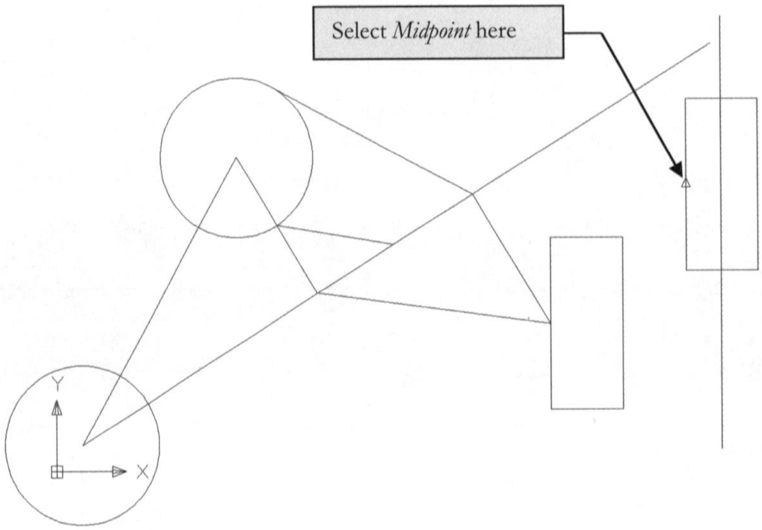

FIGURE 2-3.6 Rotate command. First Step - Select *Midpoint* of left vertical line.

You are now prompted: 

18. Type **90** and then press **Enter**.

As in the rotation-angle examples recently discussed, the previous step rotated the rectangle 90 degrees counterclockwise (Figure 2-3.7).

19. Select the **Undo** command. 

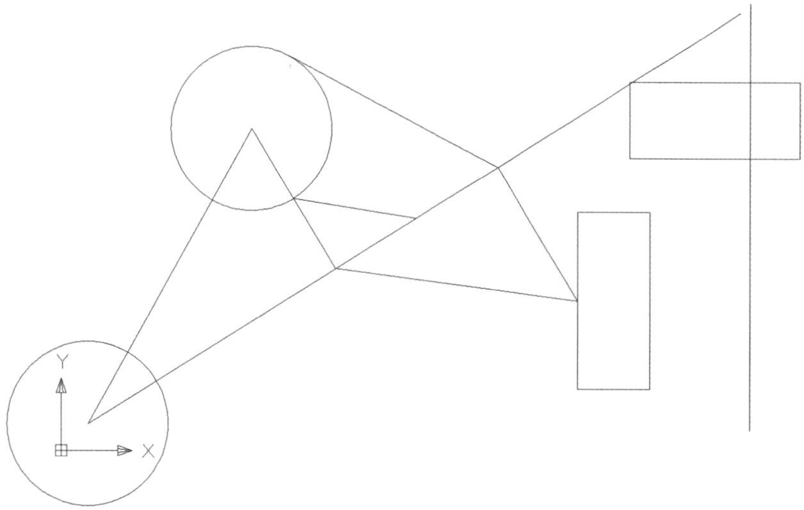

FIGURE 2-3.7 Rotate command – Rectangle rotated

Now you will do the same thing, except with a different angle. A negative angle rotates the entities clockwise.

20. After selecting *Undo* in the previous step, use the **Rotate** command, **select the rectangle**, and then **pick the same *Midpoint*** as in Step 17.

21. This time, for the *Rotation Angle,* type **-45** and **Enter**.

Notice, now, that the rectangle rotated 45 degrees in the clockwise direction (Figure 2-3.8).

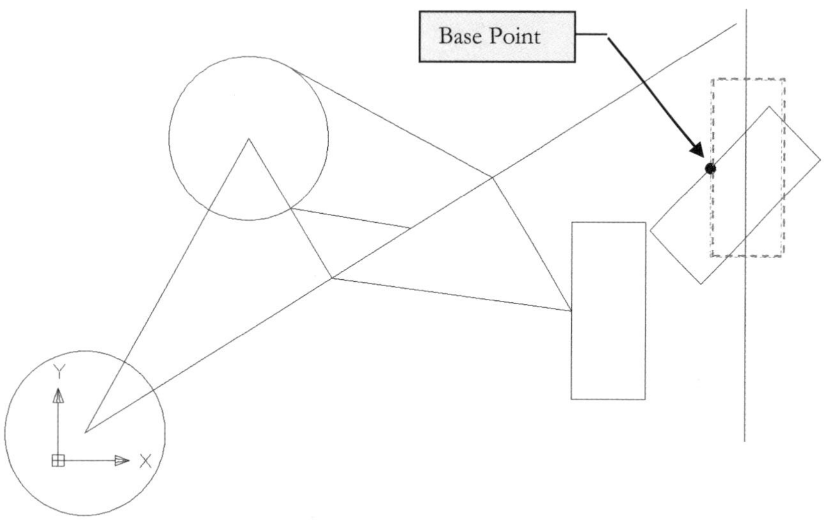

FIGURE 2-3.8 Rectangle rotated. Dashed rectangle represents original position.

Scale Command:

The **Scale** command has steps similar to the **Rotate** command. First, select what you want to scale and then specify the base point. Then, instead of entering a rotation angle, enter a scale factor (e.g., 2 or .5; where 2 would be twice the original size and .5 would be half the original size).

Next, you will use the **Scale** command to adjust the size of the circle near the bottom.

Before you scale the circle, you should use the ***Properties*** dialog box to note the **radius** of the circle. After scaling the circle, you will refer back to the *Properties* palette to note the change. This step is meant to teach you how to verify the accuracy and dimensions of entities in AutoCAD.

> ***TIP:*** *You can double-click on most objects to view their quick properties.*

22. Select **Scale** (*Modify* panel, *Home* tab). 

23. **Select the circle** (the one at the bottom) and then **right-click**. *(Again, this tells AutoCAD you are done selecting items to scale.)*

    You are now prompted: 

    TIP: *The numbers shown in the prompt above are X and Y values from the Origin; you will pick a point, not type values.*

The *Base Point* is the point about which the entity (or entities) will be scaled; see the examples on the next page.

24. Pick the center of the circle. *(In this case, you can use one of three OSNAPs: Center, Endpoint, or Intersection.)*

    You are now prompted: 

25. Type **.5** (as shown in the previous prompt) and press **Enter.**

Now use the ***Properties*** palette to note the change in the size of the circle, from $6\frac{5}{8}$" to $3\frac{5}{16}$" radius. A *Scale Factor* of .5 reduces the entities to half their original scale (Figure 2-3.9).

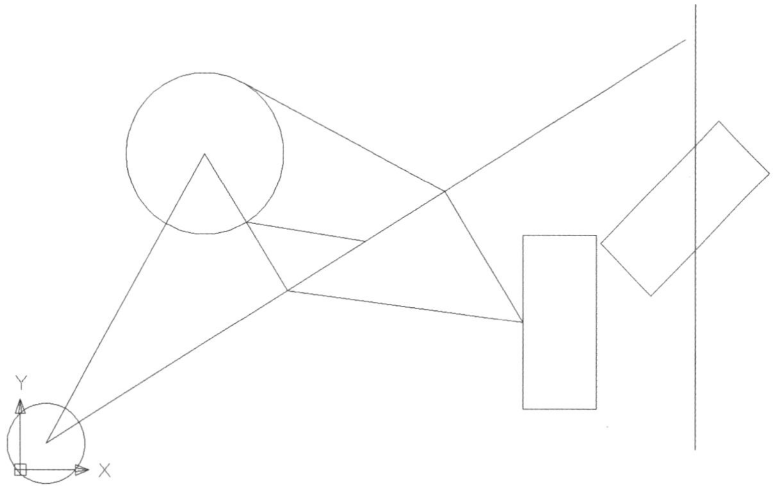

FIGURE 2-3.9 Scaled circle. Notice it is half the size of the other circle.

Selecting the Correct Base Point:

To get the desired results, you need to select the appropriate base point for both the *Scale* and *Rotate* commands. A few examples are shown in Figure 2-3.10. The dashed line indicates the original position of the entity being modified. The black dot indicates the base point selected.

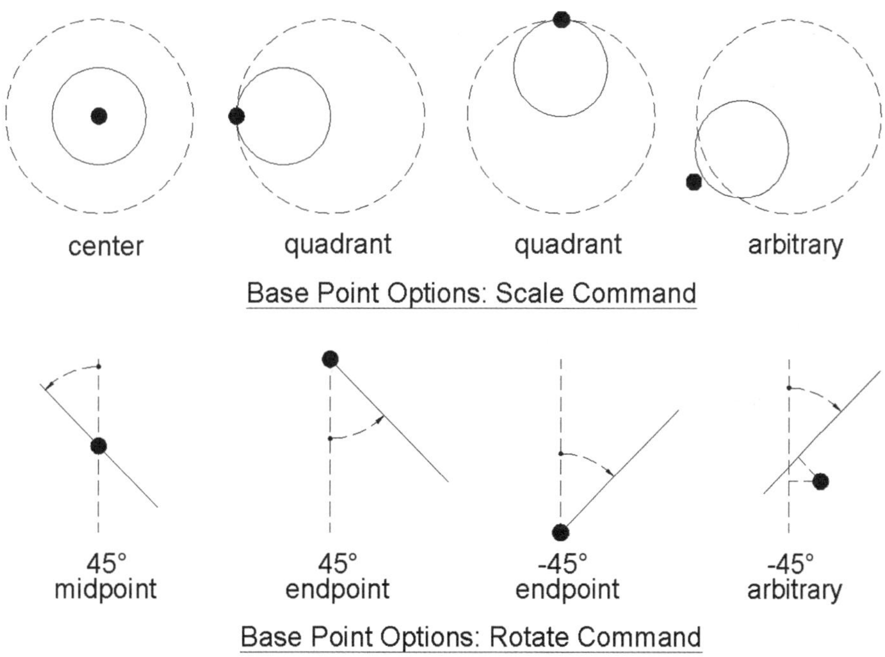

FIGURE 2-3.10 Base Point Options. The various results when different base points are selected.

This will conclude the brief tour of the *Modify* panel.

As you may have noticed, the Modify panel includes a few other icons that have not yet been investigated. Most of these will be covered later in this book.

26. **Save** your drawing. (Your drawing should already be named **ex2-3.dwg** per step number 2 of this exercise.)

Carter Residence

Images courtesy of LHB
www.LHBcorp.com

Exercise 2-4:
Annotations

Annotations (text, notes) allow designers and drafters to accurately describe the drawing. You will take a quick look at this feature now.

Annotations:

Adding annotations to a drawing can be as essential as the drawing itself. Often, the notes (i.e., annotations) describe something about a part of the drawing that would be difficult to discern from the drawing alone.

For example, a wall section drawing showing a bolt may not indicate, graphically, how many bolts are needed or at what spacing (because the spacing of the bolts is perpendicular to the view). The note might say "*5/8" anchor bolt at 24" O.C.*" (O.C. = on center)

Next, you will add text to your drawing.

1. **Open** drawing **ex2-3.dwg** from the previous lesson.

2. **Save-As ex2-4.dwg**.

3. **Zoom** out, if required; your screen should look like Figure 2-4.2.

4. Select the **Multiline Text** - referred to as **Mtext** (*Annotation* panel, *Home* tab). Click *OK* to any prompts about selecting an *Annotation Scale.*

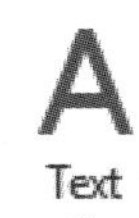

   a. Just click the top part of the split button to start the **Multiline Text** command.

Notice the current *Command* prompt; you are prompted to "**Specify first corner.**" Basically, you are specifying a window (or box) that will contain the text, which is easily adjusted later as well (Figure 2-4.1).

FIGURE 2-4.1 Command prompt for Mtext command

5. Pick your first point and then your second point to define a box as shown in **Figure 2-4.2**.

   TIP: *You rarely click and drag your mouse button in AutoCAD; mostly, you click and release the mouse button, position the cursor at the second location, and then click again.*

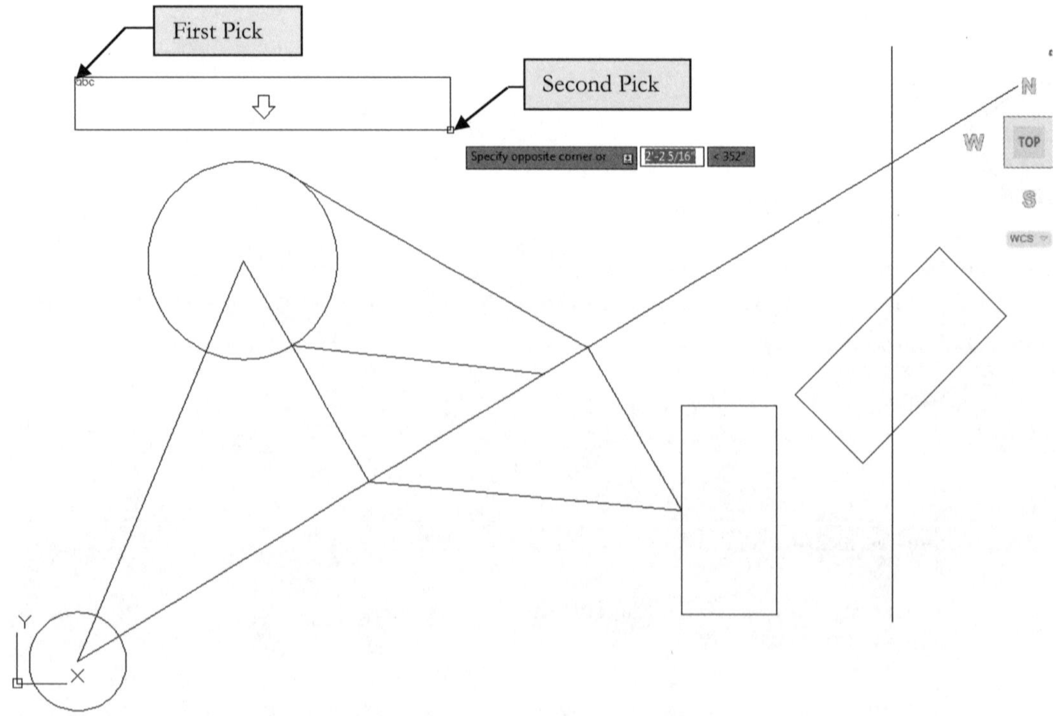

FIGURE 2-4.2 Mtext; defining the window that contains the text (first point picked; picking second)

When picking the *Mtext* window, the width is all that really matters. The width of the selected window is what controls the text wrapping feature. AutoCAD will never hide text, so as you type, if the line of text becomes longer than the width of the *Mtext* window you specified, the text will return to the next line (just like a word processor). AutoCAD will create as many lines as are required to show all the text you typed, regardless of the initial height of the *Mtext* window.

> ***TIP:*** *In the Mtext editor, you can right-click to see a pop-up menu that gives you access to several tools like Select All, Change Case (which is an easy way to make previously typed text all upper case), and Find and Replace. See the image to the right for an example.*

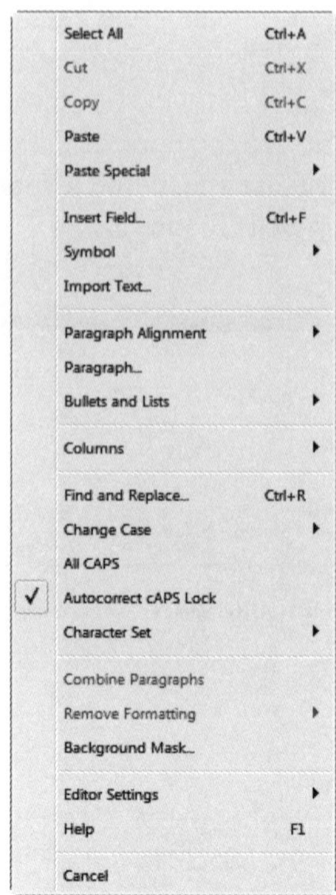

You can now enter text in the *Mtext* window. This window will not be visible when you are done typing. The *Mtext* tool is similar to text editors like MS Word or WordPerfect; you can make text bold, italic, centered, underlined, etc.

Next, you will enter some text.

6. In the *Mtext Editor,* you will type the following text (Figure 2-4.3):
   a. Set the height to **1"**. (You will have to type it in.)
   b. Set the *Columns* option to **No Columns**.
   c. Type **Learning AutoCAD is fun!**

   FYI: Do not add the second line (i.e., your name) yet.

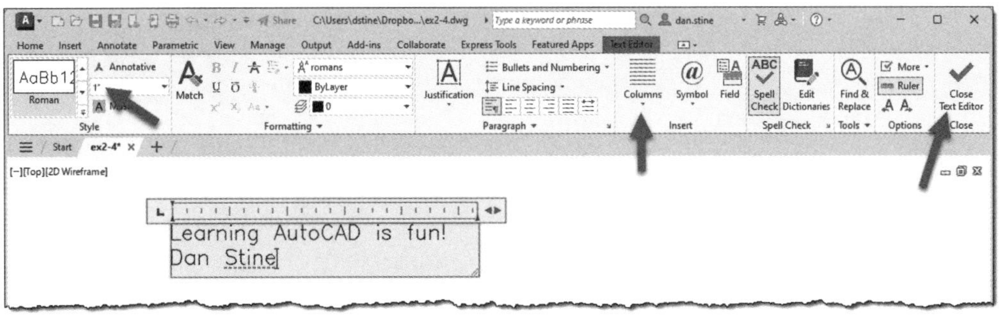

FIGURE 2-4.3 Mtext; text typed in text editor window; Text Formatting ribbon displayed

7. When finished typing text, click the **Close Text Editor** button on the *Ribbon* shown in Figure 2-4.3 above; notice the *Ribbon* changes while in text edit mode.

   TIP: If you ever want to cancel the Text Editor window without typing text, you can simply press the Escape (Esc) key on the keyboard.

Your text should look similar to Figure 2-4.4. Text can be Moved and Rotated with the tools on the *Modify* toolbar.

TIP: Whenever you select an Mtext *object, AutoCAD displays a grip in each corner to represent the* Mtext *window. A grip can be moved to increase or decrease the width of the window. The height will automatically adjust accordingly. Try it.*

Whenever you want to edit text, you double-click on it.

8. Double-click on the text, position the cursor at the end of the sentence, press **Enter** (to start a new line) and then type *your* name (not the author's).

   FYI: Pressing Enter within the text editor should only be done when you want to insert a "hard return," which will ensure the following text always starts on a new line. Otherwise, changing the text box size will adjust the length of each line; this is called a "soft return."

9. **Save** your drawing.

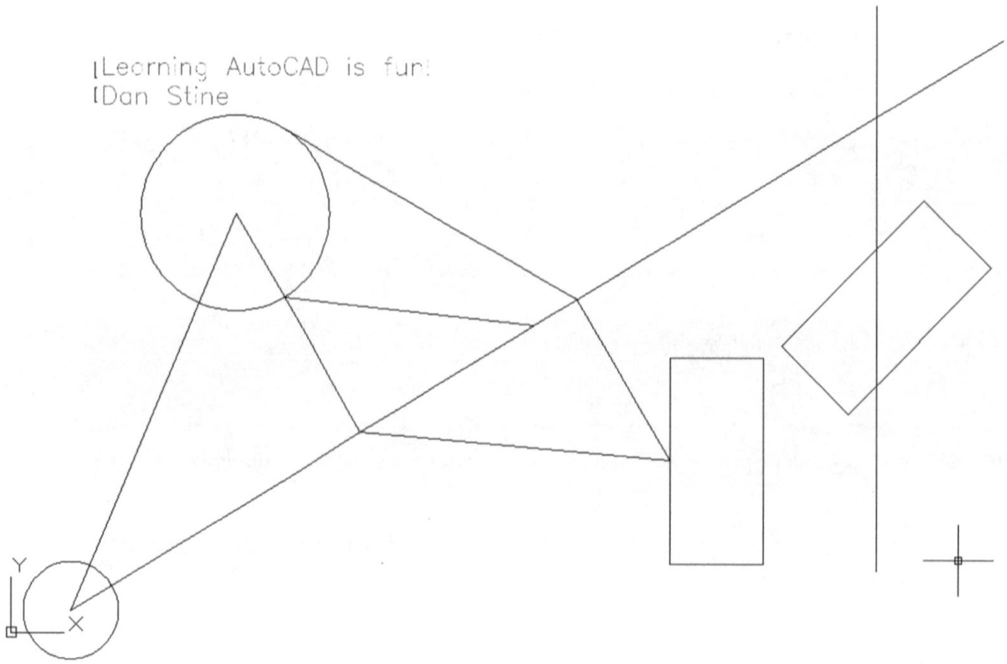

FIGURE 2-4.4 Mtext; final results of text entered

When modifying previously typed text (i.e., bold, underline, text height, etc.) you must select the text within the text edit window. To do this you drag the cursor over the desired text until it is highlighted.

> ***TIP:*** *With the* Mtext Editor *open (Figure 2-4.3), you can Copy/Paste text in from other programs such as MS Word. Most of the formatting (e.g., font, bold, underline, etc.) will be preserved.*

Exercise 2-5:
Printing

The final exercise in this lesson will cover another essential feature in CAD, which is printing. Printing takes some time to fully understand. It will be covered more later in this book (Lesson 10).

Print Room in a large architectural firm

Image courtesy of BWBR Architects
www.bwbr.com

In this exercise you will print to an 8 ½″ x 11″ piece of paper with the drawing filling the paper (i.e., not to scale).

1. Open drawing **ex2-4.dwg**.

2. Use the **Zoom** tools if required to display the portion of the drawing shown in Figure 2-4.4.

3. Select the **Plot** icon from the *Quick Access* toolbar (called *print* in other programs). 

    a. You can also select *Print* → *Plot* from the *Application Menu.*

You are now in the *Plot* dialog box. This is where you tell AutoCAD what printer or plotter to use, what scale and what size paper, to name a few examples (Figure 2-5.1).

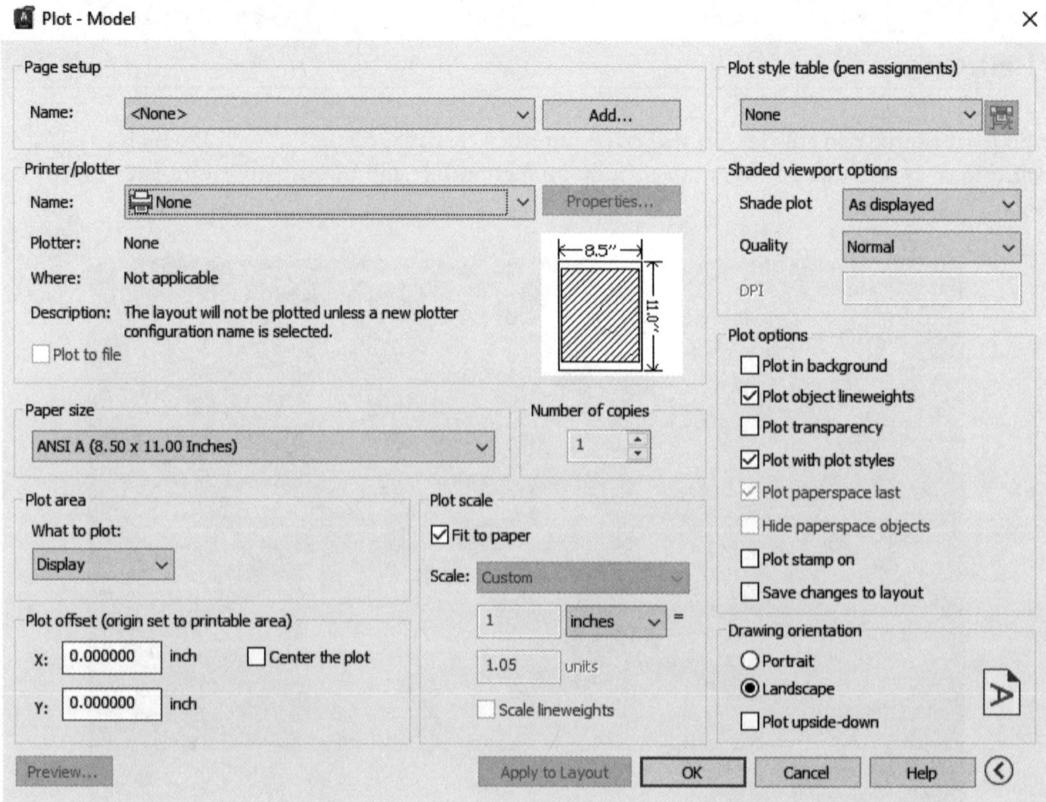

FIGURE 2-5.1 Plot Dialog Box; basic options

4. Make the following adjustments (Figure 2-5.1):
   a. Select a **Printer** you have access to.
   b. Paper size: **Letter (8.5 x 11 in.)**
   c. What to plot: **Display**
   d. **Center the plot**: *checked*
   e. Plot scale: **Fit to paper** *checked*
   f. Drawing Orientation: **Landscape** *checked*

FYI: The Display option (item 4c above) will only plot what is visible on screen; that is why you need to zoom in or out per Step 2.

It is possible to hide some information in this dialog. You typically wouldn't want to do this. But in case you accidentally do this, we will take a quick look at this before plotting.

5. Click the **Less Options** arrow in the lower right corner of the *Plot* dialog box (Figure 2-5.1).

6. Now, to restore the hidden information, click the **More Options** arrow.

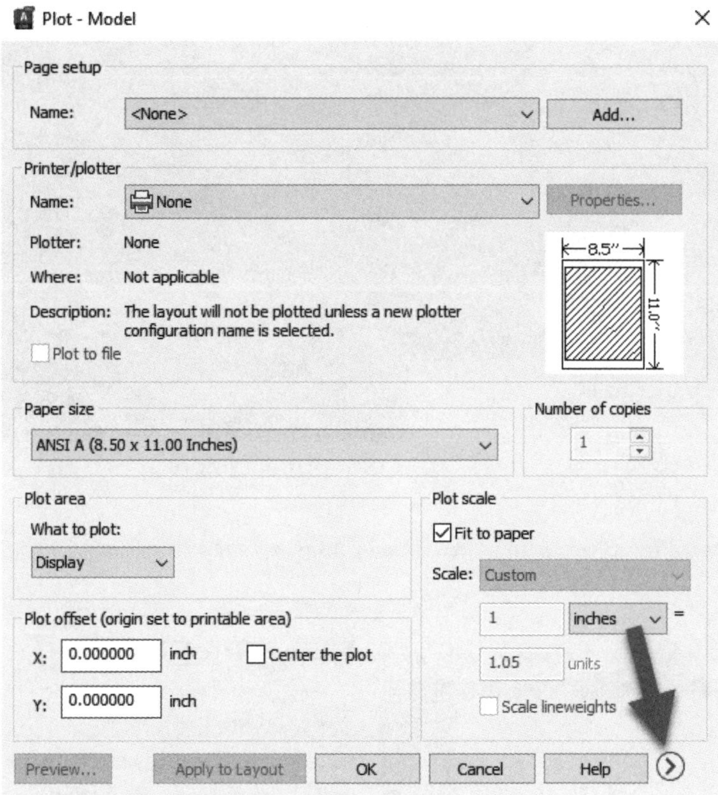

FIGURE 2-5.2 Plot Dialog Box; less options

AutoCAD can print to any printer/plotter installed on your computer. AutoCAD provides a few extra options in the device list for creating PDF and Image files. Selecting **DWG to PDF** will create a high-quality PDF of your drawing, which can be emailed to a client or contractor, for example.

A Printer is an output device that uses smaller paper (e.g., 8 ½″x11″ or 11″x17″). A Plotter is an output device that uses larger paper; plotters typically have one or more rolls of paper ranging in size from 18″ wide to 36″ wide. A roll-feed plotter has a built-in cutter that can, for example, cut paper from a 36-inch-wide roll to produce 24″x36″ sheets.

Plotter with three paper rolls

Color **printer** / copier

7. Click **OK** to send the plot (print) *if you actually want to print a page now.*

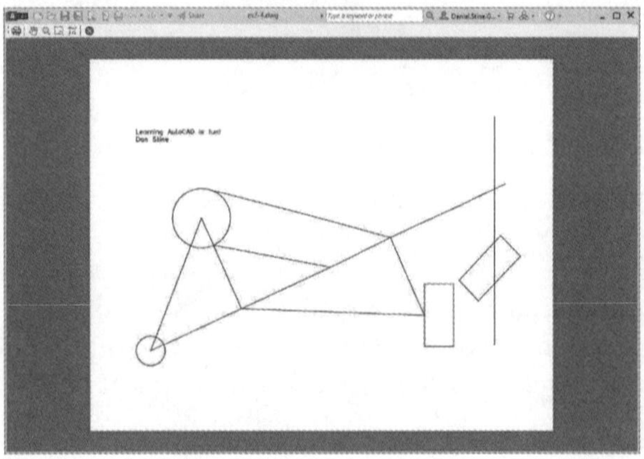

Using PREVIEW...

Before you click **OK**, it is a good idea to click the **Preview** button first. This will show how your drawing will look at the selected paper size.

Previewing first will save time and paper.

Lesson 2 Recap:

In this lesson, *Crash Course Introduction (the Basics)*, you learned how to draw accurate lines and circles, use the *Object Snap* feature for precise pick points, and use a handful of *Modify* tools (e.g., Copy, Move, Rotate, and Scale). You also had a brief introduction to creating text and plotting. You should have a well-balanced amount of base knowledge to begin creating more meaningful objects, which is what you will do in the next lesson!

Self-Exam:

The following questions can be used as a way to check your knowledge of this lesson. The answers can be found at the bottom of this page.

1. AutoCAD is only accurate to 3 decimal places. (T/F)
2. The diamond shaped *OSNAP* symbol represents the *Midpoint* snap. (T/F)
3. "Full Preview" in the *Plot* dialog WILL save you time and paper. (T/F)
4. Use the ______________ command to duplicate objects.
5. When selecting entities, use the ________________________ to select all the entities in the selection window and all entities that extend through it.

Review Questions:

The following questions may be assigned by your instructor as a way to assess your knowledge of this section. Your instructor has the answers to the review questions.

1. AutoCAD is a raster-based program. (T/F)
2. The Base Point you select for Rotate and Scale is not important. (T/F)
3. Entering 16 for a distance actually means 16′-0″ to AutoCAD. (T/F)
4. Use the _________________ command to create squares.
5. You can change the height of the text while in the *Mtext* editor. (T/F)
6. Selecting this icon  allows you to _______________ one or more entities in a drawing.
7. What is the name of the *template* file you are to use when creating a new drawing in this book? ____
8. With the **Rotate** command, typing 45 for the degrees prompt rotates the entities in the ______________ direction, whereas -45 rotates the entities in the ____________ direction.
9. List all the *OSNAP* points available on a circle (ex. Line: endpoint, midpoint, nearest): ____
10. The **OSNAP** button on the *Status Bar* must be "pushed in" (i.e., on) to automatically and accurately select snap points while drawing. (T/F)

SELF-EXAM ANSWERS:
1 – F, **2** – F, **3** – T, **4** – Copy, **5** – Crossing Window

Notes:

Lesson 3
Drawing Architectural Objects (Draw & Modify):

This lesson is meant to give you practice drawing in AutoCAD. While doing so, you will become familiar with the various shapes and sizes of the more common symbols used in a residential set of drawings.

Each drawing will be created in its own drawing file. The drawings (i.e., symbols) will be used later to automate drafting.

For some of the symbols to be drawn, you will have step-by-step instruction and/or a study on a particular command that would be useful in the creation of that object. Other symbols to be drawn are for practice by way of repetition and do not provide step-by-step instruction.

Do NOT draw the dimensions; they are for reference only.

Exercise 3-1:
Rectilinear Objects

Overview:

All the objects you will draw in this exercise consist entirely of straight lines, either orthogonal (i.e., horizontal or vertical) or angular. As previously mentioned, **all the objects MUST BE drawn in SEPARATE drawing files**. Each object will have a specific name provided, which is to be used to name the drawing file. All files should be saved in your personal folder created for this course.

Each object drawn will have the lower left corner located at the origin (0,0,0). This will be discussed further in a moment.

Each new drawing created for this course should be done using the **Architectural Imperial.dwt** template file. Remember to use the *Architectural Imperial* template in the SheetSet sub-folder. **Do NOT use the default drawing that opens automatically as it is based on a different template.**

ALL entities drawn in Exercises 1 and 2 should be drawn on the default layer, that is, *Layer 0* (zero). So just make sure the *Layers* panel displays *Layer 0* similar to the *Layers* panel shown on page 1-6.

filename: Bookcase.dwg

This is a simple rectangle that represents the size of a bookcase. Do not add the dimensions.

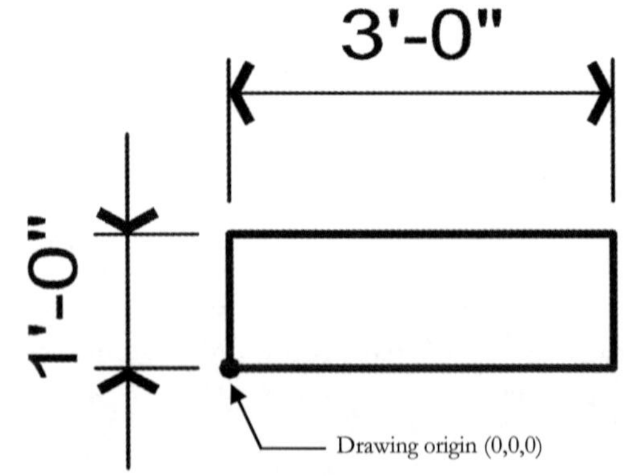

1. Start a new drawing; be sure to start from the correct template (**Architectural Imperial** in the *SheetSets* folder).

2. Switch to ***Model Space***.

   TIP: *If you did not start on a Layout Tab (next to the Model tab) named Arch D, you did not start with the correct template.*

3. Select the **Rectangle** command.

4. For the first point, enter **0,0** *(include the comma).*

   NOTE: *When entering an X,Y,Z coordinate, AutoCAD assumes Z equals 0 if you only enter X and Y values.*

5. At the **Specify Other Corner** prompt, type **3′** and then press the **Tab** key (this is for the *Width*, or the "X" value). See tip below if you have any problems.

6. Enter **1′** and **Enter** (this is for the *Height*, or the "Y" value).

7. **Save**, and then **Close**, your drawing per the name listed above (bookcase.dwg).

filename: Coffee Table.dwg

8. Similar to the steps listed above, plus the suggestions mentioned below, create the coffee table shown to the left.

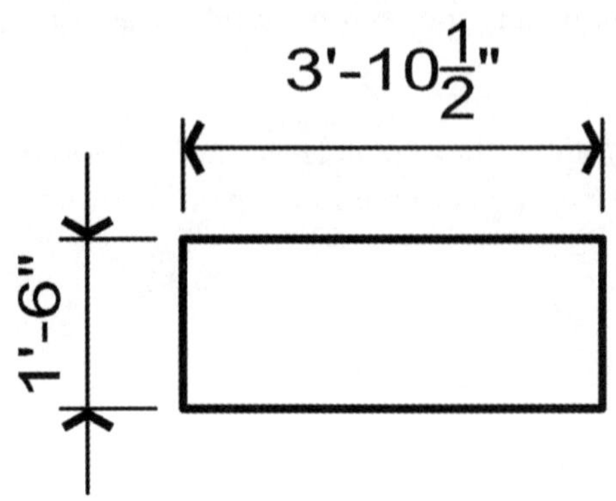

Entering fractions: The 3′-10½″ can be entered in one of three ways.

- 3′10.5
  Notice there is no space between the feet and inches.
- 3′10-1/2
  Note the dash location; it separates the inches: whole–fraction.
- 46.5
  This is all in inches; that is 3′- 10½″ = 46.5″

filename: **Desk-1.dwg**

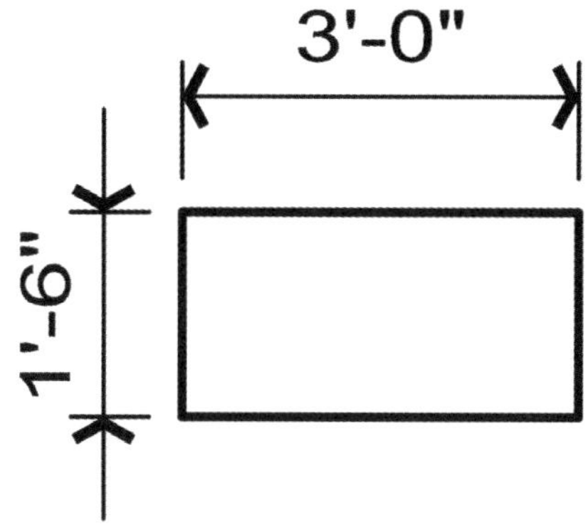

9. Draw the *Desk* in its own file, similar to the steps outlined above.

10. **Save**. After completing *desk-1.dwg*, select **Save-As** from the *Application* menu *(the large red "A")*.

11. Enter **Night Table.dwg** for the name and then click **Save**.

You are now in a new file and *desk-1* is closed.

filename: **Night Table.dwg**

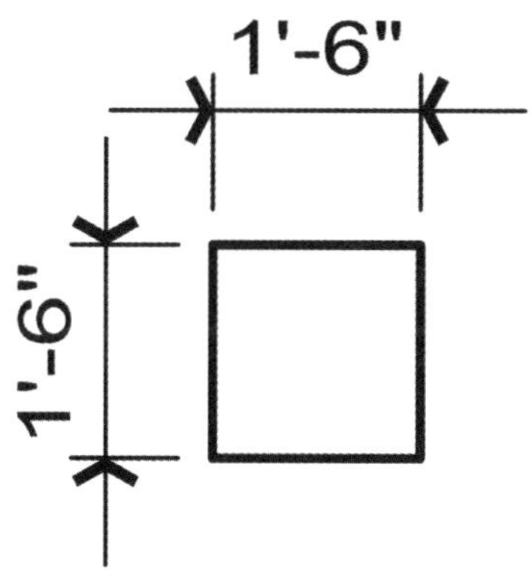

Obviously, you could draw this quickly per the previous examples. However, you will take a look at the **Stretch** command now.

You will use the **Stretch** command to stretch the 3′-0″ wide desk down to a 1′-6″ wide night table; you don't want to move the lower left corner which aligns with the *Origin*.

12. Select **Stretch** from the *Modify* panel. 

13. Select a ***Crossing Window*** (or *Crossing Lasso*) as shown in **Figure 3-1.1**.

TIP: Pick your window from right to left; refer back to page 2-23 for more on Crossing Windows.

14. Press **Enter** and then pick any point on the screen (Figure 3-1.2).

15. Make sure ***Polar Tracking*** is turned on *(TIP: Status Bar as shown in image below)*. Move your cursor to the left, with the *Polar Tracking* locking into the horizontal position, as shown in Figure 3-1.2.

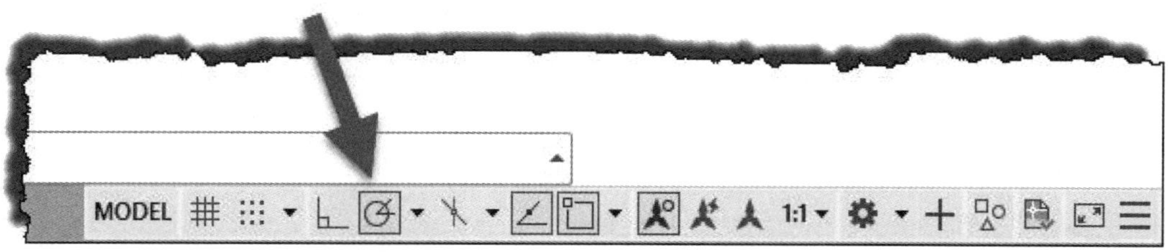

Polar Tracking turned on – with blue highlight

16. Type **1′6** *(dash and inch symbol are not required)* and press **Enter**.

17. **Save** your drawing.

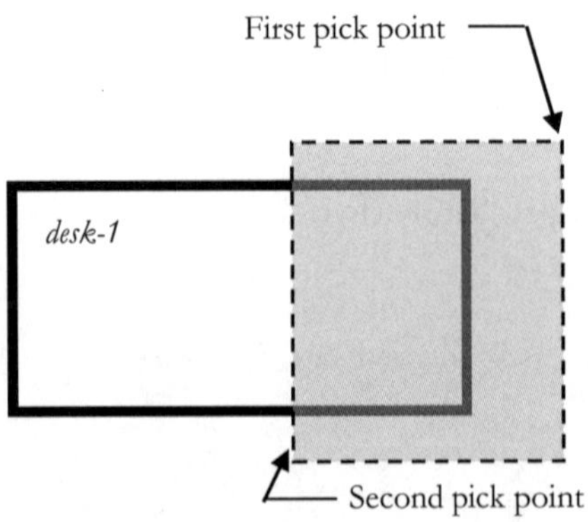

FIGURE 3-1.1 Stretch command – *Crossing Window* selection shown

Which Objects Get Stretched and Which Objects Don't?

When you select a portion of a drawing to be stretched, like the example to the left, some entities are stretched while others are moved.

Notice in the example to the left, (Figure 3-1.1), the two horizontal lines are stretched, whereas the vertical line simply moves 1′-6″ to the left.

<u>You can think of it this way:</u>
Any lines that pass through the *Crossing Window* are stretched. Any lines that are completely within the *Crossing Window* are moved.

TIP: For the *Stretch* command, always pick a crossing-window (from right to left).

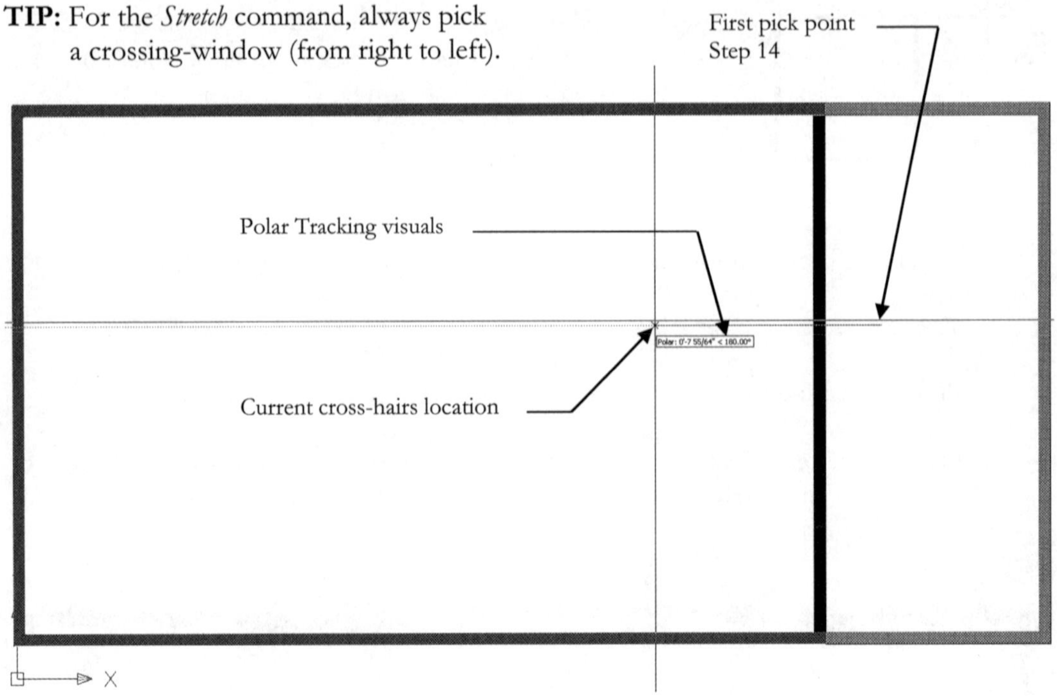

FIGURE 3-1.2 Stretch Command – Stretch in progress; first point picked

filename: **Dresser-1.dwg**

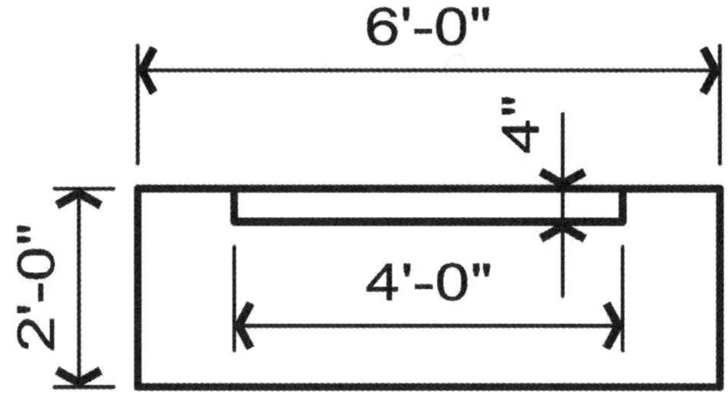

18. Draw the dresser using the following *TIP*.

TIP: Simply draw two rectangles. Make sure the large rectangle is at the Origin. Move the smaller rectangle into place using the Move command and OSNAPs.

filename: **Dresser-2.dwg**

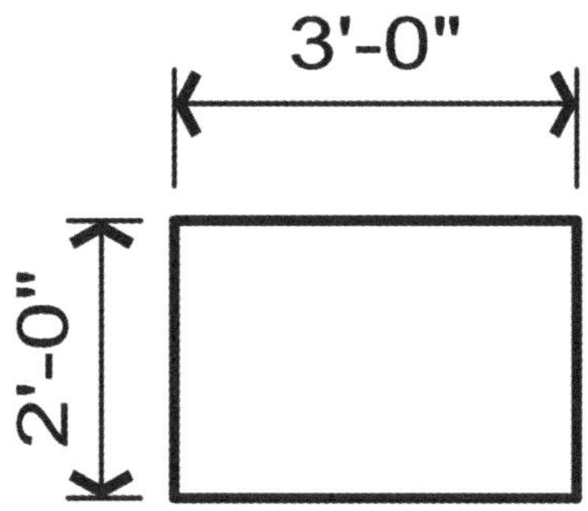

19. Draw this smaller dresser.

filename: **Desk-2.dwg**

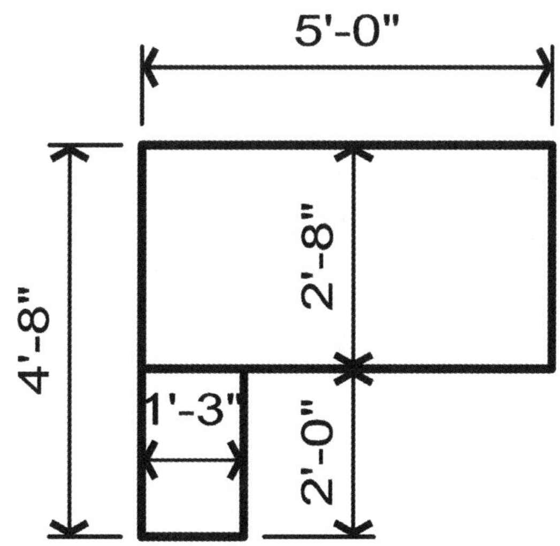

20. Draw this desk in the same way you drew dresser-1 (i.e., two rectangles). Make sure the lower left is at the *Origin*!

filename: **File Cabinet.dwg**

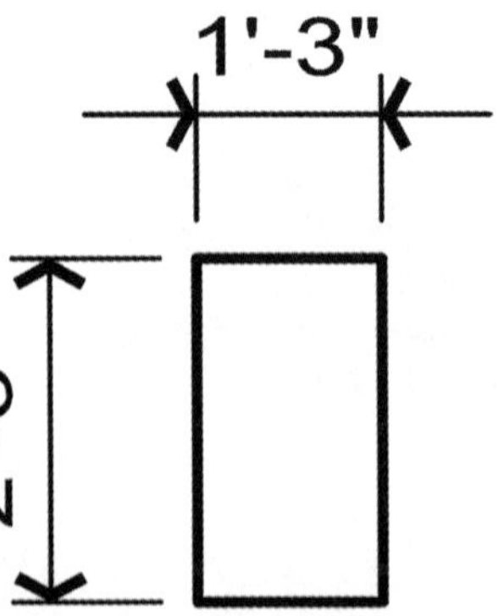

21. Draw this file cabinet.

filename: **Chair-1.dwg**

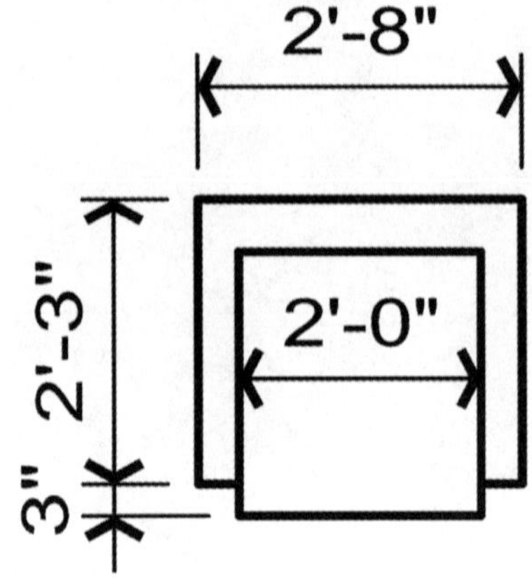

22. Draw this chair per the following *TIP*.

> ***TIP:*** *Draw the 2'x2' square first, and then draw three (temporary) rectangles as shown to the right. If necessary, move them into place with Move and OSNAPs. Next, draw a line for the arms and backrest and then delete the three temporary rectangles.*

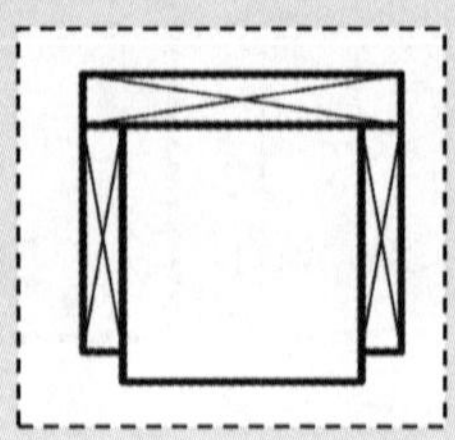

filename: **Sofa.dwg**

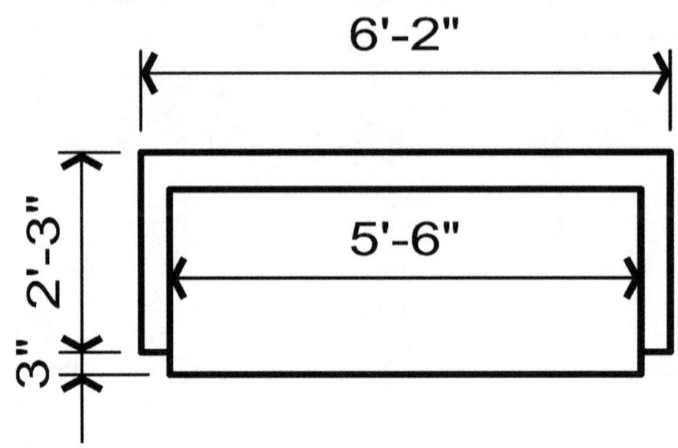

23. Do a **Save-As** from the chair-1 file and **Stretch** to create the sofa.

filename: **Bed-Double.dwg**

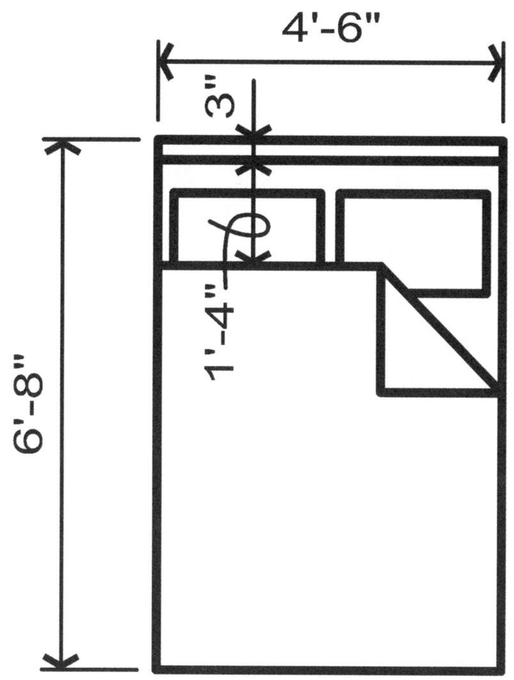

24. Draw the following **three** beds using lines and rectangles; the exact size of items not dimensioned is not important. Use **Stretch** to create the two larger beds.

filename: **Bed-Queen.dwg**

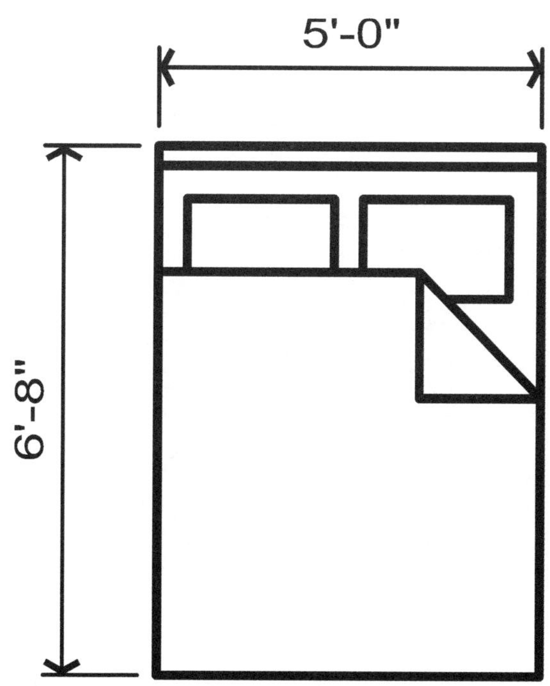

filename: **Bed-King.dwg**

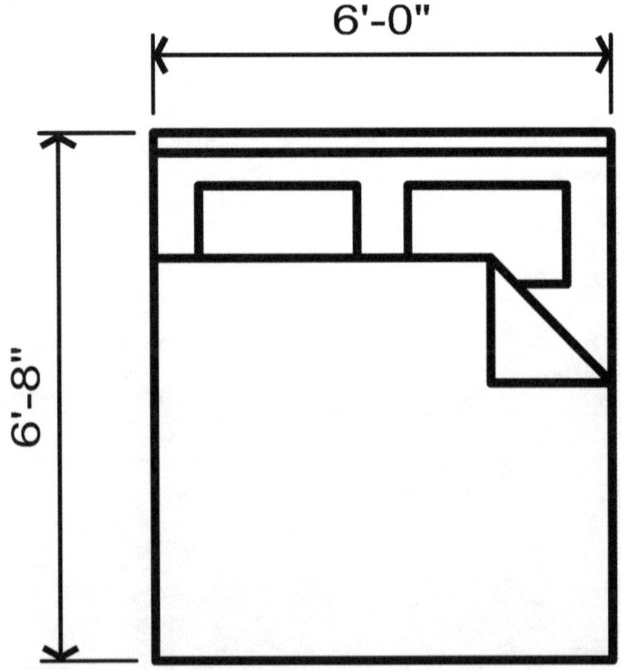

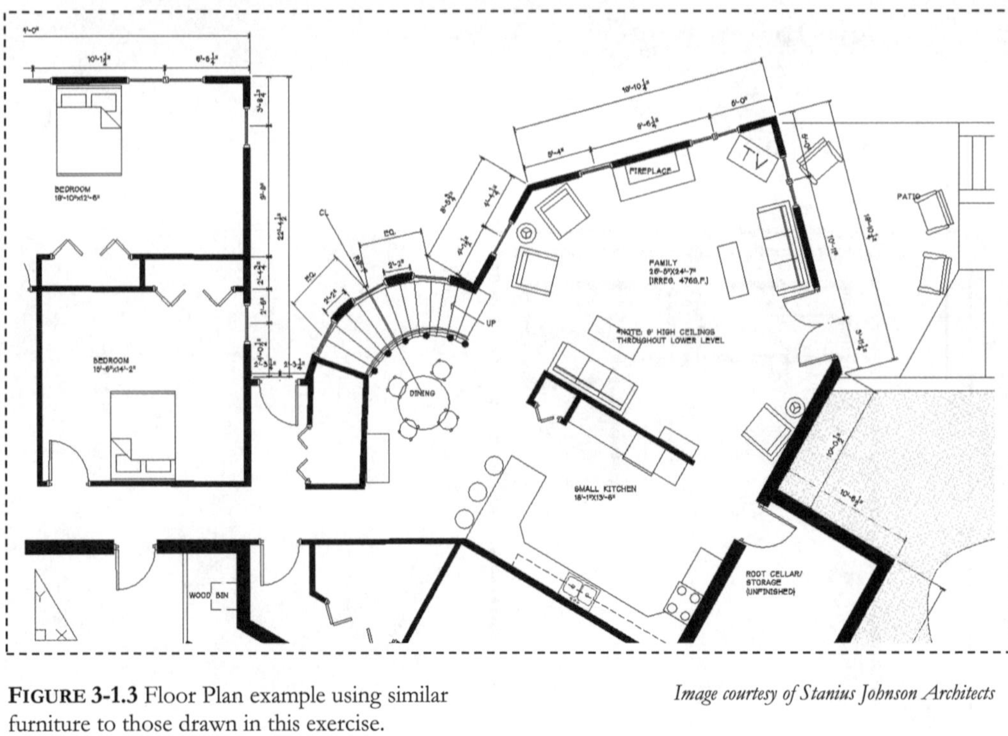

FIGURE 3-1.3 Floor Plan example using similar furniture to those drawn in this exercise.

Image courtesy of Stanius Johnson Architects

Exercise 3-2:
Objects with Curves

Similar to the previous exercise, you will draw several shapes; this time the shapes will have curves in them. You will look at the various commands that allow you to create curves, like Arc, Circle and Fillet.

Again, you will not draw the dimensions as they are for reference only. Each drawing should be drawn in its own drawing file; save the drawing with the filename provided.

One more thing about *Layers*: they all occupy the same space. *Layers* are similar to a stack of transparencies in that you can slip one out of the stack (i.e., turn a layer *off*). However, in AutoCAD, all the transparencies in the stack would occupy the space as if there were only one and not a stack. Everything in this exercise should also be drawn on *Layer* zero (i.e., *Layer0*).

Finally, the black dot on each of the drawings is for reference only. This dot represents the location of the *Drawing Origin* (0,0).

filename: Laundry-Sink.dwg

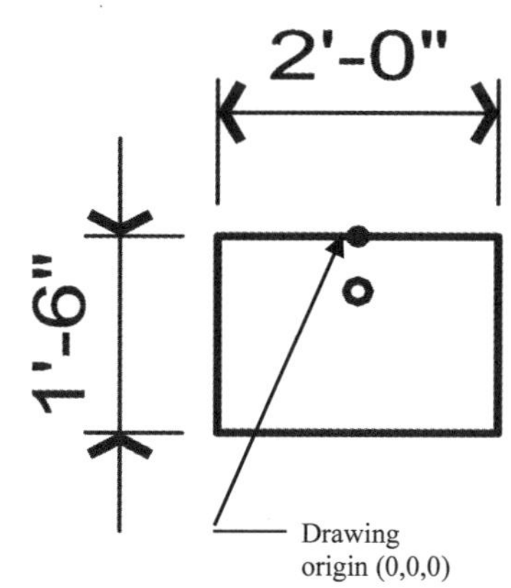

This is a simple rectangle that represents the size of a laundry sink, with a circle that represents the drain.

1. **Open** a new drawing.
2. Select the **Rectangle** command.
3. Draw a rectangle, per the dimensions shown, anywhere in the drawing (you will reposition it in the next step).
4. Use the *Move* command to position the rectangle relative to the *Origin.*
   a. Pick the **Move** icon
   b. Select the rectangle
   c. Pick the midpoint of the top horizontal line for the first point
   d. Type ***0,0** for the second point (be sure to add the asterisks at the beginning)
   e. Press **Enter**.

Next you will draw a circle for the drain. The drain needs to be centered left and right, and 5″ from the top edge. The following steps will show you one way in which to do this.

5. Start the **Circle** tool.

6. Type **0,0** to locate the center point of the circle. *(This is the midpoint of the top edge of your rectangle.)*

7. Type **1** for the radius and press **Enter**. *(This creates a 2″ diameter circle.)*

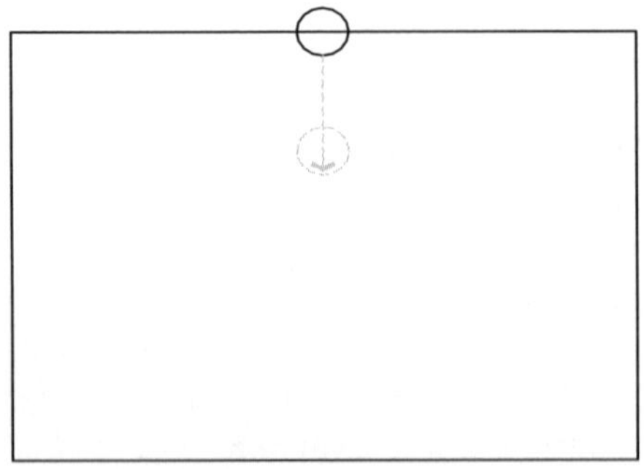

FIGURE 3-2.1 Creating a circle and moving it into place.

Next you will use the *Move* command to reposition the circle.

8. Select the **Move** icon.

9. Pick the circle. *(Press* ***Enter*** *to tell AutoCAD you are done selecting entities to move.)*

10. For your **First point of displacement**, pick anywhere in the *Drawing* window; in this example, the first point is irrelevant.

11. For your **Second point of displacement**, move the cursor in the direction you want the circle moved (*downward on the screen*) until *Polar Tracking* locks in, and then enter **5**.

12. If you haven't already done so, press **Enter** to complete the **Move** operation (Figure 3-2.1).

13. **Save** the file per the name listed above.

REMEMBER: *The black dot shown on the previous page represents the drawing's* Origin *and is* *__not__* *to be drawn. This may be a little confusing on the* Laundry Sink *example because you drew a circle at that same location. But, if you recall, you* Moved *the circle (as opposed to* Copying *it). So the circle should not be there anymore.*

filename: **Dryer.dwg**

Process Snapshot

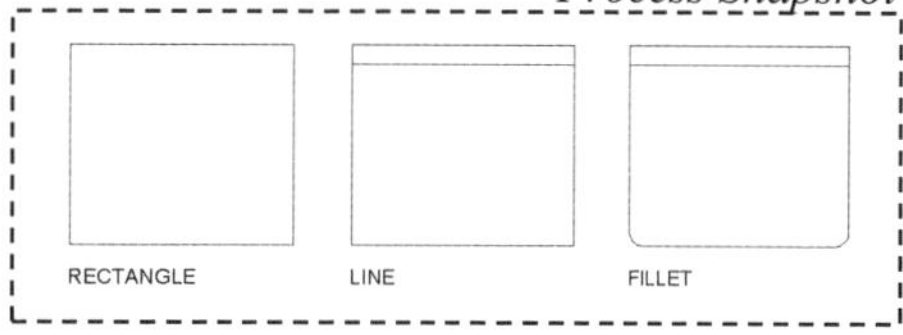

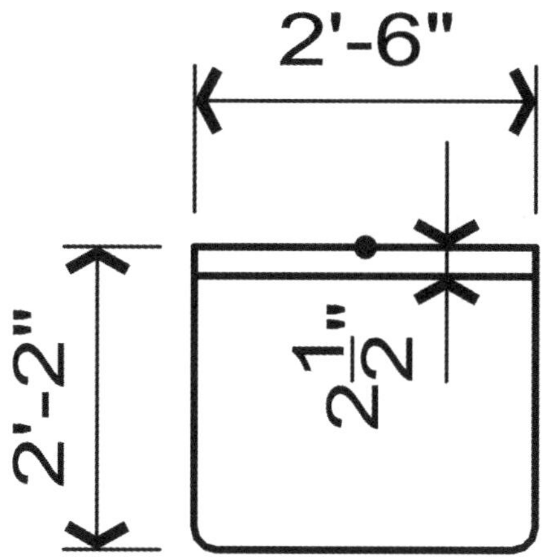

Here you will draw a dryer with rounded front corners. This, like all the other symbols in this lesson, is a plan view symbol (i.e., as viewed from the top).

14. Draw a 30″x26″rectangle.

15. **Move** the rectangle into place as described in the previous drawing (*Laundry Sink*).

Next you will draw the line that is 2½″ from the back of the dryer.

16. Make sure the following features are enabled on the *Status Bar*: ***Polar Tracking***, ***Object Snap***, ***Object Snap Tracking***.

17. Select the **Line** icon.

18. Hover the cursor over the upper left corner and then, without clicking, move the cursor straight down; type **2.5** and then press **Enter**.

TIP: Nearest OSNAP must be off.

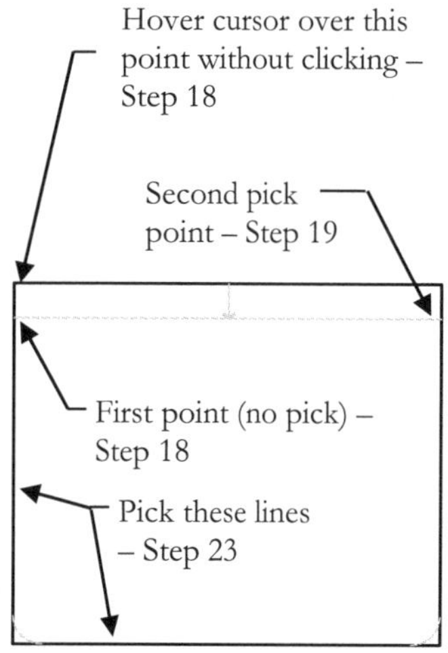

FIGURE 3-2.2 Drawing a line

You should have seen a small "x" snapped to the vertical line as you moved the cursor down. Typing 2.5 and pressing Enter tells AutoCAD the first pick point is to be 2½″ over from the reference point (i.e., the point you paused the cursor over). You may have to try this a few times to get the hang of it; if you are having problems, make sure you are not creating short vertical lines. Remember you do not actually click the first point of the line, only the second point.

19. Move the cursor to the right and use the *Perpendicular* snap on the right-hand vertical line; this is the endpoint of the new horizontal line.

Notice that you did not have to tell AutoCAD (by entering a number) how long the line needed to be. Instead, you picked two points that you knew were 30″ apart.

Next you will round-off the front corners of the dryer.

20. Select the **Fillet** icon from the *Modify* panel. Fillet

21. Type **R** and then **Enter.** *(This runs the sub-command* **Radius.***)*

Notice the prompt in the *Command Window* (Figure 3-2.3). The default *Radius* is set to zero; you will need to change that to 2″.

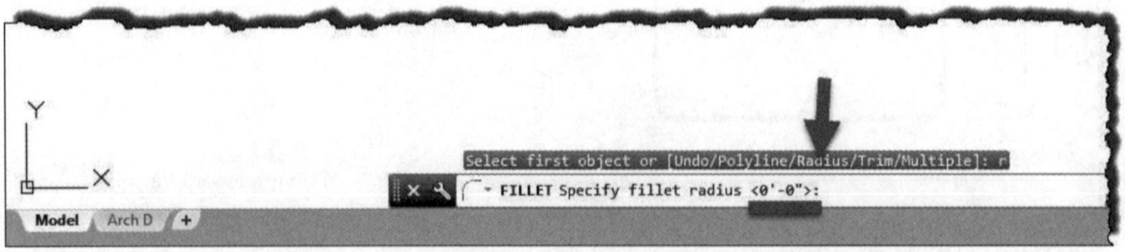

FIGURE 3-2.3 Fillet command – *Command Window* prompts after initiating the command

22. Type **2** and then **Enter.**

Next you will select the two lines whose intersection you want filleted.

23. Select the vertical line on the left and then select the horizontal line on the bottom (front). See Figure 3-2.2.

    a. Notice as you hover your cursor over the second line, a preview of the fillet is shown. This allows you to see what the fillet is going to look like before committing to it. If it is too big or too small, you can type "R" again and change the radius before finalizing the change. Do not change the radius at this time.

24. Repeat the previous step to **Fillet** the other "front" corner.

25. **Save** your drawing.

filename: **Washer.dwg**

Process Snapshot

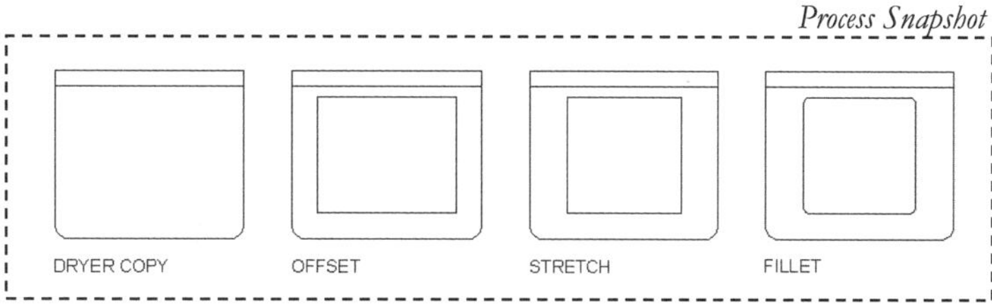

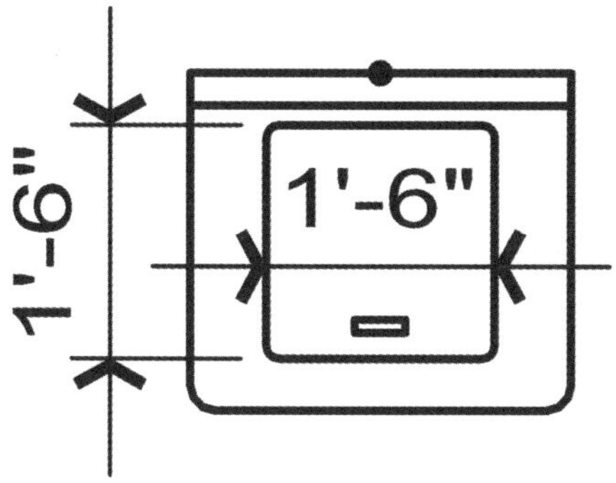

This drawing is identical to the dryer except for the door added to the top. You can open the dryer drawing and do a *Save-As* to get a jump start on this drawing.

To draw the door, you will use the *Offset* command on the *Modify* panel, found on the *Home* tab.

The *Offset* command is easy to use. To use it you…

- o Enter the distance you want to offset a line.
- o Select the line you want to offset.
- o Pick which side of the line you want to offset to.

26. Select the **Offset** icon on the *Modify* panel, *Home* tab. 

27. Type **4** and then press **Enter**.

28. Select the rectangle (that represents the perimeter of the washer) as the line you wish to offset.

29. Pick anywhere inside the rectangle.

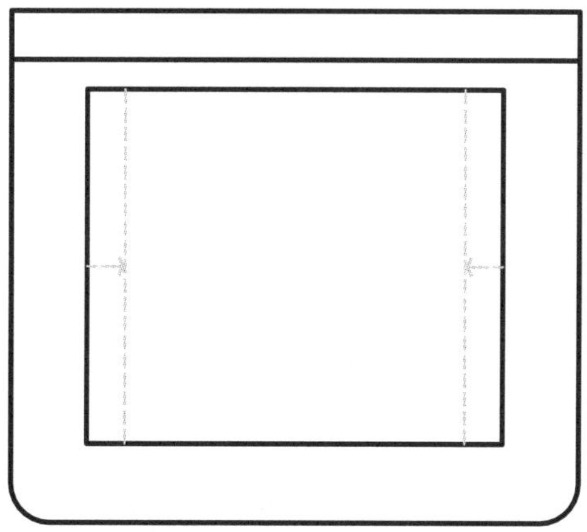

FIGURE 3-2.4 Outer rectangle offset inward 4″. Note that the dashed lines are the location of the "door" after it is stretched in Step 31.

Picking within the rectangle caused the rectangle to offset towards the inside. You are encouraged to **Undo** at this point and see what happens when you click on the outside of the rectangle. Obviously, the rectangle will offset to the outside of the existing rectangle. When finished experimenting with the **Offset** command, make sure to restore the proper rectangle per Step 29 above.

Next you will stretch the rectangle to adjust its width.

30. Use the **Stretch** techniques previously covered to stretch the right side of the inner rectangle **2″** to the left (Figure 3-2.4).

31. Repeat the previous steps to **Stretch** the left side **2″** to the right (Figure 3-2.4).

You should now have a properly sized door (1′-6″ x 1′-6″).

You should occasionally double check your dimensions; it is easy to accidentally type the wrong distance. Next you will verify the door is the correct size using the **Distance** tool (there are other ways to do this, but this is the best one for this task).

32. Use the **Distance** command (*Home* tab, *Utilities* panel, Measure drop-down) from the *Ribbon* and pick two points shown (i.e., dimensioned) for the washer drawing on page 3-13.

    TIP: *Make sure you use the OSNAPs to accurately pick the points to which you are dimensioning.*

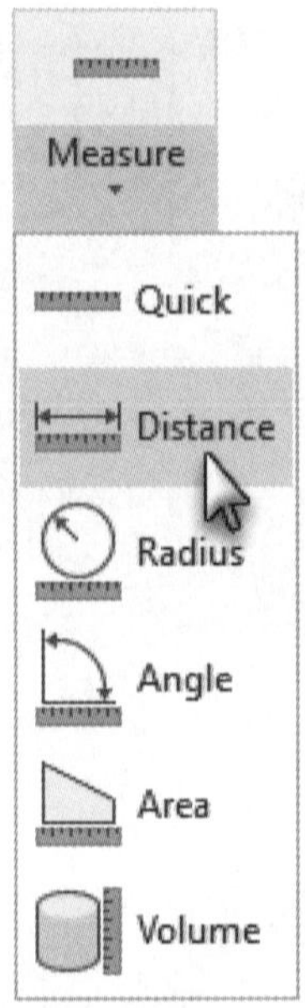

33. Note the distance listed in the *Command Window.*

    a. The distance will also show up next to your cursor if you have *Dynamic Input* turned on.

    b. Notice the additional information shown in the *Command Window.* The Delta X and Delta Y values tell you the relative change in the X and Y directions for a diagonal measurement. This would give you the overall size of a rectangle with one measurement.

Next you will **Fillet** the corners of the door. AutoCAD provides a sub-command for Fillet that will round all the corners at once. You will try this option now.

NOTE: *This option only works on polylines, which is what the* **Rectangle** *command creates. If you simply drew the rectangle with individual lines, you would have to fillet each corner separately.*

34. Select the **Fillet** icon and set the radius to **1″**.

35. Type **P** (for **Polyline**) and press **Enter** (refer back to Figure 3-2.3).

36. Select the washer door (i.e., the rectangle).

All four corners should now be rounded off. The image below shows the various results when using the **Polyline** sub-command for *Fillet*. Try it!

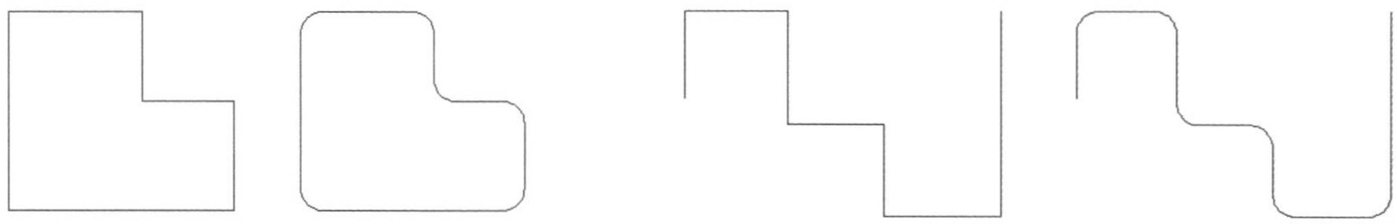

37. Draw a small 4″x1″ rectangle to represent the door handle; draw it anywhere. Using *OSNAPs*, move it to the midpoint of the bottom door edge, and then move the handle 2″ up.

38. **Save** your drawing (make sure the name is *Washer*).

filename: Range.dwg

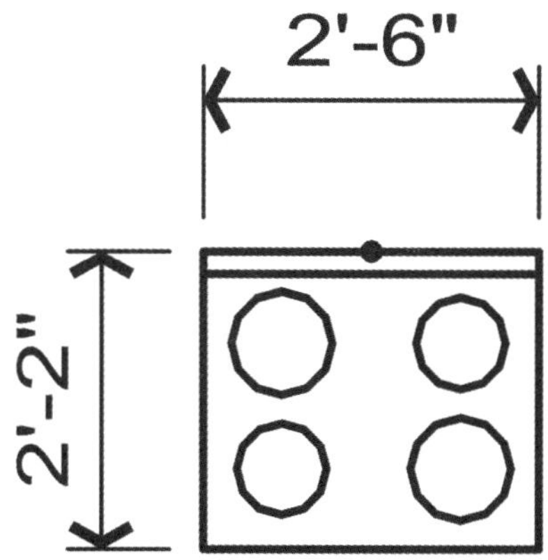

Now you will draw a Kitchen Range with four circles that represent the burners.

In this exercise you will have to draw temporary lines (called construction lines) to create reference points needed to accurately locate the circles. Once the circles have been drawn, the construction lines can be erased.

39. Draw the *Range* with a 2″ control panel at the back. Refer to the steps described to draw the *Dryer*, if necessary.

40. Draw the four construction lines shown in Figure 3-2.5. (They do not need to be dashed lines.)

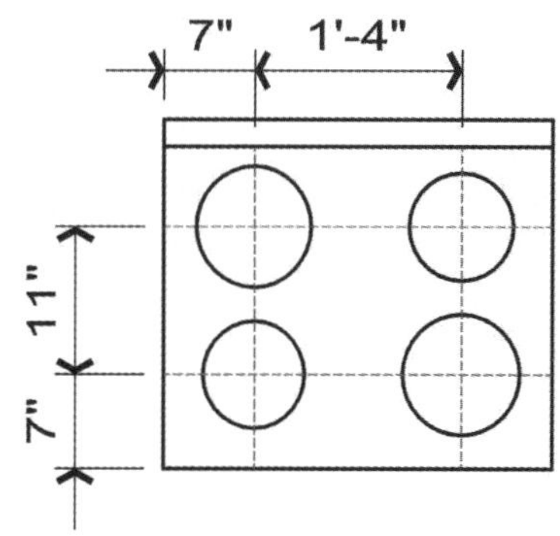

FIGURE 3-2.5
Range with four temporary construction lines (shown dashed)

41. Draw two **9½″** circles and two **7½″** circles using the intersection of the construction lines to locate the centers of the circles (Figure 3-2.5).

42. **Erase** the four construction lines.

43. **Save** your drawing.

filename: Chair-2.dwg

Process Snapshot

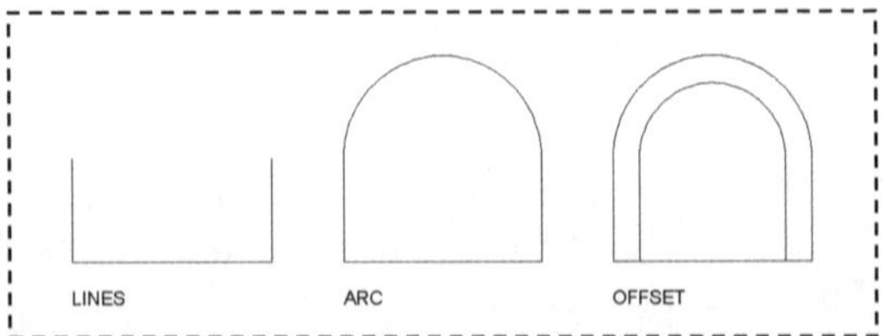

Now you will draw another chair. You will use the Line and Offset commands as well as the Arc command.

First you will draw the three straight lines at the perimeter.

44. First draw the **2′-6″** line across the bottom. Use one of the following methods to accurately position the line relative to the drawing *Origin* (0,0); these are your options:
    a. Drawing the line, type **0,0** for your first point and then type **2′-6″** (with *Polar Tracking* on; to the right). Finally, move the line **1′-3″** to the left. (This will position the line such that your 2′-6″ line's midpoint is at the *Origin*.)
    b. Anywhere in the drawing, draw a horizontal line **2′-6″** long. Now use the **Move** command. Pick the *Midpoint* of the line for the first point and type ***0,0** for the second point.

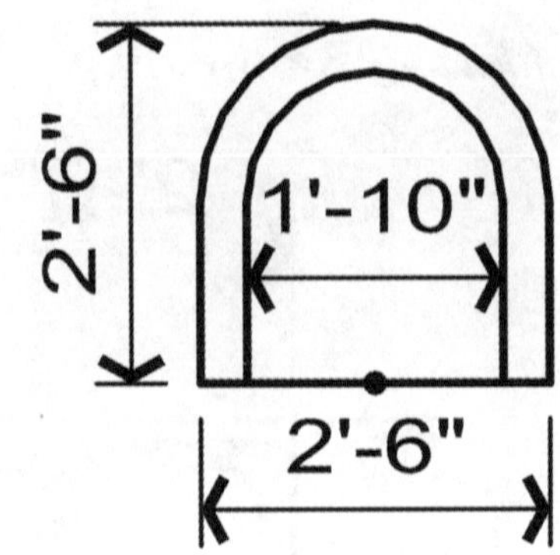

45. Using *Polar Tracking* (or *Ortho*) draw two vertical lines **1′-3″** long (Figure 3-2.6).

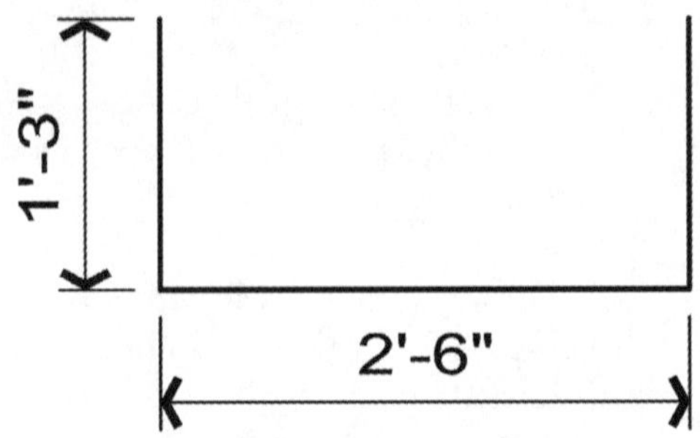

FIGURE 3-2.6 Three lines drawn for Chair-2

Next you will draw an arc to complete the chair's perimeter.

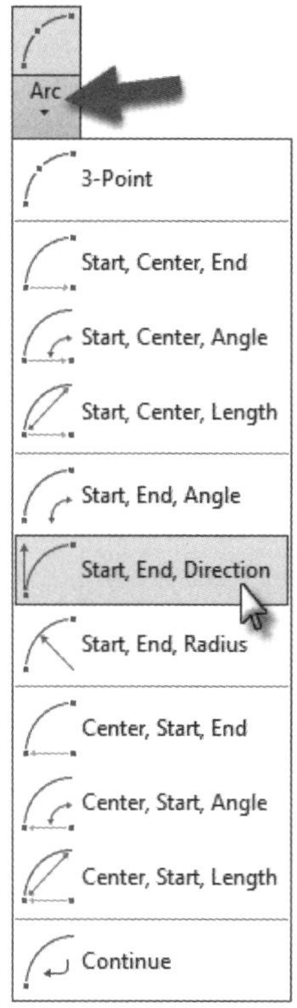

46. Select the **Arc** tool named **Start, End, Direction** from the *Draw* panel, via the down-arrow.

    Notice you are prompted to **Specify start point of arc**.

TIP: If you press the down arrow on the keyboard, you get access to the Center/End options that you see listed in the Command Window.

47. Pick the upper *Endpoint* of the vertical line on the <u>right</u>. (See Figure 3-2.7A.)

You are now prompted in the *Command Window* **Specify end point of arc**:

The on-screen prompt says:

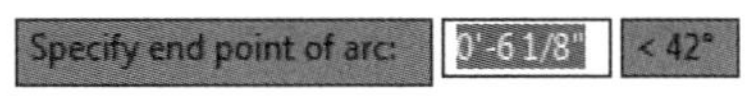

48. Pick the upper *Endpoint* of the vertical line on the <u>left</u> for the arc's endpoint (Figure 3-2.7A).

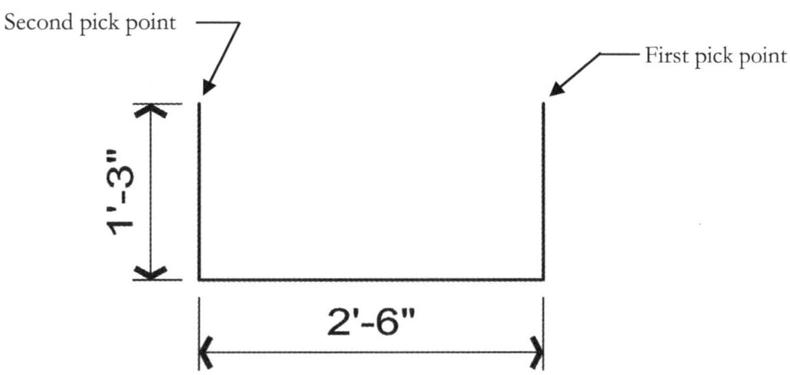

FIGURE 3-2.7A Pick points for **Arc** command

49. Move your cursor straight up with *Polar Tracking* snapped to the vertical plane (Figure 3-2.7B).

50. Once snapped to the vertical plane, click to create the arc.

You have now completed the perimeter of the chair. In previous versions of AutoCAD, you had to pick the right side first, and then the left side to get the arc to be created in the correct direction; that is not a problem in this version.

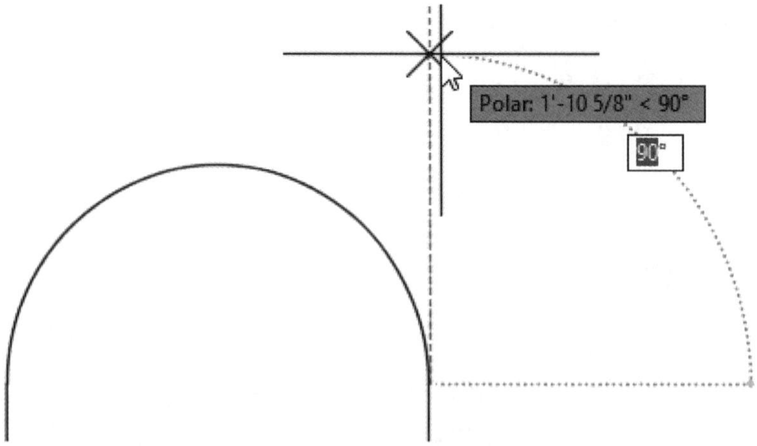

FIGURE 3-2.7B Picking direction for arc command

51. Use the **Offset** command to offset the arc and two vertical lines the required distance.

Notice that because you drew the perimeter with individual lines, the entire outline did not offset like the rectangle did. This would work if you turned these lines into polylines (which will be covered later).

52. **Save** your drawing.

filename: Love-Seat.dwg

Process Snapshot

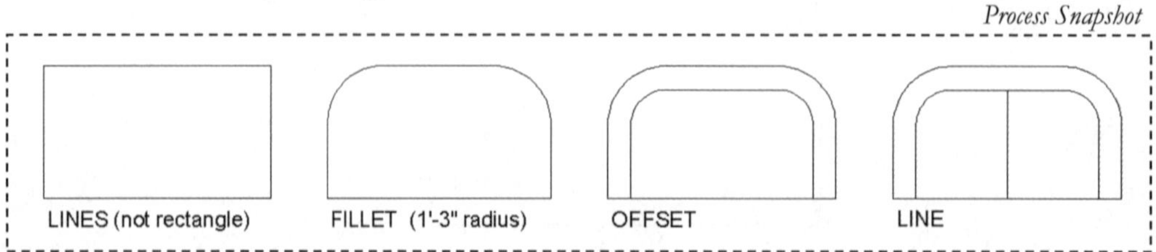

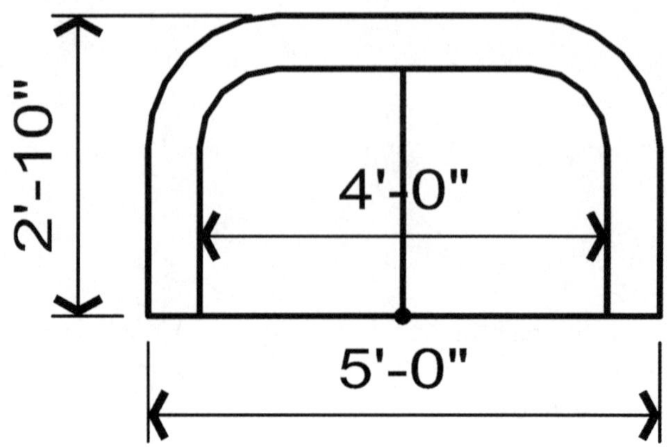

You should be able to draw this *Love Seat* without any further instruction. You can do so using a combination of the following commands:

- Line
- Fillet
- Offset
- Move

> *TIP: When starting the* Love Seat *drawing above, you might initially get the idea to draw a 2′-6″ line from the* Origin *to the right and then another 2′-6″ line from the* Origin *to the left. This would give the appearance of a 5′-0″ line with the center at 0,0. Typically that should be avoided. Anything that looks like one line should actually be only one line in AutoCAD. It is considered sloppy drafting when you have several smaller lines make up one line or to have several overlapping lines.*

filename: **Tub.dwg**

Process Snapshot

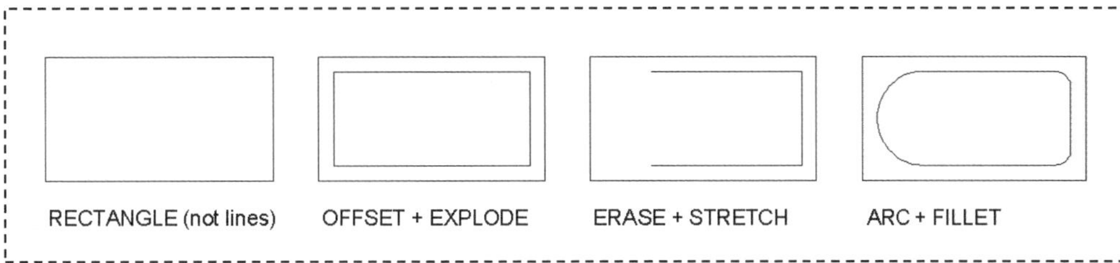

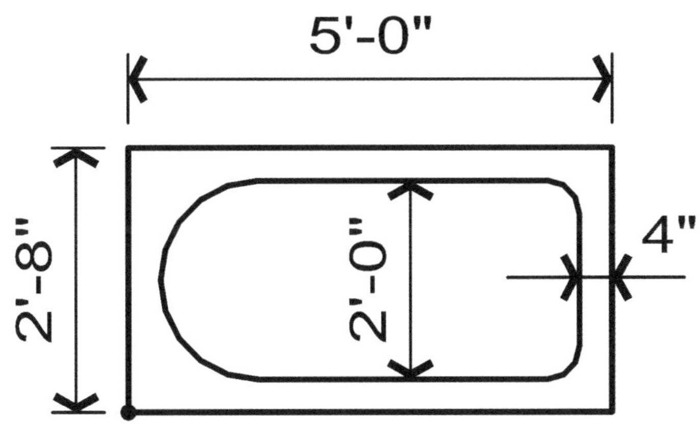

Now you will draw a *bathtub.* You will use several commands previously covered. You will also be introduced to another command called **Explode**; this command allows you to turn a polyline (e.g., rectangle) into individual lines.

53. **Draw** the rectangle.

54. **Offset** the rectangle inward **4″**.

Next you will use the **Explode** command to change the smaller rectangle from a *polyline* to *individual lines* so you can edit them separately.

55. Select the **Explode** icon on the *Modify* panel. 

56. **Pick** the smaller rectangle and then **Enter**.

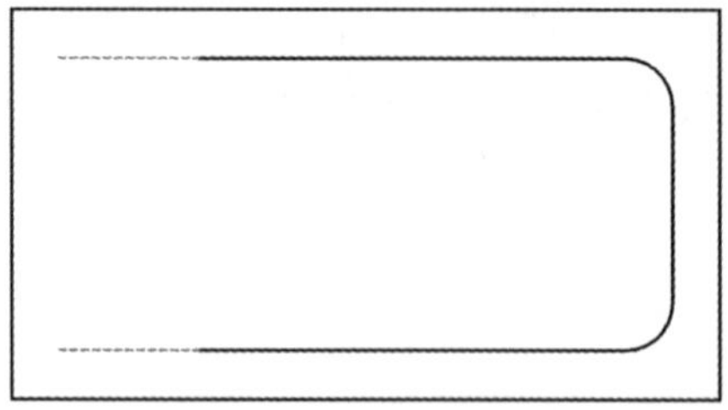

FIGURE 3-2.8 Horizontal Lines stretched 1′-0″ to the right

Select one of the lines to see that only one line is selected, rather than the entire rectangle (i.e., all four lines). Press **Escape** to unselect the line and proceed to the next step.

57. **Erase** the vertical line on the left (Figure 3-2.8).

58. **Stretch** the two horizontal lines 1′-0″ to the right (Figure 3-2.8).

59. Draw an **Arc** with a **1′-0″** radius (refer back to *Chair-2* if you need help with this step).

60. **Fillet** the two corners to have a **4″** radius.

61. **Save**.

You can start to see how the small handful of commands you have learned thus far can be used to draw many different things!

filename: Lav-1.dwg

Draw this *Lavatory* per the following specifications:

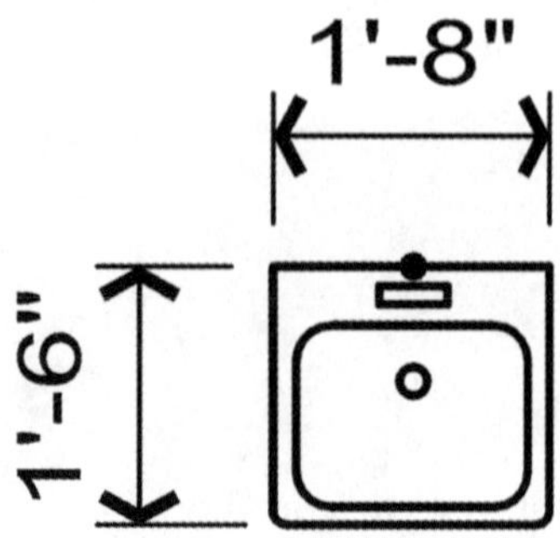

- Larger arcs shown shall have a 2½″ radius.
- Smaller arcs shown shall have a 1″ radius.
- Sides and Front of sink to have 1½″ space (offset).
- Back to have 4″ space (offset).
- Small rectangle to be 4½″ x 1″ and 1½″ away from the back.
- 2″ Dia. Drain, 8″ from Origin.

filename: **Lav-2.dwg**

Process Snapshot

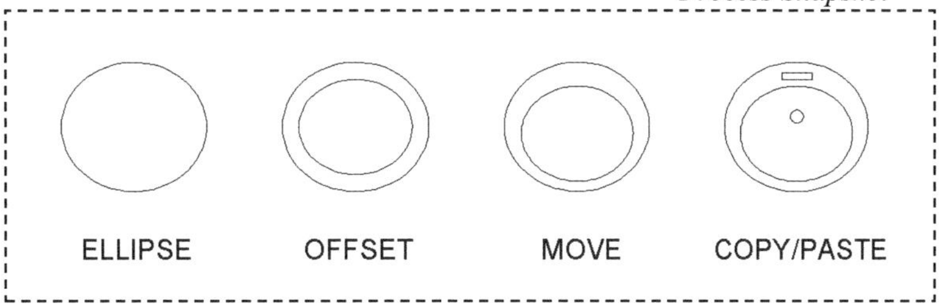

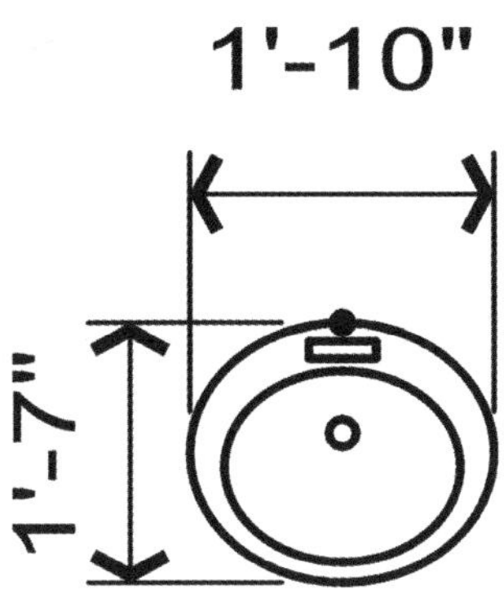

Next you will draw another lavatory. This time you will use the **Ellipse** command.

62. Open a new drawing.

63. Select the **Ellipse** tool **Axis, End** in the *Draw* panel on the *Home* tab via the down-arrow (see image below).

First you will specify the vertical axis for the ellipse.

64. Type **0,0** for the axis endpoint.

65. With ***Polar Tracking*** (or *Ortho*) turned on, point the cursor straight down (i.e., vertical in the negative direction) and then type **1'7**; press **Enter**.

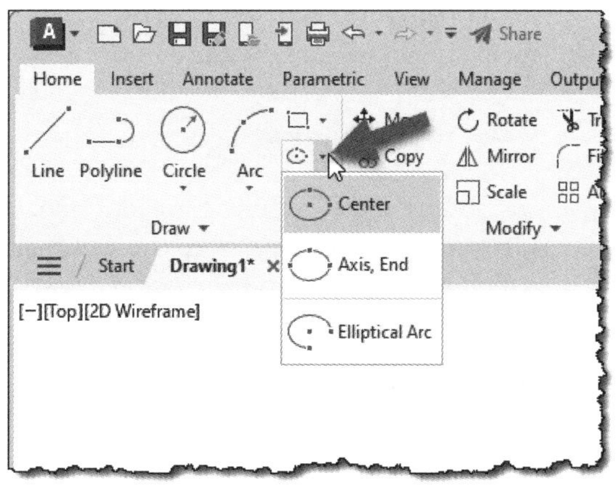

Now you need to specify the horizontal axis of the ellipse.

66. Again, with ***Polar Tracking*** on, position the cursor towards the right until it snaps to the horizontal plane and type **11** and then **Enter**.

NOTE: 11" is half the width, 1'-10".

That's all it takes to draw an ellipse!

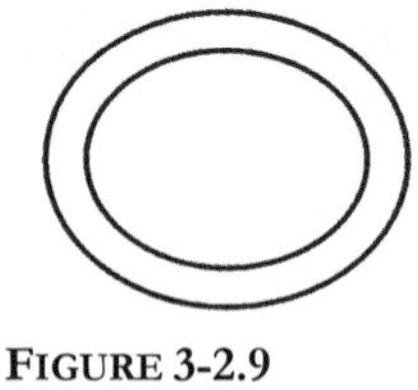

FIGURE 3-2.9
Ellipse offset inward 2½″

67. **Offset** the ellipse inward **2½″** (Figure 3-2.9).

68. **Move** the inner ellipse downward (towards the front of the sink) **1″**.

Next, you need to draw the faucet and drain. As it turns out, the faucet and drain for *Lav-1.dwg* is in the same position relative to the *Origin*. So, to save time, you will Copy/Paste these items from the *Lav-1.dwg* drawing into the *Lav-2.dwg* drawing.

69. **Open Lav-1.dwg**.

The command you will use next is not located on the *Ribbon,* so you have to type it in the *Command Window*. The command allows you to specify the insertion point before copying entities to the *Windows Clipboard,* allowing you to more accurately place the geometry when pasted in later. If you were to just use the *Copy Clip* icon on the *Home* tab, the insertion point would just be the lower left corner of the extents of the geometry in the clipboard.

70. Click in the *Command Window* and type **copybase** (with no spaces) and then press **Enter**.

71. Type **0,0** and then **Enter**.

72. Select the faucet (i.e., the small rectangle) and the 2″ drain, then press **Enter**.

73. **Close** the **Lav-1.dwg**.

74. In the **Lav-2.dwg** drawing, select **Paste to Original Coordinates** from the *Clipboard* panel on the *Home* tab *(see image to the right).*

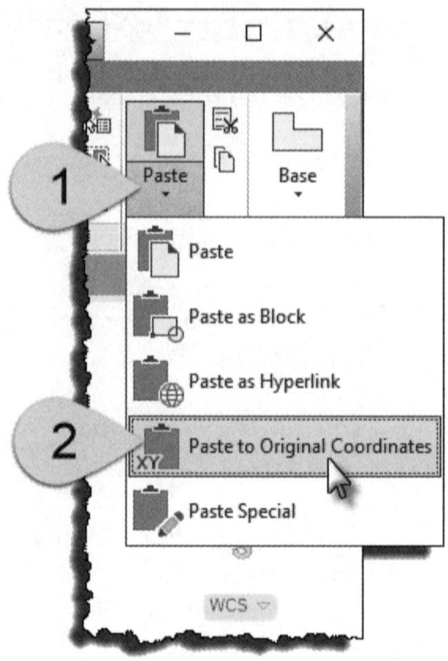

You should now have the faucet and drain correctly positioned in your *Lav-2.dwg* drawing.

75. **Save** your drawing.

filename: Sink-1.dwg

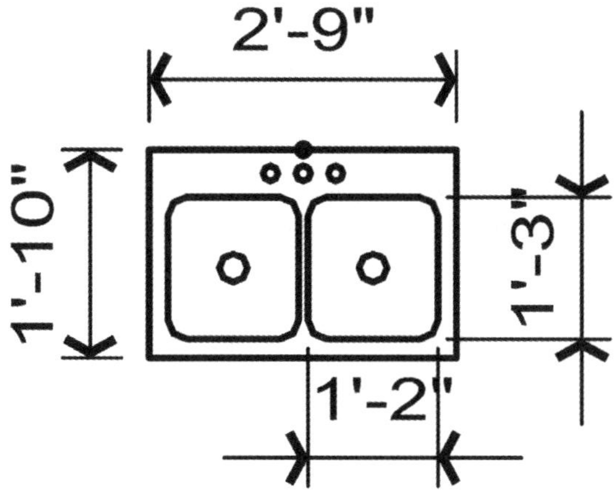

Draw this lavatory per the following specifications:

- 2″ space (i.e., offset) at sides and front.
- 3″ Dia. Circles centered in sinks.
- 2″ rad. for Fillets.
- 1½″ Dia. at faucet spacing 3½″ apart.

filename: Water-Closet.dwg

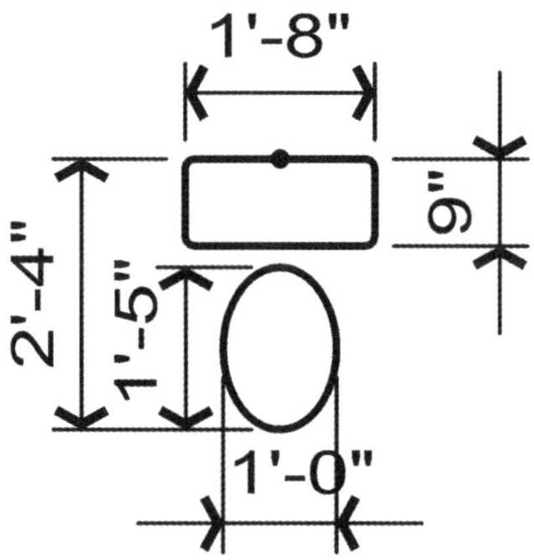

You should be able to draw this symbol without any help.

> ***TIP:*** *Draw a construction line from the Origin straight down 11″ (2′4″ – 1′-5″ = 11″). This will give you a point to pick when drawing the ellipse.*

> ***NOTE:*** *You could also start the* **Ellipse** *command and type 0,-11 for the first point. These are coordinates relative to the* Origin.

filename: Tree.dwg

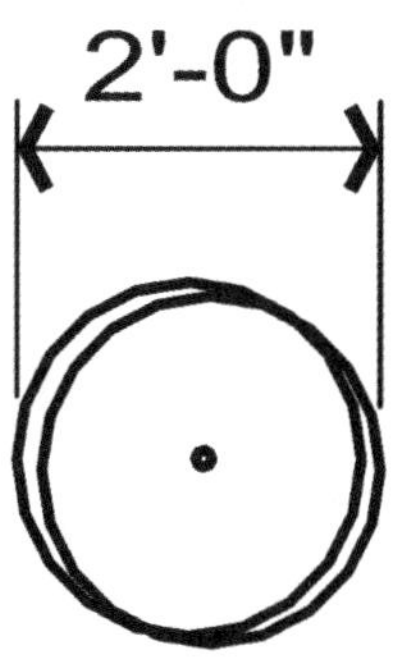

76. Draw one large circle and then copy it similar to this drawing.

77. Draw one small circle (1″Dia.) with the center at the *Origin.*

78. **Save** to Tree.dwg.

filename: **Door-36.dwg**

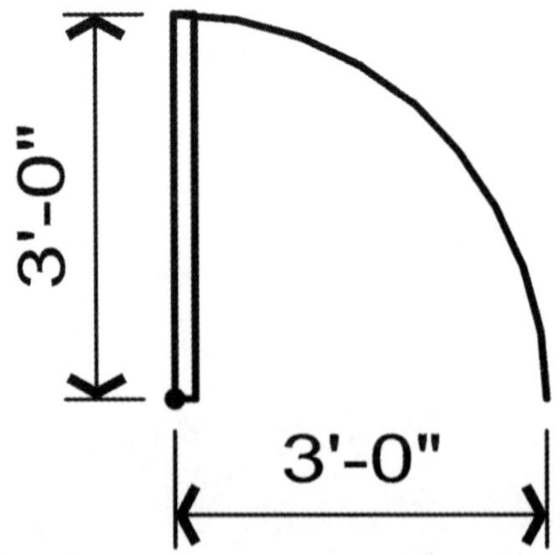

This symbol is used to show a door in a floor plan. The arc represents the path of the door as it opens and shuts. The hinges are at the origin in this example.

A symbol like this, 90 degrees open, helps to avoid the door conflicting with something in the house (e.g., cabinets or toilet).

79. Draw a **2″ x 3′-0″ rectangle.**

FYI: The rectangle represents a 2″ thick x 3′-0″ wide door.

80. Draw an **Arc** using **Start, Center, Angle** with a 3′-0″ radius.
    a. First point: type **3'**, press **Tab,** type **0**, and then press **Enter.**
    b. Second point: **pick** lower left corner of the rectangle (which is at 0,0).
    c. Last point: **pick** upper left corner of the rectangle.

filename: **Door-30.dwg**

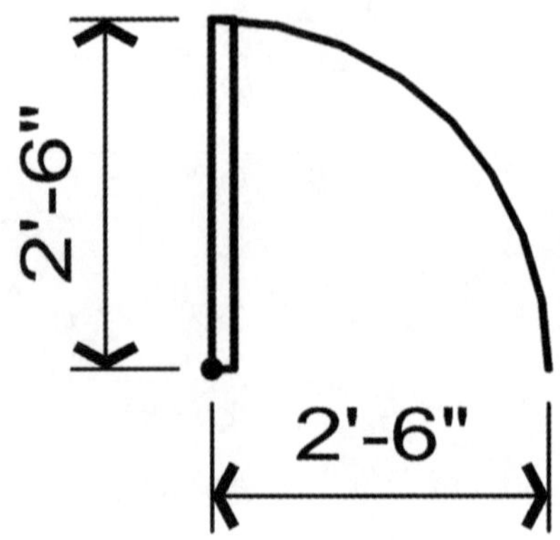

Using the previous two steps as an example, draw this smaller door.

NOTE: A door's thickness does not usually change graphically, so leave it at 2″.

AutoCAD has a feature called Dynamic Blocks. They are advanced symbols that allow visual edits via grip-like controls. One example is a door block that lets you flip or mirror the door swing or adjust the door size, all via special on-screen grips.

filename: **Door2-36.dwg**

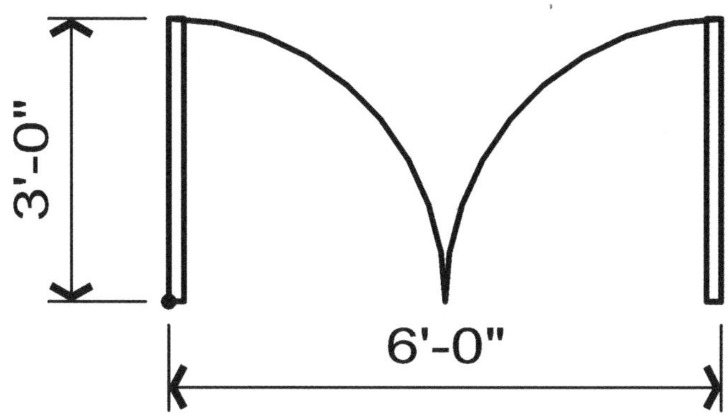

Here, you will use a previous drawing and the Mirror command to quickly create this drawing showing a pair of doors in a single opening.

81. **Open** drawing **Door-36.dwg**.

82. **Save-As** to drawing **Door2-36.dwg**.

Next, you will mirror both the rectangle and the arc.

83. Pick the **Mirror** icon from the *Modify* panel, *Home* tab.

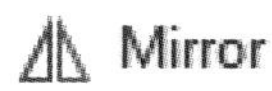

84. Select the rectangle and arc, and then press **Enter**.

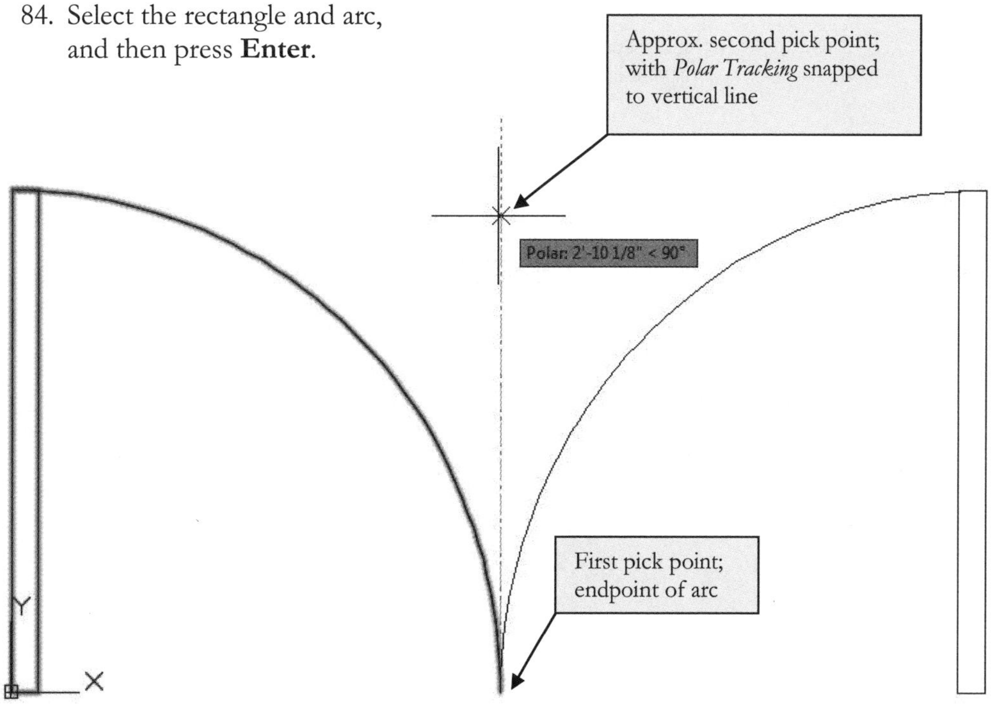

Notice the current prompt: 

FYI: Remember that Dynamic Input needs to be toggled on to see the on-screen prompts as shown above.

85. Pick the two points described in the figure on the previous page.

Basically, you drew an imaginary line that is a plane about which to mirror the selected entities.

The figure below shows several examples of mirror lines and their results (each has the same first pick point). Notice the mirrored image is symmetrical about the mirror line.

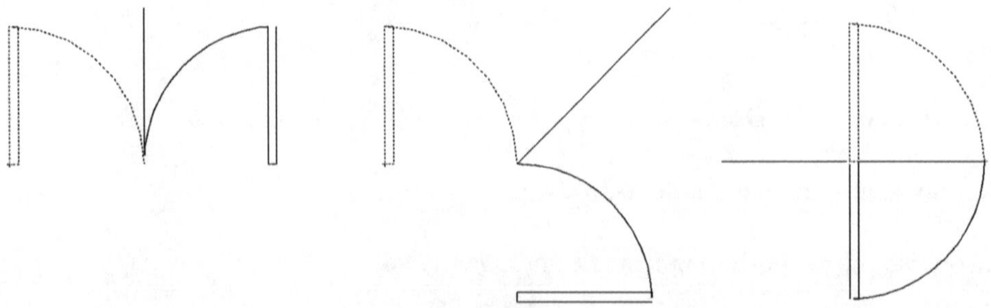

Vertical Mirror Line *Angled Mirror Line* *Horizontal Mirror Line*

FIGURE 3-2.10 Mirror command; door being mirrored, first point picked, in process of picking second point

Notice the *Command* prompt **Erase source objects? [Yes/No] <N>:**

And the on-screen prompt reads: 

You do not want the original door to be deleted here so…

86. Type **N** and press **Enter.**

TIP: Both the graphic and text prompts above indicate a default for the yes/no option; it is No. If the default is the setting you want, you can just press Enter instead of typing a Y or an N.

87. **Save** your drawing.

filename: **Clg-Fan-1.dwg**

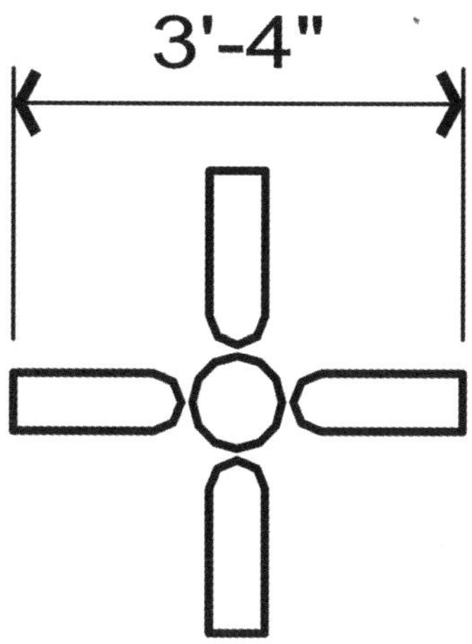

You will use the **Array** command while drawing this ceiling fan.

The **Array** command is used to copy entities in a rectangular pattern (e.g., steel columns on a grid) or in a polar pattern (i.e., in a circular pattern).

You will use the polar array to rotate and copy the fan blade all in one step!

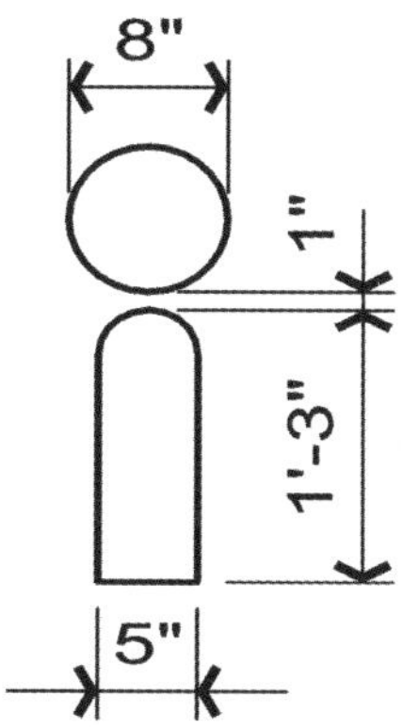

FIGURE 3-2.11
Dimensions for first part of fan to be drawn

88. Start a new drawing and create the portion of the drawing shown in Figure 3-2.11. *(The drawing origin should be the center of the circle.)*

89. Select **Array→ Polar Array** on the *Modify* panel on the *Home* tab.

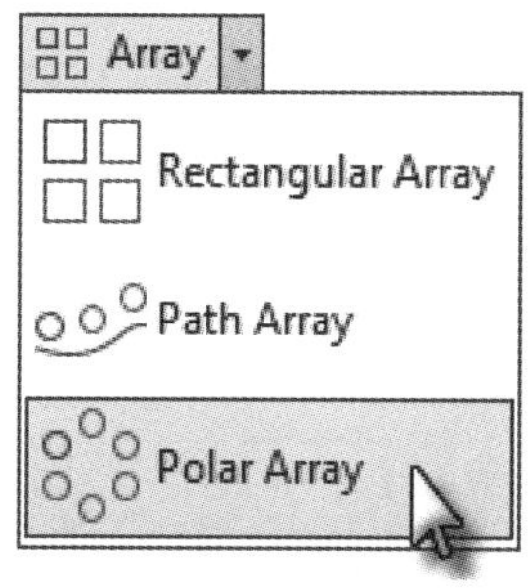

You are now prompted to select the items to array. You will only select the fan blade, not the center circle. If you selected the center circle, you would end up with several circles copied on top of it.

Next, you will tell AutoCAD which entities you would like to array.

90. Select the entities that make up the fan blade.

91. Press **Enter** (to indicate you are done selecting).

TIP: You can also right-click rather than press Enter.

Now you will specify the *center point* about which the fan blade will be rotated (which is the drawing origin and the center of the circle).

92. Using the *Center OSNAP*, **select** the center of the circle.

Notice the fan blade arrays around the center with a default of six items. All you have to do now is change the number of items to four (Figure 3-2.12).

93. On the *Ribbon*, for *Items* type **4**.

94. Press **Enter** to apply the change.

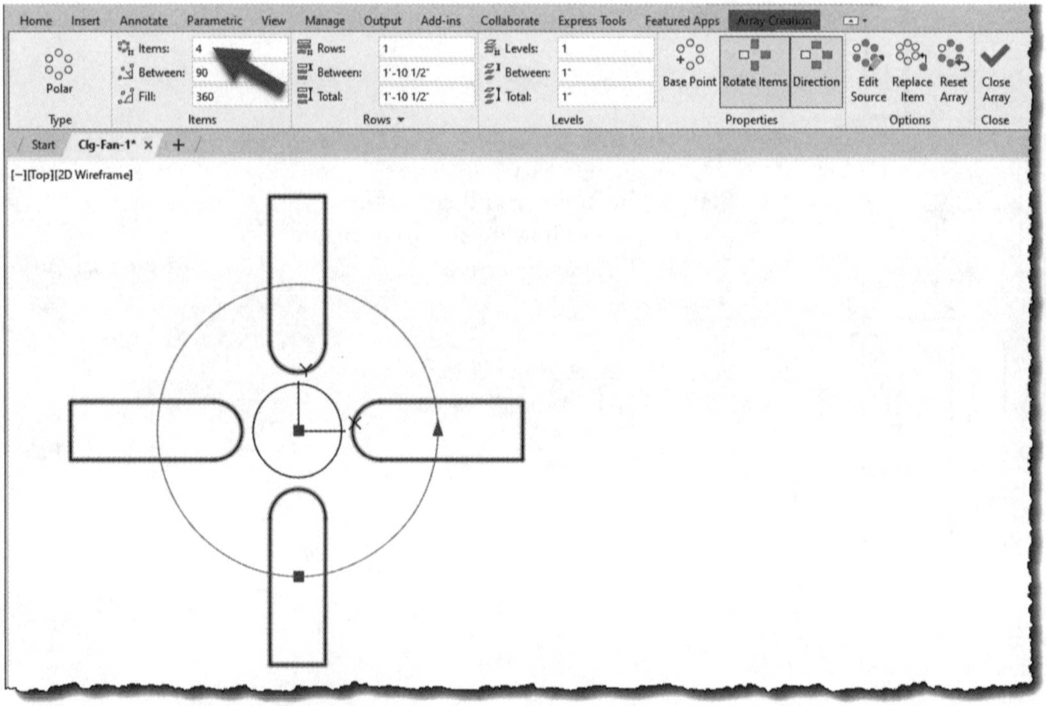

FIGURE 3-2.12 Arraying the fan blade.

95. To finish the *Polar Array* command, click **Close Array** on the Ribbon.

96. **Save** your drawing.

In the next exercise, you will see how AutoCAD can be used to parametrically adjust the number of fan blades!

filename: Clg-Fan-2.dwg

You could easily start this drawing from scratch, but instead, you will learn how to edit an array. You will create a copy of the previous fan and edit it to have five fan blades.

97. Open the **Clg-Fan-1.dwg** file.

98. Select **Application Menu → Save-As**.

99. Name the new file **Clg-Fan-2.dwg**.

100. **Select** one of the ceiling fan blades.

You should now see the *Array* tab and a few grips appear as shown in Figure 3-2.13.

101. Change the number of *Items* to **5**.

102. Click the **Close Array** button on the *Ribbon*.

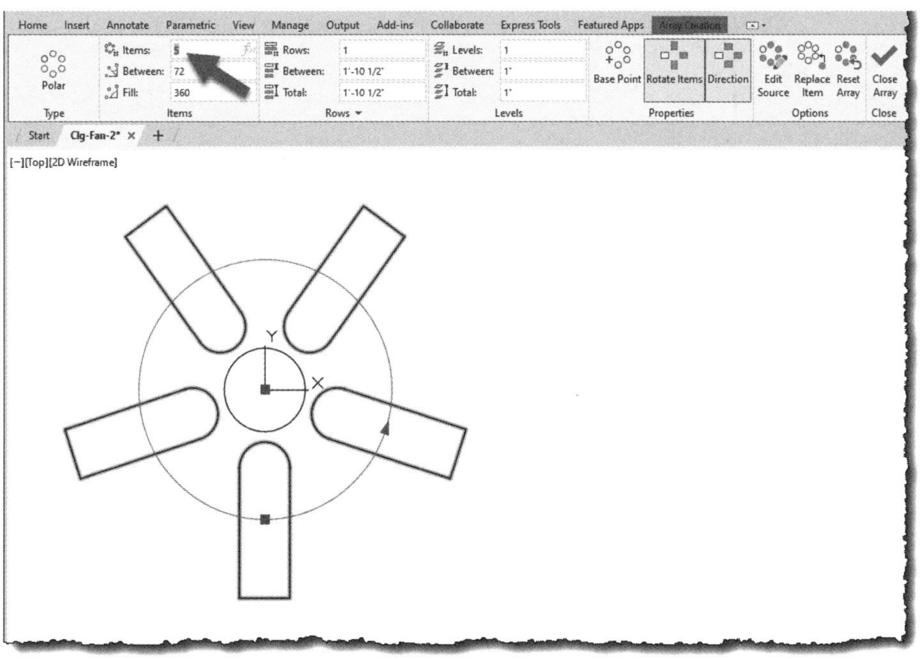

FIGURE 3-2.13 Modifying a polar array

The *Array* tab and the array grips should now be gone, and your fan should now have five blades!

103. **Save** your drawing.

filename: HC-Symbol.dwg

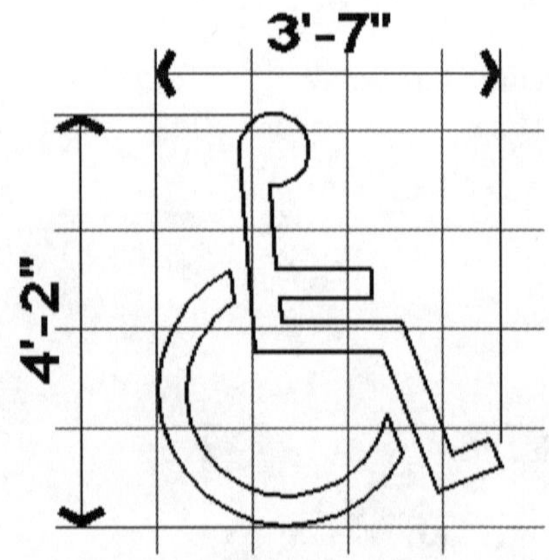

You may have some trouble drawing this symbol at this point. However, this will make you reflect on many of the commands you have covered thus far in this book (e.g.,Line, Rotate, Offset, Arc).

The distance between parallel lines should be 3½".
This is for the graphic, not the gridlines.

All other dimensions can be approximated so that your drawing looks as close to this one as possible.

You can draw the grid shown to help make your drawing more proportionally accurate. The lines are 1′-0″ apart in each direction. When finished, erase the grid lines.

Exercise 3-3:
Using Layers

Using *Layers* in AutoCAD helps to separate different types of data. Mostly, you will use *Layers* to make things visible or invisible and to control lineweights.

In a Floor Plan, for example, you will draw all the walls on one *Layer* and the doors on another *Layer.* You will also draw items such as windows, stairs, furniture, appliances, etc., each on its own *Layer.*

Many architectural firms have an Office Standard for *Layers*. This means that everyone in the firm uses the same *Layer* name (e.g., A-WALL) to draw walls on, for example. This helps make sharing drawings between projects more efficient; if you Copy/Paste from one drawing to another, and each project uses a different *Layer* name for the walls, then you would have both *Layer* names in the drawing you pasted into (e.g., *A-Wall* and *AR-Wall*).

Example:
To see a quick example of how layers work, you will open the *A1 First Floor Plan* drawing again and adjust some of the layer settings, and then notice the effect those changes have on the drawing.

1. **Open** the *Residence\A1 First Floor Plan.dwg* from the online exercise files (see page 1-17). *Reminder:* Download instructions on the inside front cover of the book.

2. Switch to ***Model Space*** by clicking the *Model* tab at the bottom of the screen; see the image below.

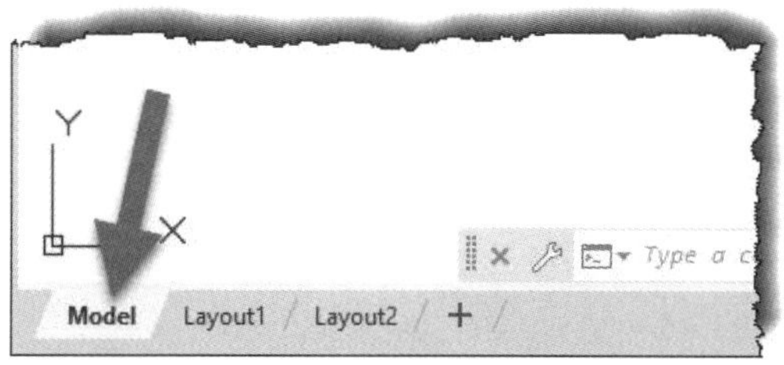

3. Select the **Layer Properties** icon from the *Layers* panel on the *Home* tab.

You are now in the *Layer Properties Manager*, where you can adjust the visibility and properties, such as lineweight, color, and linetype, of the entities on a particular layer.

All drawings have a *Layer* named 0 (i.e., zero). You can add as many layers as you wish in a drawing file. Notice in **Figure 3-3.1** that the *current* drawing has several *Layers* (34 to be exact). Many of the layer *names* are descriptive enough for you to tell what information is drawn on each layer.

Clicking a column heading sorts the list by that column. Right-click on the column heading, and you can hide columns you never typically use (do not hide any columns at this time). Next, you will freeze (i.e., turn off the visibility of) three *Layers.*

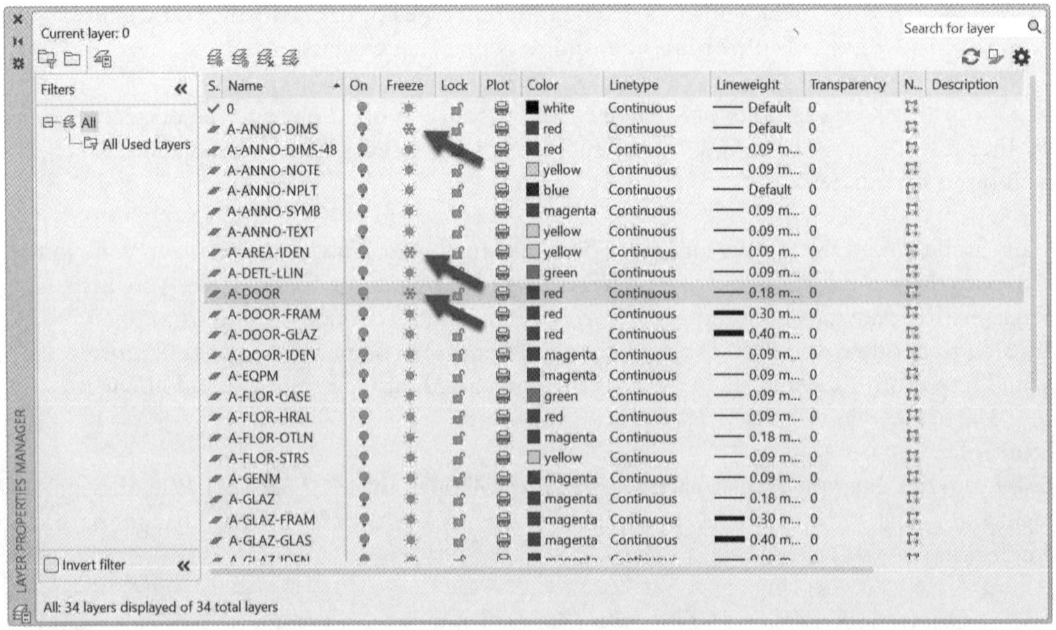

FIGURE 3-3.1
Layer Properties Manager; three layers set to frozen (Step 4)

4. In the column labeled "**Freeze**" click the *Sun* symbol (which will change the symbol to a B&W *Sun*) for the following *Layers (See Figure 3-3.1)*:
   - A-Anno-Dims
   - A-Area-Iden
   - A-Door

TIP: The "Freeze" column may not display the full label; instead, you will see a portion of the label (e.g., Fre…) as in the image above, which means the column is not wide enough to display the full label. You can, if you wish, stretch the column(s) wider with your mouse. You simply place the cursor between two labels and drag the mouse. This is helpful when the Layer *names are long as well.*

5. Click the "X" in the upper corner of the *Layer Properties Manager* to close the palette; there is no "OK" or "Apply" button as changes are made instantly.

Notice the changes to the *A1 First Floor Plan* drawing. Compare the "before" on the left to the "after" on the right in the image on the next page. The dimensions, doors, and room names are no longer visible. However, it is important to realize that they still exist in the drawing file.

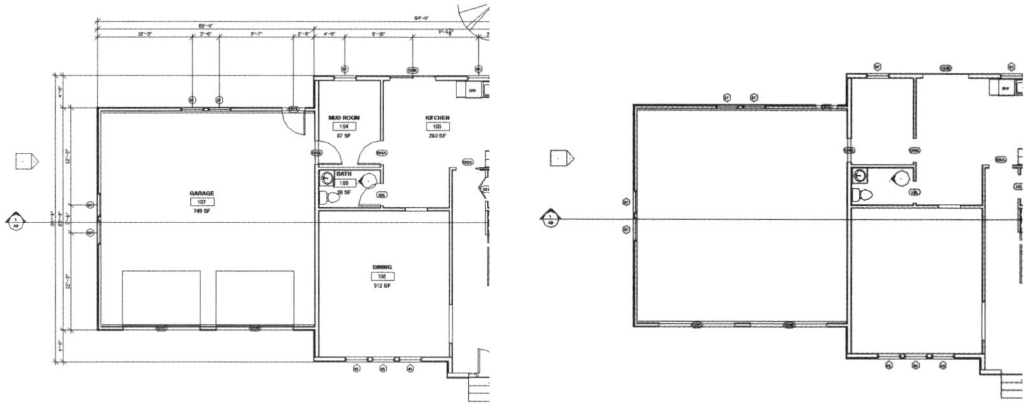

FIGURE 3-3.2
Sample drawing with layers frozen – original on left; notice doors, text and dimensions are hidden on the right

You should be able to see how this functionality is useful. If the electrical designer links the architectural designer's floor plan drawing into their drawing, they will want to turn off a few of the architectural *Layers* to "clean up" their drawing. For example, the electrical drawings might not need to include dimensions, window tags, or trees. When drawings are set up correctly, this task is easy!

Next, you will change the color of a *Layer* to see the effect it has on the current drawing.

6. **Open** the **Layer Properties Manager** again.

7. Locate the *Layer* named **A-Wall**, and then in its *Color* column, **select the colors watch** listed for this *Layer* (which should be yellow).

You are now in the *Select Color* dialog box (Figure 3-3.3).

8. Select color ***Blue*** (color #5) shown selected in Figure 3-3.3.

9. Click **OK** to exit the *Color Selector* and then click **X** (in the upper left or upper right corner – shown in the upper left in the image below) to close the *Layer Properties Manager.*

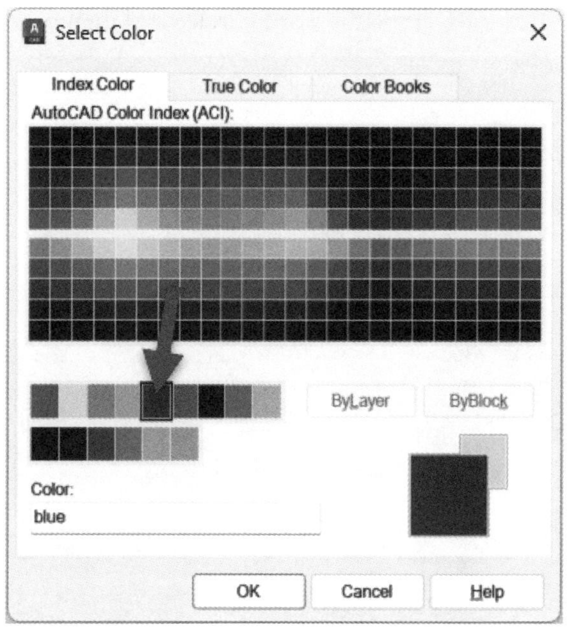

FIGURE 3-3.3 Select Color dialog *(part of the Layer Properties Manager)*

Notice the walls are now blue.

10. **Close** the *Sample* drawing without saving any changes.

Now you will open a new drawing and walk through the basic steps of creating and using *Layers* in a drawing.

Creating Layers:

11. **Open** a new drawing and switch to *Model Space.*

    TIP: Remember to start with the correct template: SheetSets\Architectural Imperial.dwt.

12. **Open** the *Layer Properties Manager.*

    TIP: Notice some Layers already exist; they came from the template file you started with.

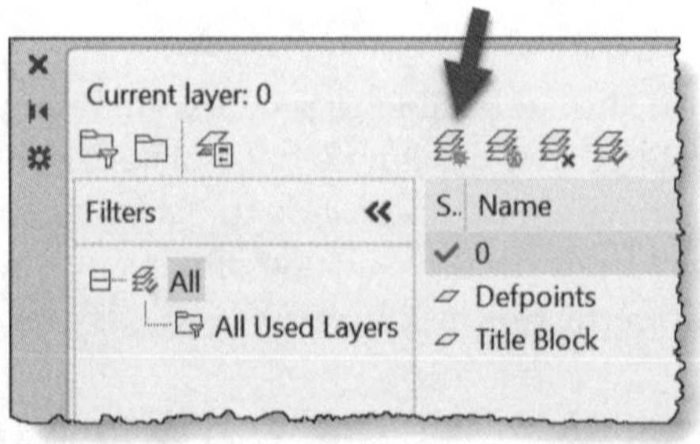

13. Click the **New** Layer icon (see image to right).

A new row has been added to the list; by default you are immediately positioned to enter the *Layer* name.

14. Type the word **Circles** and then press **Enter**.

15. Repeat steps 13 and 14 to create the following layers:
    a. **Lines**
    b. **Rectangles**
    c. **Text**

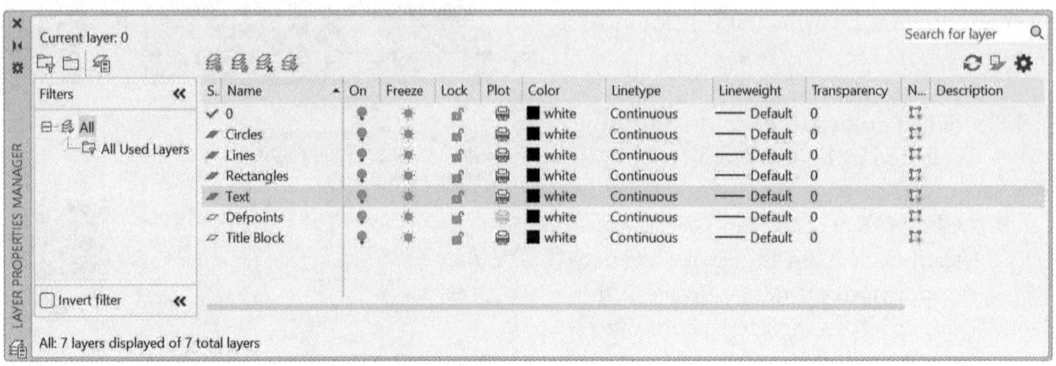

FIGURE 3-3.4 Layer Properties Manager; with 4 new layers created

Next you will assign a new color to three of the new Layers.

16. Set the *Layer* colors as follows:
    a. **Circles** Green *(color #3)*
    b. **Rectangles** Red *(color #1)*
    c. **Text** Cyan *(color #4)*

17. Click the **X** to close the *Layer Properties Manager. **FYI:** This can remain open while you work.*

You now have four new *Layers*, each with a different color.

> ***FYI:** The Layer named Title Block is from your template file. Additional Layers can be added to template files to reduce new drawing setup steps.*

Drawing on Layers:

Now that you have *Layers* you will learn how to draw on different *Layers*. The easiest method is to set a *Layer* Current, and then all entities drawn after that will automatically be placed on that *Layer* (i.e., the current layer). Looking at Figure 3-3.4, notice in the upper left is the drawing's *Current Layer* (which is set to 0).

AutoCAD provides a few different ways to change the *Current Layer*. One is in *the Layer Properties Manager* (Figure 3-3.4). You simply click on the *layer name* you want to set to current and then click the **Current** icon (a green check mark). Another method is described next.

You can quickly set the *Current Layer* via the *Layers* panel (Figure 3-3.5); this is a dynamic toolbar. The toolbar will change its display per the following three scenarios:

- No entities in the current drawing are selected (no grips visible).
  - The *Current Layer* is displayed.
- One or more entities selected which are on the same *Layer*.
  - Displays which layer the selected entities are on.
- A group of entities selected which are on two or more *Layers*.
  - Display is blank to indicate multiple layers.

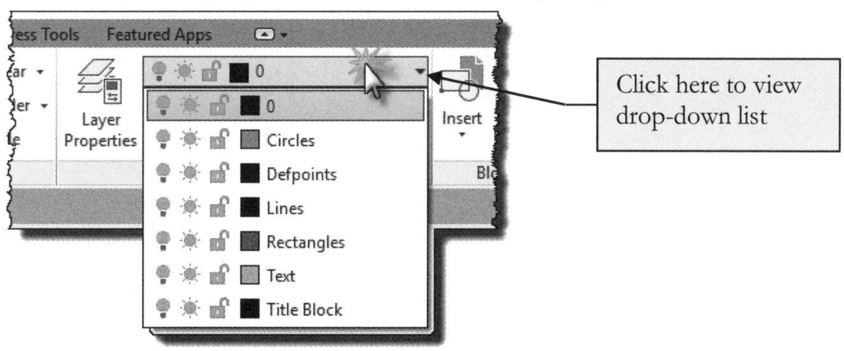

FIGURE 3-3.5 Layers panel; Figure shows layer drop-down list in the dropped-down position

So, to change the *Current Layer*, you click the down arrow to the right of the display in the *Layers* panel (on the *Home* tab of the Ribbon) to view the drop-down list (which lists all the layers in the current drawing). Next, you click on the name of the layer you want to be current, and that's it! *This only works if nothing is selected; otherwise, you are changing which Layer the selected entities are on.*

Next, you will change the *Current Layer* to *Rectangle,* so when you draw rectangles, they will automatically be drawn on the Rectangle layer.

18. Press the **Esc** key twice on the keyboard. This ensures that no entities are selected.

19. Click the **Down-Arrow** on the *Layers* panel (Figure 3-3.5).

20. Move the cursor over the *Layer* named *Rectangle* and click.

The *Rectangle* layer is now set current, which means that anything drawn from now on (until the current layer is changed again) will be drawn on the *Rectangle* layer.

Be aware that the layer name in no way implies that only rectangles can be drawn on the *Rectangle* layer. That is the intention and the drafter's responsibility to make sure only rectangles go on the *Rectangle* layer. *Note that we could rename the* Circle *layer to* Ellipse *and it would have no effect on the circles previously drawn on that layer.*

21. **Draw a Rectangle** that is **28″** wide and **48″** tall (*with the lower left corner at the Origin*).

22. **Draw** two more rectangles per the dimensions provided in **Figure 3-3.6**. *(This can be accomplished using a combination of the following commands: Offset, Stretch, and Move.)*

Next, you will draw several lines, so you will need to change the *Current Layer.*

23. Making sure no entities are selected, use the *Layers* toolbar to make ***Lines*** the *Current Layer.*

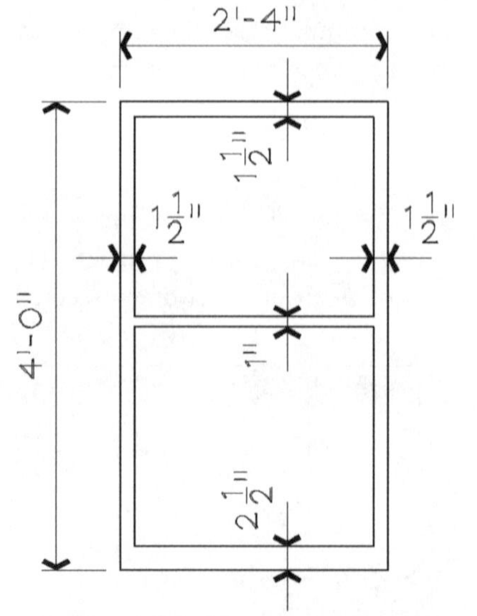

FIGURE 3-3.6 Three Rectangles drawn

24. Using the dimensions provided in **Figure 3-3.7**, draw the vertical lines shown. (*This can be achieved using either the Move or Offset commands.*)

You may already have figured out what you are drawing: a double-hung window in elevation view.

You have two more lines to draw.

25. **Draw** the two short horizontal lines shown in Figure 3-3.8. *(The lines are near each side towards the middle; compare with Figure 3-3.7.)*

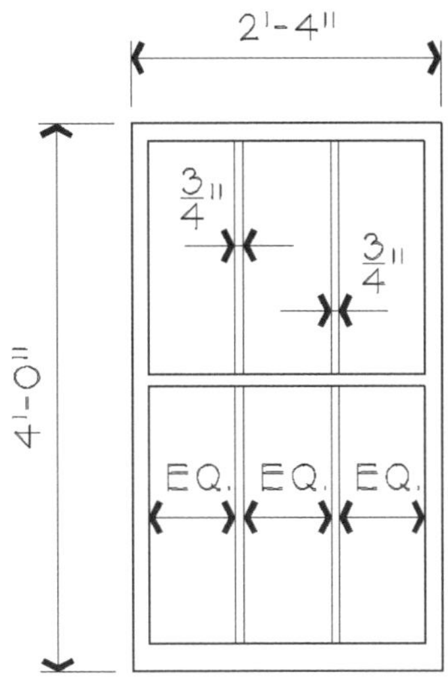

FIGURE 3-3.7
More Rectangles drawn

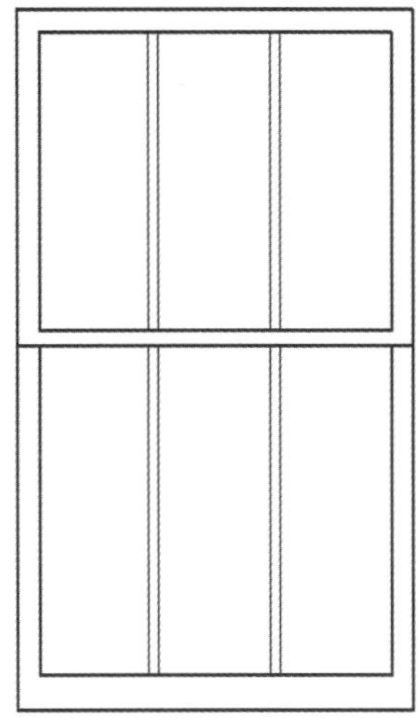

FIGURE 3-3.8
Two short horizontal lines drawn (cf. Figure 3-3.7)

26. Use the **Mtext** command to enter the text "**Double-Hung Window**" directly below the window. Make the text 2¼" high (Figure 3-3.9).

Oops:

If you were following the directions step by step, you missed a step. You forgot to change the *Current Layer* to *Text.*

You should notice one visual clue that the text is on the wrong layer; it's the same color as the lines previously drawn (*White*). If the text were on the correct layer, it would be *Cyan* (the color you assigned to the text layer).

Next, you will take a quick look at how to change which layer an entity is on without the need to erase and redraw.

FIGURE 3-3.9 Text added

Moving Entities from One Layer to Another:

Remember, when nothing is selected, the *Layers* toolbar shows the *Current Layer*, and when something is selected, it shows which *Layer* the selected entity is on.

27. **Select the text**, make sure nothing else is selected (*press Esc key*), and click on the text. *(Notice the* Layers *panel is indicating that the text is on the* Lines *layer.)*

28. From the *drop-down* list, on the *Layers* panel, select **Text**.

Notice now, with the text still selected, the *Layers* panel indicates that the text is on the *Text* layer (Figure 3-3.10). The text should also now be the proper color: *Cyan*.

29. Now press the **Esc** key to unselect the text.

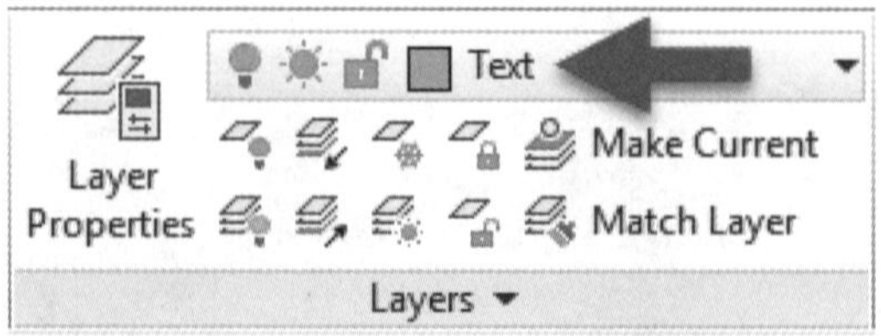

FIGURE 3-3.10 Text currently selected

Notice the *Layers* panel is now showing the *Current Layer* again. Try selecting and unselecting the various entities in your drawing to see the *Layers* panel change.

30. Make the *Circle* layer current and then draw a large circle around the window/text, similar to Figure 3-3.11.

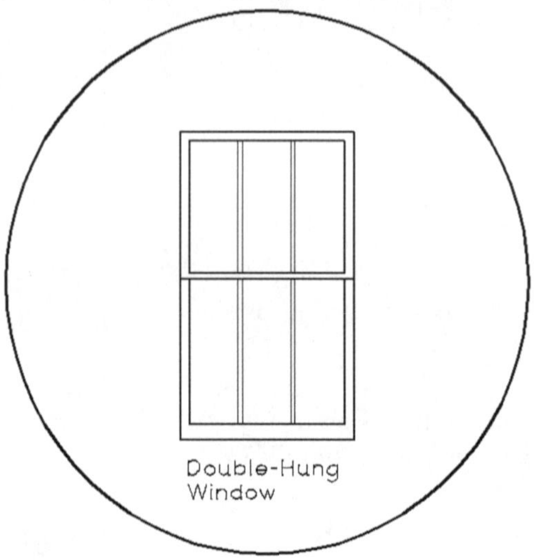

FIGURE 3-3.11 Circle added

One More Look at Controlling Layer Visibility:

Before concluding this chapter, you will take one more look at *Freezing* and *Thawing* layers, this time using your own drawing.

31. **Freeze** the *Lines* layer *(via the Layer Properties Manager).*

Notice the lines all disappear from the screen.

32. **Thaw** the *Lines* layer.

33. **Freeze** the *Circle* layer.

You should have received a message stating that AutoCAD "cannot freeze the current layer" (Figure 3-3.12). To freeze the *Circle* layer, you would have to set another layer as current first.

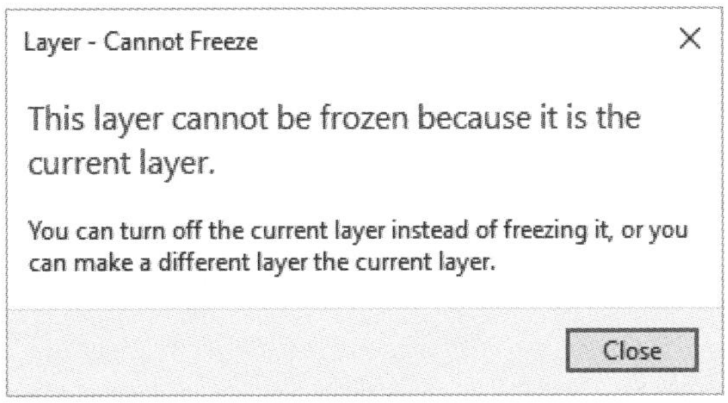

FIGURE 3-3.12 AutoCAD message

34. Set the *Rectangle* layer as *Current.*

35. Now *Freeze* the *Circle* layer.

Try a few more variations on the Freeze/Thaw scenarios before proceeding to the next step.

36. Make sure all *Layers* are turned **On** and **Thawed**.

37. **Print** the drawing showing all entities (including the circle).

38. **Save** the drawing as **Ex3-3 Layers.dwg**.

What's the Difference between Freeze and Off?

On the surface, there is no difference between Freeze and Off when it comes to controlling layer visibility. If you Freeze a layer, its contents are not displayed; the same is true when you turn a layer Off.

The difference relates to display memory. When a layer is Frozen the information required to display it onscreen is not loaded into your graphics card's memory. On the other hand, when a layer is only turned Off, all the information required to display the entities on that layer is loaded into your graphics card's memory.

The Pros and Cons:
The main benefit to turning a layer Off rather than Freezing it is:

> When you turn a layer back on, it will instantly display (without a regeneration).
> [*Negative:* slower panning and zooming on large / complex drawings]

The benefit to Freezing a layer rather than turning it Off:

> Faster Panning and Zooming without the extra baggage required in the graphics card.
> [*Negative*: requires a time-consuming Regen whenever a layer is Thawed]

Recommended use:
Freeze the following layers in your drawing if:

> The layer will typically "never" be on in the current drawing (e.g., doors and furniture in a reflected ceiling plan).

Turn a layer Off in your drawing if:

> The layer is generally always on, but you want to make it invisible for a short period of time (e.g., hiding the *Text* and *Dimension* layers to print a "clean" floor plan).
>
> When using this method, you can confidently select all the layers in the *Layer Properties Manager* and turn them all On without worrying about making a layer show up that shouldn't.

Self-Exam:

The following questions can be used as a way to check your knowledge of this lesson. The answers can be found at the bottom of this page.

1. There is no difference between *Freeze* and *Off*. (T/F)
2. A drawing's *Origin* is 0,0. (T/F)
3. Construction lines are useful drawing aids. (T/F)
4. Use the ______________ command to create an oval shape.
5. When you want to make a previously drawn rectangle wider you would use

   the ______________ command.

Review Questions:

The following questions may be assigned by your instructor as a way to assess your knowledge of this section. Your instructor has the answers to the review questions.

1. Use the *Offset* command to quickly create a parallel line(s). (T/F)
2. The *Explode* command will reduce a polyline (e.g., rectangle) to individual lines. (T/F)
3. With the *Stretch* command, lines completely within the *Crossing Window* are actually only moved, not stretched. (T/F)
4. You have to select entities and a center point when using *Polar Array*. (T/F)
5. Occasionally you need to draw an object and then move it into place to accurately locate it. (T/F)
6. Selecting this icon  allows you to ____________ two intersecting lines.
7. If an AutoCAD line looks like one line it should only be one line. (T/F)
8. Use the ______________ command to create a reverse image.
9. You can use either ____________ or ____________ in the *Layer Properties Manager* to control the visibility of a layer.
10. When no entities are selected, the *Layers* toolbar displays the _______ layer.

Self-Exam Answers:
1 – F, **2** – T, **3** – T, **4** – Ellipse, **5** – Stretch

Notes:

Lesson 4
FLOOR PLANS

In this lesson, you will jump right in and get started drawing your floor plans for the residential project. Throughout the lesson, you will be introduced to a few new commands, and you will study common methods used to draw floor plans.

Exercise 4-1:
Walls

Introduction:

Two lines, a certain distance apart, represent the walls in a floor plan. In AutoCAD, these walls are drawn on a layer named *A-WALL*. The distance between the two lines is the same as the actual thickness of the wall (or very close to it); wall thicknesses are usually rounded off to the nearest ¼″.

The following is an overview of how walls are typically dimensioned in a floor plan. This information is intended to help you understand the dimensions you will see in the exercises, as well as prepare you for the point when you dimension your plans.

Stud walls (wood or metal) are typically dimensioned to the center of the walls. This is one reason the walls do not need to be the exact thickness. Here are a few reasons why you should dimension to the center of the stud rather than to the face of the gypsum board:

- The contractor is laying out the walls in a large "empty" area. The most useful dimension is to the center of the stud; that is where they will make a mark on the floor. If the dimension was to the face of the gypsum board, the contractor would have to stop and calculate the center of the stud, which is not always the center of the wall thickness (e.g., a stud wall with 1 layer of gypsum board on one side and 2 layers of gypsum board over resilient channels on the other side).
- The extra dimensions (text and arrows) indicating the thickness of the walls would take up an excessive amount of room on the floor plans—space that would be better used by notes.

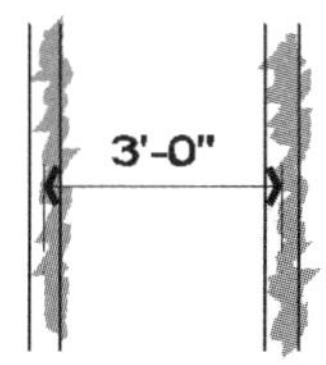

Dimension Example – Two Stud Walls

Occasionally, you should dimension to the face of a wall rather than the center. Here's one example:

- When indicating design intent or building code requirements, you should reference the exact points/surfaces. For example, if you have uncommonly large trim around a door opening, you may want a dimension from the edge of the door to the face of the adjacent wall. Another example would be the width of a hallway; if you want a particular width, you would dimension between the two faces of the wall and add the text "clear" below the dimension to make it known, without question, that the dimension is not to the center of the wall.

Dimensions for masonry and foundation walls:

- Foundation and masonry walls are dimensioned to the nominal face and not the center. These types of walls are modular (e.g., 8″x8″x16″), so it is helpful, for both designer and builder, to have dimensions that relate to the masonry wall's "coursing" (which helps reduce waste).

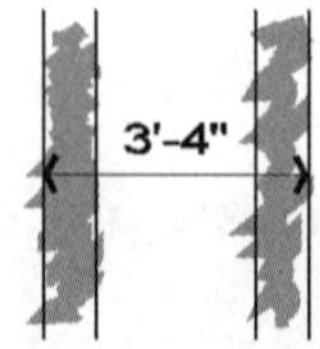

Dimension Example – Two masonry Walls

Dimensions from a stud wall to a masonry wall:

- The rules above apply for each side of the dimension line. For example, a dimension for the exterior foundation wall to an interior stud wall would be from the exterior face of the foundation wall to the center of the stud on the stud wall.

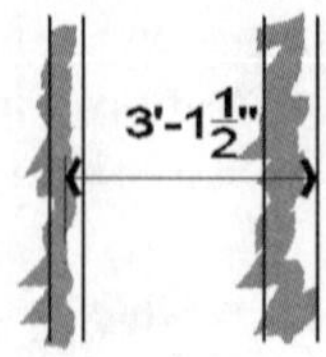

Dimension Example – Stud to masonry

Contos Residence

Image courtesy of Anderson Architects
Alan H. Anderson, Architect, Duluth, MN

Overview of the plans you will be drawing:

The following sketches will give you an idea of the floor plans you will draw in this lesson.

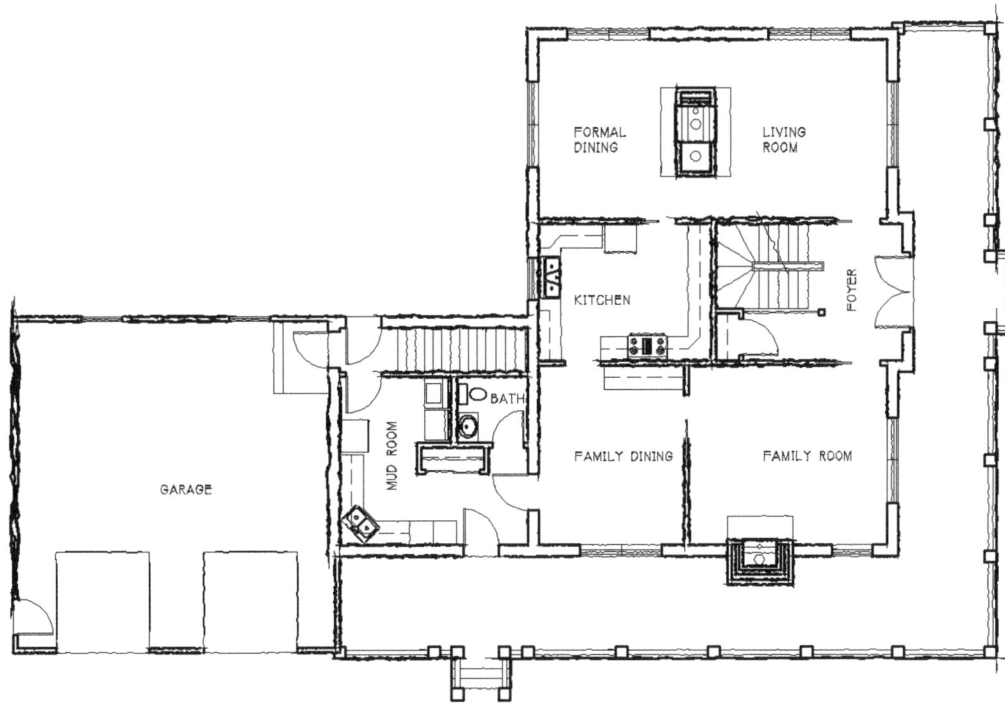

FIGURE 4-1.1 Sketch – First Floor Plan

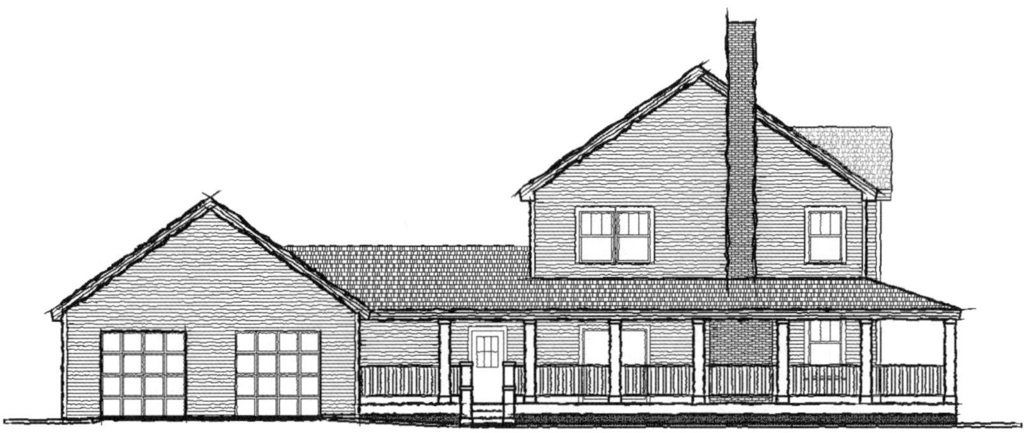

FIGURE 4-1.2 Sketch – South Elevation

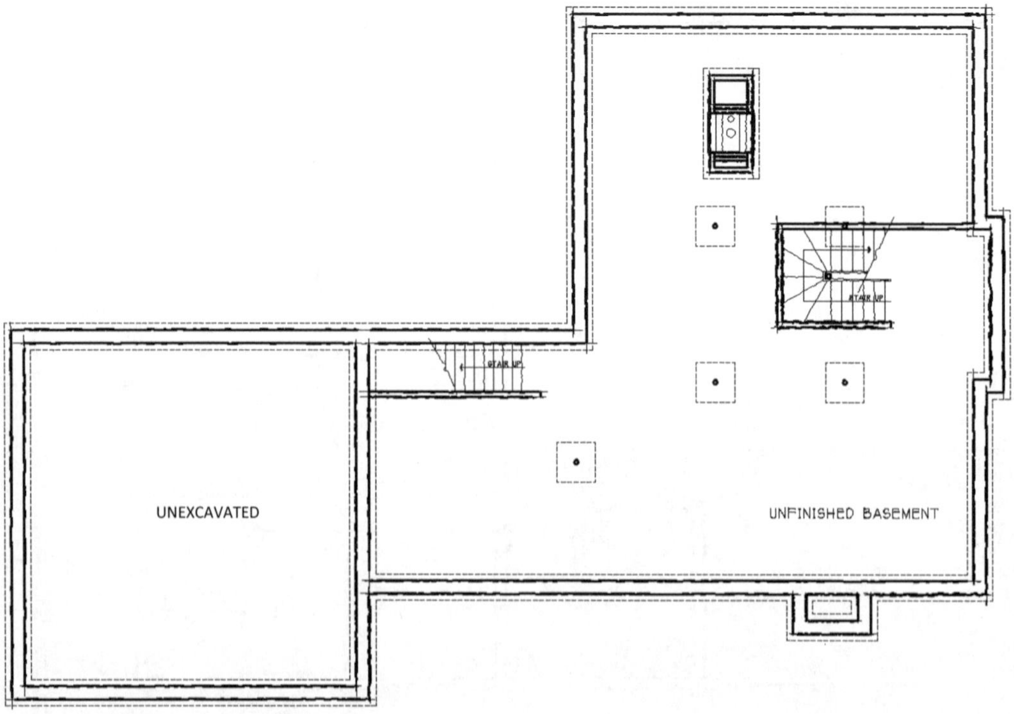

FIGURE 4-1.3 Sketch – Basement Floor Plan

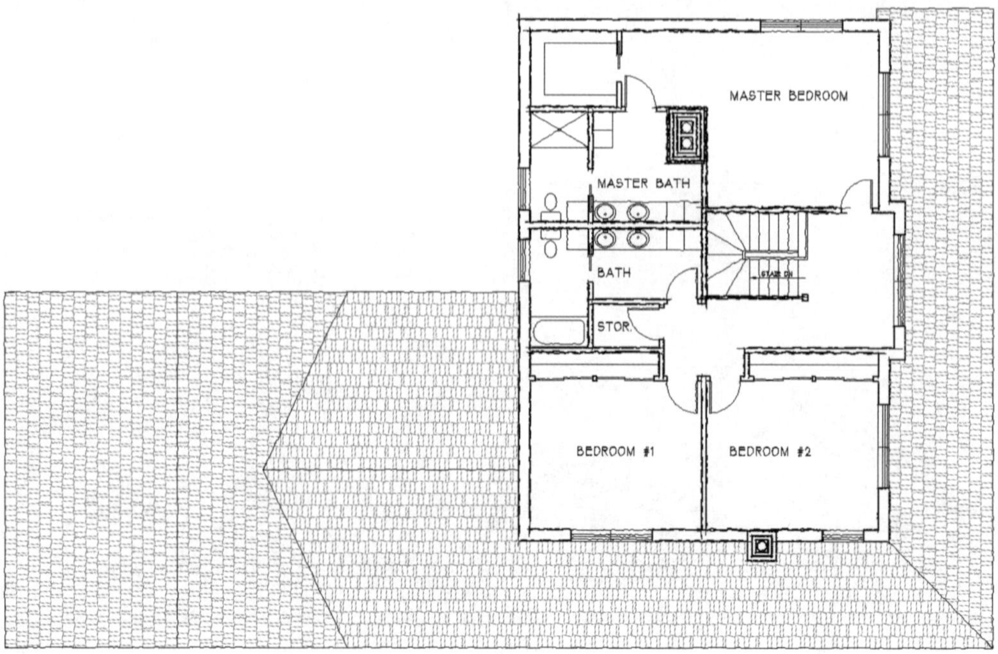

FIGURE 4-1.4 Sketch – Second Floor Plan

Getting Started:

In this exercise, you will draw just the walls for all three floor plans. Similar to the exercises in Lesson 3, you will draw each floor plan in a separate drawing.

Additionally, each drawing will share a common origin, making it easy to copy/paste, and overlay the plans to ensure things line up from floor to floor. You will use the upper left corner of the two-story portion of the residence as the origin.

Drawing walls involves extensive use of just a handful of commands, most of which you already know how to use. The most typical commands used in drawing walls are:

- Line
- Offset
- Stretch
- Trim
- Extend

The last two commands, Trim and Extend, have not been covered yet. You will study these commands in this exercise.

You will now start drawing the basement floor plan walls.

1. Start a new drawing named **Flr-B.dwg**.
   Don't forget to use the correct template: App. Menu→ ***New*** *and then* ***SheetSets \Architectural Imperial.dwt****.*

2. Switch to *Model Space.*

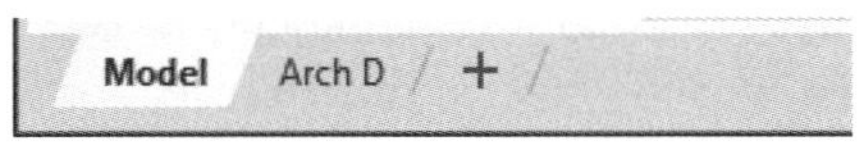

Setting the Drawing Limits

Next, you will set the *Model Space* drawing limits. The drawing space does not actually have limits; this setting relates more to zooming and drawing regenerations.

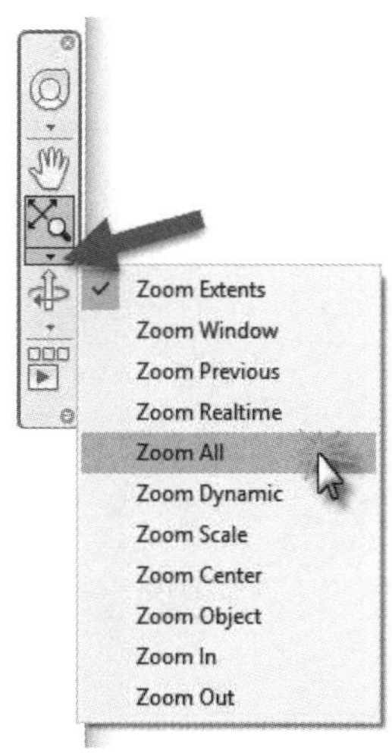

3. Type **Limits** and then **Enter** *(make sure Dynamic Input is on; F12 toggles it on and off).*

4. In the *Command Window*, type **-150′, -130′**; **Enter**.

   a. Don't miss the minus sign in the two values above.

   b. FYI: If *Dynamic Input* is on and you are typing in the drawing window (canvas), press Tab between lengths rather than a comma.

5. Type **150′, 130′**; **Enter**.

6. Select **Zoom All** from the Zoom icon flyout *(see image to the right).*

FYI: The Zoom All command will zoom to the drawing's extents or the drawing's Limits (whichever is greater). In this case, nothing has been drawn, so you have no drawing extents; thus, the drawing limits are used. You are now viewing a drawing area 300′ wide and 260′ tall (based on the limits just set), with the drawing's origin (i.e., 0,0) centered in the view. This will allow you to start drawing the floor plan without having to stop and zoom (and regenerate the drawing). Try drawing a diagonal line as you did at the beginning of Lesson 2 and list the properties to verify this (see Page 2-4); be sure to erase the diagonal line before moving on.

7. Create the layer ***A-WALL*** (color: *White*; linetype: *Continuous*).

8. With *A-WALL* layer *Current*, draw the lines shown in **Figure 4-1.5** with either *ORTHO* or *Polar Tracking* turned on.

   TIP: For drawing the first line, enter ***0,0 Enter*** *for the first point and then enter* ***24′*** *with Polar Tracking on and the cursor pointing down and snapped to the vertical.*

   a. Make sure *Dynamic Input* is toggled on (*Status Bar*).
   b. You do not need to draw the dimensions yet.

All the dimensions shown in the foundation perimeter drawing (Figure 4-1.5) relate to masonry coursing. See the ***TIP:*** on the next page.

9. Use the **Measure \Distance** command (located on the *Utilities* panel under the *Home* tab) to double-check your dimensions before moving on. Now is the time to make corrections.

FYI: Ortho *is toggled on and off from the Status Bar, near Polar Tracking. When Ortho is toggled on, you are only able to draw horizontal and vertical lines. Ortho needs to be turned off in order to draw angled lines.* Polar Tracking *gives you the "best of both worlds," i.e., angled lines and orthogonal lines. Sometimes, Polar Tracking needs to be turned off when drawing angled lines that are really close to horizontal or vertical.*

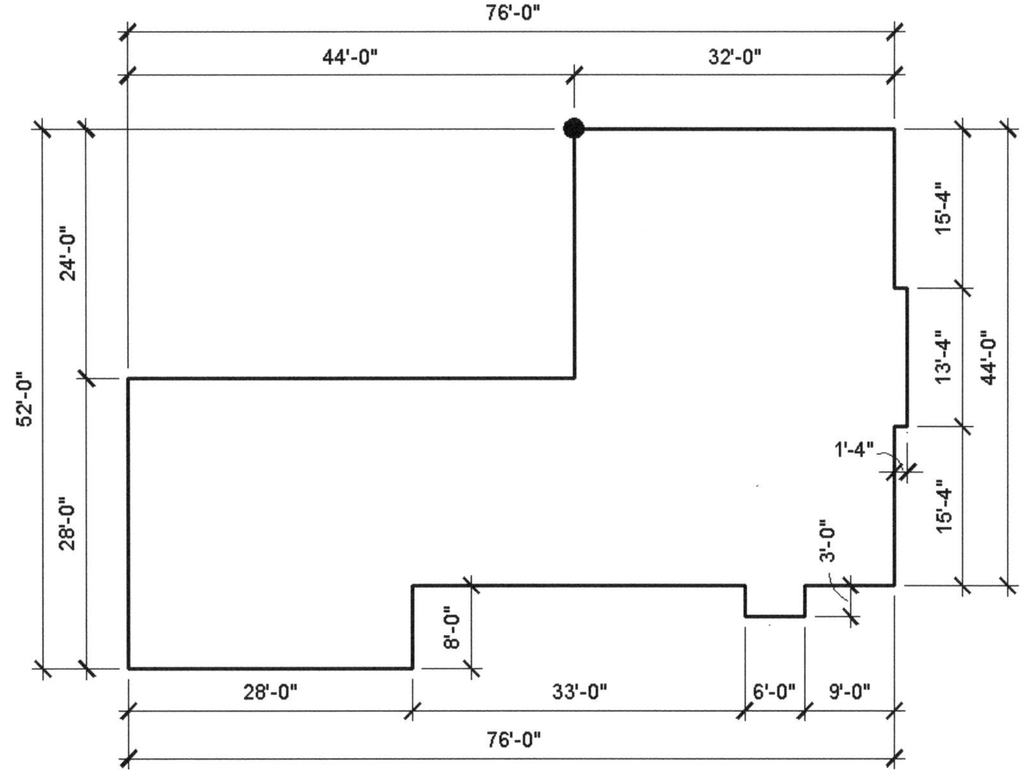

FIGURE 4-1.5 Foundation perimeter – Basement Floor Plan
The black dot represents the Origin (i.e., 0,0)

> ***TIP:*** *Concrete blocks come in various widths, and most are 16″ long and 8″ high. When drawing plans, keep a simple rule in mind to ensure you design walls to masonry coursing. This applies to wall lengths and openings within CMU walls.*
>
> *Dimension rules for CMU coursing in floor plans:*
>
> - E′-0″ OR E′-8″ — *where* e *is any even number* (e.g., 6′-0″ or 24′-8″)
> - O′-4″ — *where* o *is any odd number* (e.g., 5′-4″)

The foundation walls consist of 8″ thick concrete blocks, so you will use the offset command to quickly create the interior side of the wall.

10. Use the **Offset** command to offset the lines previously drawn toward the center of the structure **8″** (Figure 4-1.6).

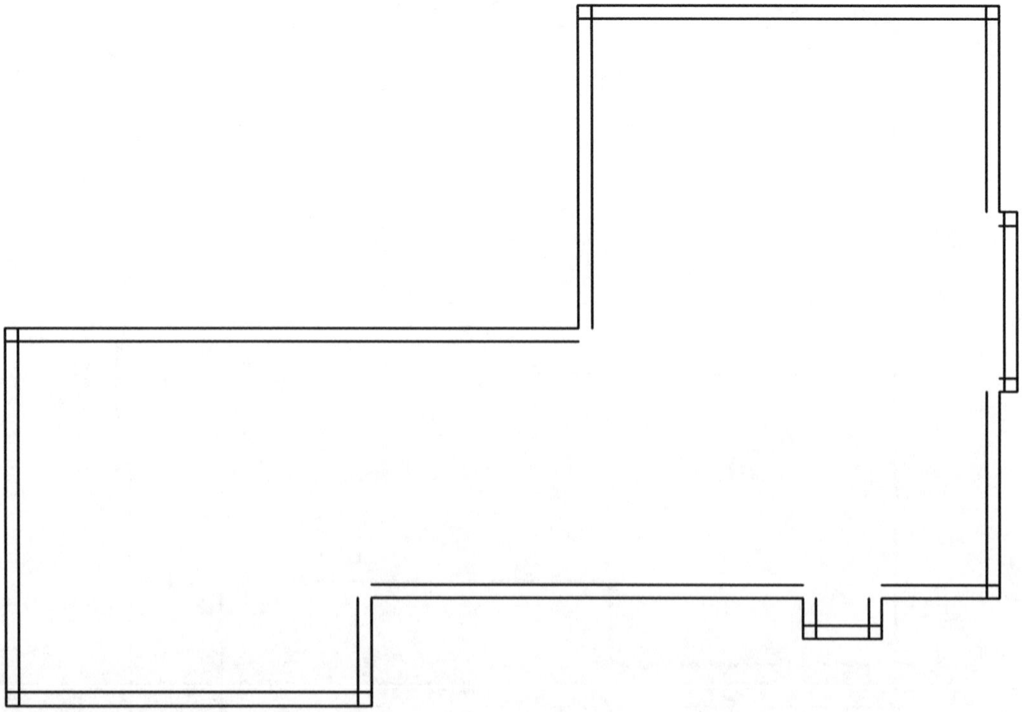

FIGURE 4-1.6 Preliminary Foundation perimeter - Basement Floor Plan

Notice in the figure above that the **Offset** command simply offsets a line of the same length as the original line. Thus, at outside corners, the lines are too long, and at inside corners, the lines are not long enough.

If you recall from the previous Lesson, the **Rectangle** command creates what is called a "closed polyline." If you had used the **Polyline** command to draw the perimeter, the entire outline would have offset with perfect corners. You would then have to explode the polyline(s) in order to create the interior walls.

11. Use the **Fillet** command with the radius set to **0** (i.e., zero) to clean up all the corners. Do <u>not</u> Fillet the corner identified in Figure 4-1.7.

    TIP: Use **Multiple,** *a sub-command of Fillet, to perform several Fillets in a row.*

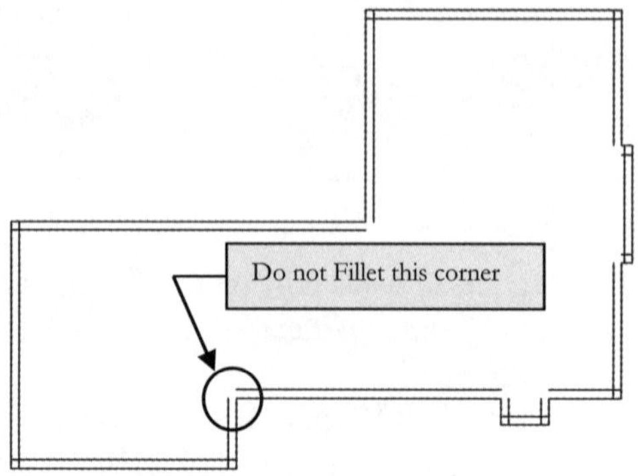

FIGURE 4-1.7 Do not Fillet this corner
Basement Floor Plan

You should now have exterior walls with all but one "cleaned-up" corner.

Using the Extend Command:

You will use both Extend and Trim to complete the other major masonry wall in the basement. Both commands are located on the *Modify* panel under the *Home* tab (on the *Ribbon*); hover your cursor over the icon to view its tool-tip, which displays the command name.

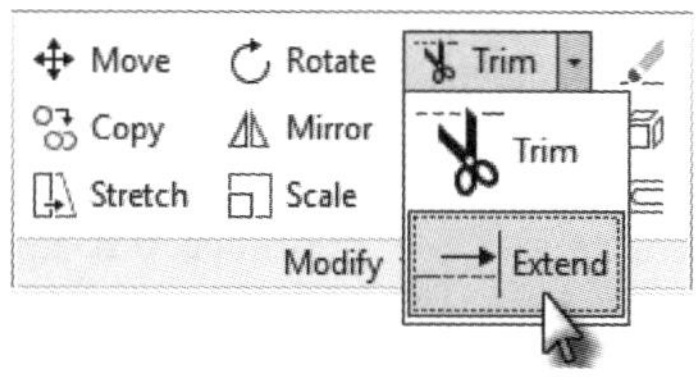

12. Select the **Extend** command (see the image to the right).

You are now prompted to **Select object to extend…**

The on-screen prompt reads:

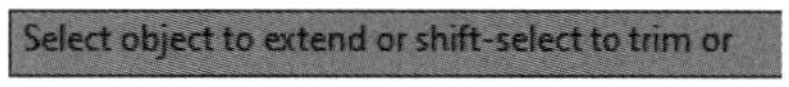

The selected object will extend to anything else nearby.

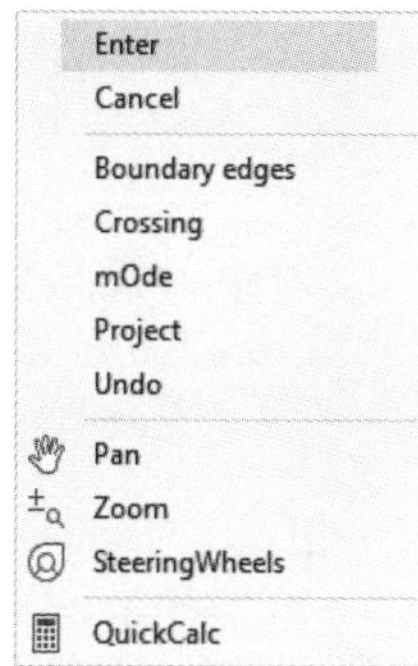

13. Pick the vertical line identified in Figure 4-1.8.

14. To complete the command, first right-click.

15. Select **Enter** from the pop-up menu (see image to the right).

16. Review the results (Problems: Use Undo and try again).

> *TIP: When you select tools from a fly-out icon, the selected tool rises to the top of the "stack." In the image above, you can see that the default icon is Trim; once Extend is used, it becomes the default (see the image below). If the one you want is on top, simply click the icon instead of the down arrow. Once AutoCAD is closed, the Ribbon reverts to the defaults.*

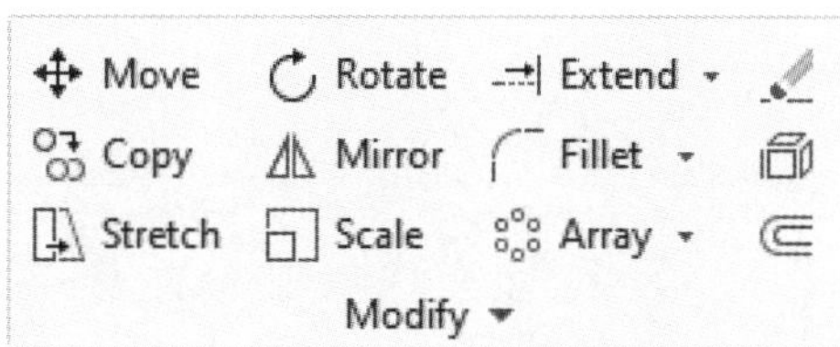

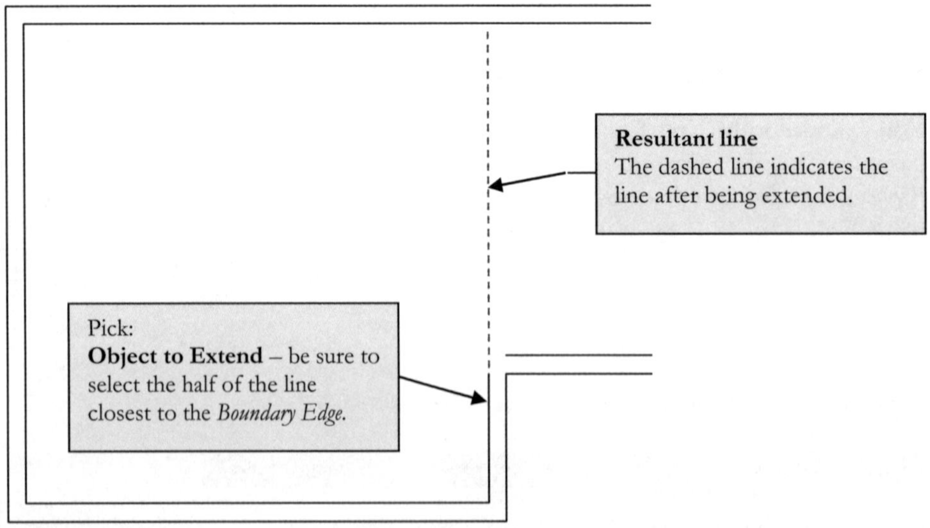

FIGURE 4-1.8 Using the Extend command to extend a line

> ***TIP:*** *When selecting a line to extend, AutoCAD is aware of which side of the line's midpoint you select. This is because you can extend a line in both directions. In the example above, you need to select the portion of the vertical line that is closest to the horizontal line you want to extend to.*

You will now draw the other line representing the 8″ concrete block wall between the basement and the unexcavated area below the garage. You have several ways in which you can draw this line. One is to Offset the line you just extended to the right 8″ and then Fillet the bottom corner. The following steps represent another option.

17. Draw a vertical **Line** from the *Endpoint* below to the *Perpendicular* point above (see Figure 4-1.9).

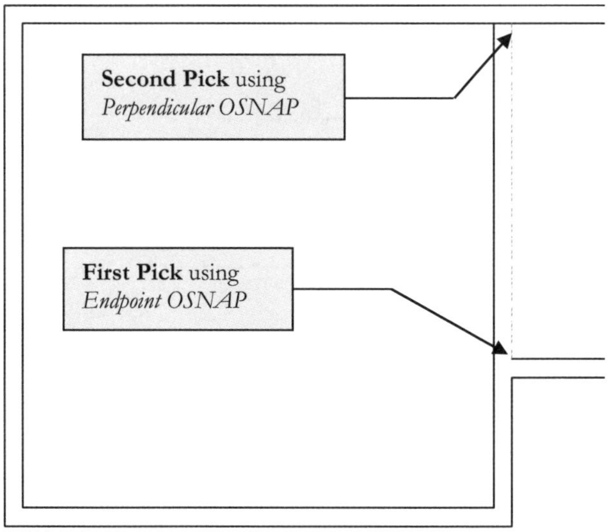

FIGURE 4-1.9 Drawing a line

Using the Trim Command:

Now you will use the Trim command to remove the portion of horizontal line between the two vertical lines you just created (at the top edge). In this example, the Trim command actually breaks one line into two lines. See Figure 4-1.10.

18. Select the **Trim** icon from the *Modify* panel.

You are prompted to **Select object to trim…**

The on-screen prompt reads: 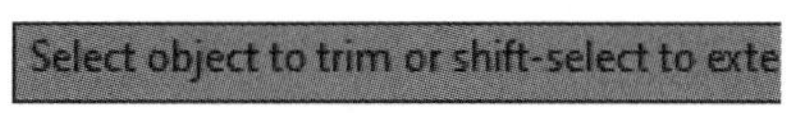

This is the line(s) you want to trim.

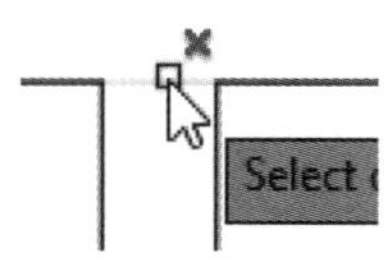

19. Click on the portion of the line to be removed (See Fig 4-1.10).

20. Press **Enter** (or right-click) to tell AutoCAD you are finished selecting cutting edges.

The horizontal line is now trimmed (see Figure 4.1-10).

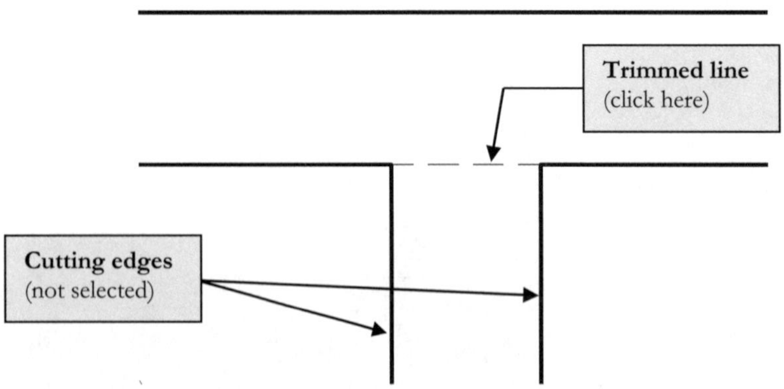

FIGURE 4-1.10 Trimming a line

Next, you will complete the foundation wall at the south fireplace (towards the bottom).

21. Modify the drawing as shown in **Figure 4.1-11**.
    a. Erase dashed line

22. Modify drawing as shown in **Figure 4.1-12**.
    a. Fillet the interior side of the wall to the corner
    b. Offset interior wall line 8" down
    c. Fillet corners
    d. See figure 4-1.14 for the end result

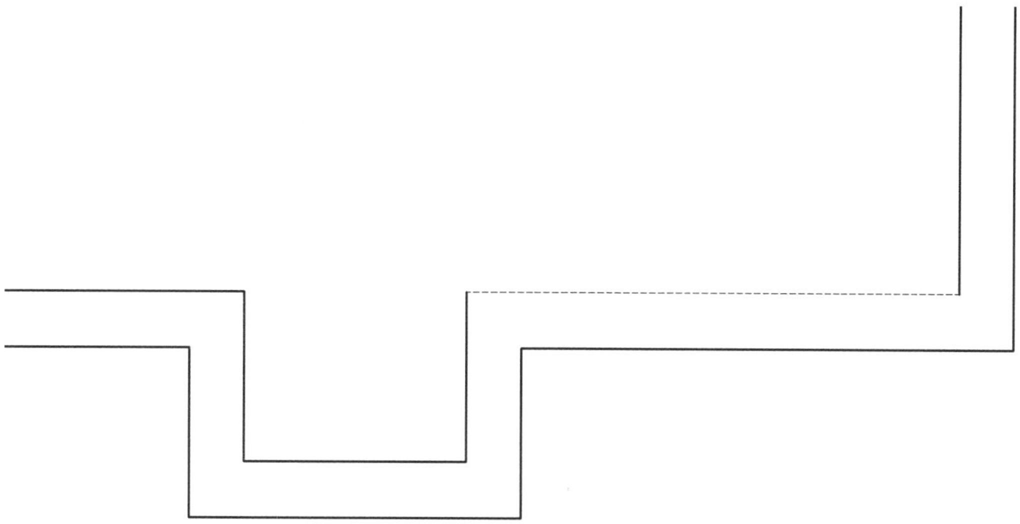

FIGURE 4-1.11 Creating and modifying walls

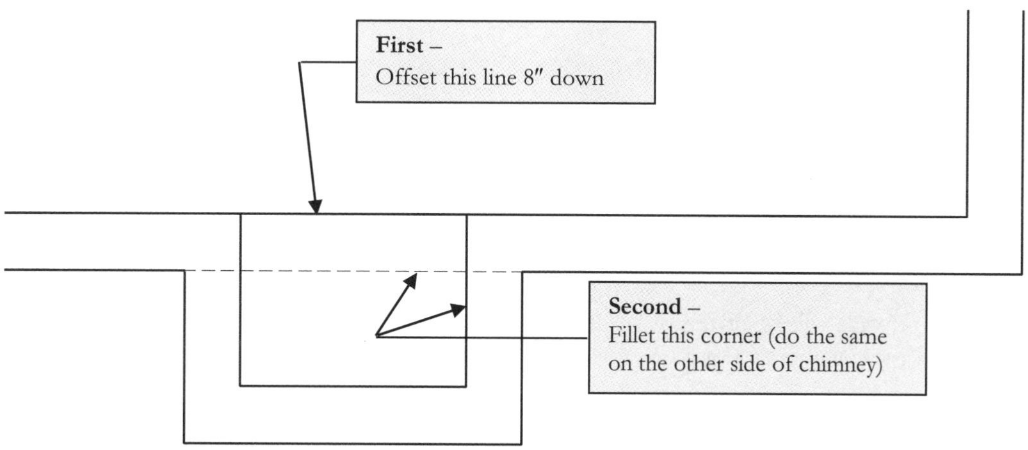

FIGURE 4-1.12 Creating and modifying walls

Drawing the Interior Walls:

Now that you have the perimeter drawn, you will draw a few interior walls. When drawing floor plans, it is good practice to sketch the various wall systems you plan to use; this will help you determine the wall thickness. Drawing the walls at the correct thickness helps when you are later fine-tuning.

The exterior walls in the basement are simply 8″ concrete block so we did not need to sketch them.

Take a moment to think about the basic interior wall in a residential project. It typically consists of the following:

- 2x4 wood studs (actual size is 1½″ x 3½″)
- ½″ gypsum board (⅝″is used for sound/fire control)

The wall system described above is sketched to the right (Figure 4-1.13).

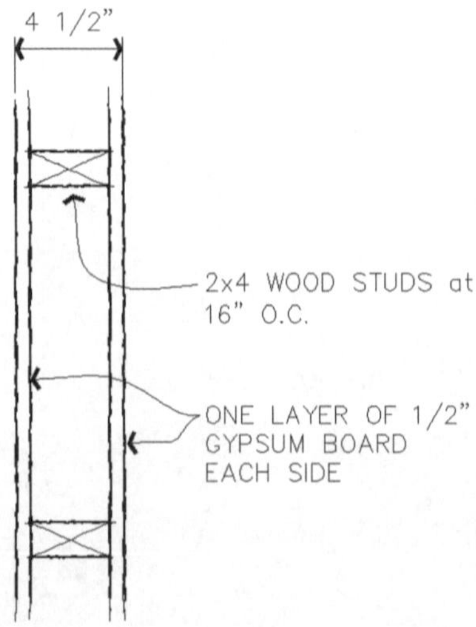

FIGURE 4-1.13
Sketch – Plan view of interior wall system

All your interior walls should be drawn **4½″** for each floor.

The exterior walls will be different for the upper floors (the concrete block does not go up to the roof); you will sketch it when you get to drawing the main level floor plan.

You will now draw the interior walls to complete the walls for the basement floor plan.

23. Draw the interior walls shown in **Figure 4-1.14** using the **Line** command. Do not draw the dimensions at this time. Use the *Measure* tool to check for accuracy.

    FYI: *The dimensions shown are <u>not</u> to the center here, for your convenience in drafting the walls.*

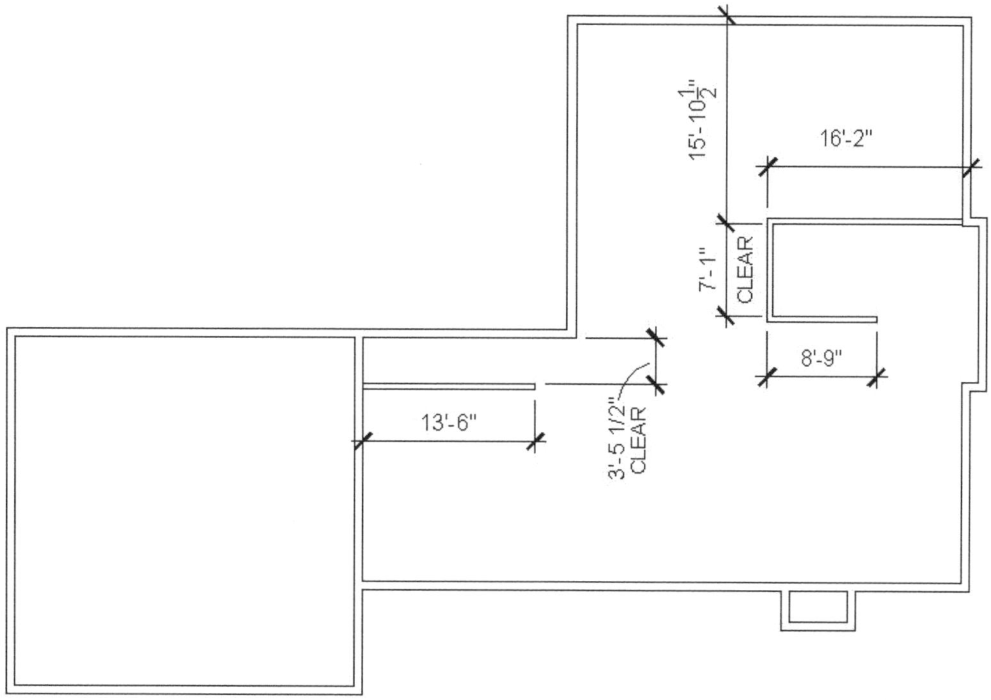

FIGURE 4-1.14 Interior walls to be drawn

Notice (in Figure 4-1.14) where one wall system meets another, the lines are not trimmed. This helps to delineate the extent of each wall. You would, however, trim the lines between two stud walls of varying thickness.

For now, you are done with the basement floor plan. You have drawn several 8″ CMU (i.e., Concrete Masonry Units, or Concrete Blocks) and a handful of interior stud partitions (i.e., walls). After saving this drawing, you will move on to the main level plan.

24. **Save** your **Flr-B** drawing file.

Drawing the Main Level Floor Plan:

Before starting the main level floor plan, you will sketch the exterior wall system (see Figure 4-1.15). Notice that the siding extends beyond the face of the concrete block foundation wall. Even though the outside face of the exterior wall is technically not aligned with the outside face of the foundation wall below, you will ignore the thickness of the siding in plan view. This allows you to draw the outside of the exterior walls in the same position as the outside face of the foundation wall below. This makes it easier to draft and for the contractor to read the dimensions on the blueprints. All the contractor needs to know is that the face of the exterior sheathing is flush with the face of the foundation wall below.

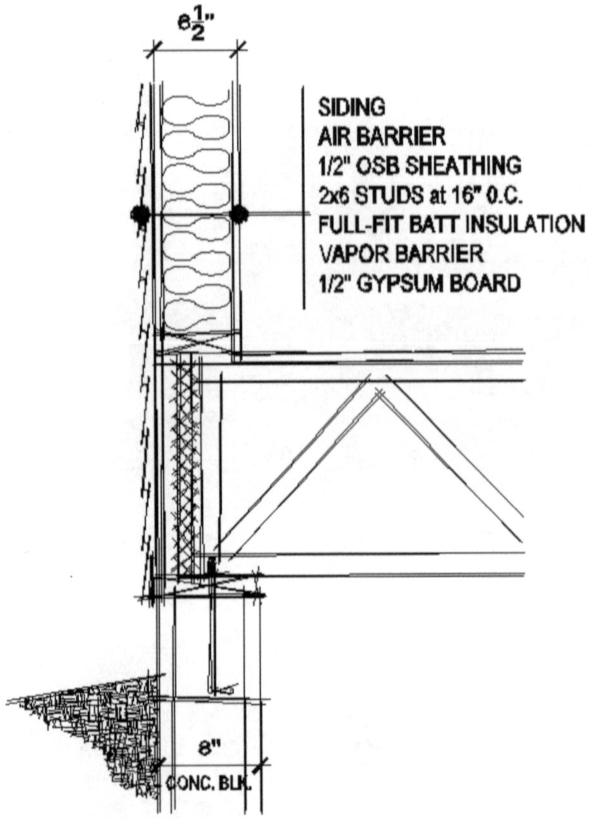

FIGURE 4-1.15 Sketch – Exterior wall in section view

This wall system will be studied more closely later in the book. However, a brief explanation will be provided. This is a fairly standard wall design. The ½″ OSB (oriented strand board) extends all the way down to the top of the foundation wall. Again, as previously mentioned, notice how the exterior face of the sheathing aligns with the exterior face of the foundation wall. Often, rigid insulation is placed on the exterior side of the foundation wall to conserve heat and protect the waterproofing.

25. Start a new drawing named **Flr-1.dwg**, set the drawing **Limits** as previously instructed (see page 4-5; i.e., template plus limits), and then **Zoom All**.

26. Using the **6½″** exterior wall dimension shown in Figure 4-1.15, draw all the walls shown in Figure 4-1.16.

NOTE: The garage is only one story in height, so the walls do not need to be constructed with 2x6's; ***draw the exterior garage walls at 4½″ thick****. The interior garage wall will still be a 2x6 wall to maintain a higher R-value in case the garage door is accidentally left open in the middle of winter!*

27. Be sure the *Origin* is in the same relative position as the basement floor plan. If it is not, use the *Move* command to move the entire first floor plan into its correct position.

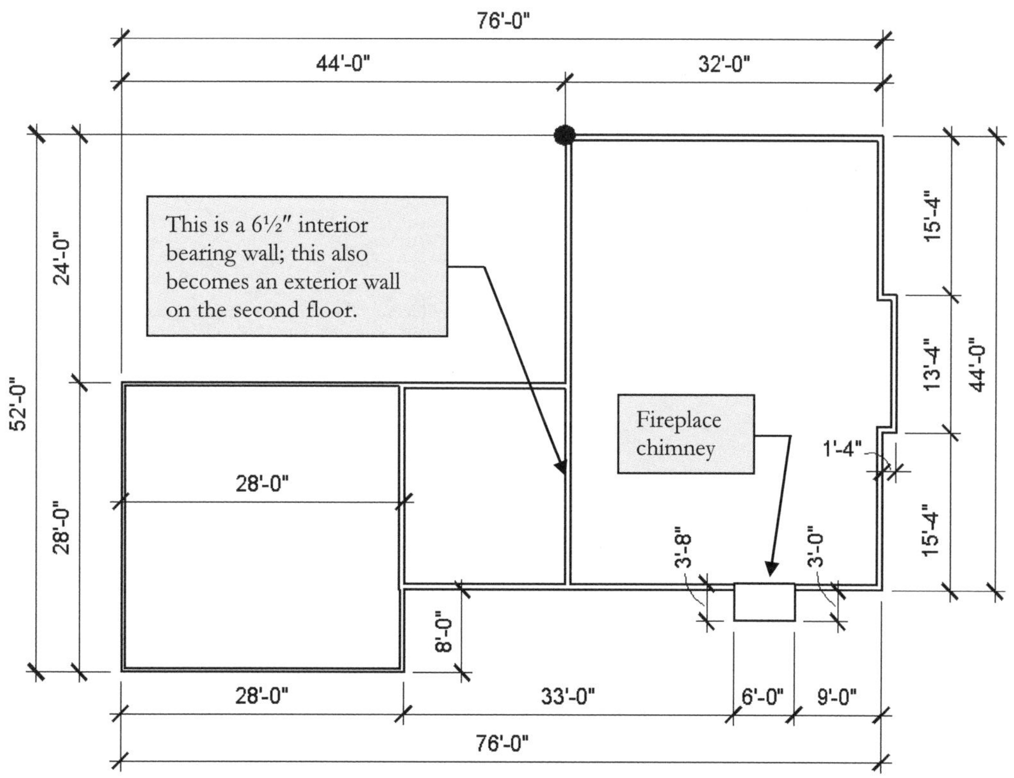

FIGURE 4-1.16 Exterior walls – First floor plan; the black dot represents the Origin

Notice that, with the exception of a few added dimensions, all the dimensions given in Figure 4-1.16 are the same as those given for the basement floor plan. (See Figure 4-1.5.)

Now, draw the interior walls.

28. Draw the interior walls shown in **Figure 4-1.17**, keeping the following in mind:
    a. Remember to use the **4½"** dimension from Figure 4-1.13.
    b. Again, the dimensions shown are to the face of the walls.
    c. Trim all intersections except at the southern fireplace.
    d. The two major horizontal interior walls are to align with the inside face of the exterior wall as shown.
    e. North is straight up as indicated by the north arrow.

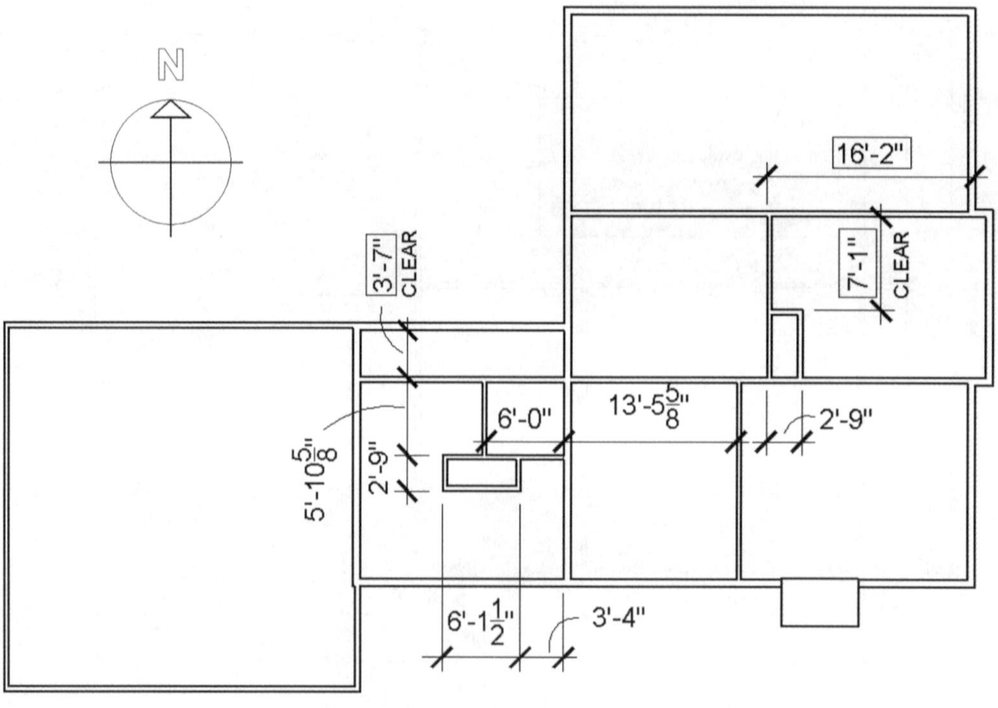

FIGURE 4-1.17 Interior walls – First floor plan

FYI: Unless there are unusual circumstances, north is always UP on architectural plan drawings (i.e., floor plans, site plans, etc.).

Notice the dimensions within the rectangles above; they relate to wall dimensions from the basement floor plan (Figure 4-1.14). Each is related to a stairway that, of course, passes between floors, so the walls, by necessity, need to align from floor to floor. (Notice the dimension changes for the stair near the garage as the exterior basement wall is thicker than the first floor exterior wall.)

Drawing the Second Level Floor Plan:

Here, you will use the same wall thicknesses previously identified.

Exterior Walls: 6½″
Interior Walls: 4½″

29. Start a new drawing named **Flr-2.dwg**, set the drawing **Limits** as previously instructed (page 4-5), and then **Zoom All**.

30. Using the same relative **Origin**, draw the second floor exterior walls shown in **Figure 4-1.18**.

FYI: The fireplace chimney is smaller at this level than below; the smaller size is centered on the larger size below. You will see this better when you draw the elevations.

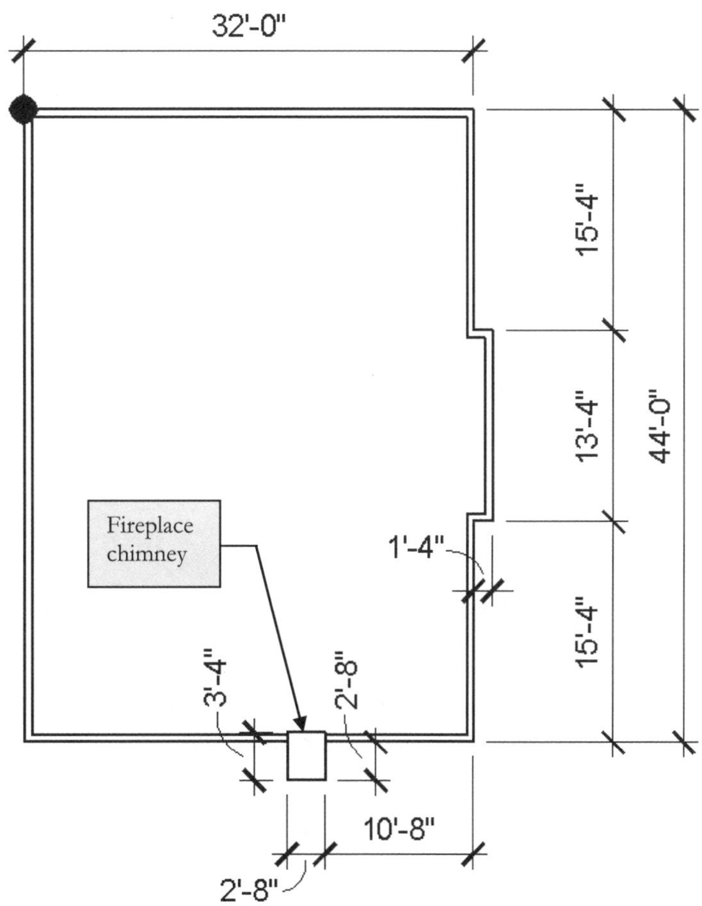

FIGURE 4-1.18 Exterior walls – Second floor plan; the black dot represents the Origin

Again, you should notice several of the dimensions in Figure 4-1.18 match dimensions shown on the two lower floor plans; this floor is considerably smaller than the other floors.

31. Draw the interior walls shown in **Figure 4-1.19**.

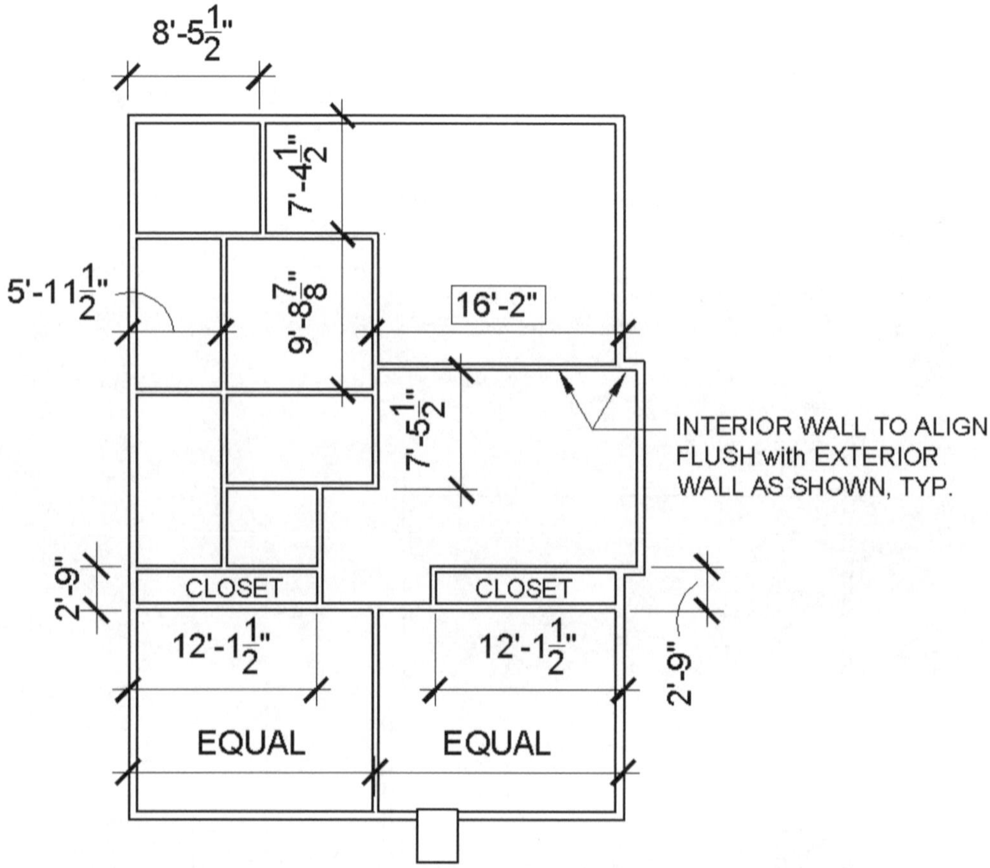

FIGURE 4-1.19 Interior walls – Second floor plan

32. **Save** your floor plan drawings.

This concludes the exercise on drawing walls for your floor plans. You should now have a good working knowledge of *Offset*, *Trim*, and *Extend*, as well as using the *Distance* command to verify your drawings.

In the next exercise, you will use *Offset*, *Extend*, and *Trim* to locate and create door openings in the walls. Additionally, you will learn how to insert pre-drawn symbols (called blocks) into your drawing. In this case, you will insert the door symbols previously drawn in Lesson 3.

Exercise 4-2:
Doors

Now that you have drawn the walls, you will add the doors. This involves locating where the door opening will be in the wall and then trimming the wall lines to create the opening. Finally, you insert a door symbol that indicates which side the hinges are on and the direction the door opens.

New doors are typically shown open 90 degrees in floor plans, which helps to avoid conflicts such as the door hitting an adjacent base cabinet. Additionally, to make it clear graphically, existing doors are shown open only 45 degrees.

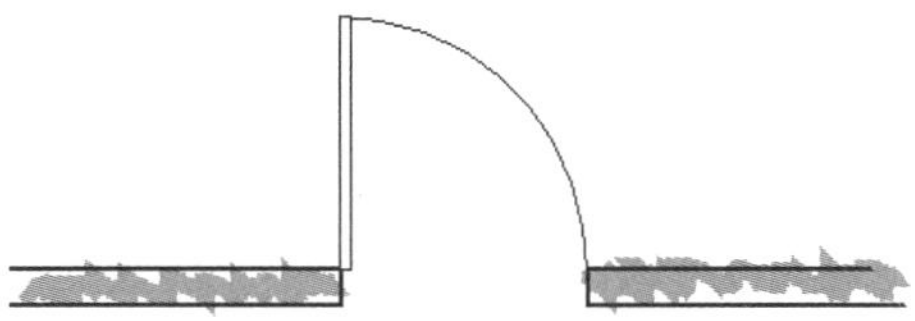

Door symbol Example – New Door drawn with 90 degree swing

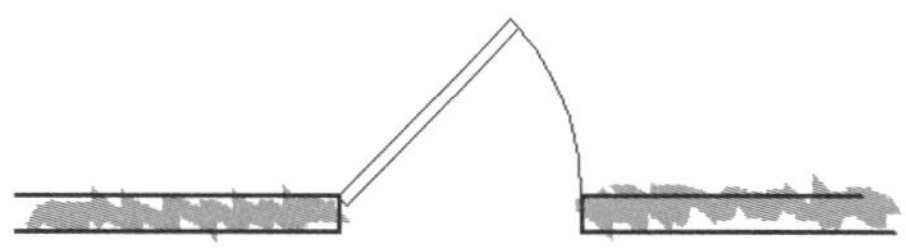

Door symbol Example – Existing Door shown with 45 degree swing

One of the most powerful features of any CAD program is its ability to reuse previously drawn content. With AutoCAD, you can insert entire drawing files as symbols into your drawing. Most of the individual drawings you drew in Lesson 3 will be inserted as symbols (AutoCAD calls them blocks) into the three floor plans.

For those new to drafting, you may find this comparison between CAD and hand-drafting interesting. When hand-drafting, one uses a straightedge or a plastic template with doors and other commonly used symbols to trace.

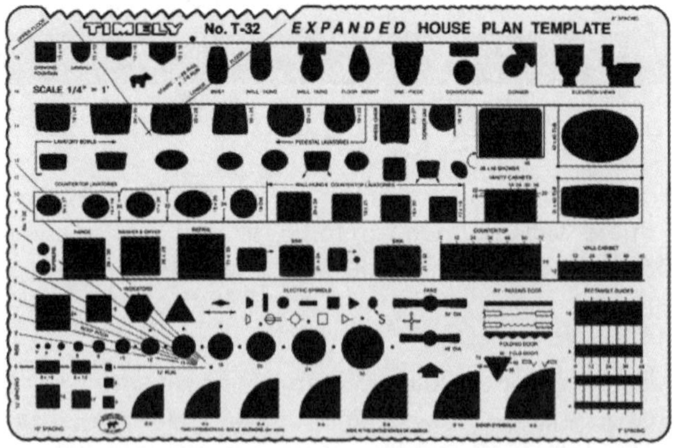

Hand Drafting Template – Plastic template with holes representing common residential shapes (at ¼″ – 1′-0″)
Image used by permission, Timely Templates www.timelytemplates.com

Doors in stud walls are dimensioned to the center of the door opening. On the other hand, and similar to dimensioning masonry walls, doors in masonry walls are dimensioned to the face (see example below).

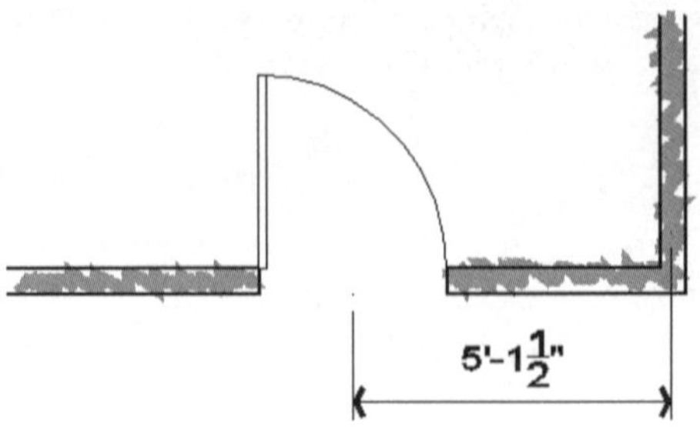

Door Dimension Example – Dimension to the center of the door opening

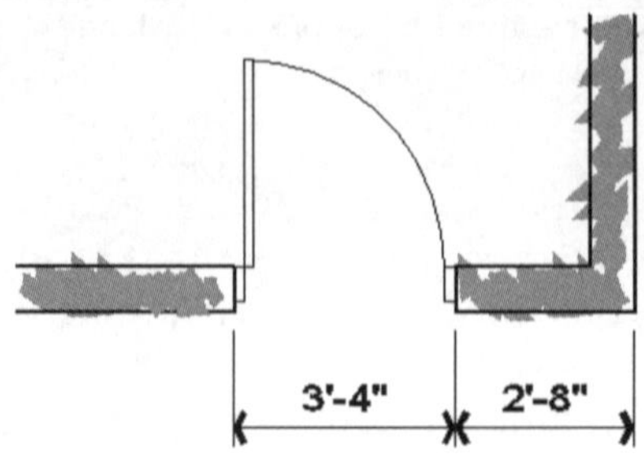

Door Dimension Example – Dimension the opening size and location

Placing a door usually involves the following commands: Offset, Extend, Trim, and Insert.

Getting Started:

First you will locate all the openings in the plans. This includes trimming the wall lines.

1. Open your **Flr-1.dwg** drawing file.

2. **Zoom** into the area shown in **Figure 4-2.1**.

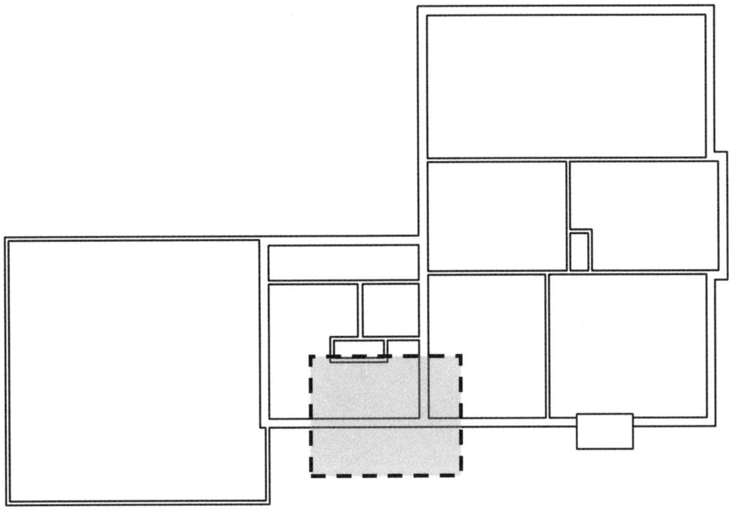

FIGURE 4-2.1 Zoom into area shown

3. **Offset** the vertical line **2′-6″** to the West (to the left) as shown in **Figure 4-2.2**.

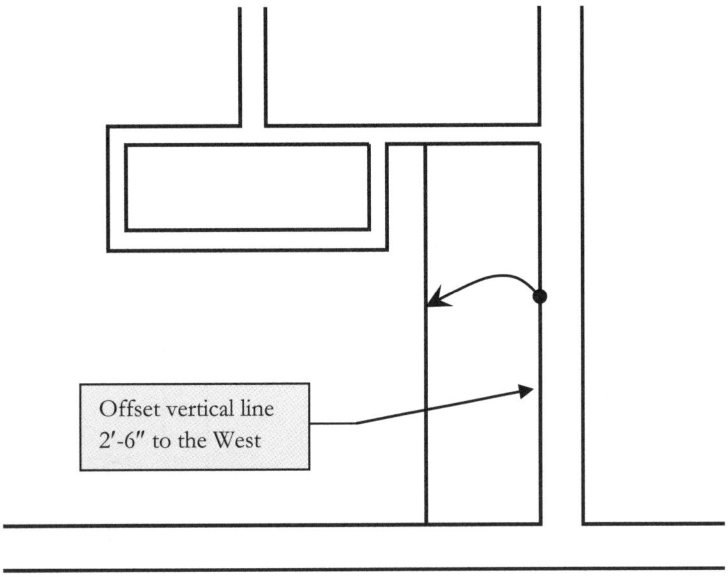

FIGURE 4-2.2 Offset vertical line 2′-6″

4. **Extend** the new line South, to the outside face of the exterior wall (Figure 4-2.3).

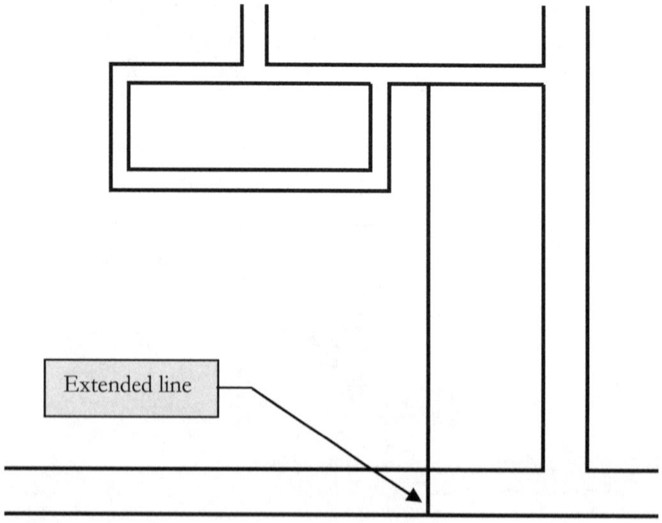

FIGURE 4-2.3 Extend new line south

5. Now **Trim** the line so its length equals the depth of the wall (Figure 4-2.4).

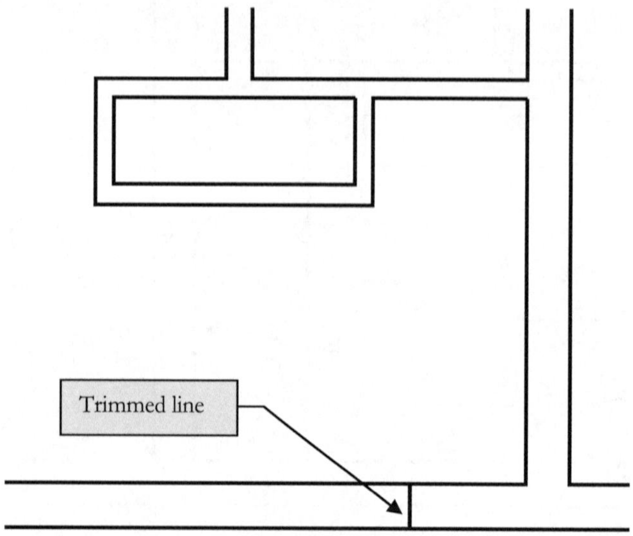

FIGURE 4-2.4 Trim the new vertical line

Next you will *Offset* the new line; the offset distance will be the width of the door.

If your line is located in the center of the door opening, you would offset it each direction with the offset distance being half the width of the door opening. Then you would delete the center line.

6. **Offset** the line **3′-0″** to the west (Figure 4-2.5).

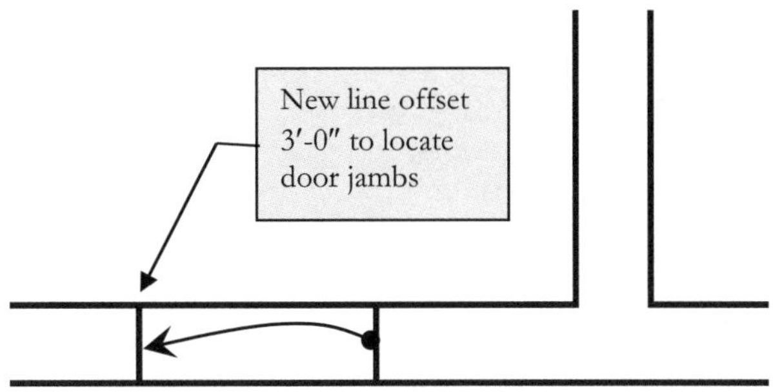

FIGURE 4-2.5 Offset to define the door opening

Finally, you will use *Trim* to remove the wall lines within the door opening.

7. **Trim** the wall lines within the door opening (Figure 4-2.6).

TIP: Select both vertical lines as the Cutting Edge and then pick the portion of the line you want to remove (the portion between the two vertical lines in this example).

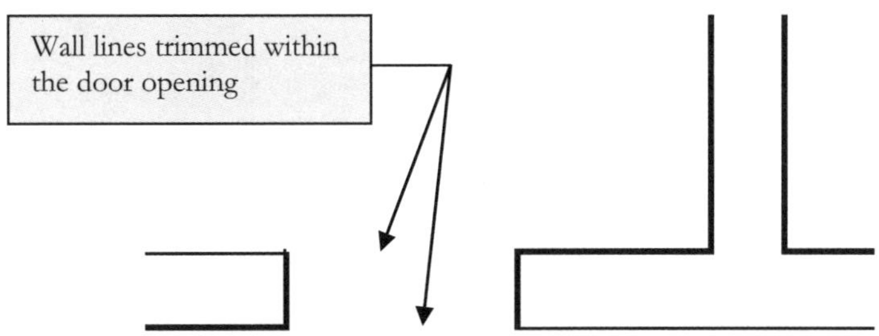

FIGURE 4-2.6 Trim the wall lines within the door opening

That completes the steps necessary to accurately locate a door opening in a wall. Next you will create the rest of the openings for both the first and second floors (the basement has no doors).

What layer do the new jamb lines go on?

The two vertical lines (jamb lines) just drawn go on the same layer as the wall.

Locate and Size the Remaining Openings:

8. Using the following four drawings (Figures 4-2.7, .8, .9, .10) and create the door openings for the first and second floors.

9. Be sure to **Save** often to avoid losing work in the event you have a power outage or the AutoCAD program crashes.

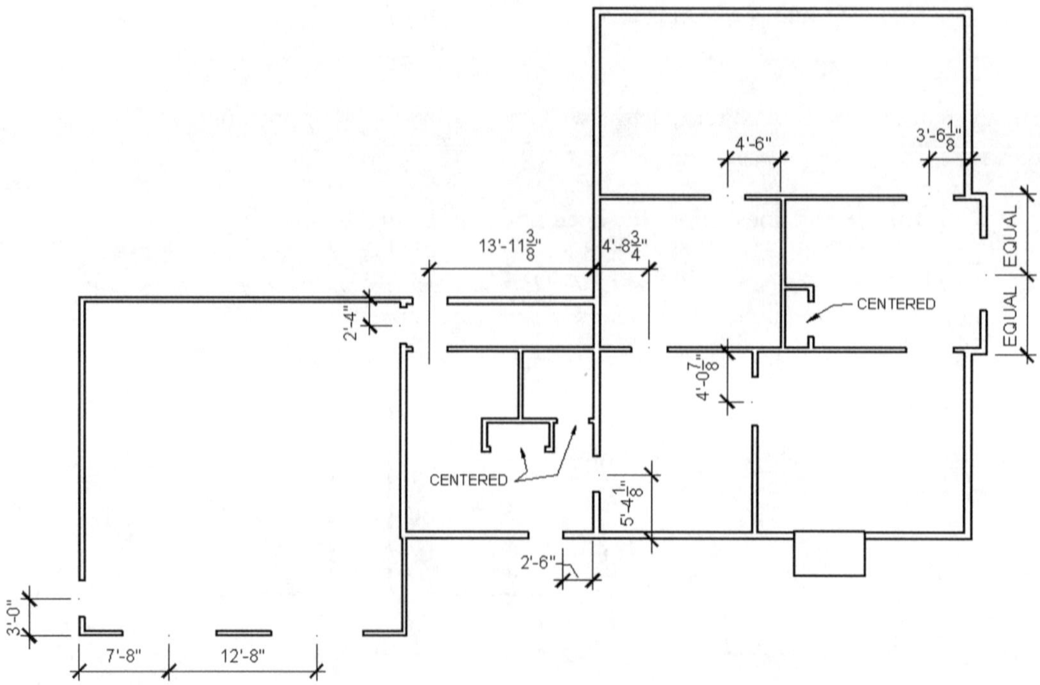

FIGURE 4-2.7 Door opening; First floor LOCATIONS

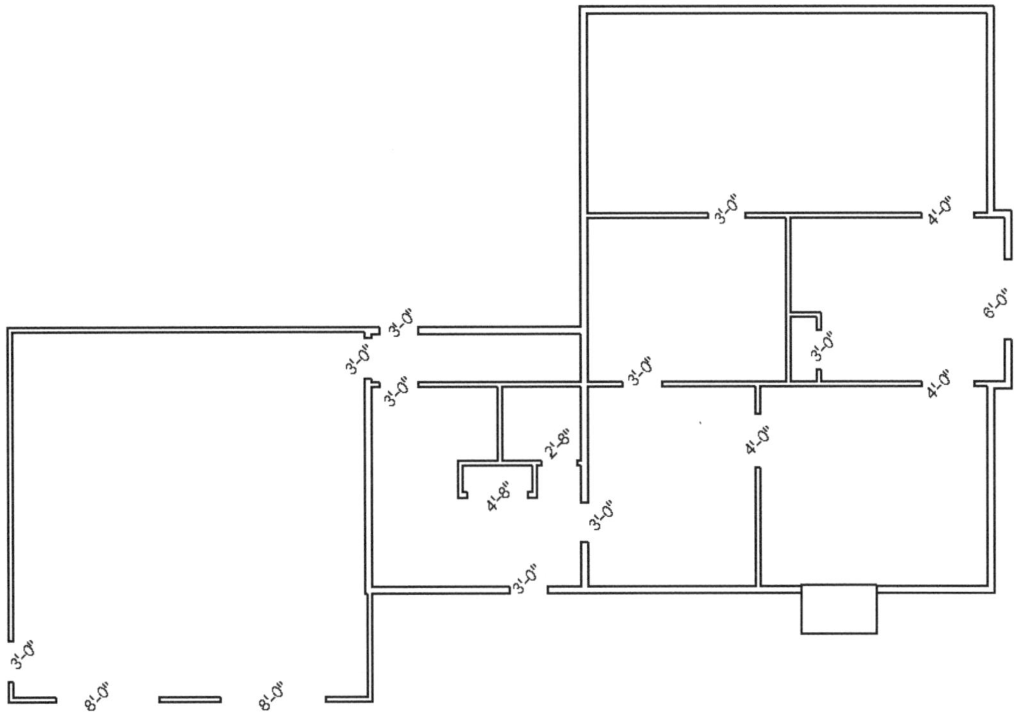

FIGURE 4-2.8 Door/opening sizes; First floor SIZES

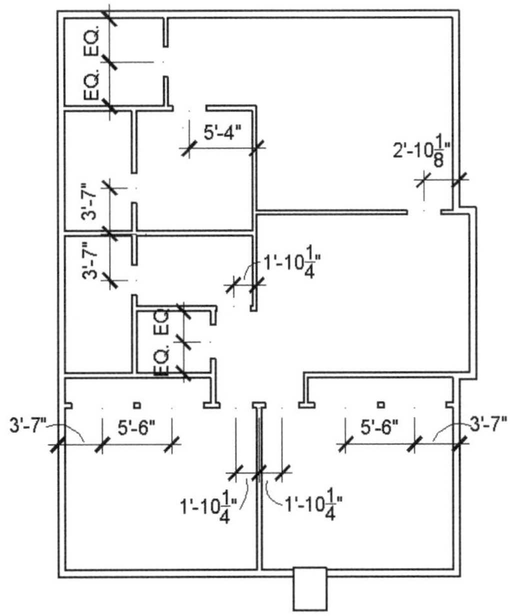

FIGURE 4-2.9 Door locations; Second floor

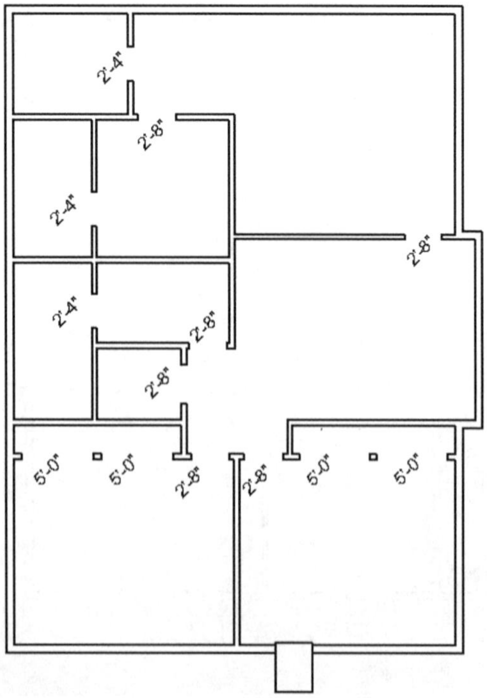

FIGURE 4-2.10 Door/opening sizes; Second floor
- angled number represents size of opening

Inserting the Door Symbols (a.k.a., Blocks):

Now that you have created all the door openings you will insert the door symbols. AutoCAD refers to these symbols as *Blocks.*

Blocks have several advantages compared to simply drawing individual lines for everything.

- A Block contains a group of entities so you can easily move it without having to meticulously select each entity that makes up the symbol.
- Blocks can also be redefined, meaning that you can add or remove the amount of detail in a block. When it's redefined, all the instances of that block in the current drawing are automatically updated.
- Blocks can consist of an entire drawing located on your hard drive. Thus, they can be used in multiple drawings as needed.
- Blocks help reduce the drawing file size.

You will insert the door *Blocks* you created in the previous lesson. You may occasionally need to Rotate and Mirror the *Block* once it is inserted. Additionally, you will need to create additional *Blocks* as needed throughout this book.

Door *Blocks* go on their own *Layer*, called *A-DOOR*. Next you will set this up.

10. In the first floor plan, create a *Layer* named ***A-DOOR*** and set its color to ***Yellow*** (Color #2).

11. Set the ***A-DOOR*** layer to be the *Current Layer.*

12. Select **Insert → Blocks from Libraries…** in the *Block* panel on the *Insert* tab (see Figure 4-2.11a).

You are now in the *Select Drawing File…* dialog, but only if you have never used this command before (more on this in a moment). This dialog allows you to insert other drawings, located on your hard drive or server, as a Block in the current drawing.

13. From the *Select Folder or Drawing File* dialog, browse to the location where you saved the **Door-36** drawing created in Lesson 3.

14. Select the file named **Door-36.dwg** and then click the **Open** button.

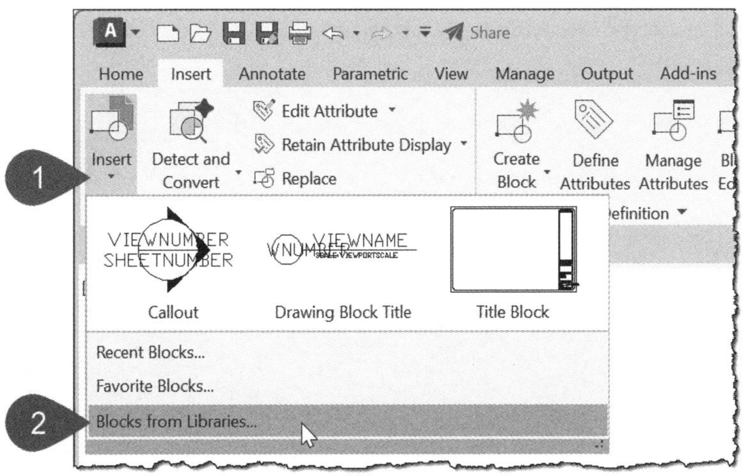

FIGURE 4-2.11A Insert, Blocks from Libraries; allows you to insert other DWG files into the current drawing as a block

15. Click the icon for the drawing you just loaded, from the **Libraries** tab, in the **Blocks** palette, that just opened - if it was not already opened (see Figure 4-2.11b, step #1).

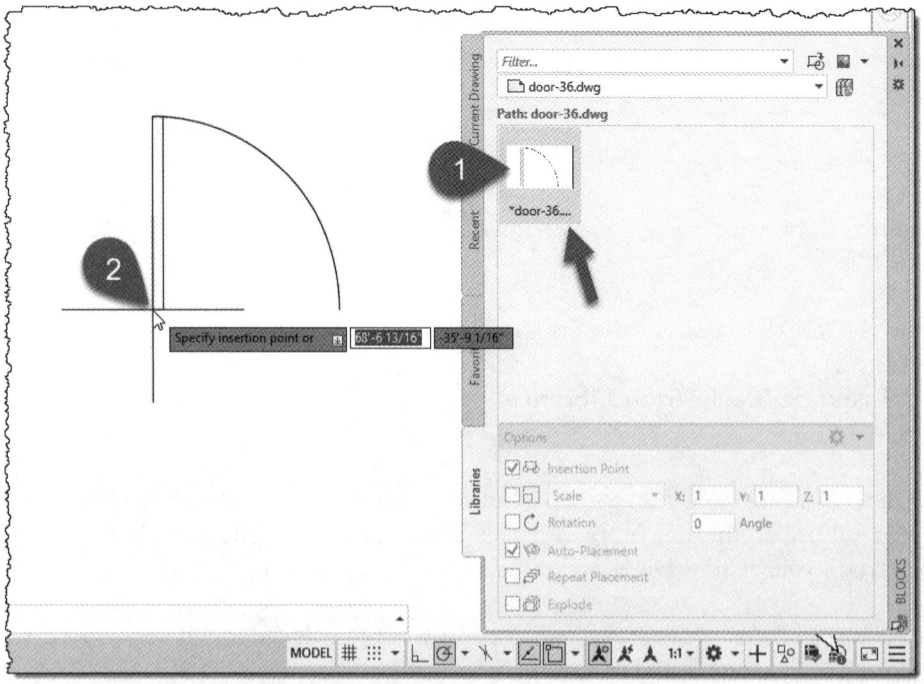

FIGURE 4-2.11B Insert, Blocks palettes; allows you to insert loaded *Blocks*

16. **Insert** the **Door-36** drawing using *OSNAPs* to accurately position the door *Block* within the opening. Insert the doors as shown in Figure 4-2.12.

    TIP #1: Use Rotate and Mirror (previously covered) as required to indicate the required swing.

    TIP #2: Doors should be yellow if the layer was set up correctly and was current when the door block was inserted.

    TIP #3: Experiment with the Rotation and Repeat Placement options within the Blocks dialog.

Notice the block insertion point?

Notice that the hinge side of the door *Block* is attached to the center of the cross-hairs. This relates to the drawing *Origin* (0,0) of the Door-36 drawing file.

If the drawing *Origin* had been located on the latch side of the door in drawing Door-36, the latch side of the door would have been attached to the cross-hairs during insert.

You may have noticed that you have not created a 2′-8″ wide door yet. Simply follow the steps outlined in Lesson 3, creating the door symbol in a separate drawing file.

17. Create the 32″ wide door drawing; name the file **Door-32**.

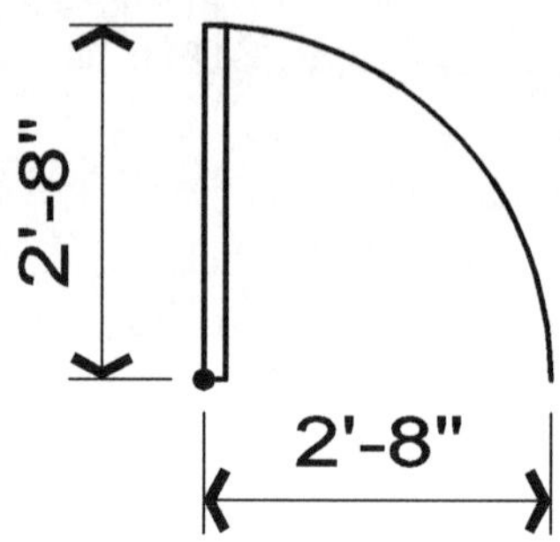

18. Insert the 2′-8″ wide doors using the **Door-32** file.

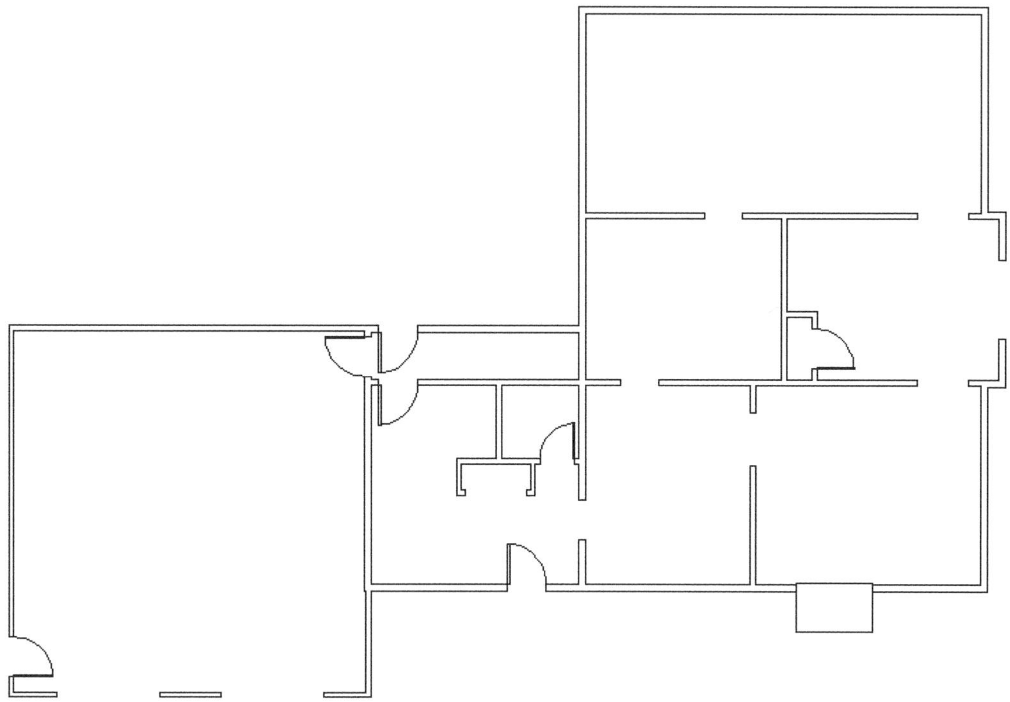

FIGURE 4-2.12 Door-36 and Door-32 blocks inserted; First floor

19. Insert the **Door2-36** drawing file as a *Block* at the main entry as shown in **Figure 4-2.13**.

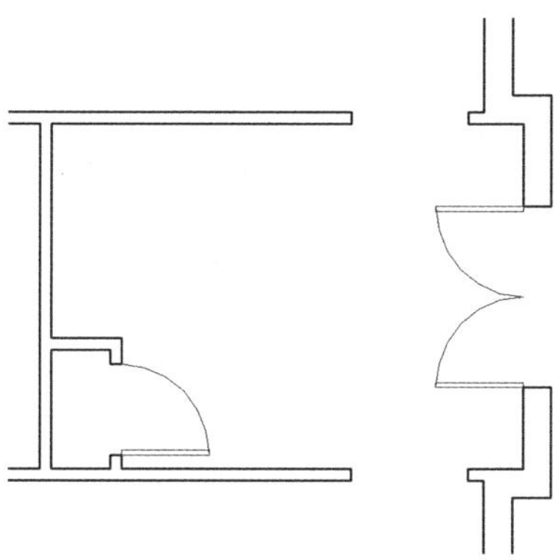

FIGURE 4-2.13 Door2-36 added

Next you will insert the doors on the second floor.

20. **Save Flr-1.dwg** and **Open** the second floor drawing file **Flr-2.dwg**.

21. Insert the doors for the second floor as shown in **Figure 4-2.14**.

NOTE: *On the second floor all swing doors are 32″ wide doors.*

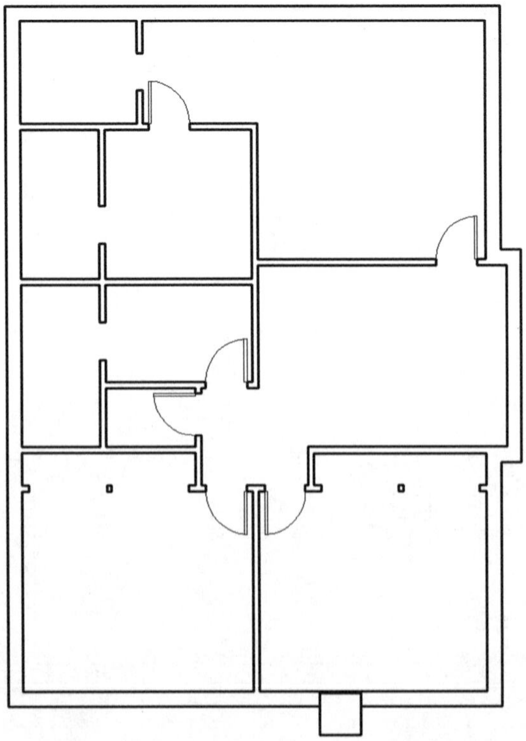

FIGURE 4-2.14 Door-32 blocks inserted; Second floor

Sliding Pocket Doors:

Sliding pocket doors are doors that slide into the wall rather than swinging open into a room. This type of door is convenient when the door will be open most of the time and you do not want, or have room for, an open door. On the other hand, if the door will be used often, like the door from the hallway into the bathroom, you should use a swinging door for ease of use and long-term durability.

One important thing to keep in mind when designing a room with a sliding door: the entire width of the door is in the wall when the door is fully open. That means you need space in the wall next to the door that equals the width of the door plus a few inches depending on the manufacturer (this includes plumbing and electrical that might be in the wall).

Next you will create the 2′-4″ and 4′-0″ wide Sliding Pocket Doors.

22. **Open** a new drawing file and name it **Pocket-28.dwg**.

23. **Create** the 2′-4″ wide pocket door (show the door 2″ thick) shown in **Figure 4-2.15**. This is basically two rectangles.

TIP: Do not draw the dimensions or the black dot. Also, the dashed lines in the figure below represent a wall (not to be drawn). Finally, make sure everything is on Layer 0 (i.e., zero).

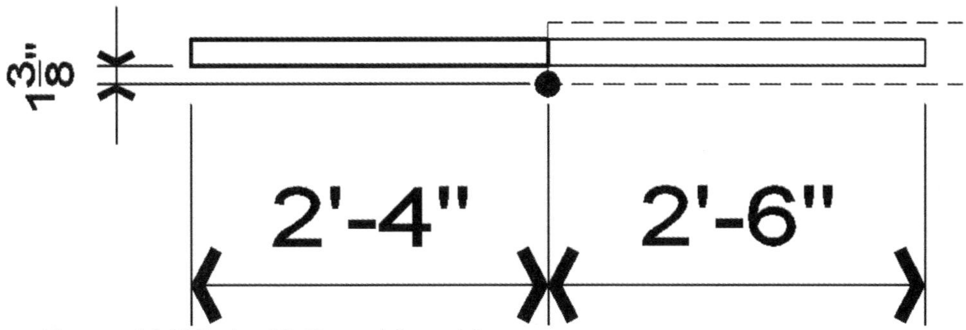

FIGURE 4-2.15 Pocket-28; First and Second floor

This *Block* (Pocket-28) will show the door in the fully closed position; you can adjust this to be partially open if you prefer.

24. **Insert** the 2′-4″ wide pocket door in the three locations shown in Figure 4-2.16 (make sure the current layer is set to *A-DOOR* before inserting the blocks; also, you may need to stretch the opening location a little so the pocket door fits in the wall).

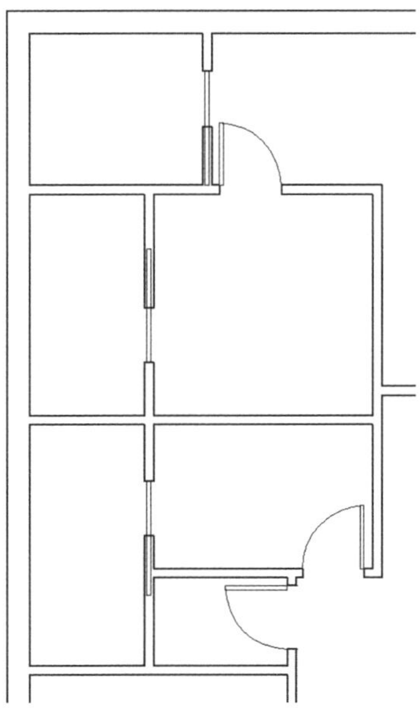

FIGURE 4-2.16 Pocket-28; three locations; Second floor

25. Do a **Save-As** to save the Pocket-28 to a file named **Pocket-48**.

26. Use the **Stretch** command to create the 48″ pocket door.

27. Insert the 48″ wide pocket door in two locations, as shown in Figure 4-2.17, on the first floor.

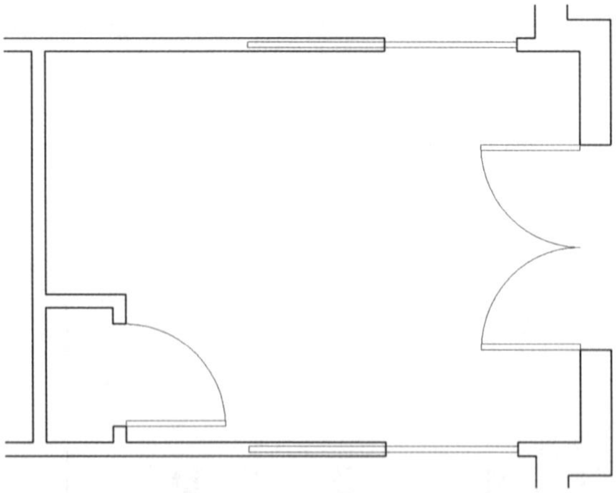

FIGURE 4-2.17 Pocket-48; two locations; First floor

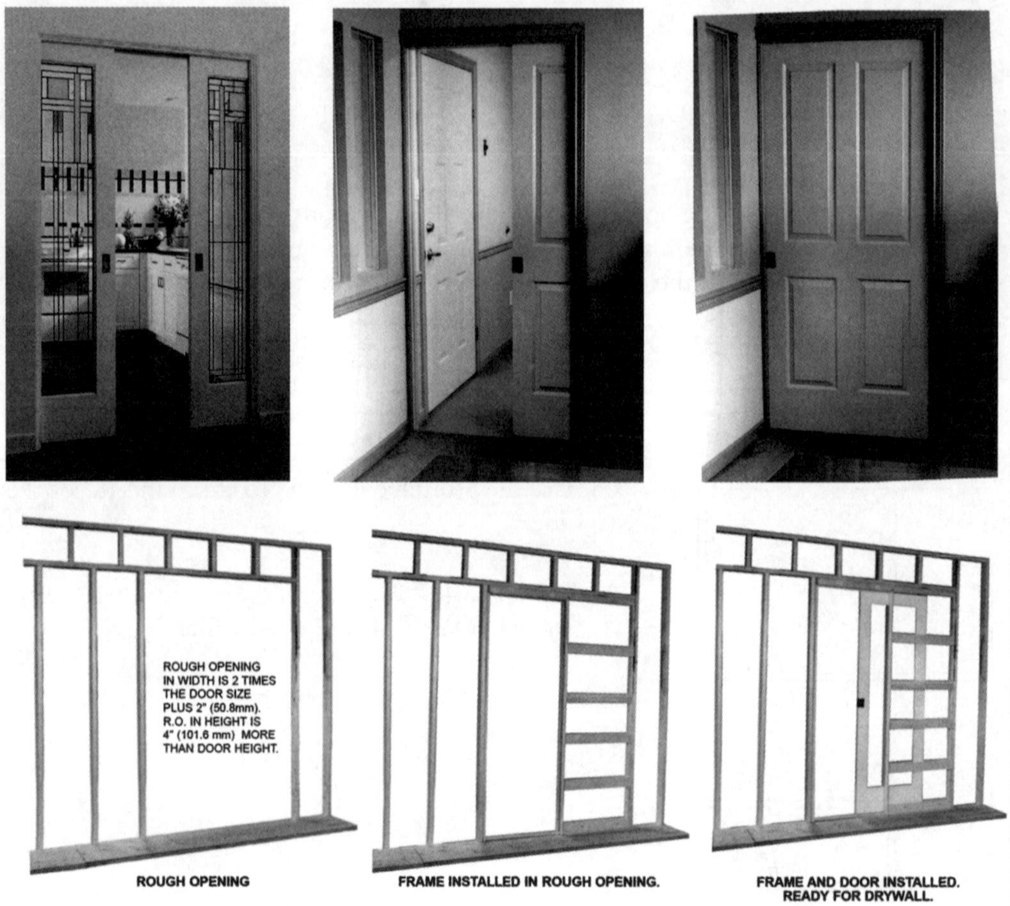

POCKET DOOR EXAMPLES – Double door and Single door photos (top); Installation illustration (bottom); *Images used by permission, KrisTrack* www.kristrack.com

Drawing Closet Doors:

These doors will be drawn right in the Flr-1 and Flr-2 drawings (on layer *A-DOOR*); not everything needs to be a *Block*.

28. **Draw** two rectangles, each 1½″ thick, per Figure 4-2.18.

29. Do the same on the second floor (4 closet openings total).

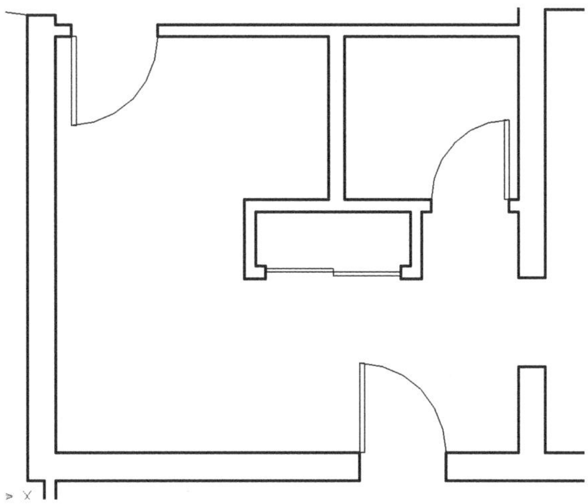

FIGURE 4-2.18 Closet door added; First floor

Garage Doors:

Now you will add the garage door. The exterior face of the door aligns with the interior face of the wall; see garage door jamb detail at right.

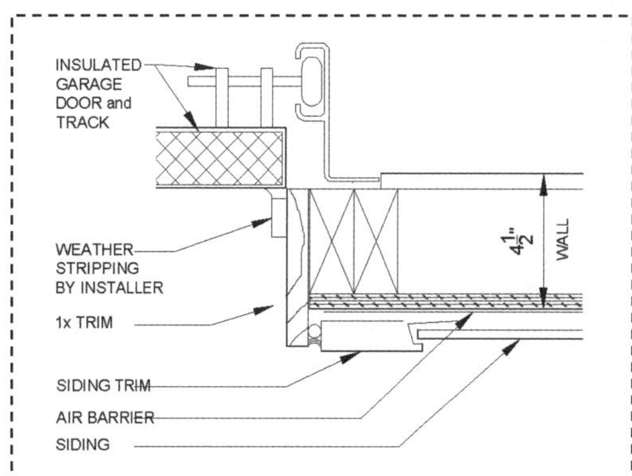

30. Similar to the closet doors, you will simply draw a rectangle (place on layer *A-DOOR*); see Figure 4-2.19.

31. **Save** your drawings.

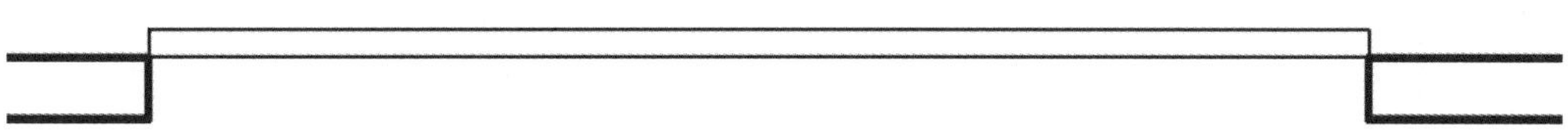

FIGURE 4-2.19 Garage door added; 2″ thick door shown

Exercise 4-3:
Windows

In this exercise you will add exterior windows to your plans. This is similar to placing doors, discussed in the previous exercise.

One difference between drawing doors and windows is that windows are drawn on two separate layers:

A-GLAZ	The window frame and glass (a.k.a., glazing) are drawn on this layer.
A-GLAZ-SILL	The sill lines are drawn on this layer. (This represents the portion of wall that continues below the window.)

Lineweights:

The primary reason that two *Layers* are used is to control lineweights. The thickness of a line (i.e., lineweight) is commonly controlled by which *Layer* it is on. One benefit to this is that you can adjust the lineweight setting in one location and all the lines on that *Layer* are updated. You will learn more about setting lineweights later in this book; for now, do not make any changes related to lineweights unless specifically instructed to do so.

When thinking about how lineweights relate to a window in plan, you need to consider whether the line is in section or not.

The diagrams below show the different components that make up a window in plan view.

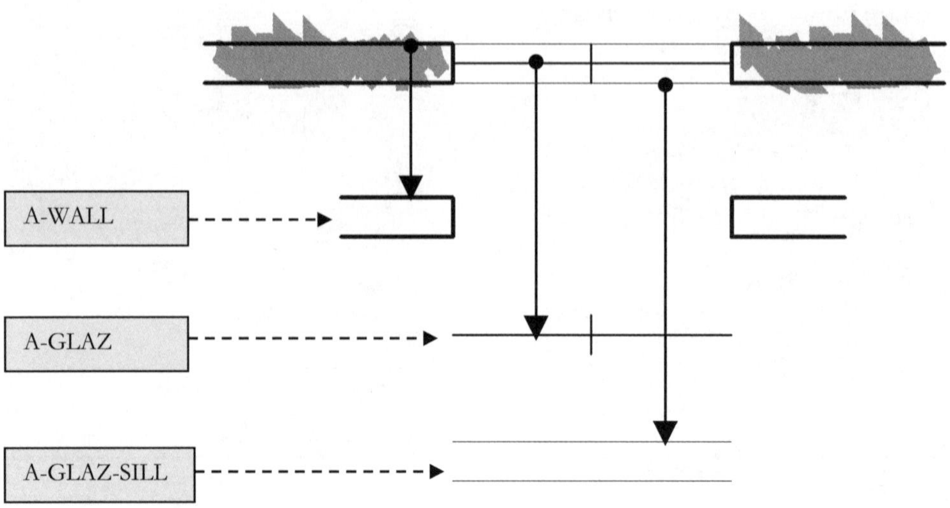

Window Opening Example Components / Layers for a window

You can think of floor plans as cutaways of the 3D building. The cutting plane is usually about 4′- 5′ above the floor level. Notice in the following illustration that the wall is in section but the window sill is not. The sill is technically in elevation (i.e., plan view) while looking down.

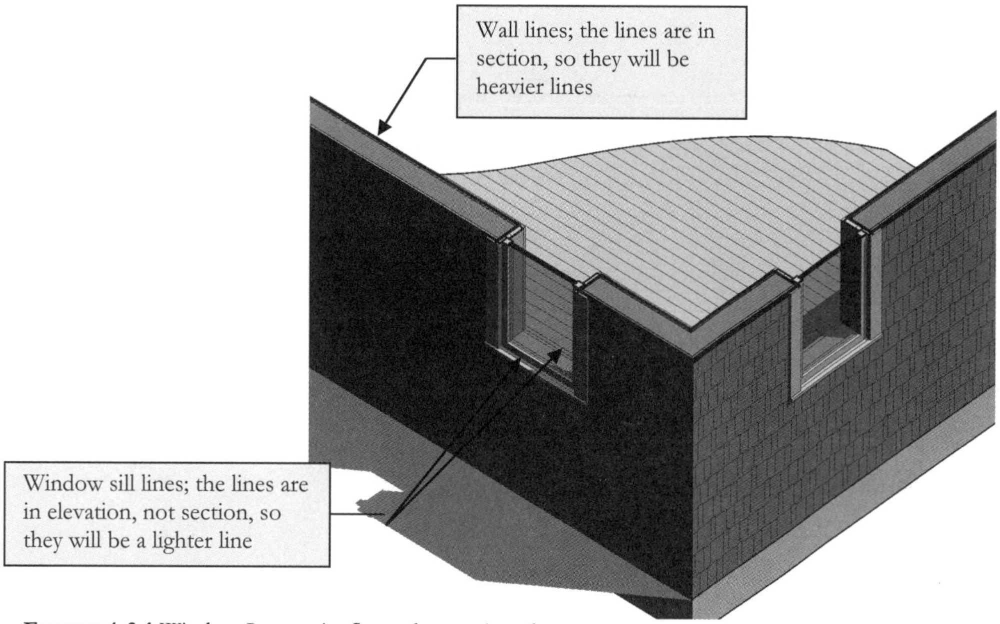

FIGURE 4-3.1 Window Isometric; floor plan cutting plane

Drawing the Windows:

The windows could be *Blocks*, similar to the doors, but you will simply draw lines to create the windows in this exercise. Again, the advantages of *Blocks* are that you can pick any part of a *Block* and the entire thing will highlight; you can also redefine a *Block* and all occurrences of it in the current drawing will automatically be updated.

1. Create the openings in your exterior walls the same way you created the door openings on page 4-20 (Figures 4-3.3, 4-3.4, and 4-3.5):
    a. The [wider] double windows are **6′-8″**.
    b. The single windows are **3′-2″**.
    c. The basement windows are as dimensioned in plan.
    d. See the *extra credit* option towards the end of this exercise (page 4-41).

2. Create the following *Layers*:
   A-GLAZ (color *Yellow*); ***A-GLAZ-SILL*** (color *Red*)

3. Draw the "window lines" per the example shown in Figure 4-3.2; draw a line in the center of the window for the double wide windows. *(This indicates two window frames mulled together.)*

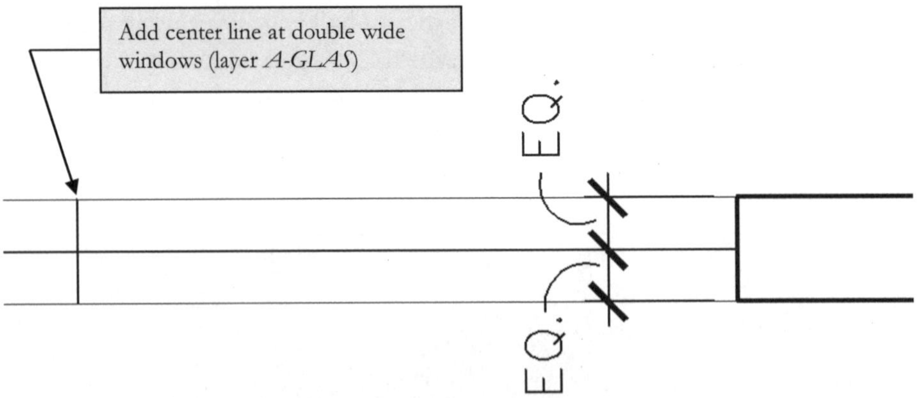

FIGURE 4-3.2 Window Lines; note that EQ. is an abbreviation of 'Equal'

4. **Save** your drawings.

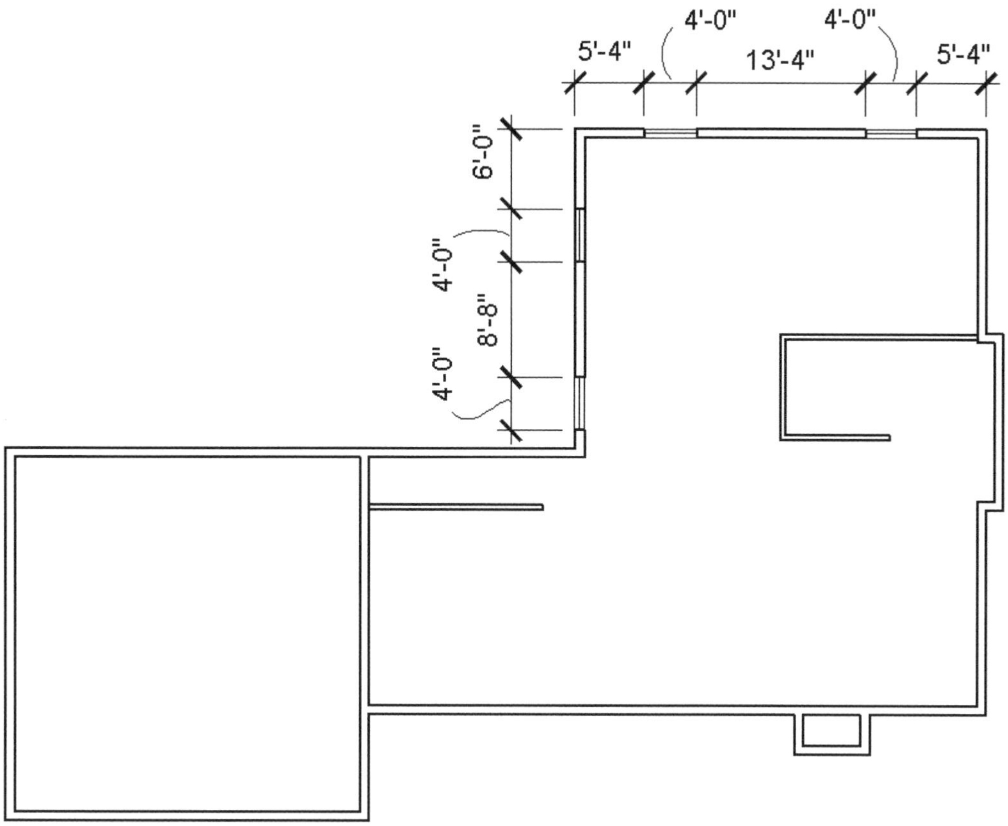

FIGURE 4-3.3 Window Locations; Basement floor

Window Dimensions in Masonry Walls?

Dimensioning windows in masonry openings is similar to dimensioning doors (discussed in the previous exercise).

The mason laying the block typically has nothing to do with the windows; they just want to know how big to make the opening and how far it is from the previous opening.

On the other hand, the carpenter typically builds the walls and installs the windows. Additionally, dimensioning windows to the center is beneficial because the window manufacturer used to draw the details may not be the one used in the project. Window sizes can vary from manufacturer to manufacturer.

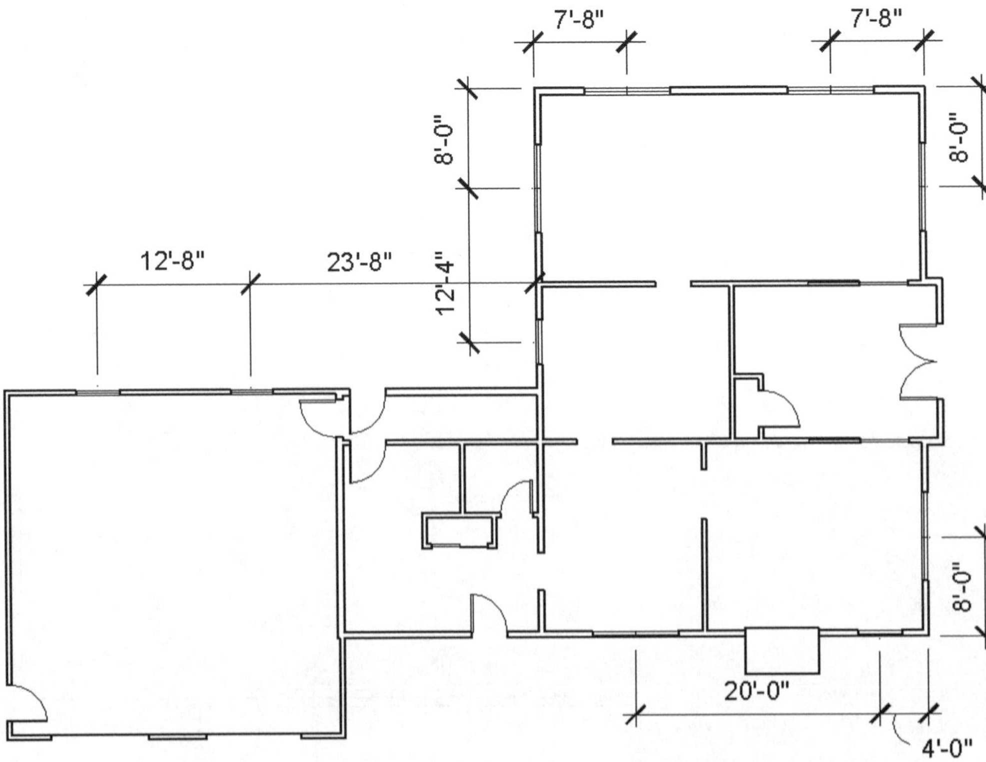

FIGURE 4-3.4 Window Locations; First floor

Double Window Example
Two Double-Hung windows

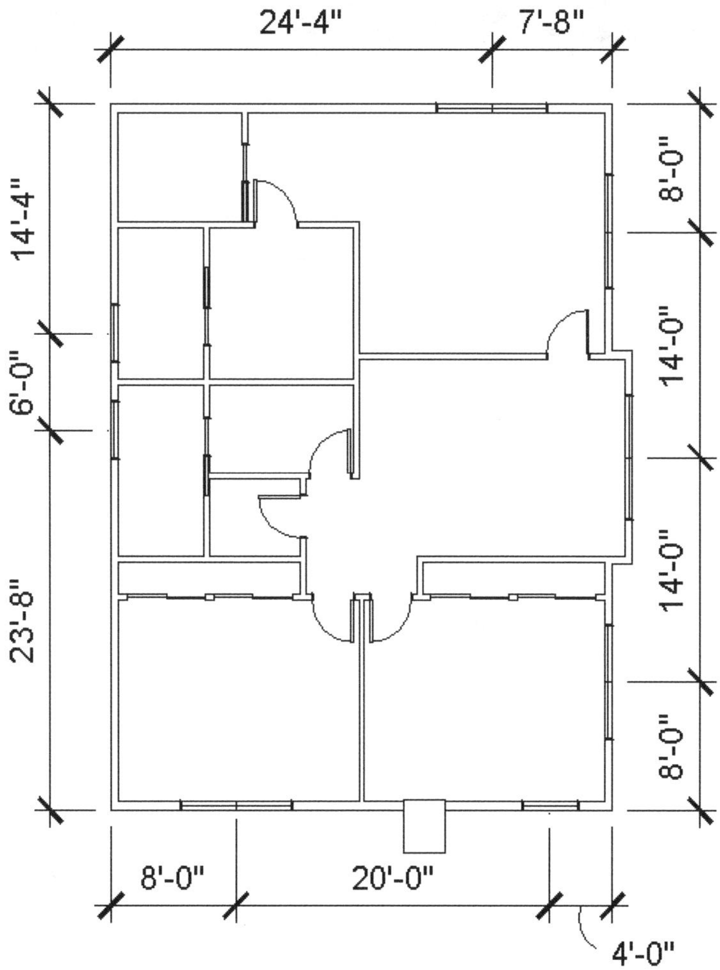

FIGURE 4-3.5 Window Locations; Second floor

Symbols Offered by Window Manufacturers?

Some window manufacturers offer CAD files of each of their windows.

Here are a few examples which can be downloaded via the following URLs:

- Andersen Windows: https://www.andersenwindows.com/for-professionals/architect/architectural-tools/
- Marvin Windows: https://www.marvin.com/support/technical-resources?rc=24&brand=marvin,integrity,infinity&prod=0&draw=65535

If you are taking this course for credit, your instructor may offer extra credit if you use this real-world content to insert your windows into the floor plans.

Exercise 4-4:
Annotation and Dimensions

As previously mentioned in Lesson 2, annotations (text; notes) and dimensions allow the designer/drafter to accurately describe the drawing.

To complete this lesson you will add room names and dimensions to your floor plans.

Room Names:

Now you will add the room names to the floor plans.

1. **Open** your basement floor plan drawing (Flr-B.dwg).

2. Create the layer ***A-ANNO-TEXT*** (color 4) and set it *Current*.

3. Using the **Text** (aka Multiline Text) command, create **9″ Arial** type text in the center of the floor plan that reads: "UNFINISHED BASEMENT." See Figures 4-4.1 and 4-4.2.

TIP: Refer back to Exercise 2-4 for more on MText.

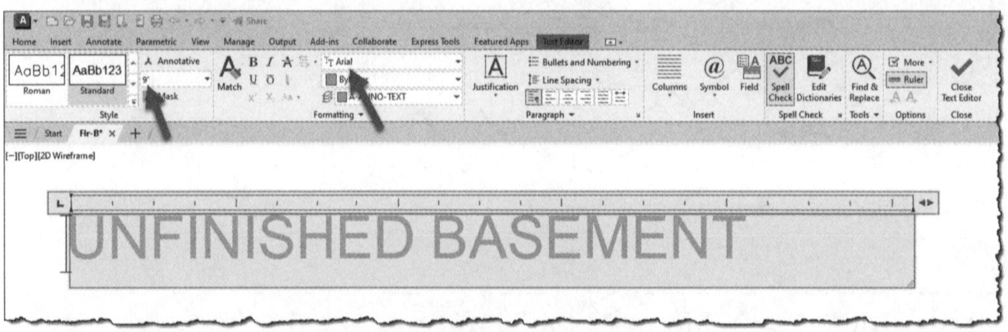

FIGURE 4-4.1 Mtext command; 9″ high Arial text

4. Looking at **Figures 4-4.3** and **4-4.4**, add the room names to the first and second floors; remember to create the appropriate text layer.

> ***REMINDER:***
> *Double-click on **Text** to edit it in **Text Editor** mode.*

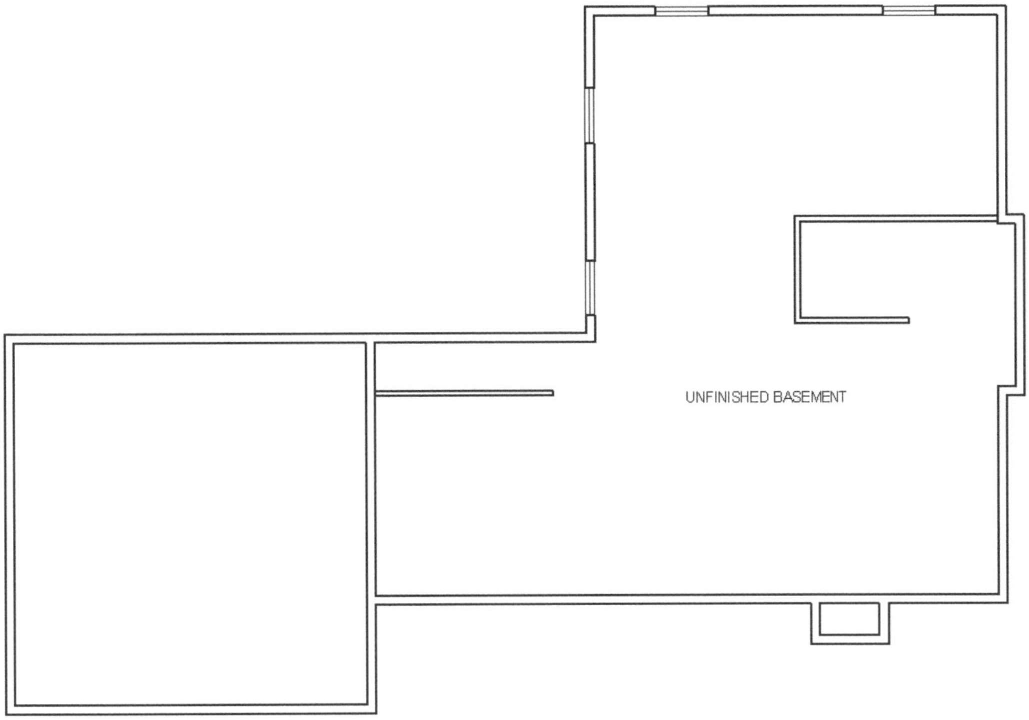

FIGURE 4-4.2 Text added; Basement floor plan

Residential project created in *Residential Design Using Autodesk Revit 2027.*

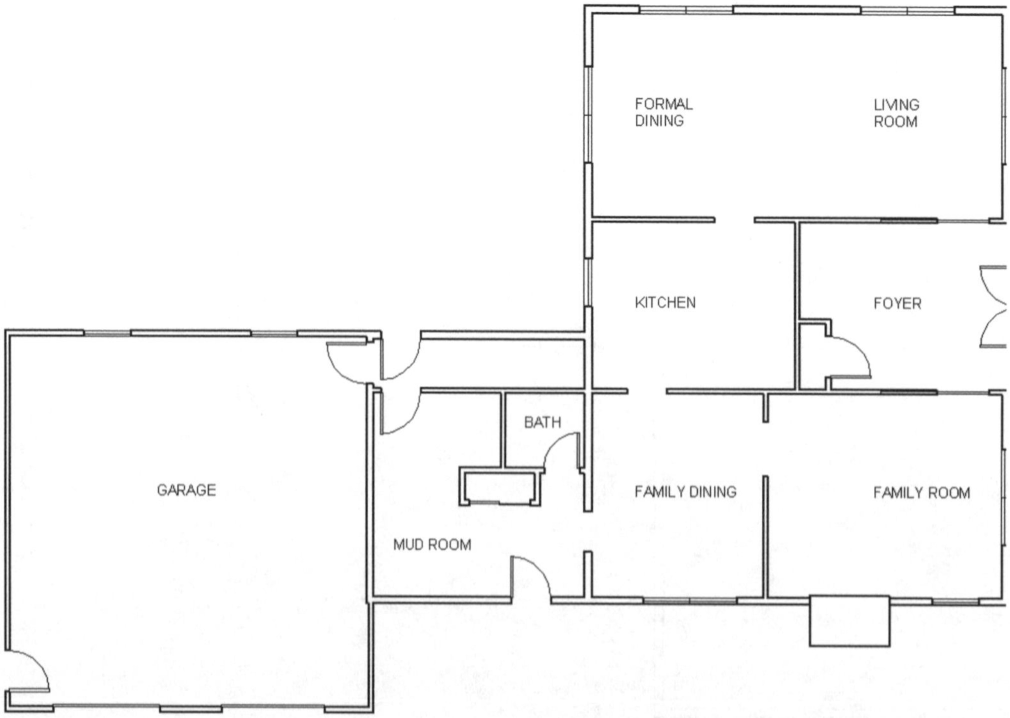

FIGURE 4-4.3
Text added; First floor plan

> **UPPERCASE vs. Lowercase text:**
>
> Text, on architectural drawings, is typically all uppercase. The lowercase letters can be hard to read, especially when they overlap lines or the printer made the strokes of the letters too thick.
>
> One exception might be a large body of general notes that are off to the side of the plans.

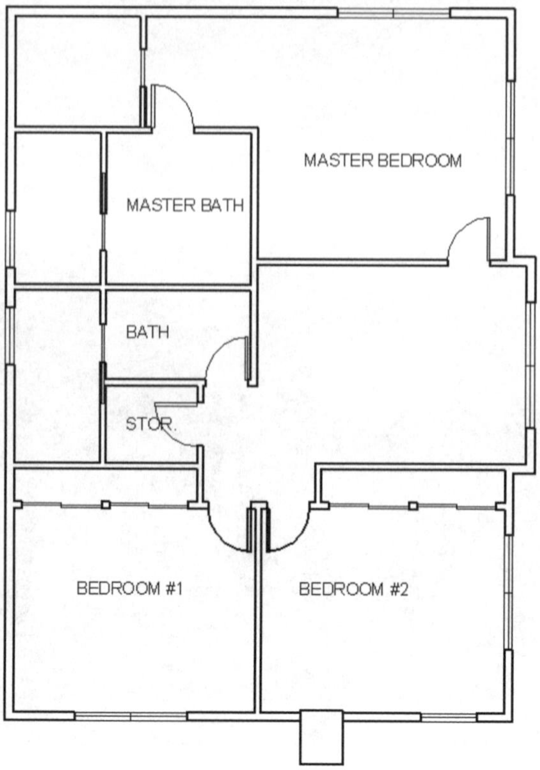

FIGURE 4-4.4 Text added; Second floor plan

Dimensions:

A floor plan shows all the major elements dimensioned. It is not desirable to leave the locations of these major components to be scaled from the blueprints; in fact, for many larger residential projects and most commercial projects, the contract prohibits the contractor from scaling the drawings and instructs them to request the information from the architect or designer.

Next, you will dimension all the Walls, Doors, and Windows on the exterior walls.

5. Type **Units**, and set the *Length Precision* to **0'-0 1/32"**.

   FYI: You need to do this so you can set the text height to 3/32" in a later step.

6. Create the layer ***A-ANNO-DIMS*** (color 30) and set it *Current.*

7. On the *Annotate* tab, click the **Dimension Style** link (small arrow in lower right).

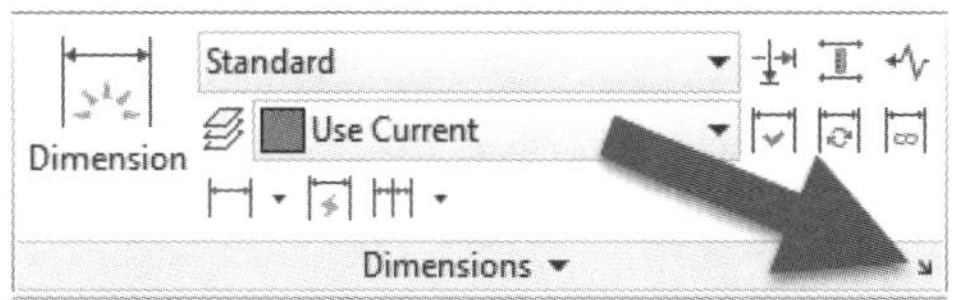

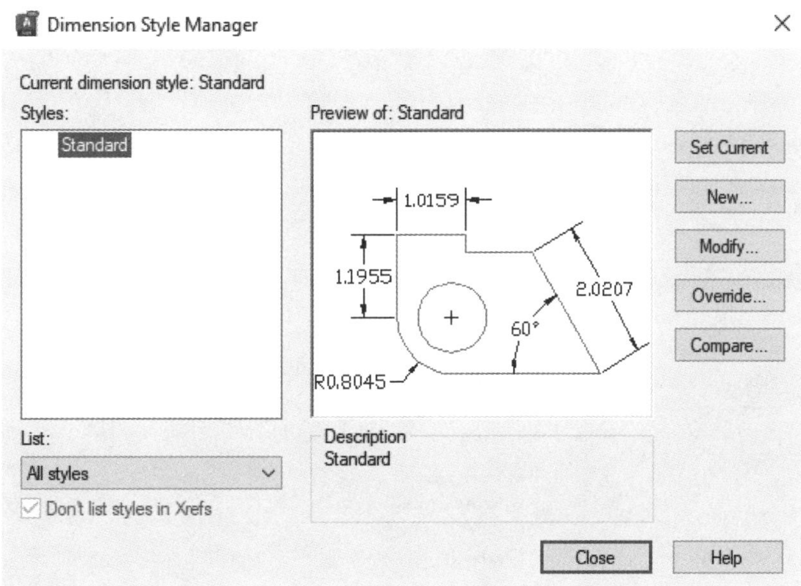

FIGURE 4-4.5 Dimension Style Manager; Standard style selected

8. Click the style **Standard** (on left), and then click **Modify…**

You are now in the dialog box that allows you to control how the dimensions look when you draw them. You will adjust a few of these settings (Figure 4-4.6A).

9. Make the changes identified with a star (★) in Figures 4-4.6A, 4-4.6B, 4-4.7, 4-4.8, and 4-4.9.

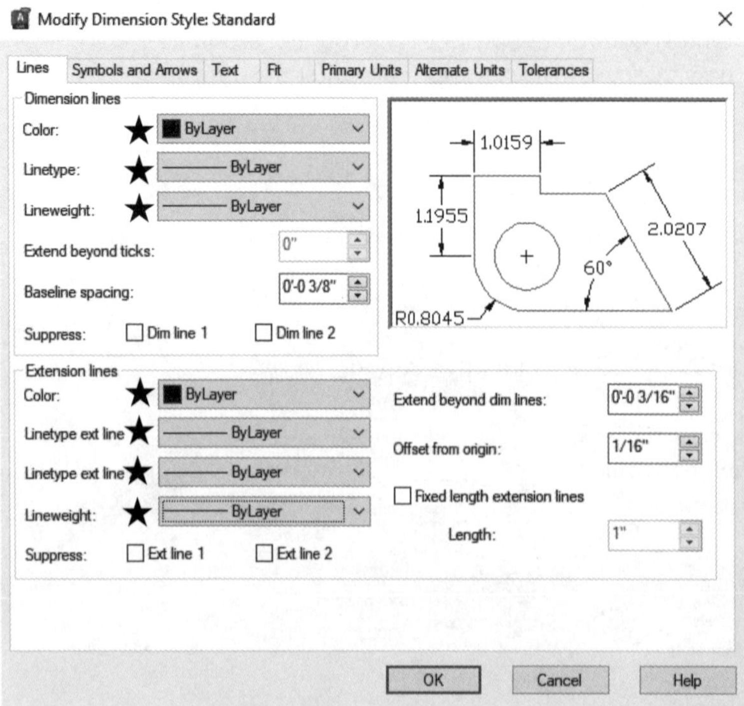

FIGURE 4-4.6A
Modify Dimension Style; *Lines* tab

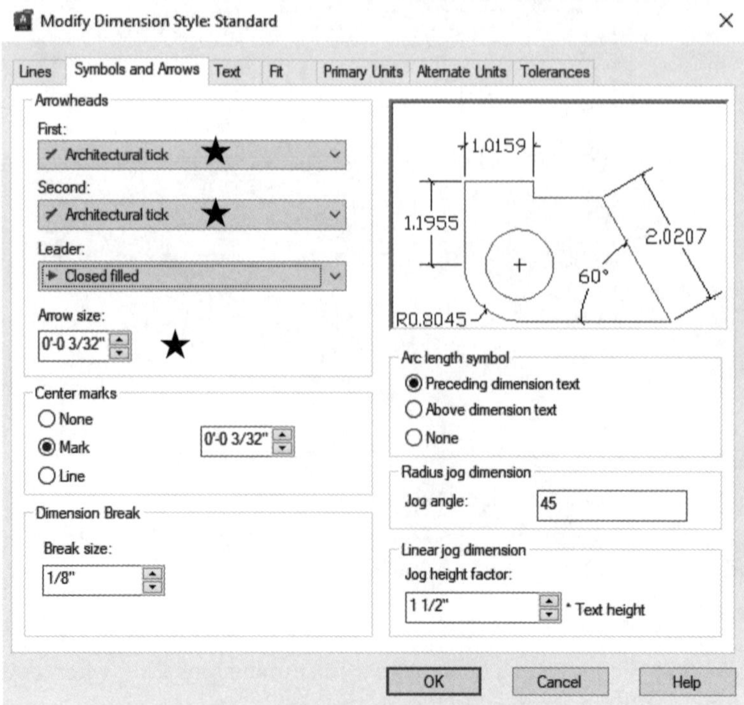

FIGURE 4-4.6B
Modify Dimension Style; *Symbols and Arrows* tab

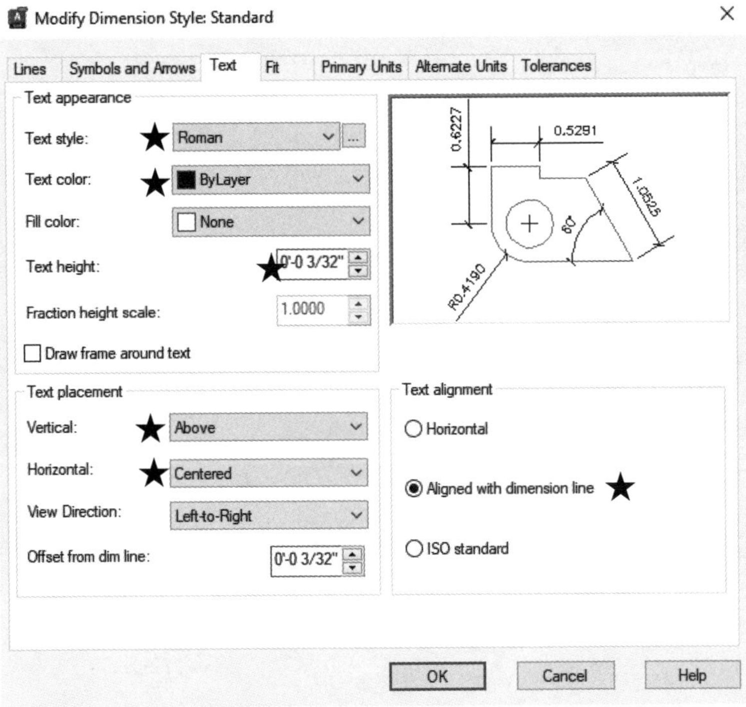

FIGURE 4-4.7
Modify Dimension Style; *Text* tab

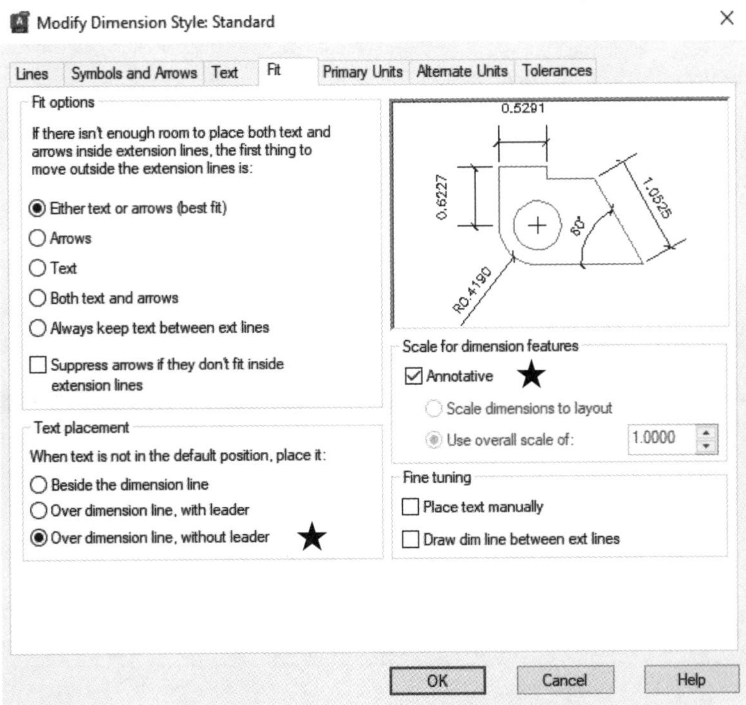

FIGURE 4-4.8
Modify Dimension Style; *Fit* tab

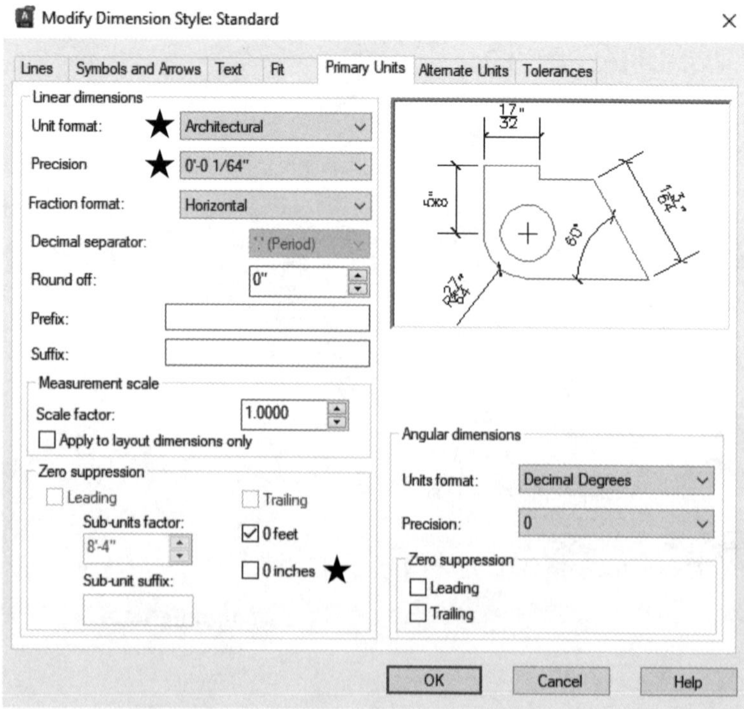

FIGURE 4-4.9
Modify Dimension Style; *Primary Units* tab

10. Click the **OK** button.

11. Click **Close** to exit the *Dimension Style Manager*.

Many of the changes you just made are self-explanatory by the description and the preview images which change as you adjust the settings.

12. At the bottom of the screen, on the *Application Status Bar* menu, click on the **Automatically Add Scales…** icon Activate that feature (see image below).

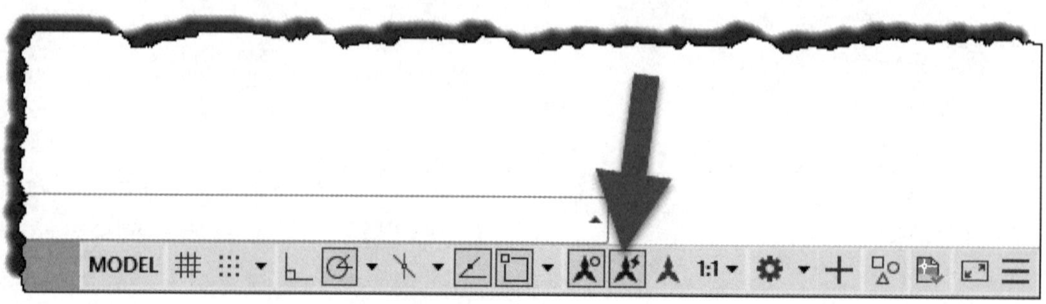

13. Just to the left of the previous item, click the *Annotation Scale* listed (should be 1:1) and select **¼″=1′-0″** from list (see image to right).

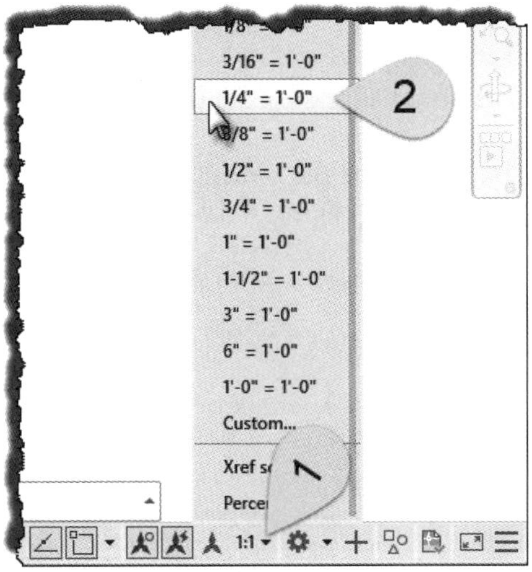

14. From the *Annotate,* or *Home,* tab select the **Dimension** command (see image to lower right).

Now when you add dimensions to this drawing, the height will automatically be set based on the scale selected at the bottom of the screen; this scale can be changed on-the-fly, instantly updating the height of all text in the drawing. You will try this next.

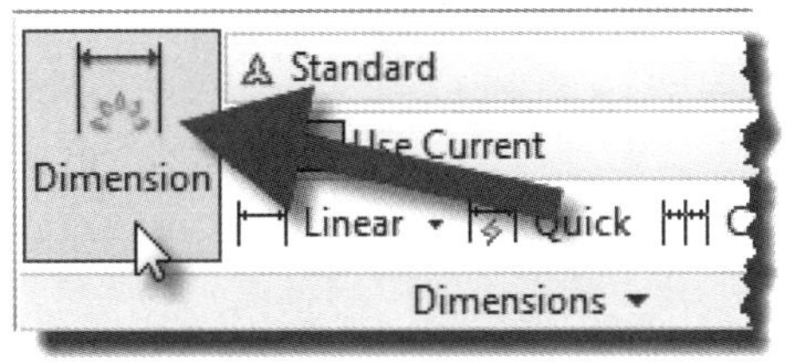

15. Draw the dimension shown in **Figure 4-4.10**.

TIP: The location of the third pick determines the look of the dimension.

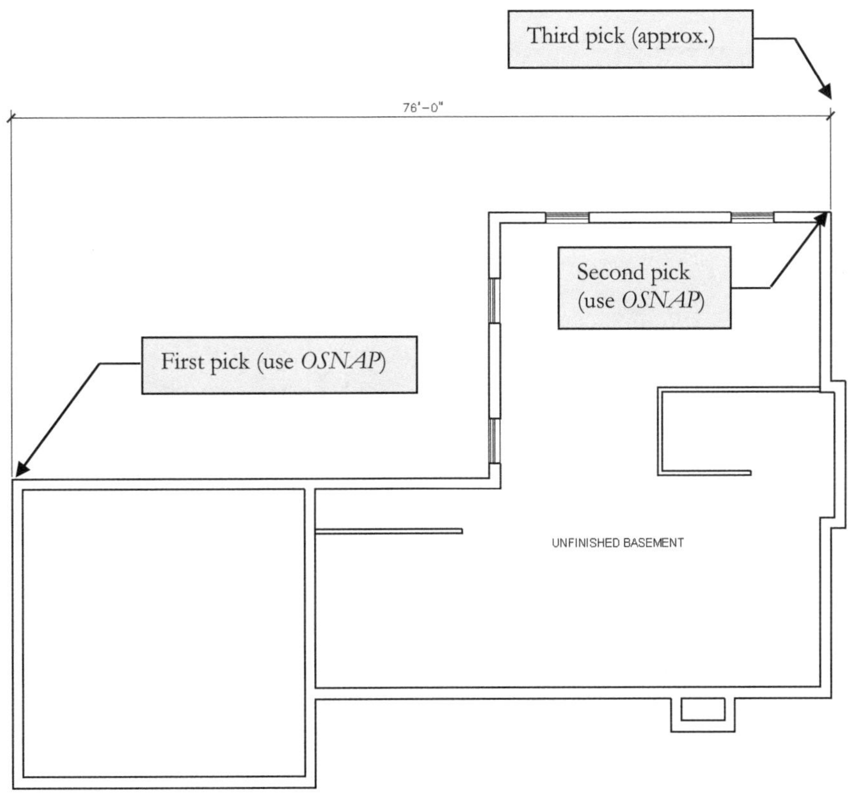

FIGURE 4-4.10 Dimension Added; Basement floor plan

Try setting the *Annotation Scale* to ½″ = 1′-0″ and notice the text and arrows on the dimensions change size. Set the scale back to **¼″ = 1′-0″** before moving on.

16. Complete the dimensioning of the exterior (for each floor plan) per the following figures (Figures 4-4.11, 4-4.12, and 4-4.13).

    ***TIP #1:** Make sure you draw on the correct layer.*

    ***TIP #2:** Use OSNAP to accurately pick points to dimension to.*

    ***TIP #3:** When creating a string of dimensions, use OSNAP for the third pick to make sure the dimensions line up perfectly.*

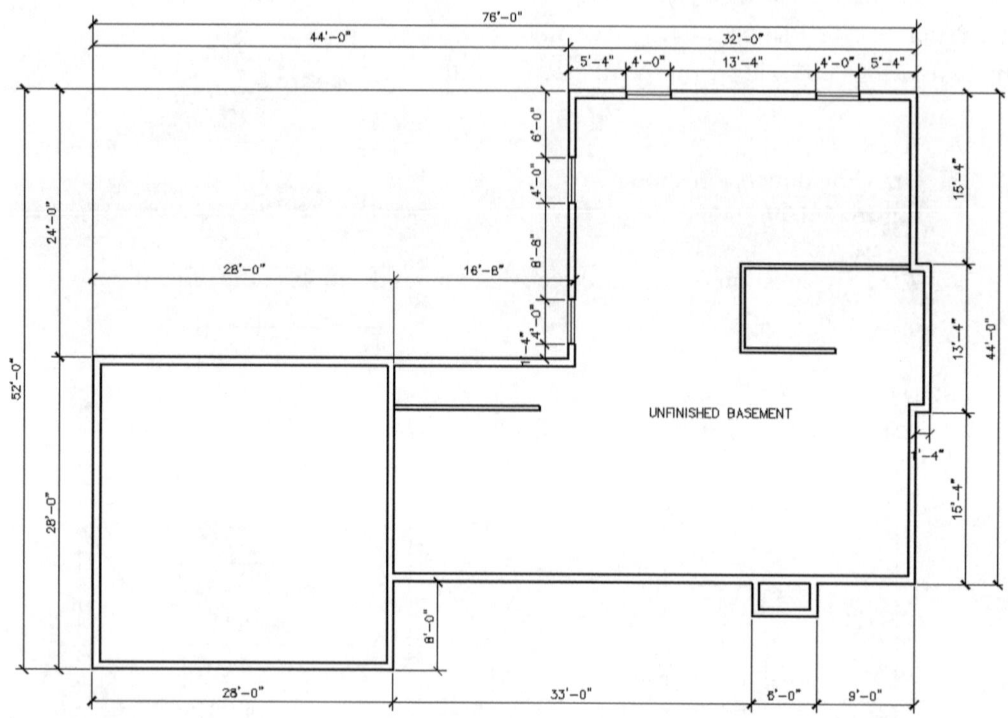

FIGURE 4-4.11 Dimensions added; Basement floor plan

TIP: If you hover over the grip of a selected dimension, you have the option of entering "Continue" mode. This mode allows you to pick points on your drawing and AutoCAD will align the dimension with the previous one.

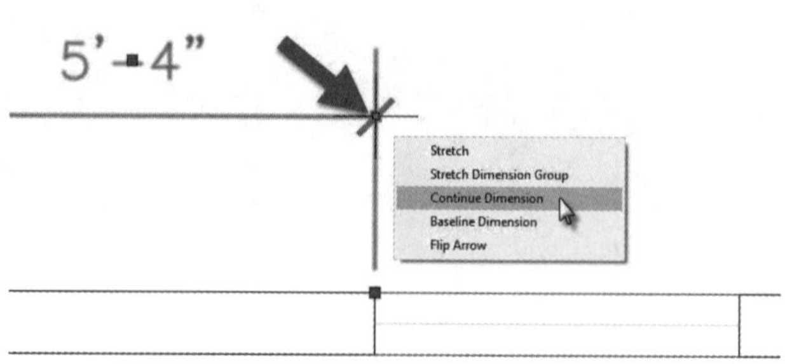

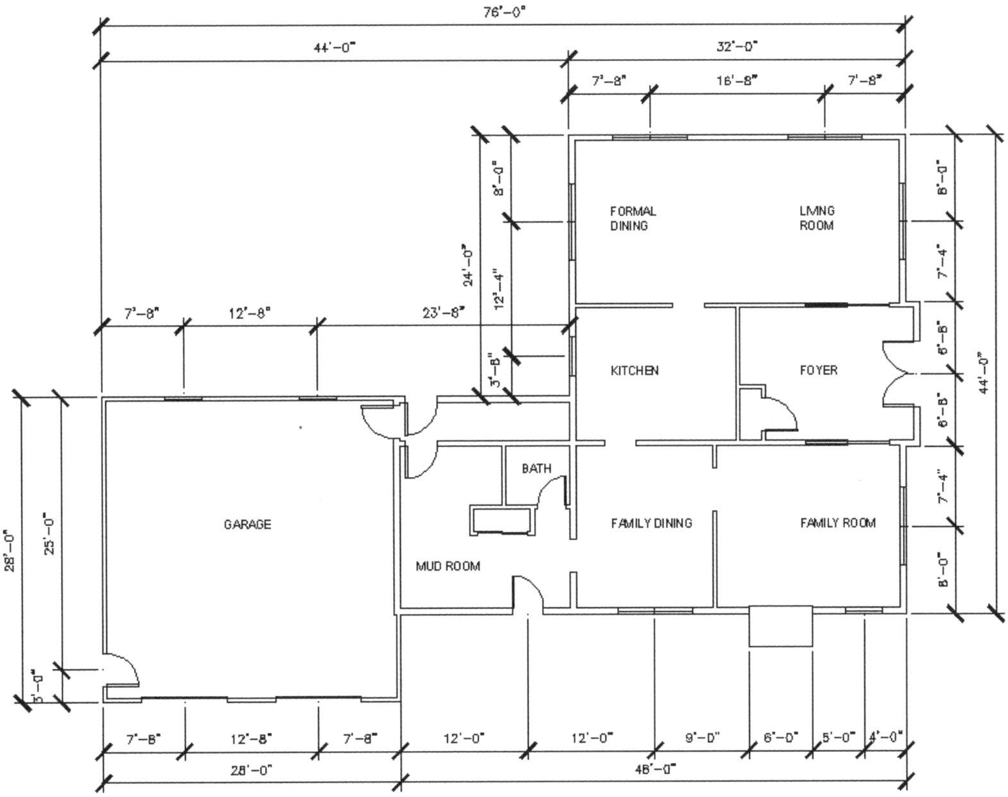

FIGURE 4-4.12 Dimensions added; First floor plan

TIP: Dimensioning Shortcut

AutoCAD has a command that allows you to quickly draw a **continuous** string of dimensions. First you add one dimension using the Linear command. Then, from the *Dimensions* panel you select the **Continue** icon. Finally, you start picking points along the wall and AutoCAD automatically places the dimension and aligns it with the first one you added! This feature can save a lot of time. Also, the drawings look better when a continuous string of dimensions aligns perfectly.

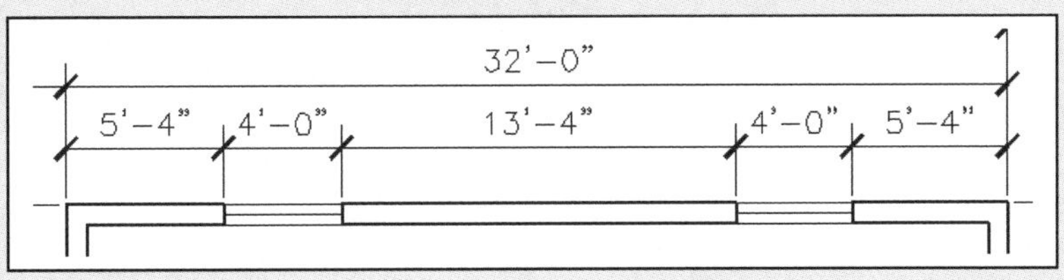

GOOD EXAMPLE

BAD EXAMPLE

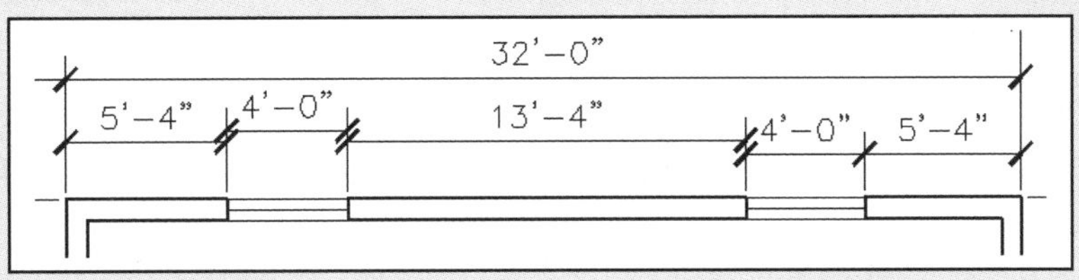

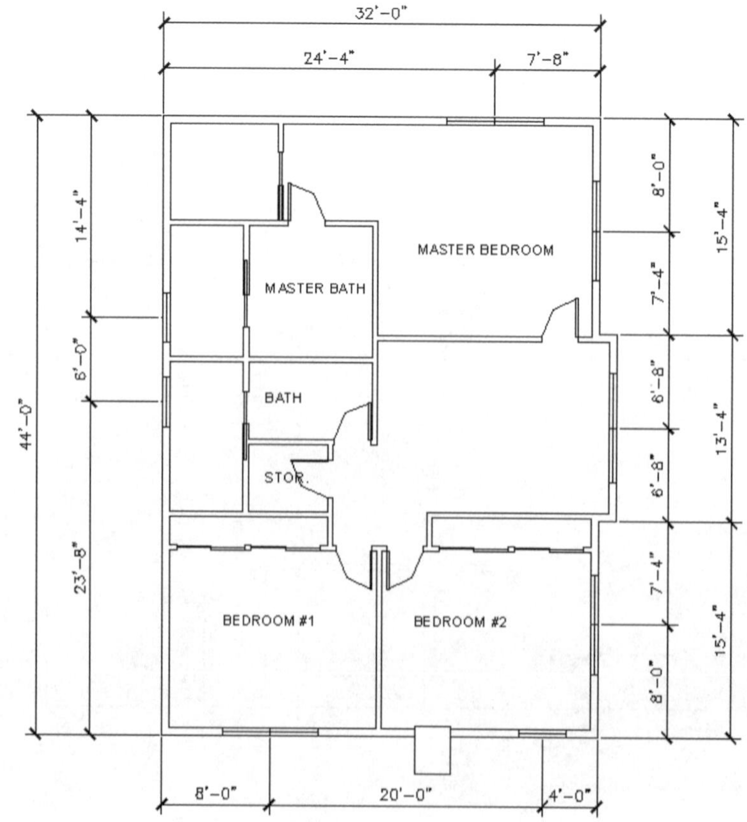

FIGURE 4-4.13 Dimensions added; Second floor plan

17. **Save** your drawings.

18. **Print** each floor plan "**scaled to fit**" on **8½ x 11** paper; refer back to Exercise 2-5 for an overview on printing.

TIP: If you use the Print Display option, per Exercise 2-5, you will need to position the floor plan as large as possible in the Drawing window. You may want to try using the Plot Window option at this point, so you can tell AutoCAD exactly what you want to print.

This concludes the "Floor Plans" exercise. Next you will develop the exterior elevations while taking a look at additional AutoCAD features like *Bhatch* (which fills an area with a pattern) and *Grip Editing* (which allows you to manipulate lines without using AutoCAD commands).

It is highly recommended that you complete the Additional Tasks at the end of this chapter.

Self-Exam:

The following questions can be used as a way to check your knowledge of this lesson. The answers can be found at the bottom of this page.

1. *Offset* is very useful for drawing floor plans. (T/F)
2. You dimension to the center of masonry walls. (T/F)
3. It does not matter which half of the line you pick when using *Extend.* (T/F)
4. Use the ______________ command to remove a portion of a line between two crossing lines.
5. All walls go on the ________________ layer.

Review Questions:

The following questions may be assigned by your instructor as a way to assess your knowledge of this section. Your instructor has the answers to the review questions.

1. Text on architectural drawings is typically uppercase. (T/F)
2. The *A-GLAZ-SILL* layer is meant to be a lighter line. (T/F)
3. It does not matter which *Layer* dimensions are drawn on. (T/F)
4. Use ________________________________ to control dimension text size.
5. You cannot mirror a *Block* such as your door blocks. (T/F)
6. These icons  allow you to _______________ and to ________________respectively.
7. For masonry coursing, what are the two options: 6′- ____″ and 6′- _____″.
8. In plan view, a door open 90 degrees is a ______________ door; and a door open 45 degrees is a_____________________________ door.
9. What *Layer* do jamb lines go on? ______________________________.
10. When inserting a drawing as a *Block*, the insertion point for the block is the same as the drawing origin (i.e., 0,0) it was created with. (T/F)

SELF-EXAM ANSWERS:
1 – T, **2** – F, **3** – F, **4** – Trim, **5** – A-WALL

Additional Tasks:

Task 4-1: Fireplace – North

Draw all the lines shown on Layer *A-WALL*. Copy/Paste this line work from the basement floor plan to the first floor plan. Do not draw the dimensions, as they are for reference only.

Commands used: Offset, Trim, Extend, Fillet, Layer Manager, Circle

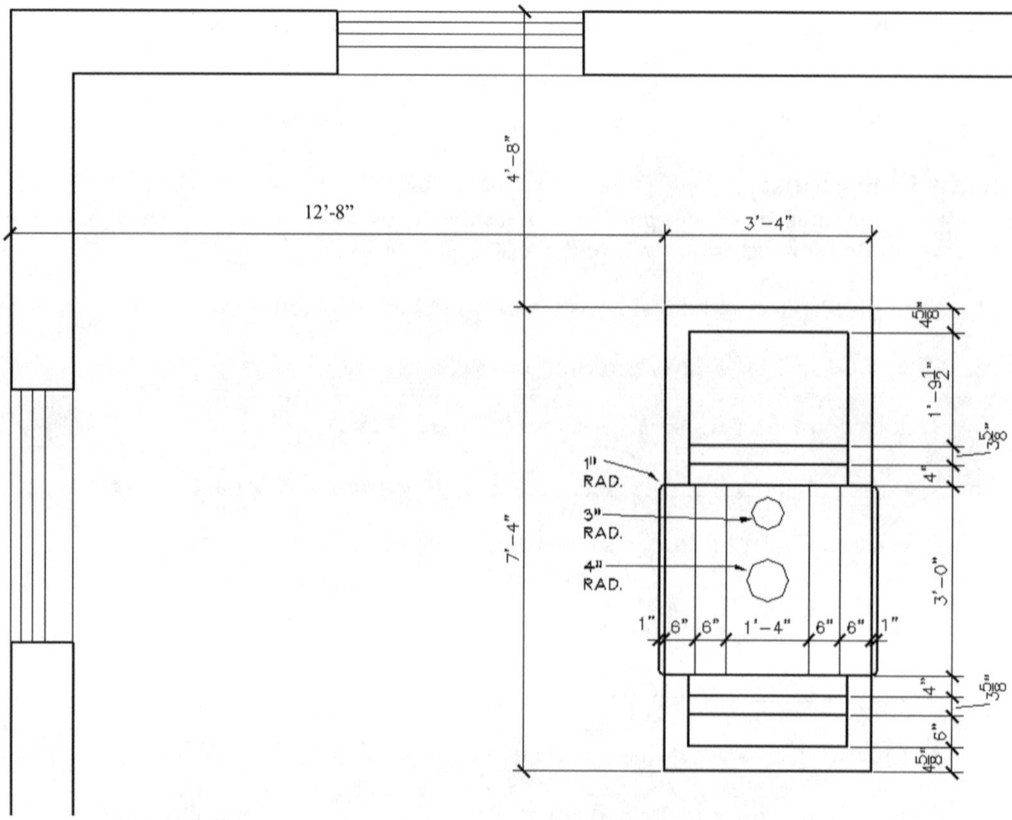

TASK 4-1 (1) Fireplace (north); Basement floor plan view (First floor is similar).

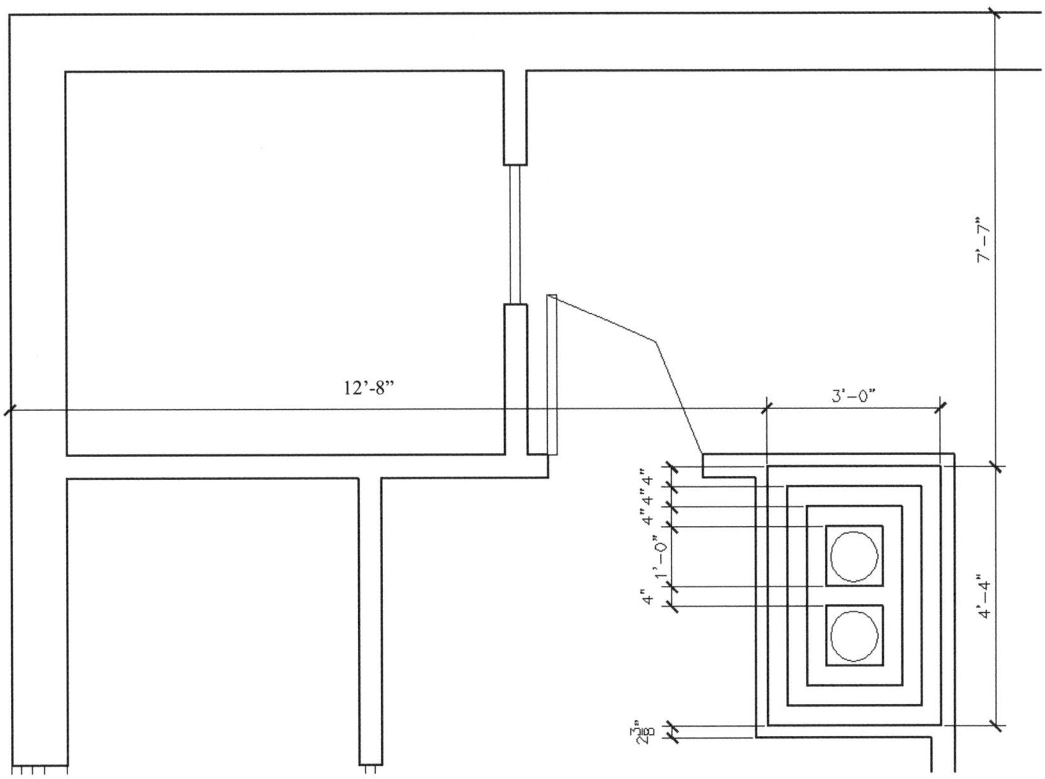

Task 4-1 (2) Fireplace (north); Second floor plan view.

Drawing Multileaders

A *Multileader* is a line with an arrow on one end and text on the other end. Multileaders are very customizable and can have various symbols on the "arrow" end, a *Block* (e.g., a circle with a number in it) or nothing at all. You will need to use this feature in the next exercise (adding notes and pointing to various parts of the drawing) so you will take a moment to learn about it now.

A *Multileader* system is similar to the dimensioning system in that you first set up the style (of which you can have several, if needed) and then draw the leader and enter the text. If the style is modified, all instances of *Multileaders* that were created using that style will be modified.

First you will set up the style; these steps could be done in a template file so you would not have to repeat them each time you created a new drawing.

1. Start a new drawing (SheetSets\Architectural Imperial).

2. On the *Annotate* tab, in the *Leaders* panel, click the **Multileader Style Manager** link—Figure Task 4-1 (3).

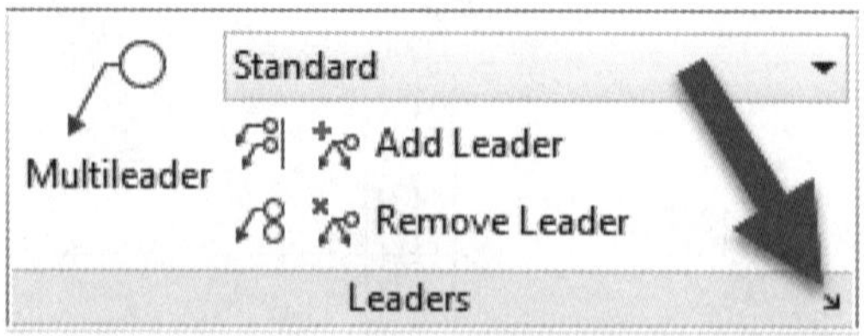

TASK 4-1 (3) Found on the *Annotate* tab

3. In the *Multileader Style Manager*, with **Standard** style selected, click the **Modify**... button—Figure Task 4-1 (4).

FYI: Notice how this looks just like the style manager for dimensions.

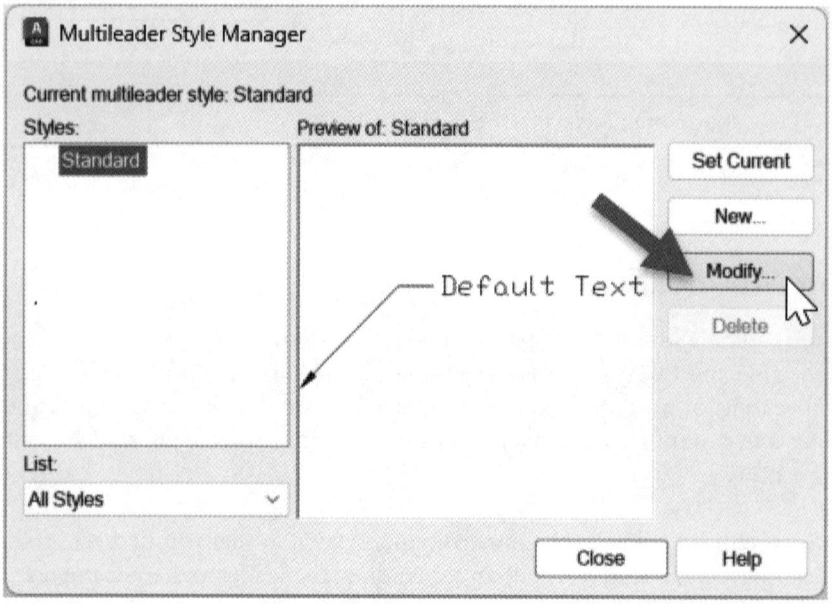

TASK 4-1 (4) Multileader Style Manager dialog

4. Make the changes shown in the following three images: Figures Task 4-1 (5)A thru Task 4-1 (5)C.

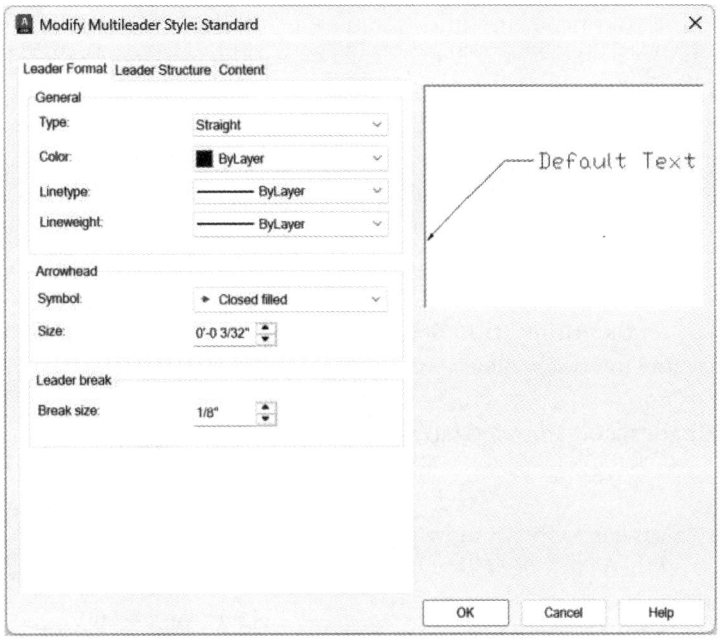

TASK 4-1 (5)A: Leader Format tab: Modify Multileader Style dialog

TASK 4-1 (5)B: Leader Structure tab

TASK 4-1 (5)C: Content tab

5. When finished, click **OK** and then **Close** to exit these two dialog boxes.

You are almost ready to use your newly modified multileader style, but first you need to set the *Annotation Scale* via the *Status Bar*. You will need to change this on a drawing-by-drawing basis according to the required plot scale of the elevation or detail. Remember, in *Model Space* everything is always drawn real-world size; only the symbols and text are scaled up or down so that a sheet with multiple details of varying scale all have the same relative text height when the sheet is printed. This is where *Annotation Scale* comes in handy!

6. On the *Status Bar*, set the **Annotation Scale** to ¼″ = 1′-0″. This is the scale of the next exercise (i.e., the interior elevations).

7. Click the **Multileader** icon, *Annotate* tab—Figure Task 4-1 (6).

8. Click three points, similar to those shown below, type some text, and then click *Exit Text Editor* on the *Ribbon* when finished.

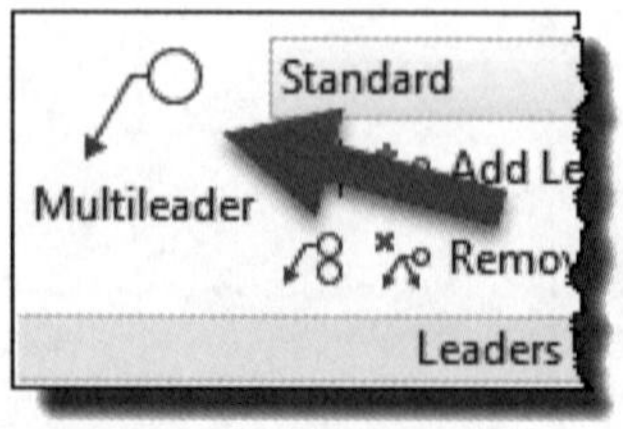

Figure Task 4-1 (6):
Multileader tool

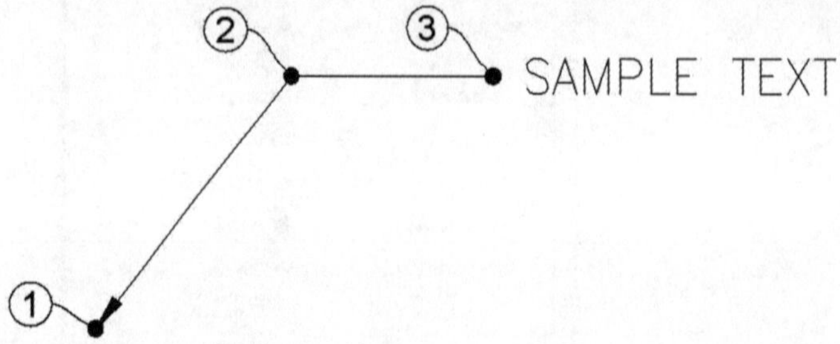

Try changing the *Annotative Scale* and notice the text and arrow size changes automatically. You can now apply this technique throughout the remaining lessons of this textbook.

Task 4-2: Main Stairway

Draw all the lines shown on Layer *A-FLOR-VERT* (color *Yellow*). Copy/ Paste this line work from the basement floor plan to the first floor plan and then modify for that condition. Handrail lines are 1½″ apart. You can use the Array (Polar) to create the angled lines (or Rotate –90 degrees divided by 3). Actually drawing the line with the arrow (i.e., Multileader) has not been covered yet but is very simple. Select the **Multileader** icon from the *Annotate* tab and pick points on the screen.

Draw the text on layer *A-ANNO-TEXT* (color 4).

The angled line that trims off part of the stair indicates where the stairs pass through the imaginary cutting plane for the floor plan; draw these lines on the *A-FLOR-VERT* layer (color 2).

Approximate the line work not dimensioned; *TYP.* means typical (i.e., they are all the same dimension).

Commands used: Line, Offset, Trim, Extend, Fillet, Layer Manager, Array, Leader, Mtext

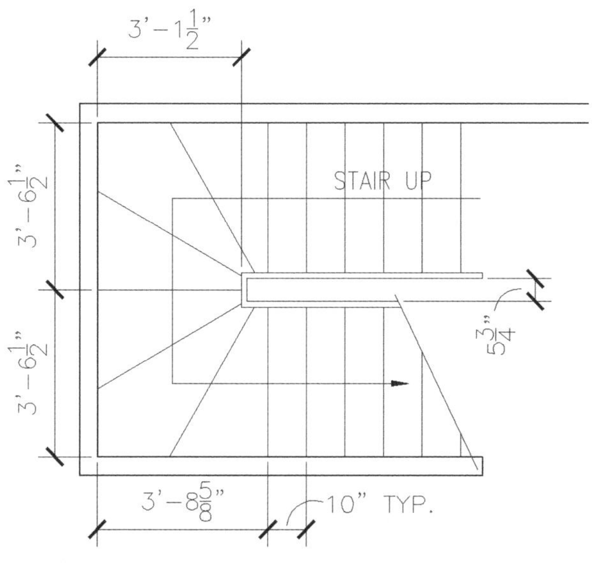

> *TIP: The 'Maximum Leader Points' within the MultiLeader properties needs to be increased to 4 to create this three legged leader.*

TASK 4-2 (1) Main Stair; Basement floor plan view.

> ***NOTE:*** *You can add the leaders with no text (just press Enter when prompted to type text) and then add regular Mtext to the position where you want it, as shown in this task. When you type the text (i.e., Up or Down) as part of the MultiLeader you are limited in where you can place the text relative to the leader.*

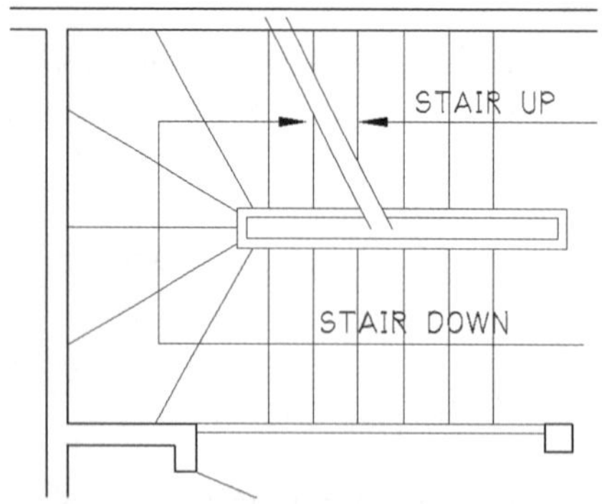

TASK 4-2 (2) Main Stair; First floor plan view.

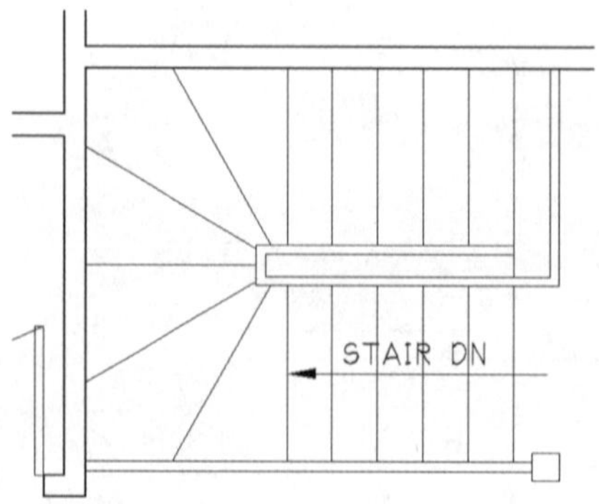

TASK 4-2 (3) Main Stair; Second floor plan view.

Task 4-3: Secondary Stairway

Similar to the previous Task; draw this stairway.

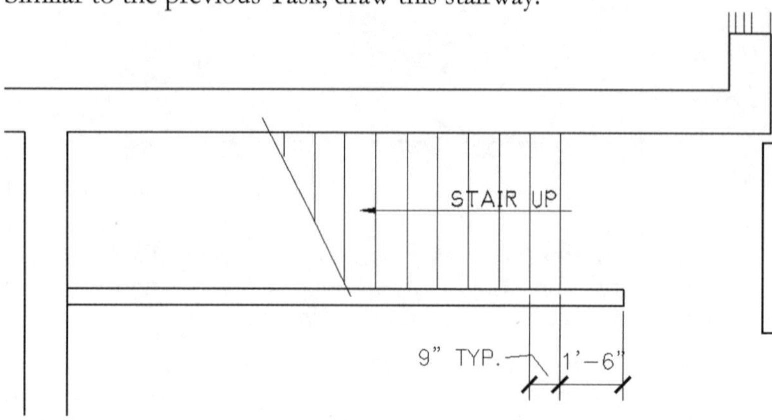

> ***FYI:*** *You will learn later, when you develop the stair section, that this stair is not in the correct location.*

TASK 4-3 (1) Secondary Stair; Basement floor plan view.

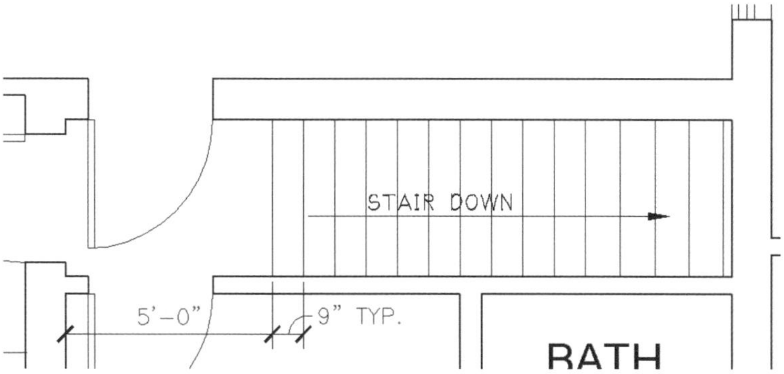

TASK 4-3 (2) Secondary Stair; First floor plan view.

Task 4-4: Porch

Draw the porch per the dimensions shown.

Draw the large columns (12"x12") and outside lines on layer *A-WALL* and the railings and steps on layer *A-FLOR-VERT*.

You do not need to draw the dimensions (unless instructed otherwise).

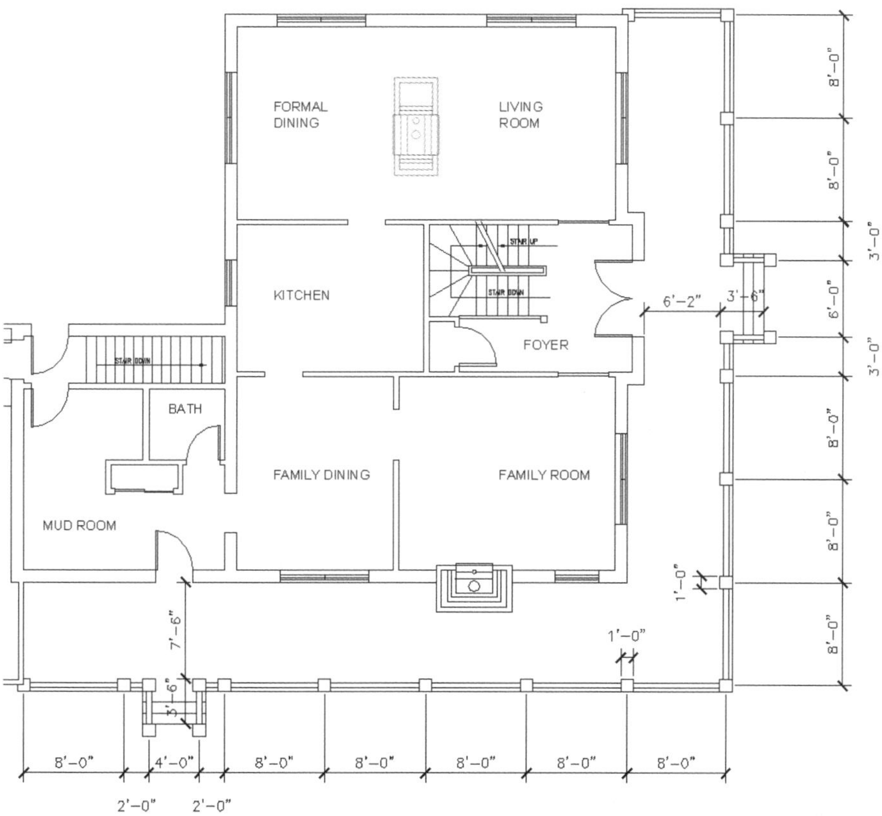

TASK 4-4 Porch; First floor plan

Task 4-5: Garage Steps

Draw the steps from the garage into the house per the dimensions shown.

> ***NOTE:*** *It is common to have the garage slab lower than the house floor to prevent any spills or snow melt from entering the house. Draw the lines on layer A-FLOOR-VERT.*

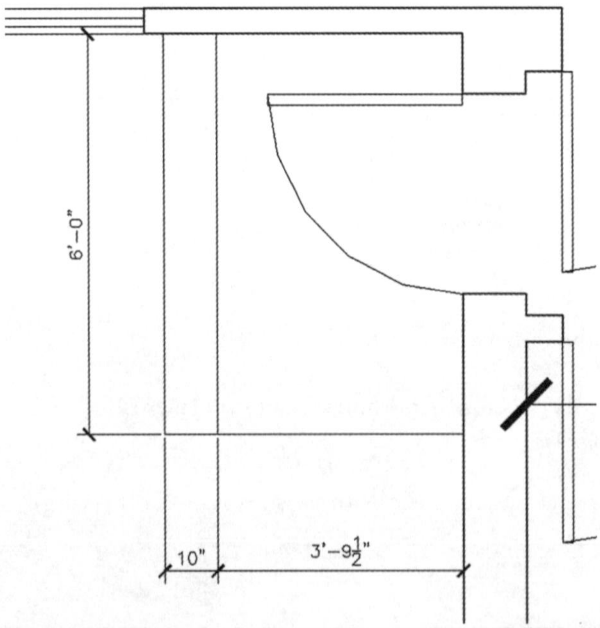

TASK 4-5 Garage Steps; First floor plan

Task 4-6: Fireplace - South

Add the following detail to the south fireplace (similar to Task 4-1).

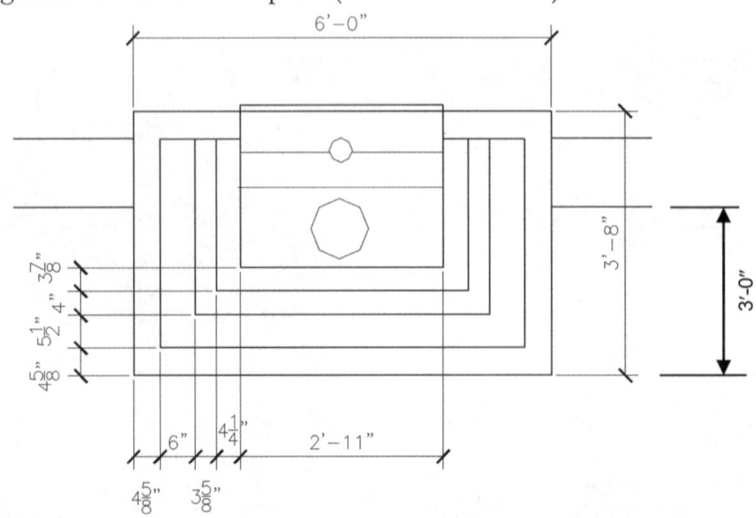

TASK 4-6 Fireplace (south); First floor plan

Lesson 5
EXTERIOR ELEVATIONS

In this lesson, you will draw the exterior elevations based on the floor plans that were previously drawn. You will also look at other commands and tools like *GRIP* editing.

Exercise 5-1:
Elevation Outlines

Introduction:

When designing a residence, one needs to be sensitive to the massing and proportions of each elevation and the various elements within. The exterior elevations are the drawings used to develop the structure's exterior aesthetic. Too often, this is not given enough thought and time, thus resulting in harsh, unappealing homes with vast amounts of siding and awkwardly sized and positioned windows.

In this section, you will look at blocking out the exterior elevations based on information previously drawn in the floor plans. The vertical dimensions will be given to you (which will also be used to draw your sections).

You will start a new drawing to draw all four elevations. Each elevation will be horizontally aligned, which helps align windows, doors, roof edges, and other elements.

South Elevation (Figure 5-1.1):

1. Create a new drawing named **Exterior Elevations.dwg**.

2. Create *Layer* ***G-Detl-Medm*** (color *Green*) and set it *Current.*

First, draw the garage outline.

3. Looking at your printed out and dimensioned floor plans (on page 4-6), notice that the garage is 28′-0″ wide.

4. Draw a horizontal line **28′-0″** long.

5. Draw a vertical line **9'-6½"** tall at each end of the horizontal line previously drawn (Figure 5-1.3).

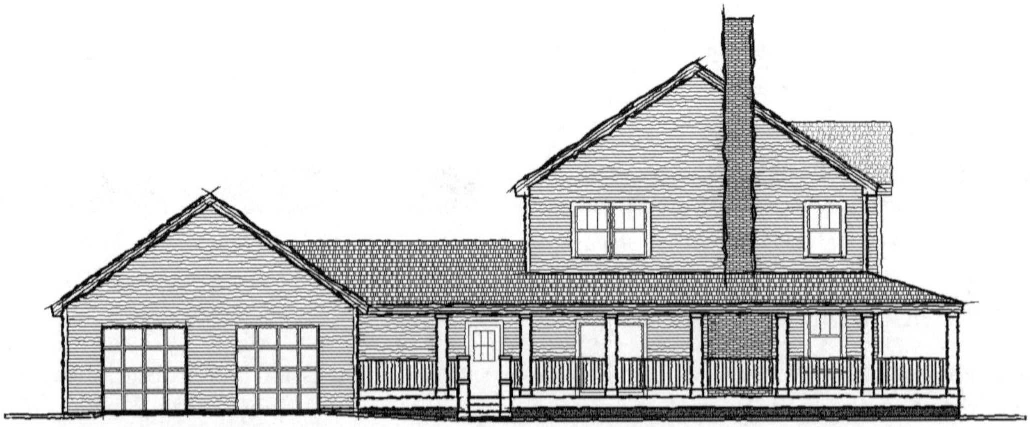

FIGURE 5-1.1 Completed South Elevation to be drawn in this lesson

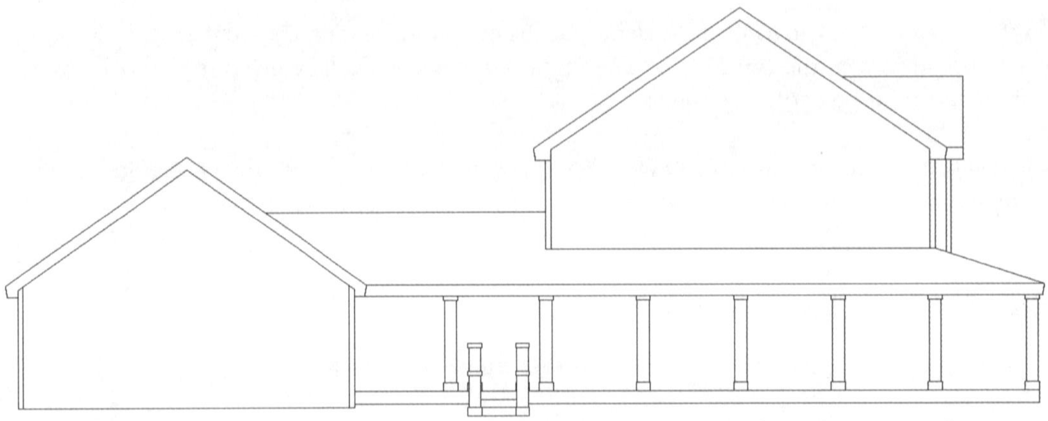

FIGURE 5-1.2 Outline of South Elevation to be drawn in this exercise

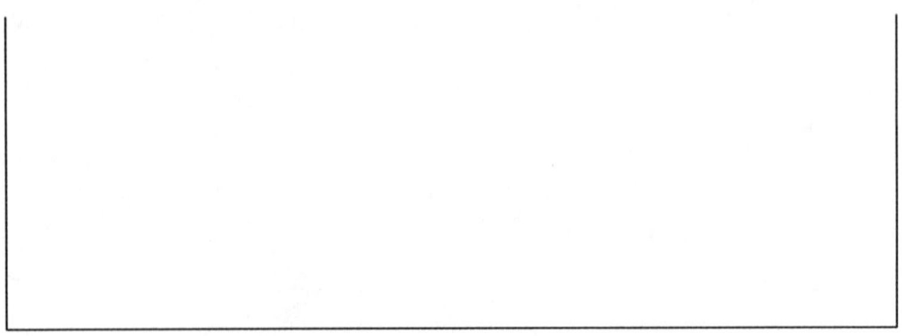

FIGURE 5-1.3 Garage elevation; first three lines

Next you will draw the angled line representing the sloped roof edge. This roof has an 8/12 pitch. That means that for every 12″ horizontally, the roof drops (or rises) 8″.

The easiest way to draw this line is to draw temporary lines per the description above and then draw an angled line that connects the dots; you will do this in the following steps:

6. At the top of the vertical line on the left, draw a horizontal line 12″ long towards the right (Figure 5-1.4).

7. Now draw a vertical line 8″ long (Figure 5-1.4).

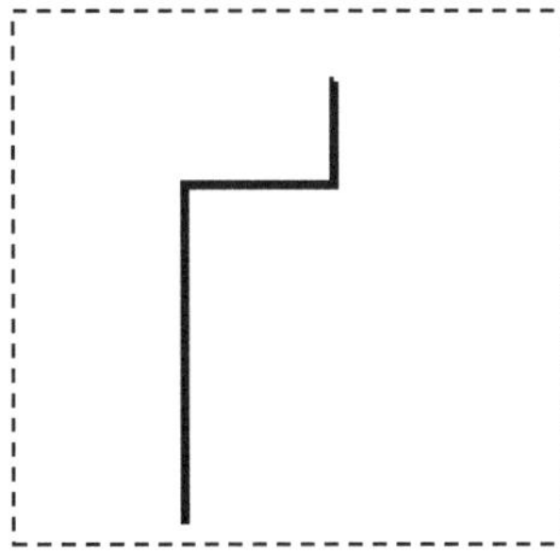

FIGURE 5-1.4
Temporary lines used to create roof edge (left side)

8. Draw the angled line using the endpoints of the temporary lines as snap points (Figure 5-1.5).

FIGURE 5-1.5
Angled line drawn using OSNAPs

9. **Erase** the temporary lines (Figure 5-1.6).

10. **Mirror** the angled line, using the Midpoint of the 28′-0″ horizontal line (Figure 5-1.7).

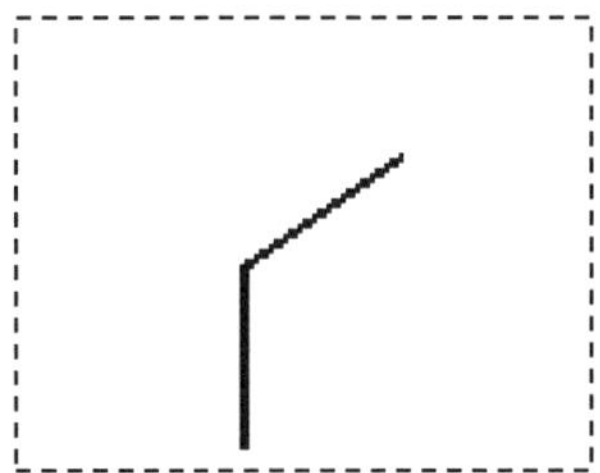

FIGURE 5-1.6
Temporary lines erased

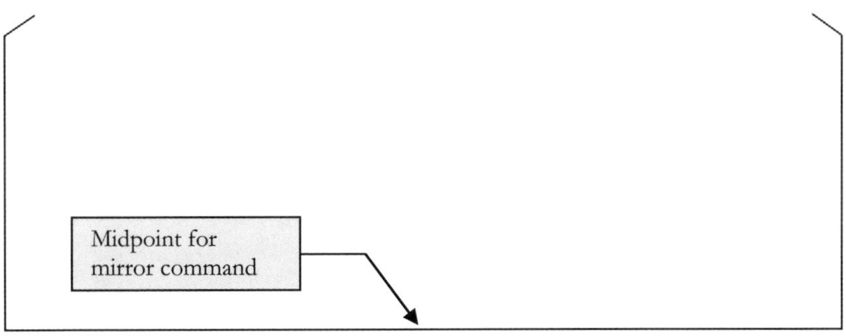

FIGURE 5-1.7 Garage elevation; angled line mirrored

You will now use the *Fillet* command to extend the two angled lines up to the peak.

11. Select the **Fillet** command. Make sure the Radius is set to **0″**, and then select the two angled lines (Figure 5-1.8).

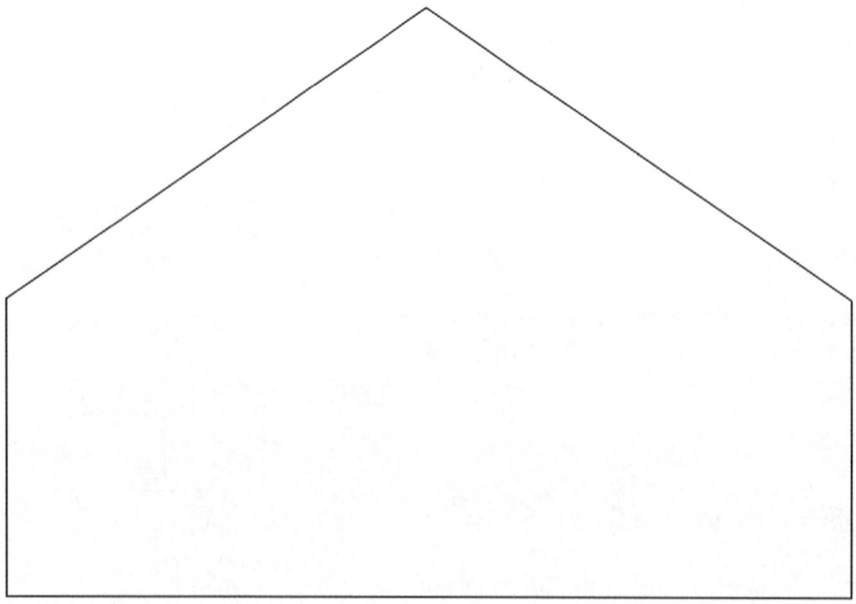

FIGURE 5-1.8 Garage elevation; roof line completed

Next you will *Offset* your two vertical lines inward. These lines will represent the vertical trim boards that the siding ties into.

12. **Offset** the two vertical lines **5½″** inward (Figure 5-1.9).

13. Use the **Extend** command to extend the trim lines up to the angled lines.

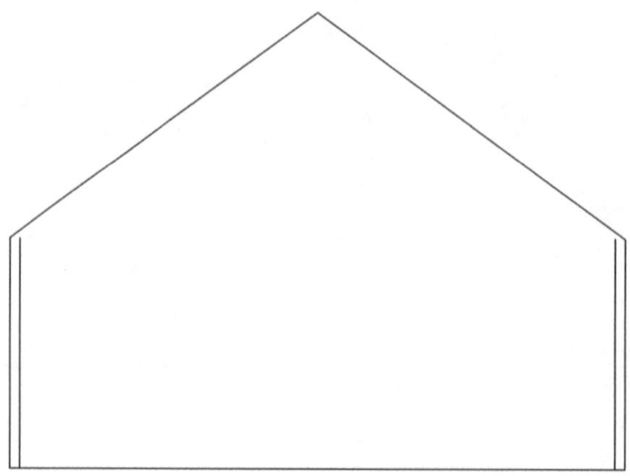

FIGURE 5-1.9 Garage elevation; corner trim

14. **Offset** the two roof lines outward **10½″** (Figure 5-1.10).

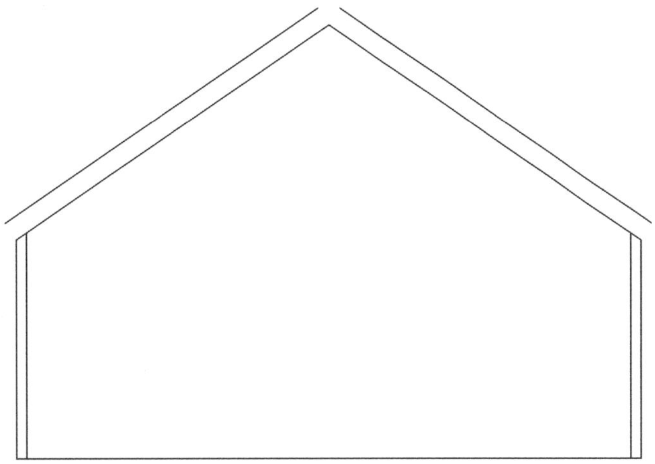

FIGURE 5-1.10 Garage elevation; fascia lines

15. **Fillet** the two new lines to form the ridge at the top.

Next you will develop the overhang. It is sometimes helpful to sketch the roof edge detail (you will draft it later in this book) so you can draw it correctly and not have to go back and tweak the elevations later. Figure 5-1.11 is our sketch, showing a total of 10½″ for the fascia and a 1′-0″ overhang.

Then you will draw the roof edge in your elevation.

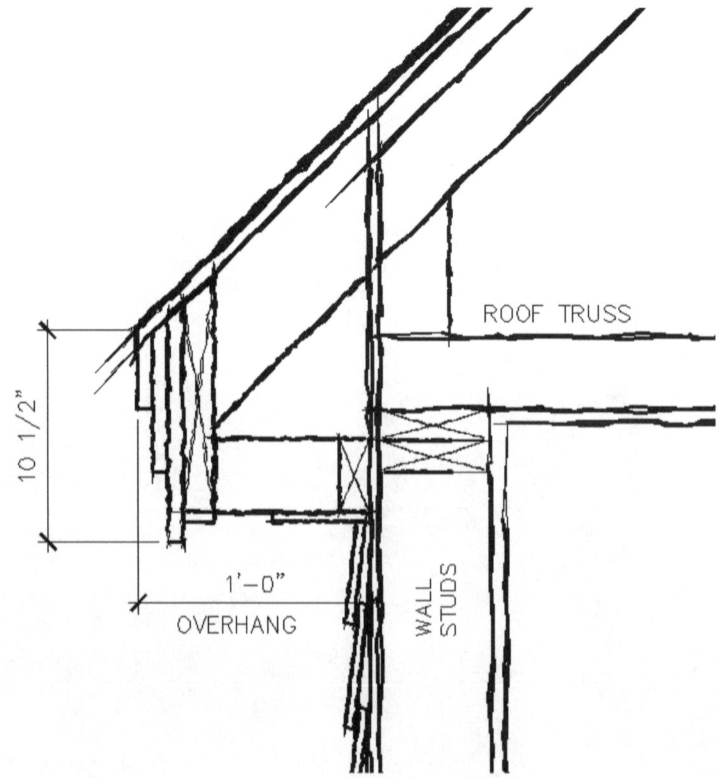

FIGURE 5-1.11 Typical Roof edge; similar condition at garage

16. Draw the roof edge profile as shown in **Figure 5-1.12.**

    a. Draw the temporary line (shown dashed in Figure 5-1.12) and *Offset* it down **5⅞"**, and then delete the temporary line.

    b. Make sure you use *ORTHO* or *Polar Tracking* to assure horizontal and vertical lines.

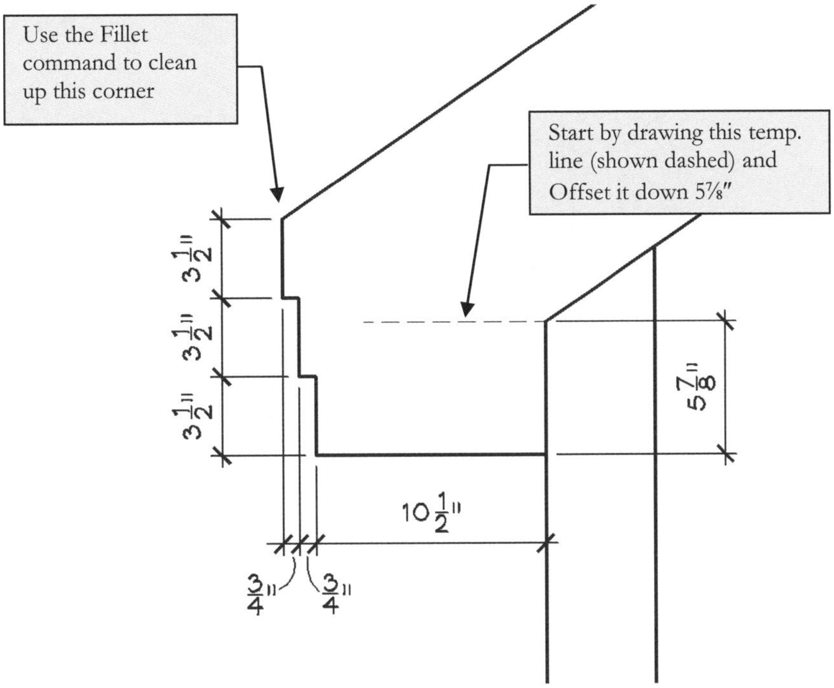

FIGURE 5-1.12 Typical Roof edge profile

17. Use the **Mirror** command to mirror the roof edge to the other side of the garage.

This completes the outline of the garage. Next you will work on the house.

Referring to your dimensioned plans (or page 4-7), notice the overall dimension is 76′-0″ and the garage takes up 28′-0″ of that dimension. So, the remaining portion to be drawn is 48′-0″.

18. Draw a line **48′-0″** to the right (Figure 5-1.13).

The first floor of the house is higher than the garage floor (to keep the snowmelt from getting into the house for us northerners!), so you need to move this line up; recall the steps drawn in Task 4-5 (page 4-62).

19. **Move** the 48′-0″ line up **1′-4″** (Figure 5-1.14).

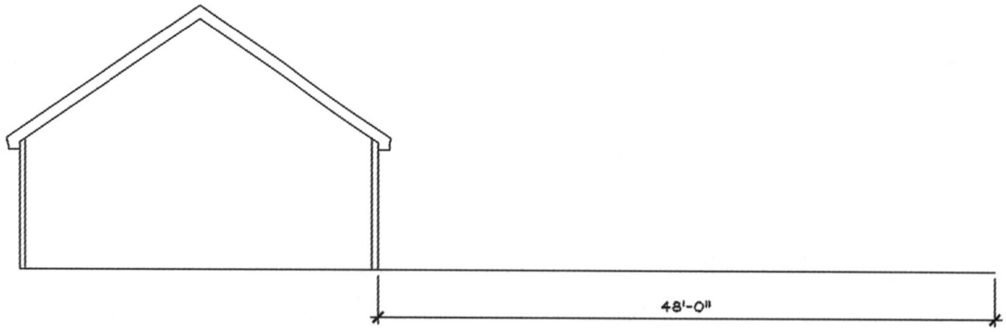

FIGURE 5-1.13 48′-0″ line drawn to the right

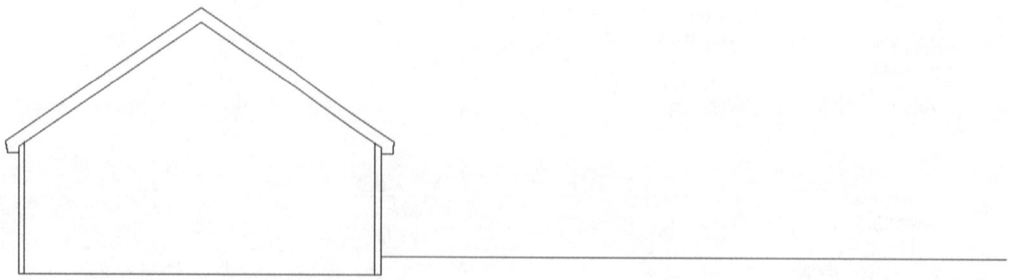

FIGURE 5-1.14 48′-0″ line moved up 1′-4″

20. Draw two vertical lines **19′-1⅝″** long and **32′-0″** apart; note the two-story portion of the building is 32′-0″ wide on your dimensioned plans.

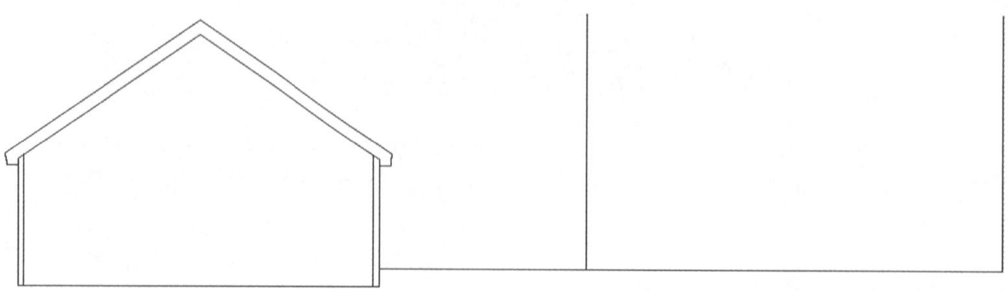

FIGURE 5-1.15 Vertical lines 32′-0″ apart; 19′-1⅝″ long lines

21. The vertical trim, roof edge and pitch are the same as the garage, so follow the same steps to complete the roof as shown in **Figure 5-1.16**.

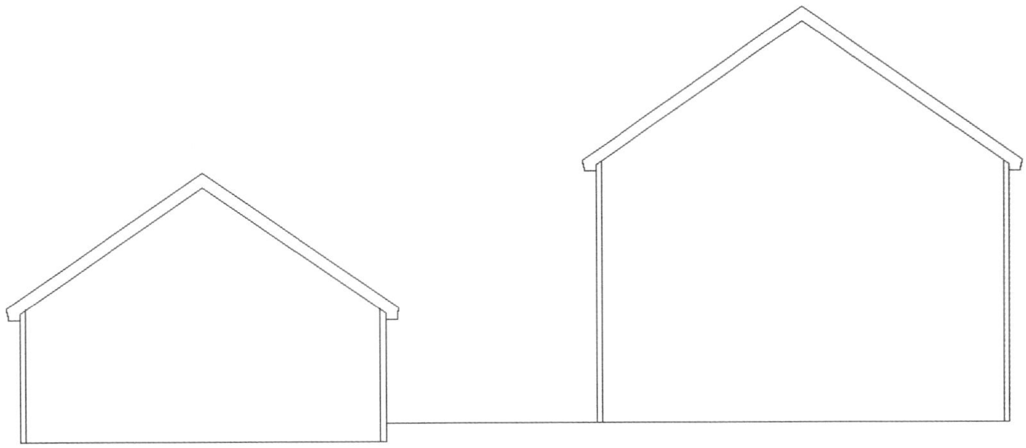

FIGURE 5-1.16 Roof outline added to two story portions of house

22. **Offset** the first floor line **14'-11"** up to establish the ridge line; extend and trim as required (Figure 5-1.17).

TIP: Knowing the building is 20'-0" wide below the portion of the roof in question, you could draw a section through this area to calculate the height of the ridge line (this roof and the porch only have a 4/12 pitch).

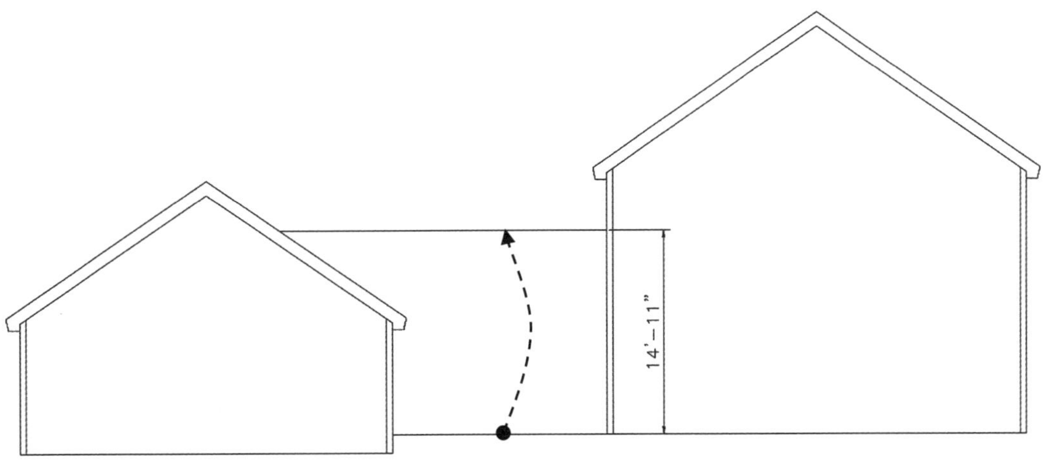

FIGURE 5-1.17 South Elevation; added roof ridge line

Taking a look back at Figure 5-1.2, you will notice that the fascia of the porch roof aligns with the garage roof. Therefore, you can draw horizontal lines extending from the endpoints of the garage roof edge.

23. Draw two horizontal lines as shown in **Figure 5-1.18**; the length does not matter at this time.

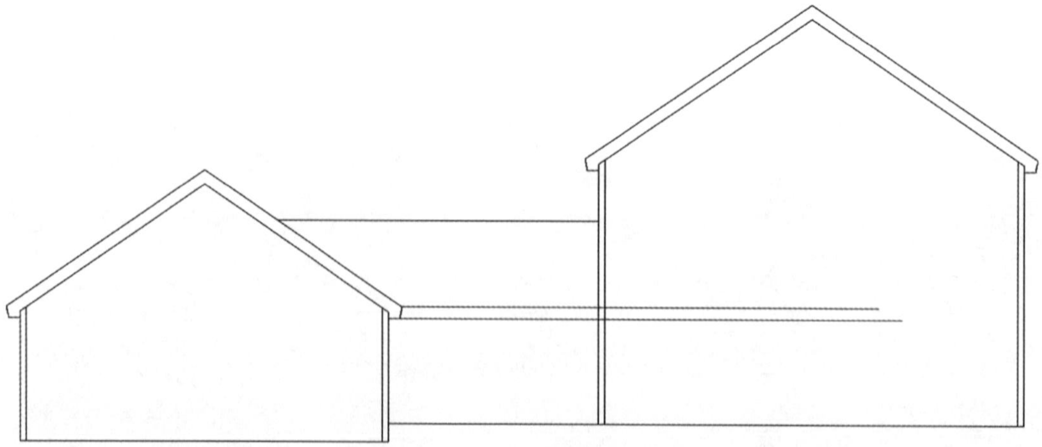

FIGURE 5-1.18 South Elevation

24. Draw an **8′-6″** line as shown in Figure 5-1.19.

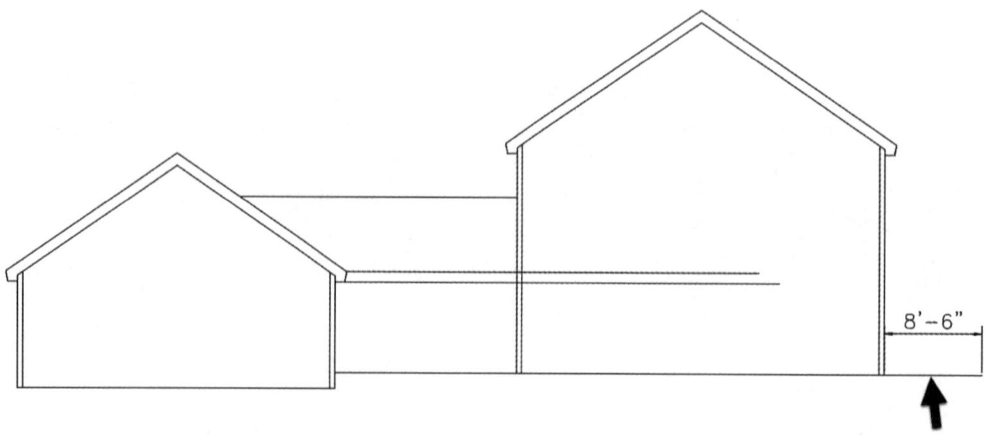

FIGURE 5-1.19 South Elevation

25. At the edge of the 8′-6″ line just drawn, you will draw one of the porch columns per the dimensions shown in Figure 5-1.20.

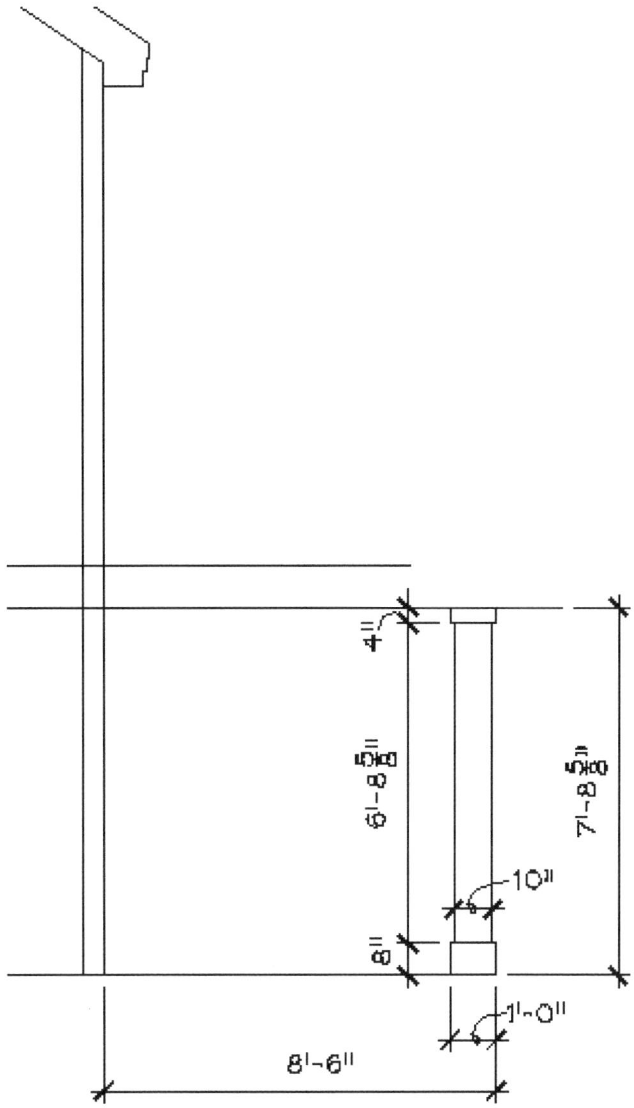

FIGURE 5-1.20 South Elevation; porch column

26. Using the same roof edge profile, draw the porch roof with a **4/12** pitch as shown in **Figure 5-1.21**. Extend the sloped roof line up to the face of the building as shown.

27. Draw the horizontal line where the porch roof meets the wall, and then trim the vertical lines to the new horizontal line as shown in **Figure 5-1.22**.

28. Draw the rest of the columns; locate them using the floor plan dimension previously provided (or use Xref, described next).

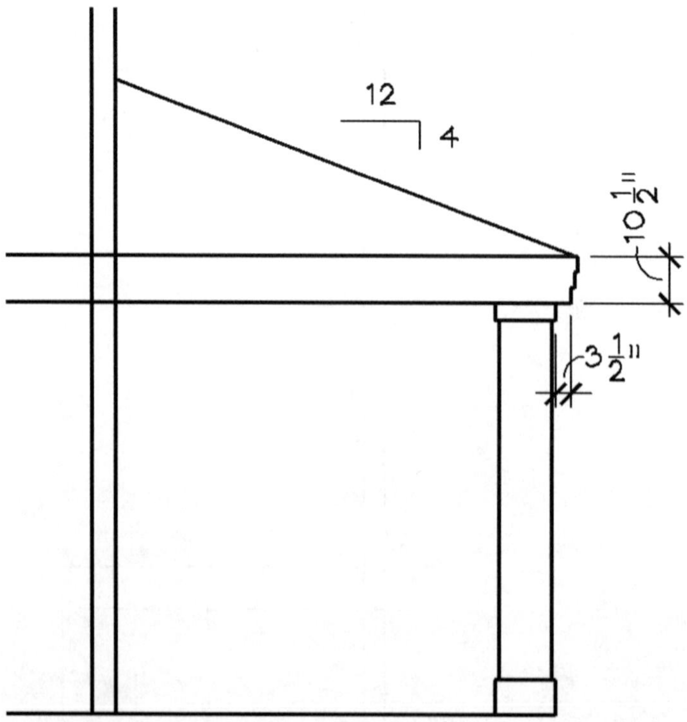

FIGURE 5-1.21 South Elevation; porch roof

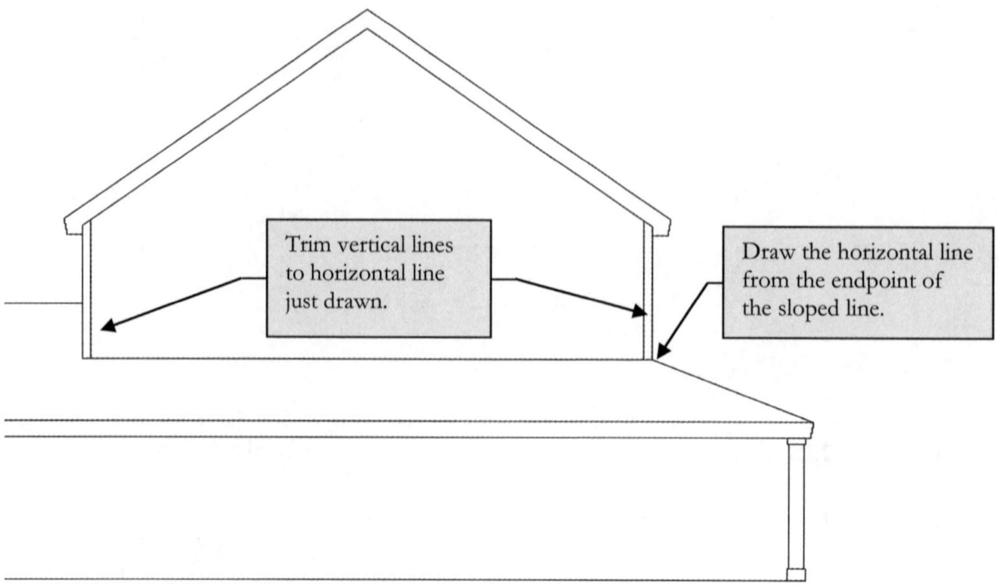

FIGURE 5-1.22 South Elevation; porch roof

External References:

We will digress for a moment and take a look at *External References*. Basically, this is a way to bring another drawing into the current drawing. AutoCAD remembers where the file is located on the computer's hard drive and reloads it every time the drawing is opened. This saves disk space and assures the referenced drawing stays current.

You will use *DWG Reference* (Xref) to bring in a floor plan so you can project lines off of it, which can speed the elevation process. When you are done you will use the *External References* palette to detach the drawing.

29. In the **exterior elevations.dwg** file select the **Attach** icon from the *Insert* tab (*Reference* panel).

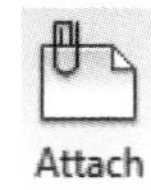

30. Browse to the location of your **flr1.dwg** file and then select **Open** (Figure 5-1.23).
    a. Make sure *Files of Type* is set to **All files (*.*)** or **Drawing (*.dwg)**.

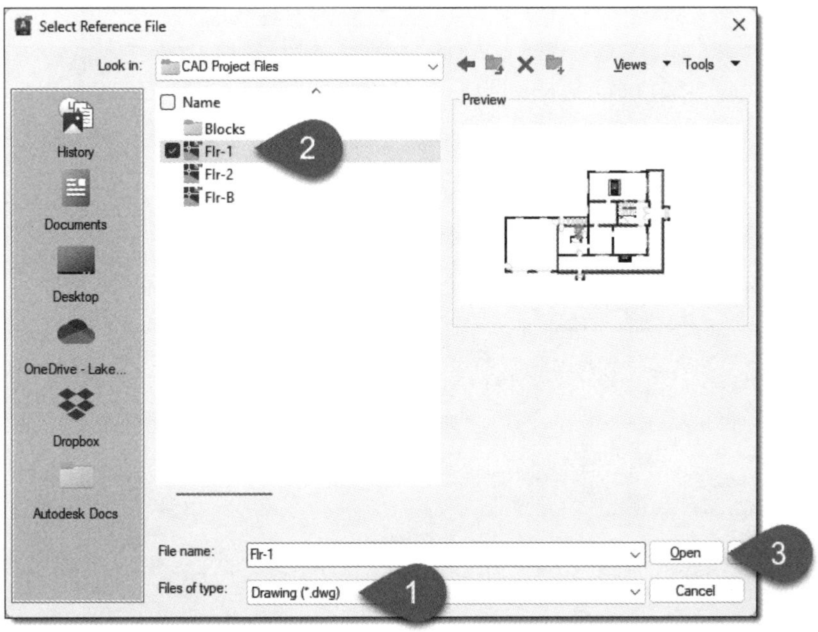

FIGURE 5-1.23 Insert External Reference (browse)

31. Next, check **Specify On-screen** under *Insertion Point* (if not already checked) and then click **OK** (Figure 5-1.24).

32. Pick a point to the <u>upper left</u> of your elevation for an insertion point.

33. **Rotate**, and **Move** if needed, the floor per **Figure 5-1.25**.

34. You can now use the floor plan and elevation to project temporary lines to quickly block out the new elevation (West).

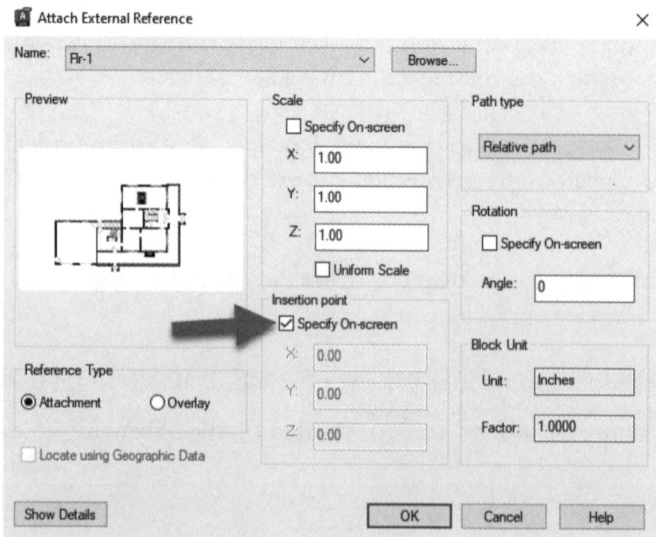

FIGURE 5-1.24 Insert External Reference dialog

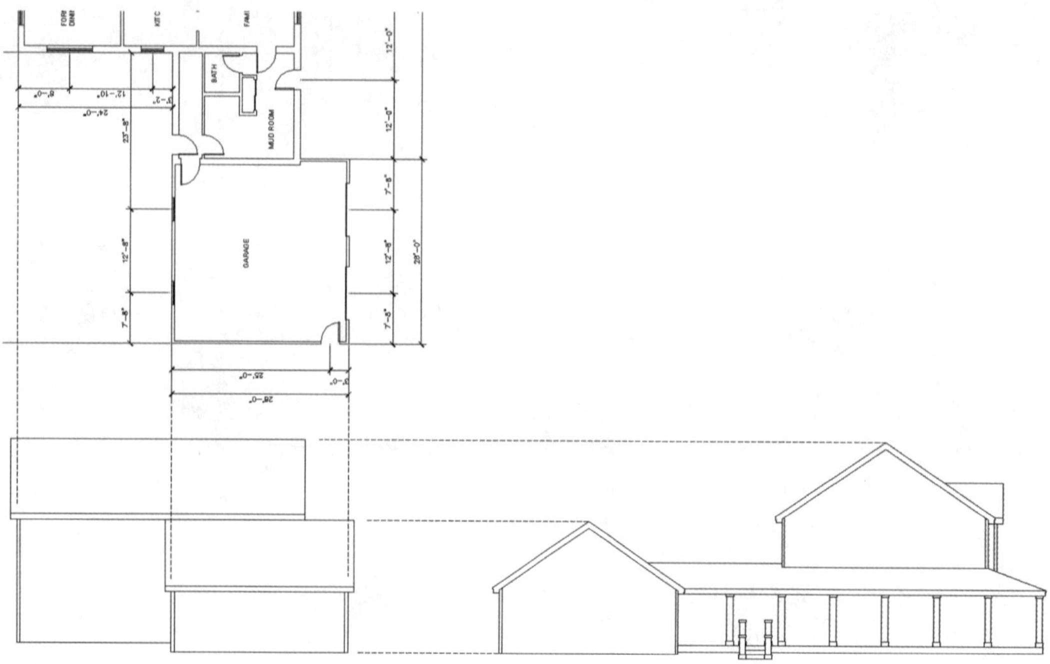

FIGURE 5-1.25 Inserted External Reference; rotated flr1 drawing

When you are finished using the *External Reference* (Xref) you can easily detach it from your drawing.

35. Select **External Reference** link from the *Insert* tab – the arrow to the right of the *Reference* panel title (or type XR and Enter).

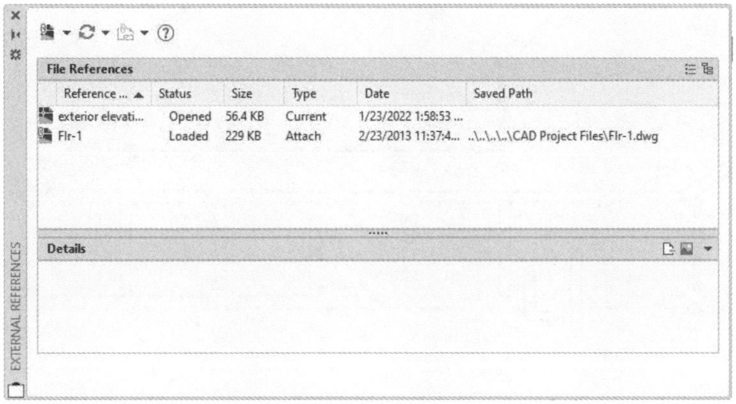

FIGURE 5-1.26A External Reference Palette

36. Right-click on **Flr1** under *Reference Name* and then click **Detach** from the context menu (Figures 5-1.26A and B).

It is also possible to select *Unload* (Figure 5-1.26B) rather than *Detach*. This gives you the ability to *Reload* the Xref whenever you want without having to pick the insertion point again. This keeps the Xref in the same location making alignment automatic.

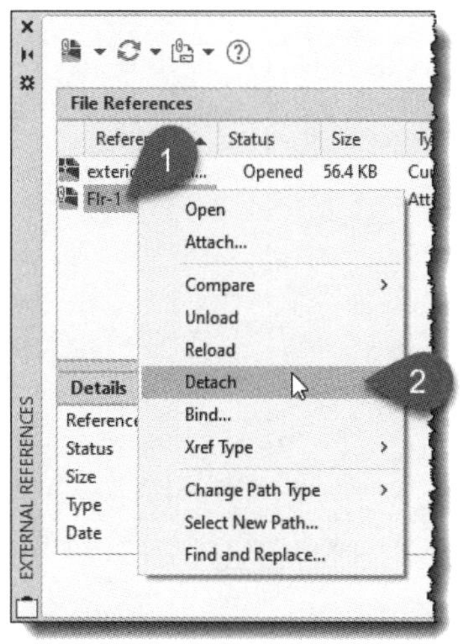

FIGURE 5-1.26B
External Reference Palette; right-click

Finishing the Exterior Elevation Outlines:

You should now have enough information to complete the outlines of the remaining exterior elevations.

37. Using the dimensions from the floor plans and the portion of elevation previously drawn, complete the outline of the four elevations per Figures 5-1.27, 5-1.28, 5-1.29 and 5-1.30.

38. **Save** your drawing.

TIP: You can find more information on how to draw the dormer-type roof, shown with dashed lines, by looking at Figure 5-1.29. ***Do NOT draw the lines dashed.***

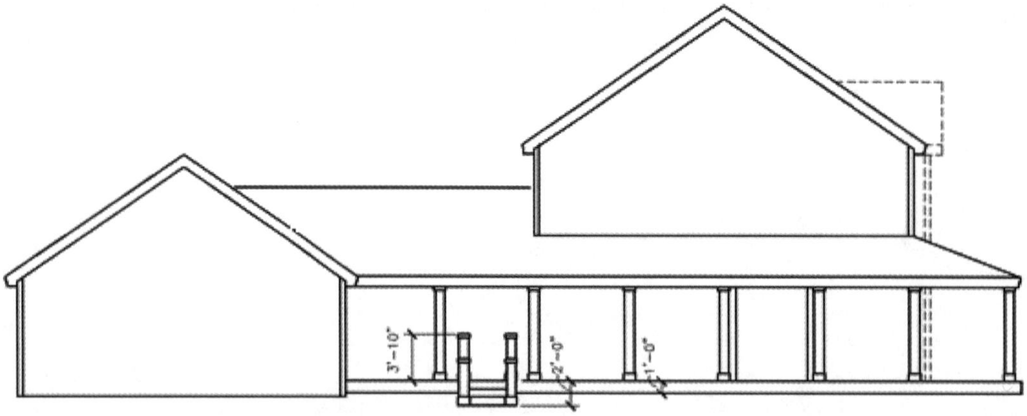

FIGURE 5-1.27 South elevation

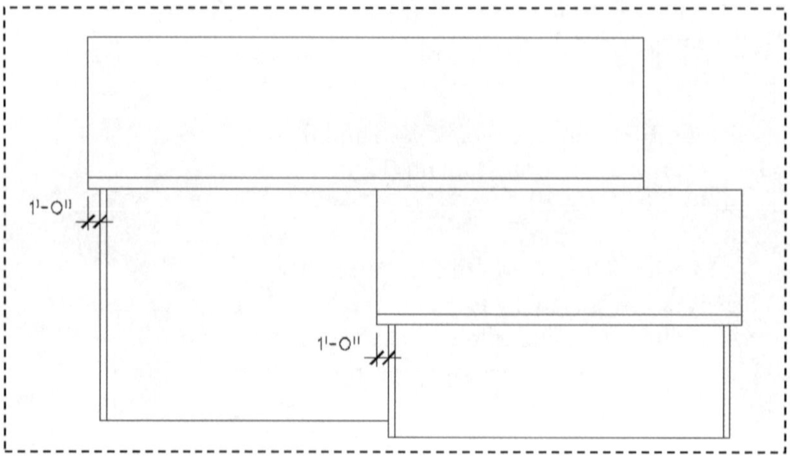

FIGURE 5-1.28 West elevation

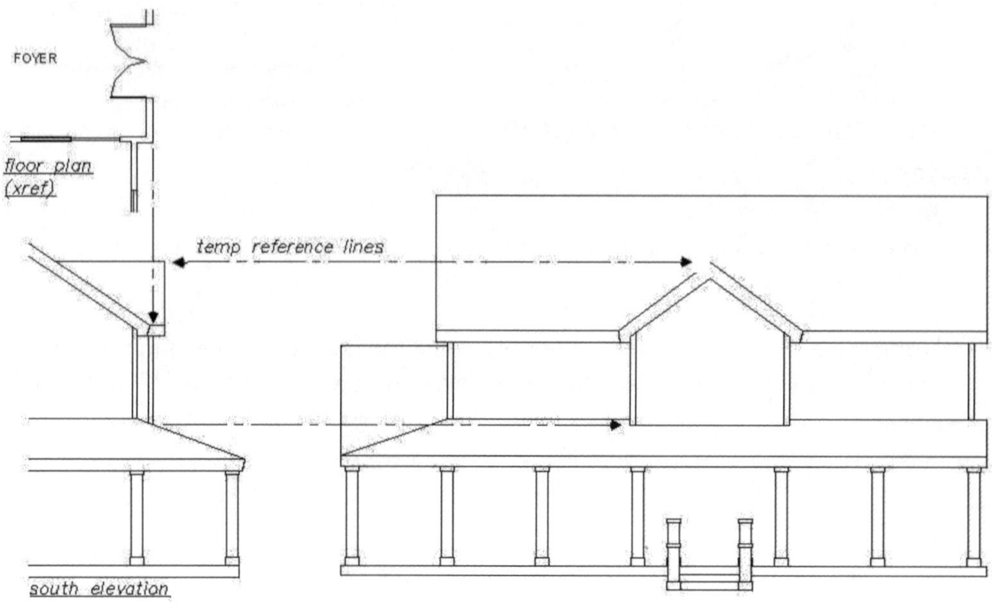

FIGURE 5-1.29 East elevation

FIND THE MISSING ELEMENT!

Comparing this elevation with the floor plan and other elevations, find the portion of elevation that is missing from Figure 5-1.30; add it to your elevation to correct the problem.

When drawing elevations, you need to thoroughly scan the plans and elevations to make sure you get everything. See Figure 5-2.7C for an image with missing elements.

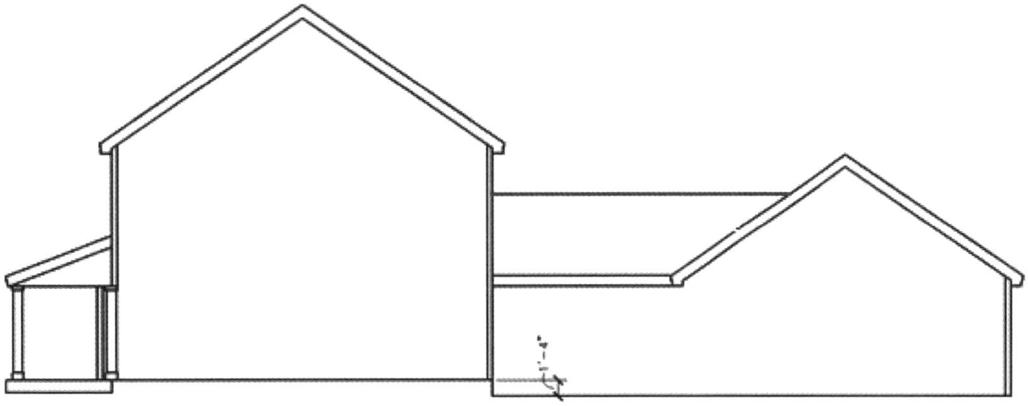

FIGURE 5-1.30 North elevation

Image courtesy of Anderson Architects
Alan H. Anderson, Architect, Duluth, MN
Interior Design, Steven W. Sanborn, A.I.A., Santa Rosa, CA

Exercise 5-2:
Windows

In this section you will add the windows to the exterior elevations. You will also study the *Block* feature a little more.

Drawing the Windows:

First, you will draw each window type in a separate drawing, similar to the drawing completed in Exercise 3-3. This method will allow you to place each drawing (of the windows) as a Block.

1. Start a **new** drawing.

2. On *Layer 0* (zero), draw the window shown in **Figure 5-2.1**. Set the bottom middle as the *Origin* (i.e., 0,0).

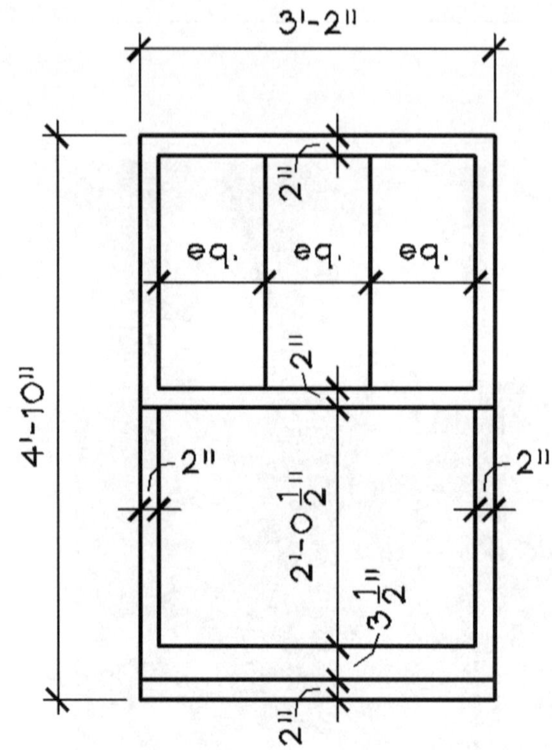

FIGURE 5-2.1 Window-1 drawing

Carter Residence *Image courtesy of LHB www.LHBcorp.com*

3. Save the window drawing as **Window-1.dwg**.

4. **Save-As** to a drawing named **Window-2.dwg**.

5. Create the window shown in **Figure 5-2.2**.

   NOTE: It is the same size as the window previously drawn so you can copy it over to create the second window.

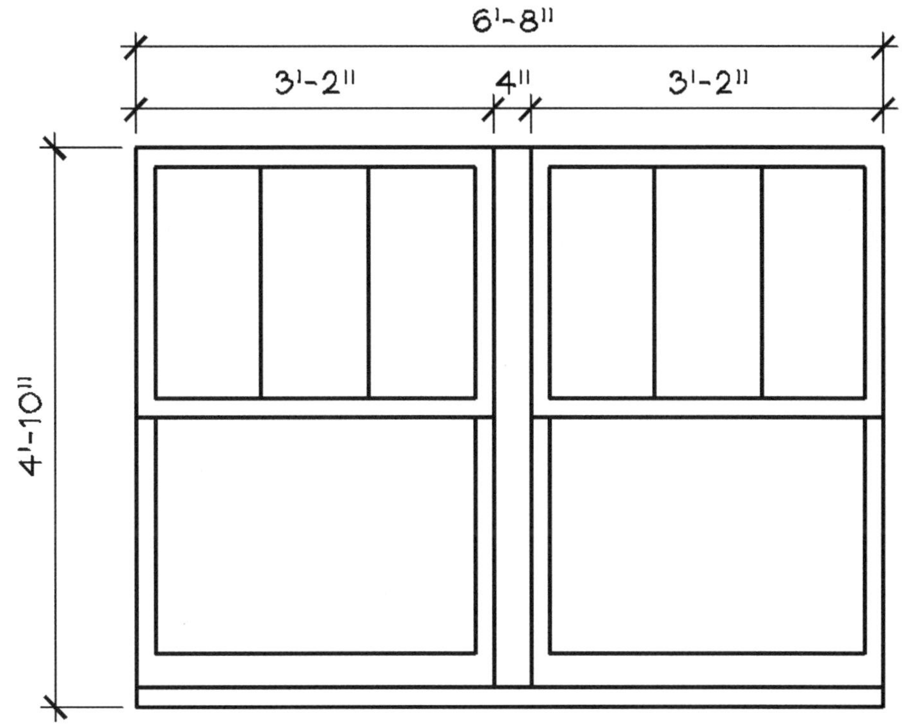

FIGURE 5-2.2 Window-2 drawing

6. **Save** your drawing (as Window-2.dwg).

The third window type is similar to Window-2 except taller. The next steps will have you save a copy and stretch the window to the correct size.

7. **Save-As** to a drawing named **Window-3.dwg**.

8. Use the **Stretch** command to quickly create the window shown in **Figure 5-2.3**.

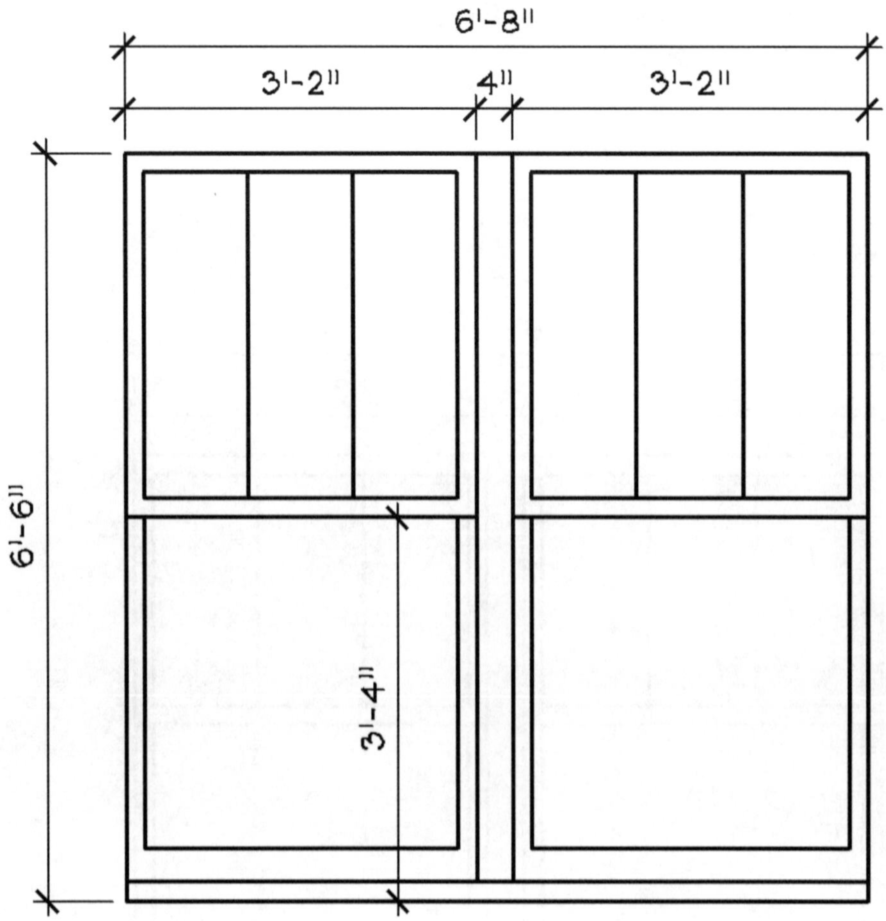

FIGURE 5-2.3 Window-3 drawing

9. **Save** your drawing.

10. **Save-As** to a drawing named **Window-4.dwg.**

11. **Erase** one of the windows and use **Fillet** to create the window shown in **Figure 5-2.4**.

You may recall from Exercise 3-3 that the vertical lines in the upper sash were more detailed in that you drew two lines, whereas here you only drew one.

Detail such as this is either added or removed depending on what scale the drawing will be printed at. Lower detail, like the window to the right, is more appropriate for smaller scale prints, such as ⅛″ = 1′-0″ or ¼″ = 1′-0″. Higher detail would be better on larger scale details, like ½″ = 1′-0″ or ¾″ = 1′-0″.

Too much detail on a smaller scale print usually produces a drawing where the lines run together, creating what looks like one really heavy line.

Now that you have created the various window types, you will insert them into the exterior elevations the same way you inserted the door symbols into the floor plans.

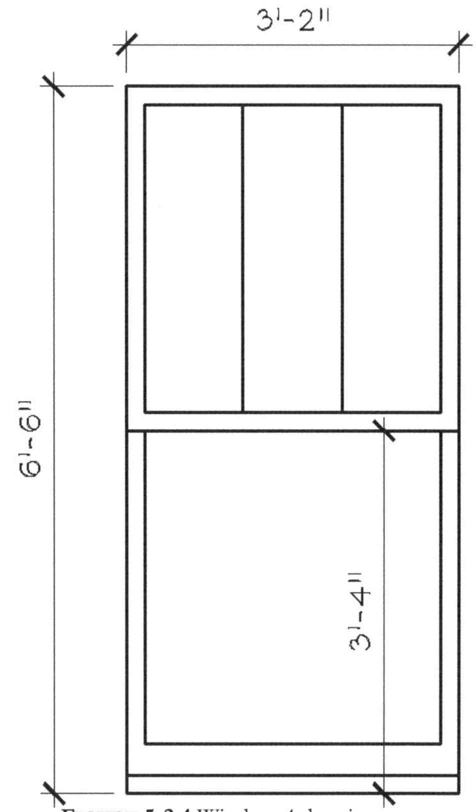

FIGURE 5-2.4 Window-4 drawing

12. **Open** the **Exterior Elevations** drawing.

13. Create a new *Layer* named ***Windows*** and set it to color *Yellow*; you will place the window *Blocks* on this *Layer*.

14. From the View tab, open the **Blocks** palette - if not already open, and switch to the **Libraries** tab.

15. Click the "**Browse Block Libraries**" icon and then **Browse** to the **Window-1** drawing.

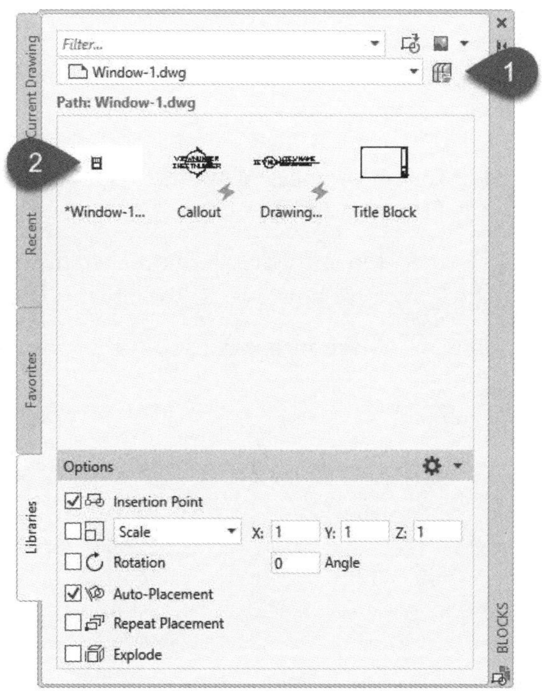

16. **Insert** the **Window-1** *Block* into the location shown in Figure 5-2.5, noting the following:
    a. The dimension shown is from the garage floor to the window sill.
    b. The horizontal dimension is to be derived from the plans; make sure you use the center of the window as a snap point if you are using an Xref'ed floor plan to locate the windows.

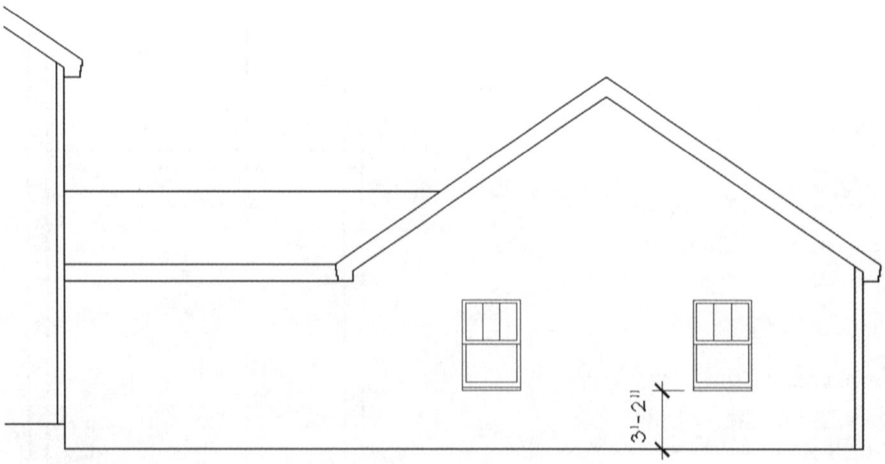

FIGURE 5-2.5 Window-1 block inserted - North elevation (garage area)

Once a *Block* (originally, an external drawing in this case) has been inserted into your drawing, you can copy it around to additional locations; you do not have to use the Blocks palette every time.

17. **Insert** instances of **Window-1, Window-2, Window-3** and **Window-4** as *Blocks* per **Figure 5-2.6.**
    a. Do not worry about the windows overlapping the porch roof and columns right now; you will adjust this later.
    b. Make sure you insert the window *Blocks* on the *Layer* named ***Windows.***

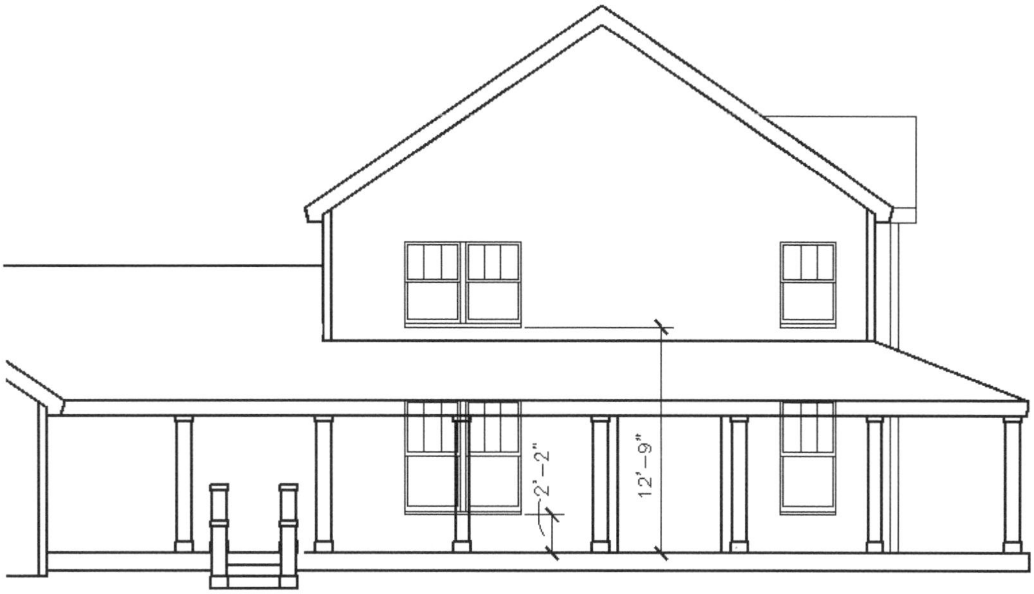

FIGURE 5-2.6 Window blocks inserted - South elevation

18. Using the sill-height dimensions and procedures previously described, insert the remaining windows based on the window locations shown in the plan (Figures 5-2.7A, B *and* C).

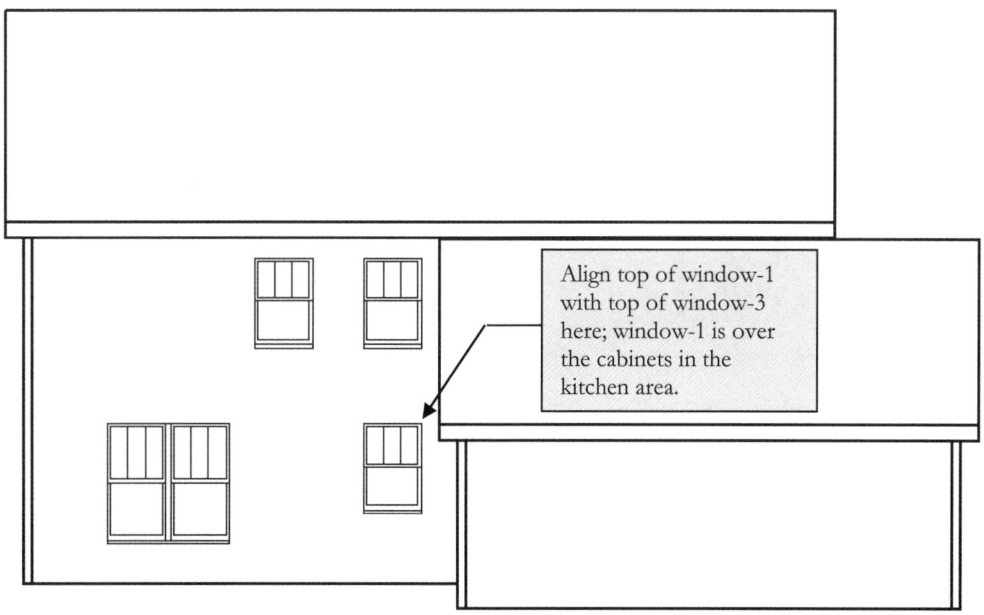

FIGURE 5-2.7A Window blocks inserted – West elevation

FIGURE 5-2.7B Window blocks inserted - East elevation

FIGURE 5-2.7C Window blocks inserted - North elevation

Advantages of using Blocks:

In addition to the window being one object when it is a *Block*, which is easy to pick and move around, you can also make changes which instantly apply to all instances of the block in a particular drawing.

Next you will modify the *Block* by adding trim, which is part of the siding. You will do this before adjusting the windows that are behind the porch roof and columns.

> **WHEN SHOULD I USE A *BLOCK*?**
>
> Anytime something is repetitive and exactly the same (or with few variations like your windows in elevation), you should use a block. This makes the drawing size smaller and any changes much quicker.

19. **Open** each of the four window type drawings and add a **5" wide trim board** to three sides and extend the sill lines as shown in **Figure 5-2.8**.

FIGURE 5-2.8 Revised windows (siding trim added)

20. **Save** each of the four window type drawings (Window-1.dwg, Window-2.dwg, Window-3.dwg, and Window-4.dwg).

21. In the *Exterior Elevations* drawing, **Zoom In** on the south elevation.

Notice the window elevations are as they were when you originally inserted them. After the next step they will all automatically update.

22. Per steps previously outlined (starting with step 14), insert the four window types again; note the following:

    a. When you are prompted to redefine the *Block*, click **Redefine Block** (Figure 5-2.9).

    b. When you are at the final stage, where you are prompted to pick a point on the screen to insert the *Block*, you can press the **Esc** key; this cancels the insert, but not before updating the block definition in the current drawing.

    c. Or, you can insert the window *Blocks* off to one side and delete them.

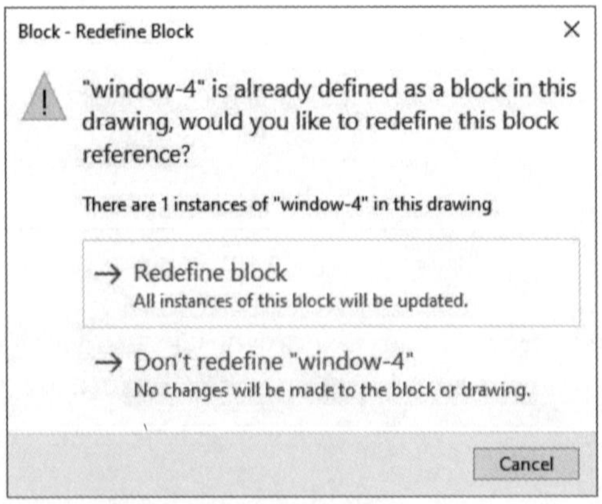

FIGURE 5-2.9 Re-define block prompt

You should review the south elevation again; notice the windows have been all updated automatically (Figure 5-2.10)! The other three elevations are updated also (because all elevations are in the same drawing file). This feature can save a lot of time.

FIGURE 5-2.10 Re-defined blocks in South elevation

Exploding Blocks:

The Explode command allows you to reduce a *Block* to its basic components (i.e., lines, arcs, text, etc.). Only the *Blocks* selected are exploded. And, even if you Explode all the instances of a particular *Block* in a drawing, the definition of the *Block* will still exist in the drawing; this allows you to insert the *Block* without having to browse to the original drawing on your hard drive (i.e., C: drive).

Next you will Explode the *Blocks* at the porch and trim the portion of window covered by the porch roof and columns.

23. Select the **Explode** icon from the *Modify* panel. 

24. Select the two windows on the south elevation and the two windows on the east elevation that are covered by the porch roof.

The four windows are now exploded to their original lines. Next you will trim the windows so you only see the lines that are not obstructed from sight by another building element.

25. **Trim** and **Erase** the window lines as shown in **Figures 5-2.11** and **5-2.12**.

FIGURE 5-2.11 Exploded windows (original lines trimmed and erased); East elevation

FIGURE 5-2.12 Exploded windows (original lines trimmed and erased); South elevation

After exploding the *Blocks* you should have noticed that the lines changed color (from *Yellow* to *White*). If you recall, you created the window on *Layer 0* in the original drawings and placed the window *Blocks* on the *Windows* layer in the 'Exterior Elevations' drawing. When a *Block* is exploded, you get the original line-work on the original *Layers*.

So, to clean house, you need to move the exploded window lines to the *Windows* layer.

26. Revise the drawing so the exploded windows are on the ***Windows*** layer.

Exercise 5-3:
Doors

In this exercise you will add exterior doors to your plans. In the process you will take a quick look at using a feature called "Grip Edit."

1. **Open** the exterior elevations.dwg drawing file.

2. Create a new *Layer* named ***Doors***; set the color to *Green.*

The elevations, as a whole, do not have more than two instances of any door; plus two of the doors need to be trimmed because they are behind other architectural elements.

Thus it is not beneficial, in this case, to create blocks of each door. So you will draw each door type in-place and then copy the entities to the second location (if applicable).

3. On the *Doors* layer, draw the door shown in **Figure 5-3.1** on the east elevation.

The door/frame elevation shown in Figure 5-3.1 represents two doors that are mostly glass and a glass transom above the doors that aligns with the tall windows on either side (not shown in Figure 5-3.1).

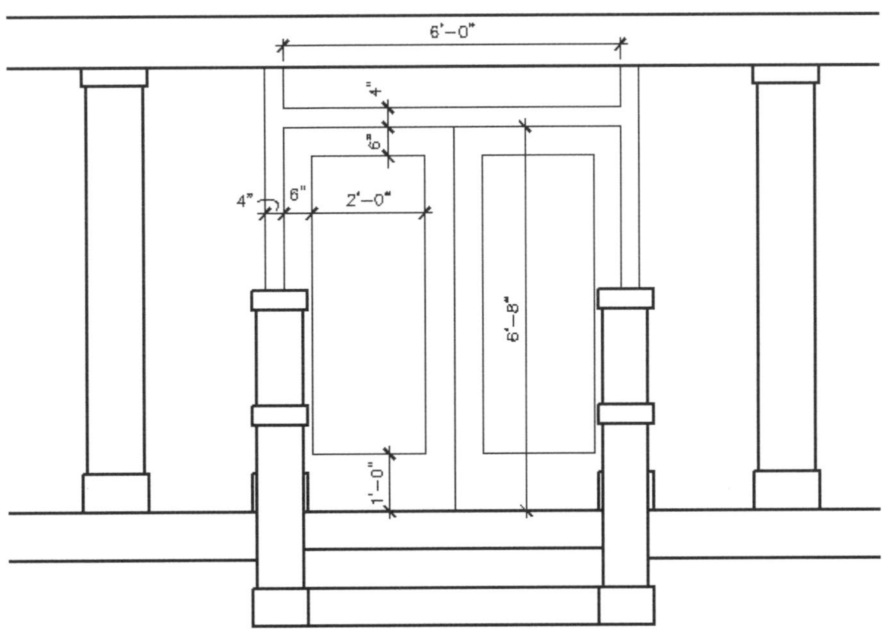

FIGURE 5-3.1 Door elevation; East elevation

Notice that the double doors you just drew correspond to the double doors you drew in the first floor plan.

4. Draw the portion of door shown in **Figure 5-3.2** on the west elevation (door into garage); you will draw more of the door in subsequent steps.

FIGURE 5-3.2 Partial door elevation; West elevation

RESIDENTIAL DOOR SIZES

Doors come in many shapes and sizes.

THICKNESS: 1⅜", 1¾" and 2¼"

The 1⅜" door is most often used in residential construction and the 2¼" door is typically only used on exterior doors for high-end projects, i.e., big budget.

SIZE: ranges from 1'-0" x 6'-8" to 4'-0" x '0"

The height of a residential door is usually 6'-8". This writer recently worked on a project where 7'-0" high doors were specified. The contractor was so used to the standard 6'-8" dimension he framed all the exterior openings at 6'-8". To top it off, the exterior walls were concrete (ICF system), so the openings could not be modified. Thus, 6'-8" doors were used.

You can find more information on the internet; two examples are

algomahardwoods.com (*wood veneer door mfr.*) and madawaska-doors.com (*custom solid wood door mfr.*)

NOTE: Do not jump ahead here; follow the next few steps closely!

5. Using the **Offset** command, offset the previously drawn lines inward, as shown in Figure 5-3.3.

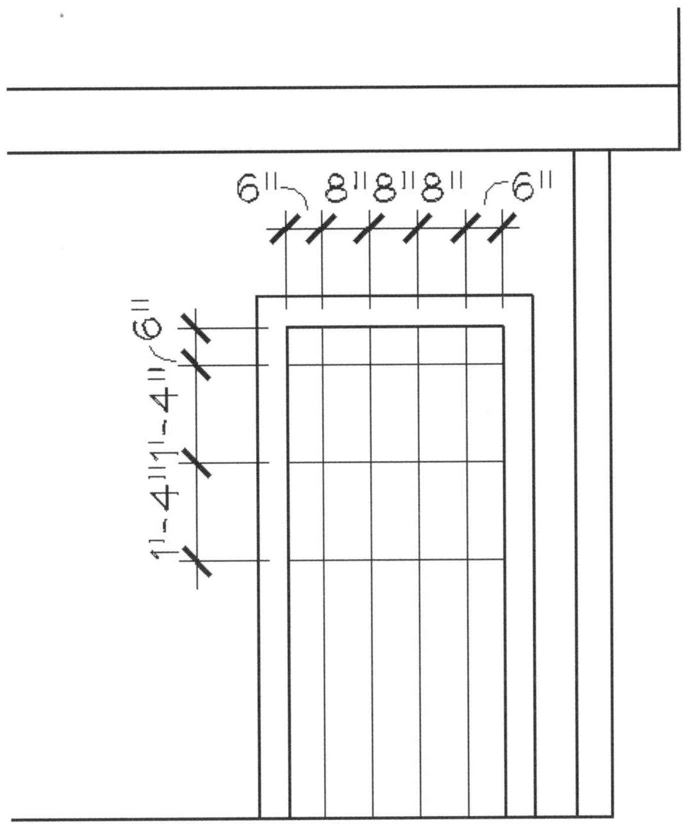

FIGURE 5-3.3 Door elevation with lines offset; West elevation

Using the Grip Edit Feature:

Next you will use the **Grip Edit** feature to modify the lines to represent the window in the door panel.

Grip Edit allows you to modify lines without having to activate a command first. Basically you select a line, then select one or more of the visible *Grips* and then reposition the *Grips* by selecting another point.

6. Without any commands active, select the horizontal line shown in **Figure 5-3.4**.

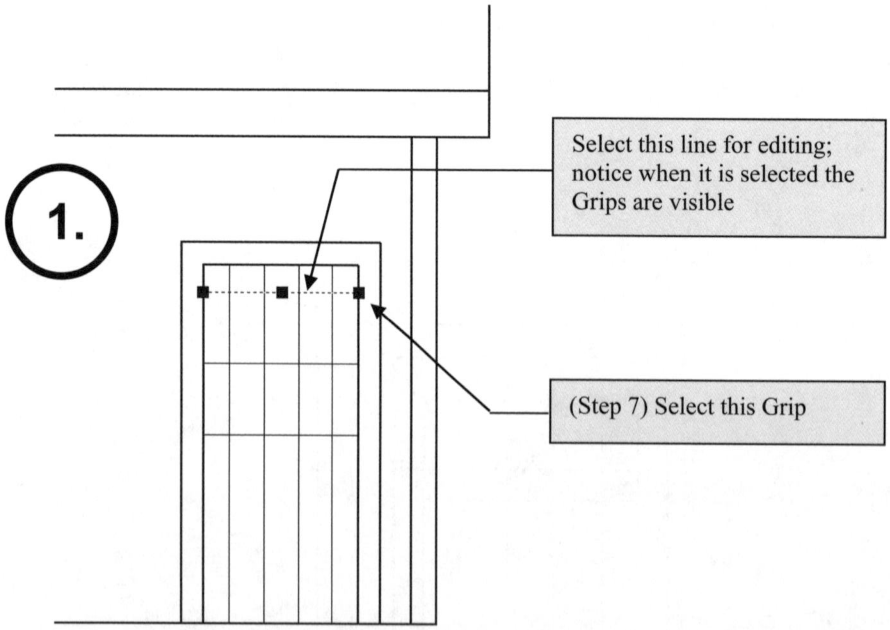

FIGURE 5-3.4 Line selected for editing; West elevation

7. Select the *Grip* on the right; simply click the mouse button with the cursor over the *Grip*. Do <u>not</u> drag the mouse button (Figure 5-3.4).

8. Move the mouse to the left. Using ***OSNAPs***, select either *Perpendicular* or *Intersection* of the vertical line shown in **Figures 5-3.5a** and **5-3.5b**.

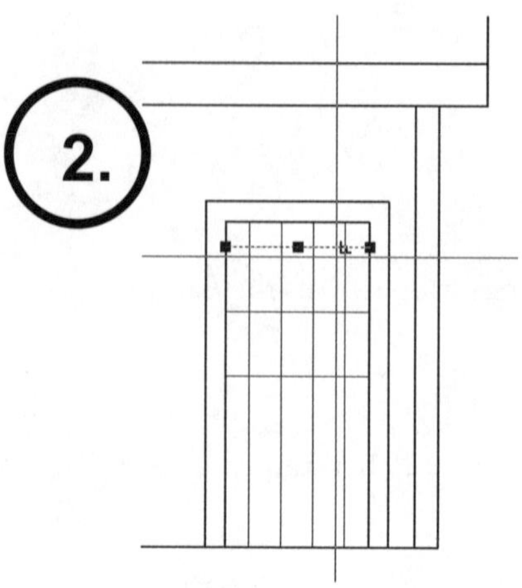

FIGURE 5-3.5A Perpendicular snap

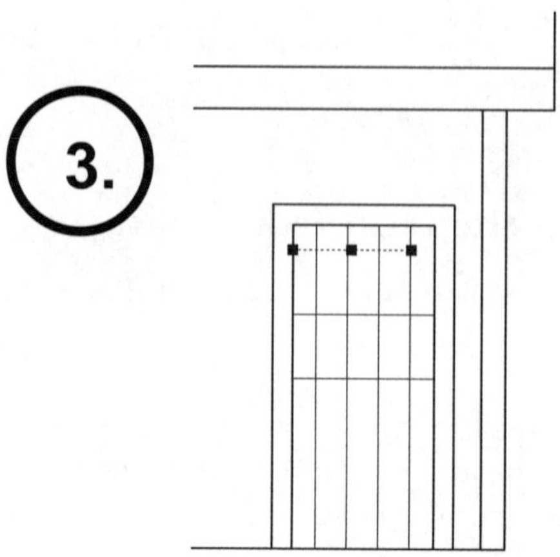

FIGURE 5-3.5B Relocated snap

9. Finally, press the **Esc** (i.e., Escape) key, on the keyboard, to clear the *Grips* (and unselect the horizontal line).

Essentially, you just trimmed a line without using the *Trim* command.

10. Using the same technique just described, modify the lines using *Grips* to look like **Figure 5-3.6**.

AutoCAD also allows you to select more than one *Grip* at a time. You will try this next to adjust the bottom of the (4) vertical lines.

11. Select the (4) vertical lines; you can click each line individually or use a *Crossing Window (by clicking right to left).*

12. Holding the **Shift** key, **click** each of the lower *Grips* on the (4) vertical lines; the selected *Grips* will turn red.

13. Releasing the **Shift** key, click the lower right *Grip*.

REMEMBER: Do not drag the mouse; i.e., do not hold the mouse button down continuously (Figure 5-3.7).

14. Moving the mouse straight up, use the *Endpoint OSNAP* to accurately select the lower horizontal line.

FIGURE 5-3.6
Lines modified with grips

Your door is now complete and should look like **Figure 5-3.8**.

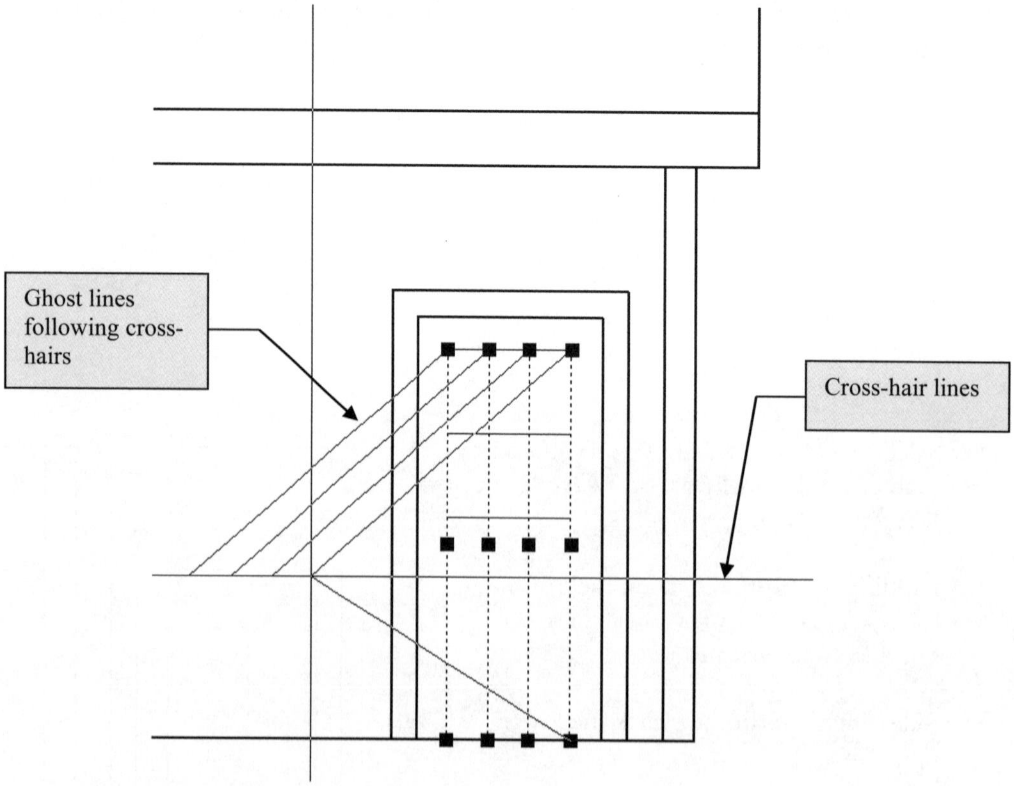

FIGURE 5-3.7 Modifying multiple grips at once

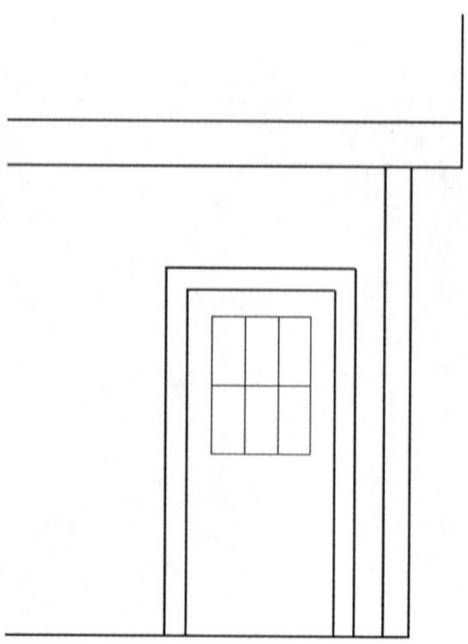

FIGURE 5-3.8 Completed door elevation

Before moving on, here are a few additional comments on the Grip Edit command that you may want to investigate further on your own.

- You select the middle *Grip* to move the entity.
- If you select a *Grip* and then right-click, you get additional modification options (Figure 5-3.9).
- The *Grip* that is selected is, by default, the base point for the *Mirror* command.

15. **Copy** the door just created to the other two locations (per the floor plans); also make sure the doors are placed in the correct floor elevation. (See **Figures 5-3.10** and **5-3.11**.)

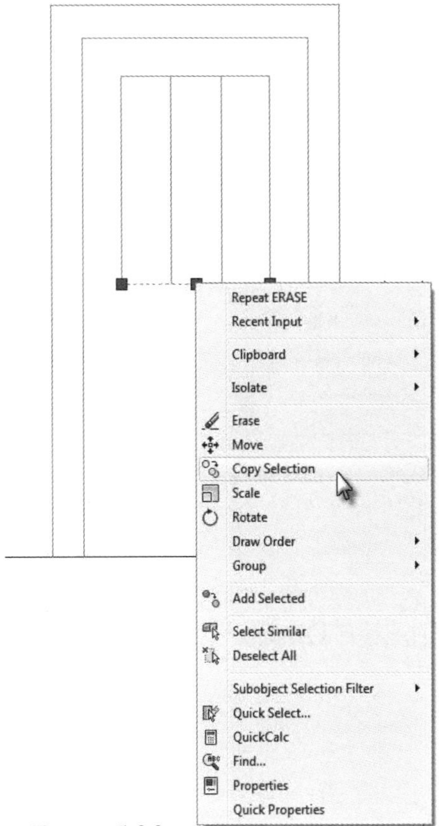

FIGURE 5-3.9
Right-click with grip selected

FIGURE 5-3.10 Door added and trimmed – South elevation

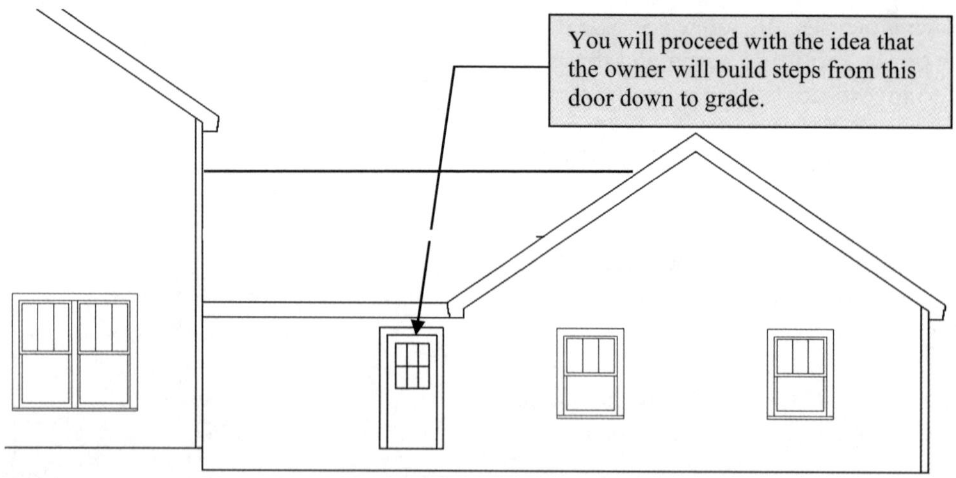

FIGURE 5-3.11 Door added - North elevation

Garage Doors:

16. Draw the **garage door** shown in **Figure 5-3.12**.
    a. All panels are to be equally spaced.
    b. **Copy** or **Mirror** the door to the other location.
    c. **Save** your drawing!

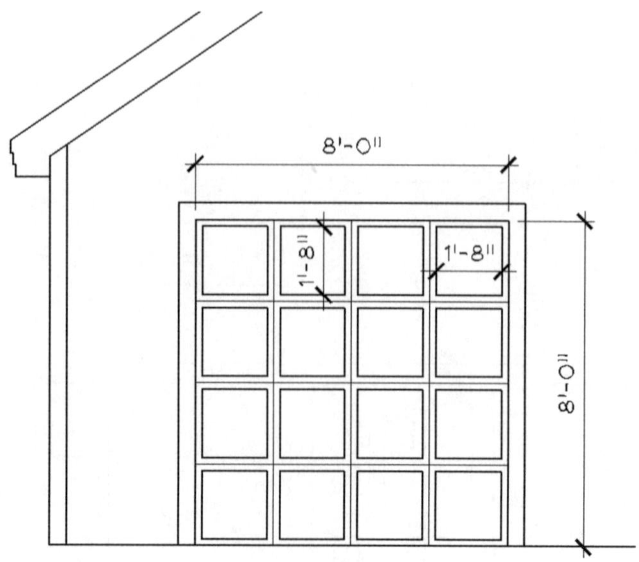

***NOTE:** This is all the information you need to draw the garage door; it requires you to do a little math.*

FIGURE 5-3.12 Garage Door

Exercise 5-4:
Chimney, Railing and Siding

In this exercise you will draw the chimneys, the railing at the porch and the siding and brick patterns.

Chimney:

1. Open your **Exterior Elevations** drawing.

2. Draw two vertical lines at the first floor that represent the width of the fireplace; refer to the first floor plan for location and width. (Place on *Layer* G-Detl-Hevy, color White.)

3. Draw the upper portion of the chimney as shown in Figure 5-4.1 (with the 2′-8″ portion centered on the first floor lines):
   a. Trim the fascia as shown.
   b. You will finish the bottom/porch roof intersection next.

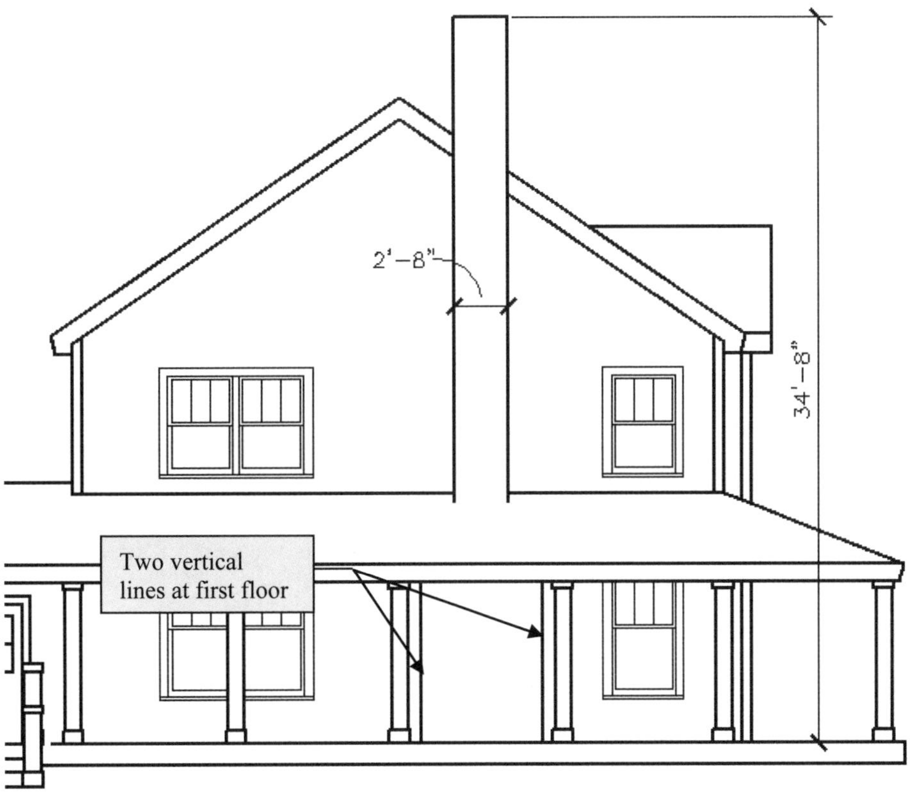

FIGURE 5-4.1 Chimney – South elevation

Next you will draw the side view of the chimney. Once you are done with this view you will be able to complete the front view.

4. On the East elevation, draw the chimney as shown in Figure 5-4.2.

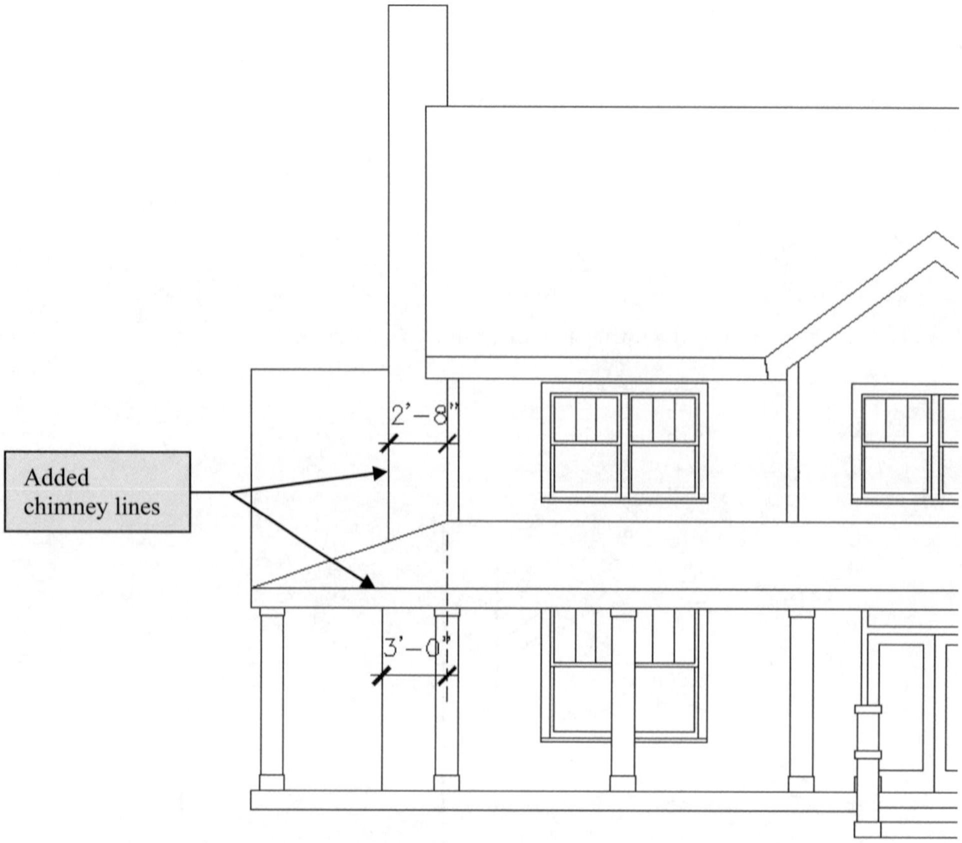

FIGURE 5-4.2 Chimney – East elevation

Now you can project a line from this elevation over to the South elevation to determine where the chimney intersects the porch roof.

5. Draw a line from where the upper chimney intersects the porch roof, over to the South elevation (Figure 5-4.3).

Notice how the side view of the chimney helps determine where the chimney intersects the porch roof in the front view of the chimney.

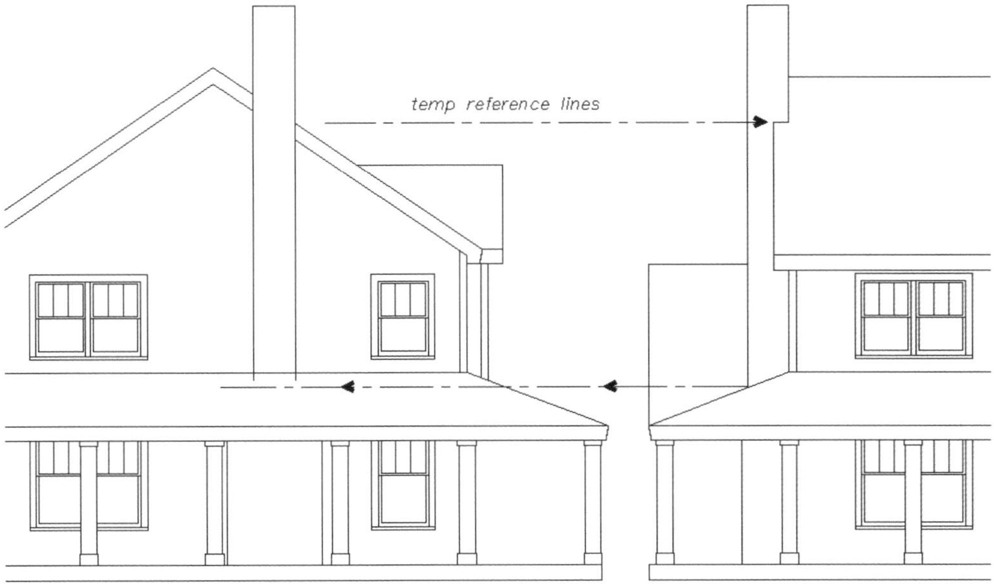

FIGURE 5-4.3 Chimney – South elevation
FYI: *This technique is called Orthographic Projection.*

6. Complete the chimney as shown in Figure 5-4.4.

FIGURE 5-4.4 Chimney – South elevation

7. Zoom into the top of the chimney and draw a concrete chimney cap shown in Figure 5-4.5.

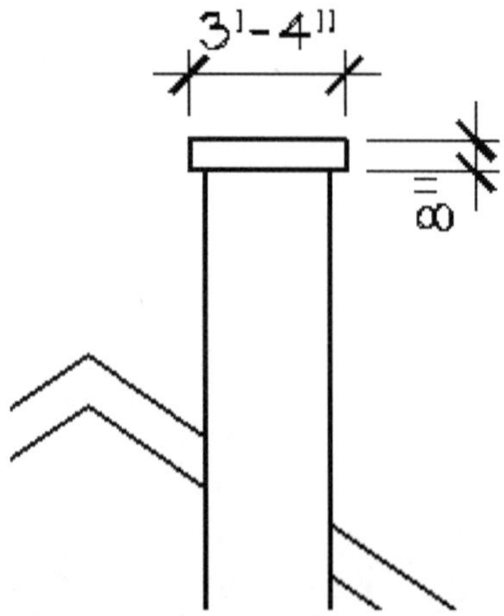

FIGURE 5-4.5 Chimney Cap

8. Copy the chimney cap to the other elevation.

9. Draw the chimney in the other two elevations (Figures 5-4.6 and 5-4.7).

FIGURE 5-4.6 Chimney – West elevation

FIGURE 5-4.7 Chimney – North elevation

You will draw the other chimney later.

> **CHIMNEY CAPS!**
>
> You can buy prefabricated chimney caps in all shapes and sizes. Here are a couple of websites that sell/make them:
>
> http://www.ejmcopper.com/chimneycaps/
> http://classiccopper.com/store
> http://chimneycapdesign.com/

Porch Railing:

10. Create a *Layer* named ***Railing*** (color *Red*).
11. **Zoom In** to the porch on North elevation.
12. Draw the railing shown in Figure 5-4.8. Do not add the shading.

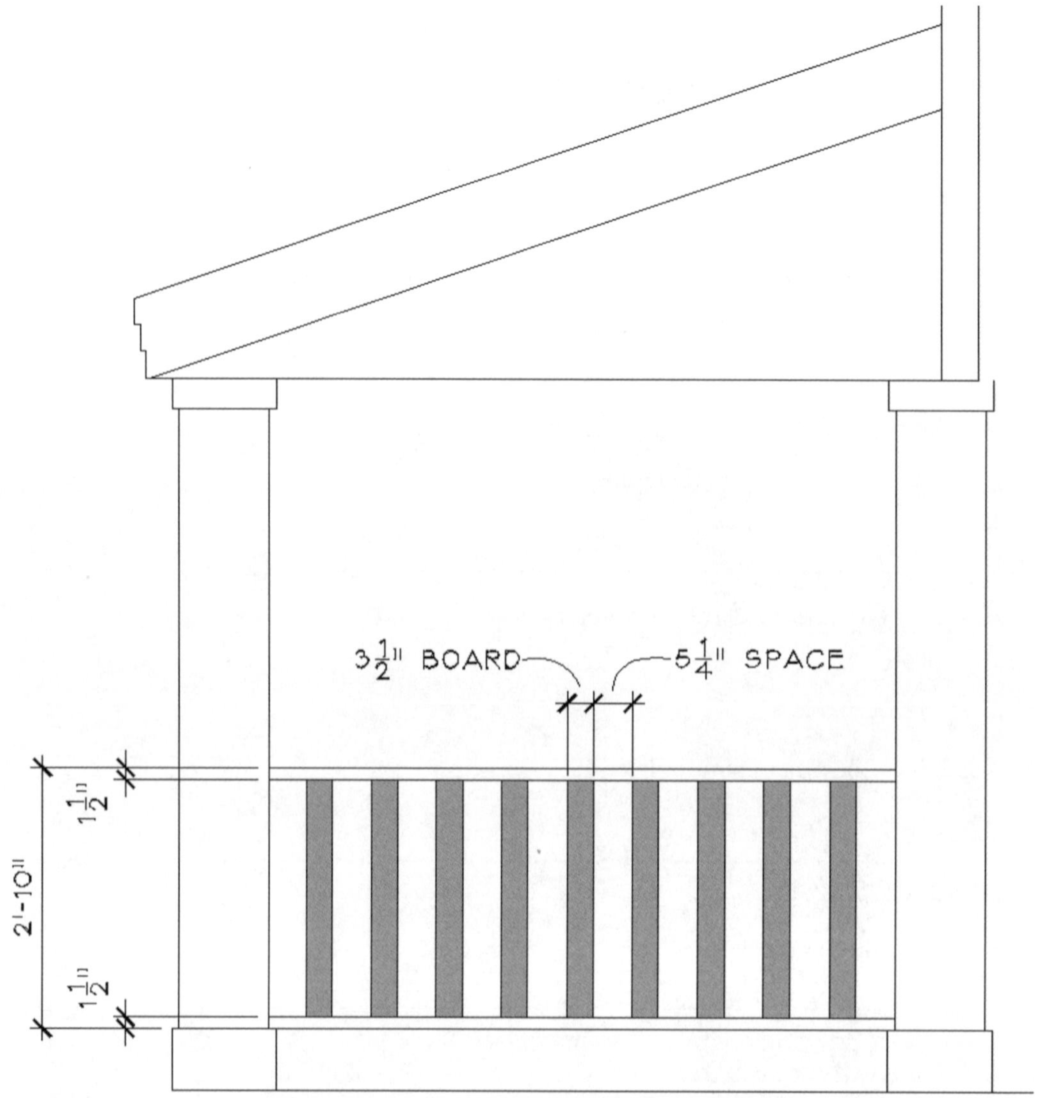

FIGURE 5-4.8 Railing – North elevation; shading added for clarity

13. Draw the rest of the railings on the other elevations (Figures 5-4.9 and 5-4.10).

FIGURE 5-4.9 Railing – East elevation

FIGURE 5-4.10 Railing – South elevation

14. **Trim** any lines that extend behind the 3½″ boards or the 1½″ top and bottom rails (Figures 5-4.9 and 5-4.10).

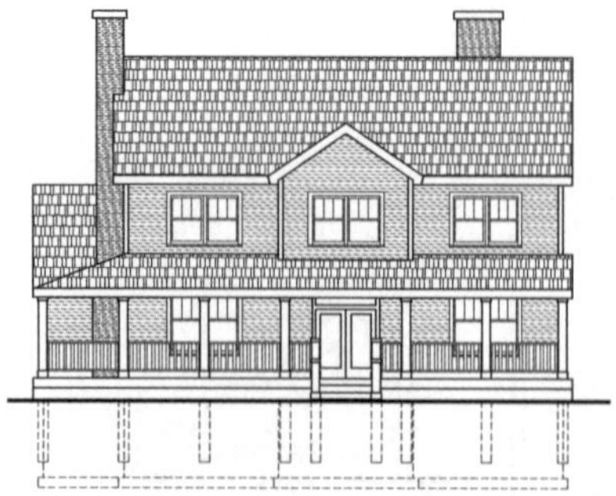

Using the Hatch Command:

The tool used in AutoCAD to draw patterns, such as bricks, siding and shingles, is called **Hatch**. This tool allows you to quickly fill an enclosed area with one of many predefined patterns. You will use this feature to add the shingles, siding and bricks to your elevations.

First you will draw the roof shingles.

15. **Zoom In** to the East elevation.

16. Create a *Layer* called ***Shingles***; color *Blue*; set it current.

17. You can start the **Hatch** command in one of the following ways:

    a. Click the **Hatch** icon on the *Draw* panel.

    b. Type **hatch** at the *Command prompt* or *On-Screen.*

You should now see the *Hatch Creation* tab on the *Ribbon* (Figure 5-4.11).

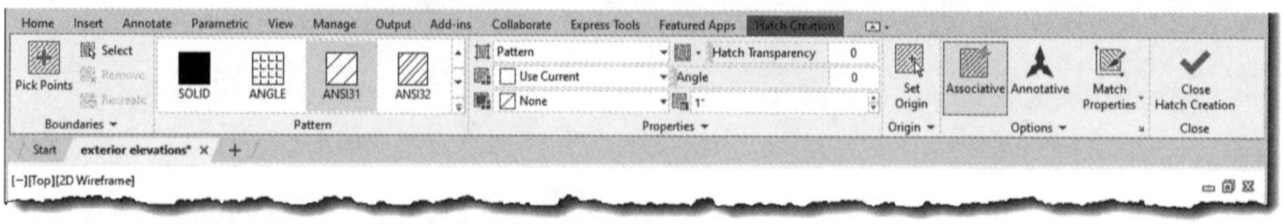

FIGURE 5-4.11 Hatch and Gradient dialog box

The Hatch Creation tab is called a **contextual tab**. It only appears while the *Hatch* command is active or when a hatch element is selected in the drawing. This tab provides access to all settings related to hatch patterns, scale, transparency, and more. With the *Hatch* command active, you set things the way you want them on the *Ribbon* and then move your cursor into the *Drawing Window*. When your cursor moves within an enclosed area, that area will automatically get a temporary hatch pattern so you can see the final result before actually clicking to create the hatch. When your cursor moves out of the enclosed area, the temporary hatch goes away. If you want to create the hatch, you simply click the left mouse button within the enclosed area. Once you are done creating hatch patterns, you click *Close Hatch Creation* on the *Ribbon*. The contextual tab goes away, and the hatch command is no longer active.

18. Click the down-arrow in the *Pattern* panel and select ***AR-RSHKE*** (Figure 5-4.12).

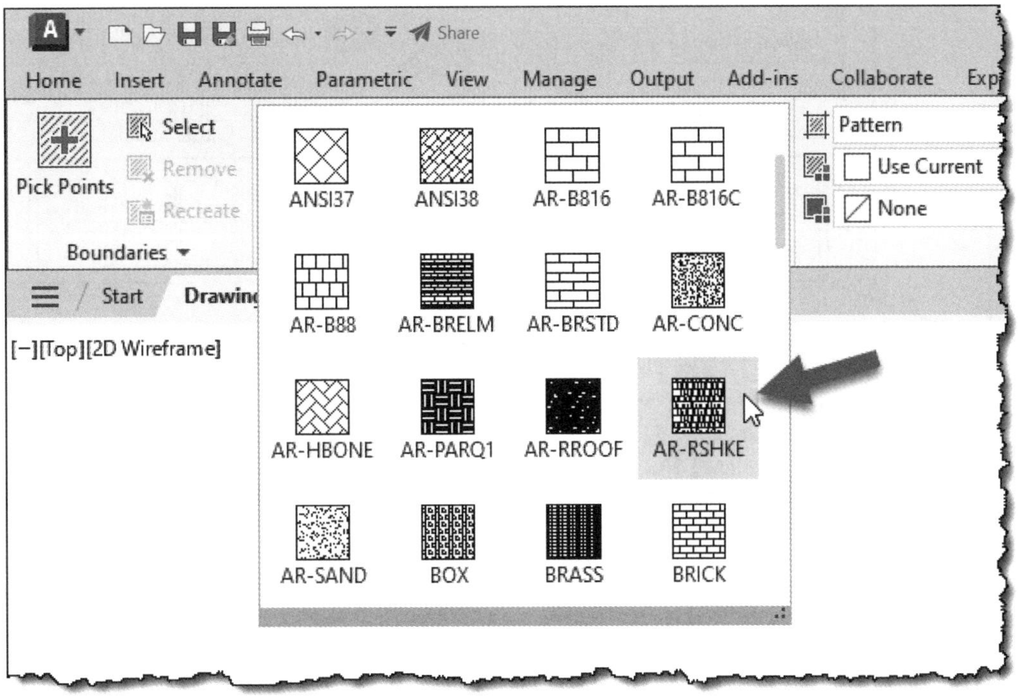

FIGURE 5-4.12 Hatch Creation tab – pattern selected

Next, you will pick a point in the drawing that is completely enclosed.

19. Click the Add: **Pick Points** button (this should be the default already).

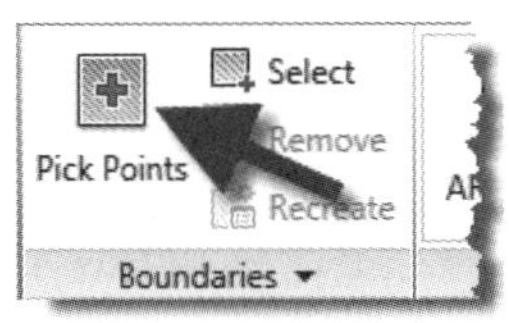

20. Click anywhere in the roof; see **Figure 5-4.13**.

21. Skip this step.

FIGURE 5-4.13 Boundary Hatch; one enclosed section hatched

22. Click the **Close Hatch Creation** button to finish the hatch creation process.

23. Use the **Hatch** tool to draw the rest of the roof shingles.

TIP: Only Hatch one area at a time; it is easier later when you have to re-hatch an area due to a change (Figures 5-4.17 – 19).

Next, you will draw the brick at the chimney.

24. Use the **Hatch** tool to draw the brick at the chimney:
    a. Do not draw the brick pattern behind the railing; this would create too much clutter.
    b. Use the pattern named **AR-BRSTD**.
    c. See fully hatched **Figures 5-4.17 – 19**.
    d. Create one *Layer* named ***Brick***; color *Blue*.

Finally you will draw the siding; this will be a little different.

25. Create a *Layer* named ***Siding***; color *Blue*.
26. Initiate the **Hatch** command.
27. Select **User Defined** next to *Type*.
28. For *Spacing* enter **4** (this means the lines will be 4″ apart). (See Figure 5-4.14.)

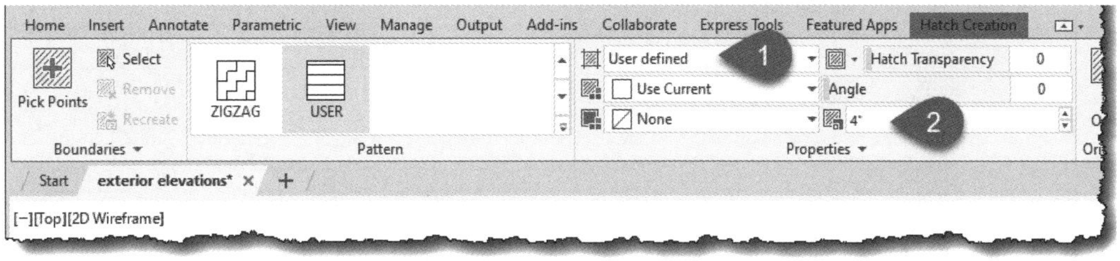

FIGURE 5-4.14 Boundary Hatch; User Defined pattern

> **TIP:**
>
> If you use the **Pick Points** button and click in an area that is not closed, you will get this error message.
>
> It may not be obvious where the opening is in the area you wish to hatch. You need to zoom in on each intersection and corner to find the opening. Finally, you "close" the opening with a line or *Fillet*.
>
> If you click on the *Options* panel fly-out, you can adjust the *Gap Tolerance* variable which allows hatch to find a valid boundary, as long as all gaps are smaller than the specified setting.

29. Zoom into the West elevation and use the **Pick Points** button to select one area at a time to hatch with the siding pattern (Figure 5-4.15).

FIGURE 5-4.15 Boundary Hatch; User Defined pattern used to draw 4″ siding

30. Use this technique to draw the rest of the siding, hatching one area at a time (see Figures 5-4.16 to 5-4.19).

    TIP: You can select several areas at one time and check the "Create separate hatches" option in the Options panel fly-out dialog box (see image to the right).

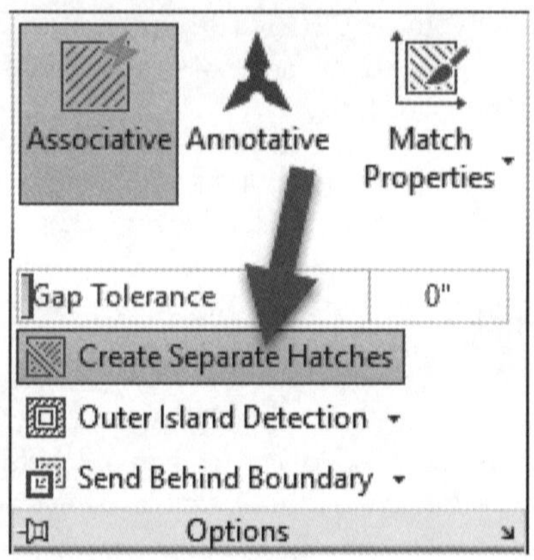

A newer hatch-related feature in AutoCAD is the ability to toggle into **Path** mode, which creates a hatch pattern at a specified width along a path defined by points picked on the screen. Consider asking the **Autodesk Assistant** how this new feature works.

The following image highlights how to enter "Path" mode when using the Hatch command. Note: this step is not required for this exercise.

> ***Tip:***
> *You can select a hatch pattern to display the Hatch Editor tab on the Ribbon. This tab is basically the same as the one used in creating the hatch pattern. Here you can change the pattern or adjust the scale and/or spacing.*

FIGURE 5-4.16 Hatching complete – East elevation

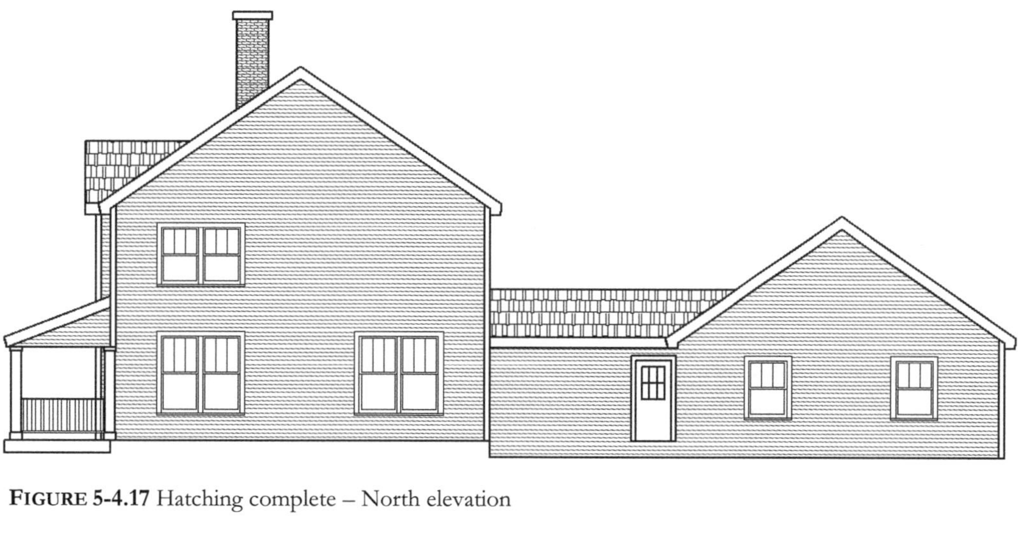

FIGURE 5-4.17 Hatching complete – North elevation

FIGURE 5-4.18 Hatching complete – South elevation

FIGURE 5-4.19 Hatching complete – West elevation

This concludes Exercise 5-4; don't forget the *Additional Tasks* at the end of this chapter. It is strongly recommended that you complete them before moving on as they contain many new concepts not yet covered.

Self-Exam:

The following questions can be used as a way to check your knowledge of this lesson. The answers can be found at the bottom of this page.

1. You do not need to create a *Block* if the item to be drawn only exists once in the drawing. (T/F)
2. You can use Grip Edit to adjust the length of a line. (T/F)
3. Use the Hatch command to draw the brick pattern in elevation. (T/F)
4. When drawing the exterior elevations, the horizontal location for the windows and doors comes from the____________________ drawings.
5. All doors go on the _______________ layer.

Review Questions:

The following questions may be assigned by your instructor as a way to assess your knowledge of this section. Your instructor has the answers to the review questions.

1. The Hatch command does not have very many patterns to select from. (T/F)
2. Redefining a *Block* causes all instances to automatically update. (T/F)
3. You can project lines from another elevation and from the plans to locate where the chimney intersects the sloping roof below it, also referred to as orthographic projection. (T/F)
4. Name the command that links a drawing to the current drawing:

   ____

5. You can select on a hatched area to edit its properties. (T/F)
6. This icon () allows you to ___________________ a *Block*.
7. A 6/12 pitch means for every 12"__________ the roof rises 6"__________
8. Name the Hatch pattern used to draw the brick: ___________________
9. What is the most often used door thickness? ______________________.
10. You should use a *Block* when something in the drawing is repetitive and exactly the same. (T/F)

Self-Exam Answers:
1 – T, **2** – T, **3** – T, **4** – Floor Plan, **5** – DOORS

Additional Tasks:

Task 5-1: Grade Line

Draw the grade lines shown in the images below.

Create a *Layer* named ***Grade*** and set its color to *Magenta.*

Use the **Polyline** command via this icon on the *Draw* panel.

After picking your first point, type **W** for width; enter **4"** (for both the starting width and end width). Alternatively, you can draw the polyline and then adjust the width afterwards using the **Pedit** command (or with the Polyline selected, by adjusting the *Global Width* option in *Properties*).

Draw the grade as close as possible to that shown below. Extend the lines at the corners of the building down to the grade line.

All grade lines should be at the same vertical location for common corners on each of the two elevations showing that corner.

Commands used: Polyline, Pedit, Layer Manager

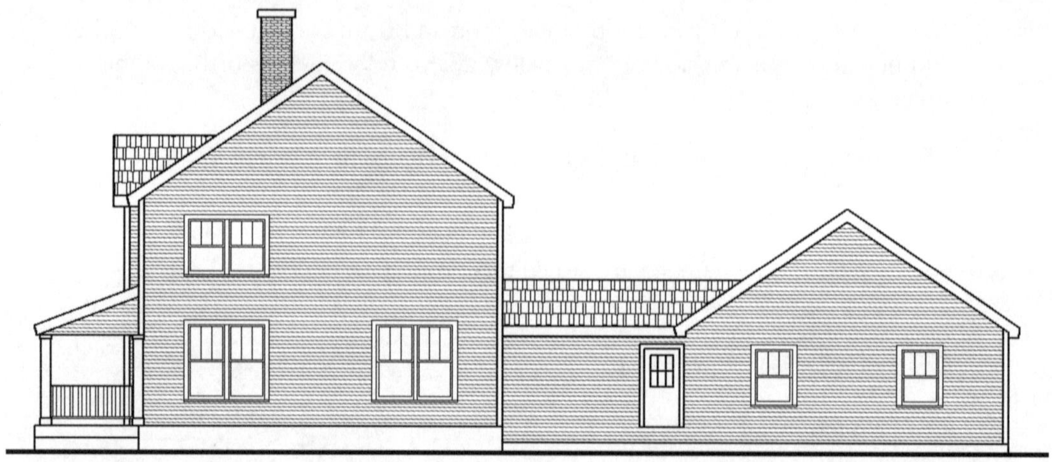

Task 5-1 (1) North elevation with grade line added; grade line is approx. 2′-2″ below porch floor

Task 5-1 (2) East elevation with grade line added; grade line is approx. 2′-2″ below porch floor

Task 5-1 (3) South elevation with grade line added; grade line is approx. 2′-2″ below porch floor

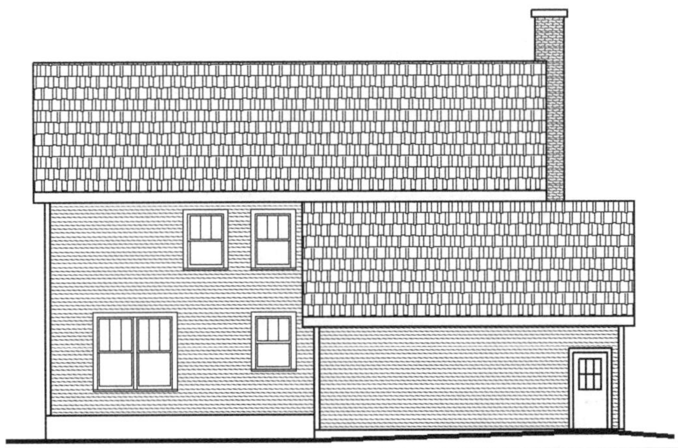

Task 5-1 (4) West elevation with grade line added

Task 5-2: Draw the Other Chimney

Draw the other chimney based on reference lines from the second floor plan and other elevations. Draw as much as you can in each elevation and then use orthographic projection to complete the task.

Draw the same chimney cap and use the same hatch pattern used to draw the first chimney. Do this for all four elevations.

Commands used: Line, Trim, Extend, Hatch

Task 5-2 (1) South elevation with other chimney added

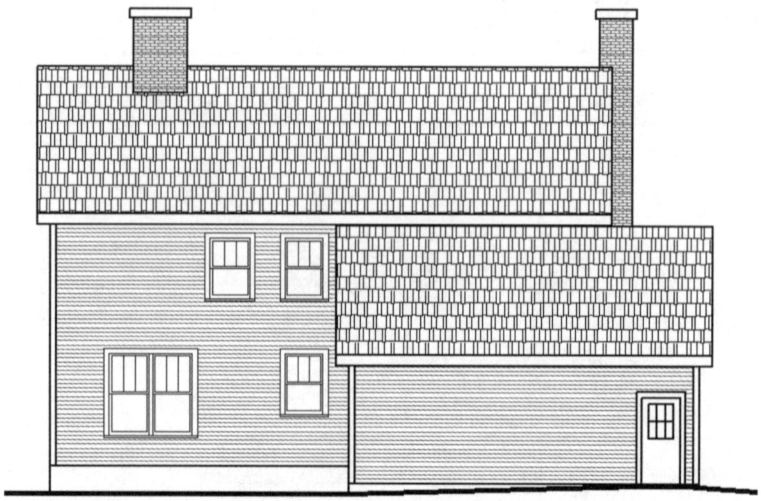

Task 5-2 (2) West elevation with other chimney added

Task 5-3: Print Content from a Website

Using your Internet web browser, print one page of information from one of the websites mentioned in Lesson 5. HAND IN ONLY ONE PAGE.

Task 5-4: Adding Foundation Lines

First you will draw the lines and then adjust the lines so they look dashed.

> *FYI: Dashed lines typically represent lines that are hidden from view but are still helpful to show. The foundation walls and footings are below the ground - so the ground is hiding them. However, they need to be seen on the drawings.*

1. Create a *Layer* named ***Foundation***; set its color to *Red*.

2. Draw the lines as shown below (4 images), and then proceed to Step 3 for instruction on making the lines dashed.

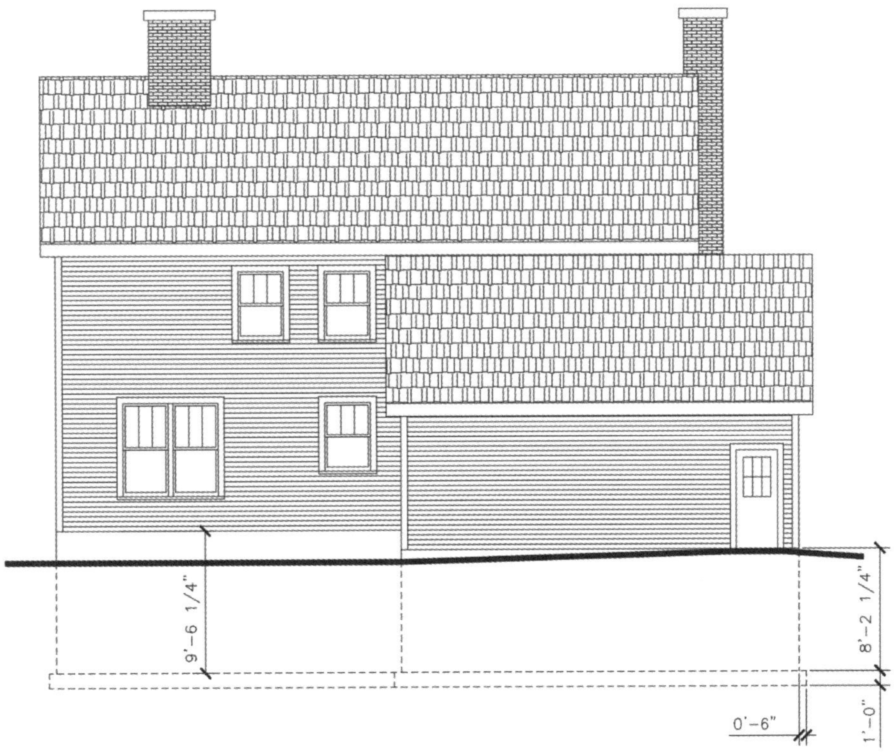

Task 5-4 (1) West elevation with foundation lines added

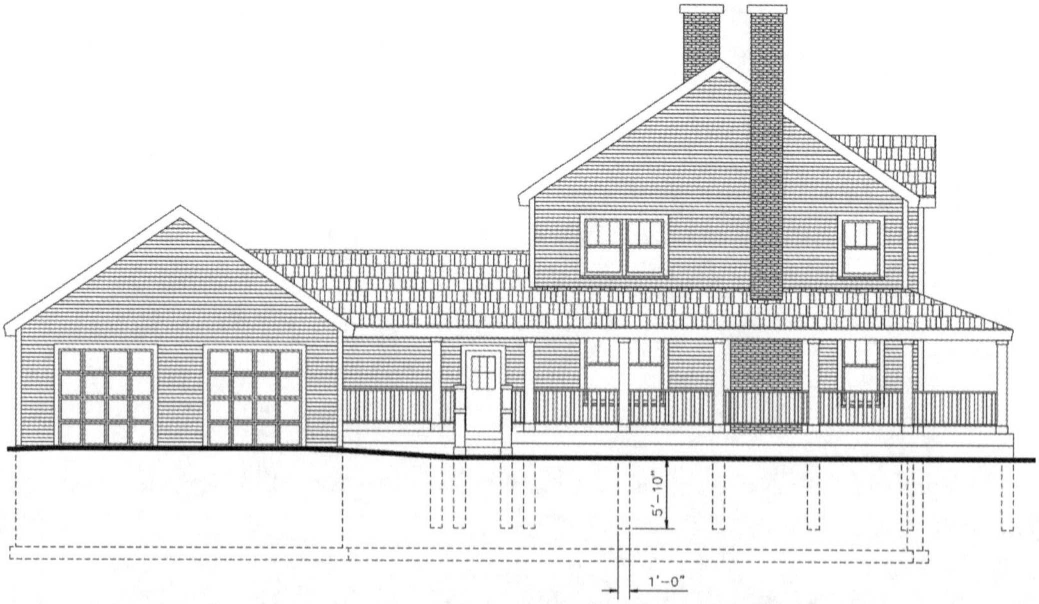

Task 5-4 (2) South Elevation with foundation lines added

Task 5-4 (3) East elevation with foundation lines added

Task 5-4 (4) North elevation with foundation lines added

Creating dashed lines:

3. Open the **Layer Properties Manager**.

4. In the ***Foundation*** (layer name) row, click the linetype name (which should be Continuous at the moment).

You are now in the Select Linetype dialog.

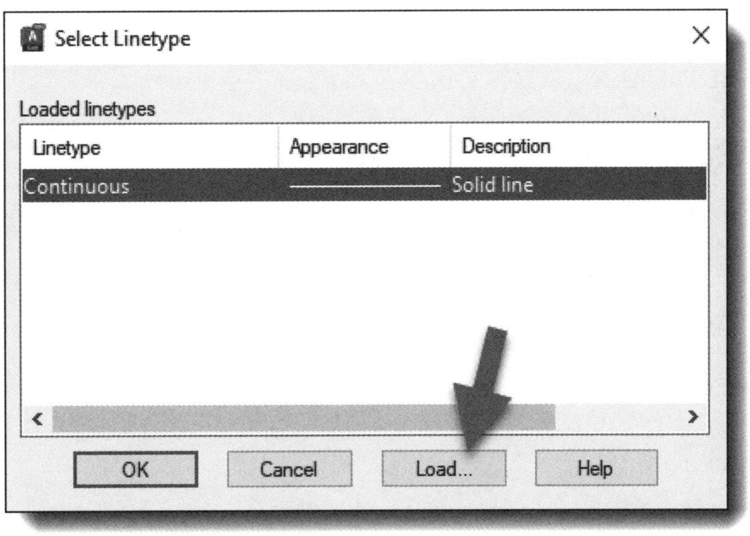

You will notice that the current drawing only has one linetype loaded. Next, you will load another linetype into the current drawing.

5. Click the **Load…** button.

You are now in the Load or Reload Linetypes dialog.

6. Scroll down to the ***HIDDEN2*** linetype; select it and click **OK**.

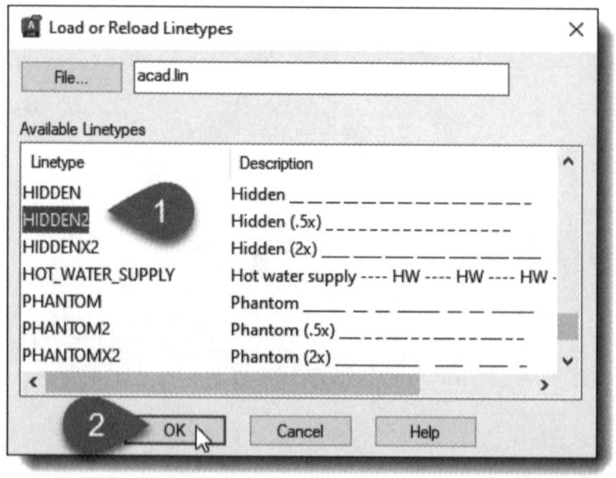

Now, back in the *Select Linetypes* dialog box…

7. Select ***HIDDEN2*** and click **OK**.

8. Click **OK** to close the *Layer Properties Manager.*

The next three system variable adjustments will make the hidden lines correct in both *Model* and *Paper Space.*

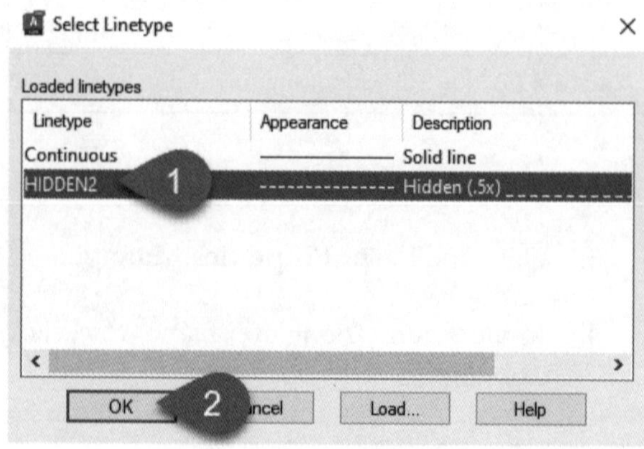

9. Type **LTSCALE** and **Enter**; then type **1** and then **Enter**.

10. Type **PSLTSCALE** and **Enter**; then type **1** and then **Enter**.

11. Type **MSLTSCALE** and **Enter**; then type **1** and then **Enter**.

Next you will set the *Annotation Scale* which controls the spacing of the lines, as well as the size of text and dimensions when set to Annotative.

12. Set the **Annotation Scale** to **1/4″ = 1′-0″**.

13. Type **REGEN** and then **Enter**.

14. **Save** your drawing.

Lesson 6
SECTIONS

In this lesson, you will create simple building and wall sections. A section helps the builder understand how the structure will be constructed and shows vertical relationships, such as the locations of floors and ceilings.

Exercise 6-1:
Building Sections

Introduction:

Building sections show an overall section through the structure.

The building sections are typically the same scale as the exterior elevations.

Because the building section generally has the same outline as one of the exterior elevations, you can copy the elevation and use it as a starting point for your building section.

You will do this next.

Building Section Outline:

1. **Open** your drawing named **Exterior Elevations.dwg**.

2. **Save-As** to a drawing file named **Building Section.dwg**.

3. **Zoom In** on the South elevation (Figure 6-1.1).

4. **Erase** and **Trim** all inner lines to create an outline of the building as shown in **Figure 6-1.2**.

   TIP: The information on the next page starts to get things set up for applying line-weights but does not actually fully implement it. This is covered in more detail later in the book. Please do not worry about adjusting the lineweights column in the Layers Properties Manager.

FIGURE 6-1.1 South elevation drawn in previous lesson

Typical Non-Plan Layers:

Non-plan drawings typically have a handful of *Layers* whose names represent the thickness of the lines drawn on that *Layer.* These drawings do not need the same level of control as floor plans so the layering system is simplified (e.g., you would never need to *Freeze* a layer that contained the steel beams).

The general concept with lineweights is this:

Things in section	Lines should be heavy
Things in elevation	Lines should be a middle-of-the-road (medium) lineweight
Hatch patterns	These are the lightest lines

5. Create the following *Layers* (do not adjust the lightweight column):
   a. ***G-Detl-Hevy*** White Heavy lines
   b. ***G-Detl-Medm*** Green Medium lines
   c. ***G-Detl-Lite*** Red Light lines

6. Modify the remaining lines (in Figure 6-1.2) to the *Layers* just created (i.e., change the outline to *G-Detl-Hevy*, the shingle hatch to *G-Detl-Lite*, etc.).

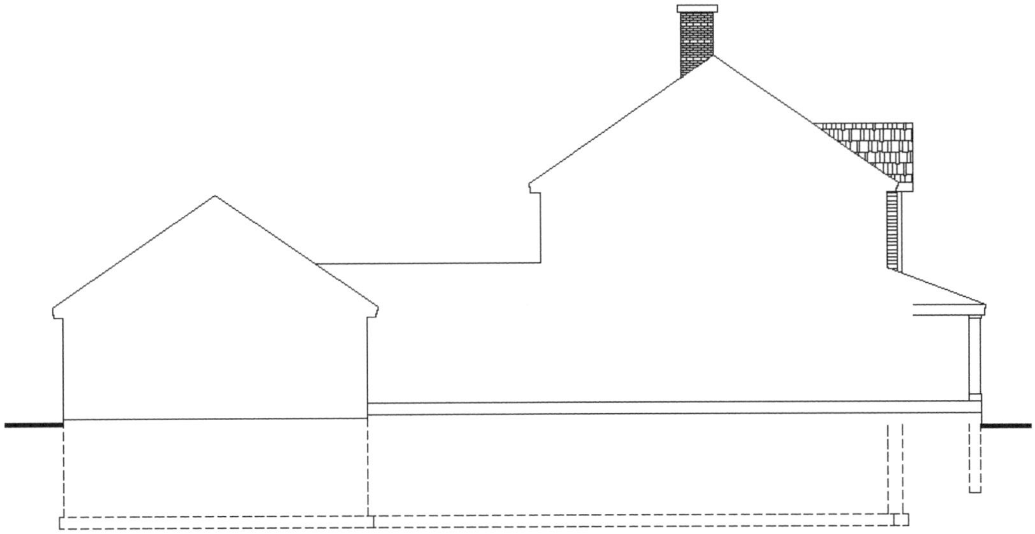

FIGURE 6-1.2 Modified South elevation; outline to start building section

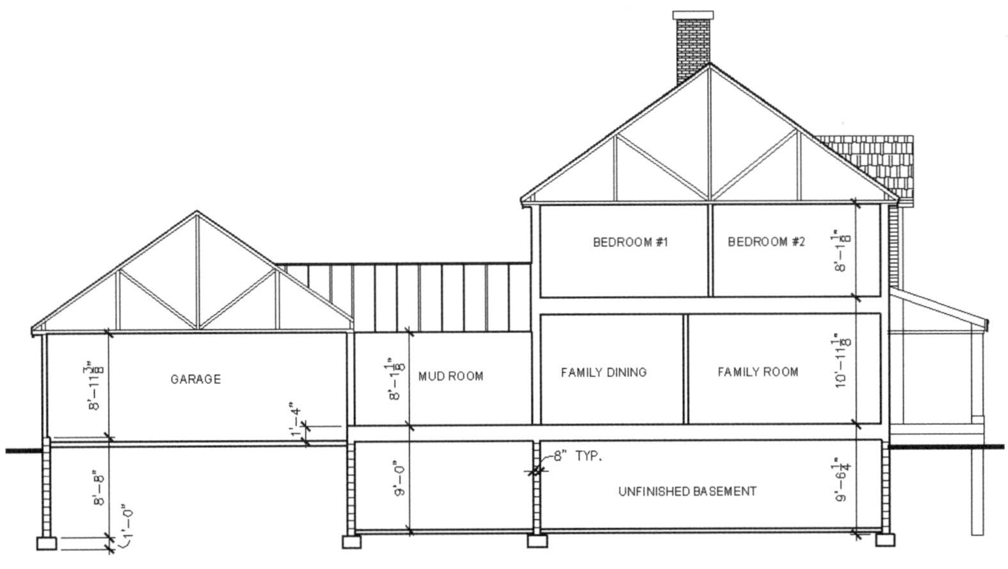

FIGURE 6-1.3 Building Section – see page 6-5 for enlarged drawing

TIP: *Once the sections are developed, you can go back and update the dashed footing and foundations line in your exterior elevations (if needed). Those lines are often approximated when first drawing the elevations and then refined as the sections are developed and other conditions arise.*

7. Begin generating the building section based on the information provided in Figure 6-1.3 and the following guidelines; see Fig. 6-1.5 for enlarged drawing:
   a. The wall thicknesses and locations are to be derived from the Xref'ed floor plans (See Figure 6-1.4).
      NOTE: *The heavy dashed line below represents the section location.*
   b. Make the footings (below the foundation walls) 1'-8" wide.
   c. The first and second floor thickness is 1-4¾"; the top of the concrete block foundation wall starts 1½" below the floor thickness (to accommodate a 2x wood nailer; see Figure 6-2.3).
   d. The two trusses (shown in elevation) have equally spaced vertical members with the diagonals drawn last (all 2x4 framing – i.e., 3½" with 2x6 top cord).
   e. Trusses shown over Mud Room: 2x4s (i.e., 1½") at 2'-0"o.c.
   f. The horizontal lines in the foundation wall are 8" apart, which represents the individual concrete masonry units (CMU).
   g. Draw the dimensions shown.
   h. Dimensions at the ceiling are to the bottom of the truss; draw a ½" thick gypsum board ceiling below the trusses.
   i. The garage/basement slabs are 5" thick.
   j. Add the room labels. ***TIP:*** *Copy them from the floor plans.*
   k. Extend the truss lines into the overhang/fascia area (simple).

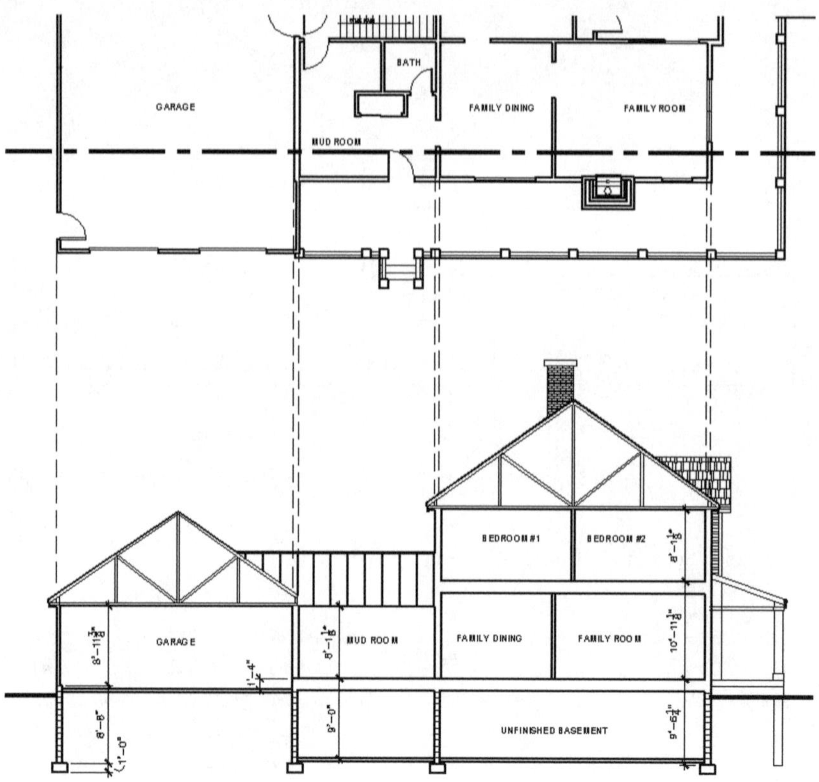

FIGURE 6-1.4 Building Section; with Xref'ed plan and temp. reference lines

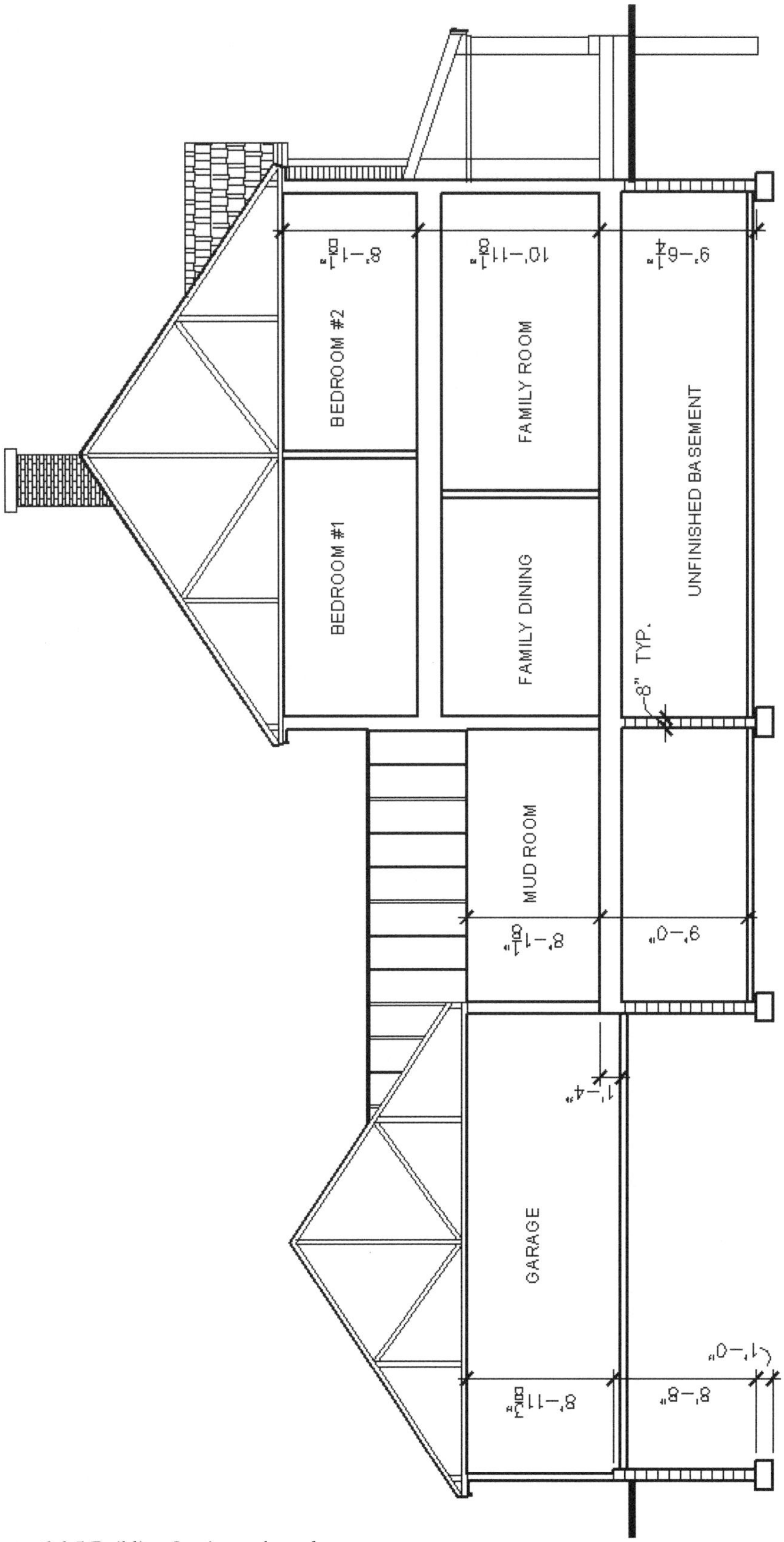

FIGURE 6-1.5 Building Section enlarged

Exercise 6-2:
Typical Wall Section

Introduction:

Wall sections are similar to building sections in that they show how a building is constructed and the vertical relationships (e.g., floor-to-floor heights). The difference between a wall section and a building section is implied by their names; a wall section is just one wall in section, and a building section is a section through the entire building. Wall sections are also drawn at a larger scale than building sections.

On smaller projects, where the building section can be drawn larger, you may not need a wall section because everything can be clearly drawn and noted on the building sections.

The wall sections are typically made as large as possible so they still fit on the sheet. Occasionally, a large repetitious area will be removed with break lines to allow the section to be larger (see Figure 6-2.1).

Wall sections are usually started after the building sections have been substantially developed. You can use the linework from the building section to start your wall section.

You will do this next.

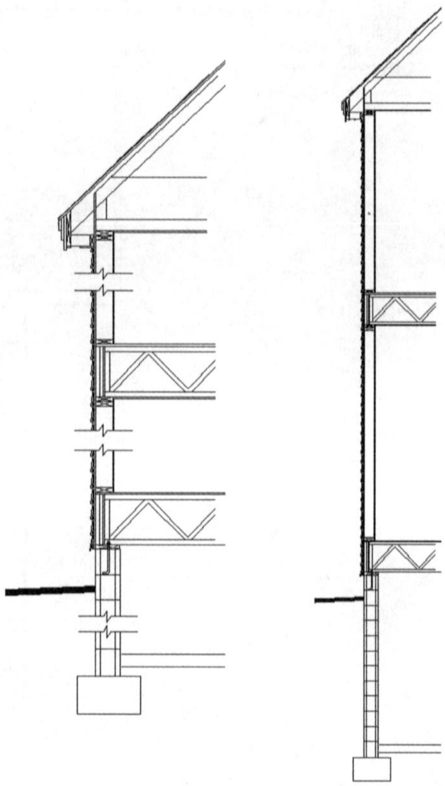

FIGURE 6-2.1 Wall section with break lines and section without. Note that section with break lines is larger.

Wall Section Linework:

1. **Open** your drawing named **Building Section.dwg**.

2. **Save-As** to a drawing file named **Wall Section.dwg**.

3. Erase and Trim portions of the building section so it looks similar to the ½″ = 1′-0″ wall section shown in Figure 6-2.1.

   TIP: Draw a temporary vertical line to trim to.

4. Use the same *Layers* as Exercise 6-1.

You are now ready to begin developing the wall section. Your section will look similar to Figure 6-2.2. You will use the information in the enlarged details, Figures 6-2.3 and 6-2.4, to draw the wall section.

5. Draw the wall section shown in **Figure 6-2.2** per the following information:

   a. Use the information in the roof edge detail (**Figure 6-2.4**) to draw items, such as the roof sheathing and gypsum board, the correct size.

   b. Use the information in the rim joist detail (**Figure 6-2.3**) to draw the joist, siding, floor sheathing and sill plate.

   c. Draw the second floor rim joist condition based on the information provided in the similar condition identified in item "b" above (Figure 6-2.4).

   d. Do not add any notes or dimensions at this time.

6. **Save** your drawing.

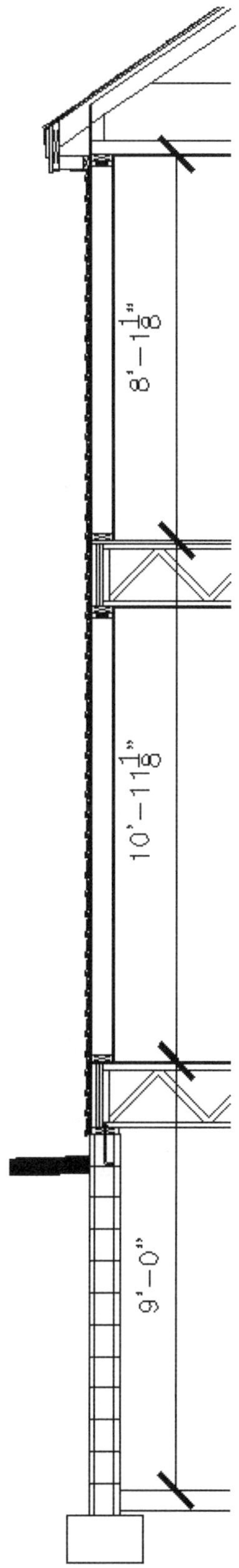

FIGURE 6-2.2
Wall section to be drawn in this exercise.

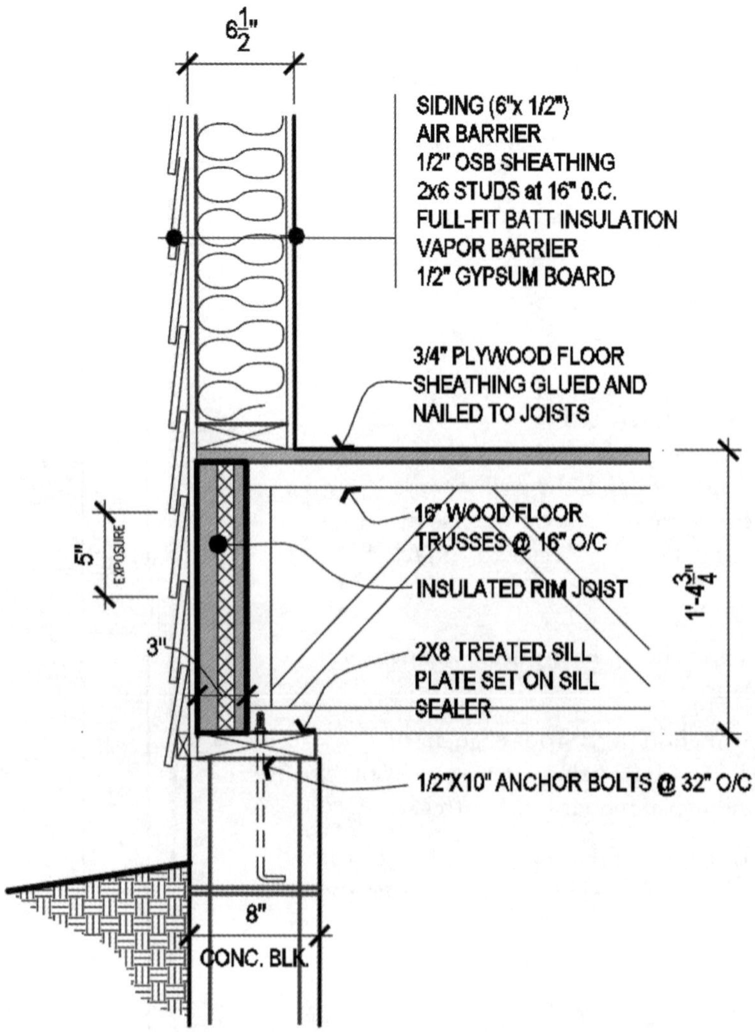

FIGURE 6-2.3 Rim joist detail

NOTES ON THE RIM JOIST DETAIL

The 2x8 sill plate creates a flat surface for the joists to sit on and be nailed to. The sill plate is set on a foam **sill sealer** that fills the voids between the irregular concrete block and the smooth wood, which helps to decrease air infiltration. The L-shaped anchor bolts are set in grout and help hold the sill plate down (with a nut and washer on top).

The first siding board rests on a "starter strip" which places the board at the correct angle (which matches the other boards above).

The air barrier goes on just before the siding; it helps to reduce air infiltration into the building. Air barriers allow moisture to pass through; this is not a vapor barrier.

The vapor barrier goes just behind the finish (on the warm side of the wall). This prevents moisture from condensing within the wall. Avoid double vapor barriers as the moisture cannot escape and creates mold. This is why air barriers are not vapor barriers.

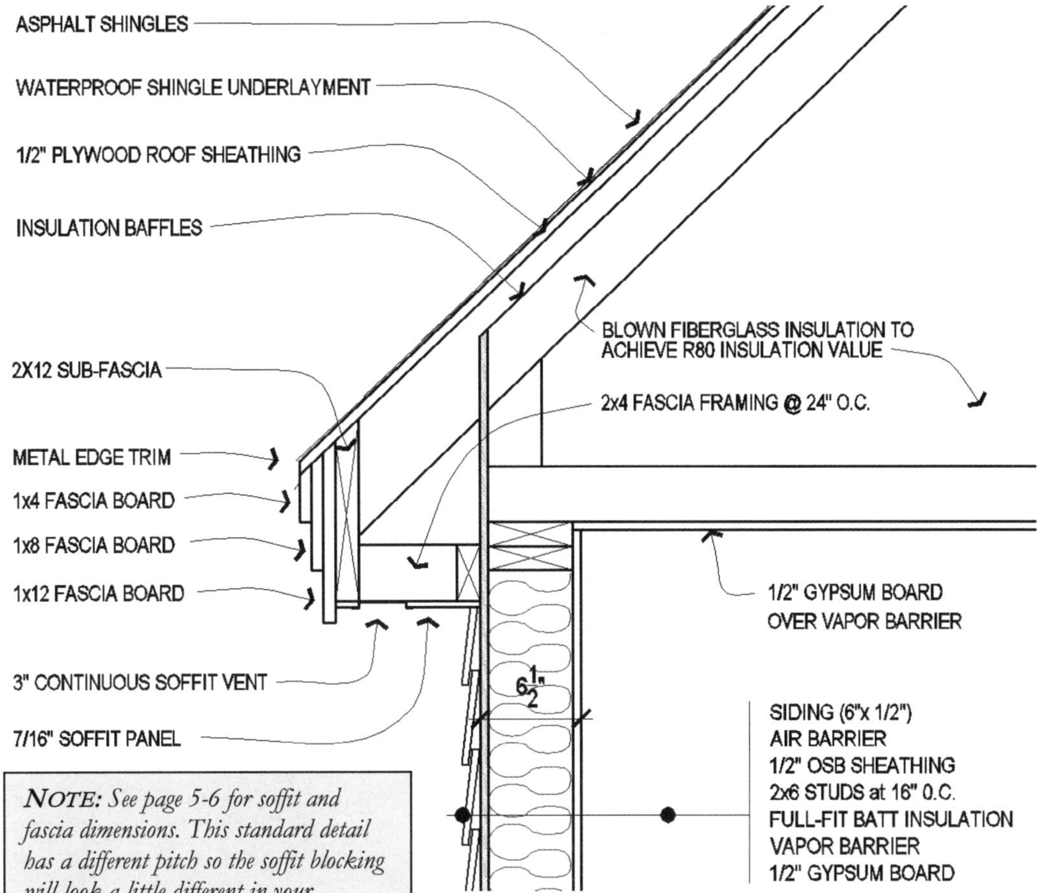

NOTE: See page 5-6 for soffit and fascia dimensions. This standard detail has a different pitch so the soffit blocking will look a little different in your drawing.

FIGURE 6-2.4 Roof edge detail

NOTES ON THE ROOF EDGE DETAIL

The "waterproof shingle underlayment" (i.e., Ice and Water Shield) is required on overhangs and valleys in colder climates. This helps prevent melted snow, which freezes at overhangs and then backs up under the shingles, from leaking through the roof sheathing. This product is occasionally applied over the entire roof in place of felt to create a second layer of waterproofing on the roof.

The insulation baffles are thin panels attached between the trusses. The baffles maintain an air space between the roof sheathing and the blown-in attic insulation. The air space helps keep the underside of the roof sheathing at the same temperature as the top side, which helps prevent ice-damming.

The soffit vent allows outside air into the attic space. This helps the attic space to maintain the same temperature as the outside air, which reduces the possibility of condensation at the shingles/sheathing plane; this helps to prevent mold.

Similar to the wall condition, the vapor barriers go just behind the finish (on the warm side of the ceiling), between the truss and the gypsum board in this case.

Exercise 6-3:
Adding Annotation to Wall Section

In this exercise, you will add notes and dimensions to your wall section.

1. **Open wall section.dwg** drawing file.

2. Create a new *Layer* named ***G-Anno-Text***; set the color to *Cyan.*

3. Setting up a drawing for text.

   - The ideal way to work with text in AutoCAD requires a few settings be adjusted first. This will have to be done in each new drawing but could be set up in an office template file in the workplace.

   - Once things are set up properly, any text added will automatically be the correct height based on the intended plot scale. If the plot scale (i.e., annotation scale) is changed, all the text in the drawing will be updated to the correct height.

   - Specific steps to perform:
     - On the *Application Menu* → *Drawing Utilities,* select the **Units** tool from the fly-out list (see image to right).
     - Set the precision to **0'-0 1/32"**.
     - Click **OK** to save the change.

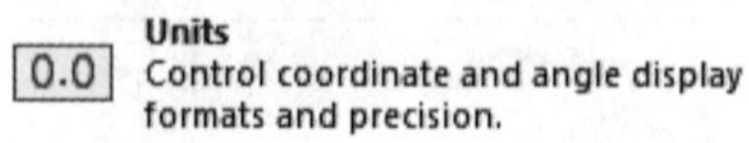

Additional steps to perform:

4. On the *Annotate* tab, in the *Text* panel, click the **Text Style** link (small arrow in the lower right corner). You are now in the dialog box shown on the next page.

   - In the *Text Style* dialog, select **Roman** under *Styles* (it should already be selected).

   - In the *Size* area, check **Annotative** and set the *Paper text height* to **3/32"**. (This is the size the text will be on paper, regardless of the drawing scale.)

   - Click **Set Current**, and then click **Yes** if prompted to save changes.
     FYI: This will make it the default text style.

   - Click **Apply** and then **Close**.
     FYI: The Cancel *button becomes the* Close *button when something changes in the dialog.*

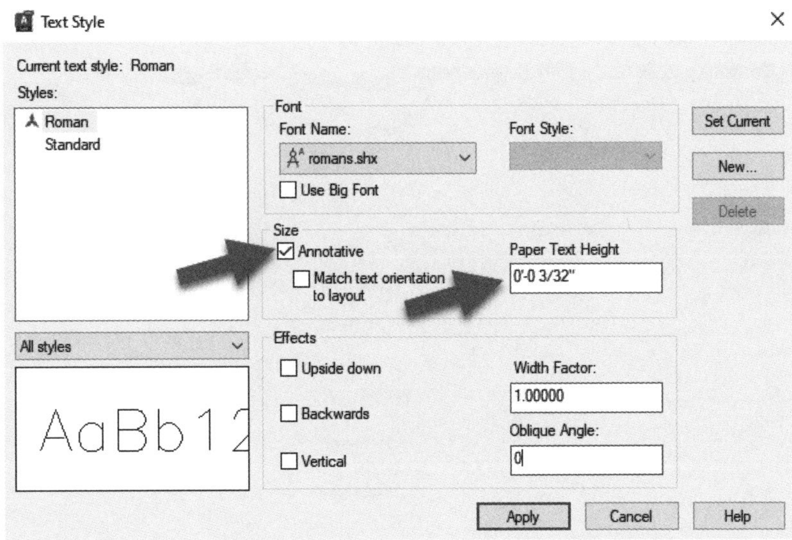

5. At the bottom of the screen, on the *Status Bar*, make sure that the **Show annotation objects** and **Add scales…** is active; when they are a glowing blue, they are active.

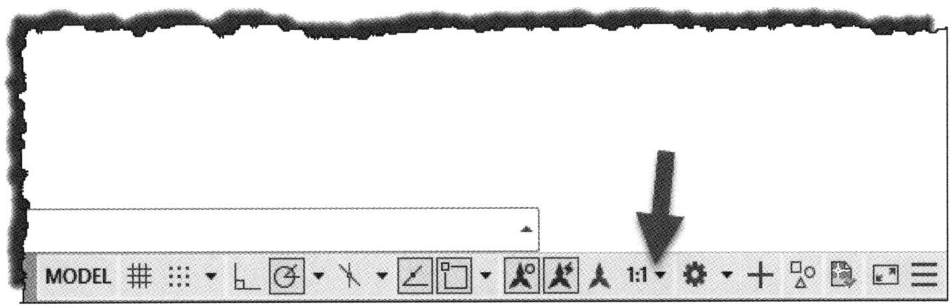

6. Just to the right of the previous item, click the *Annotation Scale* listed (should be 1:1) and select **½″=1′-0″** from the list (see image on next page).

Now, when you add text to this drawing, the height will automatically be set based on the scale selected at the bottom of the screen; this scale can be changed on-the-fly, instantly updating the height of all text in the drawing. You will try this next.

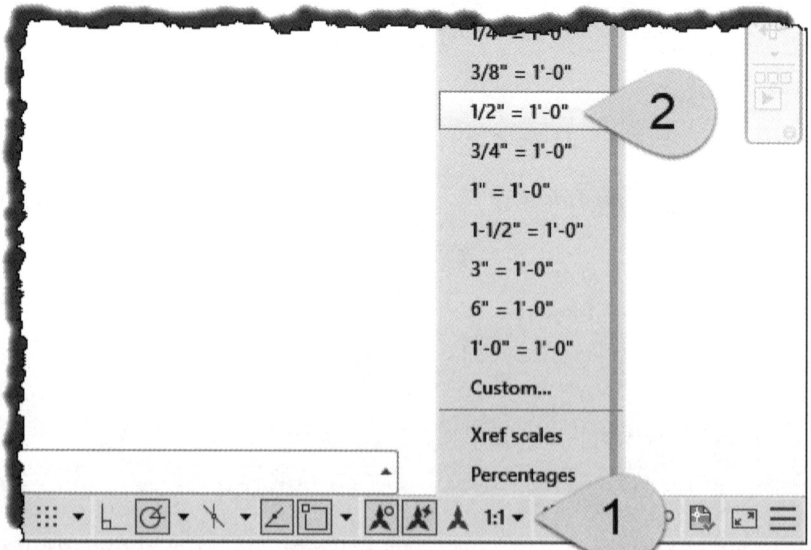

The previous steps allow you to add text to your wall section at the proper scale. This is meant for any *Multiline Text* (without leaders). For notes that point to something, you will use a *Multileader,* which allows you to add the arrows, lines, and text all as one object. You can also use the *Multileader* align tool (see icon to the right) to make sure the notes line up.

7. Add the notes for the wall construction shown in **Figure 6-3.1**:
    a. Use the **Multileader** command (Annotate tab).
    b. Place all text on *Layer **G-Anno-Text**.*
    c. All text to be aligned as shown.
    d. Adjust the *Multileader Style* settings; refer back to page 4-55 if needed for more information.

8. Add the four dimensions shown in Figure 6-3.1; draw them on *Layer **G-Anno-Dims*** (color 30). Be sure to set up the *Dimension Style*; see page 4-45 if needed.

9. **Save** your drawing.

Try changing the *Annotation Scale* (see image above) to see the notes and dimensions update automatically; make sure to Undo these changes before moving on (i.e., set the Annotation Scale to ½″ = 1′-0″).

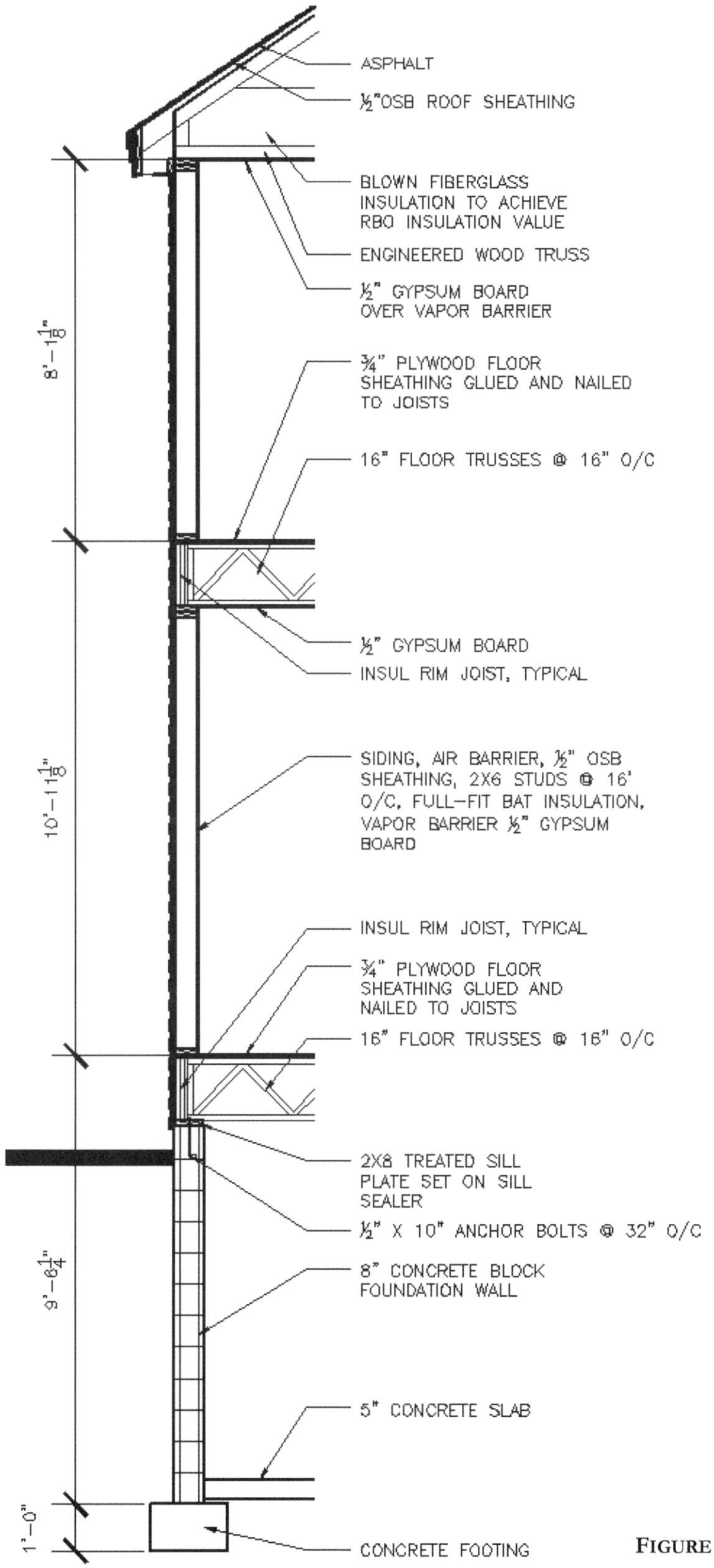

FIGURE 6-3.1 Wall Section

Exercise 6-4:
Stair Section

In this exercise, you will draw and dimension a simple stair section.

1. **Open** the **building section.dwg** drawing file.

You will draw a simple profile of a stair in this exercise. Unless the stair is very complex or unique in some way, you do not need to draw a large-scale section because contractors build stairs regularly, and lumber yards sell standard treads and risers that simplify the construction process.

First, you will use an Xref'ed first floor plan to locate the first riser.

2. Align the first floor plan with your building section and extend a line from the top riser (in plan) to the building section (Figure 6-4.1).

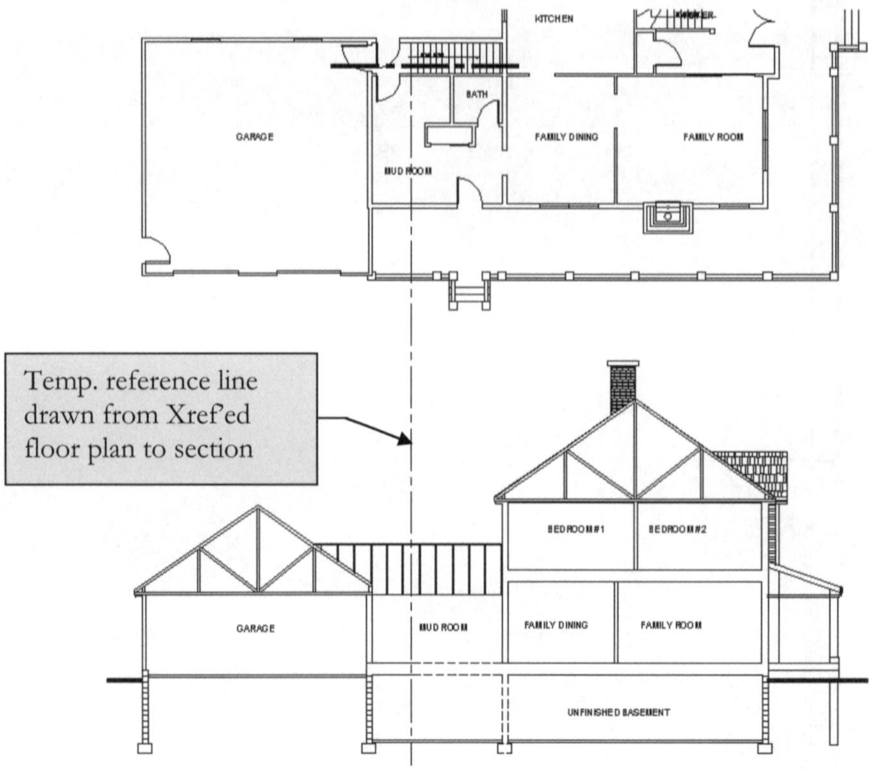

FIGURE 6-4.1 Building section with line extended from plan to locate top riser

3. Erase the portion of floor and wall shown dashed in Figure 6-4.1.

   ***FYI:** Looking back at the basement floor plans, you will notice there is no wall where you are deleting the basement wall; the floor and wall above will be supported by a steel beam due to the heavy load.*

4. Modify the remaining linework to look like Figure 6-4.2; draw the steel beam per the following information:

   a. Add the steel beam on *Layer G-Detl-Hevy.*

   b. Use the enlarged beam drawing for dimensional information only; do not draw the larger beam.

   c. Center the beam on the wall above.

   d. The top of the beam should be directly under the floor sheathing, i.e., ¾″ below the first floor line.

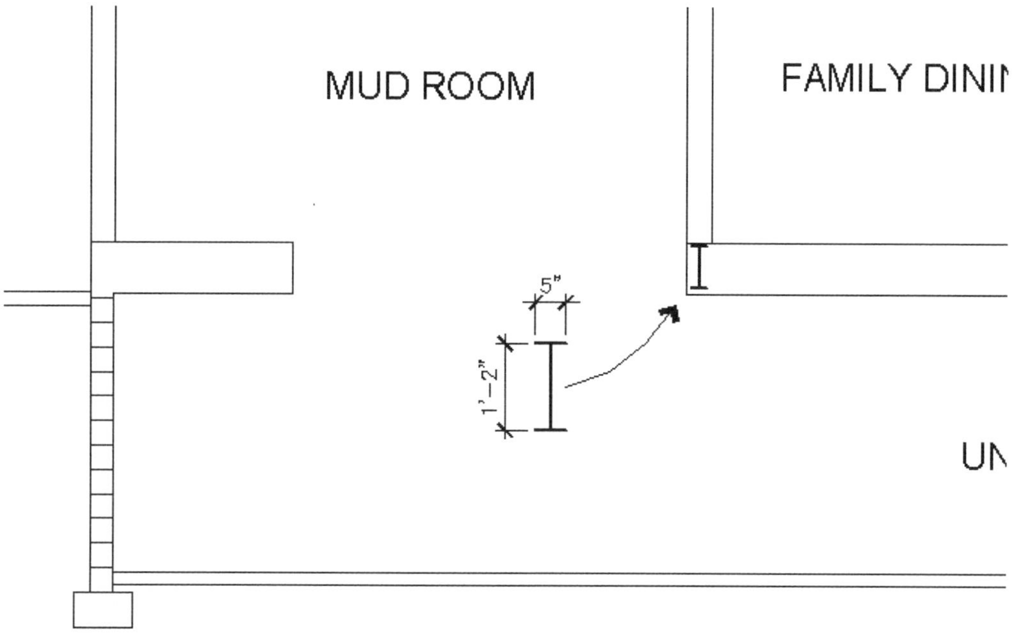

FIGURE 6-4.2 Building section with line extended from plan to locate top riser

Sizing the beam and floor trusses is beyond the scope of this tutorial. The same is true for the vertical position of the beam, but note the following points. The beam is either below the floor truss (or joist) so the floor truss can bear on it similar to the way it bears on a wall, or the beam is "upset" within the floor truss system as in our example above. An "upset" beam creates a special bearing condition for the floor truss. The floor truss needs to be top cord bearing or steel brackets can be hung off the steel beam that supports the bottom edge of the floor truss. This condition allows for more headroom.

Calculate Tread/Riser Size:

The *riser* is typically calculated to be as large as building codes will allow. Occasionally, a grand stair will have a smaller riser to create a more elegant stair.

Similarly, the *tread* is usually designed to be as small as allowable by building codes.

The largest riser and shortest tread results in the steepest stair allowed. This takes up less floor space (see **Figure 6-4.3**). A stairway that is too steep is uncomfortable and unsafe.

Building codes vary by location; for this exercise, you will use 7″ (max.) for the risers and 9″ (min.) for the treads.

Codes usually require that each tread be the same size, likewise with risers.

Calculate the number and size of the risers:

Given:
 Risers: **7″** max.
 Floor to floor height: **9′-0″** (from Exercise 6-1)

Calculate the number of risers:
 9′-0″ divided by 7″ (or 109″divided by 7″) = 15.429

Since each riser must be the same size, we will have to round to a whole number. You cannot round down, as that would make the riser larger than the allowed maximum (9′-0″ / 15 = 7.2″). Therefore, you have to round up to 16. Thus: 9′-0″ divided by 16 = 6.75.

So you need **16** risers, each 6¾.

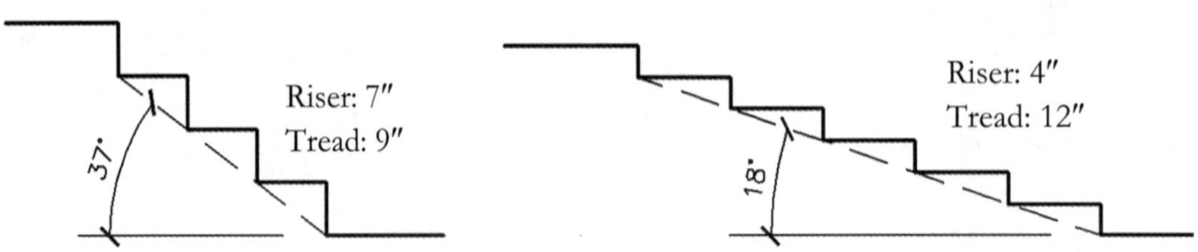

FIGURE 6-4.3 Stair rise / run comparison

Drawing the Tread/Riser Profile:

Next, you will use the Array command to create several lines appropriately spaced.

5. Use the **Array** command to "copy" the top concrete slab line up to create the tread lines:
    a. Select the **Rectangular Array** icon.
    b. **Select** the top line of the concrete basement floor slab.
    c. **Right-click** (to indicate you are done selecting items to array).
    d. On the *Array Creation* contextual tab:
        i. Type **16** for number of *Rows.*
        ii. Type **6.75** for the row *Spacing.*
        iii. Type **1** for number of *Columns.*
        iv. Click **Close Array**.

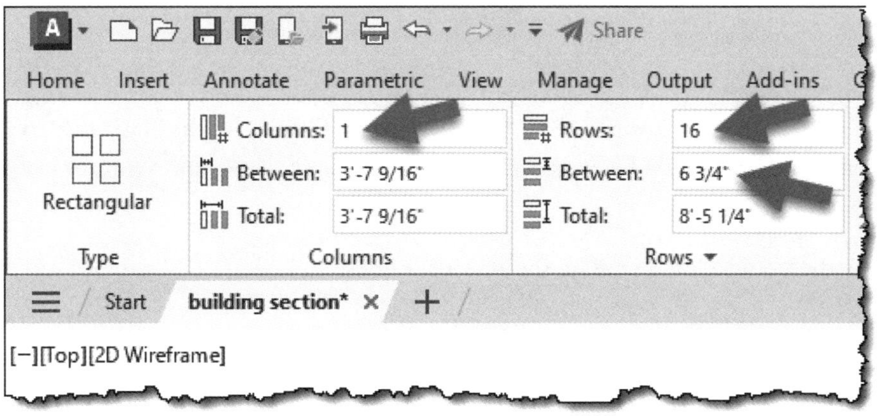

FIGURE 6-4.4 Array options on the Ribbon

You should now have horizontal lines as shown in Figure 6-4.5.

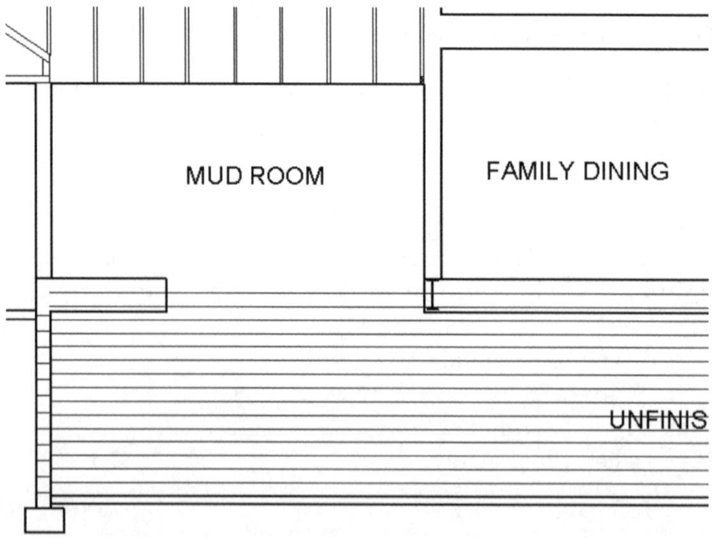

FIGURE 6-4.5 Horizontal lines arrayed to aid in creating stair profile

Here is an example of another use for the *Array* tool: Notice that if you set the *Row Offset* to 8″ in the Array command, you could have drawn the concrete block in elevation (on the foundation wall beyond).

Next you will array the vertical line to create the stair riser lines.

6. Array a vertical line to the right (you will need to draw one first):
   a. Columns: **16**
   b. Column offset: **9″**
   c. See Figure 6-4.6

Your drawing should now have the lines necessary to create the stair profile (see Figure 6-4.6).

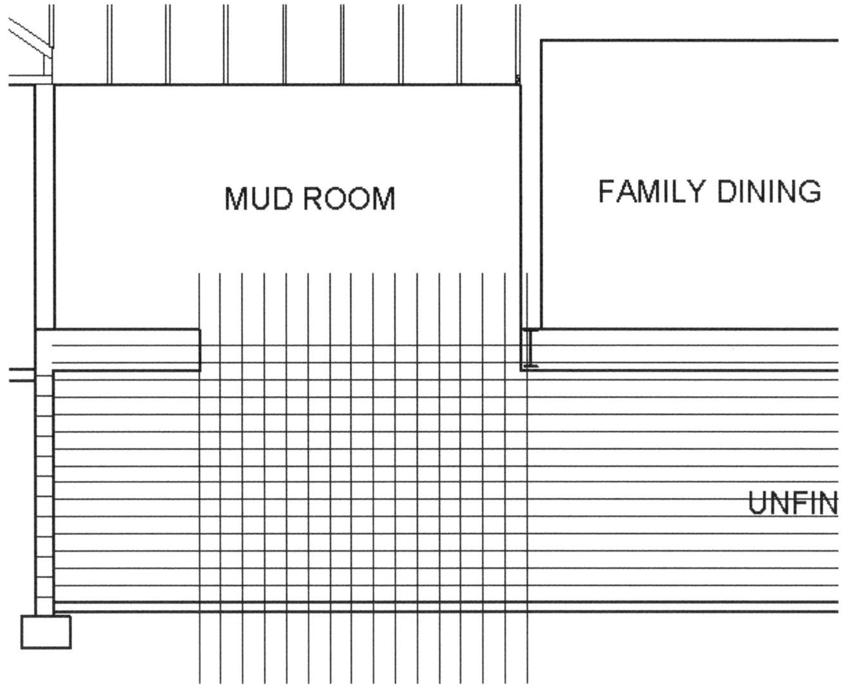

FIGURE 6-4.6 Vertical lines arrayed to aid in creating stair profile

Before you can modify the lines produced by the *Array* you need to explode it. Currently selecting any line will bring the *Array* tab back on the *Ribbon*. Once exploded, you will just have lines and not an *Array*.

7. Select **Home → Modify → Explode**, and then select one of the lines in the array (see image to the right).

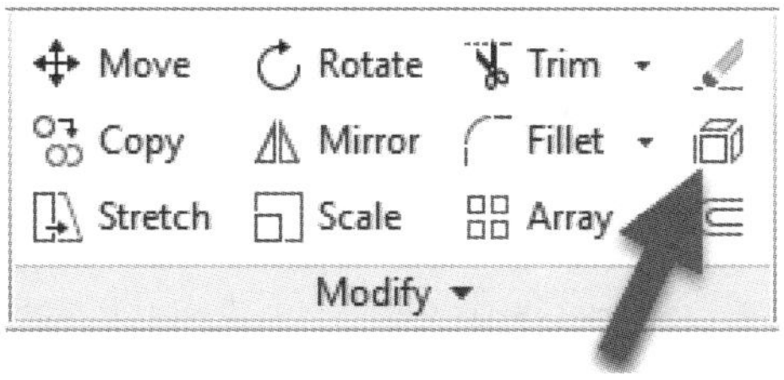

Finally, you need to modify the linework so it looks like a stair. The following image has the stair profile superimposed over the temporary reference lines to help you understand the task at hand (Figure 6-4.7).

8. Use the **Trim** or **Fillet** command to create the stair profile shown in **Figure 6-4.7**.

FYI: The original grid has been left as a background underlay (in Figure 6-4.7) so you can see the start point (i.e., the grid), and the end point (i.e., the stair profile). When you are done using the Trim command, only the stair profile will remain.

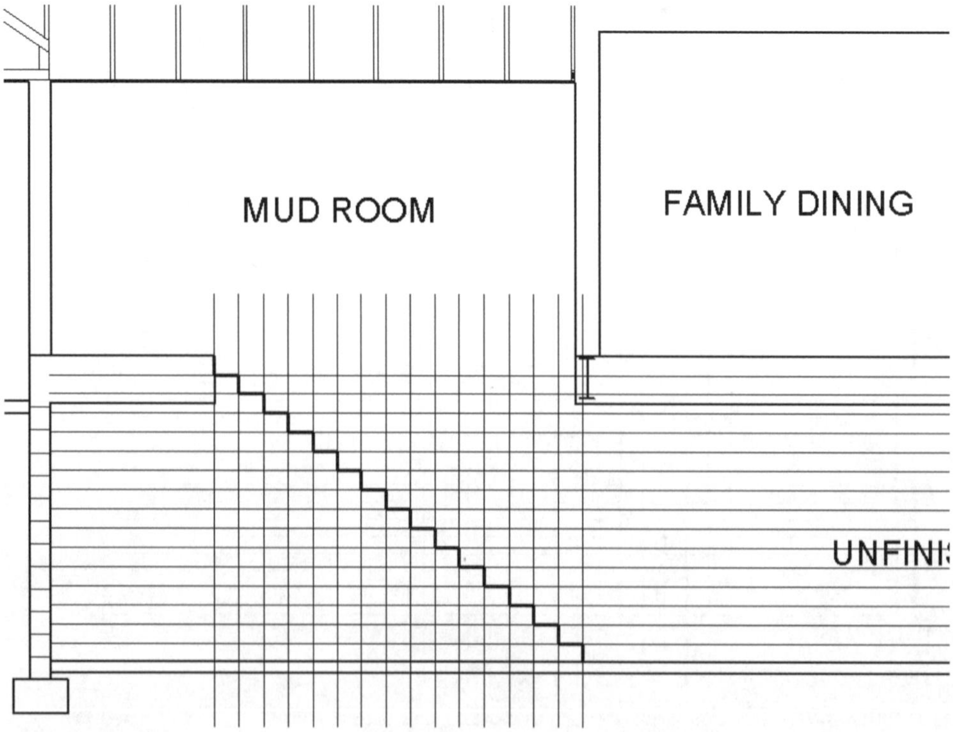

FIGURE 6-4.7 Vertical and Horizontal lines with desired stair profile superimposed

If you want to show more detail in the stair section, you can do so by using the following information as a guide (also see the Additional Tasks for even more detailed information):

- **Tread** thickness: 1⅛″ (offset the profile line downward)
- **Riser** thickness: ¾″ (offset the profile line, horizontally, in the up-run direction)
- Show a **stringer** line below the stair profile, usually cut from a 2x12 (***FYI:*** *Actual size of a 2x12 is 1½″ x 11¼″*). Draw a Line from the top nosing to the bottom nosing, Offset it downward 11¼″ and then Erase the first line. (See Additional Task 6-4 for more information.)
- Before erasing the line mentioned in the previous item, you can also Copy (not Offset) that line vertically, and upward 6′-8″ to make sure you have plenty of **headroom** (code minimums vary on this).
- A 1½″ **handrail** can be shown 30″–34″ above the treads (check local code; many also require that the handrail ends return to the wall).

Stair Annotation and Dimensions:

To complete this exercise you will create a note and two dimensions.

9. Add the **Multileader** shown in Figure 6-4.8:
    a. Set the **Annotation Scale** to **¼″ = 1′-0″**
    b. You can modify the *Multileader Style* if you would like to use curved leader lines as shown.
    c. Text should read **WOOD STAIR WITH THREE 2x12 STRINGERS AND A WALL MOUNTED HANDRAIL**.

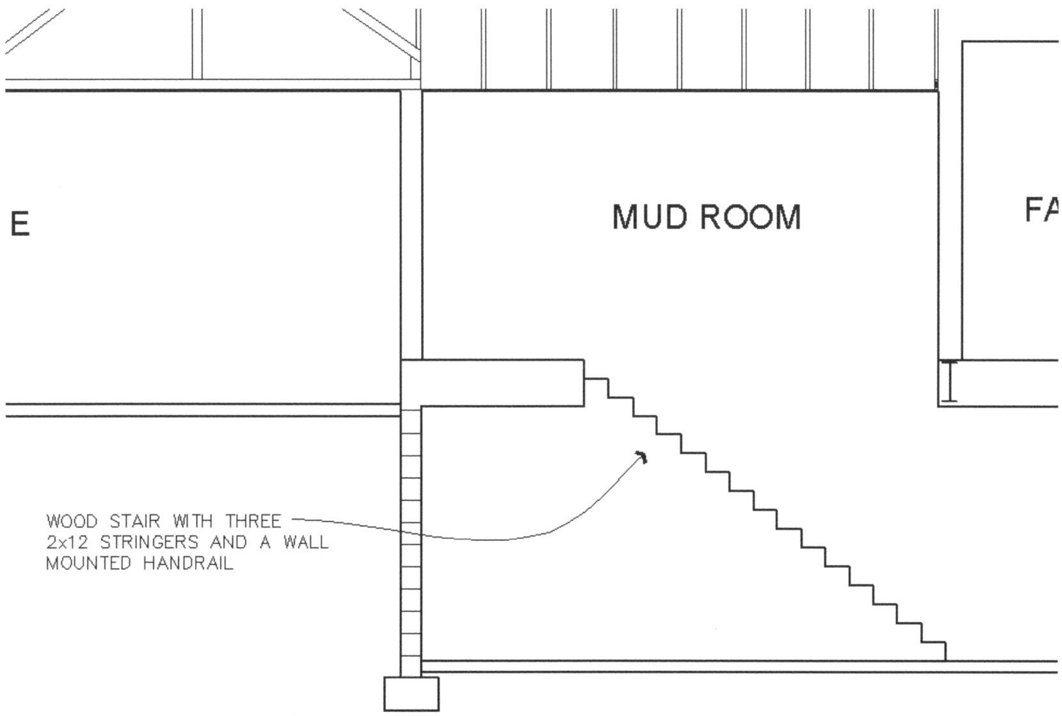

FIGURE 6-4.8 Annotation added to section

Next you will add dimensions to your stair and learn how to add additional text to the dimension line.

10. Add a horizontal and vertical dimension (linear), as shown in Figure 6-4.9.

Next you will modify the dimension line text.

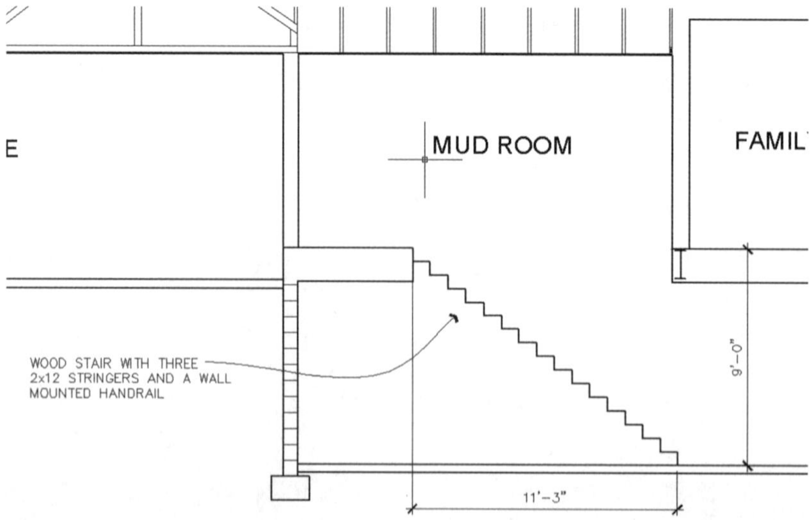

FIGURE 6-4.9 Two dimensions added to section

11. Select the horizontal dimension line.

12. Right-click and select **Properties**.

13. Locate the *Text Override* field and enter the following (Figure 6-4.10):
    15T. @ 9" = <>

    NOTE: *The line just typed means the stair has 15 treads that are 9"; all added together you get 11'-3". The <> symbol tells AutoCAD to insert the current dimension (try stretching the dimension to see the number change).*

14. Similarly, modify the vertical dimension to read (Figure 6-4.11):
    16R. @ 6¾"= <>

    TIP: *If you double-click on the dimension text you can edit it there as well (see image below).*

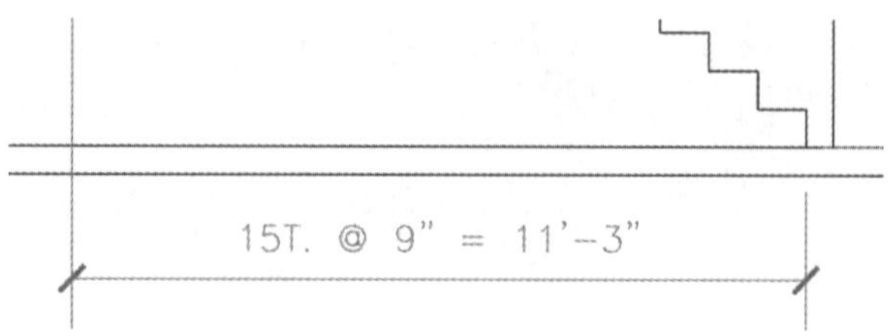

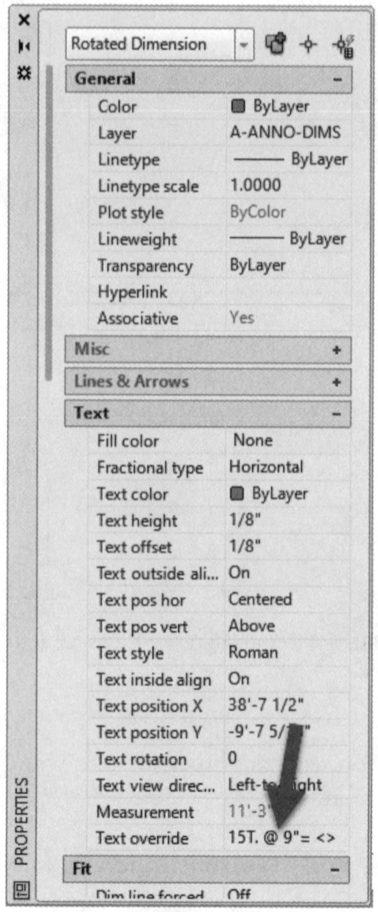

FIGURE 6-4.10 Properties; horizontal dimension selected

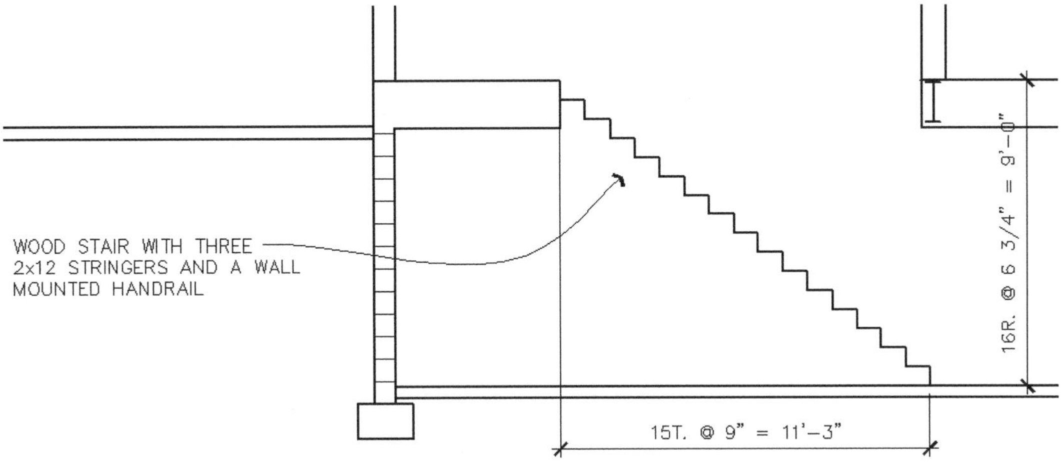

FIGURE 6-4.11 Stair with modified dimensions

15. **Save** your building section drawing.

16. Now go back and update your basement floor plan so the first riser coincides with the stair section just developed. This is not unusual, as you may not know the floor to floor height when you start designing the floor plan. A corrected version of the plan is shown below (Figure 6-4.12). Note the wall has not been modified, which is fine as sometimes having the last few steps open helps with moving furniture.

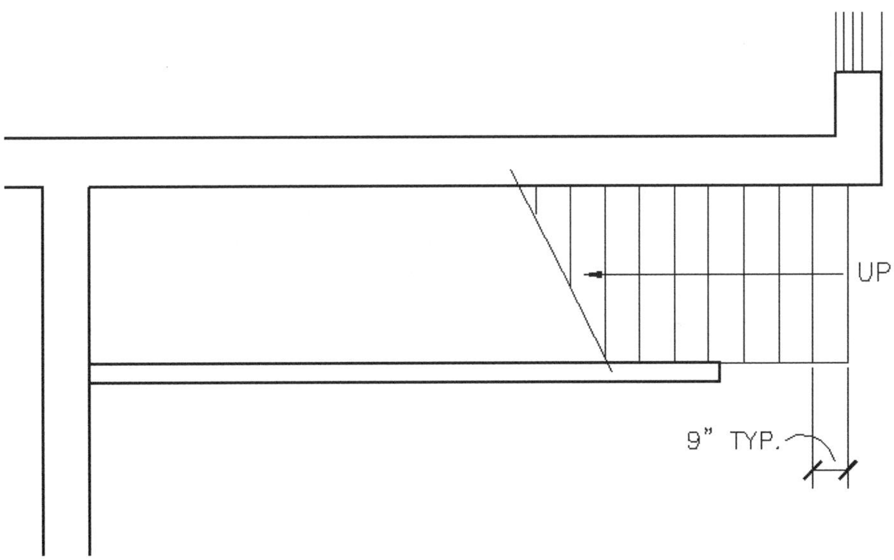

FIGURE 6-4.12 Basement floor plan updated to match stair section

Self-Exam:

The following questions can be used as a way to check your knowledge of this lesson. The answers can be found at the bottom of this page.

1. The *Layer* name in non-plan drawings relates to the thickness of lines on that *Layer*. (T/F)
2. You can Xref the plans to locate interior walls in your building sections. (T/F)
3. You should know what scale a wall section will be printed at before adding text and dimensions so its size is correct. (T/F)
4. What is the feature that controls the size of dimensions?_______________.
5. The Leader command can also add text. (T/F)

Review Questions:

The following questions may be assigned by your instructor as a way to assess your knowledge of this section. Your instructor has the answers to the review questions.

1. A vapor barrier is installed on the cold side of a wall. (T/F)
2. A wall section is typically as large as possible and still fit on the sheet. (T/F)
3. Lineweights help drawings to be more readable. (T/F)
4. Name the three non-plan *Layers* created in this Lesson:

   _______________ _______________ _______________.
5. A *Sill Sealer* helps to reduce air infiltration into a building. (T/F)
6. What command was used to locate the stair treads quickly?_______________.
7. What command creates an arrow with a line behind it? _______________.
8. What command allows you to set the drawing precision? _______________.
9. What *Layer* should text go on in section drawings? _______________.
10. Things in section are the lightest lines in a drawing. (T/F)

SELF-EXAM ANSWERS:
1 – T, **2** – T, **3** – T, **4** – Annotation Scale, **5** – T

Additional Tasks:

Task 6-1: Additional Building Sections

Draw additional building sections, using the exterior elevations as a starting point similar to exercise (Task 6-1). This section is through the front entry. The image below shows a double-stud super-insulated exterior wall system. (You can use the typical exterior wall in your building section.)

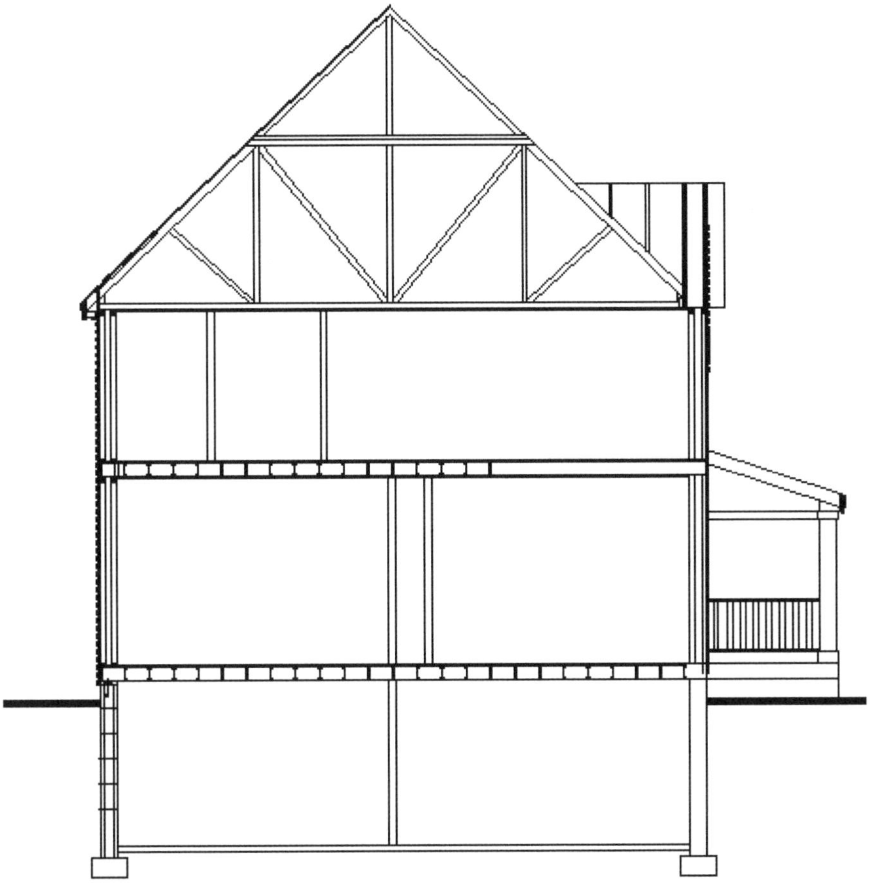

Task 6-1 Building Section (section centered on front door / dormer)

Task 6-2: Wall Section at Garage

Draw a wall section at the garage (similar to exercise 6-2).

> *TIP: Remember the exterior garage walls only have 2x4 walls.*

Task 6-3: Hatch Wall Sections

Per your instructor's direction, add hatching to your section (e.g., concrete block, concrete footing, and batt insulation).

Task 6-4: Stair Detail

In a new drawing file, draw the stair detail shown below; add the notes and dimensions shown. For the purpose of determining the text height and *Dimscale* setting, the drawing will be printed at 1½″ = 1′-0″.

The dashed line and 11¼″ dimension are provided for your information only and do not need to be drawn.

This is how you draw the stringer: Draw the dashed Line (it is a temporary line), Offset it 11¼″ (this is the size of the 2x12), and Erase the temporary line.

> ***COMMENTS:*** *The treads and risers may have different finishes depending on where the stair is in the house. The basement stair may be plain/painted wood or carpeted. The upstairs may be a high-end stained wood (maybe with a carpet runner) or simply all carpet. The basement stair may have no finish on the bottom (like the detail below), whereas the upper stairs would likely have gypsum board attached to the bottom of the stringers and joists to create the finished ceiling for that area (additional wood blocking should also be called out in the notes).*

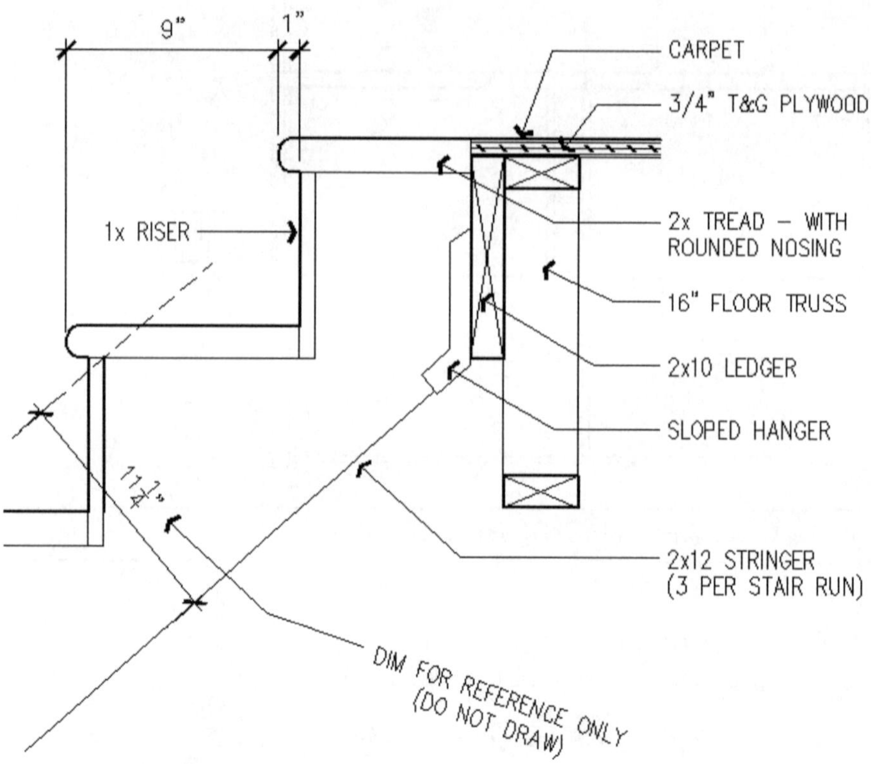

Task 6-4 Stair detail; to be printed at 1½″ = 1′-0″ scale

Lesson 7
PLAN LAYOUT & ELEVATIONS

In this lesson, you will continue to develop the floor plans and create interior elevations. You will add plumbing fixtures to the bathrooms and add furniture to the plans.

Exercise 7-1:
Bathroom Layout

Introduction:

In this exercise, you will lay out the bathroom fixtures. This typically involves considering where the plumbing is coming from and how it will reach each fixture without interfering with or compromising the design; also, factors such as circulation and door swings should be considered.

Like your floor plan, all fixtures are drawn (or inserted) into *Model Space* at full scale.

1. **Open** your second floor plan drawing **Flr-2.dwg**.

2. **Zoom In** to the bathroom area shown in **Figure 7-1.1**.

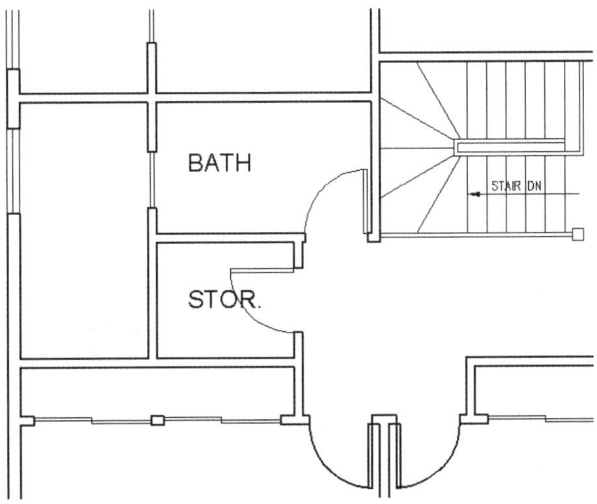

FIGURE 7-1.1 Second floor plan; zoomed into bathroom area

The first plumbing fixture you will insert is the tub, but first, you will double-check your wall locations to make sure it will fit. If you refer to the tub you drew in Lesson 3 (pages 3-18), you will notice the tub is 5′-0″ long. This is a standard size for a tub.

3. Use the **Distance** command (or draw a dimension and then erase it) to verify you have exactly **5′-0″** between the exterior wall and the interior wall as shown in Figure 7-1.2. If you do not have exactly 5′-0″, use the *Stretch* command to adjust the interior wall location.

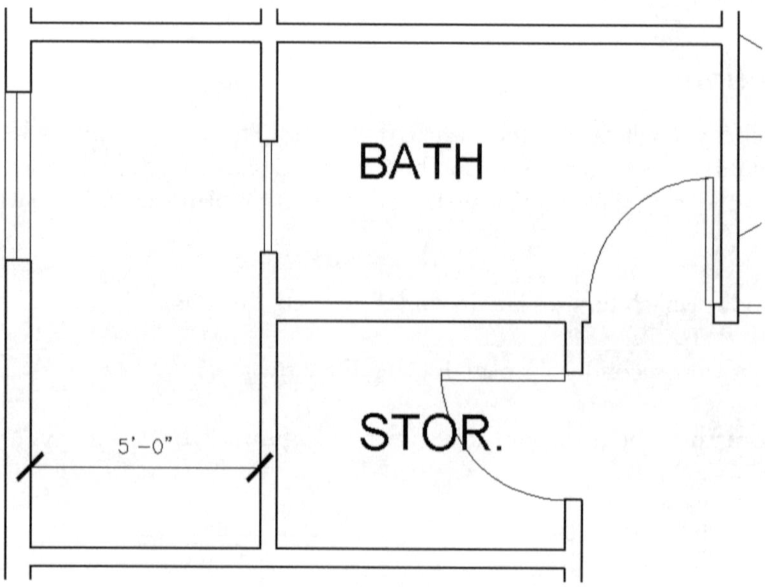

FIGURE 7-1.2 Second floor bathroom; verify wall locations

As you have already seen, when you insert an external drawing file, like you are about to do with the *Tub* drawing, it comes in as a *Block* (i.e., a named group of entities). The *Block* will be inserted on the current *Layer.*

You can easily change the *Layer* by selecting the *Block* and then picking the desired *Layer* from the *Layer Control* drop-down list on the *Ribbon.*

However, in anticipation of inserting several plumbing fixtures, you will create a *Layer* and set it to current before inserting the *Blocks.*

4. Create a *Layer* named ***A-Flor-Pfix*** and set its color to ***Green***.

5. Set the *A-Flor-Pfix* layer to be the ***Current Layer***.

6. Use the **Blocks** palette, from the **View** tab, to insert the **Tub.dwg** file you previously created (Figure 7-1.3).
    a. Make sure you use *OSNAPs* to accurately pick the corner of the wall.
    b. The more rounded side of the *Tub* is the back; the other side is where the faucet/piping is; make sure the faucet is on the interior wall as shown in Figure 7-1.3.

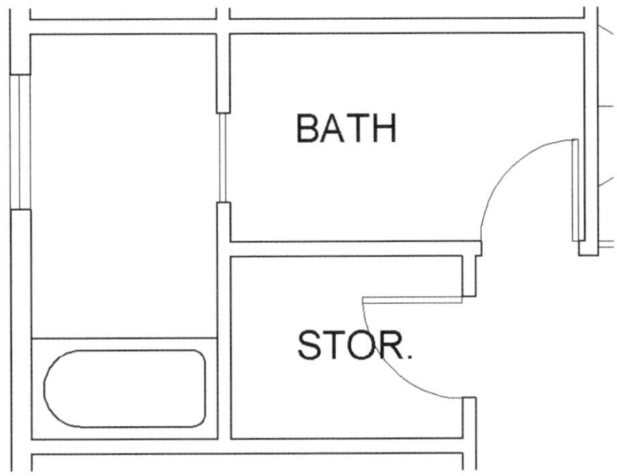

FIGURE 7-1.3 Second floor bathroom; tub block added

FIXTURE LOCATIONS IN COLD CLIMATE REGIONS

As you know, whether you live in a cold climate or not, water expands when it freezes. When this happens in a pipe, the pipe bursts under the extreme pressure exerted by the expanding water/ice. The problem is further compounded by the fact that the pipe is usually buried in the wall behind cement board and ceramic tile.

Therefore, whenever possible, you should avoid placing plumbing fixtures on exterior walls in cold climates (at least the faucet/piping side of a tub).

The problem usually occurs only when the heating system fails, residents don't notice right away, the property is vacant, or the residents are on vacation. However, the problem can still occur under extreme weather conditions (e.g., temperatures such as -40°F or colder).

If you must place the fixtures on an exterior wall, build a second wall in front of the insulated exterior wall and install grilles at the top and bottom to allow warm room air to enter the wall cavity.

7. Use the **Blocks** palette to insert the **Water-Closet.dwg** file you previously created (Figure 7-1.5).

   a. Insert a *Toilet* (aka, water closet) at a corner of the room (see Figure 7-1.4); this puts the fixture in a known location, which then can be moved.

   b. Locate the fixture 18″ away from the side wall; also, move the toilet so there is 1″ between the fixture and the backwall (Figure 7-1.5).

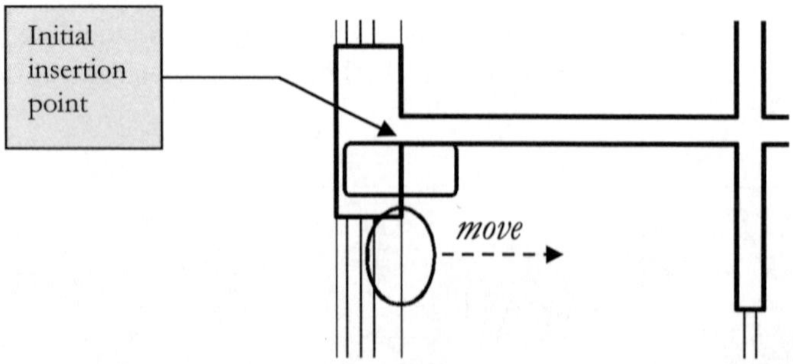

FIGURE 7-1.4 Second floor bathroom; *Toilet Block* inserted with *OSNAP*

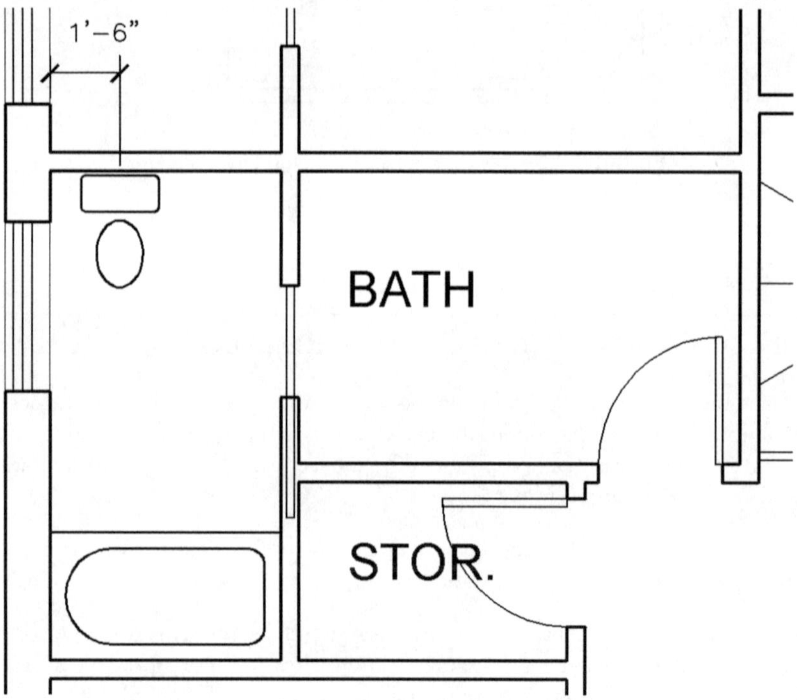

FIGURE 7-1.5 Second floor bathroom; *Toilet Block* moved into place

Next, you will add two sinks to the plans. The sinks are in base cabinets, so draw the lines representing the cabinets first.

Also, remember that in floor plans, you should separate each building element onto different Layers; this helps you have better control over the visibility and lineweights of those elements. So, you will create a *Layer* to draw the base cabinets on as follows:

Name	Color	Linetype	Descriptions
A-Flor-Case-L	Yellow	Continuous	Base cabinets
A-Flor-Case-U	Red	Hidden2	Wall cabinets

8. Create the two *Layers* described above.

Now, draw the countertop/vanity. The top is typically 21″ deep.

9. Draw the base cabinets on *Layer* ***A-Flor-Case-L***, as shown in **Figure 7-1.6**.

   TIP: Offset the wall lines to create the countertop in plan and then use Trim to clean up the lines; finally, change the lines to the correct layer.

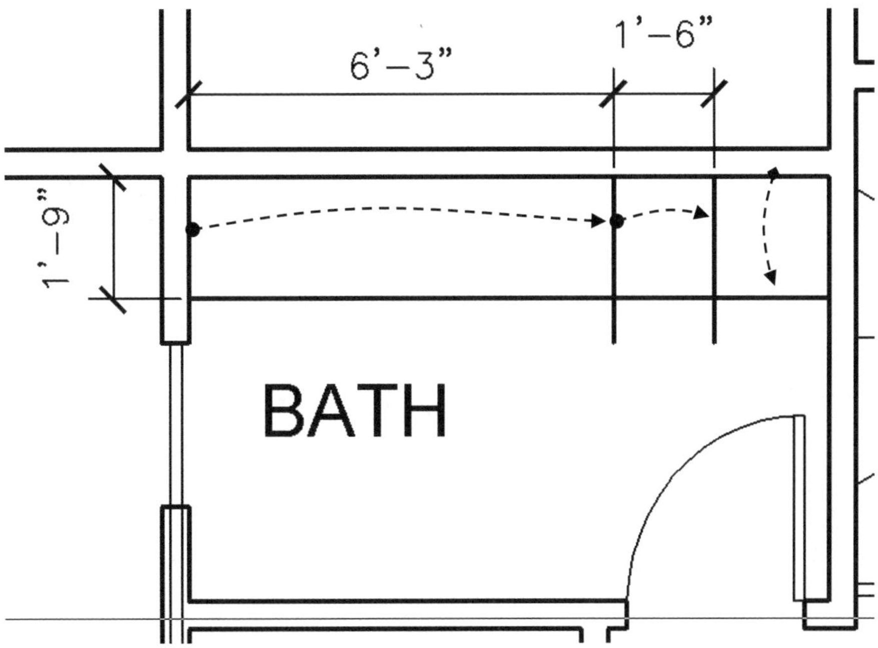

FIGURE 7-1.6 Second floor bathroom; offset wall lines to create vanity/countertop

10. **Offset** the wall line as shown in Figure 7-1.7; these lines will be erased after the sinks have been inserted.

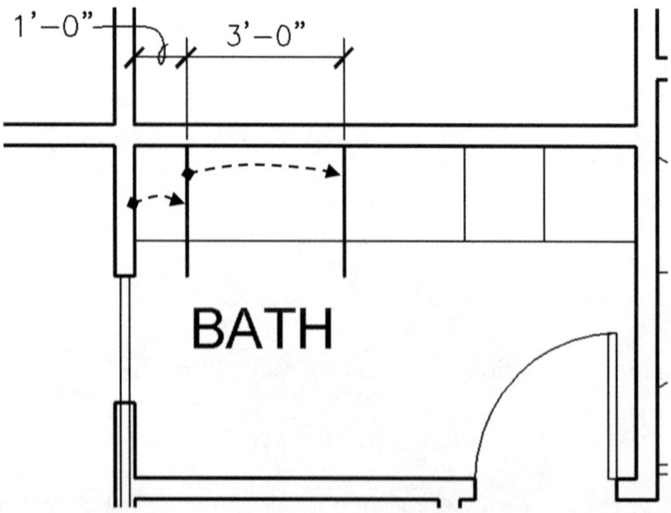

FIGURE 7-1.7 Second floor bathroom; offset wall lines to help locate sinks

11. Insert the **Lav-2** drawing file, previously created, using the **Blocks** palette, then move the sink down **1"** with *ORTHO* turned on. (See Figures 7-1.8 and 7-1.9.)

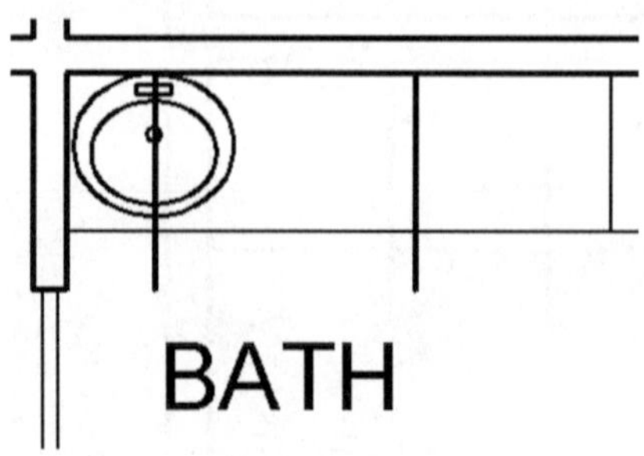

FIGURE 7-1.8 Second floor bathroom; *Sink* inserted at intersection of temp. line and wall

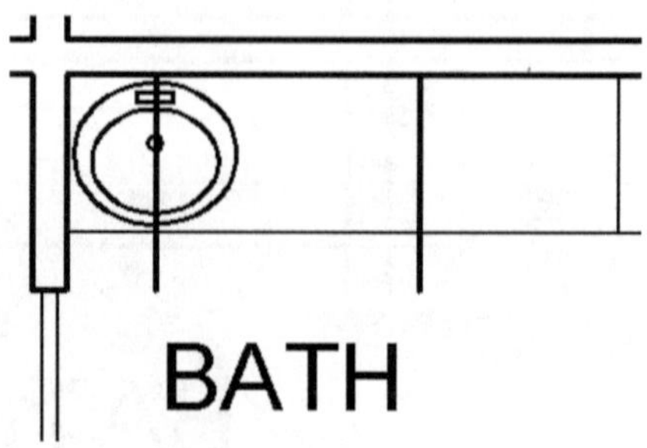

FIGURE 7-1.9 Second floor bathroom; *Sink* moved 1" out from wall

12. Repeat these steps to insert the other sink (Figure 7-1.10).

13. **Erase** the temporary lines (Figure 7-1.10).

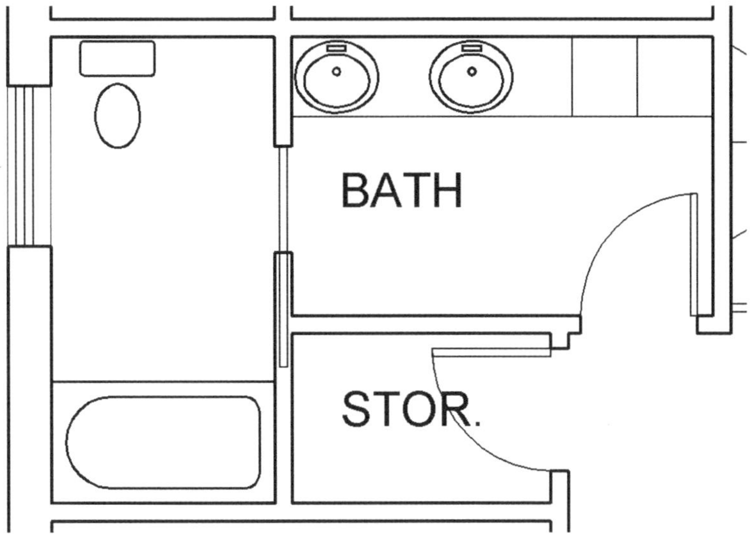

FIGURE 7-1.10 Second floor bathroom; with tub, toilet and sinks added

This completes the bathroom layout.

In the next exercise, you will draw the interior elevation of the cabinets.

> ***FYI:*** *You will see why the sinks are spaced the way they are.*

Image courtesy of Anderson Architects
Alan H. Anderson, Architect, Duluth, MN
Interior Design, Steven W. Sanborn, A.I.A., Santa Rosa, CA

Exercise 7-2:
Bathroom Elevation

Introduction:

The purpose of interior elevations is to convey information that cannot be easily shown on a floor plan. For example, you can show how high a countertop is, how tall a door is, or the layout of wall and base cabinets.

Floor plans typically show horizontal dimensions, and interior elevations typically show all vertical dimensions. However, interior elevations are usually drawn larger than the floor plan (¼″ = 1′-0″ floor plans and ½″ = 1′-0″ interior elevation), so you may have additional horizontal dimensions that would be hard to read on a smaller plan.

In this exercise, you will draw the interior elevation for the bathroom. You will use an *Xref* of the floor plan to get started and learn how to use a feature called *DesignCenter* to insert blocks contained in other drawings.

1. **Open** AutoCAD.

2. Start a new drawing named **Bathroom Elevation.**

3. **Xref** your second floor plan (**Flr-2**) into the drawing.

Next, you will use a feature called **Clip**, which allows you to crop an Xref (i.e., external reference drawing). This will allow you to position the bathroom area close to your interior elevation drawing.

4. **Zoom Extents** so you can see the entire drawing.

5. Zoom **In** to the bathroom area (Figure 7-2.1).

6. **Select** the Flr-2 Xref.

7. Click **Create Clipping Boundary** from *External Reference* contextual tab (only visible while an Xref is selected).
    - Via the on-screen prompt, select **Rectangular.**

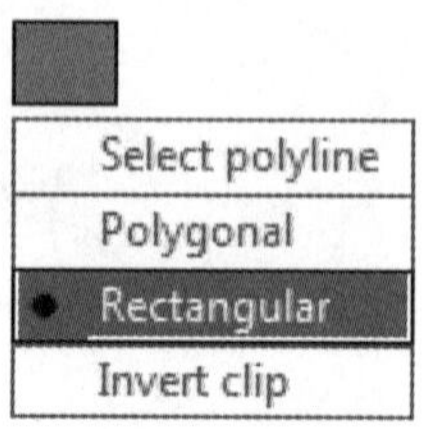

8. Click twice to select a window as shown in **Figure 7-2.1**.

TIP: You should turn OSNAP off so it does not interfere with your picks.

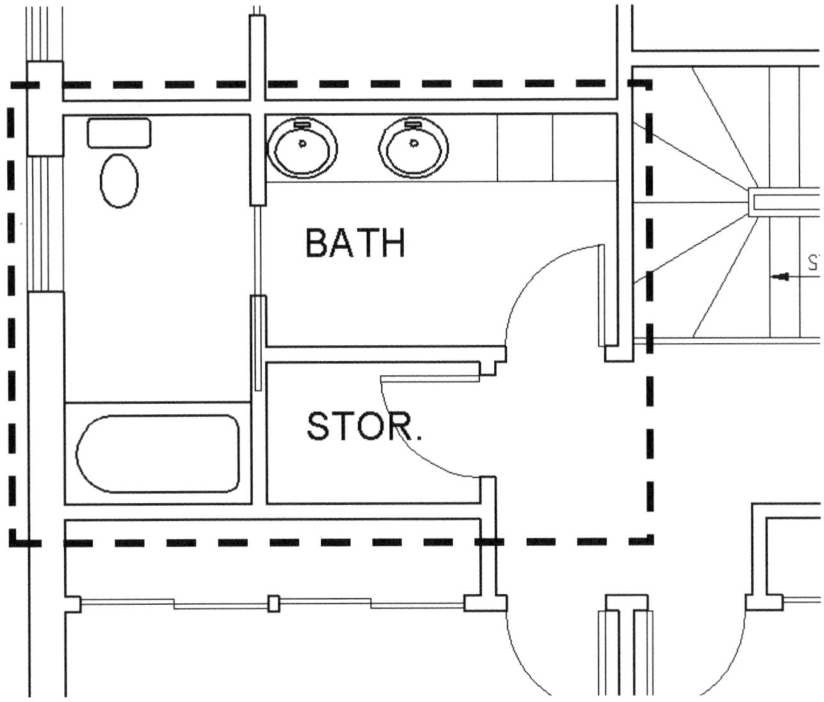

FIGURE 7-2.1 Second floor plan; bathroom area to select for Clip

MORE ABOUT CLIP

This section is meant to give you a little more information about the **Clip** command (found on the *Insert* tab). You can also Clip Blocks and Images (i.e., photos).

Removing a Clip from an Xref
Click **Clip**, select the Xref, and then type **D** (for the **Delete** sub-command), then press **Enter**. You will now see the entire Xref again.

Irregular shaped clips
You can either create the outline before using the **Clip** command or after.

> If you create it before, you need to create a *Polyline*; you can even use **Pedit** to smooth (spline) the outline. Once the *Polyline* is created you enter the **Clip** command, select the Xref, and then press **Enter** twice.
>
> Now enter **S** for the **Select Polyline** sub-command. Finally, select your *Polyline* and you are done.
>
> Or, you can also follow the prompts and create the outline within the Clip command. However, you cannot get a smooth outline like you can with the method previously described.

You can experiment with the other sub-command features by looking at the prompts while the Clip command is active.

Now that the Xref is in place, you can use it to quickly locate several lines in your elevation; you will do this next.

9. Arbitrarily draw a horizontal line and then draw the 8 vertical lines (snapping to the *Xref* for position), as shown in Figure 7-2.2.

Looking back at the *Wall Section* from Exercise 6-3, you can see the 8′-1⅛″ dimension represents the floor to truss bearing height. If you subtract ½″ for the ceiling gypsum board, you have the ceiling height for your elevation: 8′-0⅝″.

10. **Offset** the horizontal line **8′-0⅝″** upward (Figure 7-2.3).

TIP: Type 8'0-5/8 at the Command prompt.

11. **Trim/Extend** the wall lines to the horizontal floor and ceiling lines (Figure 7-2.3).

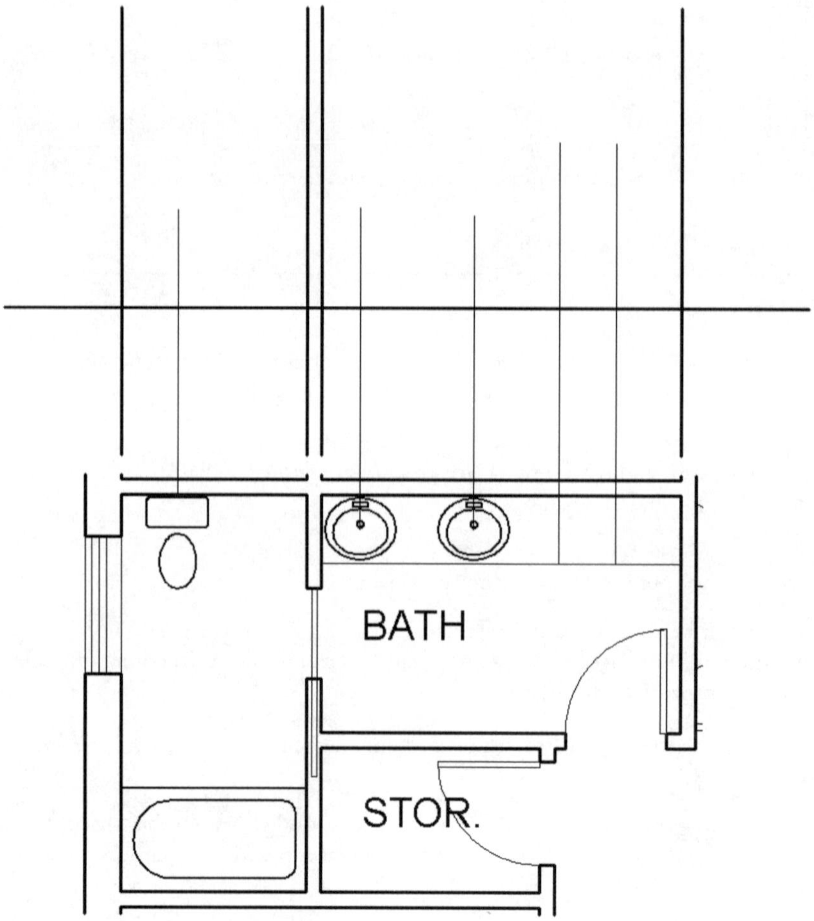

FIGURE 7-2.2 Interior Elevation: lines extended from Xref

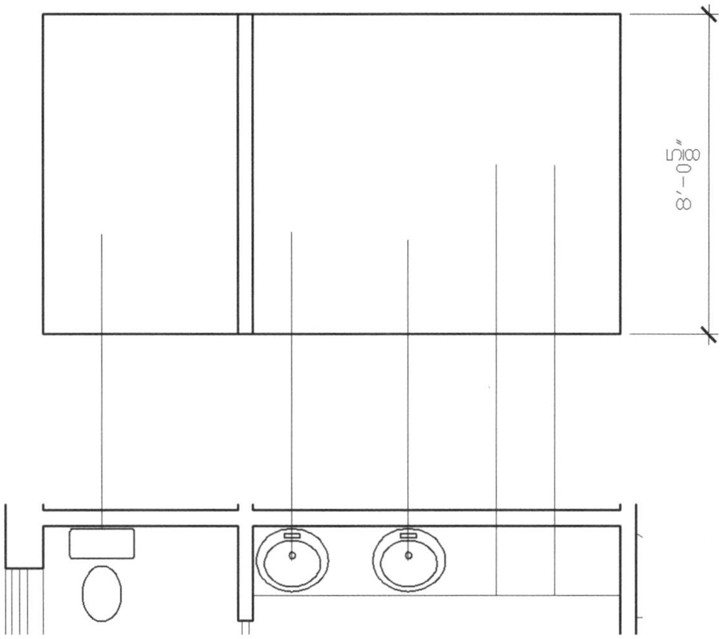

FIGURE 7-2.3 Interior elevation: lines trimmed and extended

Using AutoCAD DesignCenter:

AutoCAD **DesignCenter (DC)** allows you to quickly access drawings (whether currently open or not), and drag items such as *Blocks*, *Linetypes*, *Layer* definitions, etc. into the current drawing. You will use the DC to insert a toilet in elevation from a preinstalled sample drawing (a file that comes with the AutoCAD software).

12. From the *View* tab select the **DesignCenter** icon (shown to the right) on the *Palettes* panel.

    TIP: You can also press Ctrl + 2.

You should now see the dialog box shown in **Figure 7-2.4**. This is the default view. Notice the full path listed at the bottom of the image; use the folder tree structure to browse to this same location if not already there (see step 13).

If you only see the vertical title bar shown to the left of Figure 7-2.4, then it is set to **Auto-Hide**. Simply hover your cursor over the title bar and the full image will show. This feature is meant to save space on your screen (i.e., larger drawing window).

To disable the Auto-Hide feature:

Right-click on the title bar and uncheck the **Auto-Hide** option (see right-click menu to the right).

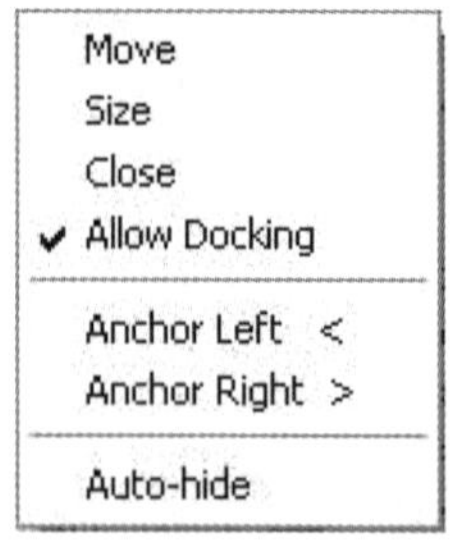

Similar to the *Properties* palette, the *DC* dialog is modeless. That means it can be open while you are drawing (whereas the *Print* dialog box must be closed before you can continue drawing).

> ***TIP:** If you are running a dual-screen system, you can drag both the Properties dialog and the DC dialog to the second screen so they remain open without sacrificing valuable drawing area.*

Also, on the title bar, right-click options include the ability to **Allow Docking**. If this is checked, the dialog will snap to the side of the AutoCAD window. Some people prefer this option, so it does not cover the drawing window in an awkward fashion.

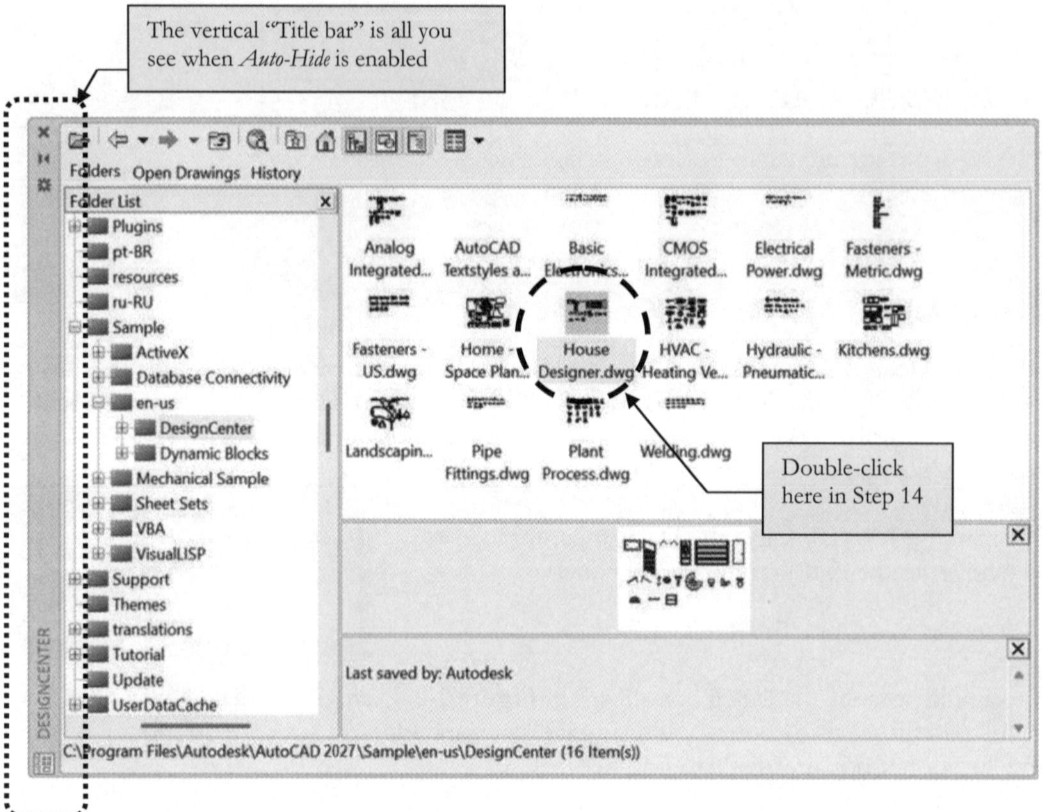

FIGURE 7-2.4 AutoCAD DesignCenter; initial view

13. First, verify you are in the correct area in *DesignCenter* (DC):
    a. Click on the **Folders** tab.
    b. In the *Folder List* pane, browse to the following folder: C:\Program Files\Autodesk\AutoCAD 2027 - English\Sample\en-us\DesignCenter.

TIP: You may have to scroll horizontally and vertically to see everything, or stretch the Folder List pane wider.

    c. Your DC should look like Figure 7-2.4.

14. In the right pane, double-click **House Designer.DWG**.

You can now see the various categories of information you have access to (see Figure 7-2.5). Notice that the selected drawing file is highlighted on the left, in the *Folder List* pane.

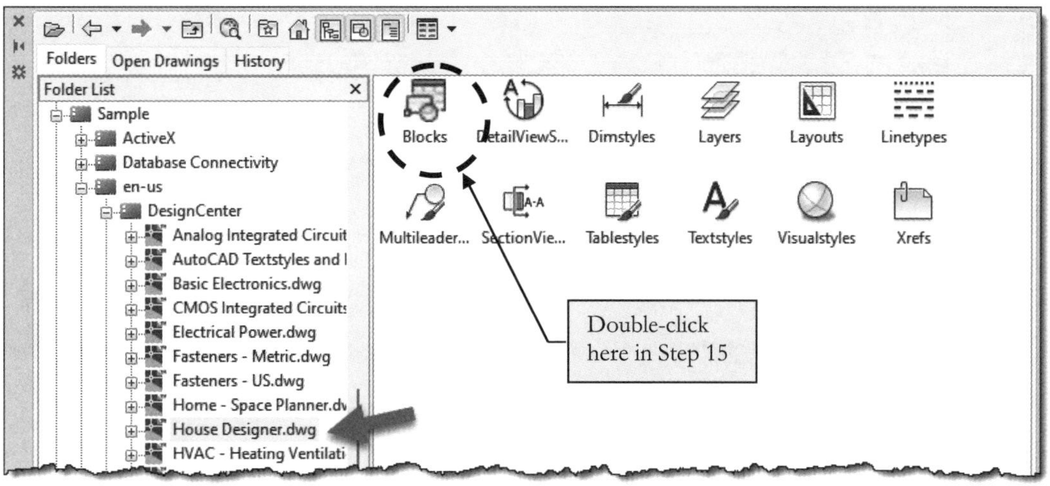

FIGURE 7-2.5 AutoCAD DesignCenter; *House Designer* sample file selected

15. Double-click on the **Blocks** icon in the right pane.

You can now see a thumbnail image of all the *Blocks* within the *House Designer* sample drawing file.

> ***TIP:*** *If you do not see thumbnail images, click the* *View* *icon and select* *Large icons.*

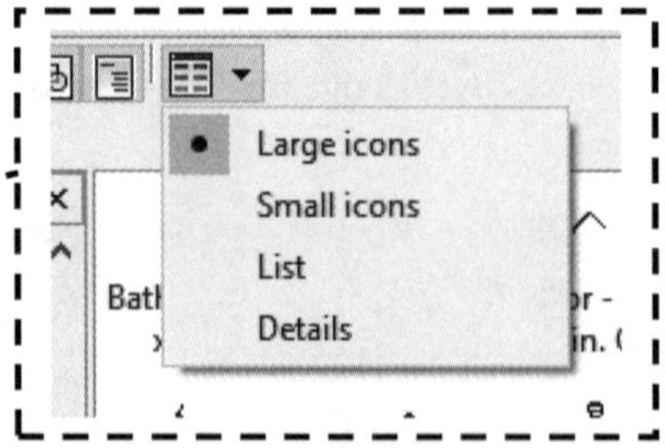

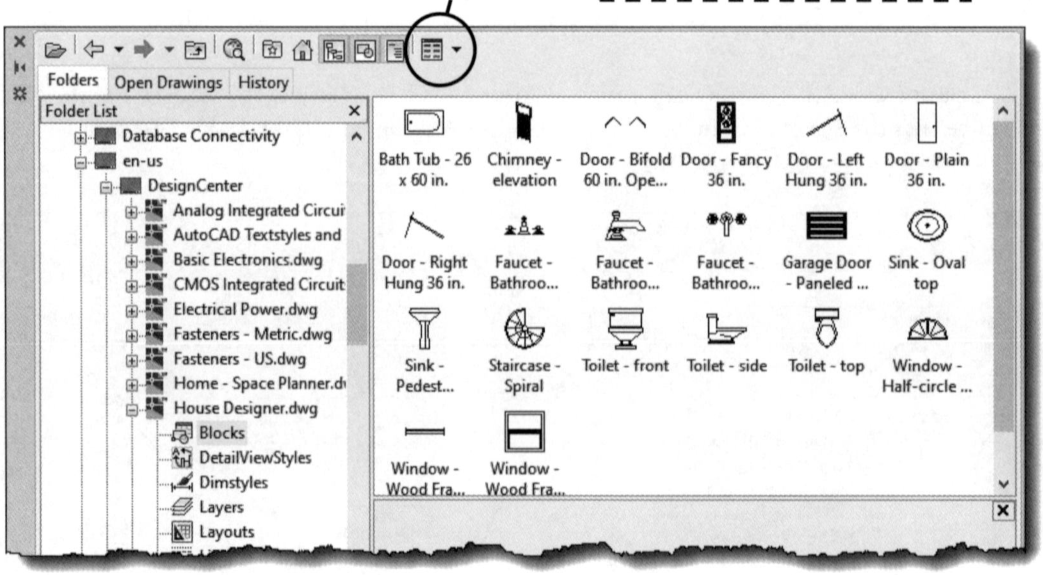

FIGURE 7-2.6 AutoCAD DesignCenter; blocks within the *house designer* sample file

Take a minute to notice the *Blocks* available for insertion into your drawing. You will only be inserting two of these *Blocks* for this drawing: the elevation of the *Toilet* and the elevation of the *Faucet.*

16. Double-click on the ***Toilet - front*** block.

You are now in the standard *Insert Block* dialog box with the *Toilet - front* block selected.

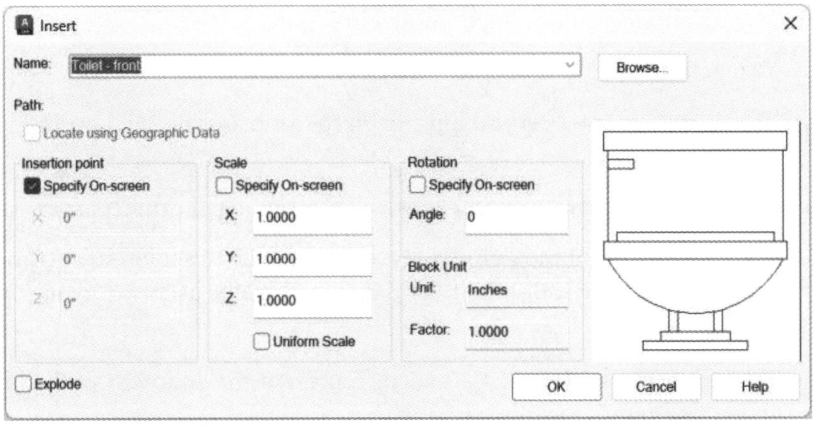

FIGURE 7-2.7 Insert dialog; initiated from DC

17. Click **OK**.

18. Using *OSNAPs*, select the *Intersection* of the floor line and the temporary vertical line projected from the toilet in the Xref'ed floor plan (Figure 7-2.8).

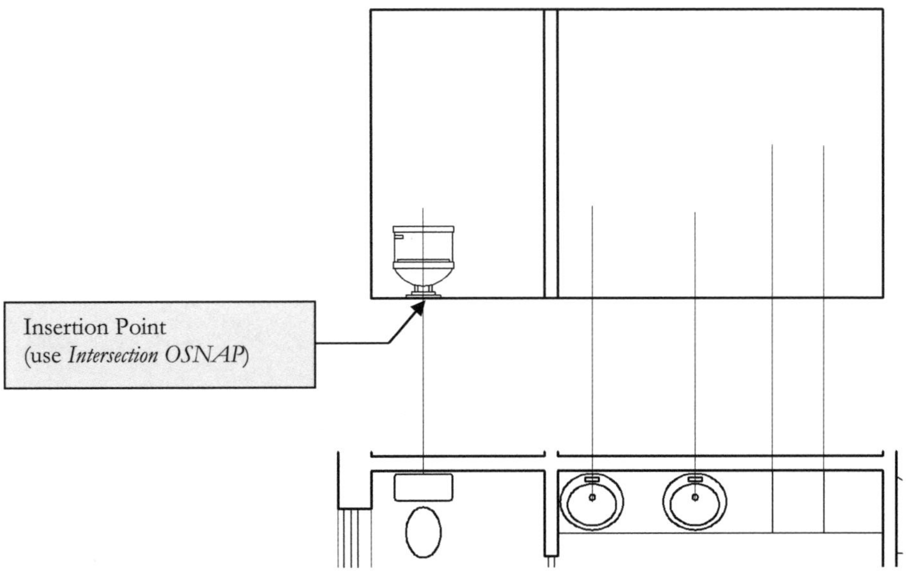

FIGURE 7-2.8 Bathroom elevation; toilet block inserted

Now you will draw the cabinets.

19. Draw the countertop and cabinets shown in Figure 7-2.9:
    a. You do not have to draw the dimensions.
    b. Notice that the two vertical lines from the sink are centered on their respective cabinets.
    c. Notice the other two vertical lines will locate the tall cabinets for you.
    d. The extra space on the right will be a filler panel; this allows for some flexibility when building the walls; the filler panel can also be ascribed to an irregular shaped wall.
    e. The two horizontal lines, 1½″ apart, represent the countertop; the line 3″ above that represents the backsplash.

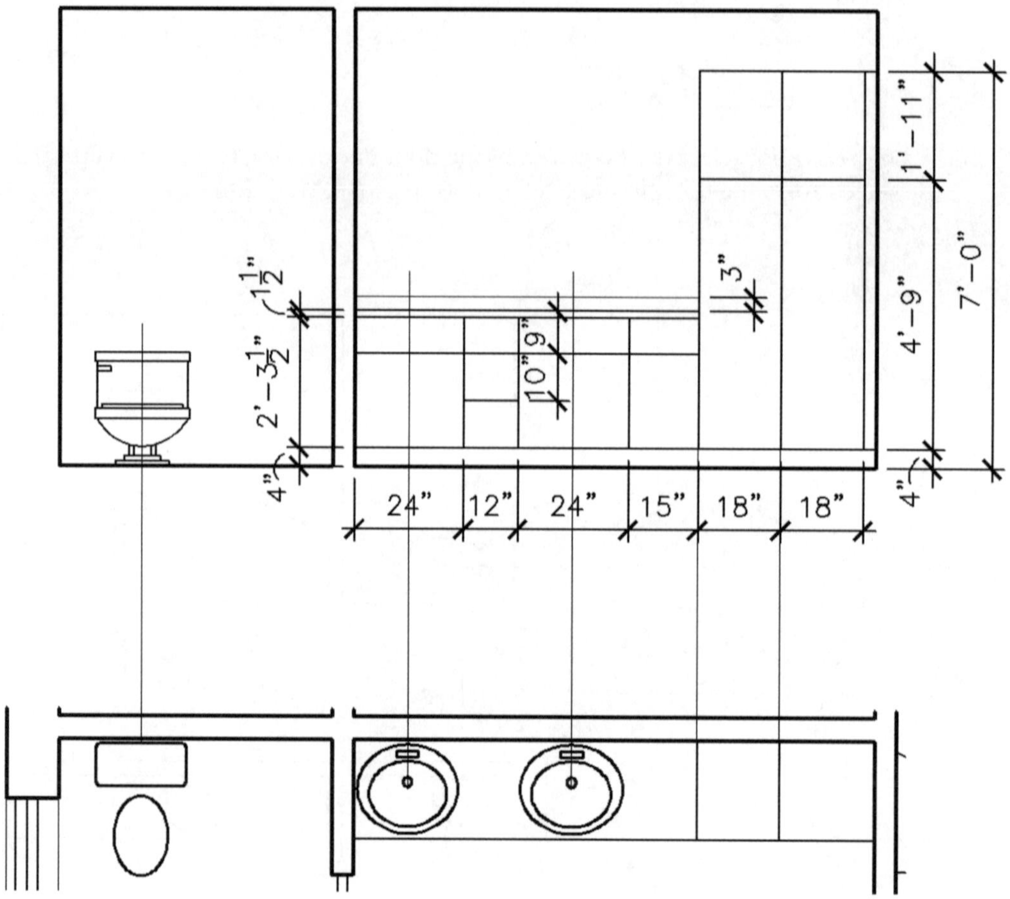

FIGURE 7-2.9 Bathroom Elevation; countertop and cabinet outlines

Next you will add more detail to the cabinets and draw the remaining elements required for this exercise.

20. Draw the remaining elements shown in Figure 7-2.10.

    a. The mirrors are 2′-0″ wide and 2′-6″ tall, centered on the sink below.

    b. The vanity lights above the mirror are the same width as the mirror and 6″ tall; draw the rest to look like the drawing.

    c. Use *DesignCenter* to *Insert* the **Faucet – Bathroom front** *Block* from the *Home Designer* drawing.

    d. Use the dimensions in the drawing below (you do not have to draw the dimensions at this time).

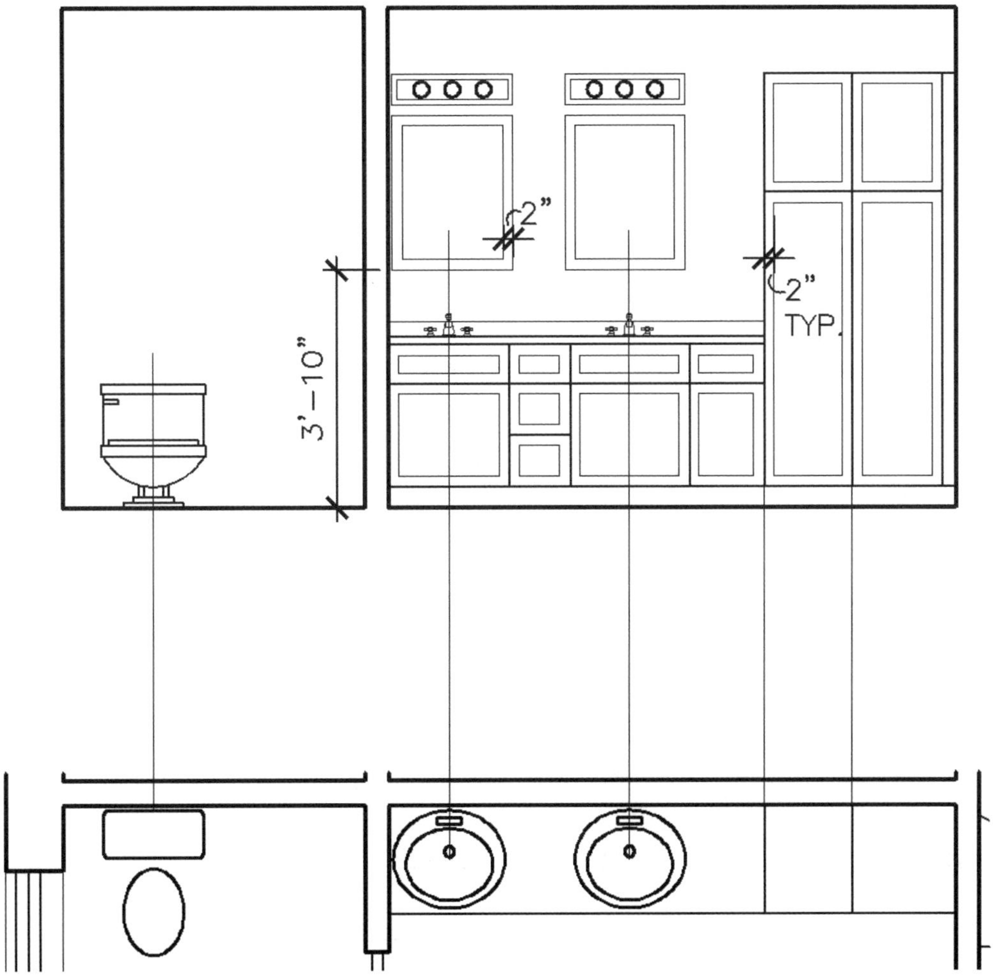

FIGURE 7-2.10 Bathroom Elevation; remaining elements to be drawn

Depending on the project you could add much more detail to the elevation.

For example, you could add:

- electrical outlets and switches to make sure they end up where you want them;
- the ceramic tile pattern and indicate the accent tile pattern as well (using hatch patterns);
- the location of the pulls on the cabinets;
- towel bars that might be in this particular elevation;
- the toilet paper holder, especially if it is recessed in a tiled wall.

NOTES ON CABINET SIZES AND DESIGN

Bathroom and kitchen cabinets come in several standard sizes. They usually start at 12″ wide and increase in size by 3″ increments.

In kitchens,

- Wall cabinets are typically 12″ deep
- Wall cabinet heights: 18″, 24″, 30″, 36″, 42″
- Base cabinets are 24″ deep with a 25″ deep countertop
- Base cabinets are 36″ high (to the top of the countertop)
- Cabinets up to 24″ wide have one door; 27″- 48″ wide have two doors

In bathrooms,

- Vanity cabinets are typically 21″ deep
- Vanity cabinets are 33″ (or 36″) high (to top of countertop)

The Internet is loaded with information on designing kitchens. A few examples to get you started are:

www.kohler.com	Major plumbing fixture manufacturer; web site is packed with kitchen and bath design information.
www.merillat.com	*National Cabinet Manufacturer*, full line of cabinets including details and specifications.
www.kraftmaid.com	Cabinet manufacturer with *Design tools*

You will now complete the elevation by adding notes and dimensions.

21. **Erase** the temporary vertical guidelines.

22. Select **External References** link *(REMINDER: small arrow in the lower right)* from the *Insert* tab (to enter the *External References* palette) and **Detach** the *Flr-2* Xref from the *Bathroom Elevation* drawing (right-click on the Xref name and select *Detach* from the pop-up menu).

23. Using ***MultiLeader*** and *Annotation Scaling*, add the notes shown in **Figure 7-2.11**.

    TIP: Make sure they go on Layer A-ANNO-TEXT.

24. Using the **Linear** *Dimension* tool, add the dimensions shown in Figure 7-2.11.

    TIP: Make sure the dimensions go on Layer A-ANNO-DIMS.

25. **Save** your **Bathroom Elevation** drawing.

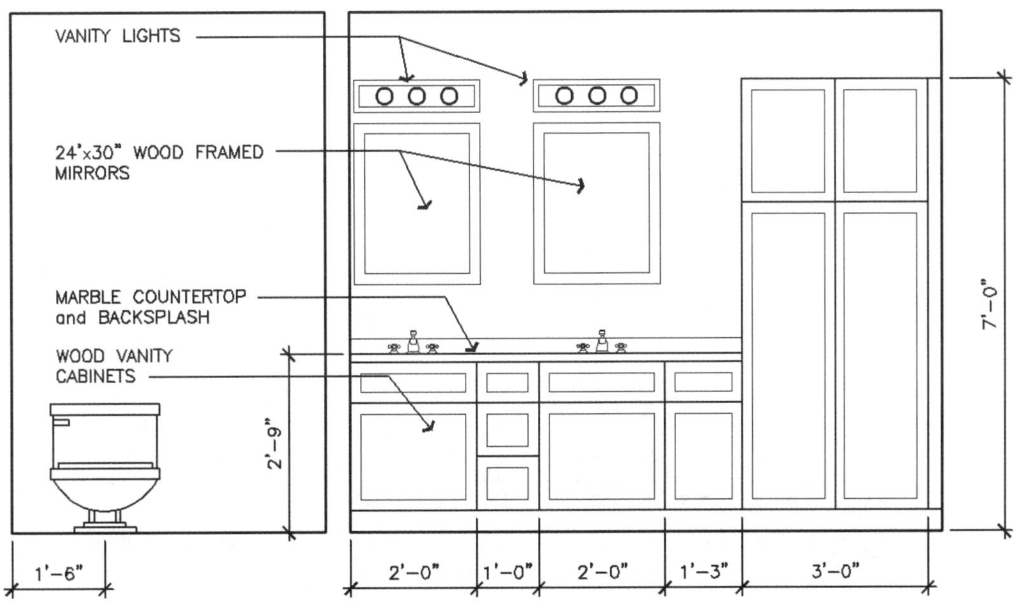

FIGURE 7-2.11 Bathroom Elevation; notes and dimensions added

Don't Forget about LineWeights:

Don't forget to draw your lines on the different non-plan *Layers* (previously discussed on page 6-2) based on how heavy the linework should be. For interior elevations:

- **Heaviest Lines**: The outline of the room should be the heaviest line.
- **Medium Lines**: Objects out from the wall, like cabinets, should be the next heaviest.
- **Lightest Lines**: Any lines on the wall (e.g., the mirror) should be the lightest lines.
- **Light Gray Lines**: Hatch patterns for ceramic tile or brick joints should be a light and gray line, so it is not too intense. (This has not been covered yet.)

The actual implementation of lineweights will be covered in Lesson 10.

Carter Residence

Image courtesy of LHB
www.LHBcorp.com

Exercise 7-3:
Adding Furnishings to Your Floor Plans

In this exercise, you will add *Blocks* that represent various furnishings. Laying out furniture helps both you and the client to verify that your floor plan design is functional. You will see that *Blocks* are available from several sources; this is in addition to the ones you drew at the beginning of this book.

First, you will start with the *Master Bedroom.*

1. **Open** the "Flr-2" drawing file.
2. Create a *Layer* named ***A-FURN***; set color to ***Red.***
3. Set the ***A-FURN*** layer *Current.*
4. Zoom **In** to the *Master Bedroom* area.

Next, you will insert a few of the symbols you created in Lesson 3.

5. **Insert** the following *Blocks*, created in Lesson 3 (Figure 7-3.1):
   a. **Bed-king**
   b. **Night-stand**
   c. **Dresser-1**
   d. **Chair-2**

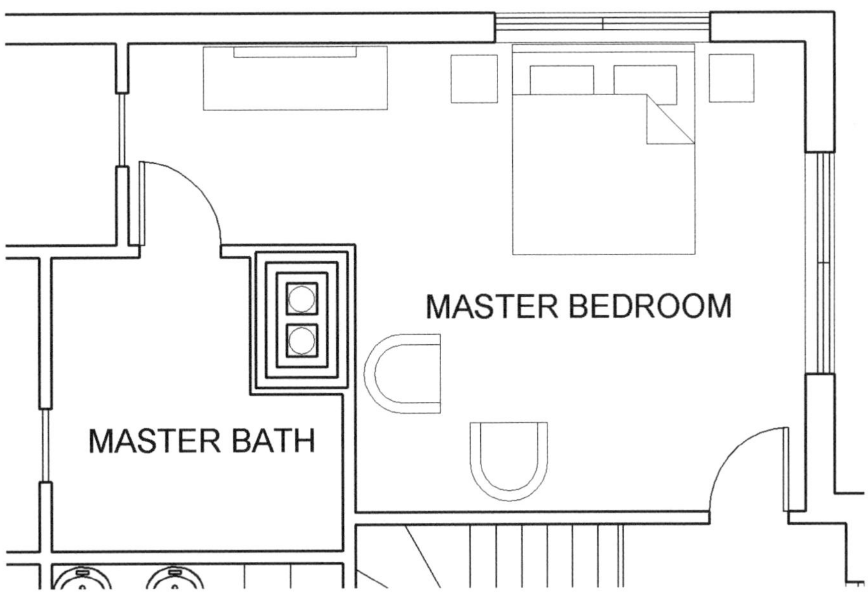

FIGURE 7-3.1 Master Bedroom; *Blocks* inserted

Now you will use *DesignCenter* to insert a *Block* located in a sample drawing file that was installed with AutoCAD.

6. Similar to Exercise 7-2, use *DesignCenter* to browse to the sample drawing file named **Home - Space Planner.dwg** (Figure 7-3.2).

7. Insert **Plant - Rubber or Philodendron** from the *Blocks* category (Figure 7-3.3).

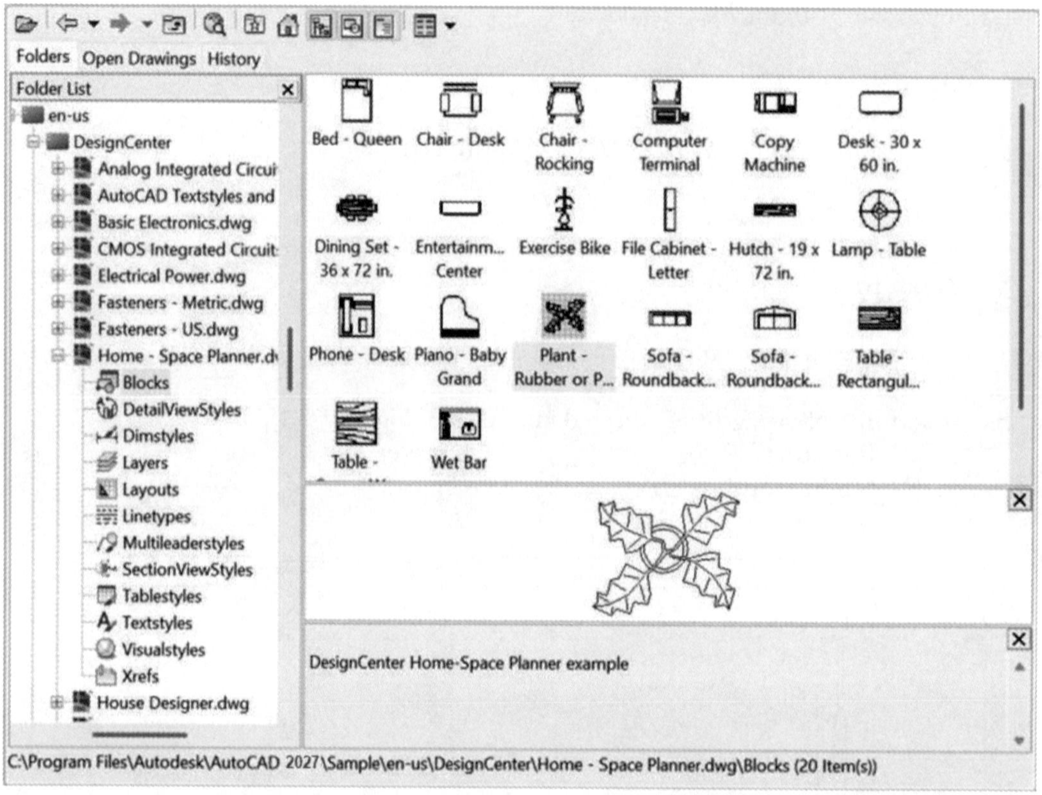

FIGURE 7-3.2 DesignCenter; *Blocks* to insert

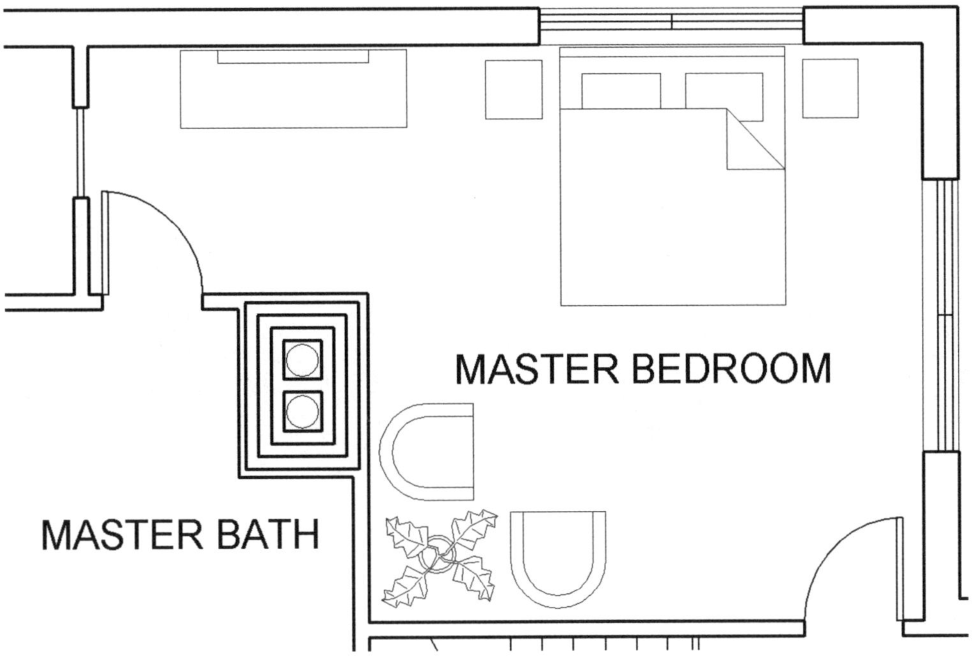

FIGURE 7-3.3 Master Bedroom; *Plant* block inserted between chairs

ADDITIONAL CONTENT RESOURCES

In addition to the design content you have drawn and have found in *DesignCenter*, you can acquire additional content from other sources. Below are a few examples:

BIMobject (see next page)	http://bimobject.com
Sweets Online:	www.sweets.com
Wood Panel Systems	www.newenglandclassic.com
General content	https://www.arcat.com/

Many manufacturers have CAD blocks on their websites for download or will mail you a CD if you ask them.

WARNING!
Keep in mind that some of the symbols available on the Internet, or elsewhere, may not be accurate for a number of possible reasons. You should verify the size and accuracy of important symbols!

BIM Object gives you access to a significant amount of online content for use in your drawings! You must be connected to the internet for this link to work.

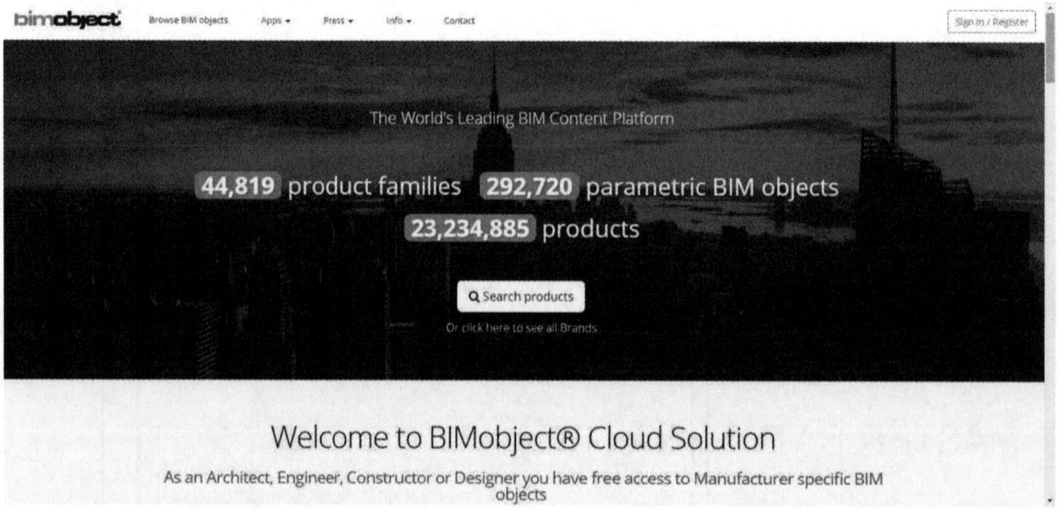

FIGURE 7-3.4A BIMobject website

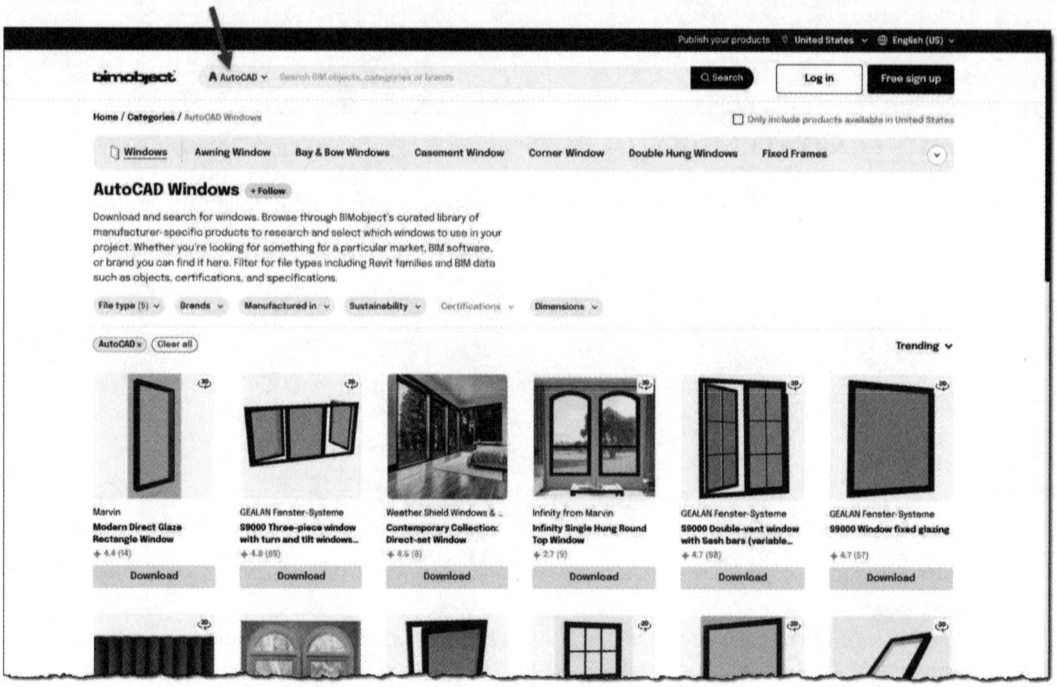

FIGURE 7-3.4B BIMobject filtered for AutoCAD

Walk-In Closet:

It is helpful to draw as much information as possible to better understand the complete design concept and make sure everything is coordinated. Drawing the clothes racks, for example, will show which walls are open and would be more accessible for an electric outlet. You will do this simple task next.

8. **ZoomIn**to the *Walk-In Closet.*

9. **Offset** both the south and west wall lines into the room **12"** (Figure 7-3.5).

10. **Trim** the two new lines and change them to *Layer* ***A-FURN*** (Figure 7-3.5).

Next, you will draw lines to represent hanging clothes.

11. Draw a line **18"** long (on *Layer A-FURN*) and randomly copy and rotate it as shown in Figure 7-3.6.

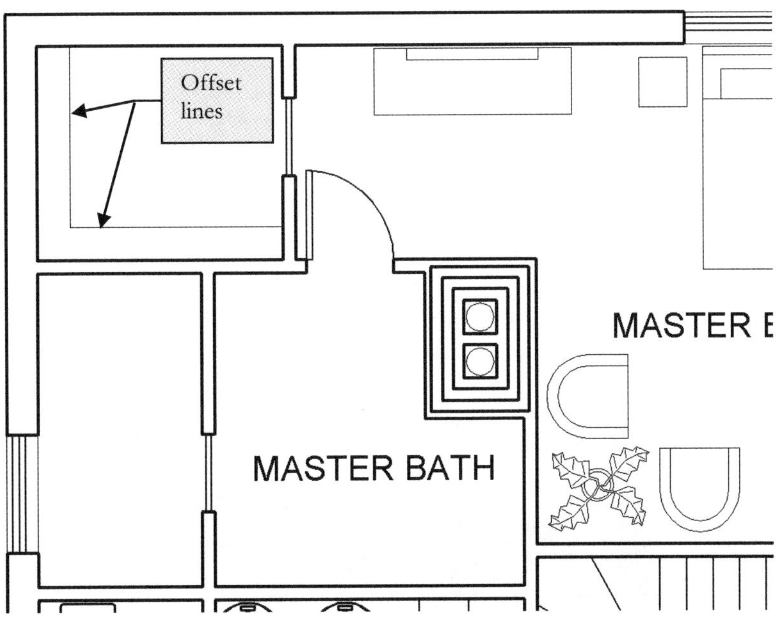

FIGURE 7-3.5 Master Bedroom Walk-in Closet; lines offset for hanging rod

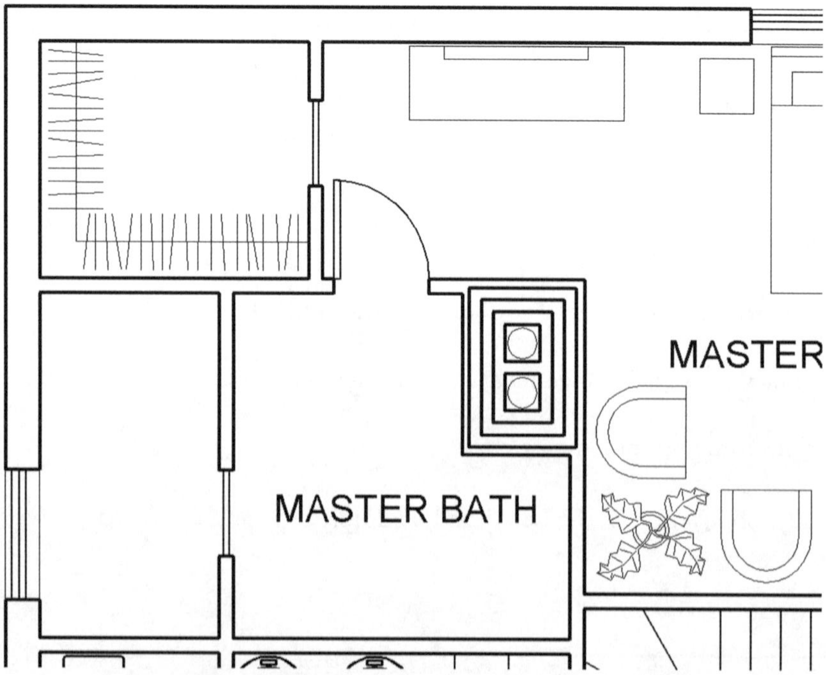

FIGURE 7-3.6 Master Bedroom Walk-in Closet; lines (i.e., hangers) added

That completes the *Master Bedroom* layout.

12. **Save** your drawing.

Image courtesy of Anderson Architects
Alan H. Anderson, Architect, Duluth, MN
Interior Design, Steven W. Sanborn, A.I.A., Santa Rosa, CA

Exercise 7-4:
Using Tool Palettes

Tool Palettes help organize content (*Blocks*) and frequently used hatch patterns. First, you will explore the standard, out-of-the-box *Tool Palettes* installed with the software. After looking at the *Tools* provided, you will learn how to customize the *Tool Palettes.*

Overview of the "Out-of-the-Box" Tool Palettes

First, you will open one of your floor plans, so you can test the *Tool Palettes.*

1. **Open** the "Flr-1" drawing file.

2. Click *View* → *Palettes* → **Tool Palette** icon if the *palette* is not currently displayed; the *Tool Palette* icon toggles the visibility on and off.

The initial view of the *Tool Palettes* should look like **Figure 7-4.1**. Notice the *Tabs* down one side, similar to file folder tabs, which allow you to organize different groups of hatches, content and commands. The current *Tab* should be the one labeled "**Architectural**"; click this *Tab* if not current.

TIP: If you only see the Title Bar show up when toggling the Tool Palettes icon, simply hover your cursor over the Title Bar and the palettes will display. This is caused by a feature called Auto-Hide (see page 7-12).

The next page consists of definitions…

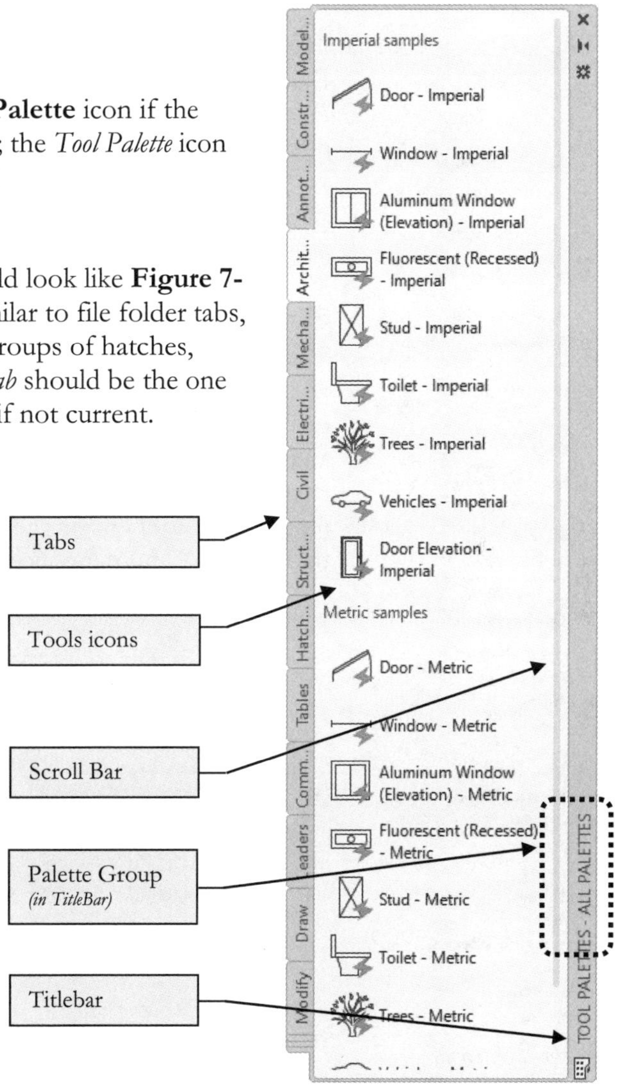

FIGURE 7-4.1 Tool Palettes; Architectural tab

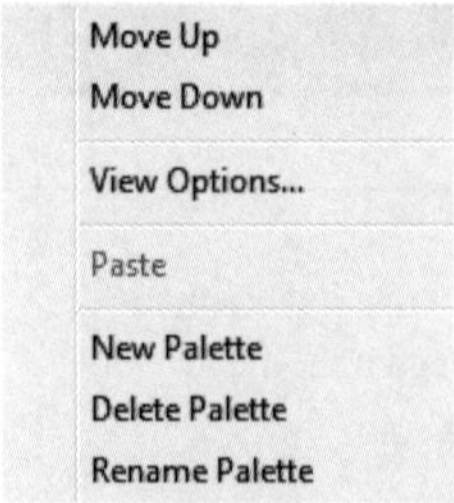

Right-click menu

Tabs:

Used to organize *Blocks*, *Hatch Patterns* and *Commands* that are used regularly. You can add new *Tabs* as well as rename and reposition existing *Tabs*. When you right-click on a *Tab* you see the menu to the left.

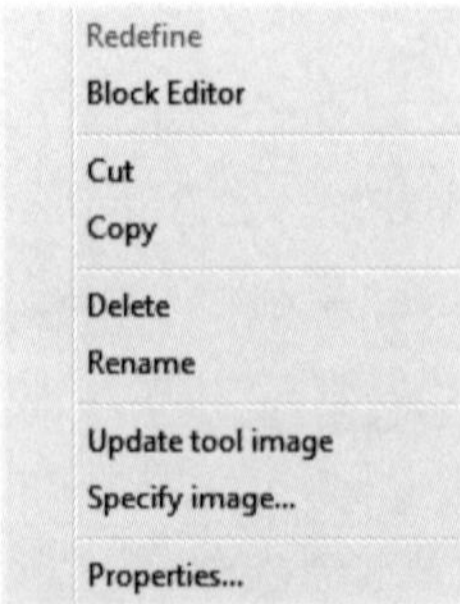

Right-click menu

Tools icons:

You can store *Blocks*, *Hatch Patterns* and *Commands* on *palettes*. Each *Icon* has various settings to control, such as the scale and where layer *Blocks* are inserted. Similarly, you can control properties like *Hatch Pattern* Scale and Color. These predefined properties will be covered next. When you right-click on a tool you see the menu to the left.

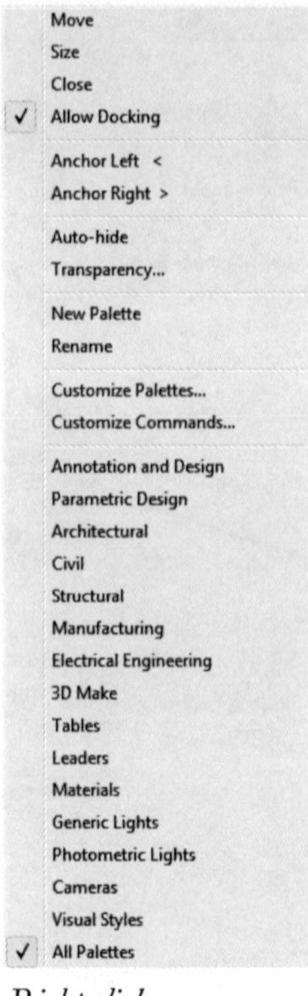

Right-click menu

Title Bar:

This is the area you select when you want to move the *Tool Palettes* window on the screen (click and drag). When *Auto-Hide* is turned on, the *Title Bar* is all you see when the *Tool Palette* is open. *Auto-Hide* and other options are set via the right-click menu shown to the left. When you have *Palette Groups* (which are several *Palette Tabs*), you can toggle between them via the list of *Groups* that would be displayed at the bottom of the right-click menu.

Inserting a Dynamic Block from a Tool Palette:

Now you will insert a *Dynamic Block* from the *Tool Palette*; you will insert a car in the garage. *Dynamic Blocks* were introduced in AutoCAD 2006. You will learn how to insert one and edit it with the special controls that are visible when the *Dynamic Block* is selected. Creating and editing *Dynamic Blocks* is beyond the scope of this tutorial.

3. **Zoom** into the *Garage* area (Figure 7-4.2).

4. From the *Architectural* tab on the *Tool Palettes*, click (not drag) on the **Vehicles – Imperial** icon.

5. Click near the center of the garage, centered on the left overhead door (i.e., garage door). See Figure 7-4.2A.

Oddly, your drawing should look like Figure 7-4.2A. One of the interesting things about *Dynamic Blocks* is that they can store multiple representations of the same or similar objects.

When you select the inserted *Dynamic Block*, a special symbol is displayed near the block. Clicking the symbol displays a list of display representations you can toggle between for the particular insertion. (This will not change any other insertions for that same block.)

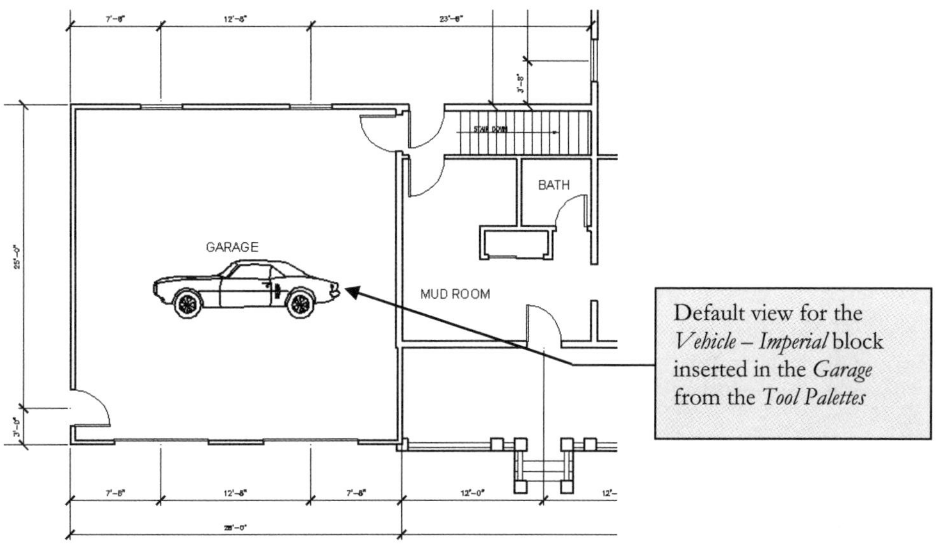

FIGURE 7-4.2A
First Floor Plan; (default view) Vehicle – Imperial block inserted in Garage

Next you will change the *Dynamic Block* to display a top view of the vehicle block.

6. Click the car symbol just inserted; notice the symbol that is now visible (Figure 7-4.2B).

7. Click on the triangle-shaped *Grip* to see a list of display options.

8. Select **Sports Car (Top)** from the pop-up menu displayed (Figure 7-4.2C).

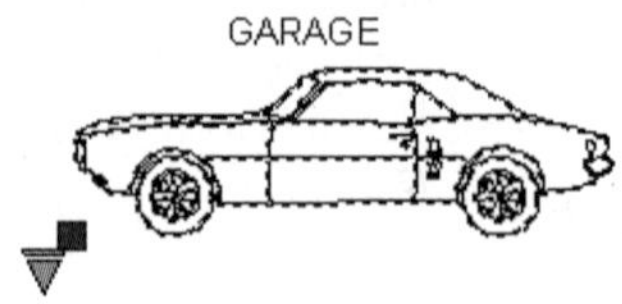

FIGURE 7-4.2B
Dynamic Block selected; notice special *Grip*

You will notice from the pop-up menu that the *Vehicle – Imperial* block has 12 different display options associated with it. The image below is the same drawing file with the same block (*Vehicle – Imperial*) inserted 12 times, and each insertion is set to display a different representation (Figure 7-4.2D).

9. Rotate the car *Block* negative 90 degrees so the front of the car points into the garage (Figure 7-4E).

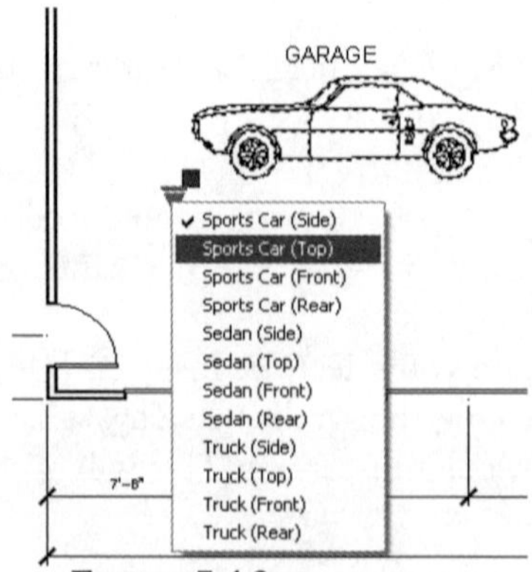

FIGURE 7-4.2C
Dynamic Block display options listed

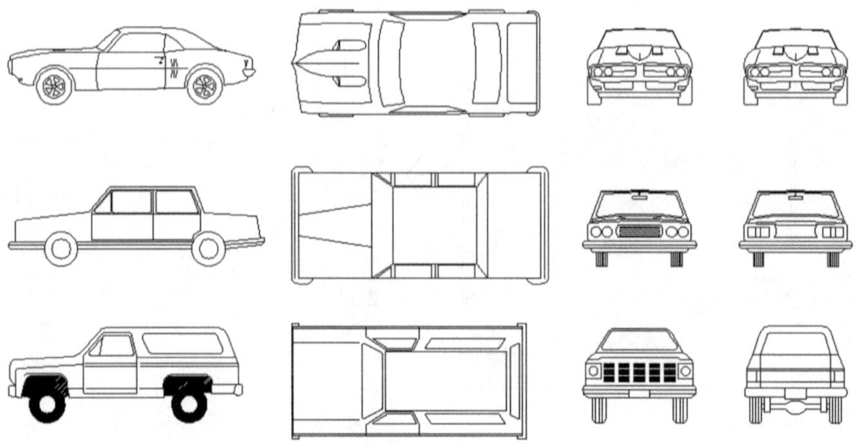

FIGURE 7-4.2D Dynamic Block display options

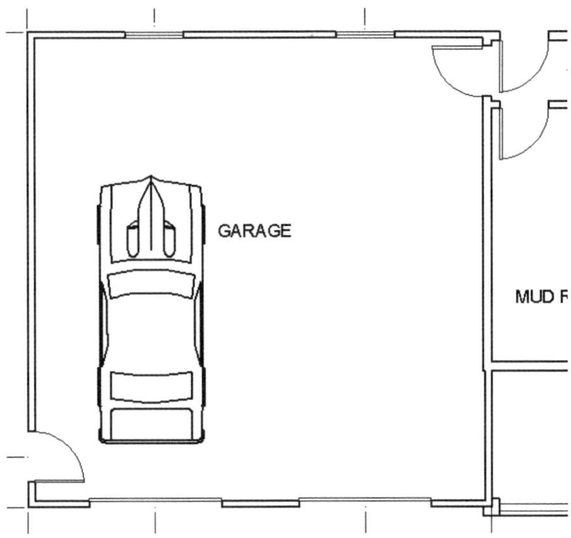

FIGURE 7-4.2E Dynamic Block rotated into place

Dynamic Blocks have many other capabilities, such as stretching a table and having additional chairs added as the table is stretched. Additional control *Grips* can be added to quickly Mirror and Rotate the selected symbol. To create and edit *Dynamic Blocks*, you use the *Block Editor* which has a *Tool Palette* loaded with tools to create complex symbols.

Another *Dynamic Block*, listed in the *Tool Palettes*, is the **Door – Imperial** block. This is a very useful *Block*. You can adjust its size between several standard door widths; you can flip, change the open angle, and rotate the symbol via the special control *Grips* (Figure 7-4.2F) to adjust the door swing. The built-in jamb lines are also adjustable to match a few predetermined wall thicknesses.

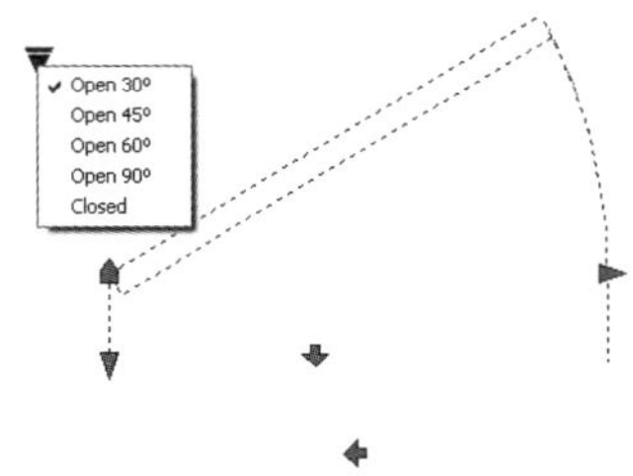

FIGURE 7-4.2F Dynamic Block: *Door - Imperial*

Notice that when you clicked the *Tool Palettes* icon, you did not see the standard *Insert* dialog (Figure 7-2.7). This is because all the settings you are normally prompted for from the *Insert* dialog have been pre-assigned to each *Block* stored in a *Palette*. You will explore these settings next.

10. Right-click on the **Vehicles – Imperial** icon (Figure 7-4.1).

11. Select **Properties…** from the pop-up menu.

Take a minute to observe some of the settings available for the selected tool (*Vehicle – Imperial*). These are the main settings:

Source file: AutoCAD imports the *Block* from an external drawing file, so the file must always exist in the location specified.

Scale: This is set to *1* for "real-world" items like furniture and fixtures; they are drawn at actual size and don't need to be scaled. However, annotation symbols (e.g., the detail bubble) need to be scaled relative to the intended plot scale.

Color: This should almost always be set to *ByLayer*, which means the *Layer* the block is inserted on controls the color of the *Block* (assuming the lines in the *Block* were drawn on *Layer0* <zero>).

Layer: When set to *use current*, the *Block* is inserted on the current *Layer*, just like the standard Insert Block command. However, unlike the standard Insert Block command, you can pre-specify a *Layer* for the *Block* to be inserted on. So in the example below, you know the *Block* should always be inserted on the *A-SITE-CARS* layer. Simply setting the *Layer* property to *A-SITE-CARS* assures you that it will always be inserted on the correct *Layer*, regardless of the *Current Layer* setting; the Layer will even be created if it does not exist in the current drawing!

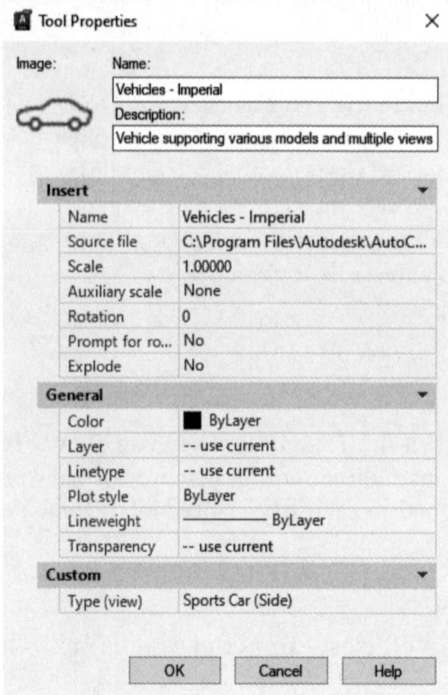

FIGURE 7-4.3
Tool Properties; Vehicle - Imperial tool

Using a Hatch Tool on the Tool Palettes:

Next, you will use one of the standard *Solid Hatch* patterns predefined on the *Hatches* tab.

You will be using the Solid Hatch tool to fill in the walls, which will make them stand out more when printed.

The first thing you will do is create a separate *Layer* for the wall fill pattern to go on; this will allow you to *Freeze* it when you do not want it to show.

12. Open the second floor plan, **Flr-2.dwg**, and create a *Layer* named ***A-Wall-Patt***; leave the color set to *7* (*White*).

    *NOTE: Do **NOT** set this* Layer *to be* Current*!*

To show how you can predefine the *Layer*, you will adjust the *Layer* setting for one of the Hatch tools before filling the walls.

13. Right-click on the third icon located on the ***Hatches*** tab (on the *Tool Palettes* darker blue swatch).
    - If you do not see the *Hatches* tab, right-click on the icon at the bottom of the title bar and select "All Palettes."

14. Select **Properties**.

15. Click on the word **"use current"** next to the *Layer Property* (this will cause a down-arrow to show up on the right).

16. Click the down-arrow to display the list of *Layers* in your drawing.

17. Select **A-Wall-Patt** and then select **OK** (Figure 7-4.4).

    TIP: The layer will not show up in the list if it has not been previously created.

Now you are ready to fill a section of wall with the Hatch tool.

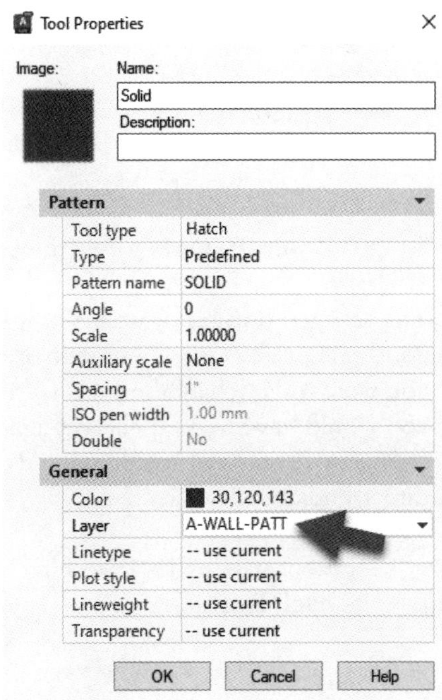

FIGURE 7-4.4 Tool Properties; Solid tool

18. Click the **Hatch** icon you just modified.

19. Click within the wall area in the upper-right corner of the *Master Bedroom* (Figure 7-4.5).

TIP: If you get the error "Valid hatch boundary not found," you should zoom in on all corner- and end-points to verify they are truly connected; AutoCAD needs to find a "perfectly" closed area in order to draw a hatch pattern.

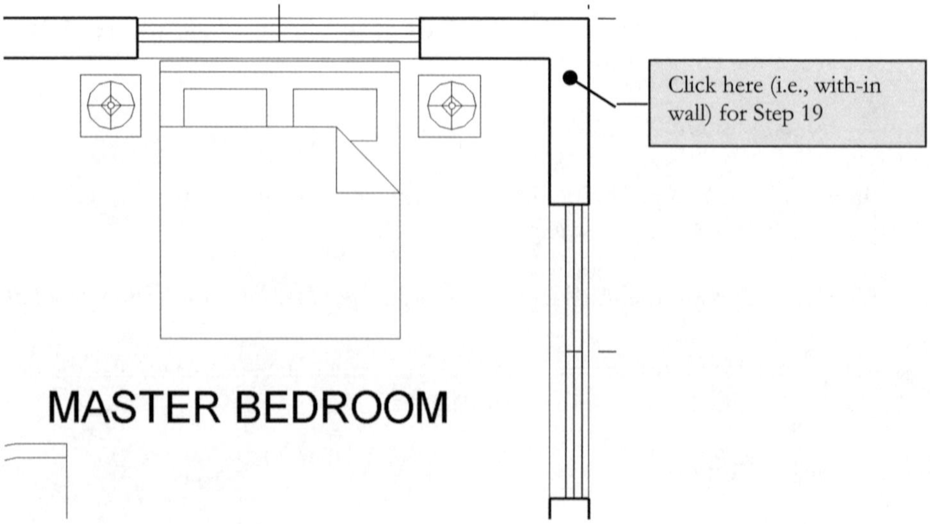

FIGURE 7-4.5
Second Floor Plan; area to click to specify area to be hatched

20. **Zoom Extents** to see the entire plan.

The selected portion of wall is now *Hatched* (Figure 7-4.6). It is good practice to only Hatch one or two closed areas at a time. If you were to Hatch all the walls for the entire floor at one time, you would have to do it all over again to accommodate one change, whereas you would only need to redo the fill pattern directly adjacent to the change.

21. Repeat steps 18-19 to Hatch the rest of the walls **on each floor**.

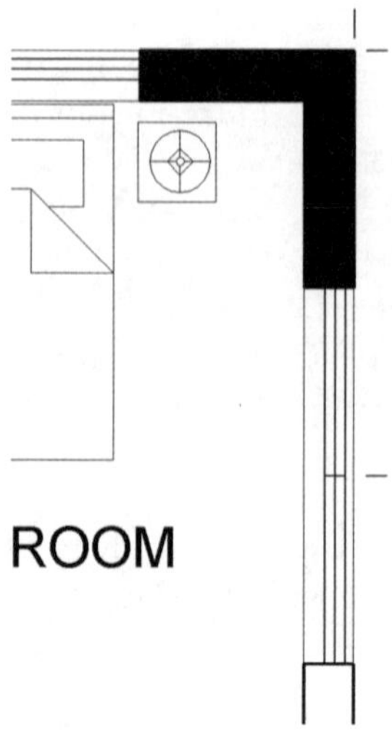

FIGURE 7-4.6
Portion of wall hatched

> *TIP: You only need to adjust the Tool Palette settings once, not for each drawing (i.e., you don't need to change the Hatch tool Layer setting for the first floor; it will even create the Layer for you).*

All your walls should now be hatched (Figure 7-4.7).

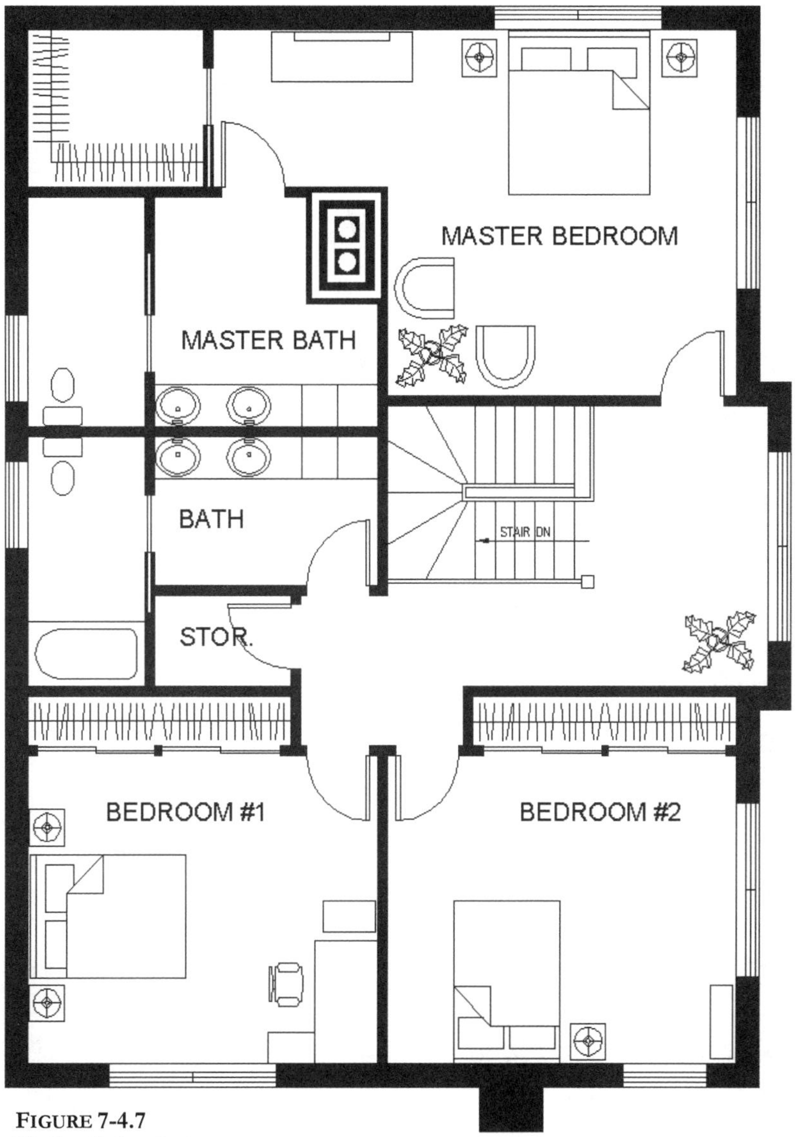

FIGURE 7-4.7
Flr-2 walls hatched

Notice how the floor plan reads more clearly with the walls hatched; there is no question where a wall starts and ends.

> *FYI: Extra furniture and toilet room layout is based on the "additional task" section.*

Next, you verify the Solid Hatch was drawn on the correct *Layer* (even though that *Layer* was not set *Current* when drawing the Hatch).

22. In the *Layer Manager*, **Freeze** layer ***A-Wall-Patt***.

All the wall hatching should no longer be visible.

23. **Thaw** layer ***A-Wall-Patt***.

You should also notice that the color for the *Solid Hatch* has been set *ByEntity* rather than *ByLayer*. So, even though the *A-Wall-Patt* layer has its color set to 7, the *Solid Hatch* is set to True Color 30,120,143 per the color property in the *Tool Properties (see Figure 7-4.4)*.

Adding Custom Content to a Tool Palette:

Now you will create a custom *tab* and add some of the *Blocks* you have previously created.

Content is added to the *Tool Palettes* by "dragging and dropping" *Blocks* from the *DesignCenter, Drawing Window* or *Windows Explorer*. So, similar to inserting *Blocks* from the *DesignCenter*, you browse to a drawing (open or closed) and open its *Blocks* category. Then you drag the desired *Block* to the *Tool Palette*. Finally, you can specify the scale, *Layer*, etc., if desired.

First, you will create a custom *Tool Palette* tab; this creates a storage area for your frequently used symbols (i.e., *Blocks*).

24. Right-click on one of the existing tabs and select **New Palette** from the pop-up menu (see page 7-28).

25. Enter the tab name ***My Symbols*** in the area provided and then press **Enter**.

You now have a custom *tab* ready to hold your *Blocks* or hatch patterns. (See Figure 7-4.8.)

Make sure your Flr-2 drawing is open before proceeding.

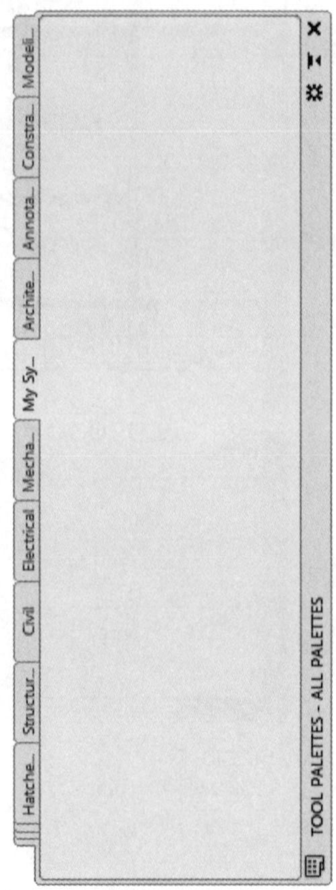

FIGURE 7-4.8
New Tool Palette tab

26. Open the ***DesignCenter*** palette.

27. Click on the ***Open Drawings*** tab (near the top).

28. Expand the **Flr-2** drawing to view its categories (i.e., click the plus symbol) *if necessary*.

29. Select the **Blocks** category (Figure 7-4.9).

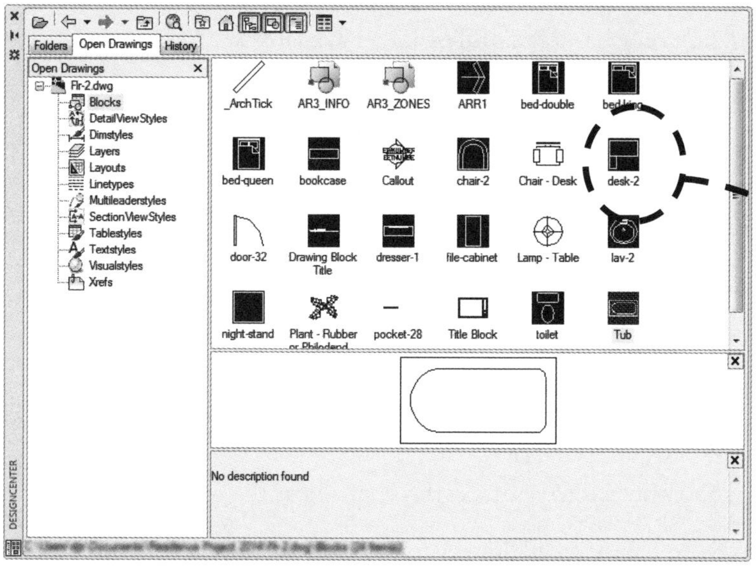

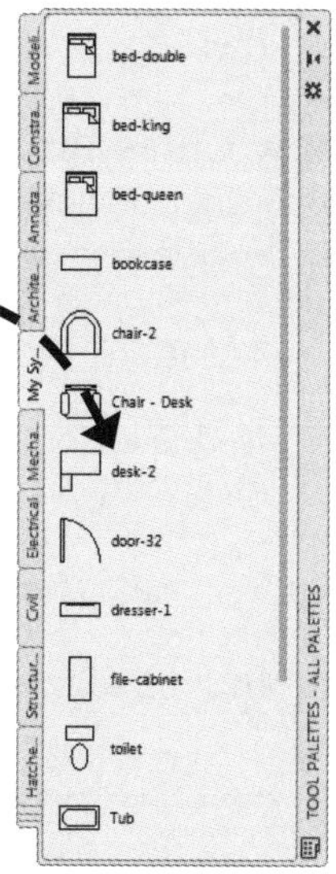

FIGURE 7-4.9
DesignCenter; *Open Drawings* tab - Flr-2\Blocks selected

FIGURE 7-4.10
Custom content added to Tool Palette

30. Drag your *Blocks* (the ones you created) from *DesignCenter* to the "My Symbols" *Tool Palette* (Figure 7-4.10).

31. Set the *Layer* to ***A-Furn*** (cf. 7-4.4) for each furniture symbol and ***A-Flor-Pfix*** for each plumbing fixture.

32. Save your **Flr-1** and **Flr-2** drawings.

Keep in mind that the Flr-2 drawing file cannot be moved or renamed as the *Tool Palette* will extract the symbols out of this file every time the symbol is needed (in other drawings).

Self-Exam:

The following questions can be used as a way to check your knowledge of this lesson. The answers can be found at the bottom of this page.

1. Base cabinets should be placed on the *Layer A-Flor-Case-L*. (T/F)
2. Interior elevations are typically drawn at ½″ = 1′-0″. (T/F)
3. You can use an irregular shaped polyline to *Clip* an external reference. (T/F)
4. What type of *Block* can have multiple graphics?_________________.
5. *DesignCenter's SEEK* link only has a handful of *Blocks* available.(T/F)

Review Questions:

The following questions may be assigned by your instructor as a way to assess your knowledge of this section. Your instructor has the answers to the review questions.

1. *Clip* permanently deletes all of the clipped lines. (T/F)
2. In this lesson you used *DesignCenter* to insert *Blocks* contained within other drawing files. (T/F)
3. You can *Offset* wall lines to quickly create a temporary reference line. (T/F)
4. In *DesignCenter*, to access drawings on your hard drive, you must have the

   _________________tab selected (one of the three tabs near the top of *DC*).
5. You can draw lines from your *Clipped* floor plan to position walls and fixtures in your interior elevation. (T/F)
6. Typing *Clip* does what?______________________________________.
7. This icon () allows you to open ______________________________.
8. All furniture should be drawn on *Layer*______________________________.
9. All *Blocks* (symbols) downloaded off the Internet are 100% accurate. (T/F)
10. You cannot create your own *tabs* in the *Tool Palette*. (T/F)

SELF-EXAM ANSWERS:
1 – T, **2** – T, **3** – T, **4** – Dynamic, **5** – F

Additional Tasks:

Task 7-1: Toilet Room Plan Layouts

Using the techniques learned in this lesson, add the plumbing fixtures to the two remaining toilet rooms. Refer back to Figures 4-1.1 and 4-1.4 for the fixture locations.

Task 7-2: Toilet Room Elevations

Using the techniques learned in this lesson, draw the interior elevations for the wall with the toilet and sink for the plans drawn in the previous task (Task 7-1).

Task 7-3: Furniture Layout

Using the techniques learned in this lesson, place furniture symbols throughout the house. Use your own ideas for this task. Imagine it is your house and decide where you would put the couch, the chair, the television, etc. Create new blocks for any symbols you may need but cannot find.

Notes:

Lesson 8
SITE PLAN

This lesson will introduce you to the basic site plan drafting concepts. First, you will draw the existing site conditions from a survey. Secondly, you will draw the building footprint, driveway, and walks on the site. Finally, you will draw new contours indicating finished grade and drainage for the site.

Exercise 8-1:
Draw Existing Survey

Introduction:

The first step you typically take when preparing a site plan is to draw the existing site conditions. A survey crew will gather site data and then draw a site plan showing the locations of any buildings, trees, and paved surfaces, as well as contours that describe the land's shape.

Ideally, you would get an AutoCAD file from the surveyor, which would allow you to pretty much start drawing the new conditions. One thing to understand, in this case, is that you will usually have to adjust the scale (i.e., size) of the drawing. The reason is that surveyors use one AutoCAD unit as a foot, whereas architects use one AutoCAD unit as an inch. Therefore, if you were to list the distance of a line (from a survey drawing) that is 48′ in a drawing (with its units set to architectural), you will get 4′-0″ (see the following chart):

Drawing	Line	Units	Length	Adjustment
Survey	48 Acad units	Decimal	48′	n/a
Site Plan	48 Acad units	Architectural	48″=4′	48x12=576″=48′

Thus, you scale the survey drawing up 12 times to make it the correct scale in your site plan file (or any file that has the units set to architectural). AutoCAD will do this automatically in most cases, but this is good for you to know when things don't work correctly.

If you do not receive an AutoCAD file of the survey, you will need to draw it from the provided blueprint. This can be more challenging than reproducing an existing floor plan drawing because curved lines are harder to create. In this lesson, you will draw a site survey from a "hardcopy only" drawing.

Create Layers:

The first thing you will do is create the required *Layers*.

1. In a new drawing file, set the *Limits* to **280′ x 160′**, and then **Zoom All**.

2. Create the following *Layers*:

	Layer Name	*Color*	*Linetype*
a.	C-ANNO-TEXT	YELLOW	CONTINUOUS
b.	C-PROP	MAGENTA	PHANTOM2
c.	C-TOPO	YELLOW	HIDDEN2
d.	C-TREE	CYAN	CONTINUOUS
e.	C-WATR	CYAN	CONTINUOUS

Draw the Property Lines:

Now you will draw the property line. This will involve entering decimal feet for lengths and degrees-minutes-seconds for angles.

3. On the correct *Layer*, draw the property line shown in Figure 8-1.1. Note the following:

   a. Entering the length 134.6254′
   You can directly enter the decimal foot property line lengths listed. Consider a similar example: when drawing a line, you can enter 1′6″ or you can enter 1.5′; in either case, AutoCAD will draw the line the same length.

   b. Entering the angle 101°56′
   Entering angles by inputting Degrees-Minutes-Seconds requires a particular format: 101d56′ (for this example). If you are in the Line command, you can enter the following to draw the line the correct length/angle: @122.653456′<78d4′. If you need to dimension angles using this format, you would change the *Units* (from *Application Menu* → *Drawing Utilities*) to Deg/Min/Sec.

4. Set the variables related to the linetype scale:
   a. **LTSCALE= 1**
   b. **PSLTSCALE = 1**
   c. **MSLTSCALE = 1**
   d. *Annotation Scale:* this will be set in a later step

   FYI: Just type 'LTSCALE' and press enter to set the system variable to 1.

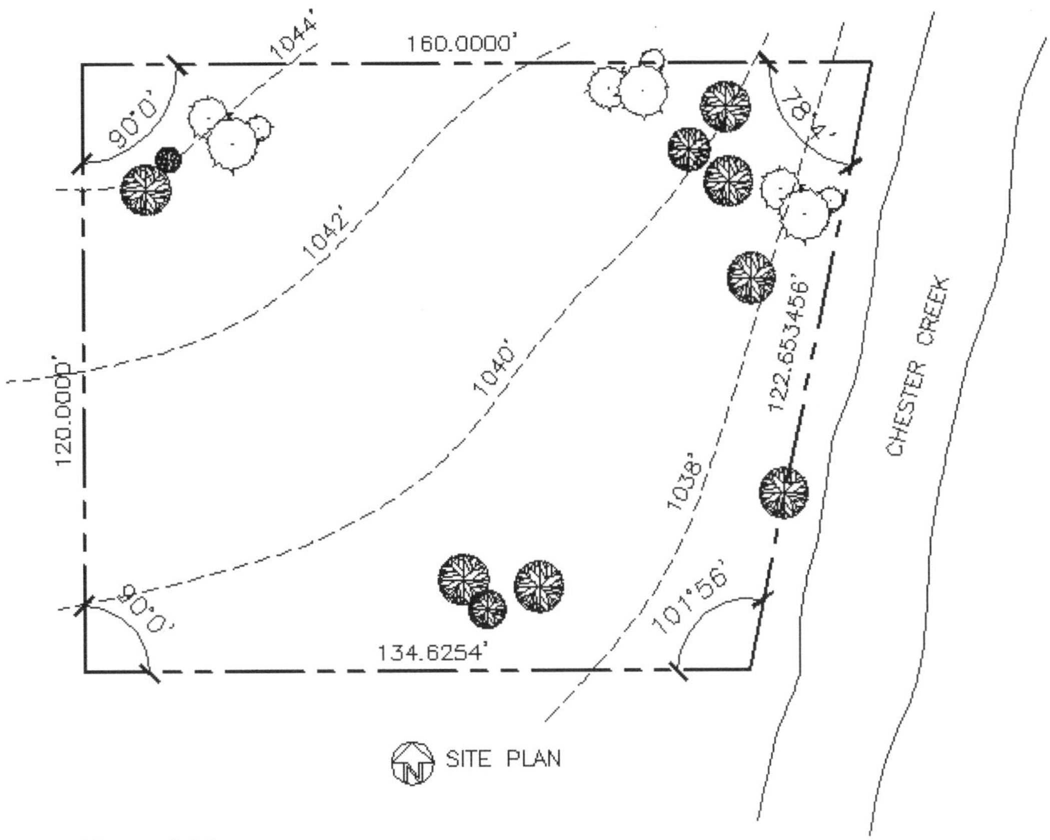

FIGURE 8-1.1
Site Survey; current/existing conditions

Drawing the Contours:

You have a few options for getting the contours into your cad file. One is to scan the drawing and place it in AutoCAD at the correct scale, then you can draw/trace over the image. The second involves using a grid to approximately transfer the curved contour lines from the "hard copy" to the drawing file; you will try this next.

Normally, you would hand-draw a 10′-0″ x 10′-0″ grid on a blueprint of the survey using an engineer's scale and a parallel bar or drafting board. However, this step will not be necessary for this tutorial; the grid is already added in Figure 8-1.3.

5. Using the **Pline** command (i.e., Polyline), draw the contours on the correct *Layer* per the comments below:

    a. Use the site plan with the 10′-0″ x 10′-0″grid overlay in Figure 8-1.3.

b. Draw a 10′-0″ x 10′-0″ grid overlay on your site plan aligned with orthographic property lines as shown in Figure 8-1.3.

c. Draw each contour using the various locations the contour crosses the 10′ x 10′ grid as a reference (Figure 8-1.2). For example:

    i. Draw one contour at a time, following and noting where the line intersects the grid.

    ii. You only need to pick points where the contour line intersects a grid line; you will smooth out the line in a later step.

    iii. Notice that the contours cross exactly at some of the grid intersections; these are the easiest points to locate.

    iv. All other intersections can be approximated to be ¼, ½ or ¾ distance between two grid lines.

d. You want to be as accurate as possible, but it is not necessary to be as accurate as you need to be when drawing the floor plans.

6. Select all the contours, then, from the *Properties* palette, set the *Linetype Generation* to **Enabled**.

FYI: This setting makes the dashes consistent in your dashed lines. When this feature is disabled, dashes are calculated for each line segment in the polyline, many of which may not be large enough to show a dash at all, making portions of the line look continuous.

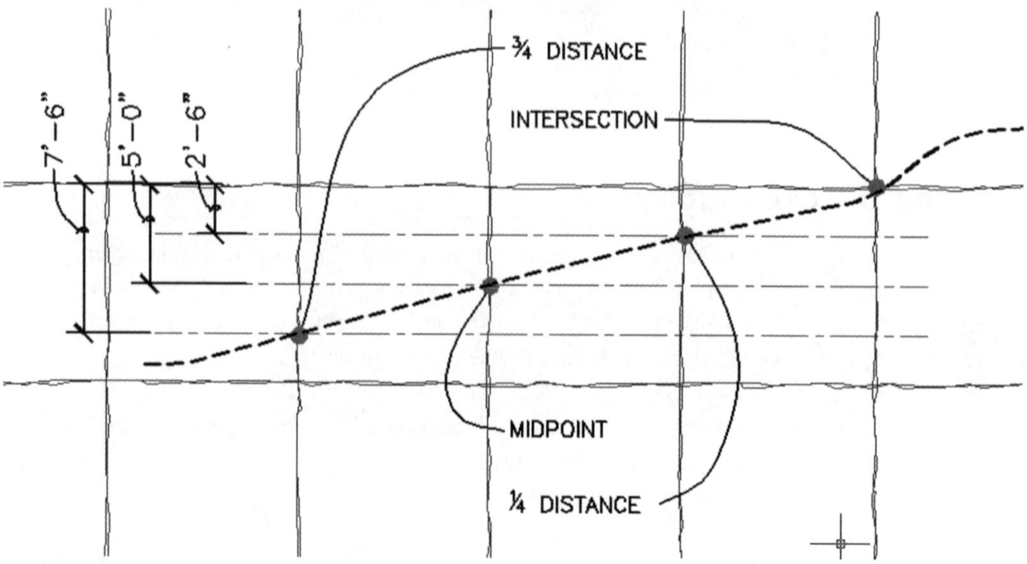

FIGURE 8-1.2 Contour layout explanation:
The image above shows the four primary points where the contour line crosses the vertical grid lines; the same process is used on horizontal grid lines.

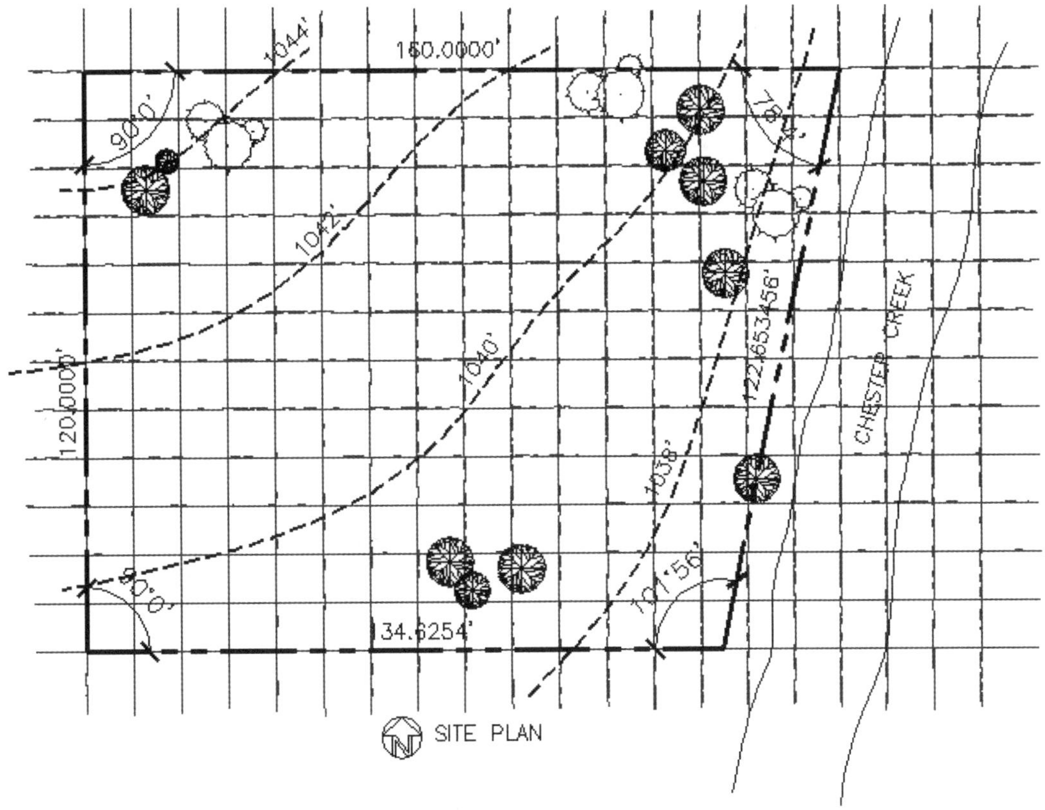

FIGURE 8-1.3
Site Survey; with 10′-0″ square grid overlay

Smoothing the Segmented Contours:

Now you will use the **Pedit** (aka, Polyline-Edit) command to smooth out the segmented contour lines. If you recall, you used the Pedit command to adjust the width of the grade line (which was a polyline) on your exterior elevations. Another sub-feature of the Pedit command is to smooth out a segmented Pline. The Pedit command has two methods available for smoothing a line: *Spline* (aka, Spline Fit) and *Fit* (aka, Curve Fit).

You can see the effect each option has on a polyline in Figure 8-1.4. The top figure indicates the original "segmented" polyline where the dots represent the points you picked while drawing the Pline. The second (or middle) image shows what happens when you use the *Spline* option of Pedit. Finally, the bottom image shows how the *Fit* option modifies a Pline.

Seeing as the points you pick to create the polyline (i.e., contour) are defining the path, you will want to use the *Fit* option on your contours.

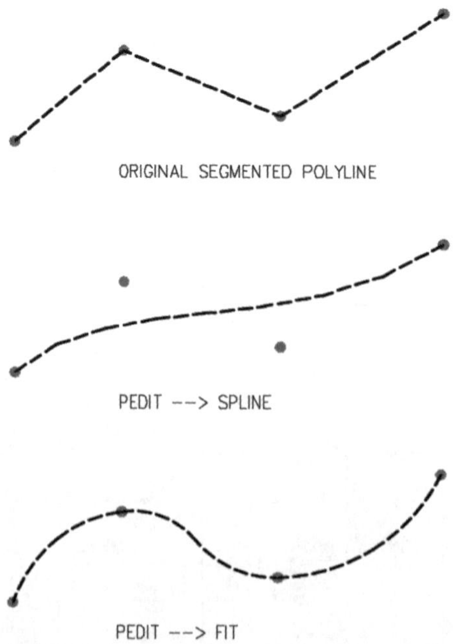

FIGURE 8-1.4
PEDIT Options; compare results of Pedit:Spline and Pedit:Fit

7. Type **Pedit**, press **Enter**, and then select one of the contour lines.

You now see the following in the *Command Window*: **Enter an option [Close/Join/Width/Edit vertex/Fit/Spline/Decurve/Ltype gen/Undo]:**

8. Type **F** (for Fit) and then press **Enter**.

The line is now smoothed and you get the same prompt as before, which would allow you to further modify the polyline if necessary.

9. Press **Enter** to complete the *Pedit* command.

You can also select the *Pline* and right-click to access the options just covered (see image to the right).

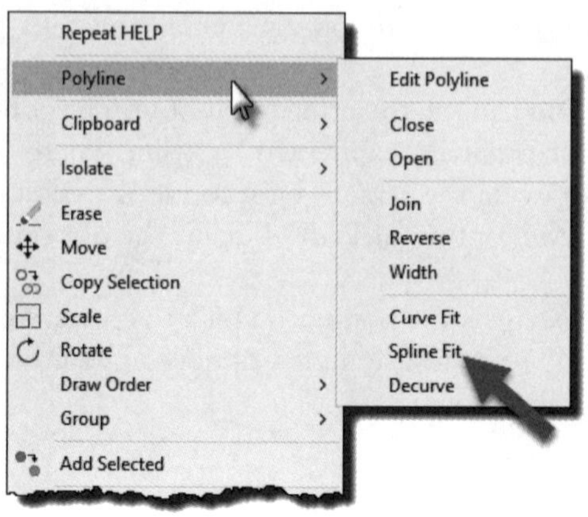

10. Repeat the previous three steps to smooth out each contour line.

11. Using the information just covered, draw the creek:

    a. Draw the lines on *Layer* ***C-WATR***.

    b. Smooth the lines using Pedit.

Adding the Trees and North Arrow:

Once again, thanks to one of AutoCAD's sample drawings you have access to the pre-drawn trees and a north arrow shown in Figure 8-1.1. You will place these items next.

12. Using ***DesignCenter*** (and steps previously covered in this book), browse to the folder shown in Figure 8-1.5.

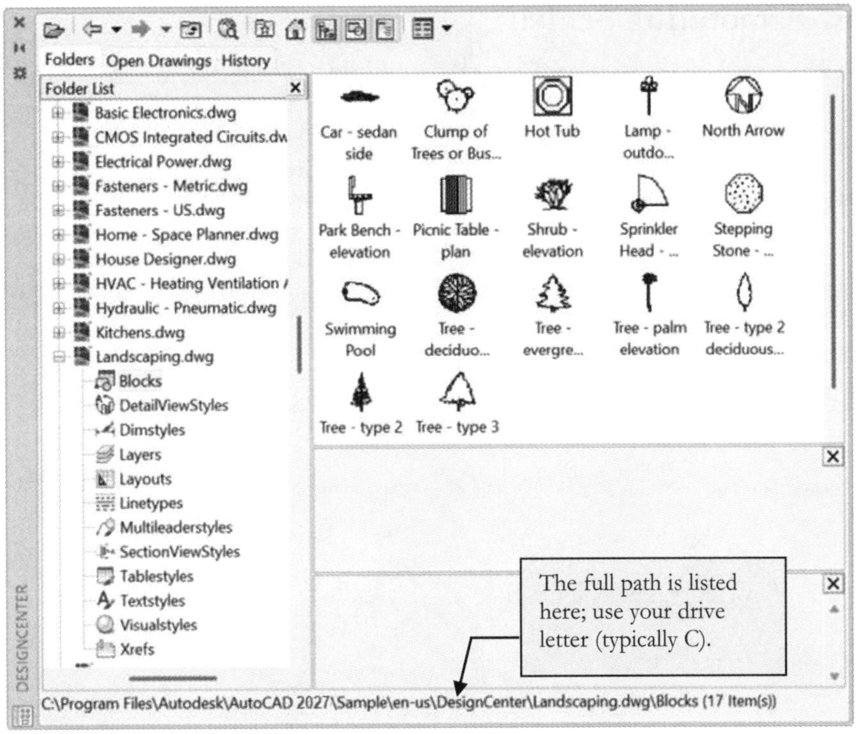

FIGURE 8-1.5
DesignCenter: landscape blocks available via the sample files

13. Drag and drop "**Clump of Trees or Bushes – plan**" and "**Tree – deciduous plan**" into your site plan; the trees should automatically be placed on the correct *Layer: C-Tree.*

14. Copy the *Blocks* around the drawing using Figure 8-1.3 as a reference for quantity and location.

FYI: You are drawing existing conditions, not designing a new site; therefore, you should not deviate from the prescribed drawing at this time.

TIP: You can (and should) Scale and Rotate the tree blocks so they don't all look the same and thus will better account for current conditions.

Insert the **North Arrow** drawing from the *DesignCenter.*

15. Draw all the text shown in Figure 8-1.1, including the contour elevation labels, property line lengths and the creek label (all of which should be on the *C-ANNO-TEXT* layer).
    a. Rotate the text to align with the contours and property lines.

Adding a New Annotation Scale:

The template you started with does not have a 1″=20′-0″ option in the list of scales (1:20 is not the same; it is 1″=20″). You will learn to add it to the list so your annotation is correct.

16. From the scale list (you may need to scroll down), select **Custom** (Figure 8-1.6).

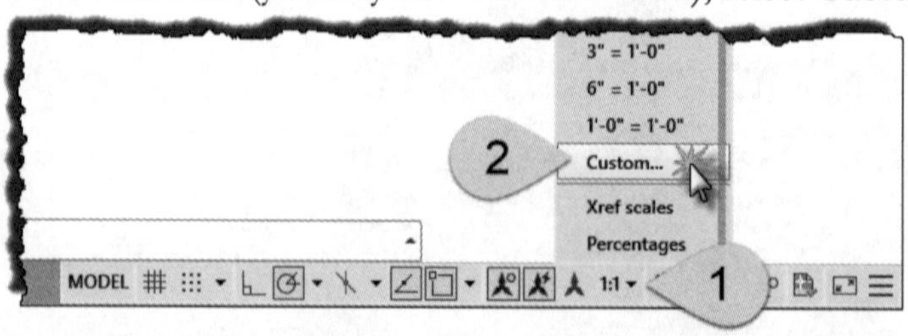

FIGURE 8-1.6 Annotation scale

17. Click **Add.**

18. Enter **1″ = 20′-0″** for the name (Figure 8-1.7).

19. Set the following:
    a. Paper units: **1**
    b. Drawing units: **20′**

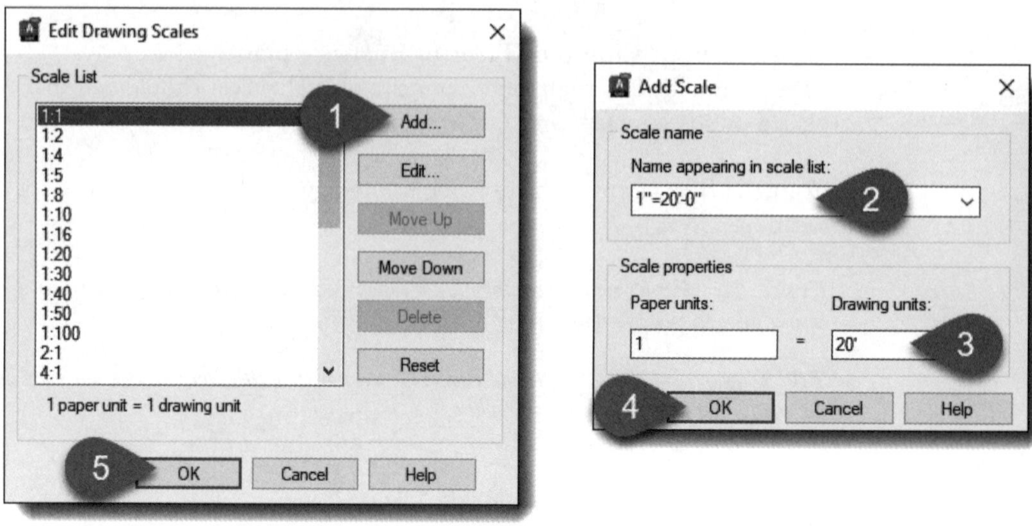

FIGURE 8-1.7 Custom scale

20. Click **OK** to close the open dialog boxes.
21. Set the annotation scale to **1″=20′-0″**.

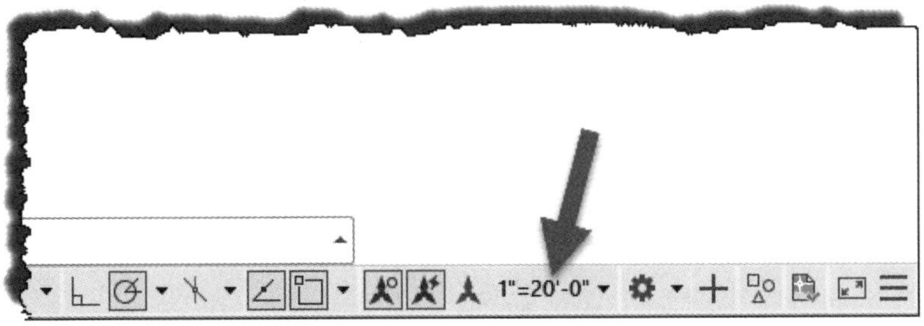

FIGURE 8-1.8 New annotation scale

In addition to the items just drawn, you might expect to find the following items on a survey/site plan:

- **Utilities**– water, gas, storm, sewer, cable, etc.
- **Land Features**– exposed ledge, rock, ponds, etc.
- **Easements/Covenants**– areas you cannot build on so access to utilities can be maintained.
- **Setbacks**– how close a building can be to the front, back and side property lines based on local zoning codes.
- **Soil Boring Locations**– where soil tests have been done to determine the footing size and depth.

The items listed above are added by the survey based on what has been contracted for when the survey was ordered. If you (or the client) only paid for property line locations, that is all you get! Typically, the client directly pays the surveyor to lessen the Architect/Designer's liability related to the survey's accuracy and potential of unknown conditions (e.g., buried foundation wall).

You now have the existing site plan drawn and ready for you to place the new elements such as the building, walks, driveway, etc.

> *TIP: It is good practice to save an unmodified copy of any original drawing. This helps if you decide to start over and have made several changes to the drawing. It also helps to quickly go back and verify existing conditions; maybe you accidentally erased a tree and did not realize it until later. You could open the archived existing drawing and copy/paste the missing tree into your new drawing. In your new drawing, once all the existing conditions have been drawn, it is a good idea to Lock the "existing"* Layers *to keep from accidentally changing existing linework. You should never erase anything existing; rather, place it on a demolition* Layer *(whose linetype is dashed).*

Exercise 8-2:
Add House, Driveway and Walks

Introduction:

This exercise locates the outline of the building on the site as well as the driveway and sidewalk.

First you will create the appropriate Layers.

1. *Layer Name* — *Color* — *Linetype*

	Layer Name	Color	Linetype
a.	C-ANNO-DIMS	Yellow	CONTINUOUS
b.	C-BLDG	WHITE	CONTINUOUS
c.	C-BLDG-PATT	254	CONTINUOUS
d.	C-BLDG-PRCH	YELLOW	CONTINUOUS
e.	C-WALK	RED	CONTINUOUS
f.	C-ROAD	RED	CONTINUOUS

Now you will temporarily Xref in your first floor plan so you can draw an outline of your building and see where the doors are.

2. **Xref** your first floor plan (flr1.dwg) into the site drawing.

3. Move the Xref'ed floor plan so it is in the proper position, as shown in Figure 8-2.1.

4. **Freeze** the *Dimension* layer in the floor plan Xref:

   a. When you Xref a drawing, all the visible *Layers* in that drawing are also visible in the Xref; you can Freeze some *Layers* in the Xref if you wish.

   b. Each *Layer* in the Xref'ed drawing shows up in the *Layer Properties Manager*, each with the Xref's **filename** as a prefix.

   c. So, to Freeze the Xref's dimension layer, you will Freeze the *Layer* named ***Flr1|A-Anno-Dims***.

Next you will draw a polyline around the perimeter of the building.

5. On the ***C-BLDG*** layer, draw a **Pline** around the perimeter of your building.

   a. Do not draw the outline around the porch, just the building.

   b. Use AutoCAD's *OSNAPs* to accurately draw the outline.

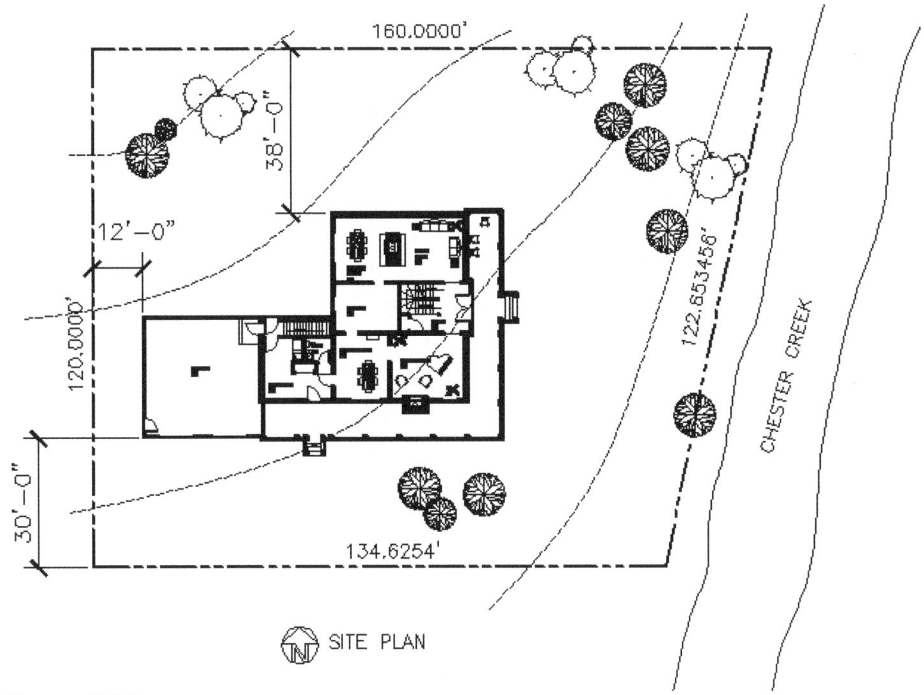

FIGURE 8-2.1
Site Plan; Xref positioned in proper location

6. Draw a **Polyline** along the exterior side of the porch on layer C-Bldg-PRCH.

7. Add the dimensions shown in Figure 8-2.1 on layer C-Anno-Dims.

   TIP: Make sure your Annotation Scale is set to 1″ = 20′-0″.

8. Draw a 22′-0″ wide driveway centered on the garage doors on *Layer C-Road.*

   TIP: Draw a line from the Midpoint of the wall between the two garage doors and then Offset the line 11′-0″ each way.

9. Now draw a 5′-0″ wide sidewalk as shown in Figure 8-2.3 on layer *C-Walk.*

   TIP: Draw one side of the sidewalk, using Fillet, and then Offset the lines 5′-0″ to create the other side of the sidewalk.

Next, you will *Unload* (not detach) the Xref. By unloading the Xref, you can quickly *Reload* it without having to browse for it, position it and adjust the *Layers*. This is handy for occasionally verifying that your building outline is still up to date.

10. In the *External References Palette*, **right-click** and select **Unload** the Flr1 drawing (Figure 8-2.2).

11. Click **X** to close the *External References Palette.*

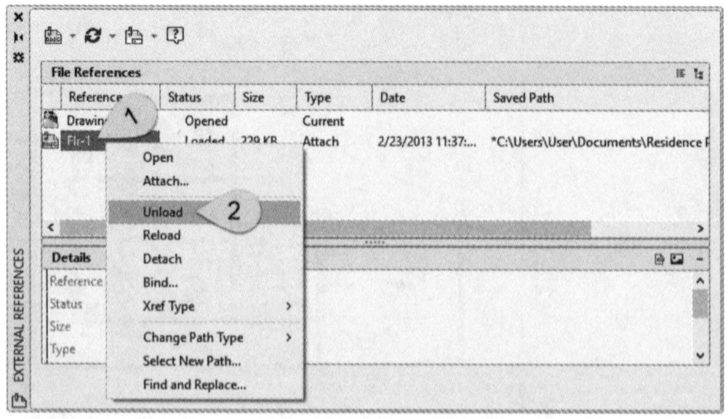

FIGURE 8-2.2
External References Palette; Flr1 drawing unloaded

Your drawing should now look like Figure 8-2.3.

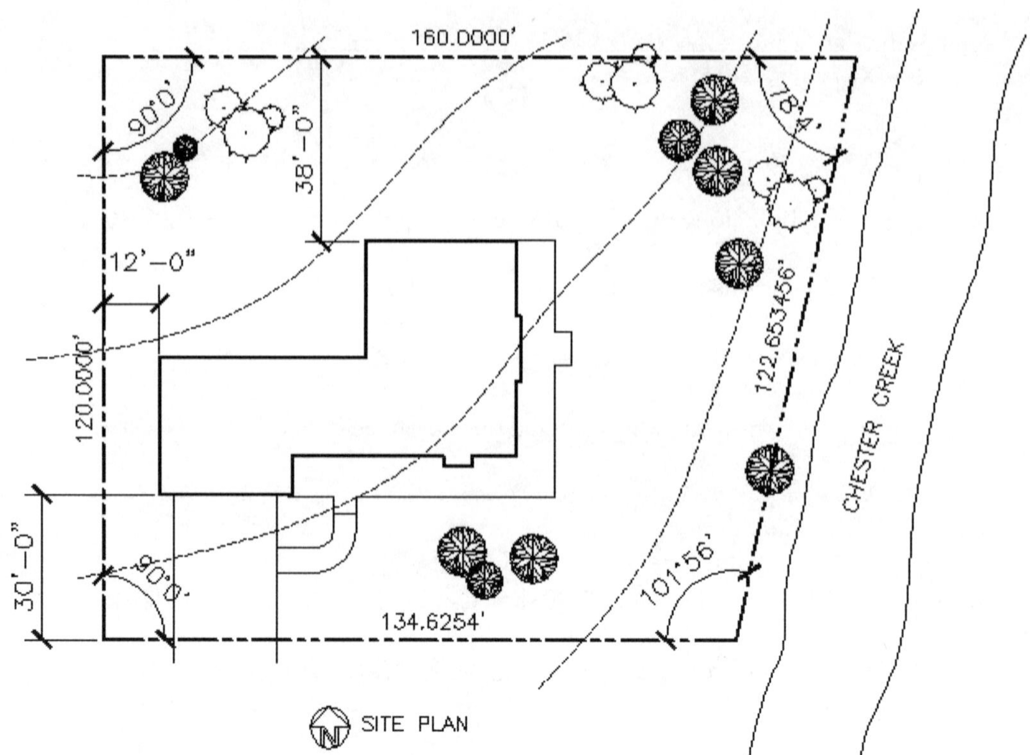

FIGURE 8-2.3
Site Plan; building outline and paved areas added

Next you will fill the building footprint with a solid shade to help it stand out.

12. Using the **Hatch** command, add a *Solid* hatch pattern to the building footprint on layer *C-Bldg-Patt.*

13. Draw a 20′-0″ x 16′-0″ patio on the back inside corner of the residence (see Figure 8-2.4).

14. Use the *Hatch* pattern "**GRAVEL**" at a scale of **48** as a symbol for stone pavers in the patio.

15. From the *Landscaping* sample drawing (discussed in the previous exercise), **Insert** the picnic table; Rotate as shown in Figure 8-2.4.

16. Save your drawing as **ex8-2.dwg**.

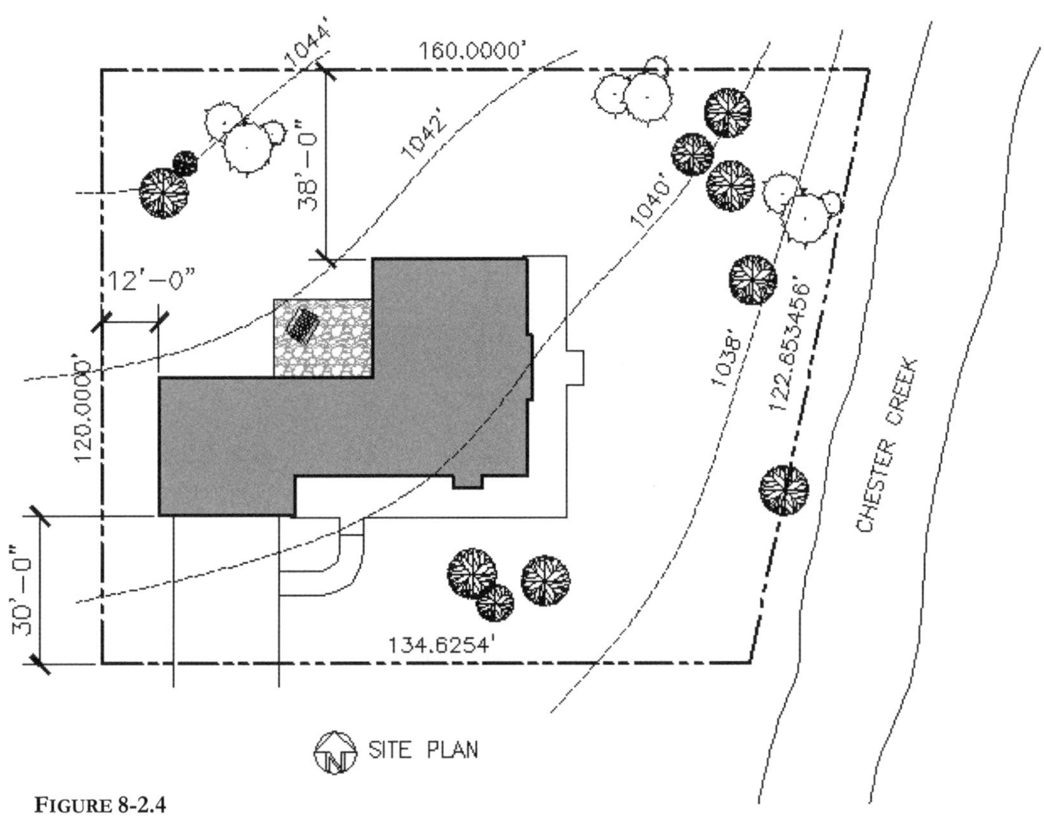

FIGURE 8-2.4
Site Plan; building fill and patio added

Exercise 8-3:
Layout New Contours

Introduction:

In this lesson, you will add new contours and take a quick look at drawing a cross-section of the grade along a line.

The site's finished grade needs to be modified primarily to improve drainage. The drainage, as currently shown in Figure 8-2.4, would dump quite a bit of surface runoff (i.e., rainwater) into the back inside corner of the residence.

To indicate modified grading, new contours are added to the site plan. These contours show the contractor the final finished grade and intended drainage for the site.

New contours are shown with solid (i.e., continuous) lines:

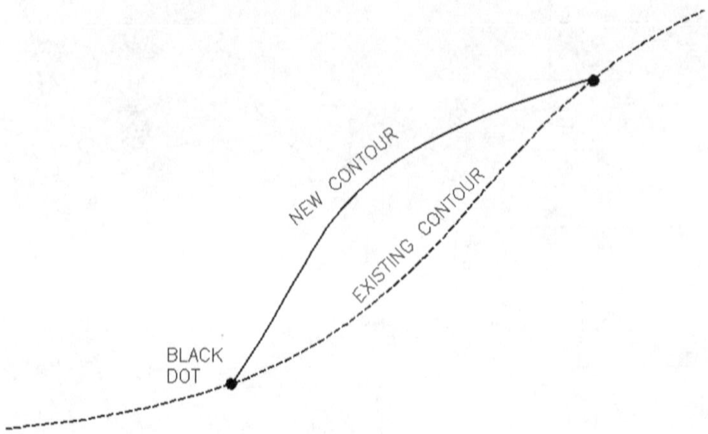

FIGURE 8-3.1
New Contour; new contour solid, existing contour dashed

As a contour with a smaller number (i.e., lower elevation) gets closer to a contour with a larger number (i.e., higher elevation), the contractor has to remove earth:

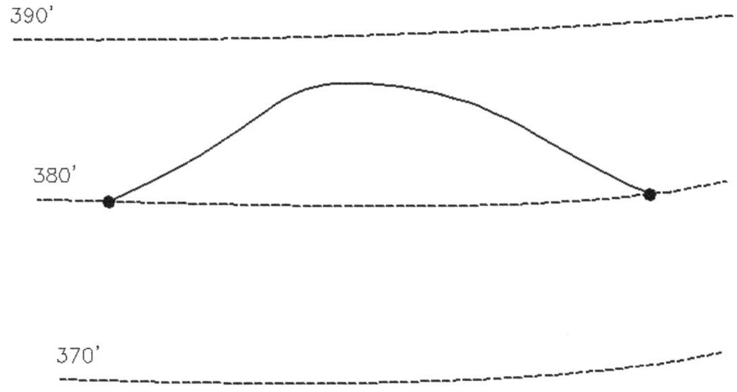

FIGURE 8-3.2 Earth Cut Example
Imagine the new contour extending straight into the existing hillside and coming back out to reconnect with the existing contour. All the earth above that line needs to be removed!

Conversely, when a higher contour is moved closer to a lower contour, the contractor has to add earth:

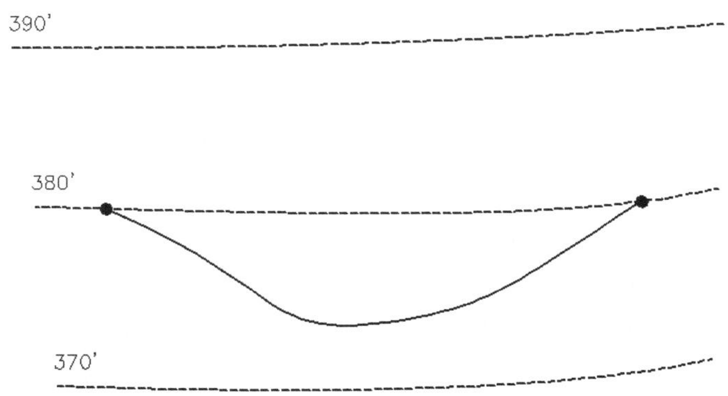

FIGURE 8-3.3 Earth Fill Example
Now imagine the new contour extending straight out into the air above the existing hillside and coming back to reconnect with the existing contour. Earth needs to be added below the line to support it!

Now you will draw new contours on your site plan.

1. Create a *Layer* named ***C-Topo-Neww***.
    a. Linetype: ***Continuous***
    b. Color: ***Green***

FYI: It looks like a mistake, but the strict National CAD Standards require four characters in their standard Layer naming conventions.

You do not need to be extremely accurate when drawing the new contours in the next step; just try to get it as close as possible.

2. Draw the **new contours** shown in Figure 8-3.4.
    a. Use the Polyline (aka, Pline) command to draw the lines.
    b. Use Pedit→*Spline* to smooth out the contours (or right-click menu).
    c. Use the *Nearest Snap* to accurately attach your new contour with the existing contour.

3. Use the **Donut** command to create the black dots at the start and end points of each new contour line (Figure 8-3.4).
    a. Set the inside diameter to **0″**.
    b. Set the outside diameter to **24″**.
    c. Draw the Donut on layer ***C-Topo-Neww***.

FYI: To the right is a donut with its inside diameter set to something other than zero.

4. Use the **MultiLeader** command to draw the "drainage flow" lines (Figure 8-3.4).
    a. Create a new *MultiLeader* style
        i. Named *Drainage*
        ii. Select *Spline*
        iii. Max. leader points = 10
        iv. Multileader type = none
        v. Linetype to **Center2**.
    b. Place the *MultiLeader* on the ***C-Anno-Text*** layer.

    FYI: You will be drawing two multileaders.

5. Add the text "DRAINAGE FLOW" (as shown in Figure 8-3.4).

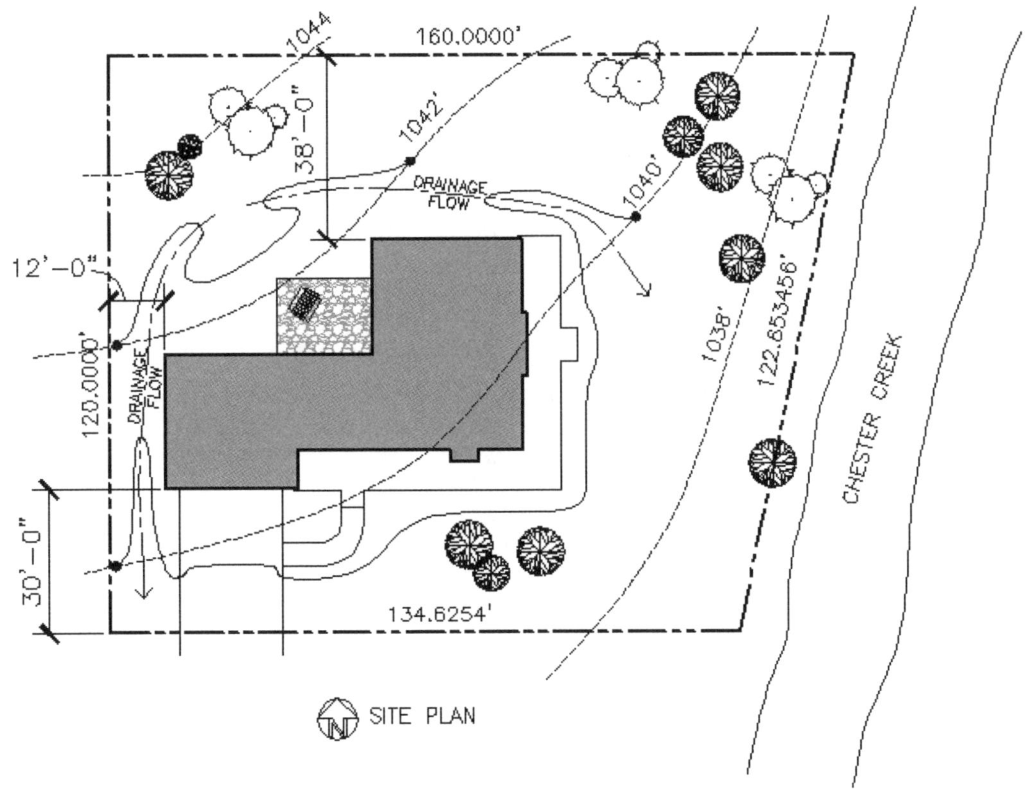

FIGURE 8-3.4
New contours added; Plines drawn and smoothed out with the Pedit command

Notice in the image above that the contour line 1040′ cuts into the earth near each end of the new contour line and requires fill to be added in between.

The new contour lines reach up toward the higher contour where it intersects the drainage flow line. This creates a swale (not unlike a river, but subtler of course) that "directs" water around the building.

A spot elevation should be called out in the back inside corner. The elevation should be high enough to allow any rainwater that falls in that area to flow away from the building.

Drawing a Grade Profile:

Now you will look at how to draw a grade profile. A grade profile is analogous to drawing a building section; you are showing what the land looks like in a section view.

The profile in this example will show both the new and existing profiles. This could then be used to calculate the amount of cut-and-fill required on the site. It can also be used to determine the building's floor elevation relative to finished grade.

In this example, you will draw a line generally perpendicular to the slope of the site. The first thing you will do is draw a line on the site plan that indicates where the profile is to be cut.

6. Draw a line on your site plan, approximately perpendicular to the contour lines as shown in Figure 8-3.5.

7. At this point, you may want to temporarily copy your entire site plan off to one side so you can rotate it, making the section line aligned with the drawing window (Figure 8-3.5).

*TIP: The most accurate way to rotate the drawing is to use Rotate and then the Reference sub-command. First, you pick your base point, then R for reference. Next, you pick one end of the section line and then the other end. Finally, you type 0 (or 180) and press **Enter**. See AutoCAD's **Help** system for more information on this feature.*

8. In the closest available empty drawing area below the section line, draw 6 horizontal lines spaced 2′-0″ apart (Figure 8-3.5).

FYI: This spacing corresponds to the vertical distance between the contours.

9. Project a vertical line down from the location where each contour intersects the section line (Figure 8-3.5).

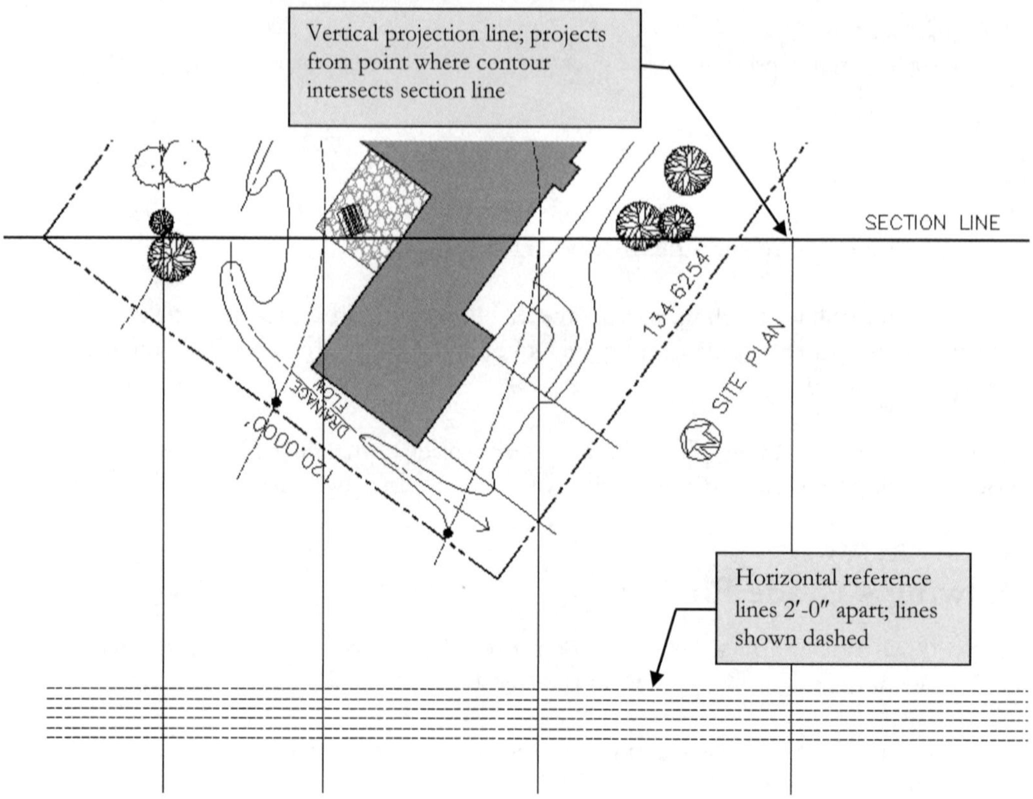

FIGURE 8-3.5
Reference lines for profile; copy of site plan rotated so section line is orthogonal

Now you simply play connect-the-dots to create the grade profile (Figure 8-3.6).

10. Draw a **Pline**, picking the points where the vertical projection lines intersect the horizontal reference lines.

11. Use the **Fit** feature of *Pedit* to smooth out the line (Figure 8-3.6).

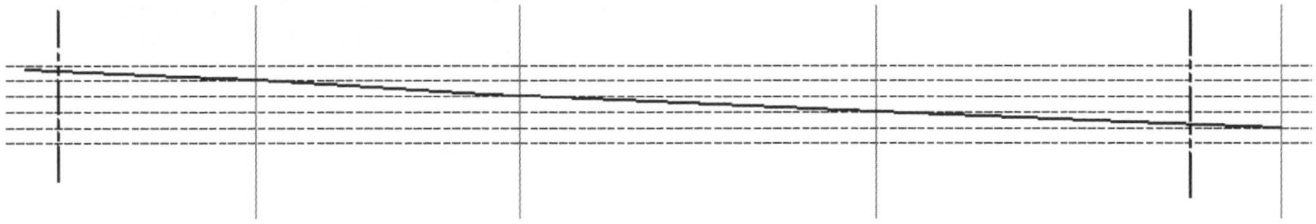

FIGURE 8-3.6
Grade Profile; property lines also added for context

12. You can now **Erase** the vertical projection lines.

13. Use the same technique just covered to draw the new grade profile, then overlay the two to see the variation.

FYI: This section does not show a significant amount of cut and fill.

The sample image shown below indicates how a profile looks with both new and existing profiles. This image can be used to estimate the amount of cut-and-fill required for the project. The ideal situation is to have equal amounts of each to avoid buying fill or paying to haul away extra fill.

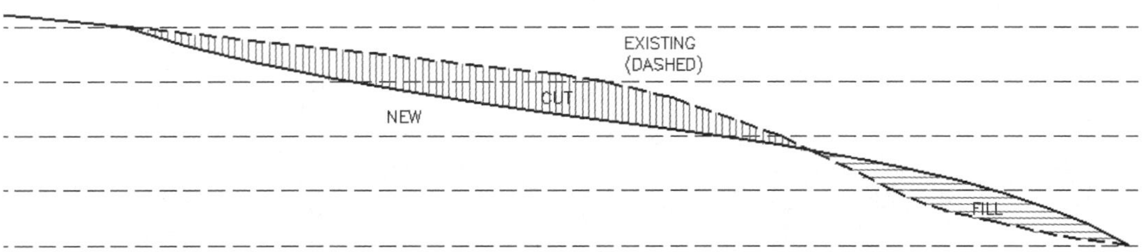

FIGURE 8-3.7
Sample Grade Profile; sample profile with both new and existing shown (existing shown dashed)

14. **Save** your drawing.

TIP: Civil Engineers sometimes exaggerate the vertical scale of sections so they are easier to read.

Defining your location on Earth:

It is possible to specify the location of your project on the Earth. This is done from the *Insert* tab, using the **Set Location** tool. The first time you click **Set Location → From Esri Maps**. This will allow you to see satellite photometry in AutoCAD. When the *Geographic Location* window appears, simply type in the city or project address to define a location. To refine your location, right-click on the map and select **Drop Pin Here**.

Once the image is displayed in AutoCAD, you will see a Geolocation tab on the Ribbon, which provides several tools to adjust or remove the location. The **Esri Imagery** drop-down provides several options shown to the right, in the image below.

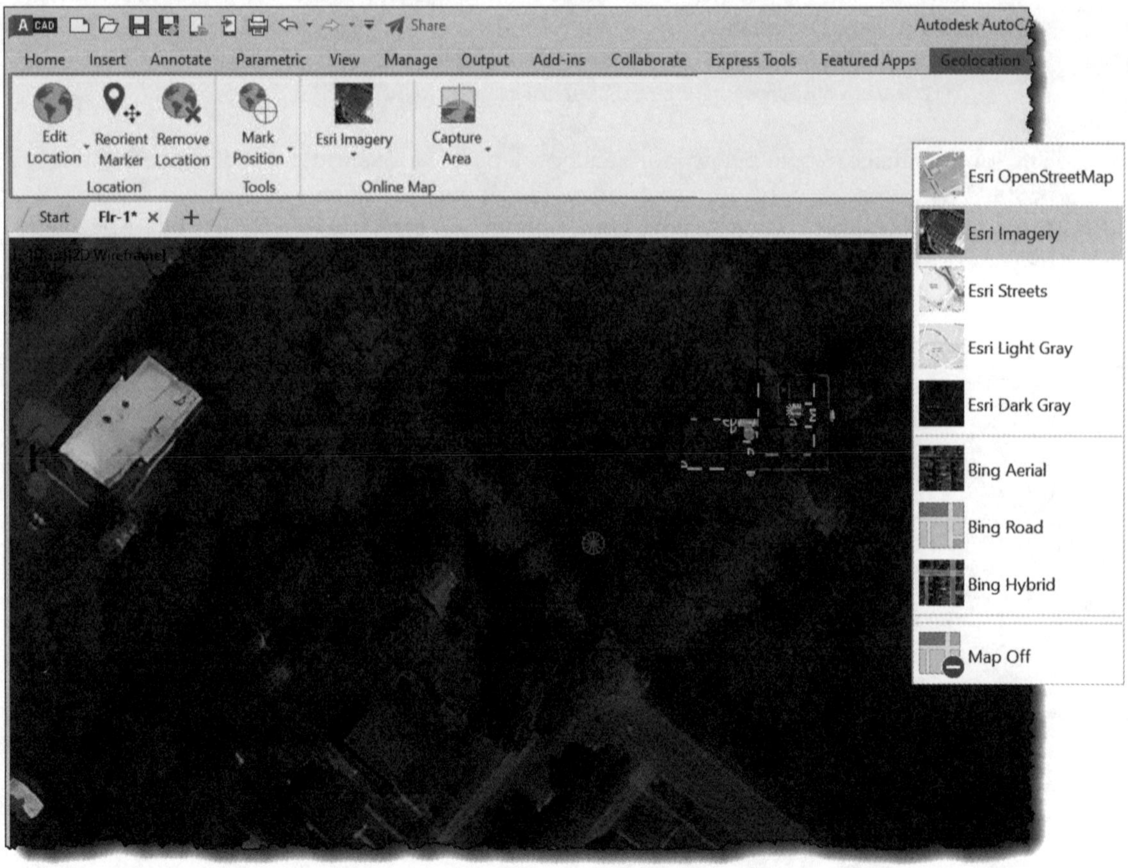

Self-Exam:

The following questions can be used as a way to check your knowledge of this lesson. The answers can be found at the bottom of this page.

1. You can use the Donut command to draw solid dots. (T/F)
2. You can "unload" an Xref and then quickly "reload" it later. (T/F)
3. You typically have to scale a survey drawing (drawn with Decimal units) down 12 times to work with Architectural units. (T/F)
4. You draw new contours on this *Layer*: ___________________________
5. New contour lines are "continuous" and existing lines are "dashed." (T/F)

Review Questions:

The following questions may be assigned by your instructor as a way to assess your knowledge of this section. Your instructor has the answers to the review questions.

1. A grade profile can help to calculate the amount of cut and fill required. (T/F)
2. Scaling and rotating the tree blocks as they are inserted helps to make the drawing look more natural (less like a cookie-cutter). (T/F)
3. A swale helps to direct the flow of surface runoff on a site. (T/F)
4. With the Pedit command, the _______________ sub-command makes a smoothed-out polyline that maintains the points you picked to draw the

   contour, whereas the __________________ sub-command allows the polyline to deviate from your original points.
5. Layers associated with an Xref have what as a name prefix? ______________
6. You need to set which property of a polyline to "enabled" to make the dashes

   consistent: __________________
7. When a "lower" (e.g., 1060′) contour is rerouted to move closer to a "high"

   (e.g., 1065′) contour, the contractor would have _______________ earth.
8. After picking your first point, type the *Command* window instructions to draw a line 321.125′ long with an angle of 43°12′ (ccw off the horizontal):

   @__________<____________.
9. To draw a solid black dot with a 24″ diameter you would use the Donut command with the "inside radius" set to 0″ and the "outside radius" set to 12. (T/F)
10. What *Layer* does the building outline go on? ___________________

SELF-EXAM ANSWERS:
1– T, **2**– T, **3**– F, **4** – c-topo-neww, **5** – T

Additional Tasks:

Task 8-1: Add Items to the Site Plan

Add additional items to the site plan, such as new trees and landscaping (labeling them as such). You can search the internet for pre-drawn blocks. Also, add notes for the new road and sidewalk (e.g., blacktop driveway; concrete sidewalk).

Task 8-2: Draw another Grade Profile

Draw a grade profile that generally follows one of the swales; this will be a more dramatic cut-and-fill profile.

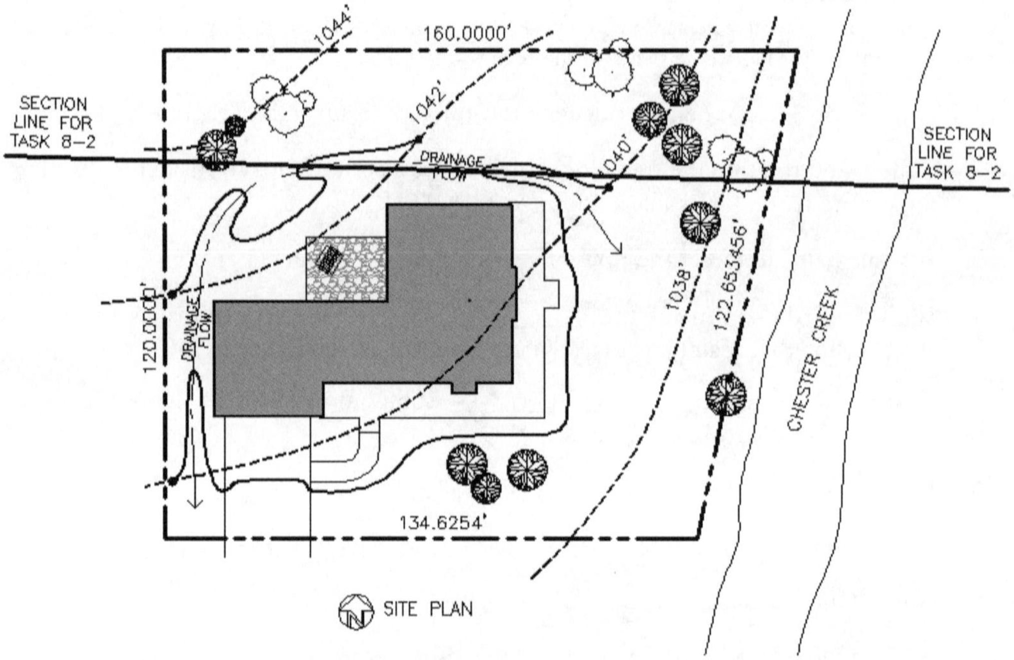

Task 8-3: Update the Grade Profile for Each Exterior Elevation

You can draw a grade profile at each side of the building and then superimpose that profile on your exterior elevations to accurately describe how the grade engages the building's perimeter.

Lesson 9
SCHEDULES & SHEET SET UP

In this lesson you will learn to use the new Table feature to create schedules in AutoCAD. You will also explore how drawings are set up on sheets so they can be plotted with a professional look and fashion.

Exercise 9-1:
Room Finish Schedule

Introduction:

A *Room Finish Schedule* indicates what finish the walls, ceiling, and floors get in each room. This information is typically organized in a grid of rows and columns, where each row represents a room and each column represents a surface to be finished. AutoCAD has a feature, called *Tables*, that is designed to accommodate this type of data (i.e., schedules).

Most rooms have both a name and a number to facilitate accurate identification on plans and schedules. Numbers are not always required on residential projects; however, it is typically done for consistency. Using a number is necessary when you have multiple rooms with the same name. In your plan, for example, you have multiple bathrooms and bedrooms. On large commercial projects, a floor plan might have 30-40 rooms all labeled "office," so it is easy to see how important numbers are.

The first step is to add the room numbers to your floor plans.

1. **Open** your **Flr-1** drawing.

2. Add the room numbers:

    a. Double-click on each room name.

    b. Click the cursor at the end of the room name.

    c. Press **Enter** to start a new line.

    d. Type the room numbers shown in Figure 9-1.1.

FYI: Having the room name and number in the same Mtext object helps to keep them aligned. It also makes moving them easier as you only have to worry about selecting one object, not two.

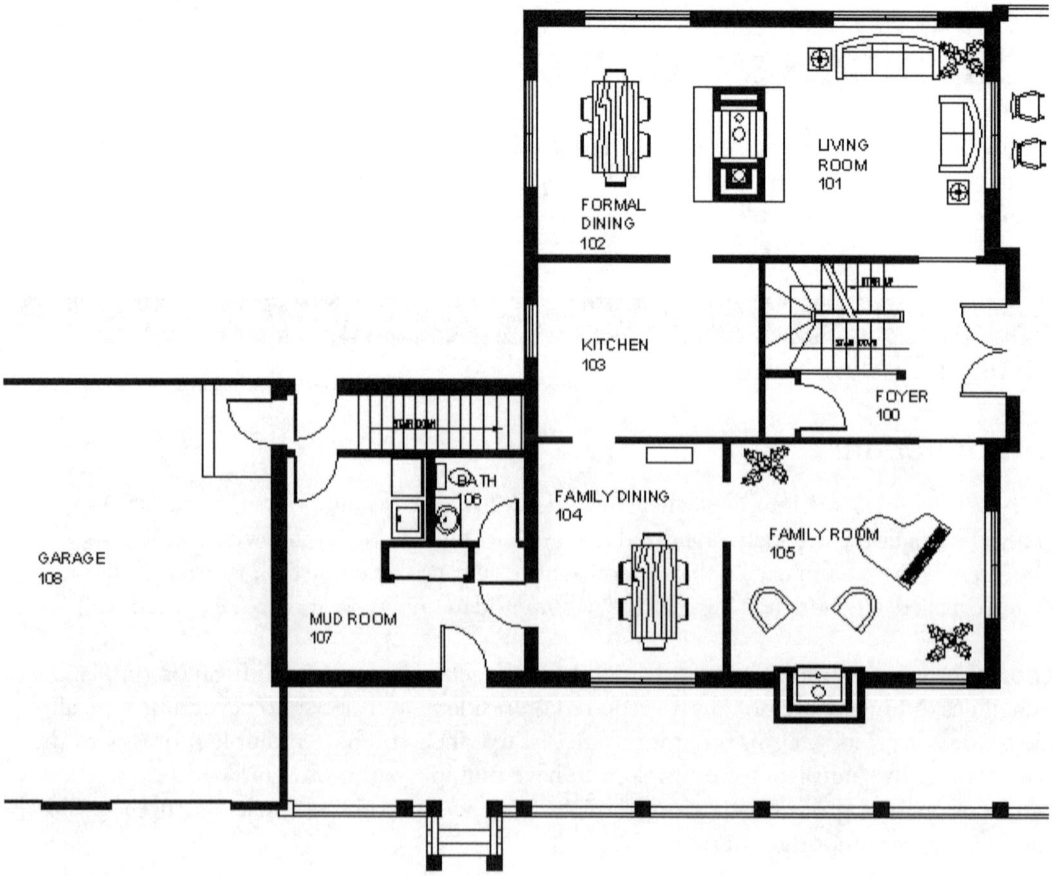

FIGURE 9-1.1
First floor plan; room numbers added

3. **Open** your **Flr-2** drawing.

4. Add the room numbers per Figure 9-1.2.

5. **Open** your **Flr-B** drawing.

6. Add the number **001** below the room name (i.e., UNFINISHED BASEMENT).

7. **Save** your floor plan drawings.

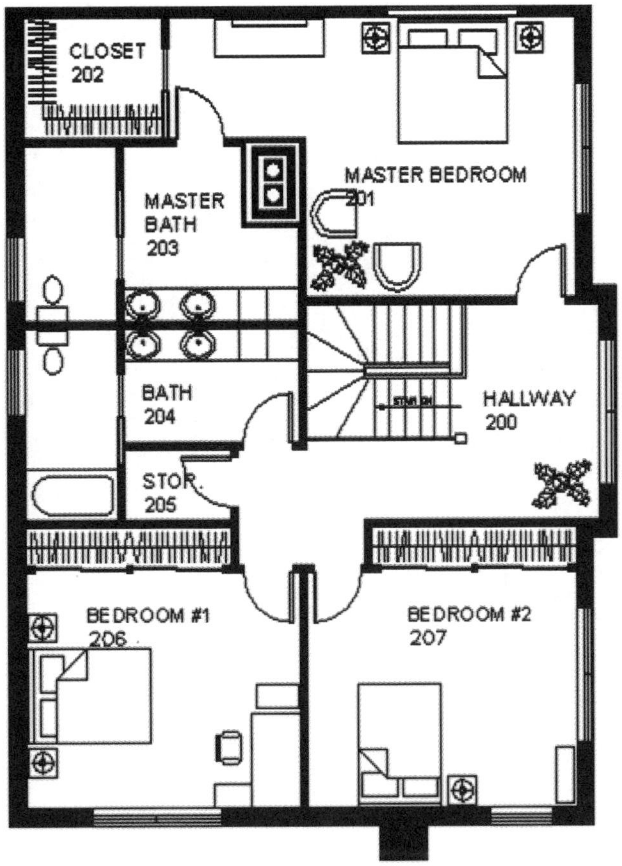

FIGURE 9-1.2
Second floor plan; room numbers added

Creating a Table:

8. Create a new drawing using **Architectural Imperial.dwt** as your template file.

9. Switch to *Model Space* and then click the **Table** icon from the *Home* panel (or type *Table* and press Enter).

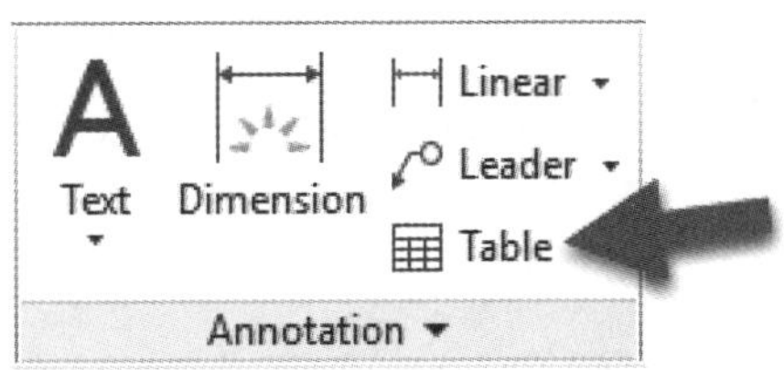

You are now in the *Insert Table* dialog box (Figure 9-1.3). At this point you could create a table using the *Standard* table style; if other styles existed, you could select one of them as well. You will create a *Table* using the *Standard* style.

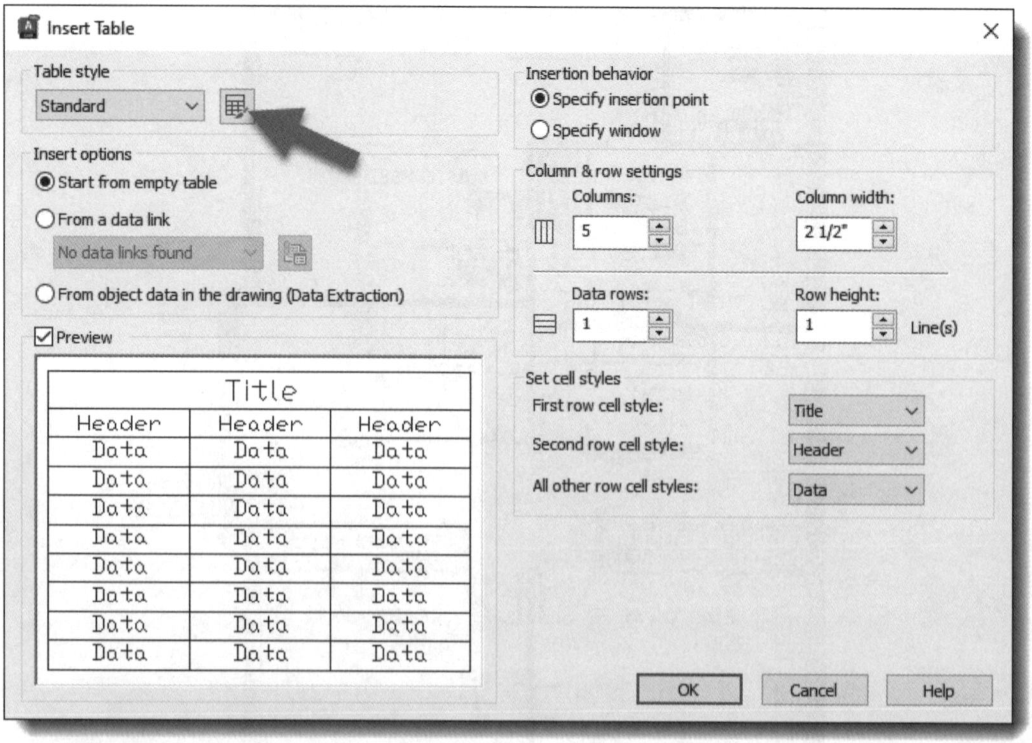

FIGURE 9-1.3
Insert Table dialog; initial view

Adjusting the Table Style Settings:

The first thing you will do is adjust the *Standard* table style. You will adjust the *Text Height* to a smaller size as well as change the *Text Style.*

10. Click on the **Table Style Settings** button (Figure 9-1.3). 

11. Click the **Modify…** button to modify the *Standard* table style.

12. Make changes shown in **Figure 9-1.4** to the **Data** *Cell styles.*

13. Make changes shown in **Figure 9-1.5** to the **Header** *Cell styles.*

    FYI: *Only the* Text *tab has changes to it (typically).*

14. Make changes shown in **Figure 9-1.6** to the **Title** *Cell styles.*

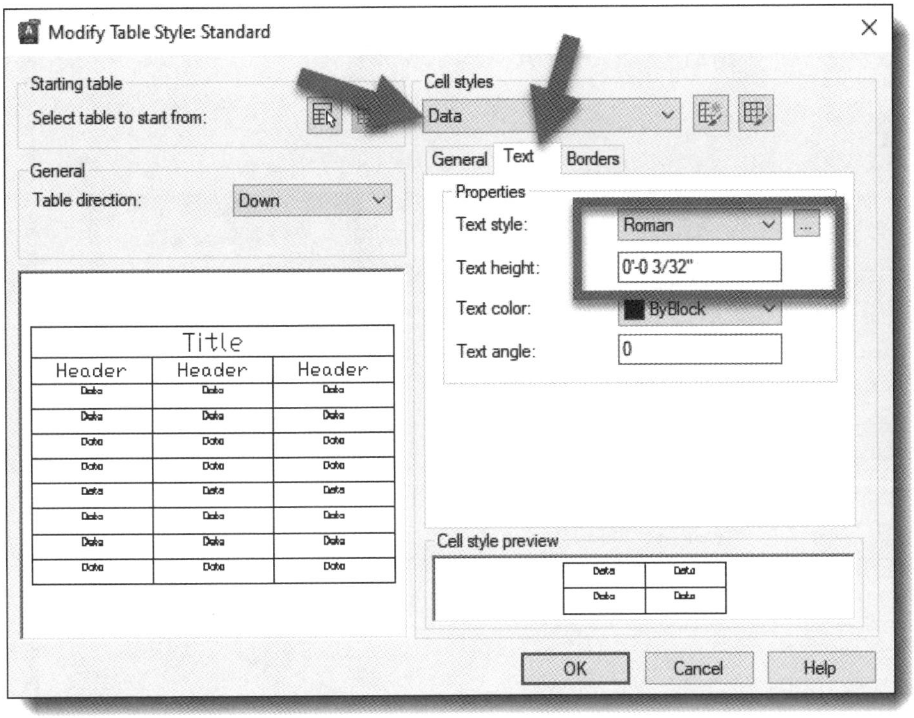

FIGURE 9-1.4
Modify Table Style dialog; Data tab

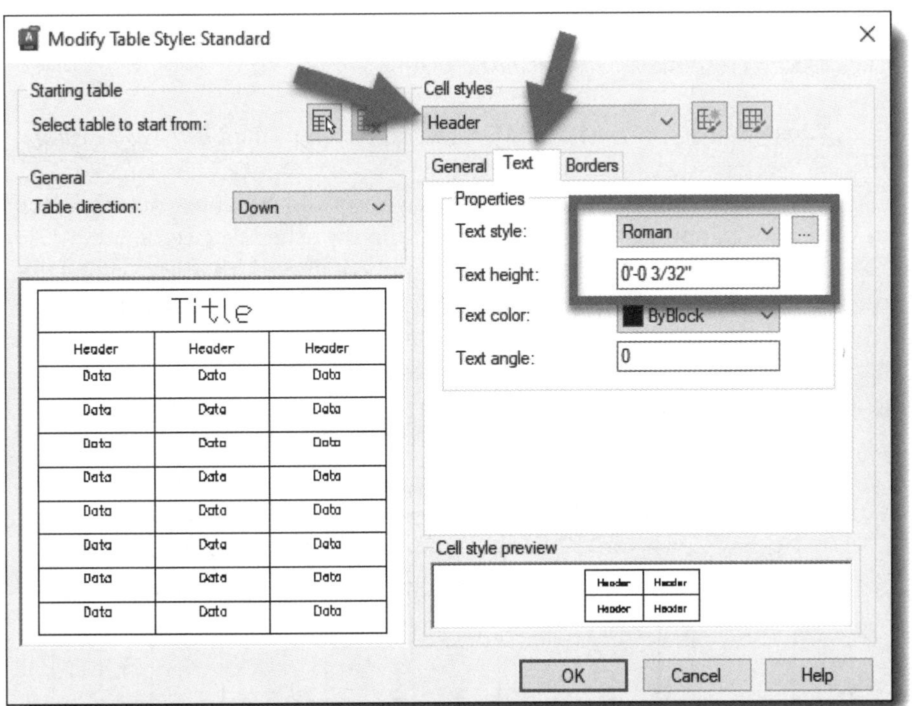

FIGURE 9-1.5
Modify Table Style dialog; Column Heads tab

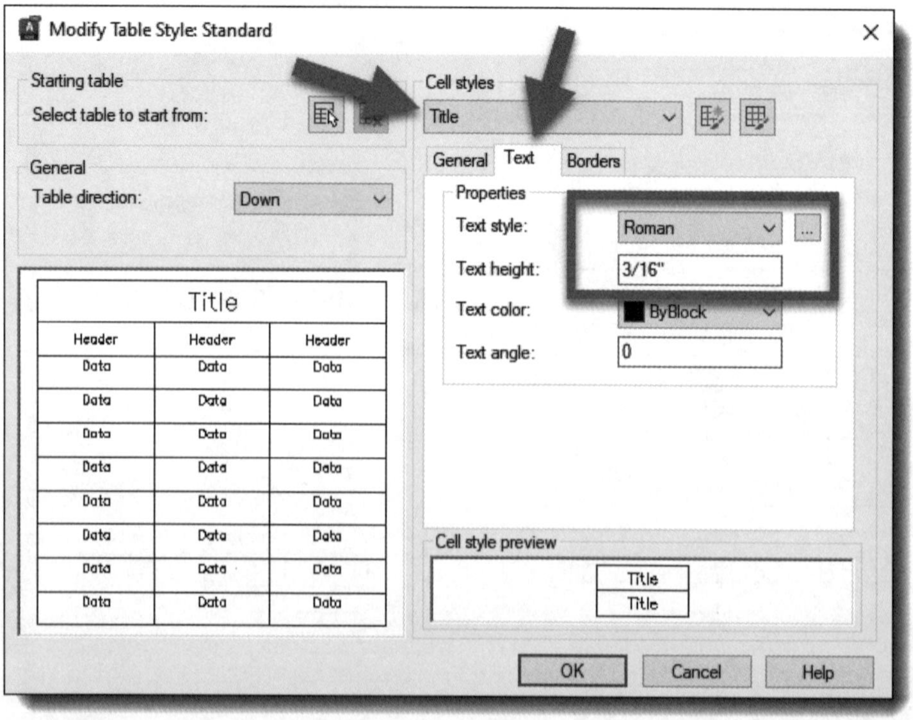

FIGURE 9-1.6
Modify Table Style dialog; Title tab

15. Click **OK** to close the *Modify Table Style* dialog.

16. Click **Close** to exit the *Table Style Manager* and return to the *Insert Table* dialog.

At this point, you need to have an idea of how many rows and columns you need. You can sketch out what information you will need to display in the schedule (see Figure 9-1.7 for an example). You also need to specify the row height and column width; these will be the default row and column sizes. You will be able to adjust the size of individual columns/rows once the *Table* has been created. You can also add rows and/or columns after creating the *Table*. Therefore, you do not need to be too concerned about forgetting a row or column at this point, as it can easily be added later.

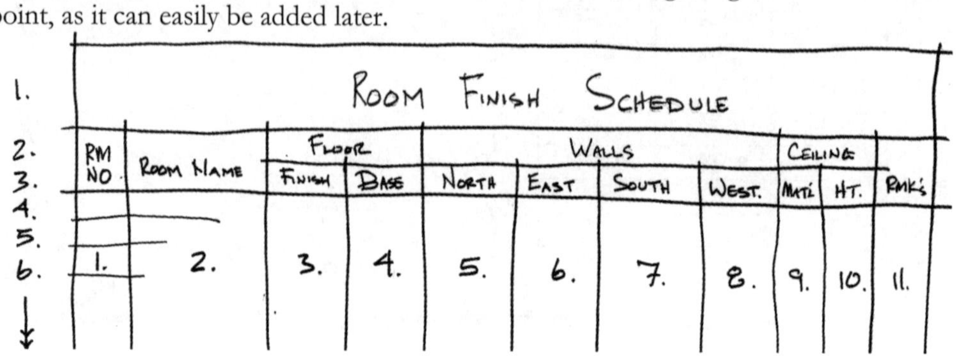

FIGURE 9-1.7
Preliminary Room Finish Schedule Sketch

Based on the sketch above, create a quick Table with 11 columns and 6 rows. You will make additional adjustments later.

17. Make the following adjustments to the *Insert Table* dialog:
    a. Columns: **11**
    b. Column Width: **1"**
    c. Data Rows: **6**
    d. *Leave everything else at the default* (Figure 9-1.3).

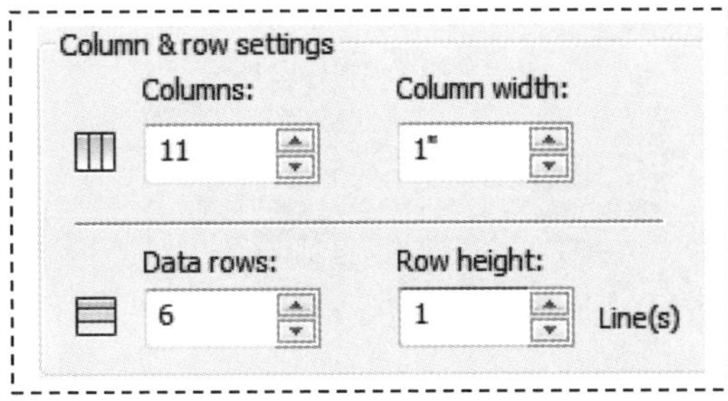

18. Click **OK** to insert the *Table.*

At this point, you will see the specified *Table* attached to your crosshairs so you can visually place it.

19. Move your cursor so the entire *Table* is visible and centered on the screen and click the mouse to place it.

You are now automatically prompted for the title of the table.

20. For the *Table* title, type "**ROOM FINISH SCHEDULE**" (Figure 9-1.8).

TIP: Just start typing; no need to click anywhere.

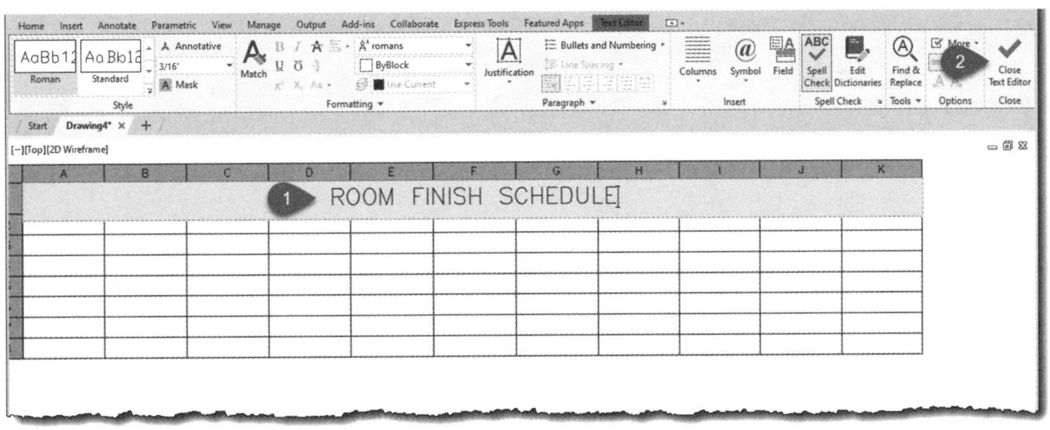

FIGURE 9-1.8
Inserted Table; entering table title text

21. Click **Close Text Editor** on the *Text Editor* tab/ribbon.

You now have a *Table* created in your drawing. Next, you will adjust the width of the columns to match the sketch.

22. Select a column to adjust its width per the following:
    a. Click and drag the mouse from the lowest cell to the highest cell (or vice versa).
    b. See Figure 9-1.9.

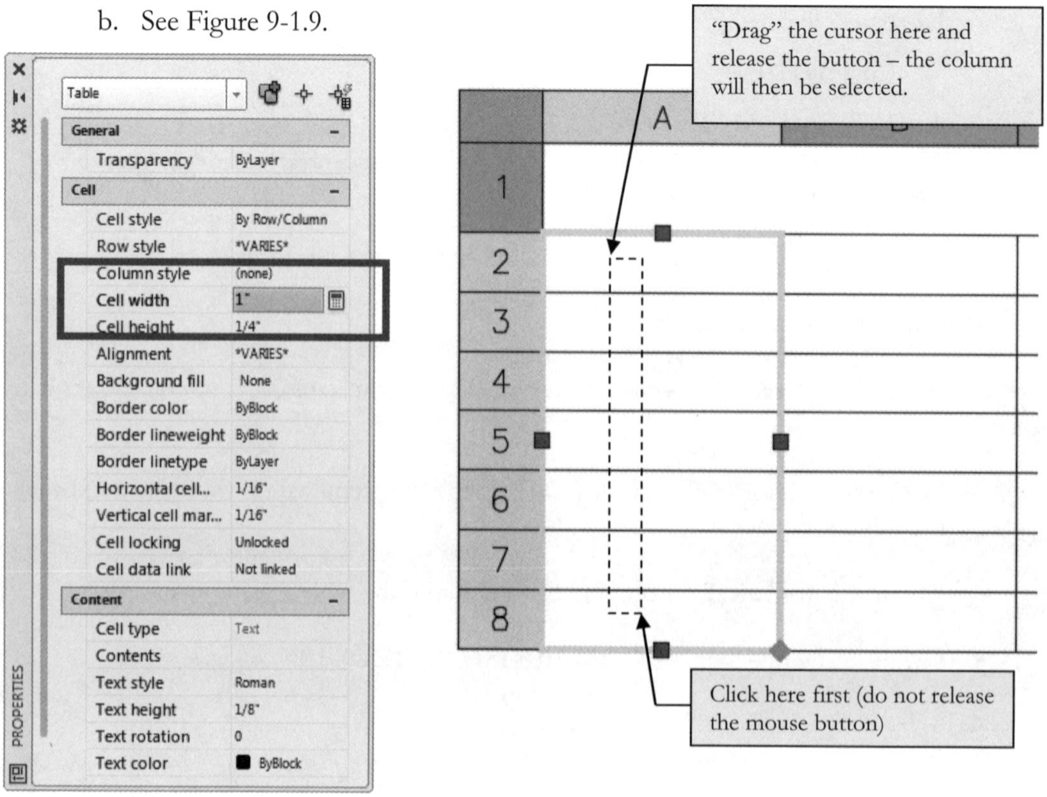

FIGURE 9-1.9
Table and its Properties; column selected (selected cells properties displayed)

23. In the *Properties Palette*, change the *Cell width* to **.5"** (for the selected column, column A) and then press **Enter**.

The *Table* column has now been updated to display the *column width* per your specifications (Figure 9-1.10).

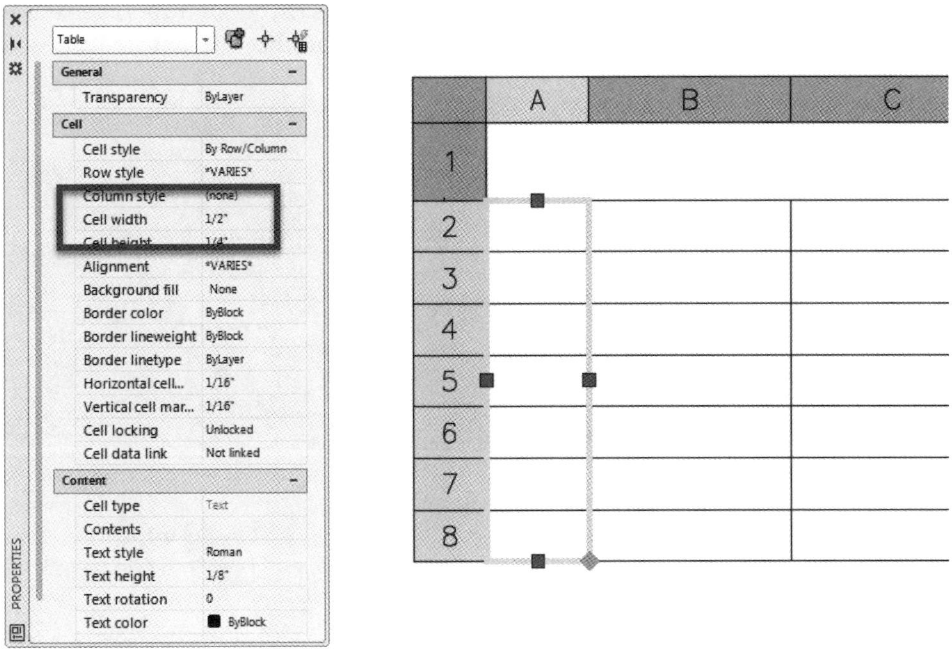

FIGURE 9-1.10
Table and its Properties; column width adjusted

24. Press **Esc** to deselect the column.

25. Adjust the remaining column widths per the following information (Figure 9-1.11):
    a. Column B (room name): **2″**
    b. Columns C – J: **1″**
    c. Column K (remarks): **2″**

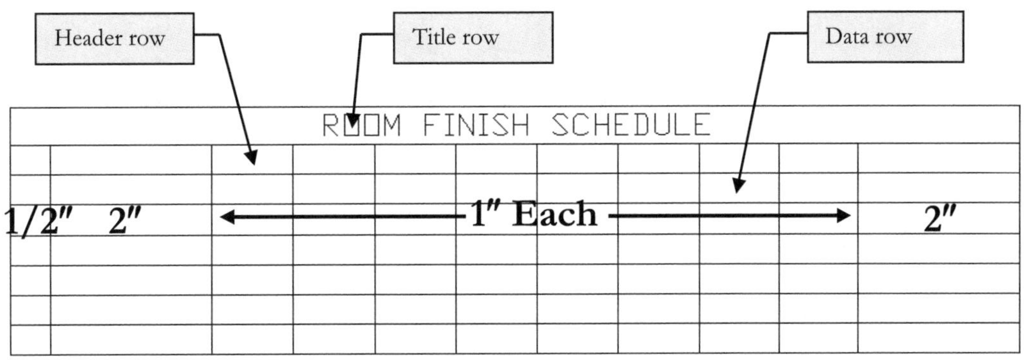

FIGURE 9-1.11
Table; all column widths adjusted

As you will recall, you specified 11 columns and six rows. In addition, a Table automatically includes a *Title* row and a *Header* row. Compare the image above (Figure 9-1.11) with the preview image in Figure 9-1.3.

Merge Cells:

Next, you will merge cells together to create larger cells within the *Table.*

26. Select the two cells identified in Figure 9-1.12.

    ***FYI:** This is where the room number label goes.*

27. Select **Merge Cells → Merge All** icon from the *Ribbon* (Figure 9-1.13).

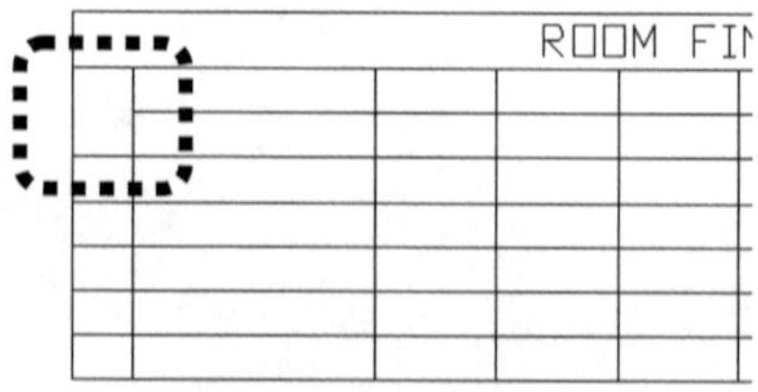

FIGURE 9-1.12
Table; two cells merged together

You now have a merged cell in your *Table*! Take a moment to notice the other commands on the *Ribbon* in Figure 9-1.13. (Hover your cursor over each icon for a tooltip of the command name.)

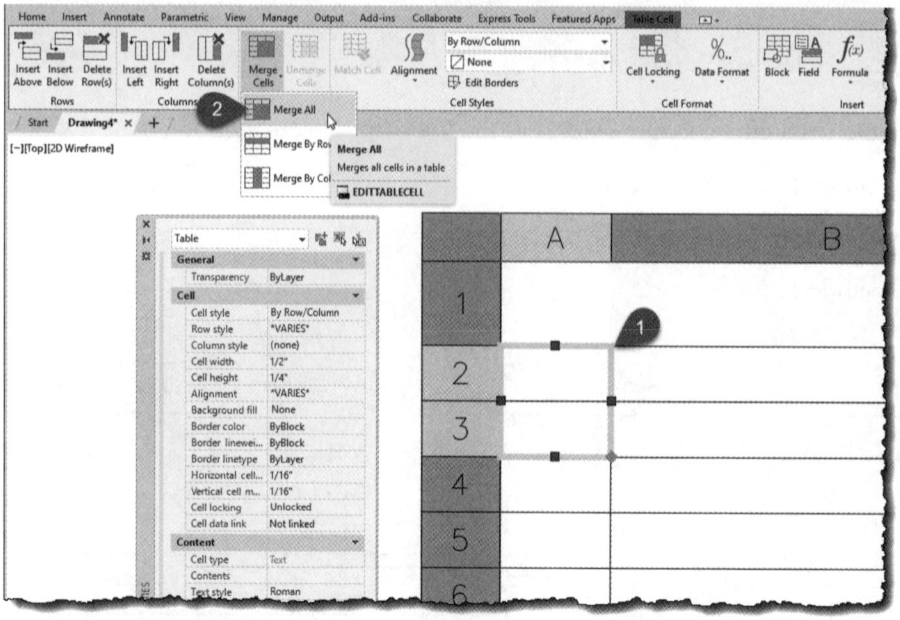

FIGURE 9-1.13
Merge Cells; two cells selected and then right-click

28. Use the **Merge Cells** feature to make your table look like the one in Figure 9-1.14.

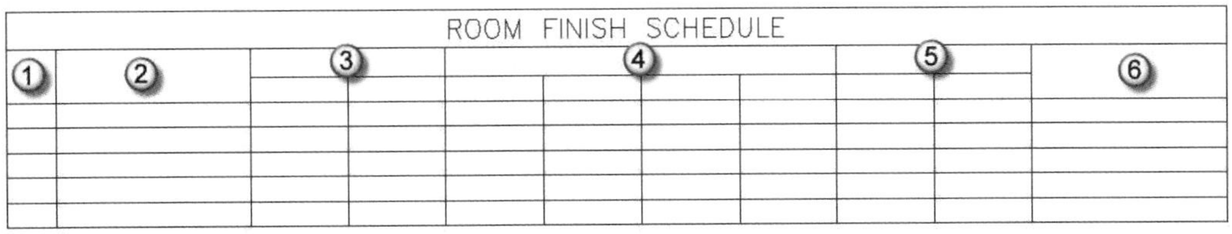

FIGURE 9-1.14
Merge Cells; several cells merged

Inserting Additional Rows:

Before adding data to the table, you will insert additional rows. A few too many will be added, so you can learn to delete rows later.

29. Click in any *Data* cell and then click and select the **Insert Row Below** icon from the *Ribbon* (Figure 9-1.15).

30. Repeat the previous step until you have **20** *Data* rows.

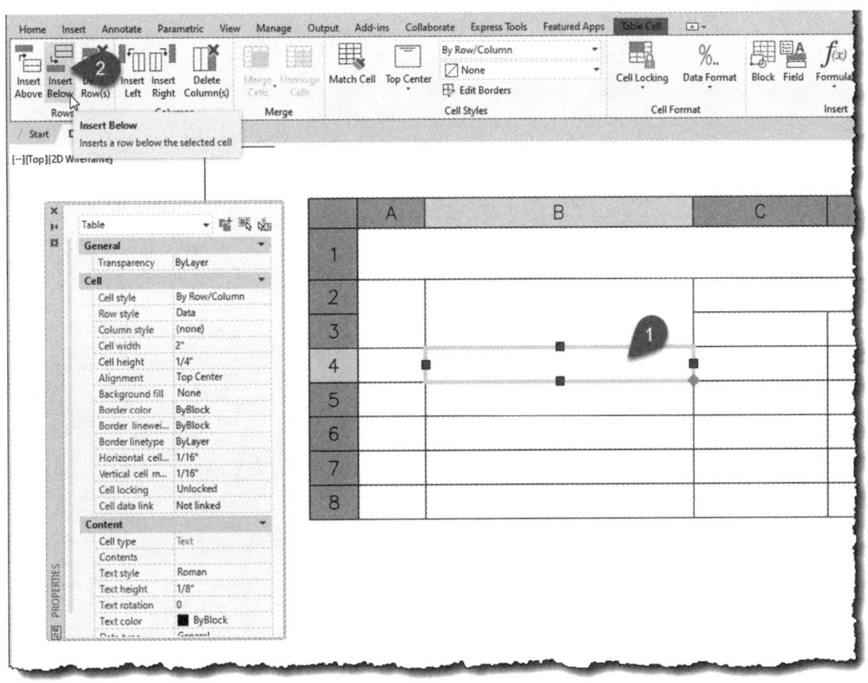

FIGURE 9-1.15 Insert rows; creates extra data lines

Now you can see why it is good to calculate the approximate number of rows you will need when creating the *Table*; you can type in the number of rows versus right-clicking for each row added later.

Adding Column Header Labels:

Now add labels indicating the information in each column of the schedule (table).

31. Click to select the cell and then double-click within each *Header* cell and type the label per the sketch in Figure 9-1.7; see Figure 9-1.16 for the finished product.

    TIP: Once in "cell edit mode" you can arrow-key between cells.

Adding Data to Cells:

It is very easy to add data to your *Table*; you simply double click in a cell and type. Next you will add the data to your table.

32. Looking at Figure 9-1.16, enter the data into your Table.

    TIP: After you double-click in a cell, you can use the Tab and Arrow keys to move between cells.

    TIP: You can Copy/Paste multiple cells. Click and drag to select the cells to Copy, and then press Ctrl+C (copy to Windows Clipboard). Next click and drag to select the cells to Paste to, and then press Ctrl+V (paste from Windows Clipboard).

ROOM FINISH SCHEDULE										
RM NO	ROOM NAME	FLOOR		WALLS				CEILING		REMARKS
		FINISH	BASE	NORTH	EAST	SOUTH	WEST	MAT'L	HEIGHT	
001	BASEMENT	SEALED	N/A	CMU	CMU	CMU	CMU	EXP.	–	
100	FOYER	Q.T.	Q.T.	WOOD PNL	WOOD PNL	WOOD PNL	WOOD PNL	GYP BD	8'-6"	
101	LIVING ROOM	WOOD	WOOD	GYP BD	GYP BD	GYP BD	GYP BD	GYP BD	8'-6"	
102	FORMAL DINING	WOOD	WOOD	GYP BD	GYP BD	GYP BD	GYP BD	GYP BD	8'-6"	
103	KITCHEN	Q.T.	Q.T.	GYP BD	GYP BD	GYP BD	GYP BD	GYP BD	8'-6"	
104	FAMILY DINING	CARPET	WOOD	GYP BD	GYP BD	GYP BD	GYP BD	GYP BD	8'-6"	
105	FAMILY ROOM	VINYL	WOOD	GYP BD	GYP BD	GYP BD	GYP BD	GYP BD	8'-6"	
106	BATH	MARBLE	MARBLE	C.T.	C.T.	C.T.	C.T.	GYP. BD.	8'-6"	
107	MUD ROOM	Q.T.	Q.T.	GYP BD	GYP BD	GYP BD	GYP BD	GYP BD	8'-6"	
108	GARAGE	SEALED	–	GYP. BD.	GYP BD	GYP BD	GYP BD	GYP BD	8'-6"	
200	HALLWAY	WOOD	WOOD	GYP BD	GYP BD	GYP BD	GYP BD	GYP BD	8'-0"	
201	MASTER BEDROOM	WOOD	WOOD	GYP BD	GYP BD	GYP BD	GYP BD	GYP BD	8'-0"	
202	CLOSET	WOOD	WOOD	GYP BD	GYP BD	GYP BD	GYP BD	GYP BD	8'-0"	
203	MASTER BATH	MARBLE	MARBLE	C.T.	C.T.	C.T.	C.T.	GYP. BD.	8'-0"	
204	BATH	C.T.	C.T.	C.T.	C.T.	C.T.	C.T.	GYP. BD.	8'-0"	
205	STORAGE	WOOD	–	GYP BD	GYP BD	GYP BD	GYP BD	GYP BD	8'-0"	
206	BEDROOM #1	CARPET	WOOD	GYP BD	GYP BD	GYP BD	GYP BD	GYP BD	8'-0"	
207	BEDROOM #2	CARPET	WOOD	GYP BD	GYP BD	GYP BD	GYP BD	GYP BD	8'-0"	

FIGURE 9-1.16
Room Finish Schedule; with data entered

Deleting Rows:

Next, you will delete one of the extra rows. The following technique works the same way for columns as well.

33. Click within the cell <u>directly below</u> BEDROOM #2.

34. Select **Delete Rows** from the *Ribbon* (Figure 9-1.17).

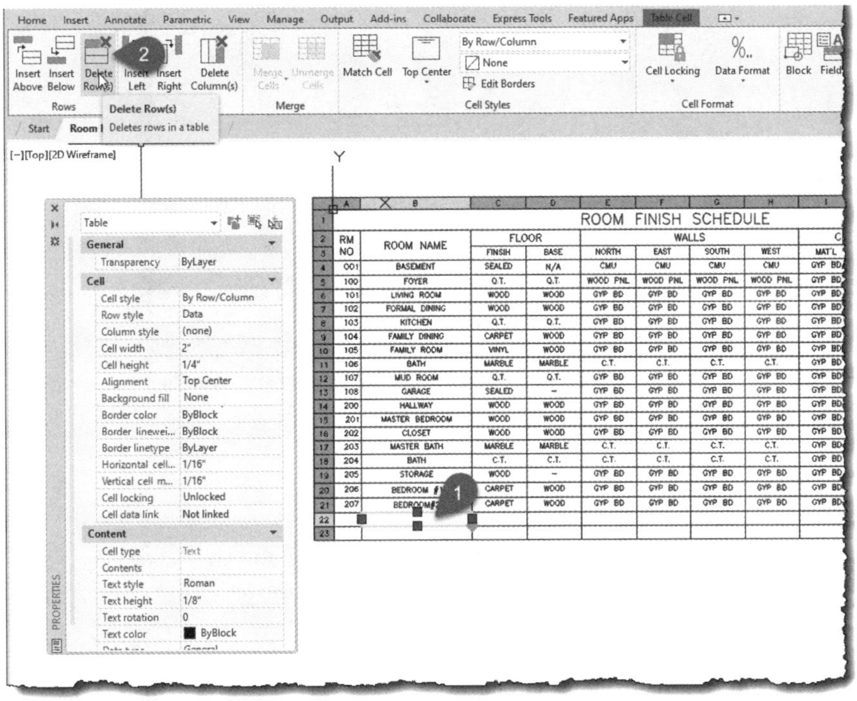

FIGURE 9-1.17
Room Finish Schedule; deleting a row

Making the Table Title Text Bold:

Finally, change the font of the Table Title (i.e., Room Finish Schedule) to Arial Black, a distinctive bold font. To do this, you will need to create a new AutoCAD *Font Style* and then modify the *Table Style* to use the new *Text Style.*

35. Press the Esc key to unselect the table, and then click the **Text Style…** link, *Annotate* tab, *Text* panel.

You are now in the *Text Style* dialog, where you manage AutoCAD *Text Styles.*

FYI: *AutoCAD Text Styles allow you to predefine several settings for a particular type of note or label. Additionally, like other "styles" in AutoCAD, if you change a style setting (e.g., the Width Factor), all the text of that style will update automatically.*

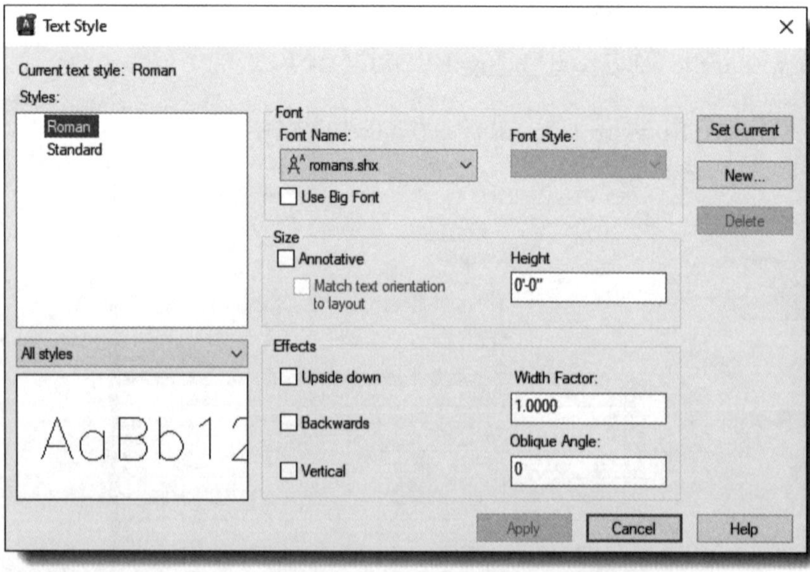

FIGURE 9-1.18
Text Style dialog; initial view

Notice, in the image above, the settings for the "Roman" *Text Style.* The *Font Name* is "Romans.shx"; the *Style Name* is similar but can be anything. The *Height* is set to 0′-0″, which means you can adjust the height for each instance in your drawing.

36. Notice under *Styles* that only two exist in the current drawing (*Standard* and *Roman*).

Now you will create a new *Text Style* named *Bold.*

37. Click the **New** button.

You are now prompted for a name (Figure 9-1.19).

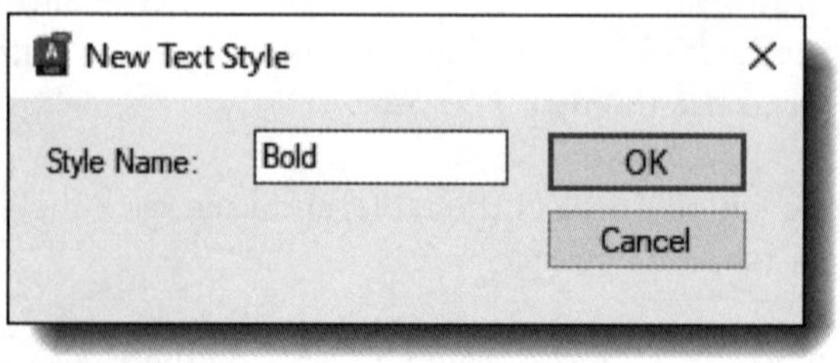

FIGURE 9-1.19
New Text Style dialog; style name Bold entered

38. Type the new *Style Name* **Bold** and then click **OK**.

39. Make the following adjustments (Figure 9-1.20):
    a. Font Name: **Arial Black**
    b. Width Factor: **0.9**

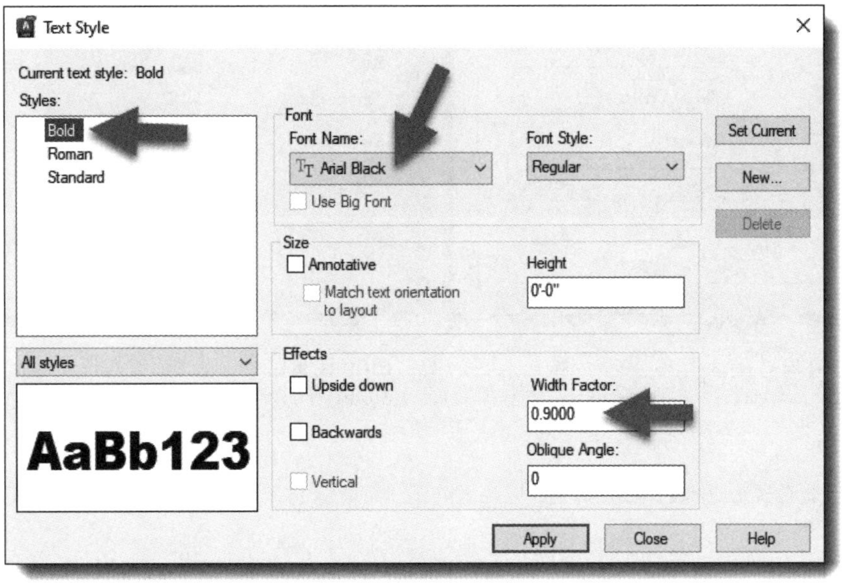

FIGURE 9-1.20
Text Style dialog; setting for text style named "*Bold*"

40. Click **Apply** to finalize your new *Text Style* settings.

41. Click **Close**.

The new *Text Style* is now available for use in the current drawing. If you want regular access to the *Bold* text style, you would add it to your *Drawing Template* file. Now you will modify the *Table Style* title text.

42. On the *Table* panel, in the *Annotate* tab, select the **Table Style** link *(see image to the right)*.

43. Click the **Modify…** button *(to Modify the Standard Table Style)*.

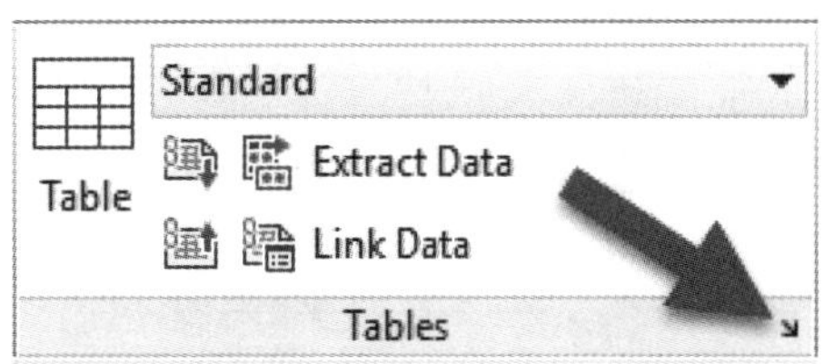

44. Under the **Title** *Cell styles*, change the following:
    a. <u>*Text*</u> tab: *Text style* to **Bold** and *Color* to **250** (Figure 9-1.21B).

b. *General* tab: *Fill color* to **Color 255** (Figure 9-1.21A).

FYI: Another option is to select the Title cell and adjust these settings in the Properties Palette.

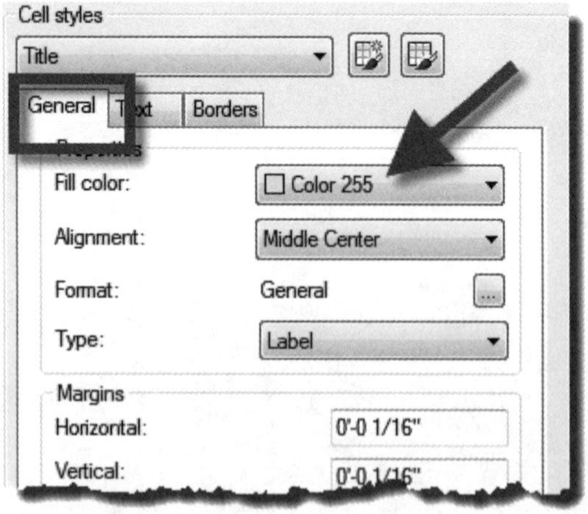

FIGURE 9-1.21A
Modify Table Style; Title – General tab

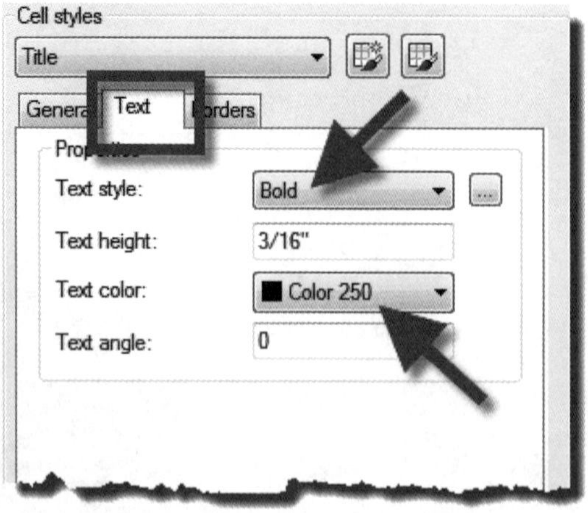

FIGURE 9-1.21B
Modify Table Style; Title – Text tab

45. Click **OK** and then **Close** to close the dialog boxes.

You should notice the text for the *Title* is now *Bold*, and the cell is filled with color 255 (a grey shade) in your *Room Finish Schedule* (Figure 9-1.22). Similarly, if you had additional tables inserted into the current drawing (and using the *Standard* style), they would all be updated to use the *Bold* font as well.

ROOM FINISH SCHEDULE											
RM NO	ROOM NAME	FLOOR		WALLS				CEILING		REMARKS
		FINSIH	BASE	NORTH	EAST	SOUTH	WEST	MAT'L	HEIGHT	
001	BASEMENT	SEALED	N/A	CMU	CMU	CMU	CMU	GYP BD	8'-6"	
100	FOYER	Q.T.	Q.T.	WOOD PNL	WOOD PNL	WOOD PNL	WOOD PNL	GYP BD	8'-6"	
101	LIVING ROOM	WOOD	WOOD	GYP BD	GYP BD	GYP BD	GYP BD	GYP BD	8'-6"	
102	FORMAL DINING	WOOD	WOOD	GYP BD	GYP BD	GYP BD	GYP BD	GYP BD	8'-6"	
103	KITCHEN	Q.T.	Q.T.	GYP BD	GYP BD	GYP BD	GYP BD	GYP BD	8'-6"	
104	FAMILY DINING	CARPET	WOOD	GYP BD	GYP BD	GYP BD	GYP BD	GYP BD	8'-6"	
105	FAMILY ROOM	VINYL	WOOD	GYP BD	GYP BD	GYP BD	GYP BD	GYP BD	8'-6"	
106	BATH	MARBLE	MARBLE	C.T.	C.T.	C.T.	C.T.	GYP BD	8'-6"	
107	MUD ROOM	Q.T.	Q.T.	GYP BD	GYP BD	GYP BD	GYP BD	GYP BD	8'-6"	
108	GARAGE	SEALED	–	GYP BD	GYP BD	GYP BD	GYP BD	GYP BD	8'-0"	
200	HALLWAY	WOOD	WOOD	GYP BD	GYP BD	GYP BD	GYP BD	GYP BD	8'-0"	
201	MASTER BEDROOM	WOOD	WOOD	GYP BD	GYP BD	GYP BD	GYP BD	GYP BD	8'-0"	
202	CLOSET	WOOD	WOOD	GYP BD	GYP BD	GYP BD	GYP BD	GYP BD	8'-0"	
203	MASTER BATH	MARBLE	MARBLE	C.T.	C.T.	C.T.	C.T.	GYP BD	8'-0"	
204	BATH	C.T.	C.T.	C.T.	C.T.	C.T.	C.T.	GYP BD	8'-0"	
205	STORAGE	WOOD	–	GYP BD	GYP BD	GYP BD	GYP BD	GYP BD	8'-0"	
206	BEDROOM #1	CARPET	WOOD	GYP BD	GYP BD	GYP BD	GYP BD	GYP BD	8'-0"	
207	BEDROOM#2	CARPET	WOOD	GYP BD	GYP BD	GYP BD	GYP BD	GYP BD	8'-0"	

FIGURE 9-1.22
Modify Table Style; Text style for title set to "Bold"

46. **Save** your drawing as **ROOM FINISH SCHEDULE.DWG**.

Exercise 9-2:
Sheet Set up and Management (Sheet Sets)

Introduction:

This exercise covers an AutoCAD feature called *Sheet Sets*, which is a powerful capability previously found only in more advanced, architecture-specific programs like Autodesk Revit.

The *Sheet Set Manager* allows one or more drafters to view a list of all sheets in the project set. Each sheet can be opened by double-clicking its label in the list. Once a sheet is open, you can place drawings on it. Reference bubbles can be placed on sheets, which are automatically updated when the drawing numbers or sheet numbers are changed.

When you have completed this section, you will have created several sheets with title blocks and will have placed your drawings on them using the *Sheet Set Manager*.

Procedural and Organizational Overview:

The following information outlines the basic procedure and organization of a *Sheet Set*. This will give you a good understanding of this feature before you actually try it.

Sheet Sets pivot around three types of files:

- ♦ Resource Drawings (Model Views)
- ♦ Sheet Files (Sheet Views)
- ♦ A Sheet Set Data File

In addition to the three types of files listed above, other files are used as well (e.g., callout blocks and template files). Next, you will take a closer look at the three file types listed above and their roles in the *Sheet Set* feature.

<u>Resource Drawings</u>:

- o Drawing files (DWGs)
    - Each floor plan, elevation, detail, etc., in a drawing file, has a *Named View* associated with it.
    - These files are the files you have created thus far in this book.
    - You will cover *Named Views* later in this exercise.
- o Any text or dimensions drawn in a *Resource Drawing* need to be scaled appropriately based on the scale at which that drawing will ultimately be plotted.

<u>Sheet Files</u>:

- Drawing files (DWGs)
  - Each of these files represents a sheet in a set of drawings (e.g., 24″x 36″ sheet)
- *Named Views*, from various *Resource Drawings*, are placed on these sheets.
- *Named Views* can be placed at various scales at the time of insertion. A drawing title tag is automatically inserted below the drawing view; the tag is even automatically filled out with the view's number (if/when one is provided in the *Sheet Set Manager*) and scale (i.e., the scale you selected when the view was placed on the sheet). The image below describes the default drawing tag:

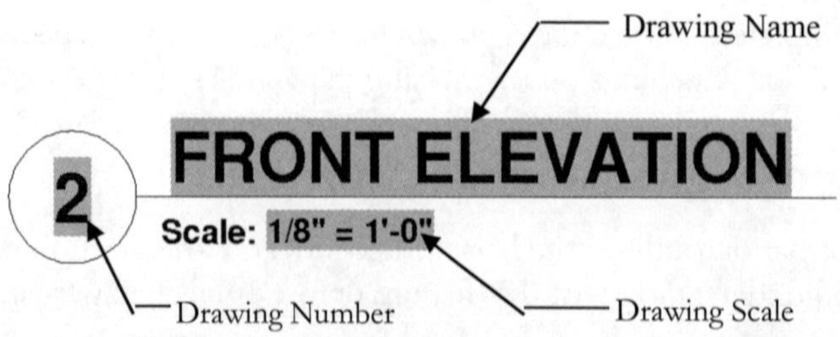

- Once a *View* has been placed on a sheet, you can specify a *Drawing Number*; you can also change the *Drawing* (view) *Name*. This must be done in the *Sheet Set Manager* to ensure all sheets and views are correctly cross-referenced.
- *Callout Bubbles* (elevation and detail) can be placed on sheets. The bubbles reference a *Named View* from a *Resource Drawing*. The reference bubble is automatically filled out with the view's number and the sheet number the view is placed on (all of which is stored in the *Sheet Set Data* file). The image below describes the basic components of a callout bubble:

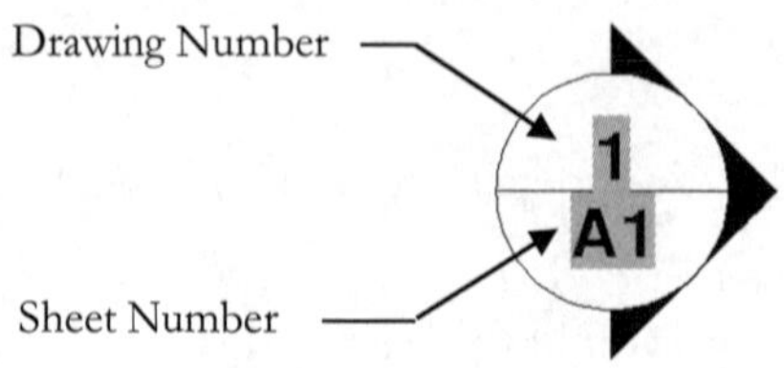

- The shaded rectangle behind the text lets you know that the text is updated automatically and should not be modified manually. Specifically, they are called *fields*, and are updated at key points while working on a drawing (e.g., Open, Save, Plot, Regen). These are similar to the *fields* in *MS Word*; the *Date* field is shaded and automatically updated.

A Sheet Set Data File:

- File name and extension: *filename*.dst.
- This file is a database that maintains information about the *Sheet Set* and detail/sheet numbering and cross-references.
- The file can be located anywhere on your system (including a network drive). This file should be stored in your project folder for easy backup.

Creating Named Views in Your Resource Drawings:

As mentioned above, each of the various plans, elevations, sections and details you wish to place on a sheet needs to be identified by a *Named View*, which is simply defined by an imaginary rectangular area within a drawing file. If you move a door detail, for example, to another part of *Model Space*, the *Named View* does NOT move and would be "looking" at an empty portion of the drawing at that point.

You will start with the exterior elevations.

1. Open your **Exterior Elevations** drawing created in Lesson 5.

If created per the tutorial outlined in Lesson 5, you have all four elevations in one drawing. You will create one *Named View* for each elevation in the *Exterior Elevation* drawing.

2. **Zoom In** to the South elevation.

3. Type **V** and **Enter** to access the *View Manager*.

   You are now in the *View Manager* dialog (Figure 9-2.1).

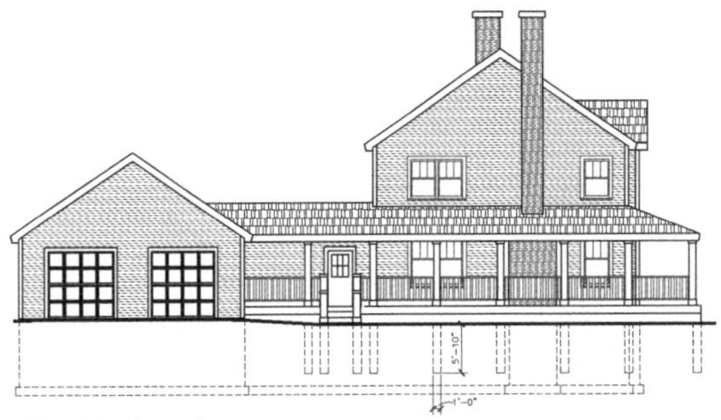

South elevation

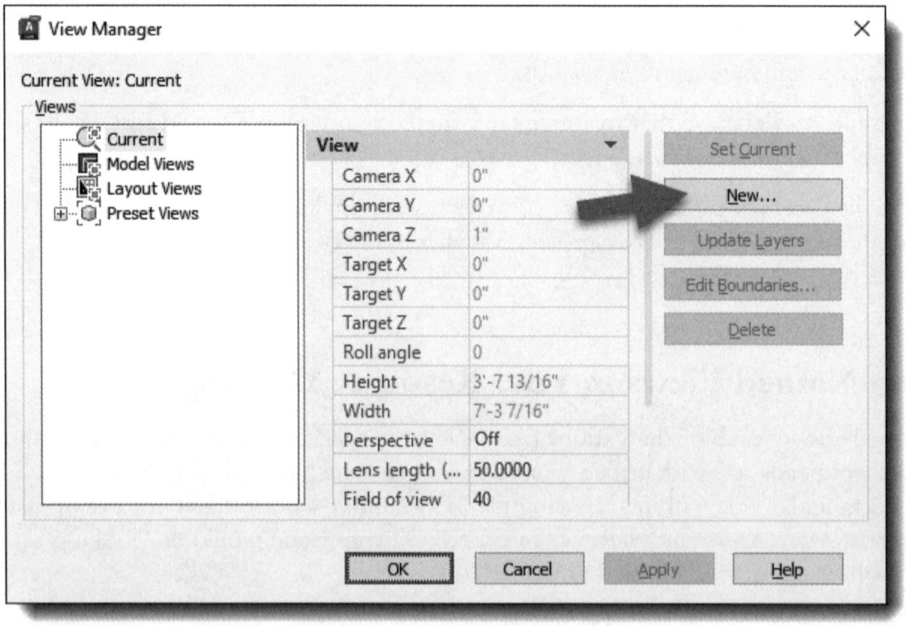

FIGURE 9-2.1
View Manager dialog box; click "New…" to create a named view

4. Click **New** to create a new *Named View*.

You are now in the *New View* dialog (Figure 9-2.2), where you can create a *Named View*.

5. Enter **South Elevation** for the *View* name (Figure 9-2.2).

   TIP: *The name entered here is the default name used in the drawing title tag when the view is placed on a sheet.*

6. Click **Define window** in the *Boundary* area (Figure 9-2.2).

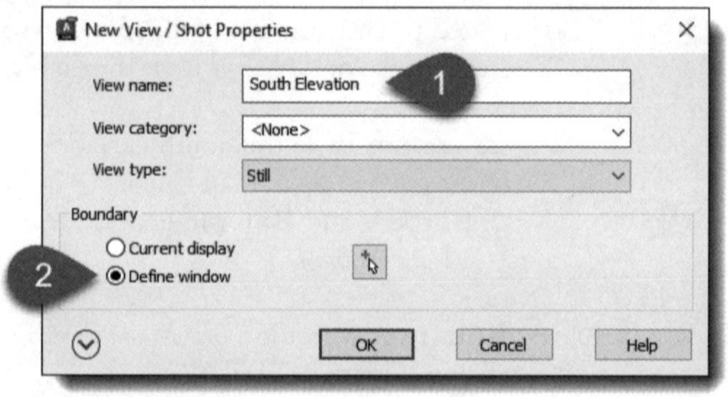

FIGURE 9-2.2
New View dialog; create a view named "South Elevation"

Immediately after clicking *Define window* you are temporarily brought back to the drawing to select a boundary window around your South elevation.

7. Select a window (rectangular area) around your South elevation (Figure 9-2.3) and then right-click to finish.

   TIP: *Note the following regarding your boundary window selection:*

   ****You should try to pick a window as tight to the drawing as possible, leaving room for any anticipated additions to the drawing (e.g., more building or notes).*

   ****By default, the drawing title tag is placed just below the lower left corner of the view when it is placed on a sheet, so too much extra space to the left of the drawing would position the title tag so that it is not under any of the drawing.*

   ****If your drawing does grow larger than the Named View's specified boundary, you can use the Edit Boundaries feature (see Figure 9-2.1) to resize the boundary.*

FIGURE 9-2.3
South Elevation; select window as shown to define view

8. Click **OK** to close the *New View* dialog and create the view.

9. Repeat the previous steps to create a *Named View* for the **North**, **East** and **West** elevations in your *Exterior Elevations* drawing.

When finished, you will see each *Named View* listed in the *View* dialog box (Figure 9-2.4).

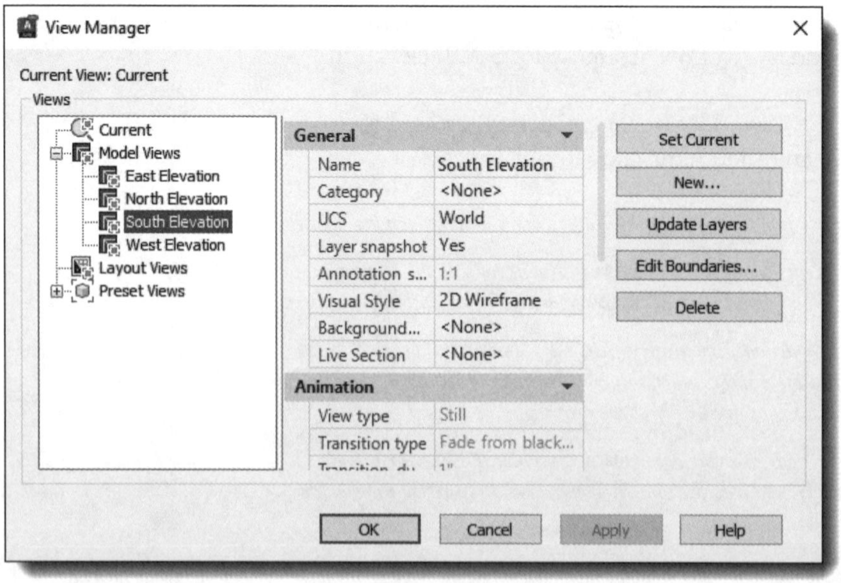

FIGURE 9-2.4
View dialog; a named view created for each elevation in the Exterior Elevations drawing

10. **Open** your other drawings and create *Named Views* per the chart below.

Drawing name	Named View to create
Flr-B.dwg	Basement Floor Plan
Flr-1.dwg	First Floor Plan
Flr-2.dwg	Second Floor Drawing
Building Section.dwg	Building Section
Wall Section.dwg	Wall Section
Bathroom Elevation.dwg	Bathroom Elevation
Room Schedule.dwg	Room Finish Schedule
Site.dwg	Site Plan
Additional Task dwg's	*Name views appropriately*

FYI: Remember, these drawings will be referred to as the Resource Drawings in the Sheet Set Manager (on the Model Views tab).

11. **Save** your drawings.

Next, you will create the *Sheet Set Data* file via the *Sheet Set Manager.*

Setting Up a Sheet Set:

You will look at one of the methods provided to set up a *Sheet Set*. This involves using the *Create Sheet Set Wizard*.

12. Make sure a drawing is open. You must have at least one drawing open to get started; it can be a blank drawing or one of your project files.

13. **Open** the **Sheet Set Manager** by clicking its icon on the *View* tab*, Palettes* panel.

14. At the top of the *Sheet Set Manager* palette, click the down-arrow and then select **New Sheet Set…** from the menu (Figure 9-2.5).

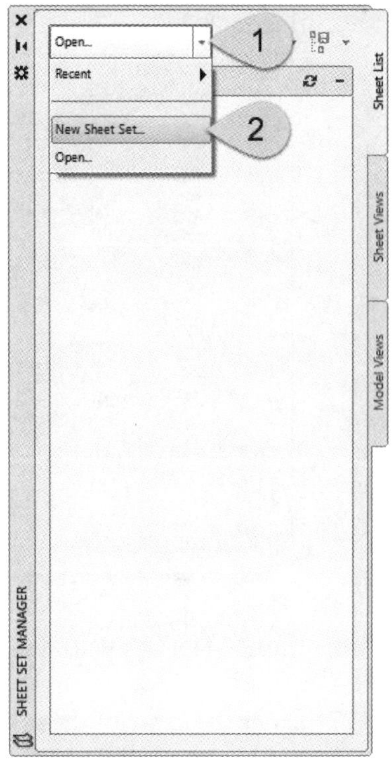

FIGURE 9-2.5
Sheet Set Manager; click the Down-Arrow and select "New Sheet Set…" to start a new Sheet Set

This starts the *Sheet Set Manager Wizard* (Figure 9-2.6).

15. Click **Next**.

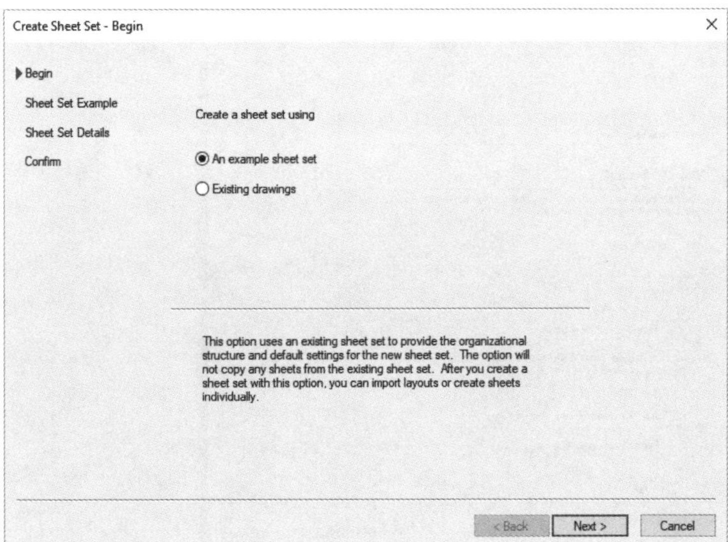

FIGURE 9-2.6
Create Sheet Set Wizard; Begin screen

16. Next, make sure **Architectural Imperial Sheet Set** is selected and then click **Next** (Figure 9-2.7).

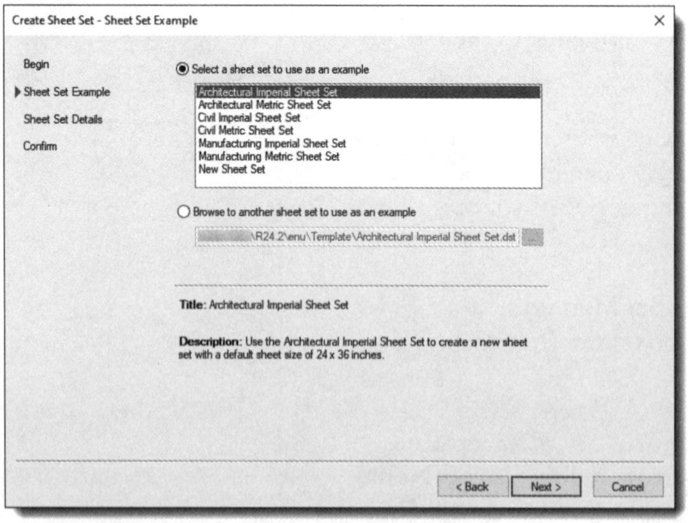

FIGURE 9-2.7
Create Sheet Set Wizard; Sheet Set Example screen

17. Enter the name of the new *Sheet Set*; use your last name (e.g., *last name* Residence). See Figure 9-2.8.

18. Click the  button to change the location where the *Sheet Set Data* file will be stored; **a.**) Create a subfolder named Sheet Set Files in the folder that contains the files you created in this book, or **b.**) Select the new folder.

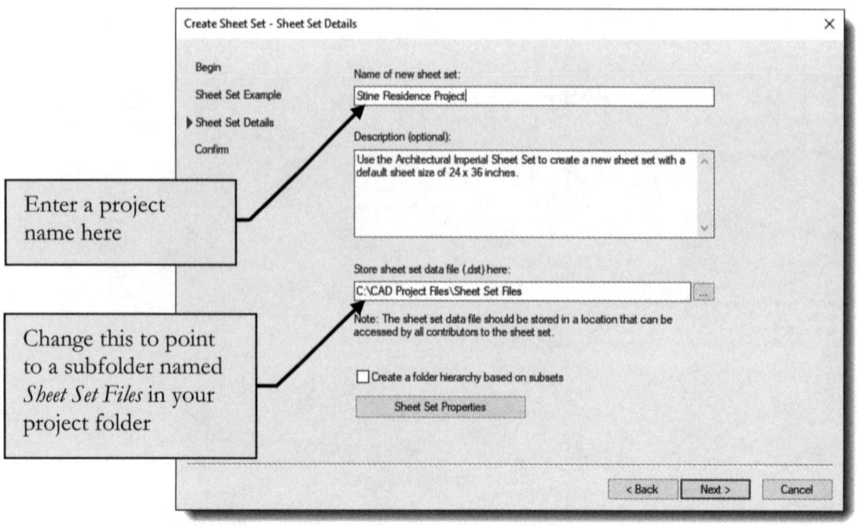

FIGURE 9-2.8
Create Sheet Set Wizard; Sheet Set Details screen

TIP: To ensure the remainder of this lesson proceeds smoothly, you should make sure all your project files are located in one folder. Only include the current files, not backup DWG (i.e., .BAK) files or old copies.

You are now at the final screen of the wizard. You are given detailed information on the "what and where" for the new *Sheet Set* about to be created.

19. Click **Next** and then select **Finish** to create the new *Sheet Set* (Figure 9-2.9).

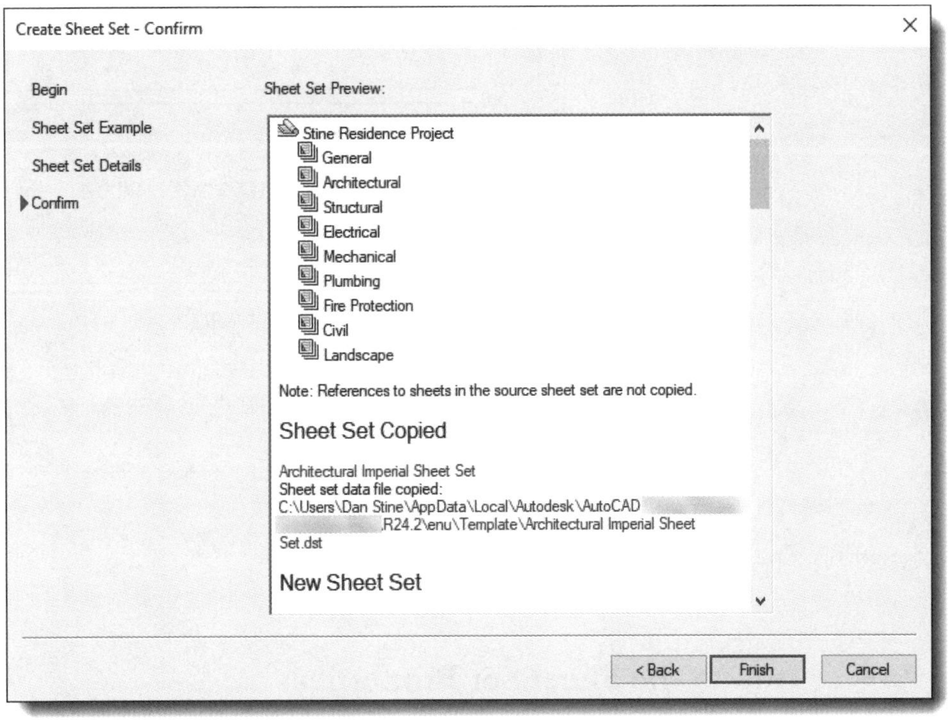

FIGURE 9-2.9
Create Sheet Set Wizard; Confirm screen

The wizard closes and the *Sheet Set Manager* is populated with the specified information. If you use *MS Windows Explorer* to browse to your *Sheet Set Files* folder, you will see a new file named "*Last name* Residence.dst"; this is the *Sheet Set Data* file previously discussed.

The *Sheet Set Example* file used contained several *Subsets* (e.g., Architectural, Structural, etc.), which are seen on the *Sheet List* tab (Figure 9-2.10). *Subsets* allow *Sheets* to be organized, by discipline in this example. The right-click menu allows you to easily add, rename or remove a *Subset* at any time.

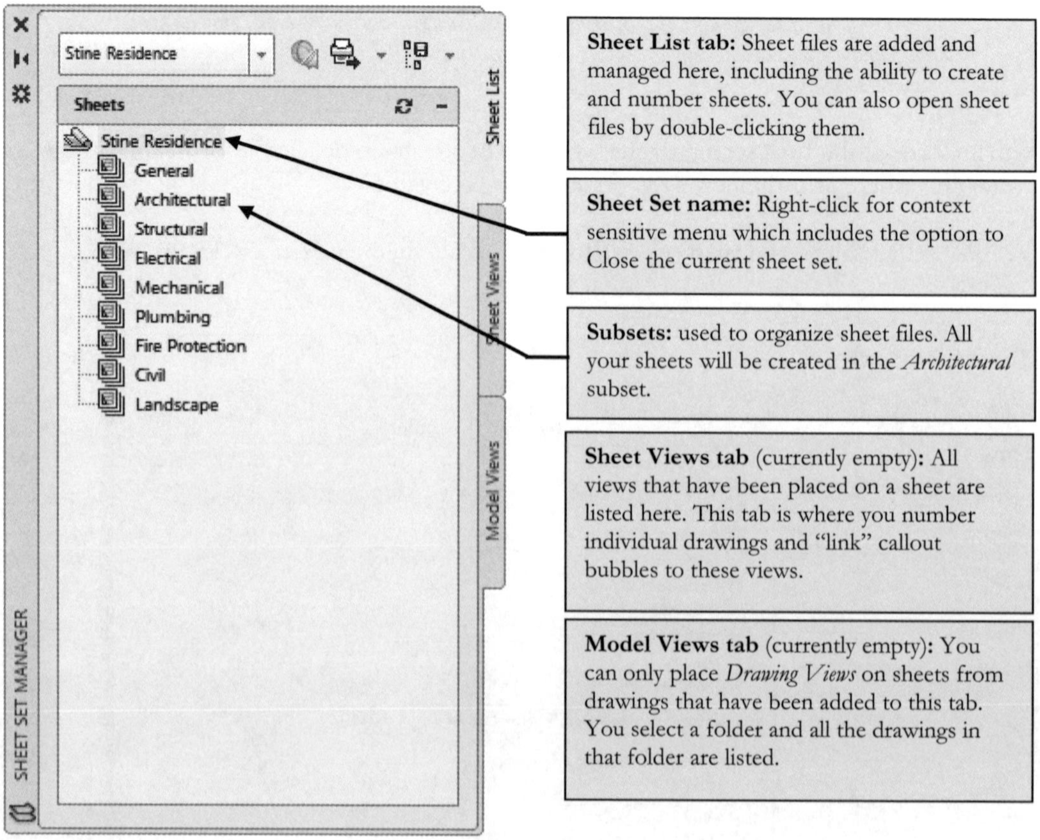

FIGURE 9-2.10
Sheet Set Manager; Sheet List tab

Adding Project Info to the Sheet Set Properties:

The *Sheet Set Properties* dialog contains key information that AutoCAD needs to properly manage and control the *Sheet Set*. Next you will enter the project name and address, which is automatically placed in the title block of each sheet in the set!

> ***NOTE:*** *For the remainder of this lesson, substitute your last name for Stine when referring to the sheet set/project name.*

20. In the *Sheet Set Manager*, on the *Sheet List* tab, **right-click** on the sheet set name (*Stine Residence*) at the top of the list – under the *Sheets* label – and select **Properties** from the pop-up menu.

21. In the *Sheet Set Custom Properties* section, add information similar to that shown in **Figure 9-2.11**.

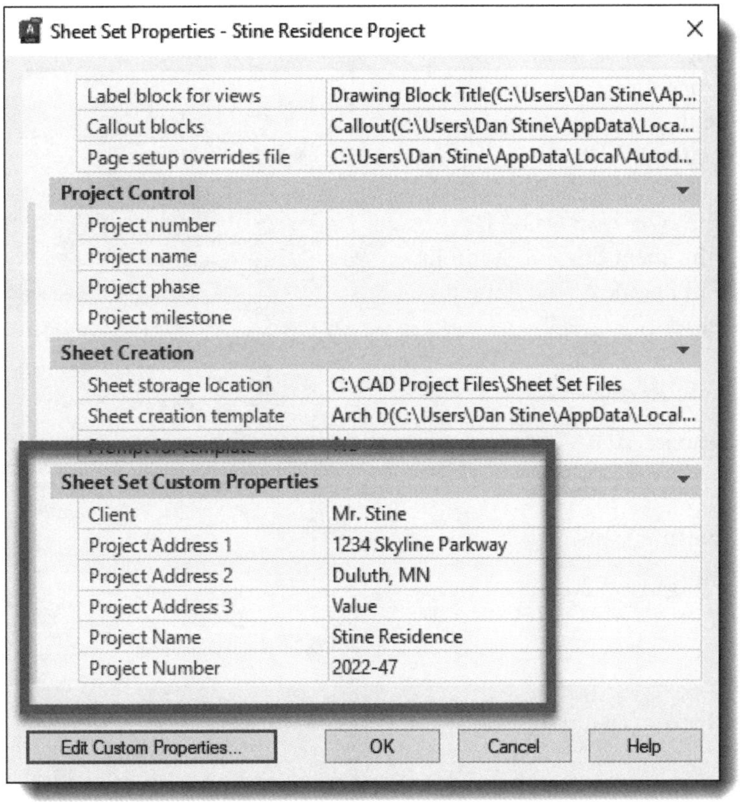

FIGURE 9-2.11
Create Sheet Set Properties; partial view of dialog

TIP: If you do not need one field, such as the "Project Address 3" line above, make it blank; otherwise any text entered will show up on the drawings.

22. Click **OK** to complete the changes.

Creating Sheets for Placing Named Views:

Creating a sheet with a title block, a number and client information has NEVER been easier in AutoCAD! In just minutes you will have all the empty sheets set up and ready for *Named Views* to be placed on them.

As you create sheets in the *Sheet Set Manager*, AutoCAD creates a drawing file in the specified folder (*Sheet Set Files* sub-folder in this example). This file IS the sheet. If the file is erased or corrupt, that sheet will no longer be available. Therefore, you should back up the files in the *Sheet Set Files* sub-folder, just as you would your *Resource Drawings* or any important files on your computer.

Next you will set up the entire set of sheets, starting with the project *Title* sheet.

23. On the *Sheet List* tab, in the *Sheet Set Manager*, right-click on the *Architectural* subset, and then click **New Sheet…** from the pop-up menu (Figure 9-2.12).

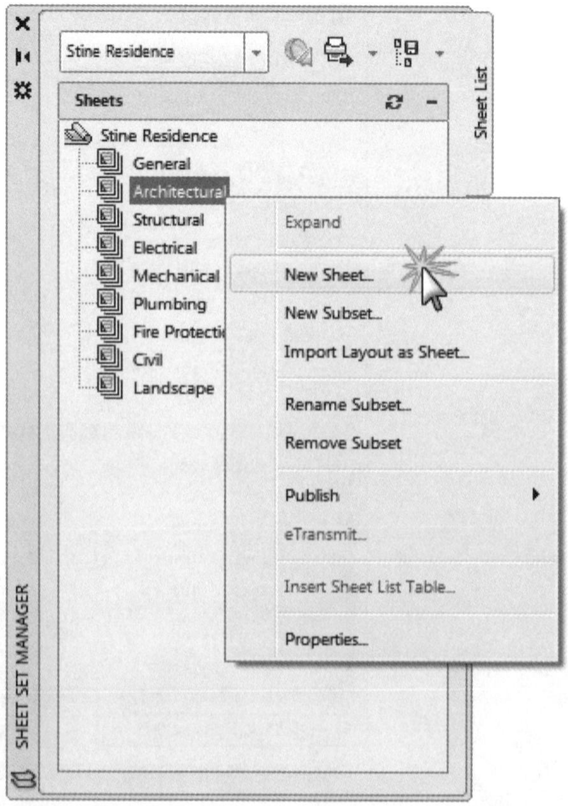

FIGURE 9-2.12
Sheet Set Manager; create new sheet

You are now in the *New Sheet* dialog box where you enter the sheet title and number, as well as specify the name of the drawing file that will be created.

24. Enter the following:
    a. Number: **A0**
    b. Sheet title: **Title Sheet**
    c. File name: *default*
    d. See **Figure 9-2.13**.

25. Click **OK** to create the sheet.

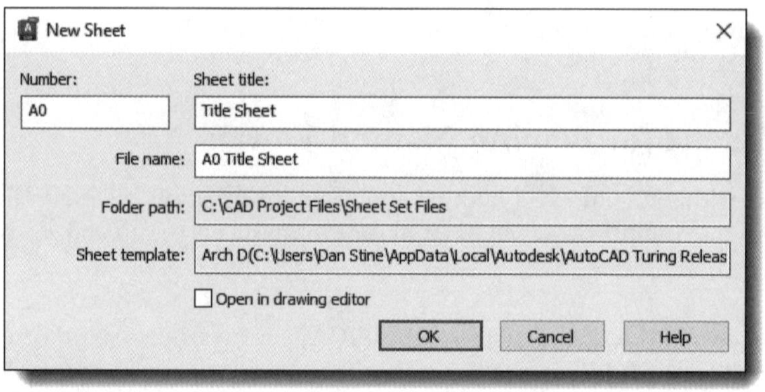

FIGURE 9-2.13
New Sheet dialog; enter sheet number, title and file name

You have just created your first sheet! You now see the sheet listed under the *Architectural* subset in the *Sheet Set Manager* (Figure9-2.14).

26. Per the steps above, create new sheets so that you have all the sheets listed in the table below.

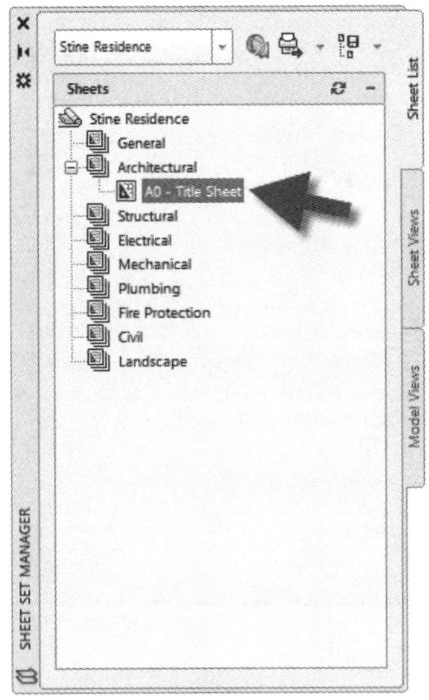

FIGURE 9-2.14
Sheet Set Manager

Sheet name	Sheet number
Title Sheet	A0
Basement Floor Plan	A1
First Floor Plan	A2
Second Floor Plan	A3
Exterior Elevations	A4
Exterior Elevations	A5
Building Sections	A6
Wall Sections	A7
Interior Elevations	A8
Schedules	A9

Once finished, all the sheets will be listed in the *Sheet Set Manager* as shown in Figure 9-2.15.

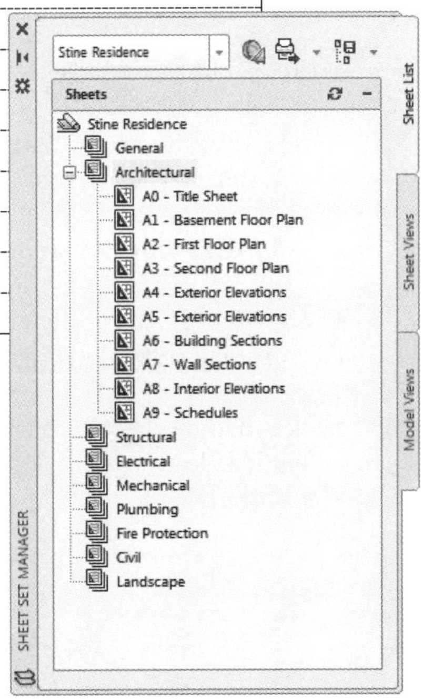

FIGURE 9-2.15
Sheet Manager; all sheets created in Architectural subset

FIGURE 9-2.16
Windows Explorer view of your *Sheet Set Files* sub-folder you created in your project folder; files automatically created with the Sheet Set Manager. Be sure to back up these files.

Take a minute to browse to the *Sheet Set* files folder you previously created and notice an AutoCAD file has been created for each sheet (Figure 9-2.16).

These files can be opened here, by double-clicking, or from *Open* on the *QAT* within AutoCAD.

Next you will see how the *Sheet Set Manager* allows you to do this.

Opening Sheets from the Sheet Set Manager:

In the *Sheet Set Manager* you can double-click on a sheet title (on the *Sheet List* tab) to open the drawing file that represents that sheet. Once the drawing is open you can save and close it just like any other drawing file.

Next you will open the exterior elevation sheet A4 to place one of your drawings on it.

27. On the *Sheet List* tab, in *Sheet Set Manager*, double-click on the sheet title **A4 – Exterior Elevations.**

The drawing **A4 -Exterior Elevations** (located in your *SheetSet Files* sub-folder) is now open.

28. **Zoom In** to the lower right corner of the sheet to see the information that was automatically entered in the title block (Figure 9-2.17).

29. Notice that the sheet number, project name and date have been automatically added to the title block.

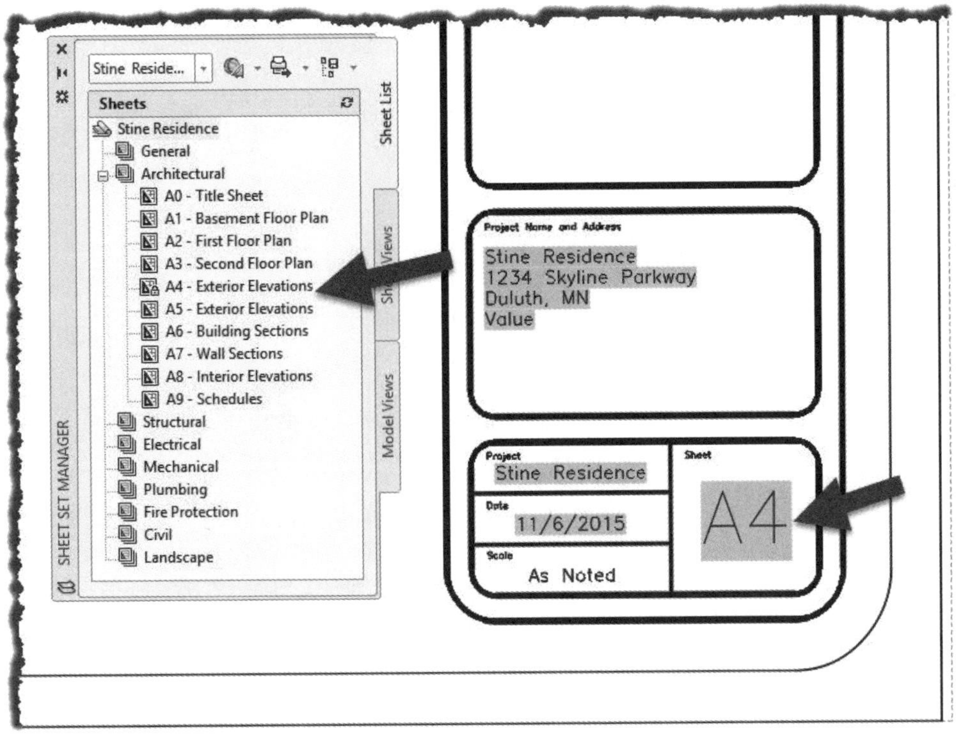

FIGURE 9-2.17
Sheet A4 – Exterior Elevations; Shaded text are fields which are modified/updated using the Sheet Set Manager

30. **Zoom Previous** so you see the entire sheet.

Contos Residence

Image courtesy of Anderson Architects
Alan H. Anderson, Architect, Duluth, MN

Specifying *Resource Drawing* Locations:

You are just about ready to start placing drawings on sheets. But first you need to tell the *Sheet Set Manager* where to look for your drawing files that contain the *Named Views*. You will do this next.

31. Click on the **Model Views** tab in the *Sheet Set Manager.*

32. Double-click the **Add New Location…** icon (Figure 9-2.18).

33. Browse to the folder where all your drawings, created in the book, are stored and then click **OK**.

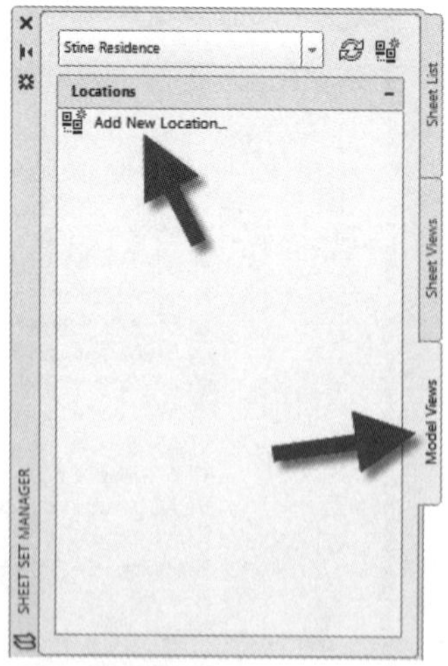

FIGURE 9-2.18
Model Views tab;
no folder listed yet

Notice in Figure 9-2.19 that the folder you selected is now listed in the *Locations* pane (on the *Model Views* tab).

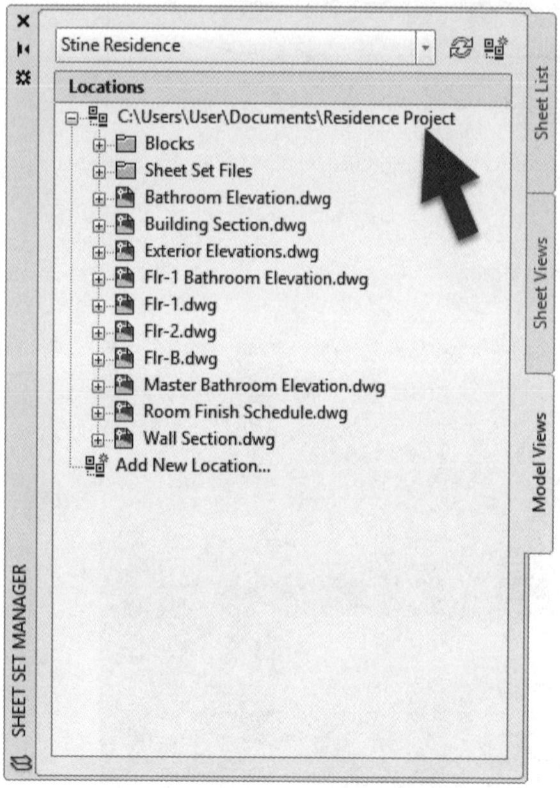

FIGURE 9-2.19
Model Views tab;
Residence Project 2027 folder and contents now listed

Notice, like other palettes, you are able to adjust the size of the palette. This is useful when the information runs past the current width of the palette. Simply place your cursor near one of the edges and drag the palette wider or narrower.

The *Refresh* button, in the upper right, will scan your hard drive to see if any files have been added or changed, and update the listing.

The "plus" symbol next to the new *Locations* folder allows you to expand the view to show the drawings listed in that folder. After clicking the plus symbol, the drawings and folders are displayed and the "plus" changes to a "minus" symbol (Figure 9-2.20).

Adding Named Views to Sheets:

You are now to the point where you can start placing drawings (*Named Views*) on your *Sheets*. Basically, you drag a *Named View* from the *Model Views* tab onto your *Sheet.*

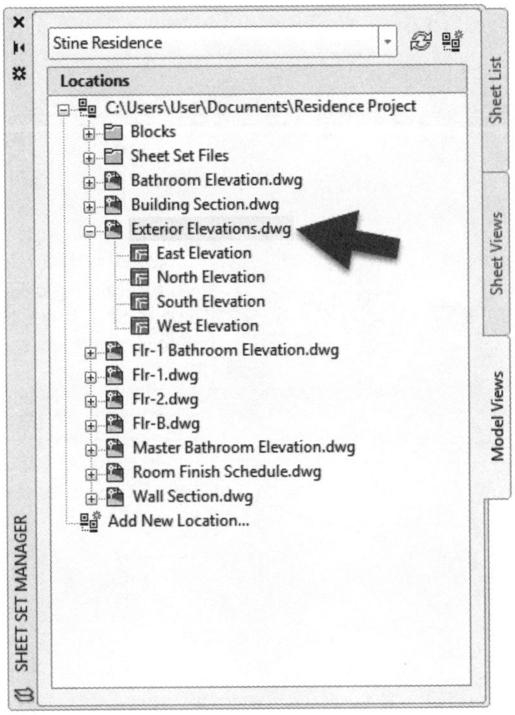

FIGURE 9-2.20
Model Views tab; Named Views in *Exterior Elevations.dwg*

Similar to the previous discussion on how the "plus" symbol expands the *Locations* folder, the "plus" symbol next to the drawings (listed in the *Locations* folder) expands that drawing's view to display its *Named Views.*

First, you will open a sheet to place a drawing (*Named View*) on.

34. On the *Sheet List* tab, double-click the **A4 – Exterior Elevations** sheet to open it (if not already open).

35. Click the *Model Views* tab to make it current.

36. Click the "**plus**" symbol next to the **Exterior Elevations** drawing to view that drawing's *Named Views.*

You can now see the four *Named Views* you created in the "Exterior Elevations" drawing (Figure 9-2.20).

37. Click and drag the **South Elevation** from the *Sheet Set Manager* onto your **A4 – Exterior Elevations** sheet (Figure 9-2.21).

Move your cursor about the screen to see how the view is attached to your cursor and AutoCAD is prompting for the location at which to place the drawing. Before you click to place the drawing, you need to specify the scale at which you want the drawing printed.

38. **Right-click** to display the *Insertion Scale* pop-up menu (Figure 9-2.20).

39. Select **¼″ = 1′-0″** from the list.

Notice how the size of the drawing changes to correspond to the selected scale. Displaying the drawing at the correct scale helps you position it correctly on the sheet. You should also notice that a drawing title tag is positioned below and to the left of your view, which you will look at more closely after the view is placed.

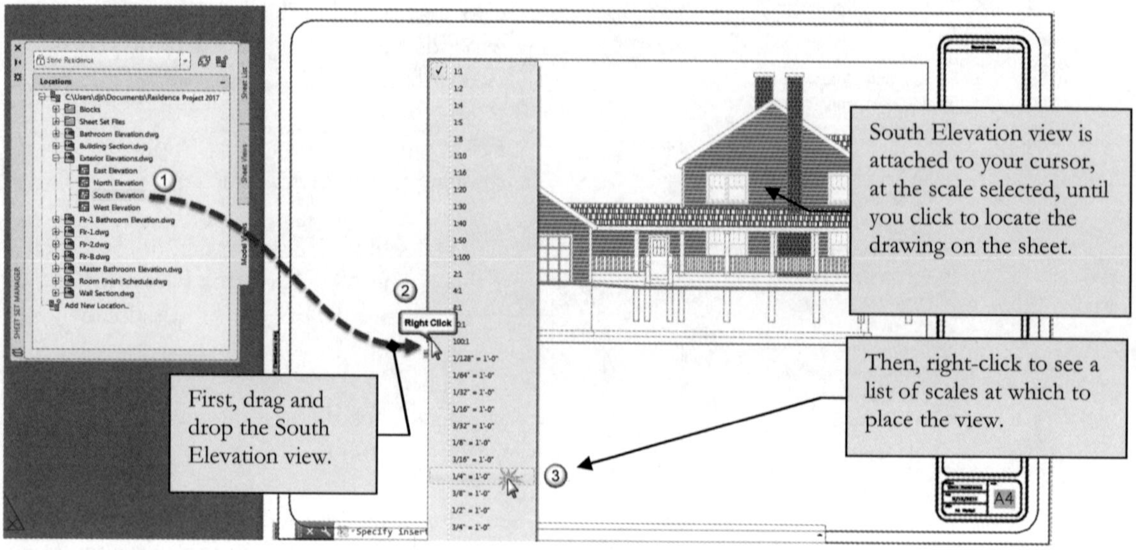

FIGURE 9-2.21
A4 - Exterior Elevations; placing the South Elevation view and right-clicking to see scale options

40. Position your mouse so the elevation is centered on the sheet and then click to place the view on the sheet.

You have placed your first drawing on a sheet (Figure 9-2.22)! In just minutes, you could have all the *Named Views* placed, but first, you will explore a few other options and see how they are affected when you change a few sheet numbers.

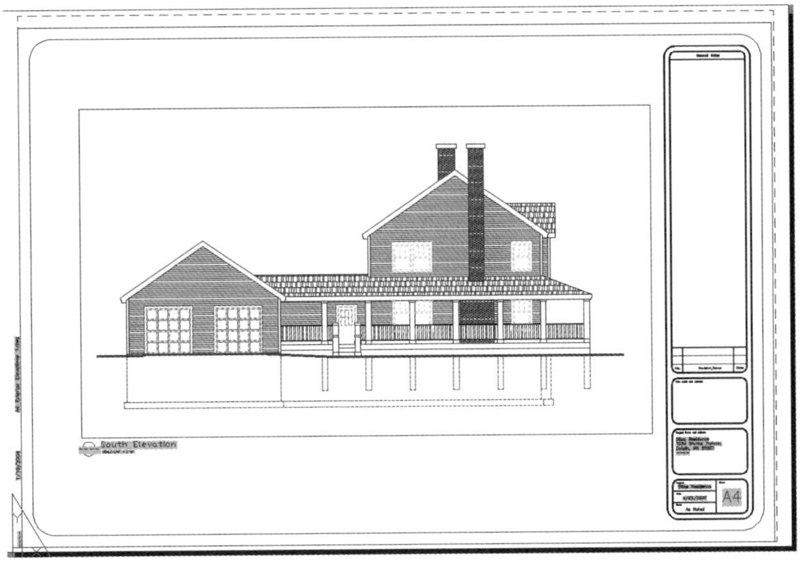

FIGURE 9-2.22
A4 - Exterior Elevations; South Elevation placed at ¼"=1'-0"

41. **Zoom In** on the *Drawing Title* tag (Figure 9-2.23).

FIGURE 9-2.23
A4 - Exterior Elevations; zoomed in on drawing title tag

Notice that the drawing name has been automatically filled in using the name you provided when you created the *Named View* in the *Resource Drawing* (exterior elevations.dwg).

Also, notice that the drawing scale has been added and, of course, corresponds to the scale you selected when you placed the view.

The only field not yet filled is the drawing number. You enter the drawing number for a view, once it is placed on a sheet, in the *Sheet Set Manager*. Next, you will provide the sheet number via the *Sheet Set Manager*.

TIP: If the fields are not visible, delete the symbol and then right-click on the view name in Figure 9-2.24 and select "place view label block."

WARNING: Do not change the number in the drawing as it will be overwritten by the Sheet Set Manager.

42. Select **Sheet Views** tab.

Notice that the *South Elevation* view is listed. Eventually, all your *Named Views* will be listed here once they are all placed on sheets (Figure 9-2.24).

43. Right-click on the *South Elevation* view and select **Rename & Renumber…** from the pop-up menu.

44. Enter number **1** in the *Number* textbox (Figure 9-2.25).

45. Click **OK** to apply the change.

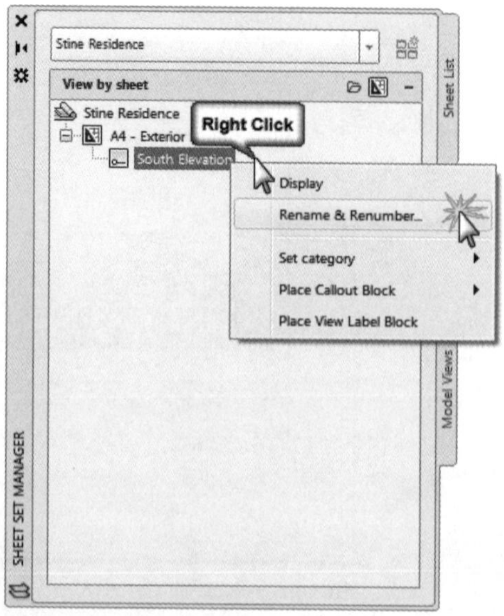

FIGURE 9-2.24
Sheet Set Manager; View List tab

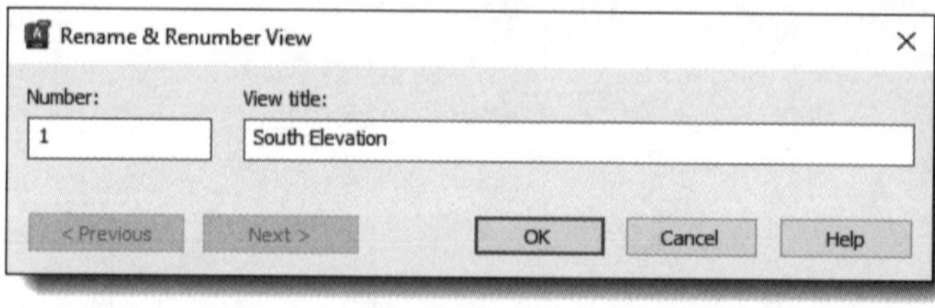

FIGURE 9-2.25
Rename and Renumber View; enter number 1

You will notice that your drawing has not updated yet. The next step will update the drawing title tag.

46. Type **Regen** and then press **Enter**.

The drawing title tag now has the number 1 in the circle (Figure 9-2.26). A few other key events trigger AutoCAD to update the tags, such as opening or plotting a drawing.

FIGURE 9-2.26
A4- Exterior Elevations; field updated automatically

Placing Callout Tags:

Another powerful feature of Sheet Sets is the ability to place Callout tags that are automatically cross-referenced to a sheet and drawing number. Next you will place an elevation *Callout* tag (that references the South Elevation) on the floor plan.

First, though, you will need to place the first floor plan on the appropriate sheet.

47. Per the steps previously outlined, place the **First Floor Plan** view at **¼" = 1'-0"** (from the Flr-1.dwg resource drawing) onto sheet **A2 – First Floor Plan** (Figure 9-2.27).

TIP: Open the sheet from the Sheet List tab and then drag the view from the Model Views tab.

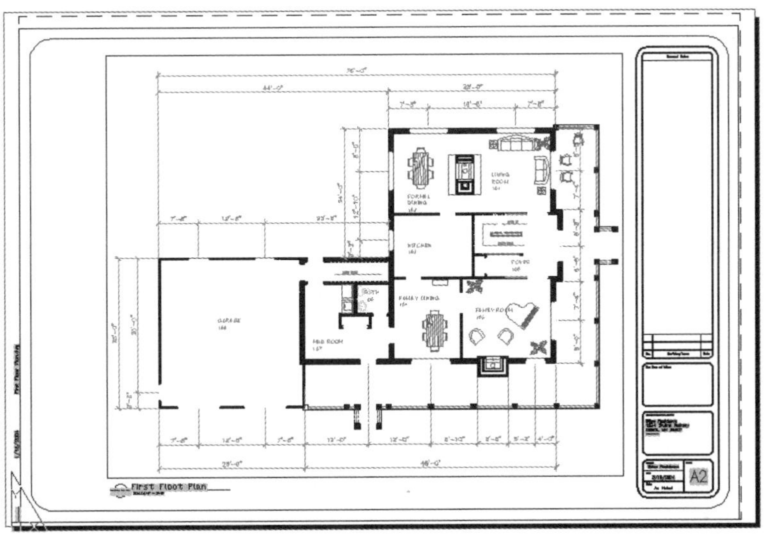

FIGURE 9-2.27
A2- First Floor Plan; First floor plan view placed on sheet at 1/4"

48. **Zoom In** to the bottom center of the floor plan sheet.

49. On the *Sheet Views* tab, right-click on the *South Elevation* view, and then select **Place Callout Block → Callout** (Figure 9-2.28).

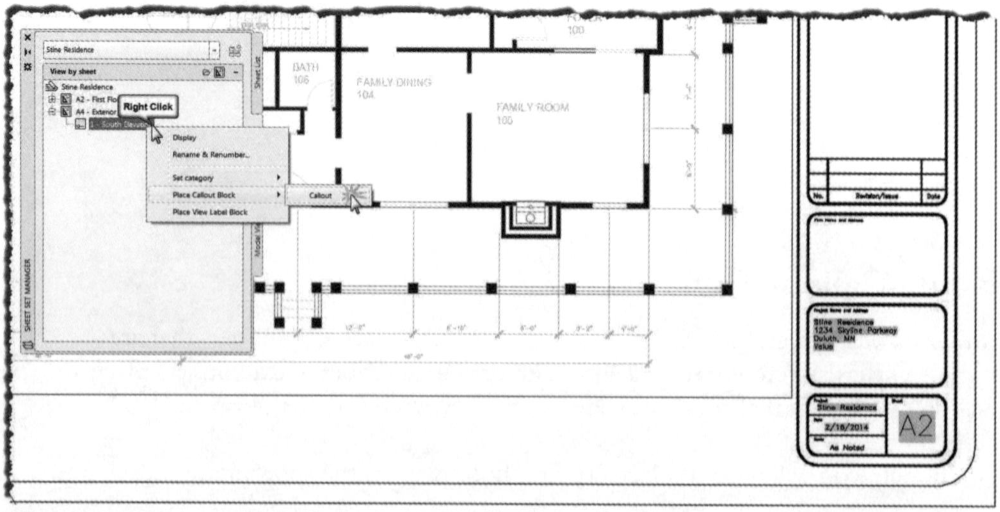

FIGURE 9-2.28
View List tab; right click on '1 – South Elevation'

50. Click to place the elevation tag approximately as shown in Figure 9-2.29 (it will be pointing to the right).

Notice that the *Elev. Indicator* has been automatically filled out. It references both the sheet and drawing numbers where the elevation (i.e., the elevation the tag points to) can be found.

The *Callout* symbol is a *Dynamic Block* that is set up to allow easy rotation of the pointer arrow (without rotating the text). The default orientation is pointing to the right, so you will adjust the arrow so it points north. The next numbered steps will walk you through this process. As you recall, selecting a *Dynamic Block* causes its special control *Grips* to display. One of these controls the rotation of the arrow (which has been set up to snap to certain angles).

51. Click to select the symbol.

52. Click the round *Grip*.

53. Move the cursor so the arrow is pointing north and then click.

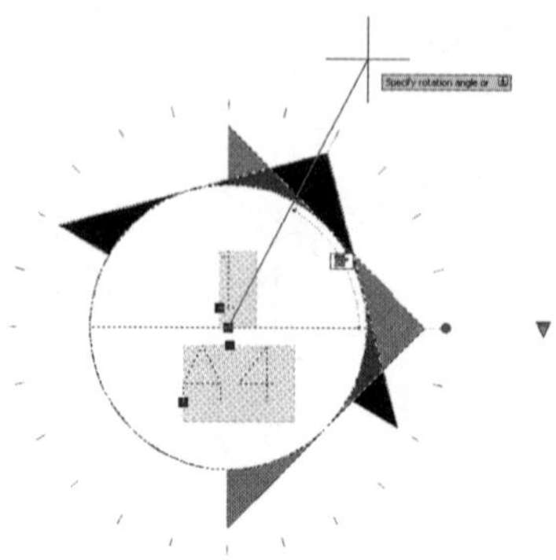

That's it; the callout has been modified.

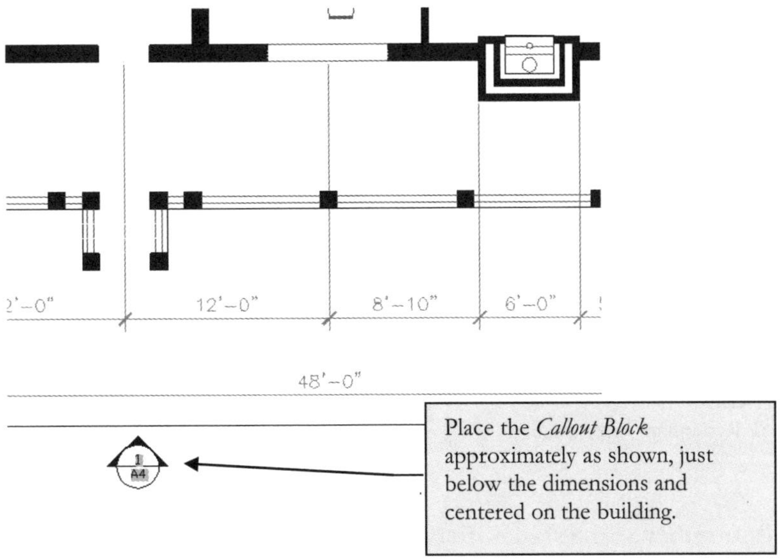

FIGURE 9-2.29
First Floor Plan sheet; elevation callout placed

54. **Save** both your elevation and plan sheet (*Save* on *QAT*); don't forget to save often so you don't lose any work.

Changing Sheet Numbers:

Looking at Figure 9-2.22, you realize that you will need two more exterior elevation sheets because one elevation takes up most of the sheet at ¼″ = 1′-0″. Next you will increment all the sheets that come after the exterior elevation sheets by 2 and then add two more exterior elevations sheets; all this is done in the *Sheet Set Manager.*

55. On the *Sheet List* tab, right click on sheet **A9 – Schedules** and select **Rename & Renumber.**

56. Make the following changes in the dialog box:
    a. Change the *Number* to **A11**
    b. Check <u>all</u> boxes under **Rename options**
       TIP: *If the rename file options are not checkable, the file is probably open and needs to be closed first.*
    c. Click **OK** (Figure 9-2.30)

This is similar to renumbering and renaming a view on the *View List* tab (look back at Figure 9-2.24).

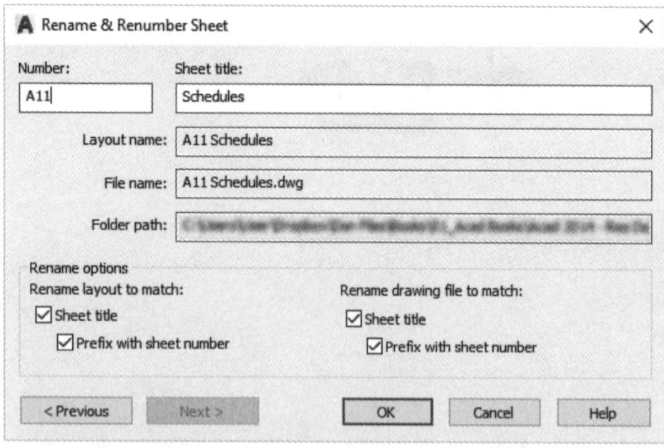

FIGURE 9-2.30
Rename & Renumber Sheet; change sheet A9 to A11

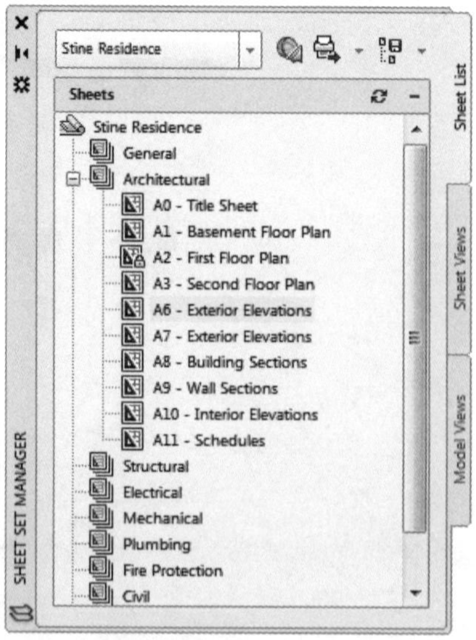

FIGURE 9-2.31
Sheet View tab; last six sheets renumbered, making room to insert two sheets

57. **Renumber** all the sheets after sheet *A3 – Second Floor* to make room to insert two new sheets numbered *A4* and *A5* (you will add the new sheets later). (See Figure 9-2.31.)

TIP: When renumbering, use the Previous *button to step back through the sheets.*

FYI: Files (i.e., sheets) must be closed before renaming can be done. Opened files cannot be renamed.

Normally, changing sheet numbers is not a good idea because, no matter how hard you look, you will usually miss one reference bubble, leaving the bubble pointing to the wrong sheet. This leads to confusion and possible loss of time and money.

AutoCAD has provided a solution to this problem. The callout bubbles, drawing titles and sheet borders are all linked to the information in the *Sheet Set Manager*. So once you changed the sheet numbers in the *Sheet Set Manager*, all the sheets were (or will be) updated automatically. You will verify this next.

58. In the **A6 – Exterior Elevations** sheet, zoom into the lower right corner to see the sheet number (Figure 9-2.32).

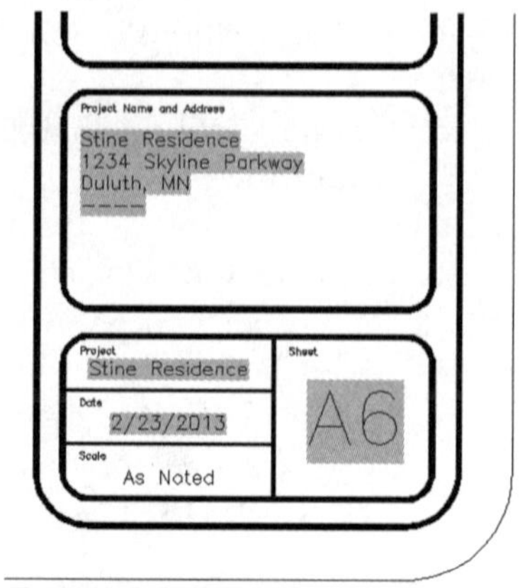

FIGURE 9-2.32
A6 – Exterior Elevations sheet; sheet number in title block has been updated automatically

TIP: You may need to Regen the drawing to see the change.

As you can see, the sheet number has been updated automatically!

What about the elevation tag you placed on the floor plan sheet?

59. On the **A2 – First Floor Plan** sheet, **Zoom In** on the callout bubble (elev indicator). See Figure 9-2.33.

    TIP: You may need to Regen the drawing to see the change. However, if the file is closed and reopened the update will be automatic.

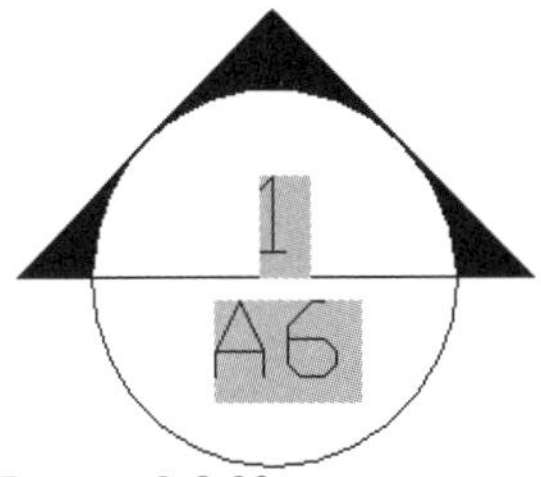

FIGURE 9-2.33
A2 – First Floor Plan sheet; sheet number in callout block has been updated automatically.

As you can see, the elevation callout tag has been updated automatically, thus eliminating the possibility of cross-reference errors when this system is used.

60. Add the following sheets to complete the set:

    TIP: You can drag the sheet labels (on the Sheet List tab) to change the listed order.

Sheet name	Sheet number
Exterior Elevations *Filename: A4 Exterior Elevations*	A4
Exterior Elevations *Filename: A5 Exterior Elevations*	A5

61. Place the remaining views (see step 36) on the appropriate sheets.

    FYI: The room schedule view should be placed at a scale of 1:1.

62. On the *Sheet Views* tab, give each view a number (see the *TIP* on the next page).

TIP:

Drawings are typically numbered in the direction indicated below. The first drawings are placed in the upper right, and fill in the sheet toward the left. The main reason for starting on the right is this: if a sheet is only half full (for example), you would not have to open the set all the way to see the drawings on that sheet.

Also, it is usually a good idea to wait until the sheet is mostly full before numbering drawings. That way you can organize the drawings neatly on the sheet and avoid a situation where the drawing numbers are not in sequence.

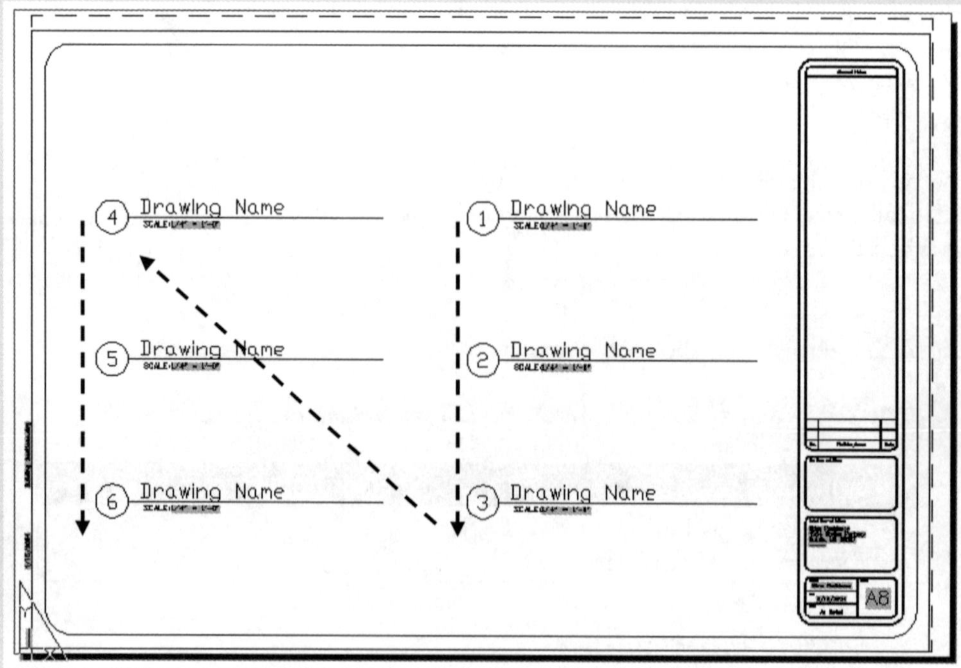

63. Place ***Callout*** blocks on your floor plan sheets to reference all your elevations (interior and exterior). See Figure 9-2.34.

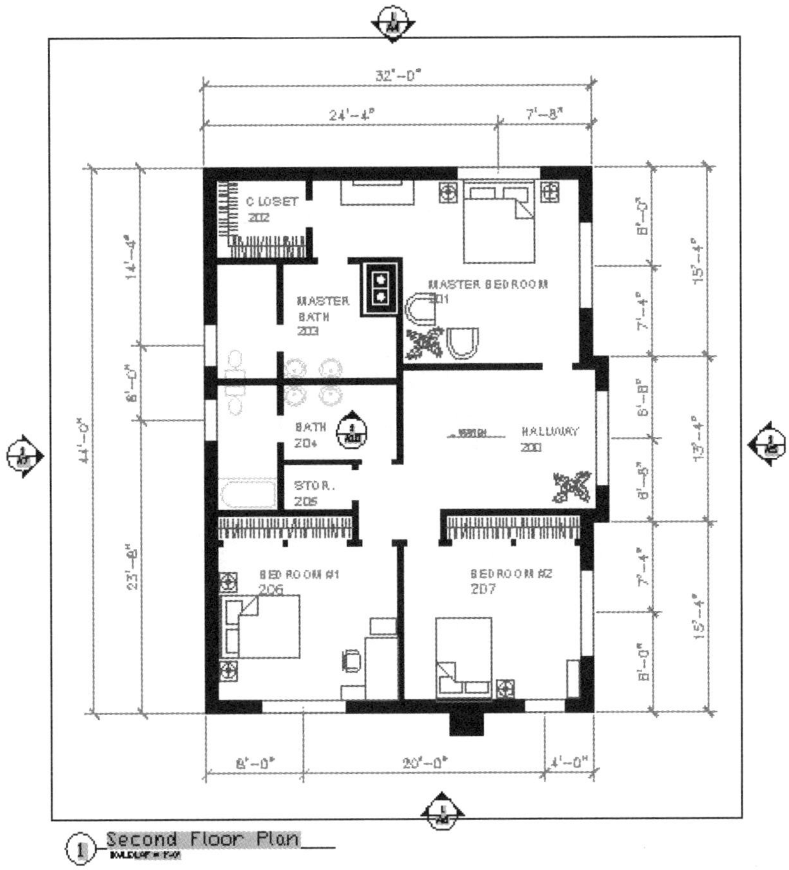

FIGURE 9-2.34
A3 – Second Floor Plan sheet; callout bubble added

> ***TIP:*** *The rectangle surrounding your drawings when placed on a sheet (cf. Figure 9-2.34) is called a viewport. This line cannot be erased, but it can be moved to its own Layer (e.g., Viewport) and then that layer can be Frozen; the drawing will still be visible but the rectangle (viewport) will not.*

64. **Save** and close all your open drawing files.

65. **Close** the *Sheet Set Data* file via the *Sheet Set Manager;* right-click on the *Sheet Set* project name (i.e., *Stine Residence*) and select **Close Sheet Set**.
    a. Any drawings opened with the *Sheet Set Manager* can be closed similar to any other AutoCAD drawing file. They can later be opened again via the *Sheet Set Manager* or using the normal *Open* command.

This concludes the study on *Sheet Sets.*

Manually Setting up a Sheet:

On occasion, you will want to know how to set up a sheet without using the *Sheet Set Manager*. This will help you better understand what the *Sheet Set Manager* is automatically doing for you every time you add a view to a sheet.

You will use the *Layout View* existing in your Flr-1 drawing. This tab came from the template that you started. Every drawing must have a *Model Space* tab and at least one *Layout View* (paper space) tab. If you recall, after creating each new drawing, you had to switch to *Model Space* because the *Layout View* tab was current.

As previously stated, *Model Space* is where all the drawing is done, and *Layout View* is where the plot sheet is set up. On the plot sheet, you draw a special rectangle, called a *Viewport*, that looks into *Model Space*. You can set the scale for the *Viewport*. Also, you can have several *Viewports* in the *Layout View*. They can each have a different scale if you need it, and they can look at the same drawing. That is, you can have one Viewport looking at the overall floor plan at ⅛″ = 1′-0″ and another looking at the toilet rooms only, at ¼″ = 1′-0″.

66. Open your **Flr-1** drawing file. You do not need to have the *Sheet Set Manager* open for this.

67. Switch to the **Arch D** *Layout View* tab (a.k.a., *Paper Space*).

68. Type **MV** to activate the *Make Viewport* command.

69. Pick two points on the screen to define the extents of the *Viewport* (Figure 9-2.35).

    You now see everything in *Model Space*, which is zoomed to fit the *Viewport*.

FIGURE 9-2.35 Manually adding a viewport

70. Select the *Viewport*, and set the scale to **¼″ = 1′-0″** via the *Status Bar* (Figure 9-2.36)

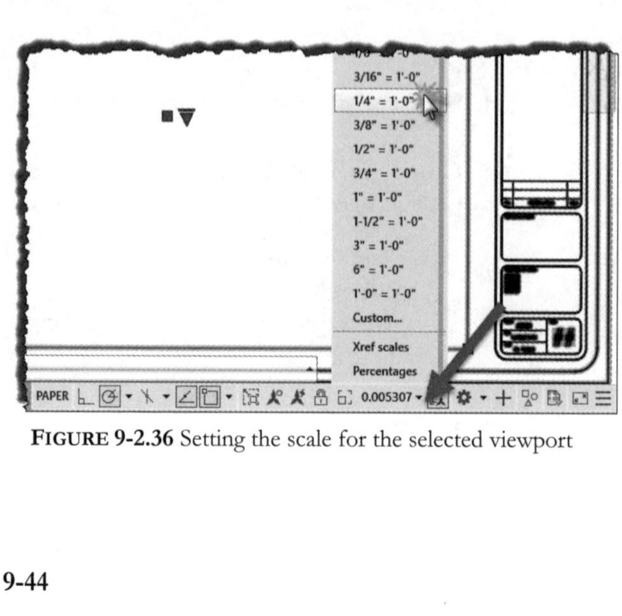

FIGURE 9-2.36 Setting the scale for the selected viewport

The scale is now set correctly. Sometimes it is necessary to pan the drawing within the *Viewport*. This can be done by double-clicking within the *Viewport* and using the *Pan* command. Be careful not to zoom as this will mess up the scale. When finished, double-click outside of the *Viewport* or select the Model button on the Status Bar (which says Paper when you are not in the Viewport).

When the *Viewport* is selected, you may also click the **Lock** icon on the Status Bar to lock the scale for the selected *Viewport* so it does not accidentally change (see image below).

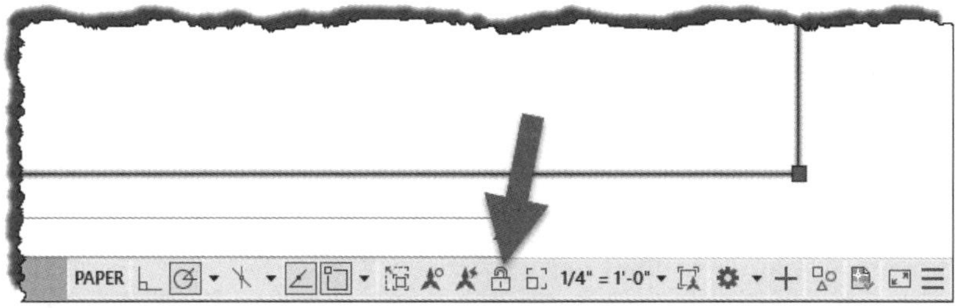

FIGURE 9-2.37 Locking the scale of a manually created viewport

71. Create another *Viewport* as shown in the image below (a smaller rectangle within the larger one), zoom in on the toilet room, and set the scale to **1/2" = 1'-0"**.

    TIP: Press Ctrl+R *to toggle between Viewports once one is active.*

72. Create a *Layer* called **Viewport**, move the two *Viewports* to this *Layer,* and turn its visibility off.

    FYI: It is not possible to place items on a layer coming from an xref (even though they are listed in the Layer Manager). You must create a Viewport layer if one does not already exist in your drawing.

73. **Save** your Flr-1 drawing file.

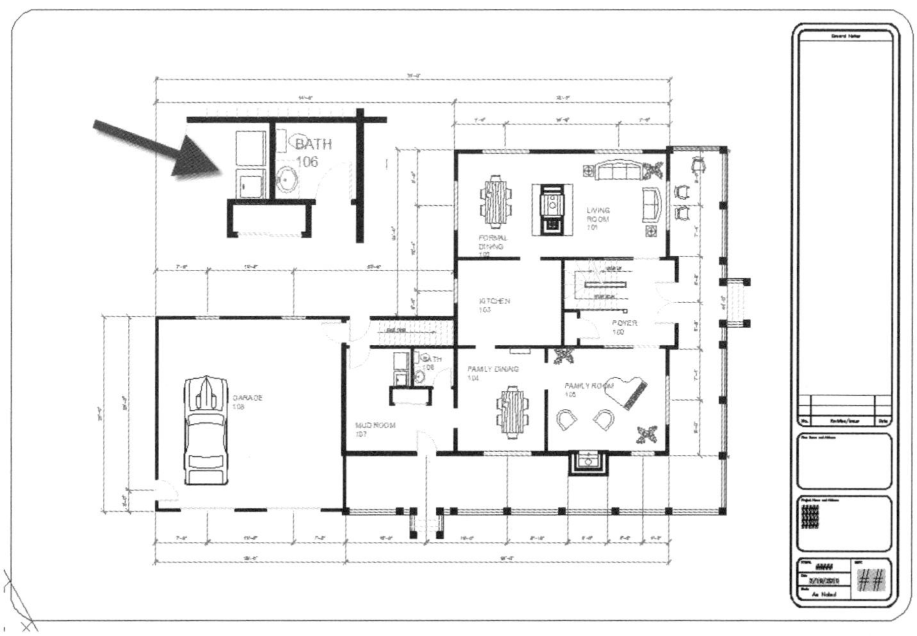

FIGURE 9-2.38 Two viewports created

Exercise 9-3:
Sheet Index

Introduction:

In this exercise, you will take a look at the *Sheet Index* feature that takes advantage of both *Sheet Sets* and *Tables*. The *Sheet Index* feature extracts information stored in the *Sheet Set Data* file (sheet name and number) and then generates a *Table* to be placed on one of your sheets in the *Sheet Set*.

The *Sheet Index* has hyperlinks embedded in each listing; thus, you can "Ctrl+click" on a sheet name or number to open that sheet. As you will see in the next *Lesson*, these hyperlinks transfer to the electronic set (DWF file), which allows a client or consultant to easily navigate the set of drawings.

Opening an existing Sheet Set via *Recent* flyout or *Open…* and browse

1. **Open** your *Sheet Set Data* file (*your name* Residence.dst).

   FYI: *The DST file can also be opened from the Application Menu → Recent Files.*

2. Open **A0 – Title Sheet** from the *Sheet List* tab.

3. Using **Mtext**, add large, bold text as shown in Figure 9-3.1.
   a. *Font:* **Arial Black**
   b. *Height:* **1″**

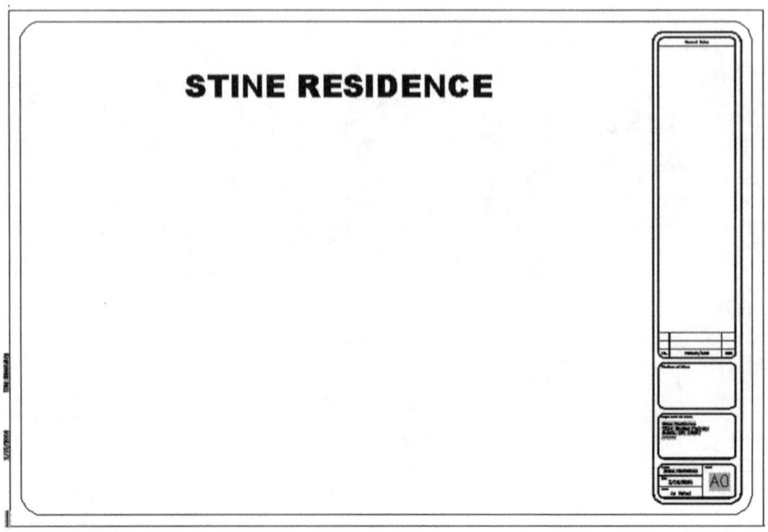

FIGURE 9-3.1
A0 – Title Sheet; text added to sheet

FYI: A Title sheet usually has the project title as its focal point. Additionally, you will typically find the following information:

- *Rendering or picture of a model of the project*
- *Sheet Index*
- *Abbreviation Legend (e.g., TYP. means TYPICAL)*
- *Symbol Legend (e.g., show a swatch of AR-CONC hatch pattern and identify it as the symbol for concrete)*
- *Building Code/ Zoning Summary*
- *Site Plan (typically on smaller projects)*

The *Legends*, which are used over and over, without modification, can be created in a separate drawing and inserted as a block on the *Title* sheet.

Next, you will insert a *Sheet Index*.

4. **Right click** on the *Sheet Set* project title (at the top of the list on the *Sheet List* tab).

5. Select **Insert Sheet List Table…** from the pop-up menu (Figure 9-3.2).

You are now in the *Insert Sheet List Table* dialog (Figure 9-3.3).

6. Click **OK** to accept the defaults and close the dialog.

7. Click anywhere on your *A0 - Title Sheet* to place the *Sheet List* table on the sheet.

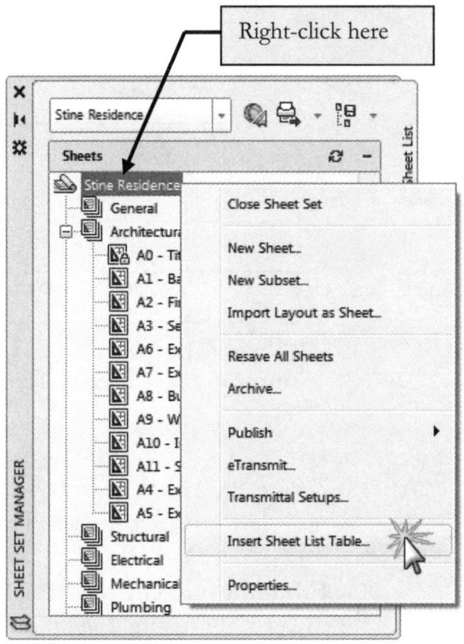

FIGURE 9-3.2
Sheet Set Manager; right click on project title (Stine Residence in this example)

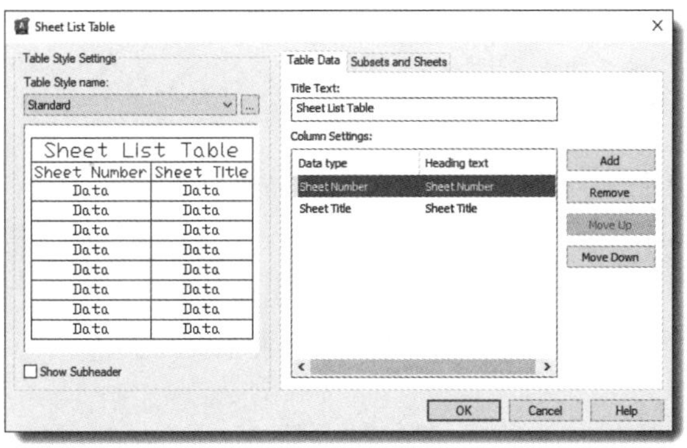

FIGURE 9-3.3
Insert Sheet List Table dialog

The table is now placed on your *Title* sheet (Figure 9-3.4).

Sheet List Table	
Sheet Number	Sheet Title
A0	Title Sheet
A1	Basement Floor Plan
A2	First Floor Plan
A3	Second Floor Plan
A4	Exterior Elevations
A5	Exterior Elevations
A6	Exterior Elevations
A7	Exterior Elevations
A8	Building Section
A9	Wall Sections
A10	Interior Elevations
A11	Schedules

FIGURE 9-3.4
A0 – Title Sheet; inserted sheet list table

After inserting the *Sheet List*, you decide to change the justification of the data cell so that everything is left-justified. You will make this change now…

8. From the *Annotate* tab, select the **Table Style** link (the small arrow in lower-right of the *Table* panel).

9. Select the ***Standard*** style and click the **Modify** button in the *Table Style Manager.*

10. On the *General* tab (for the **Data** *Cell styles*), set the *Alignment* to **Top Left**.

11. Click **OK** and **Close** to close all the open dialog boxes.

As you can see, this is the same process previously described in the *Room Finish Schedule* exercise because the *Sheet List* is a table!

Sheet List Table	
Sheet Number	Sheet Title
A0	Title Sheet
A1	Basement Floor Plan
A2	First Floor Plan
A3	Second Floor Plan
A4	Exterior Elevations
A5	Exterior Elevations
A6	Exterior Elevations
A7	Exterior Elevations
A8	Building Section
A9	Wall Sections
A10	Interior Elevations
A11	Schedules

FIGURE 9-3.5
A0 – Title Sheet; modified sheet list table

If you add a sheet or change a sheet number via the *Sheet Set Manager*, the *Sheet List* can be updated by selecting the edge of the table, right-clicking, and then selecting *Update Table Data Links*.

Inserting Raster Images into a Drawing:

While you still have your *Title* sheet open, you will take a quick look at inserting a raster image into a drawing. This can be done in any drawing file. The process is similar to Xref-ing a drawing.

This example adds a raster image to the *Title* sheet. Ideally, you would be adding a raster image that contains a rendering of the exterior of your building. However, because you do not have one at the moment, you will insert an image that is installed with AutoCAD 2027.

12. From the *Insert* tab, select the **Attach** icon (on the *Reference* panel).

Attach

13. Browse to the following folder: **C:\Program Files\Autodesk\AutoCAD 2027\Sample\VBA**.

14. Set the *Files of Type* to **All Image files**, and then select the file **WorldMap.TIF** and click **Open** (Figure 9-3.6).

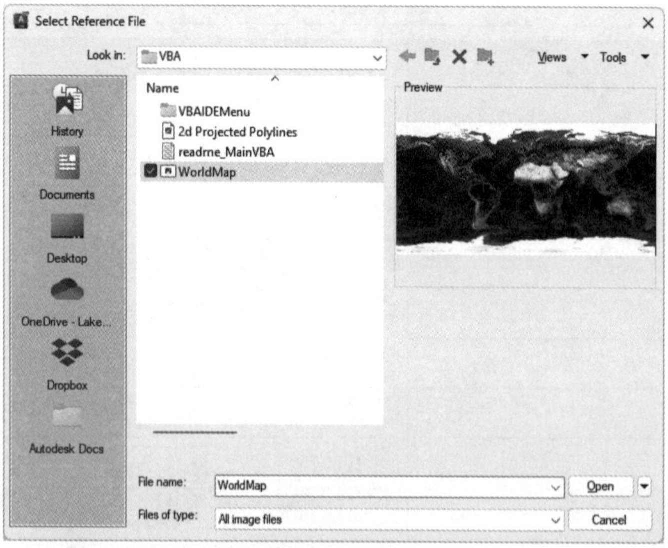

FIGURE 9-3.6 Select Reference File dialog

You are now in a dialog that is similar to inserting external references (Xref's).

15. Accept the default settings and click **OK** (Figure 9-3.7).

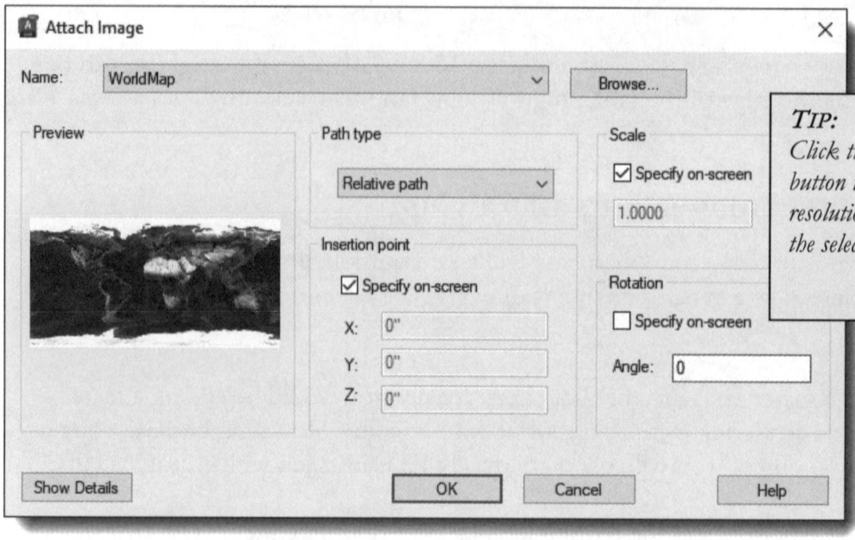

> ***TIP:***
> *Click the Show Details button to view size and resolution information for the selected image file.*

FIGURE 9-3.7 Image dialog

You now see the image outline near your cursor for insertion.

16. Click to place the image approximately centered below your large text.

17. At this point you can visually move the mouse to adjust the image size or type a value (you will accept the default value of 1).

18. Press **Enter** to accept the default scale of 1.

FYI: The image can be moved, rotated, scaled, or erased at any time (after insertion) using the standard AutoCAD commands.

TIP: If you don't want the rectangle around the image, you can turn it off using the **image frame** *variable. The default value is* ***1****, which makes the outline show and plot;* ***0*** *makes the outline invisible, and the image is not selectable (i.e., you cannot move, scale, etc.);* ***2*** *makes the outline show but not plot.*

19. **Move** the *Sheet Index* to center it under the image.

The *Title* sheet should now look like Figure 9-3.8.

FYI: You can detach or unload images via the External References Palette… (see the next page).

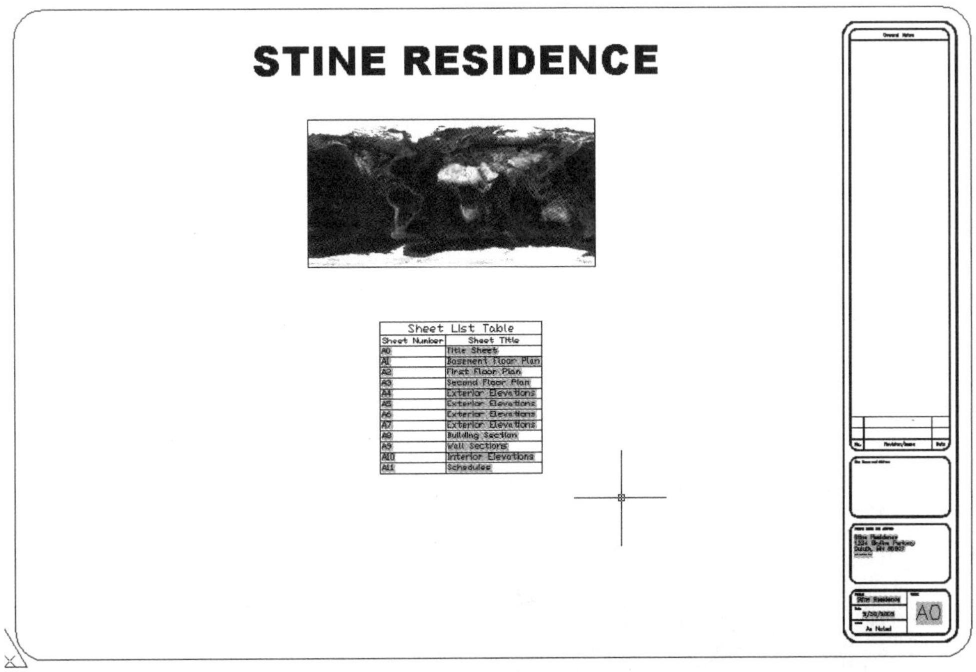

FIGURE 9-3.8

If you select the image and then right-click you will see a few options for editing the selected image; also, selecting External References… from the *Insert* tab loads a *Palette* that shows all referenced files. Notice the Ribbon has several settings related to the image when it is selected (see images at the top of the next page).

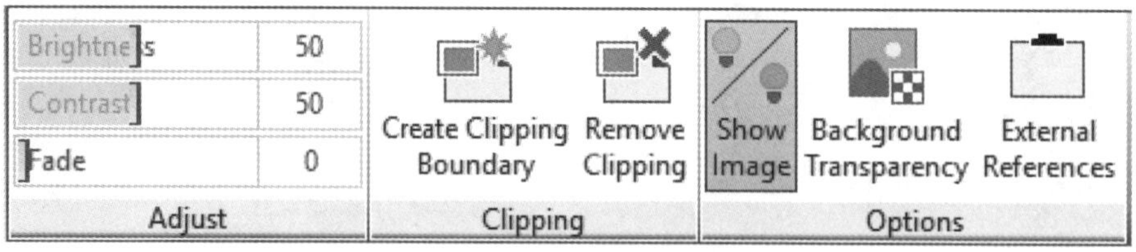

Ribbon; image selected

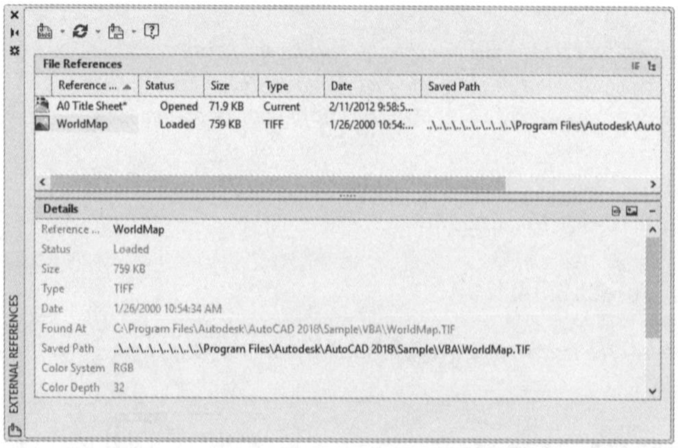

External References Palette

You can also scan a blueprint of a floor plan (or anything else) and use the scanned file to trace over with AutoCAD lines. You need to use *Scale* and its subcommand *Reference* to accurately adjust the size of the image before tracing.

You can also place photos of existing conditions on a sheet and add (AutoCAD) notes and leaders on top of the photo. For example, point out an entry roof to be removed on the front of a building (see example image below from an AutoCAD drawing).

For more advanced raster placement and editing tools check out **Autodesk Raster Design**. This is an add-in to AutoCAD which allows you to select, move, delete and erase portions of an image and much more. It is often used to manipulate scanned hand drawn sheets.

20. **Save** your **A0 – Title Sheet** drawing.

That completes the introduction to *Sheet List* tables and raster images.

Self-Exam:

The following questions can be used as a way to check your knowledge of this lesson. The answers can be found at the bottom of this page.

1. The *Table Manager* is where you change a table's text height. (T/F)
2. You need to create *Named Views* for each drawing/detail that you want to place on a sheet. (T/F)
3. Once a *Sheet List* table is placed you have to manually update it if you add or remove any sheets. (T/F)
4. When dragging a view from the *Sheet Set Manager* onto a sheet, you ______________ to get a listing of scales to insert the view at.
5. In the *Named Views* dialog, you can change the view's boundary. (T/F)

Review Questions:

The following questions may be assigned by your instructor as a way to assess your knowledge of this section. Your instructor has the answers to the review questions.

1. Once a *Table* is created, you cannot add rows or columns. (T/F)
2. It is not possible to combine two or more table cells into one. (T/F)
3. AutoCAD creates a drawing file each time you create a new sheet in the *Sheet Set Manager*. (T/F)
4. Views are placed on sheets by dragging the view name from the ______________tab; views are numbered (and renamed) on the ________________ tab in the *Sheet Set Manager*.
5. You cannot specify where the *Sheet Set Data* file is stored. (T/F)
6. The bottom number, in an elevation callout bubble, indicates the ________________ number the elevation is located on.
7. This icon () allows you to insert a __________________________.
8. In a *Sheet Set*, sheets can be organized using __________________.
9. You should not move or rename the files created by the *Sheet Set Manager* (except what you are able to do in the *Manager* itself). (T/F)
10. You right-click on the ___________ to see the *Insert Sheet List* option.

SELF-EXAM ANSWERS:
1 – T, **2** – T, **3** – F, **4** – right-click, **5** – T

Additional Tasks:

Task 9-1: Create a Door Schedule

Using the techniques learned in Lesson 9-1, create a door schedule and place it on the *Schedules* sheet. You will need to number the doors in your plans. Typically, a door has the same number as the room it swings into. If a room has more than one door (like the *Master Bedroom*), you add letters to the number (i.e., 201A and 201B). Include the following columns in your schedule: Door Number, Door Size, Door Material, Door Type, Frame Material, Frame Type, Jamb Detail, Head Detail, Sill Detail, Fire Rating, Remarks.

Task 9-2: Place All Your Views on Sheets

If you have been creating the drawings suggested in the previous "additional tasks," you can place them on the appropriate sheets, adding sheets if necessary.

Task 9-3: Place Callout Blocks to Reference Your Drawings

You can add additional callout blocks:

- Any other interior elevations you may have drawn.
- Building Section: you can draw a line through your floor plan, where your building section is cut, and place an elevation callout block at one end of the line to reference the building section.
- You can add a note to your floor plan that says, "For room finish schedule see" and place the "basic" callout block next to the note.
- Wall Section: draw a rectangle (Fillet its corners and change the linetype to dashed) around a portion of your building section that represents the extents of your wall section and then place a "basic" callout bubble with a line drawn from the bubble to the rectangle.

Task 9-4: Add Additional Raster Images to Your Drawings

Add additional images to your drawings. If you have a scanner, you may try sketching a perspective of your building, scan it to a raster file and then place it on your *Title* sheet.

Lesson 10
LINEWEIGHTS & PLOTTING:

In this final lesson, you will examine how lineweights work in AutoCAD. Finally, you will take another look at plotting, this time plotting to scale from the *Sheet Set Manager*.

When you finish this chapter, you will have a formidable part of a set of residential working drawings.

Exercise 10-1:
Lineweights

Introduction:

As previously discussed, lineweights are an important part of an architectural drawing set. They help differentiate among the many lines in a drawing; more specifically, lineweights indicate which parts of the drawing are in section versus elevation.

Hand drafters would create different line thicknesses as they drew, whereas CAD drawings typically don't show the actual lineweight until the drawing is printed.

AutoCAD has three primary ways to handle lineweights. This book will describe all three and give an overview of two methods. Then, you will use one method on your floor plan drawings.

Three Methods Described:

Color Dependent Plot Style:
With this method, the line thickness is determined by the line color and whether the color is set to ByLayer or ByEntity. This used to be the only method available in AutoCAD and is probably still the most used.

Named Plot Style:
With this method you assign a Named Plot Style to each Layer (and even ByEntity – not recommended). A Named Plot Style has a name, like Heavy, and has several settings assigned to it (i.e., line thickness, screened, etc.). A group of Named Plot Styles are stored in a file called a "Named Plot Style Table."

Lineweight ByLayer:
With this method, a Plot Style Table is not used (neither color nor named). Rather, the lineweight is set by the Lineweight column in the Layer Manager (or ByEntity in the Properties Dialog – not recommended). Note that the Lineweight column only applies when a Plot Style Table is not selected in Page Setup (Page Setup will be covered shortly).

Example of the "Lineweight ByLayer" Method:

Here you will take a look at a sample drawing, located on the Autodesk website, that uses this method. Because of the nature of this sample drawing, it has the lineweights set *ByEntity* rather than the preferred *ByLayer* method. However, we will use this drawing to understand this method of applying lineweights and why the *ByLayer* method is more preferable.

1. In your web browser (e.g. MS Internet Explorer), go to http://www.autodesk.com/autocad-samples, right-click **Line Weights**, and then click **Save Link As**. Save the file to your desktop and then open it.

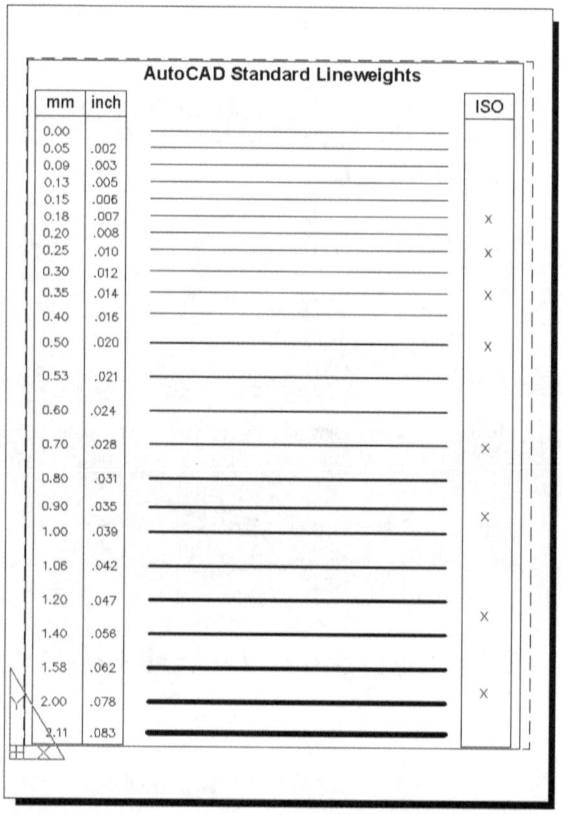

FIGURE 10-1.1
Sample Drawing; Lineweights.dwg

By default, you should be on the layout titled "**Letter Size**" and see the image shown in Figure 10-1.1. However, you may not yet see the actual line thickness for each line; if not, you will set this next.

2. To toggle the *Lineweight* on-screen visibility on or off:
   a. Click the *Customization* icon (the last one on the right) on the *Status Bar*, and then select **LineWeight**. This will add a new option to the *Status Bar*.
   b. Click the **Show/Hide Lineweight** (LWT) button on the *Status Bar* if not already activated (Figures 10-1.2a&b).

The **LWT** button works for any of the methods of defining lineweights discussed.

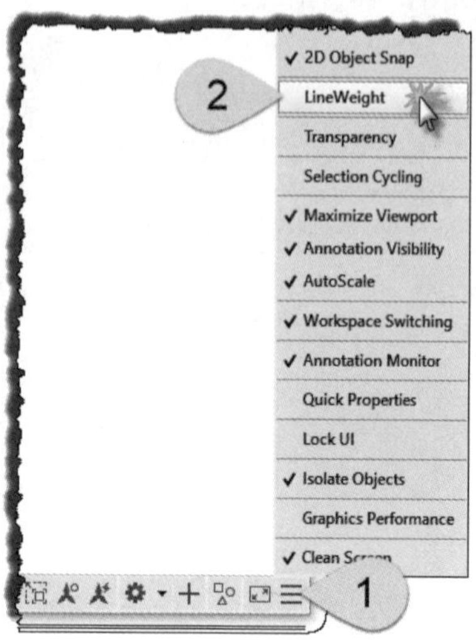

FIGURE 10-1.2A
Status Bar; Customization options

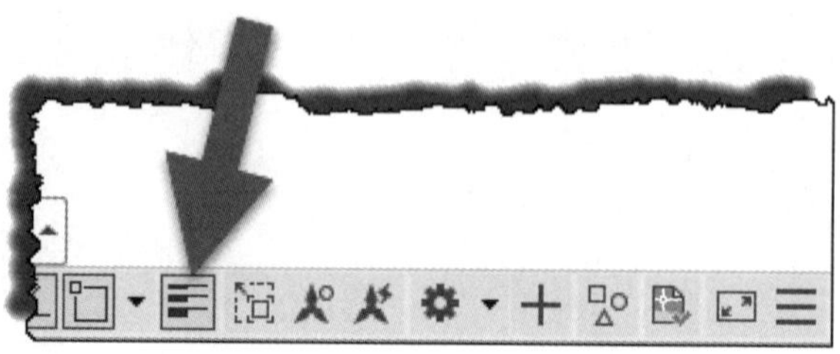

FIGURE 10-1.2B
Status Bar; LWT stands for Lineweights

3. Switch to *Model Space.*

The line thicknesses in *Model Space* are exaggerated. Most users do not typically have lineweight visibility turned on during day-to-day drafting.

4. Click the **Show/Hide Lineweight** button on the *Status Bar* to turn **off** the onscreen lineweight visibility; the blue highlight will go away.

The Lineweight column in the *Layer Properties Manager* controls the lineweight for each *Layer.* So anything drawn on a *Layer,* which has its lineweight property set to 0.13mm, will always print at 0.13mm (unless the lineweight has been changed for one or more lines in the *Properties* dialog; this overrides the *Layer* setting).

5. **Open** the ***Layer Properties Manager*** (Figure 10-1.3).

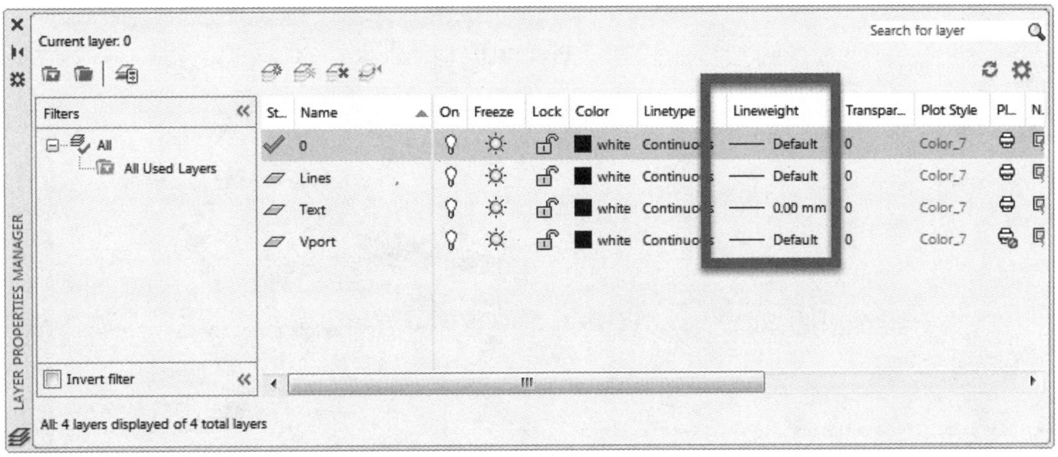

FIGURE 10-1.3
Lineweights Sample Drawing; Lineweight column used when a Plot Style Table is not used.

The highlighted area in Figure 10-1.3 is the *Lineweight* column that you would adjust to various lineweights. So if you want everything drawn on layer *Lines* to be 0.70mm, you would adjust the *Lineweight* setting for the *Lines* layer to 0.70mm. This drawing actually has an override set for each line via the *Properties Palette*; you will look at these values in a moment.

As mentioned earlier, for AutoCAD to use these settings you need to make sure that a *Plot Style Table* is not selected in *Page Setup*. You will verify this next.

6. Right-click on the *Model Space* tab and then select **Page Setup Manager…** from the menu.

7. Click **Modify…** to adjust the default settings for the *Model* tab (Figure 10-1.4).

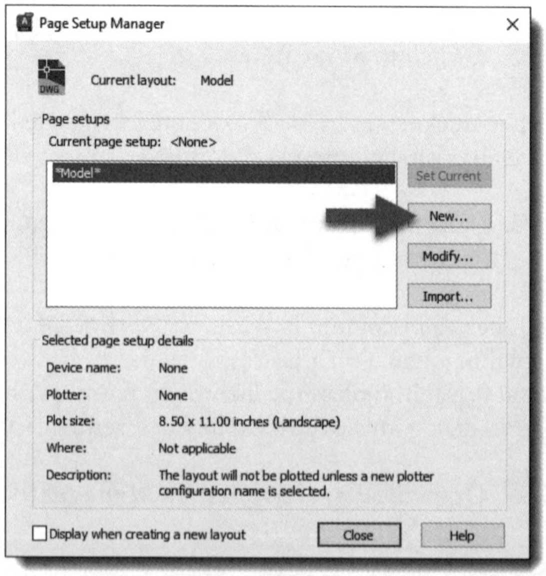

FIGURE 10-1.4 Page Setup Manager

Notice in the image below (Figure 10-1.5) that a *Plot Style Table* is not specified; that is, it is set to ***None***.

8. **Close** the open dialogs.

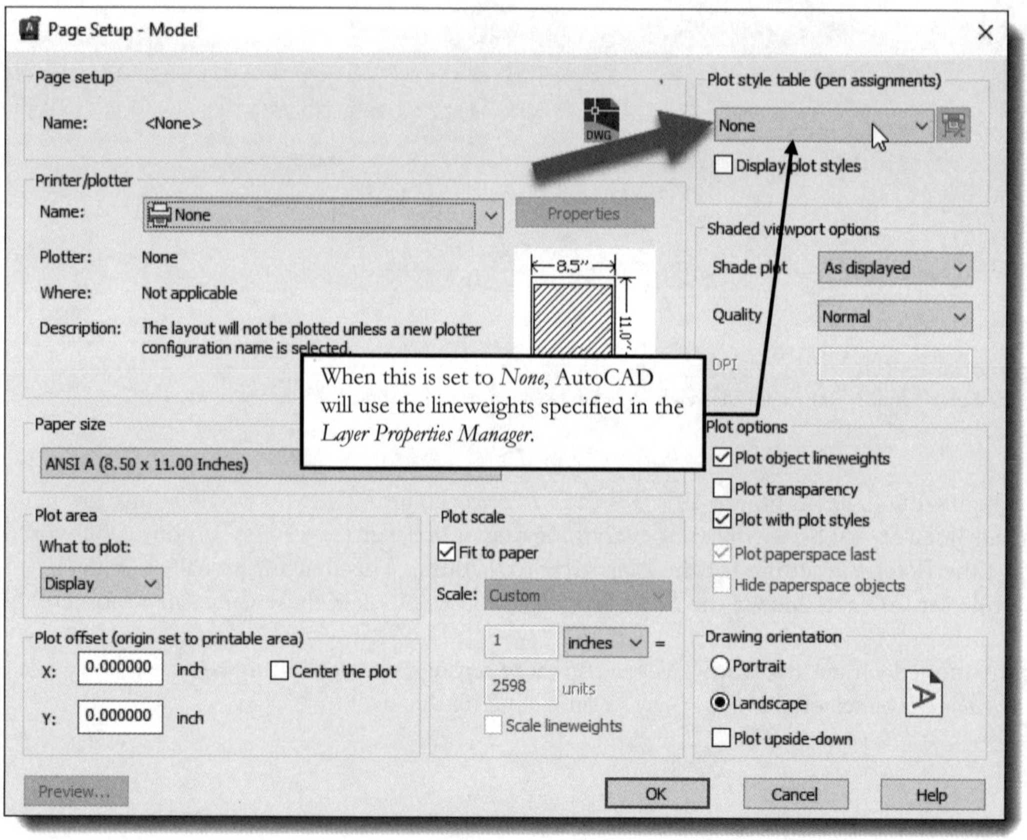

FIGURE 10-1.5 Lineweights Sample Drawing; Page Setup

The last variation on this method is setting the lineweight *ByEntity*, which overrides the setting in the *Layer Manager*. It is generally recommended that you do not change settings (such as color, lineweight, etc.) *ByEntity*. The reason for this is that it is difficult to change the settings of several lines that have been changed *ByEntity*, whereas when you want to change the color of all the lines on layer *A-Wall*, all you have to do is change the color one time in the *Layer Manager*. Finally, having all the settings for an entity set to *ByLayer* allows for more control over *Externally Referenced* drawings.

Even though changing settings *ByEntity* is not recommended, the sample drawing is set up this way. Next you will look at this *ByEntity* type of modification to better understand what has been described.

9. Select the **0.35mm** line (i.e., the horizontal line to the right of the 0.35mm label). (See Figure 10-1.1.)

10. Right-click and select **Properties** (Figure 10-1.6).

Notice that the *Lineweight* setting for the selected line is set to 0.35mm, so no matter which *Layer* this line is on, it will always print 0.35mm thick.

The lineweight for the selected entity could be changed via the *Properties* dialog shown in Figure 10-1.6. In addition to several other lineweights, you can select *ByLayer*; this setting uses the lineweight assigned to the *Layer* and is generally the preferred method of assigning lineweights (i.e., *ByLayer*).

11. Select a few other lines and look at their properties; notice that each line has its *Lineweight* setting changed (to match its corresponding label in the case of this drawing).

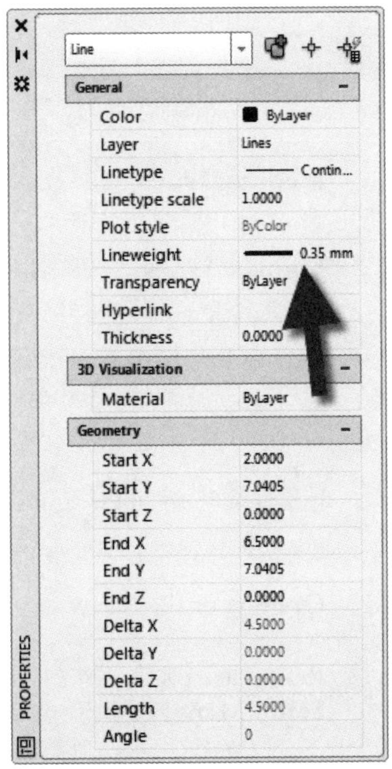

FIGURE 10-1.6
Properties; 0.35mm line selected

> *TIP: You may want to print the Lineweight.dwg sample drawing so you have a reference sheet showing what each line thickness really looks like printed on paper. Switching to the Letter Size Layout, you should be all set to print to an 8½" x 11" paper; you should only have to select the printer.*

12. **Close** the Lineweight.dwg drawing file without saving.

Applying the "Color Dependent Plot Style" Method to Your Drawings:

Now you will apply lineweights to your floor plans. Below, you will take a minute to study lineweight theory; that is, what should be drawn with a heavy line and what should be drawn with a light line.

For floor plans:

- **Heaviest Lines**: Wall lines and openings in floor; any major building component in section (e.g., column) **0.60mm.**
- **Medium Lines**: Objects like cabinets, doors and windows should be the next heaviest **0.30mm.**
- **Lightest Lines**: Any lines on the floor (e.g., furniture) and windowsill lines should be the lightest lines **0.05mm.**
- **Light Gray Lines**: Hatch patterns, such as ceramic tile or a recessed slab area, should be a light gray line so it is not too intense (use one of the screened plot styles) **0.10mm.**

For interior elevations lineweight descriptions, see page 7-20.

13. **Open** your **Flr-2** drawing.

14. Right-click on the *Model* tab and select **Page Setup Manager…** from the pop-up menu.

15. Click the **Modify…** button.

16. From the *Plot Style Table* drop-down list, select **New…** (Figure 10-1.7).

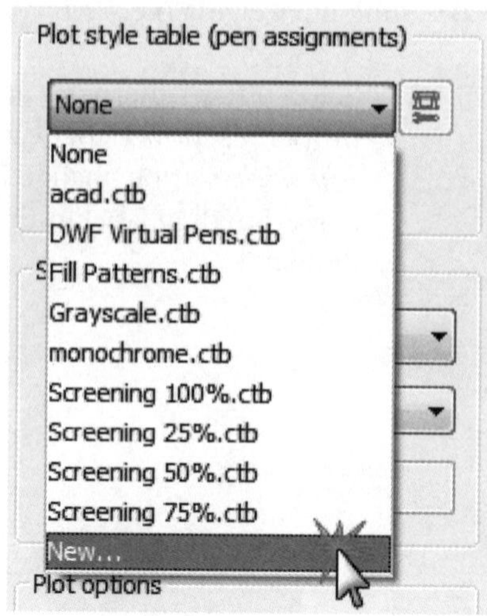

FIGURE 10-1.7
Page Setup; creating a new Plot Style Table

> ***TIP:*** *If you only see tables that end with .STB, you started your drawing with the wrong template. You need to copy/paste your drawing into the correct template file per Lesson 3 – page 3-1.*

You are now in the *Add Color-Dependent Plot Style Table Wizard*, which will walk you through the steps and information necessary to create a *Plot Style Table.*

17. Select **Start from scratch** and then click **Next >**.

18. Type **your last name** for the *Plot Style Table* file name and then click **Next >**.

19. Accept the default settings and click **Finish**.

Your new *Plot Style Table* is now selected as current in *Page Setup*. Next you will modify your new table so that each of the first seven AutoCAD colors equals a particular lineweight.

20. Click the **Edit Plot Style Table** icon. 

21. Click on the ***Form View*** tab.

22. Modify each of the first seven *Plot Styles* (i.e., Color 1 thru Color 7) so the *Color Property* is set to ***Black***.

23. Assign each of the first seven colors a lineweight (ranging from 0.1000mm to 1.0000mm). See Figure 10-1.8 for an example; also see the *TIPS* below:

    TIP #1: *Divide 1mm by seven and pick the closest lineweight available in the list for each of the 7 colors.*

    TIP #2: *On a separate piece of paper, write down the color number and then the lineweight you assigned to that color; this list will be useful shortly.*

    TIP #3: *If you prefer, you can use the color/lineweight settings shown in Figure 10-1.9 rather than coming up with your own. This is not the "standard" by any means but is arranged so the "brighter" lines are heavier lineweights and the "dimmer" lines are lighter lineweights (based on a black drawing area background).*

24. Assign each of the last six colors (250-255) the lineweight **0.1500mm**; leave the *Color* property set to **Use Object Color.**

TIP: When you set a Layer's color to 250-255, the objects on those Layers will print in five shades of gray (depending on which of the five colors are used). This is used for building lines that are very far back in the elevation/ or existing. Another use would be for a patch pattern that represents brick coursing (which are lines that are close together and can be overpowering if not printed with grayscale lines). One more use might be for a solid hatch that might indicate circulation (i.e., hallways) or sidewalks and driveways.

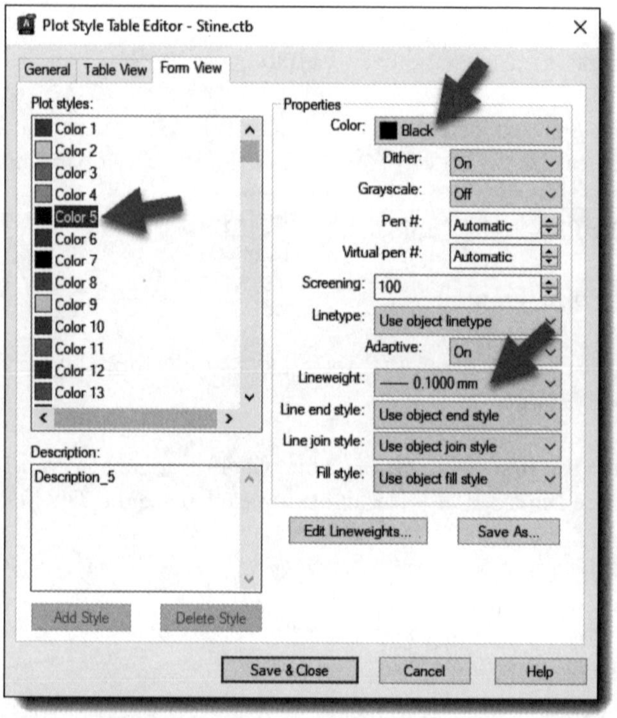

FIGURE 10-1.8
Plot Style Table Editor; plot style "Color 5" selected

25. Click **Save & Close** to apply these changes to your *Plot Style Table* (Figure 10-1.8).

26. Click **OK** to close *Page Setup* and then **Close** to exit the *Page Setup Manager.*

Now in any drawing file, when your *Plot Style Table* is selected in *Page Setup*, any entity that is Color 5 (*Blue*) will print as a fairly light line (0.1000mm) using the example in Figure 10-1.8.

Once you create a standard and use it for a while, you will instinctively know which color corresponds to which lineweight.

27. **Open** the ***Layer Properties*** palette.

28. Adjust the **Color** for each *Layer* (Figure 10-1.9).

    TIP: Based on your Plot Style Table, each color now corresponds to a particular lineweight.

When you are finished, every *Layer* should be assigned a color ranging from 1 to 7; you should never use any other colors (except the "shade" colors discussed above) as they will print with unexpected results.

29. **Save** your **Flr-2** drawing.

30. **Make the same changes to your other floor plans.**

AutoCAD's seven named colors:

FYI: AutoCAD has 255 standard colors (AutoCAD Color Index – ACI), of which the first seven also have names (see the chart below).

AutoCAD also has a *True Color* system which allows for millions of colors. *True Colors* are great for presentation drawings. They are not controlled by a *Plot Style Table*; they will always print in the color specified (only on a color printer, of course).

Color number	*Color name*
1	Red
2	Yellow
3	Green
4	Cyan
5	Blue
6	Magenta
7	White (or black when background is white)

Back up Your Plot Style Table:

You should back up your Plot Style Table to a CD or Thumb Drive because you will need it on each computer you print from to get accurate lineweights. You also need to send this file with the drawings, if providing consultants or owners with the drawing files.

31. Back up your *Plot Style Table* file; this file is located at (see *TIP* below, if you have problems here):

    C:\Users*your_login_name*\AppData\Roaming\Autodesk\AutoCAD 2027\R24.1\enu\Plotters\Plot Styles

    TIP: *Substitute your login name for the "your_login_name" placeholder above. Also, the Application Data folder may be hidden; see your system administrator for help.*

    TIP: *If the Application Data folder is not visible, go to Windows Explorer, select View (tab) → Options → Folder and search options → View (tab) and check Show hidden files, folders and drives.*

    FYI: *In an office environment, these files can be shared on a network. This ensures everyone is using the same lineweight standards.*

Create a Lineweight Reference Chart:

Until you learn which color equals which lineweight, you will benefit from using a reference chart. If you want a line to be thin, you look at the chart, find a thin line you like and then look at what color is associated with that lineweight, then you modify the line to that color (by changing or creating *Layers*).

32. In a new drawing named **Reference Chart.dwg**, create the drawing shown in **Figure 10-1.9**.
    a. Adjust the drawing to match your color/lineweight settings.
    b. Make all the text set to one of your medium lineweights.
    c. Print the chart, making sure your *Plot Style Table* is selected in *Page Setup*.
    d. The lines should be arranged from heaviest to lightest.
    e. Draw everything within a 6"x6" square.

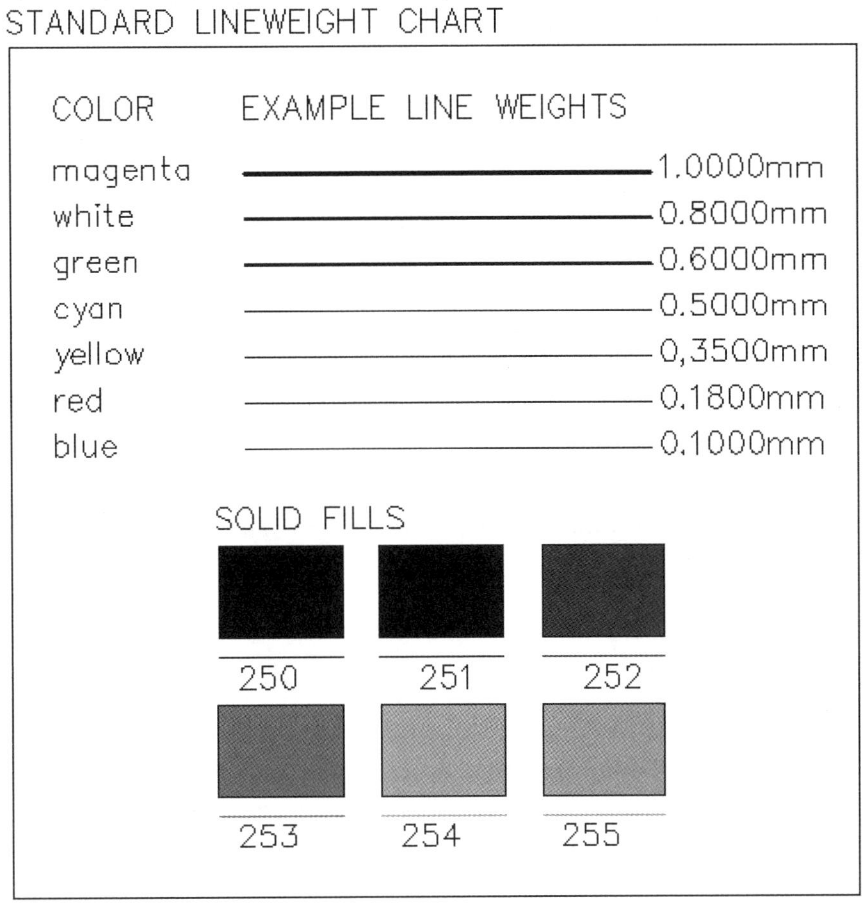

FIGURE 10-1.9 Lineweight reference chart

33. **Save** and **Close** any open drawings.

Summary:

Most people still use the *Color Dependent Plot Style Tables* because, no matter what Drawing/Layer a line is in/on, if it is green (for example), it will always print the same lineweight, whereas the *Named Plot Style Table* requires extra settings in the *Layer Properties Manager* and entities that are green (again, for example) could be different lineweights, even in the same drawing. The visual color/lineweight relationship is very useful, especially when multiple people (or multiple firms) are working on the same set of drawings.

Exercise 10-2:
Plotting: Digital Set

Introduction:

In this exercise you will learn how to quickly and easily publish your entire set of drawings to a single file that can be viewed by downloading a free viewer from Autodesk.

The file is referred to as a *Design Web Format* (DWF). A DWF is smaller than the drawing file because it is only for viewing and printing, not editing. It can even be password protected. In fact, one of the best things about DWFs is that they cannot be edited. Thus, you can share the DWF set with a client or contractor and not have to worry about them accidentally (or intentionally) changing the drawings. You can also create a PDF, which most everyone can open and view as Adobe Reader is a free download and used by many.

The first thing you need to do is adjust the *Page Setup* in each *Sheet* drawing, so the *Sheets* are ready to plot.

1. **Open** your sheet **A1 – Basement Floor Plan** from the *Sheet Set Manager.* (See Exercise 8-2 for instruction on this.)

2. Right-click on the **A1 Basement Floor Plan** layout tab (Figure 10-2.1).

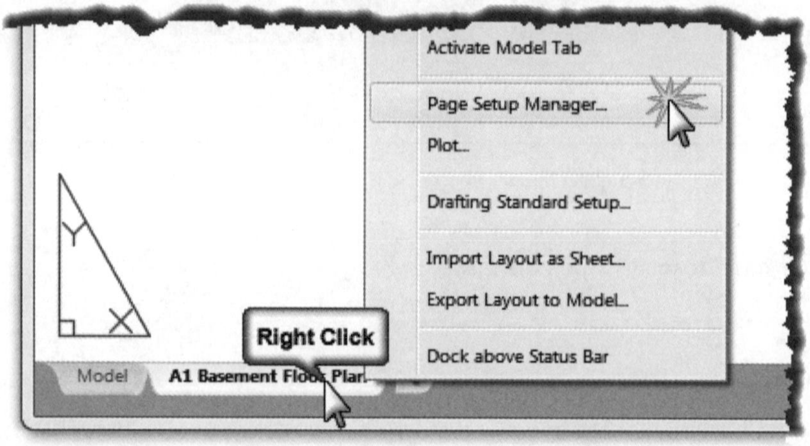

FIGURE 10-2.1 A1 – Basement Floor Plan; right-click on layout tab

3. Select **Page Setup Manager…** from the pop-up menu.

4. With ***A1 Basement Floor Plan*** selected, click the **Modify…** button (Figure 10-2.2).

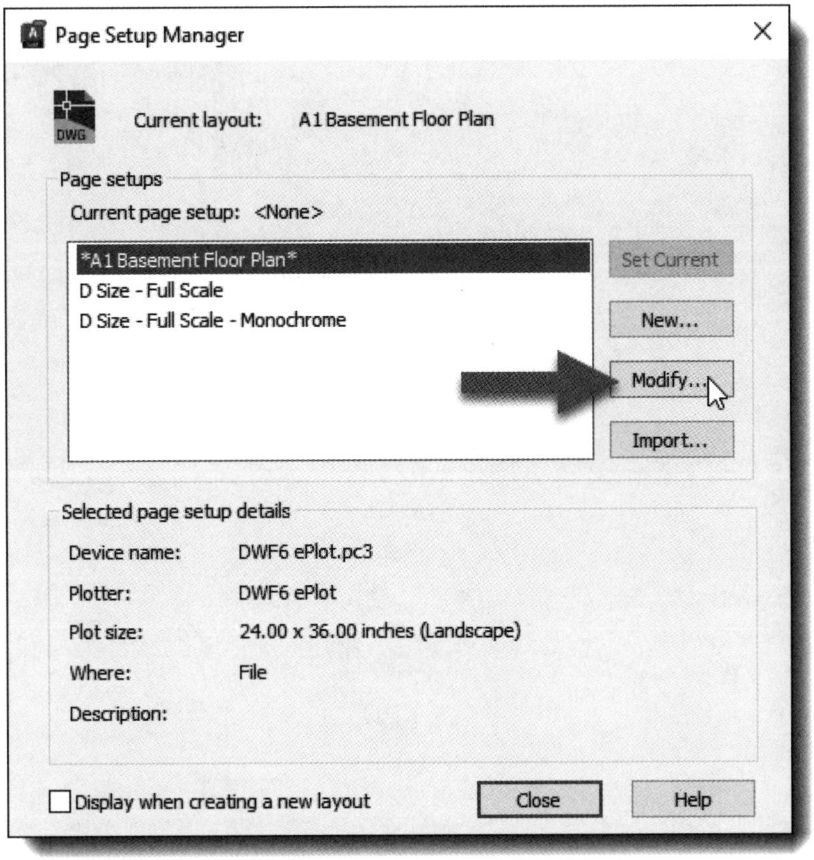

FIGURE 10-2.2
Page Setup Manager; modify the default layout settings

5. Select your *Plot Style Table* (created in Exercise 10-1): *yourname*.ctb (Figure 10-2.3).

6. **Check** the "*Display Plot Styles*" option just below the selected *Plot Style Table* (Figure 10-2.3).

TIP: Selecting "Display Plot Styles" will cause AutoCAD to display your Layout View *in black and white rather than color. This is more of a "what you see is what you get" type of view – even more so when LWT is toggled on from the* Status Bar.

NOTE: The lines are only black if you are using colors 1-7.

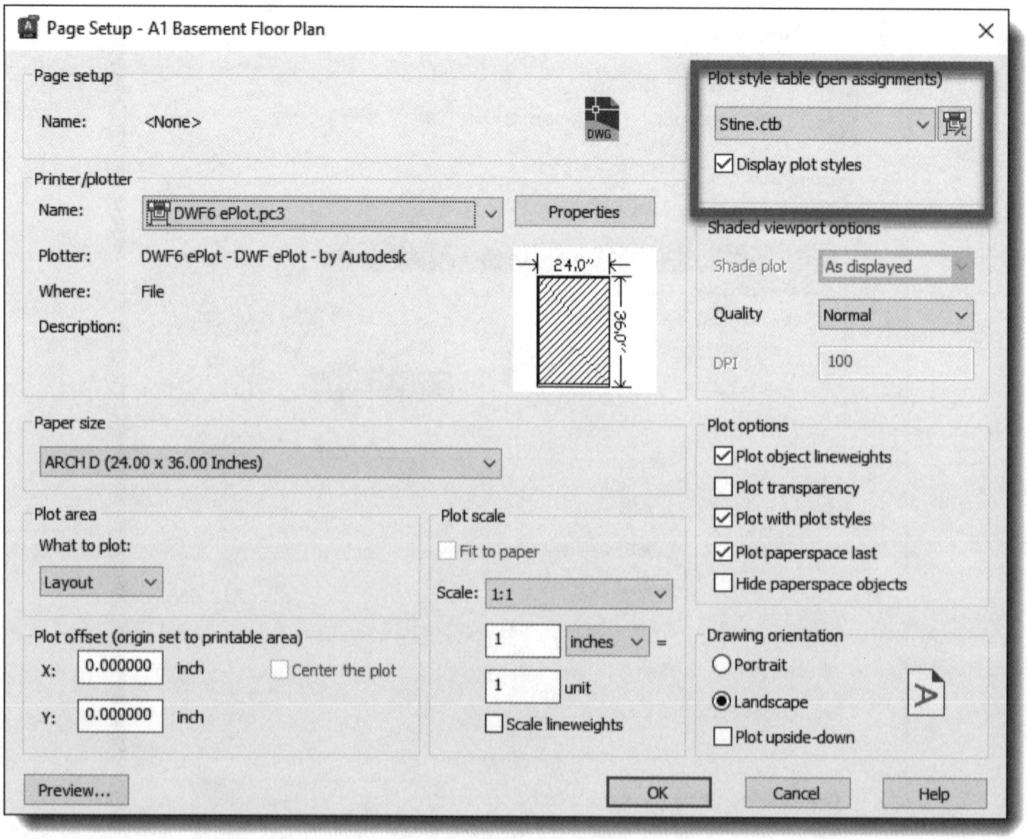

FIGURE 10-2.3
Page Setup – Basement Floor Plan; select your plot style table

7. Click **OK** and then **Close** to exit the open dialog boxes.

8. **Save** and **Close** the *Basement Floor Plan* sheet drawing.

9. Now open each sheet in your *Sheet Set* and make the same modification; **Save** and **Close** each drawing when done.

Now you will look at the *Options* related to *Publishing* "sheets" from the *Sheet Set Manager*.

10. If not open, **Open** your *Sheet Set Data* file. (See Exercise 8-2.)

11. **Right-click** on the *Sheet Set* project title (*Stine Residence* in this example). (See Figure 10-2.4.)

12. Select **Publish → Sheet Set DWF Publish Options…**(Figure 10-2.4).

    FYI: At least one drawing needs to be open, not just the NewTab.

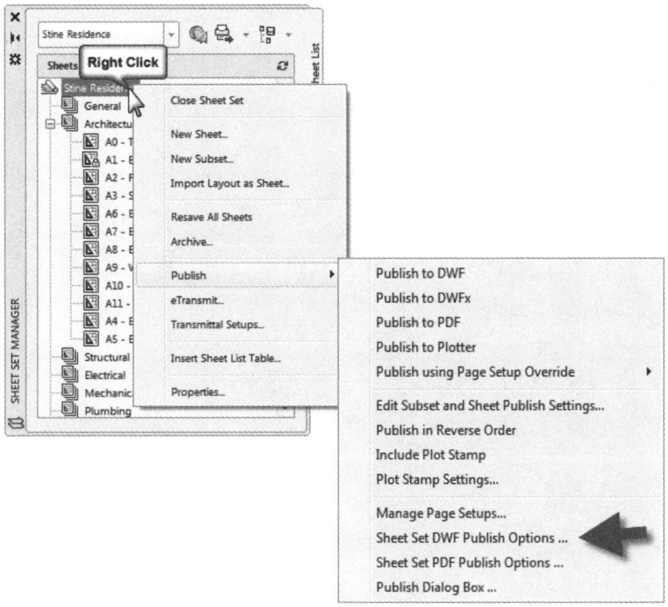

FIGURE 10-2.4
Sheet Set Manager; right-click menu for sheet set label (Stine Residence in this example)

Take a minute to notice the various options available for publishing sheets from the *Sheet Set Manager*; see Figure 10-2.5.

- **Default output location (plot-to-file)**
  Here you can specify a default location to save a file to.
- **General DWF options**
  When **Single-sheet** is selected, each sheet is created as a separate DWF file. When **Multi-sheet** is selected, all sheets are published into one DWF file.
- **Naming**
  Here you can specify the file name or have AutoCAD prompt you for the name each time you publish; this option is only available if **Multi-sheet** is selected above.
- **Layer information**
  Allows you to include the AutoCAD layers in the DWF file. With this option selected, you can control *Layer* visibility in the DWF file viewer; for example, turn off dimensions and notes to print a clean plan. For PDFs *Adobe Reader* can control the visibility of Layers when they are present in a PDF.
- **3D DWF**
  Controls settings related to 3D drawing information.

FYI: You are only drawing 2D information in this book.

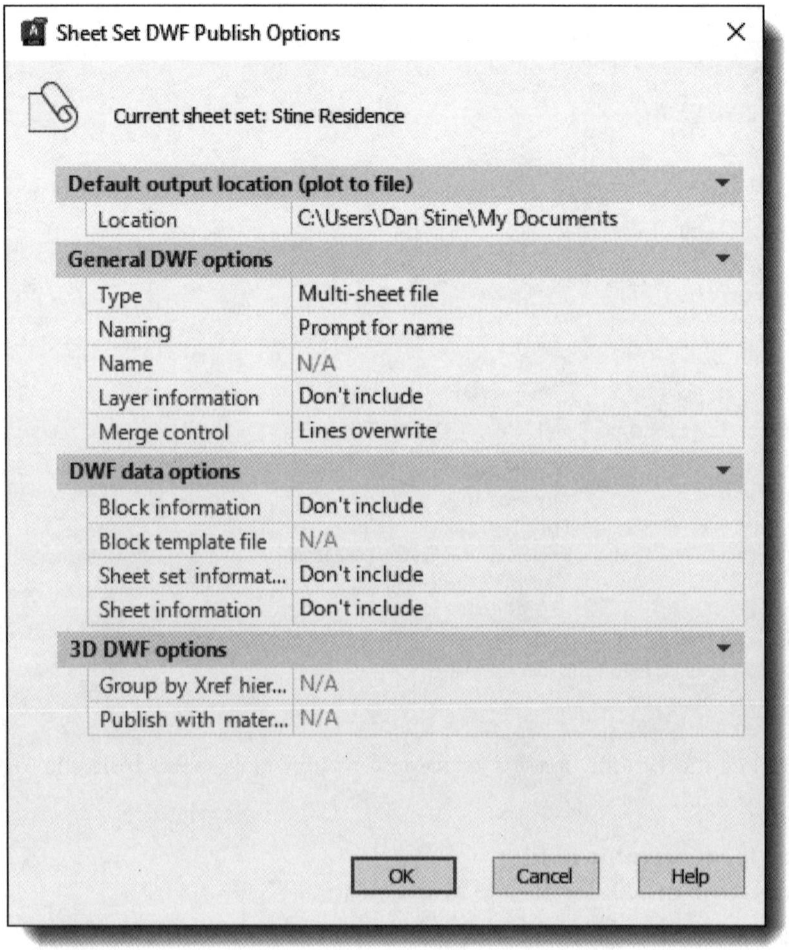

FIGURE 10-2.5
Sheet Set Publish Options – default settings shown

13. Accept the default options and click **OK**.

14. **Right-click** on the *Sheet Set* project title again (*Stine Residence* in this example). See Figure 10-2.4.

15. **Publish → Publish to DWFx** (Figure 10-2.4).

You are now prompted to specify the name and location for the DWF file. Notice, though, that the default location is "Documents," which is the specified folder in the *Publish Options* dialog.

AutoCAD suggests the *Sheet Set* project name for the file name; you will accept that name next.

16. **Browse** to your project folder and accept the suggested file name and click **Select** to start the publishing process (Figure 10-2.6).

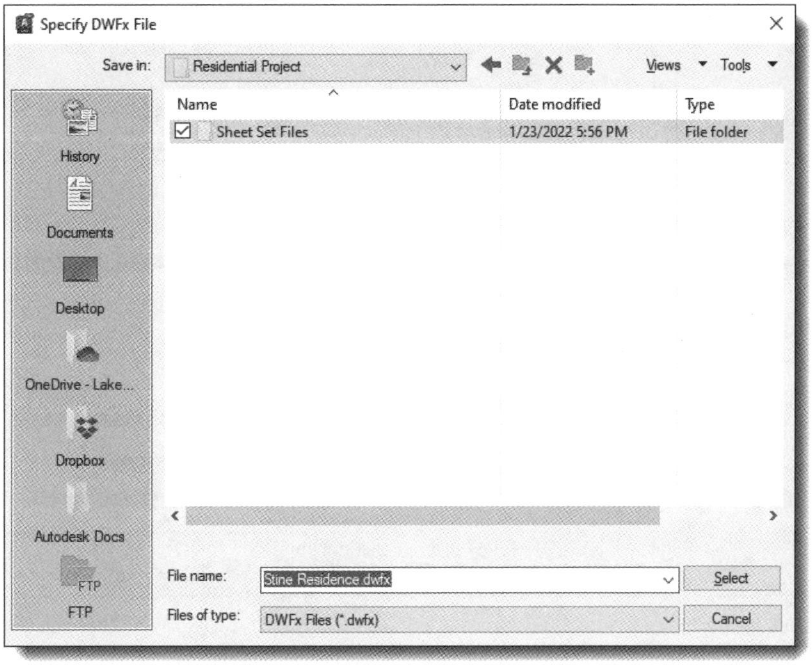

FIGURE 10-2.6
Select DWF File dialog– specify DWF file name and location

AutoCAD now begins to publish each drawing to the DWF file you specified. The *Publish* routine runs in the background, so you can continue to work. Depending on your computer speed, a set this size might take 5 – 15 minutes. AutoCAD has to open each file and plot it.

AutoCAD provides a small "plotter" icon on the right-hand side of the *Status Bar*. You can hover your cursor over this icon to display a tooltip showing the status of the background *Publish* project (Figure 10-2.7).

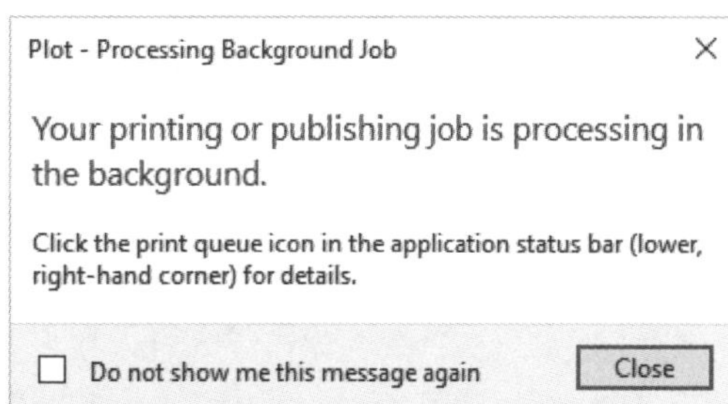

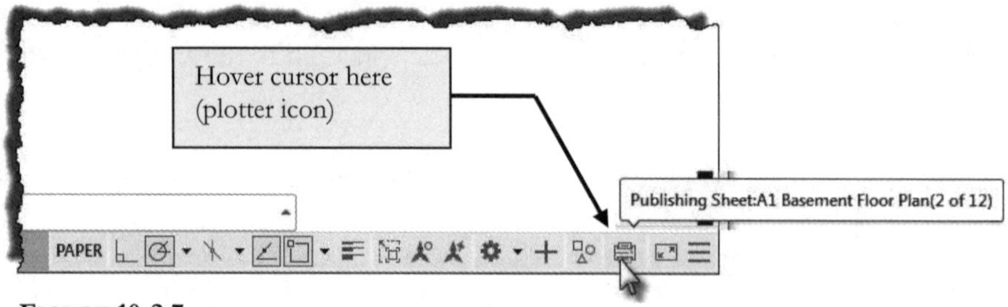

FIGURE 10-2.7
Plot and Publish Status Icon
Hover cursor over icon to display status tooltip.

When the publishing process is complete, a balloon message will be displayed indicating such (Figure 10-2.8), and it also provides a link to a report. You will take a quick peek at the report before viewing the DWF file.

FIGURE 10-2.8
Plot and Publish Status Icon; Balloon notification that job is complete.

17. Click on the link "*Click to view plot and publish details…*" in the *Plot and Publish* balloon notification message (Figure 10-2.8).

Notice the report lists the date, number of sheets, the location of each plotted file and the location of the DWF file (Figure 10-2.9).

18. Click **Close** to close the *Plot and Publish* window.

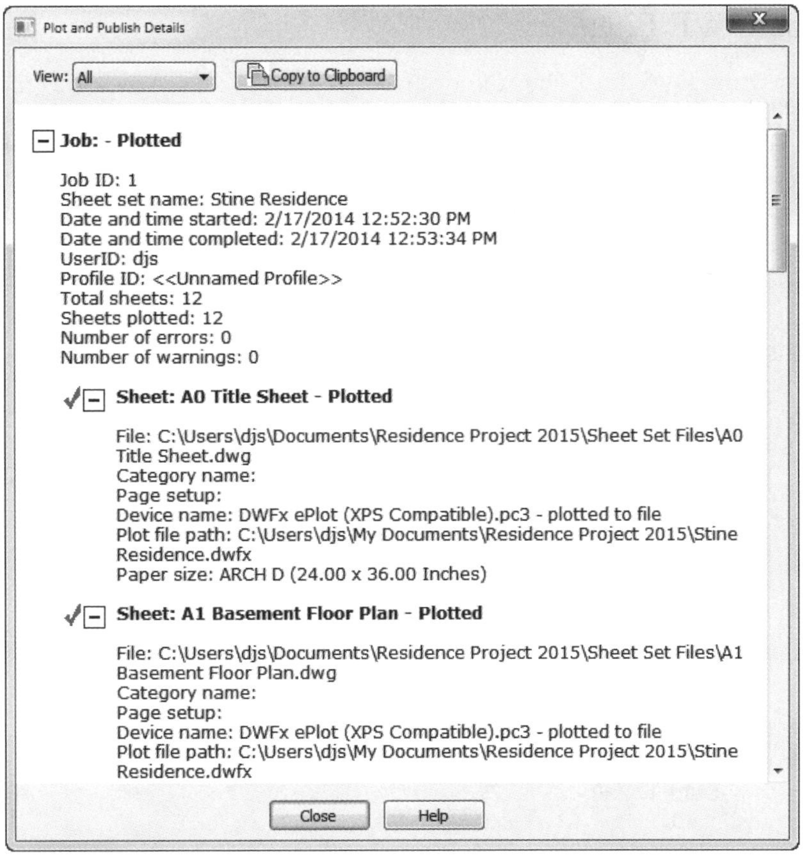

FIGURE 10-2.9
Plot and Publish Details; report on job just completed

Downloading the Autodesk DWF Viewer:

This free software is no longer installed by default with AutoCAD. However, the software can still be installed separately.

If you will be sharing your DWF files with someone who does not have a *DWF Viewer* (*NOTE: AutoCAD cannot open DWF files directly*) installed on their computer, you can give them instructions on downloading the free program from Autodesk's website.

Using an internet browser, such as *Microsoft Internet Explorer*, go to https://www.autodesk.com/products/design-review/overview. Next, click on the **Download** link.

As mentioned in Chapter 1, Autodesk is developing many Cloud-based tools. These include DWG and DWF viewers. You can view these files on your tablet or smartphone.

Viewing the DWF File:

Next, you will view the DWF file using Autodesk *Design Review*. You can view this file by double-clicking the file in *Windows Explorer*, or you can access the file from the **Plot and Publish** icon.

19. The next several steps require *Autodesk Design Review* be installed on your computer. If you do not have it, download it and install it. If you are not able to install it, skip to the next exercise.

20. Right-click on the **Plot and Publish** icon on the right side of the *Status Bar*.

21. Select **View Plotted File…** from the pop-up menu (Figure 10-2.10).

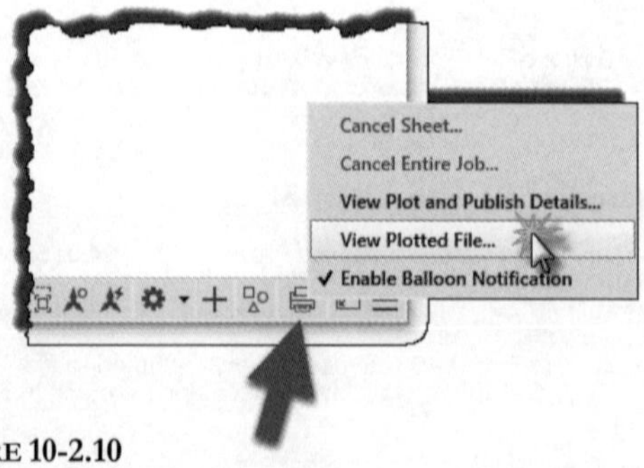

FIGURE 10-2.10
Plot and Publish Icon Menu; right-click on icon to see menu

A totally separate program (*Autodesk Design Review*) now opens with the DWF project you just created (Figure 10-2.11); this program is typically installed with AutoCAD – it is also a free download.

The *Viewer* allows you to zoom, pan and print the sheets in the multi-sheet DWF file.

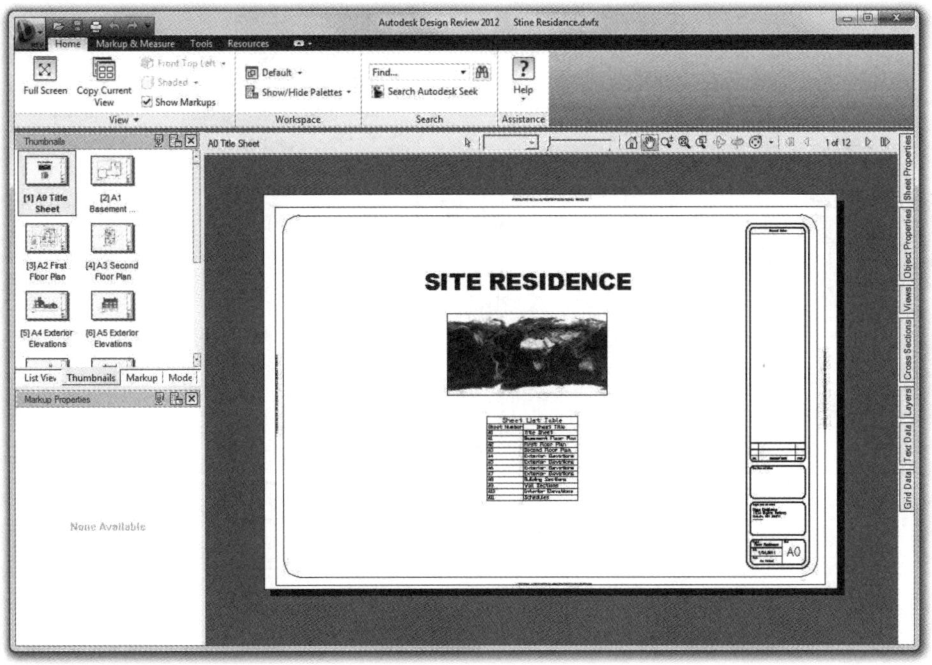

FIGURE 10-2.11
Autodesk DWF Viewer; your residential project loaded

You can view the various sheets in the DWF file by either clicking on one of the *Thumbnail* images on the left or by clicking the right/left arrows on the toolbar (at the bottom).

A DWF file is still a vector-based file, so, like a DWG file, you can zoom in really far without seeing any pixelation. These drawings also include all your lineweights, so your drawings will print accurately.

Next, navigate to another sheet and zoom in to view the drawing's lineweights.

22. Scroll down in the *Thumbnails* pane until you see your **A6 Exterior Elevations** sheet.

23. Click on the **A6 Thumbnail** image to select it.

24. Using your wheel mouse (or the Zoom icon), **Zoom In** on the elevation as shown in Figure 10-2.12.

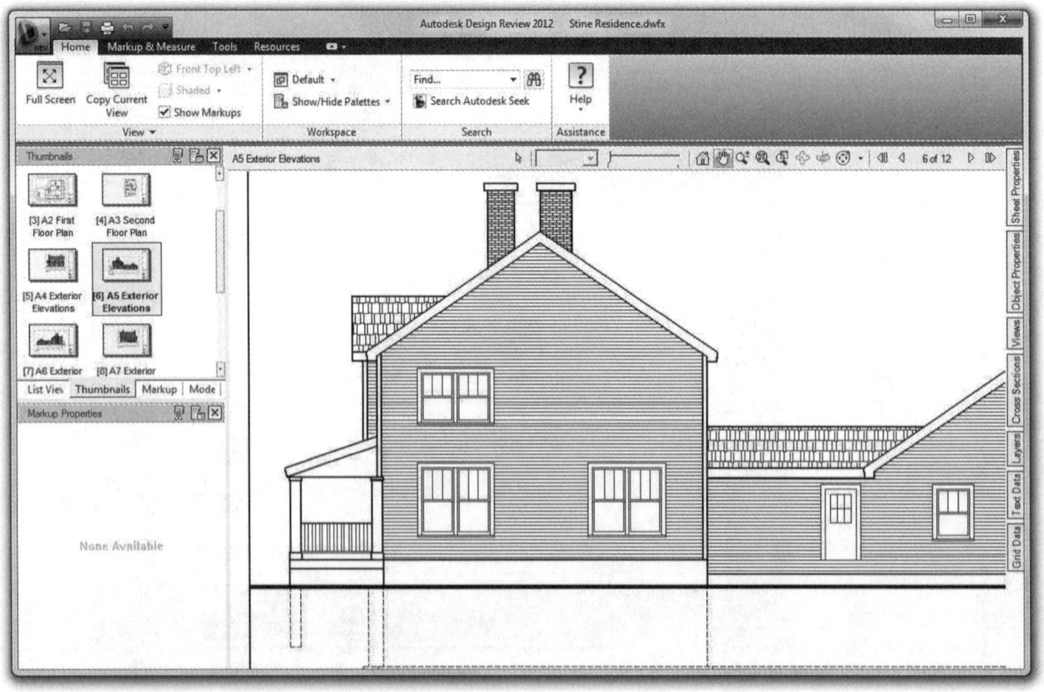

FIGURE 10-2.12
Autodesk DWF Viewer; sheet A6 – Exterior Elevations displayed

NOTE: In Figure 10-2.12, various lineweights are visible in the elevation drawing.

Try repeating this process to create a PDF file.

Linking Feature in the Multi-Sheet DWF File:

Another great feature associated with *Sheet Sets* and *Multi-sheet DWF* files is the hyperlinking embedded in the *Sheet List* and *Callout Bubbles.*

25. In your DWF file, switch back to the *Title Sheet* and zoom in on the *Sheet List.*

26. Hover your cursor over the "A2 – First Floor Plan" text to see the pop-up tooltip (Figure 10-2.13).

The pop-up tooltip displayed in Figure 10-2.13 indicates you can follow a link by CTRL + clicking the text. You will try this next.

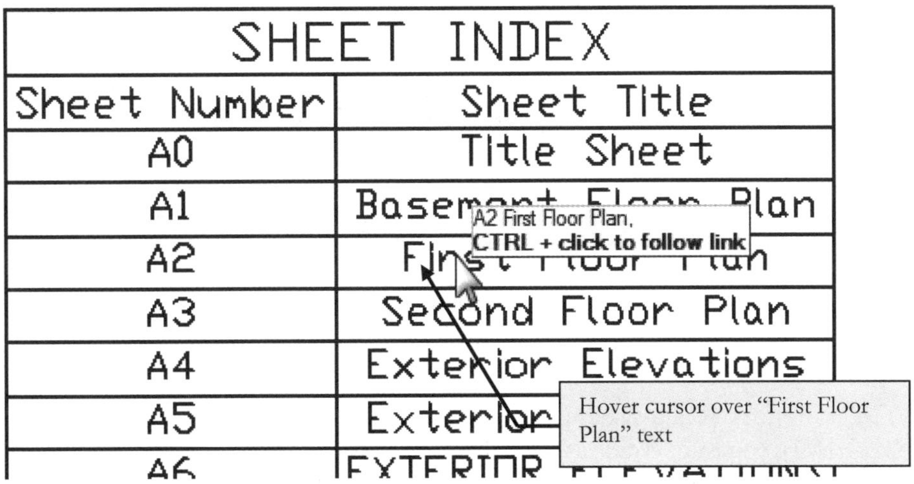

FIGURE 10-2.13
Multi-sheet DWF file; hyper linked text in Sheet List

27. While pressing the Ctrl key, click the "**First Floor Plan**" text in the *Sheet List Table* location on the *Title Sheet.*

As you can see, this is an easy way for you or a client to navigate a set of drawings (Figure 10-2.14).

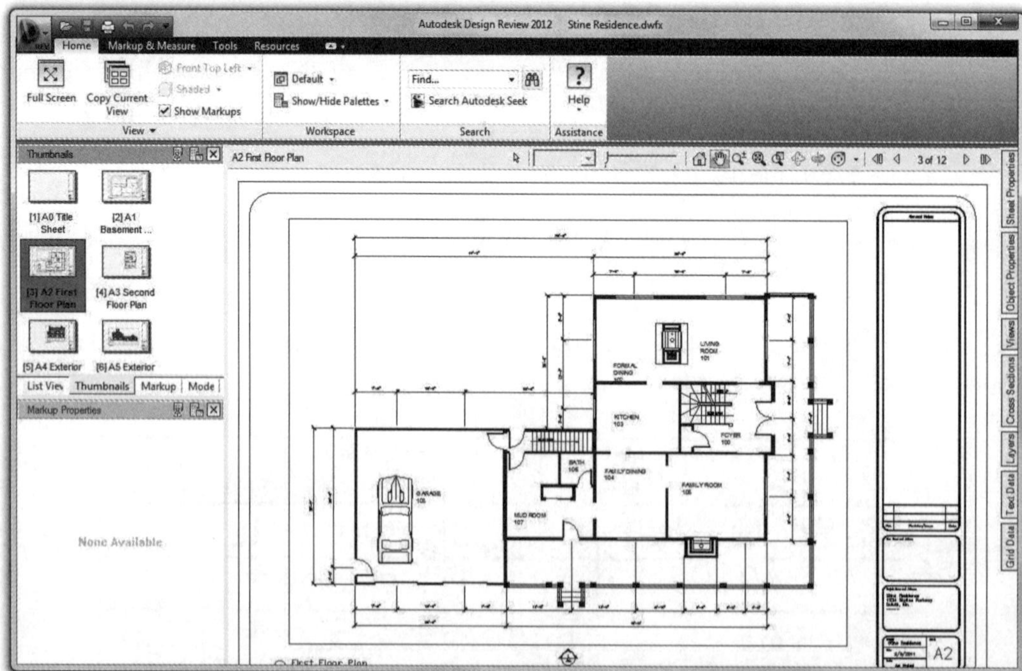

FIGURE 10-2.14
Multi-sheet DWF file; view displayed by clicking hyper-linked sheet index on title sheet

DWF files do not typically take up a lot of disk space. The DWF file just created should only be about 1MB; you can verify this with *Windows Explorer.* Given the file's small size, it can easily be emailed or loaded on a web site.

The *Viewer's Print* dialog (Figure 10-2.15) allows you to print one sheet of the entire set to *Scale* on 24"x36" paper or *Fit to page* on 8½" x 11"paper as you can see in Figure 10-2.15.

> ***FYI:** If you plan to create a DWF file on a project, you can print your hard copy set(s) from this DWF file, eliminating the need to complete the steps outlined in the next section (10-3), which shows how to print directly to the plotter rather than to a DWF file.*

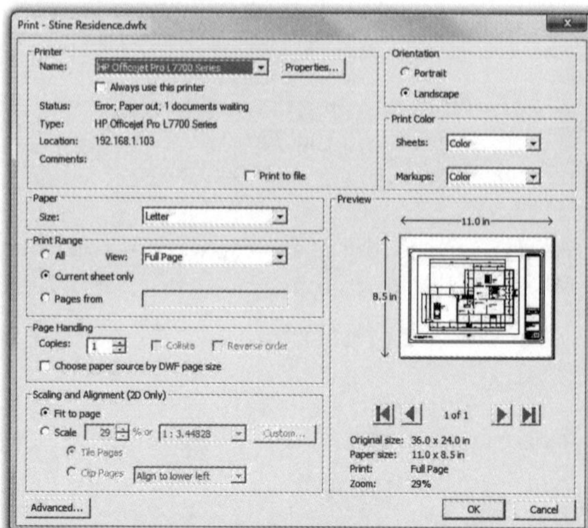

FIGURE 10-2.15
Autodesk DWF Viewer; print dialog box

28. **Save** and **Close** all files and programs to complete this exercise.

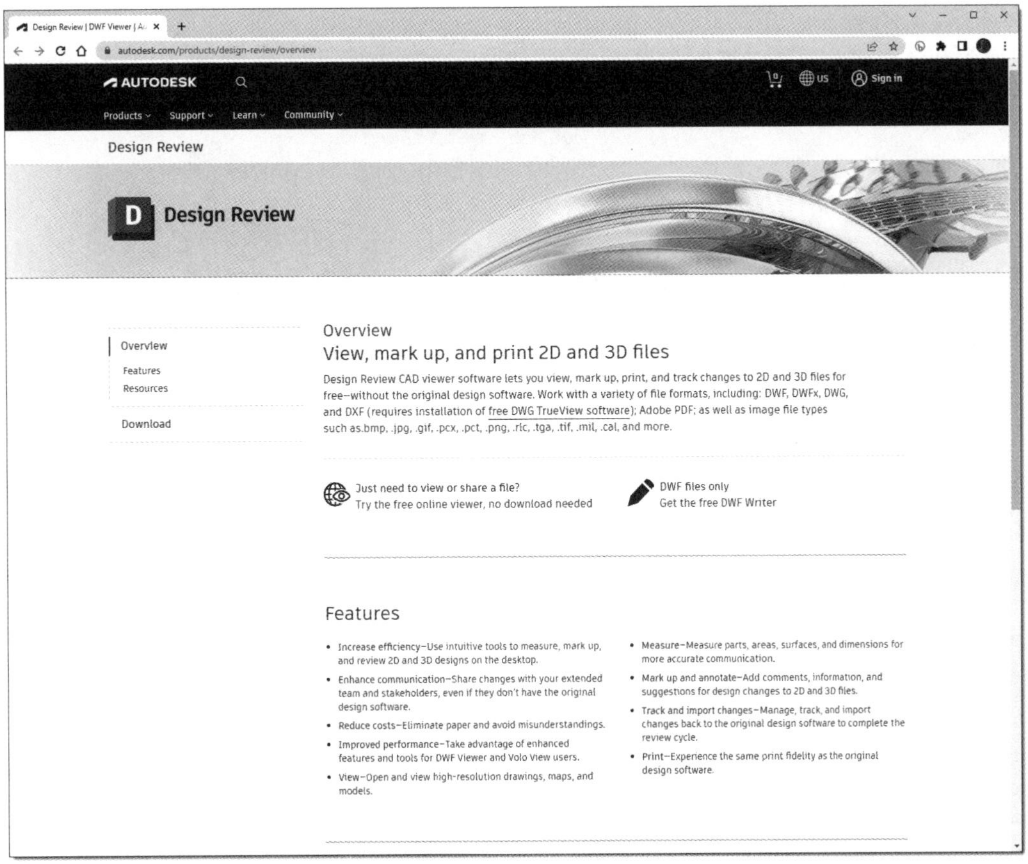

FIGURE 10-2.16
Autodesk Web Site; DWF Design Review page

Exercise 10-3:
Plotting: Hardcopy Set

Introduction:

In this final exercise you will look at a few settings that you should be aware of to create high quality printouts (i.e., plots). You will look at plotting both from an individual sheet and from the *Sheet Set Manager.*

Xerox 8850 Digital Solution
High speed B/W plotter + scanner

HP Designjet 1000 series
High quality color and B/W plotter

Page Setup Settings for Your Layout View:

Page Setup allows you to pre-set things like scale and paper size. Each tab has its own *Page Setup* settings. The *Page Setup* dialog looks almost exactly like the *Plot* dialog. In fact, the *Plot* dialog box gets its initial settings from the current *Page Setup* settings. Again, each drawing file has its own *Page Setup* settings for each *Layout View* tab; this saves time when plotting because each drawing/*Layout View* tab can be pre-set and ready to plot.

1. **Open** your **A3 – Second Floor Plan** sheet from the *Sheet Set Manager. (This can be opened directly with the Open command as well.)*

2. **Right-click** on the *Layout View* tab and select **Page Setup Manager...**

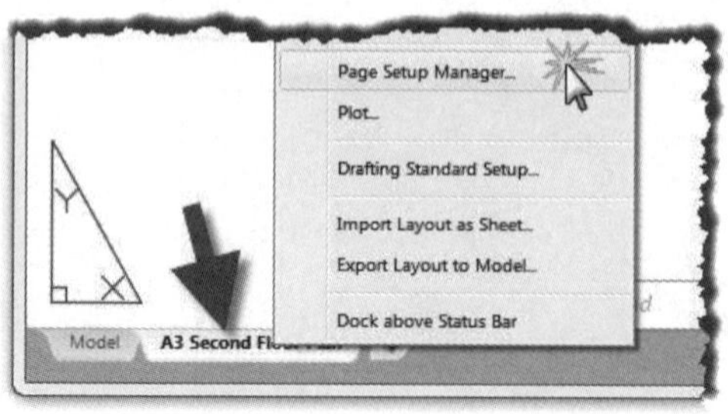

You are now in the *Page Setup Manager.* Here you can create/modify named *Page Setups*, and apply one to the current *Layout* and *Import Page Setups* from other drawings. You will modify an existing *Page Setup.*

3. Select **D Size – Full Scale** from the list and then select **Modify…** (Figure 10-3.1).

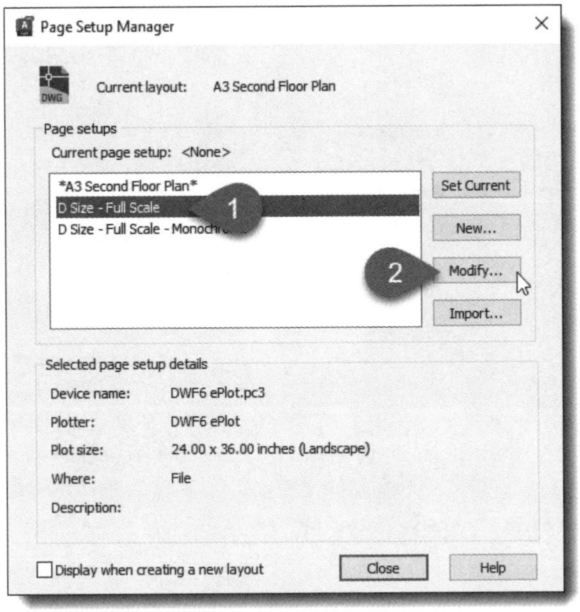

FIGURE 10-3.1
Page Setup Manager; Page Setup "D Size – Full Scale" selected

You are now in the *Page Setup* for "D Size – Full Scale."

4. Note and adjust the following settings (**Figure 10-3.2**):
   a. *Select your plotter.* In this case, select one that is capable of printing a large sheet like 24″x36″.
   b. Make sure your *Plot Style Table* is selected, **Stine.ctb** in this example.
   c. Check the box next to **Display plot styles**.

   FYI: *This setting will make the on-screen display look more like the plotted version of your drawing. (You can also click the LWT toggle on the Status Bar to see the lineweights on-screen as well.)*

   d. Check the box next to **Scale Lineweights**.

   FYI: *If the drawing is printed half-scale, for example, the lineweights are adjusted.*

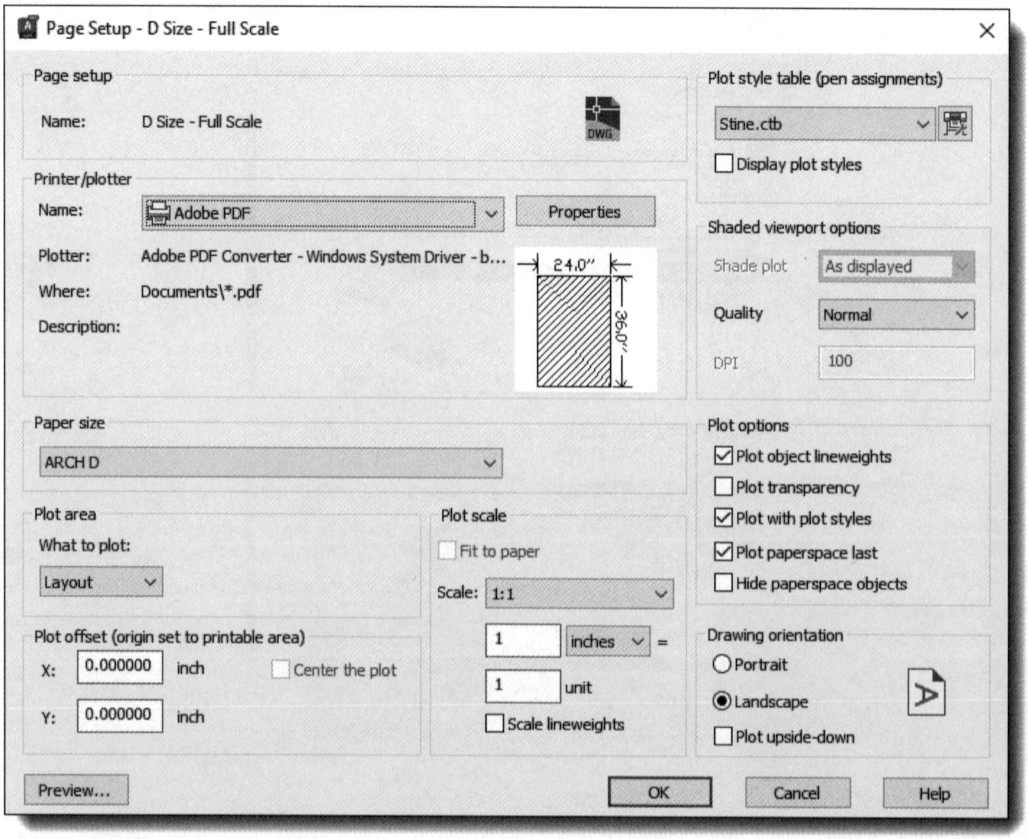

FIGURE 10-3.2
Page Setup; "D Size – Full Scale" modifications to be made

e. Note these settings as well; they should be set already as they are the default (Figure 10-3.2).

   i. The paper size is set to **24″x36″**.

      FYI: *This setting controls the size of paper you see on the screen in each Layout View.*

   ii. The *Plot Area* is set to **Layout.**

      1. *Layout* = *the paper size selected*
      2. *Extents* = *all lines selected to print*
      3. *Display* = *only lines displayed on screen*
      4. *Window* = *user selected area to be plotted*

   iii. The *Plot Scale* is set to **1:1.**

      FYI: *The 1:1 scale means the 24″x36″ sheet will print 24″x36″.*

   iv. **Plot with plot styles** is checked.

5. Select **OK** to close the *Page Setup* dialog box.

6. Click **Close** to exit the *Page Setup Manager.*

Next you will explore the *Plot* dialog box.

7. From the *Quick Access* toolbar, select **Plot…**

Notice the similarities between the *Plot* dialog and the *Page Setup* dialog (Figure 10-3.3). You should also notice that the settings previously set in *Page Setup* are NOT the defaults in the *Plot* dialog. Your modifications are not the default settings because you did not set the "D Size – Full Scale" page setup to be current (see Figure 10-3.1). However, you can select this on the fly in the plot dialog.

Additional settings on the *Plot* dialog box (vs. *Page Setup*):

- **Plot to File**: Creates a "plot file" that can be copied to disk and brought to a print shop (if you don't have a large format or color printer). You need to call the print shop and ask which printer driver to use because the "plot file" is printer specific.
- **Number of copies**: You can specify the number of prints here.

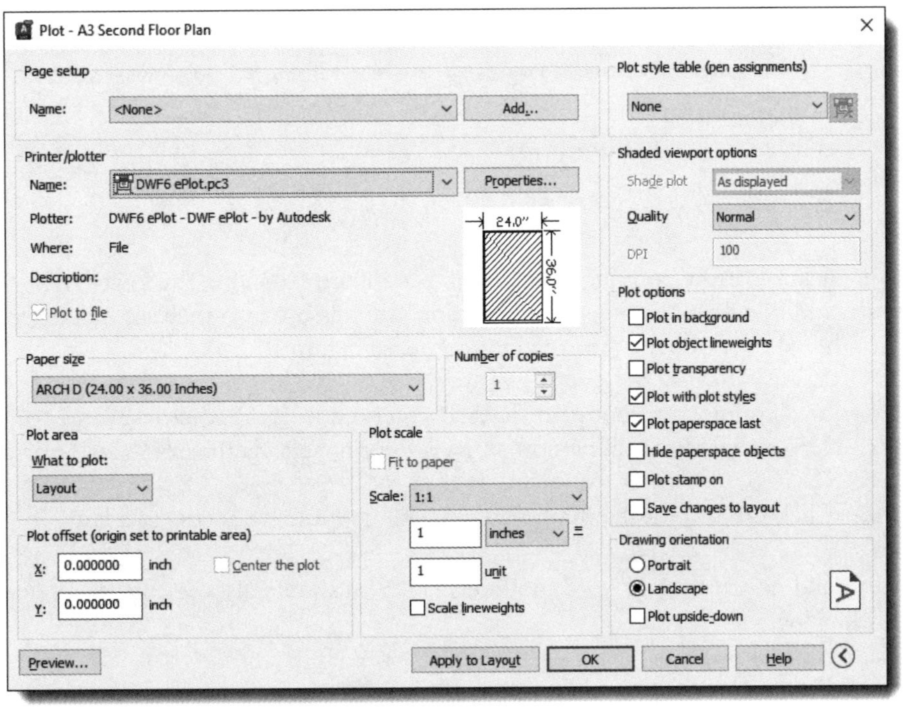

FIGURE 10-3.3
Plot dialog; initial settings; no page setup selected

8. Select **D Size – Full Scale** from the *Page Setup* drop-down list near the top of the dialog box (Figure 10-3.3).

Notice how all your settings change to correspond with the selected *Page Setup* (Figure 10-3.4 – fully expanded dialog view).

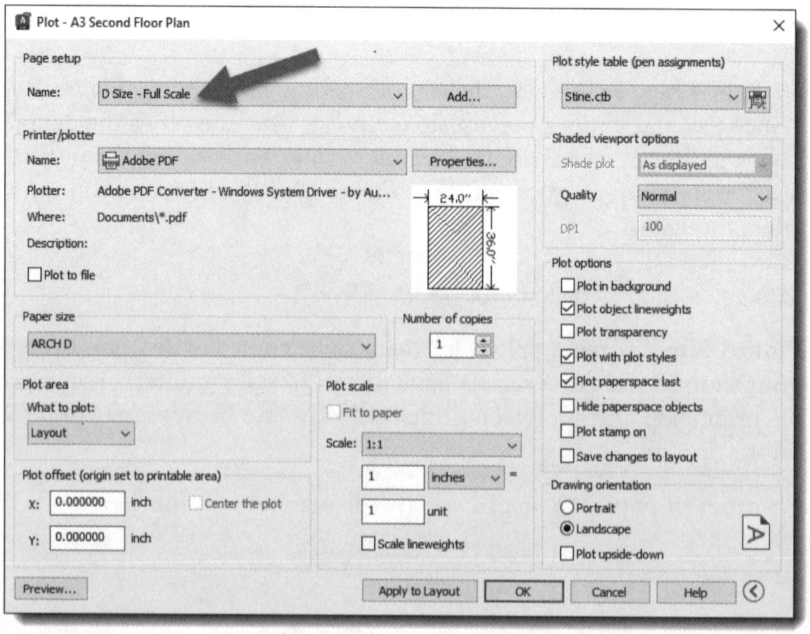

FIGURE 10-3.4
Plot dialog; page setup applied

If you click the arrow pointing to the right (see Figure 10-3.3) in the lower right corner, you will see additional plot settings. These settings are less used, so they are hidden so the user is not bothered by too much information (compare Figure 10-3.4).

Next you will print your floor plan sheet. If you do not have access to a large format plotter, you can skip ahead to the discussion on how to print sets via the *Sheet Set Manager.*

9. Click **OK** to plot the floor plan drawing (if you have access to a large format plotter).

You should now have a 24″x36″ plotted sheet. You should also be able to see lineweights in your drawing.

10. Plot the basement and first floor plans per the previous steps.

Plotting Sets Using the Sheet Set Manager:

The previous steps are useful when printing one or two sheets. However, on large projects with 20-30 sheets it would take a lot of your time to open and plot each sheet. Large commercial projects can have hundreds of sheets.

The *Sheet Set Manager* allows you to print the entire set of drawings at one time. When printing large sets, it can still take quite a while. However, anytime the computer can do the work and save the user time is well worth the effort. Also, the plotting occurs in the "background," which means you can still work in AutoCAD during this process.

11. Open your *Sheet Set* via the *Sheet Set Manager* (see Exercise 8-2 for information on how to do this).

Similar to the first part of this exercise, the *Sheet Set* has a *Page Setup Manager*. Here you can prepare a *Page Setup* that can be used for all *Sheets* in your *Sheet Set*; this is called a *Page Setup Override*. The *Override* option ensures consistency and eliminates the need to open every drawing if a *Page Setup* change is required.

12. Right-click on the *Sheet Set* title (*Stine Residence* in the book example).

13. Select **Publish → Manage Page Setups…** from the pop-up menu (Figure 10-3.5).

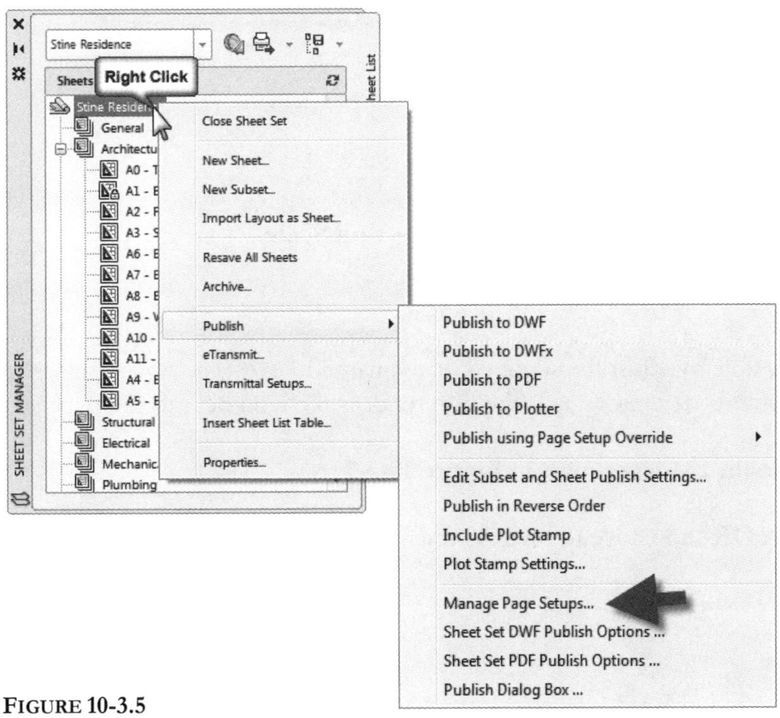

FIGURE 10-3.5
Sheet Set Manager; Select Manage Page Setups…

You are now in the *Page Setup Manager* (Figure 10-3.6). This is almost identical to the one previously discussed (see Figure 10-3.1). The difference is this *Page Setup Manager* applies to the current *Sheet Set* (*Stine Residence*), whereas the previous one applied to the *Layout View* (*Paper Space*) in that drawing. Notice one reads *"Current sheet set"* and the other *"Current layout"* at the top of the dialog box.

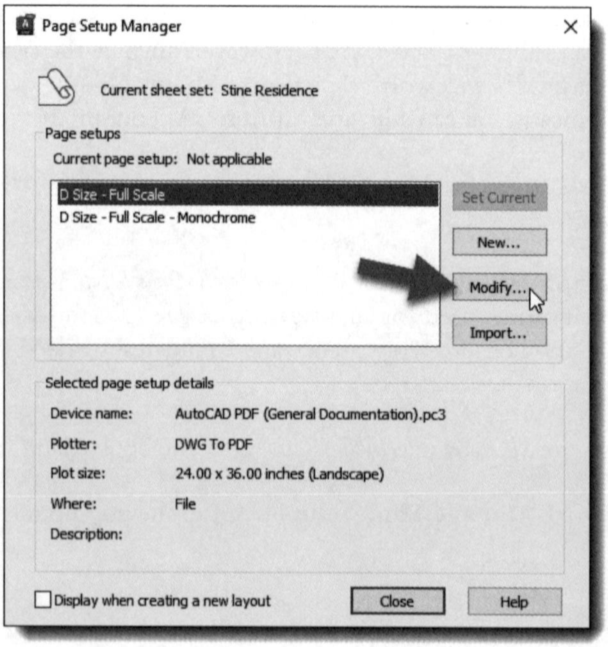

FIGURE 10-3.6
Page Setup Manager; D Size – Full Scale selected

14. Select the *Page Setup* named "**D Size – Full Scale.**"

15. Click the **Modify…** button.

You are now able to adjust the settings for the named *Page Setup*. Again, this is identical to what you just did a few pages ago (the difference is the icon next to the page setup name).

16. Make the changes shown in **Figure 10-3.7**.

17. Click **OK** and **Close** to save the changes and exit the *Page Setup Manager.*

TIP: Select a plotter you have access to.

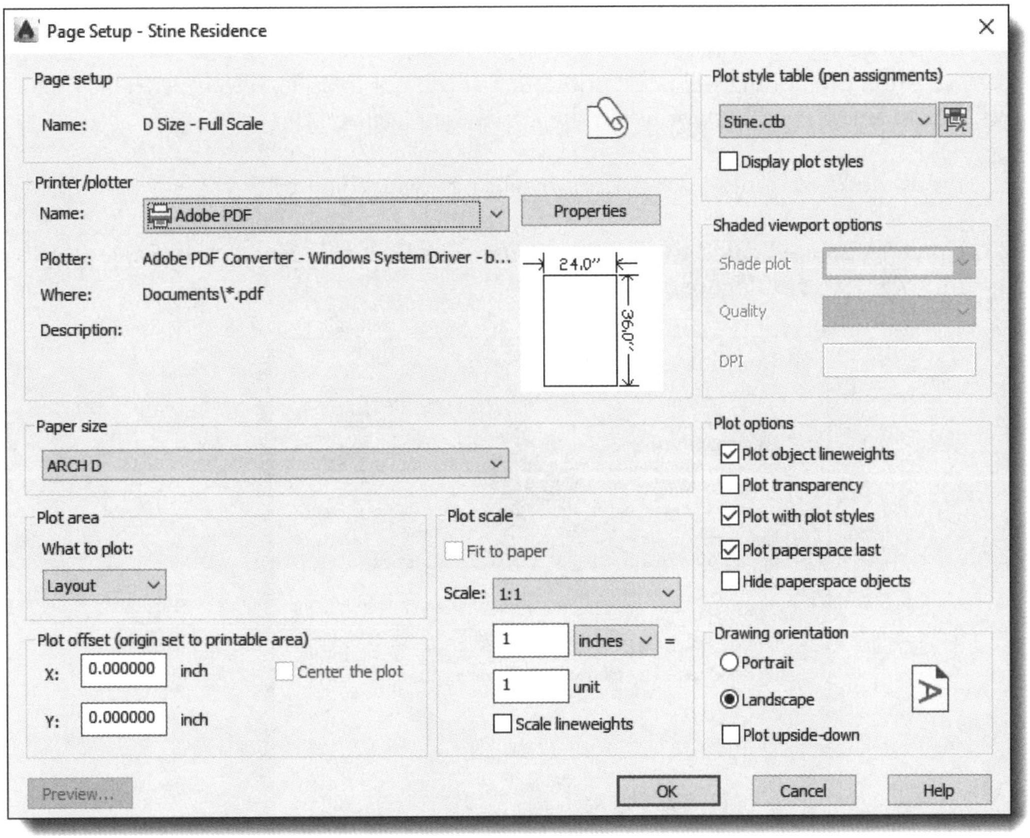

FIGURE 10-3.7
Page Setup; adjust settings for the selected named page setup

Publishing the Sheet Set:

Looking back at Figure 10-3.5, notice two things: under the *Publish* fly-out menu, you have **Publish to Plotter** and **Publish using Page Setup Override**. The former uses the current *Page Setup* settings in the *Sheet* file, whereas the latter uses the specified *Page Setup* from the *Sheet Set Manager*. You will try the **Override** option next.

18. Right-click on the sheet set title and select **Publish → Publish using Page Setup Override** (Figure 10-3.5).

    FYI: This step will actually print sheets if you have a plotter. From the Override fly-out, select ***D Size – Full Scale****.*

The plotting process now begins in the background. You will notice the **Plot and Publish** icon on the right side of the *Status Bar*.

FYI: You can right-click on it to cancel the current print job at any time.

Drawings should start printing shortly after the process begins!

Publishing a Small Review Set:

The last variation on plotting will be to print out a small, not to scale, review set. This time you will create a new *Page Setup* for use in the *Page Setup Manager.*

19. From the *Sheet Set's Page Setup Manager* select **New…** (Figure 10-3.6).

20. Enter "**A Size – Scaled to Fit**" for the name and select **D Size – Full Scale** from the *Start with* area (Figure 10-3.8).

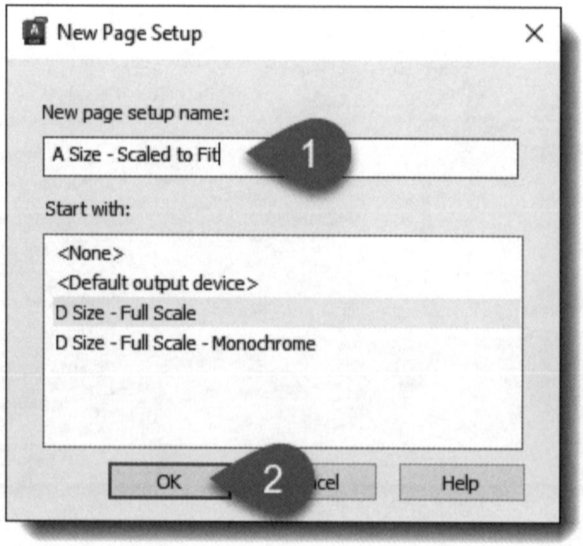

FIGURE 10-3.8
New Page Setup; creating a new page setup

21. Select **OK** to continue.

22. Make the changes shown in Figure 10-3.9.

FYI: Notice the "What to plot" is set to Extents; this is a work-around necessary to plot a layout setup for 24x36 onto an 8½ x 11 piece of paper.

TIP: If you have access to a printer that has 11"x17" paper, you can select that paper size; sets are a little larger and easier to read. Also, one nice thing about using 22" x 34" sheets (rather than 24"x36") is that 11"x17" sets are half-scale which is better than scaled to fit.

23. Select **Save** and then **Close** to complete the open dialog boxes.

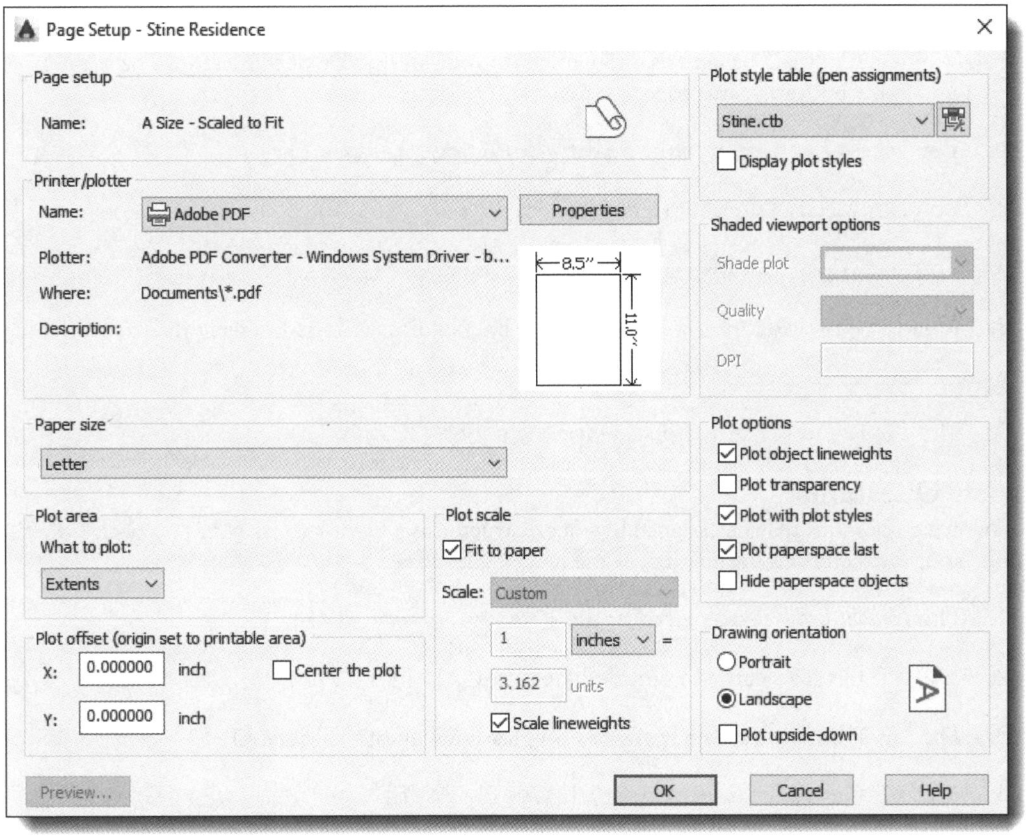

FIGURE 10-3.9
New Page Setup; make changes shown

24. Now, simply *Publish* using a *Page Setup Override* as previously reviewed, selecting the new *Page Setup*: "A Size – Scaled to Fit."

Your drawing will begin to print in a moment.

25. **Save** your drawings and close your sheet set.

You have now completed this book (except for the *Additional Tasks*)! You should possess the fundamental skills required for most tasks necessary to complete a set of residential drawings.

With the solid foundation you have built using this book, you should be able to explore and develop additional commands and techniques on your own. Using the Help system, News Groups and a little "trial and error," you can draw just about anything. **Good luck with your CAD drafting endeavors!**

Self-Exam:

The following questions can be used as a way to check your knowledge of this lesson. The answers can be found at the bottom of this page.

1. You access *Plot Styles* to your plan *Layer Properties Manager.* (T/F)
2. You can specify "number of copies" via *Page Setup.* (T/F)
3. You access page setups via the *Page Setup Manager.* (T/F)
4. What type of *Plot Style Table* associates a line's color with its lineweight?

   ____

5. The *Layout* tab is real-word scale for the paper. (T/F)

Review Questions:

The following questions may be assigned by your instructor as a way to assess your knowledge of this section. Your instructor has the answers to the review questions.

1. The *Callout Bubbles* are placed in the *Resource Drawings.* (T/F)
2. A DWF file is a vector-based file like AutoCAD files. (T/F)
3. The LWT button on the *Status Bar* toggles lineweight visibility. (T/F)
4. A DWF file is a little larger than a DWG file. (T/F)
5. You specify which *Plot Style Table* to use in the *Page Setup* dialog. (T/F)
6. In a *Layout* view's *Page Setup*, the plot scale should be set to __________.
7. Autodesk *Design Review* is a free download with which you can view and redline DWF files. (T/F)
8. Which lines should be light gray in a plan drawing?______________________
9. You can plot an entire set of drawings from a *Multi-sheet* DWF file. (T/F)
10. You can organize *Sheets* in subsets within the *Sheet Set Manager.* (T/F)

SELF-EXAM ANSWERS:
1 – F, **2** – F, **3** – T, **4** – Color Dependent, **5** – T

Additional Tasks:

Task 10-1: Apply Lineweights to All Your Drawings

Using the techniques learned in Lesson 10-1, apply lineweights to all your other drawings (or per your instructor's direction), including the exterior elevations, sections and interior elevations.

Task 10-2: Plot All Your Drawings Full Size

Using the techniques learned in Lesson 10-3, plot each of your drawings that have been set up on a sheet. Plot them full size if your plotter supports large format paper.

Task 10-3: Email a DWF File

Create a *Multi-view* DWF file and email it to your instructor or friend and verify that they were able to open it and view the drawings.

Task 10-4: View your files in the Cloud

Log in to your Autodesk 360 account and view your files using the Cloud-based viewers.

Image courtesy of Anderson Architects
Alan H. Anderson, Architect, Duluth, MN

Interior Design, Steven W. Sanborn, A.I.A., Santa Rosa, CA

Notes:

Index

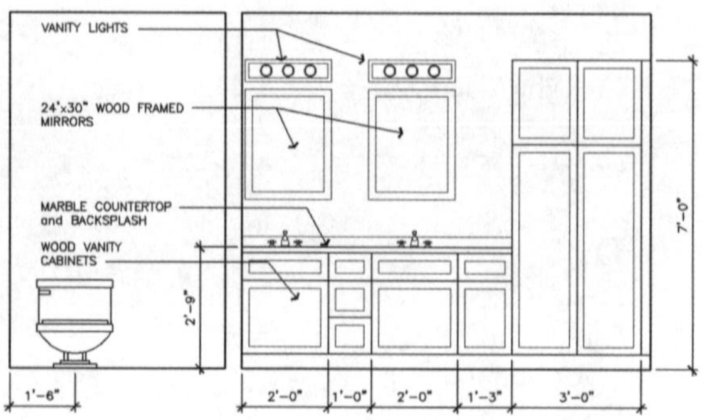

Interior elevation created while working through this textbook; see page 7-19. The floor plan is referenced in and clipped so lines could be projected onto the elevation (orthographic projection) and used to locate items…